S0-BCY-563

DEVELOPMENT
BY PEOPLE

DEVELOPMENT BY PEOPLE

Citizen Construction of a Just World

by

Guy Gran

Foreword by
Mary Racelis Hollnsteiner

PRAEGER SPECIAL STUDIES • PRAEGER SCIENTIFIC

Library of Congress Cataloging in Publication Data

Gran, Guy.
  Development by people.

  Bibliography: p.
  Includes index.
  1. Economic assistance. 2. Economic assistance,
American. 3. Economic development projects.
4. Community development. 5. Rural development.
I. Title.
HC60.G645   1983   338.9′009172′4   82-22442
ISBN 0-03-063294-3
ISBN 0-03-063296-X (pbk.)

Figures 12.1 and 12.2 reproduced from Branco Horvat *The Political Economy of Socialism* (1982) with permission of M. E. Sharpe, Inc.

Published in 1983 by Praeger Publishers
CBS Educational and Professional Publishing
A Division of CBS Inc.
521 Fifth Avenue, New York, New York 10175, U.S.A.

© 1983 by Praeger Publishers

All rights reserved

456789 052 9876543
Printed in the United States of America

. . . that any human on earth, who will, may escape the peonage of ignorance, the inhumanity of a power structure, and the stunting illusions of shamanism.

Foreword
by Mary Racelis Hollnsteiner

With publications on development flooding the reading publics of North and South America, Africa, Asia and Europe, why should Guy Gran's book be singled out for special attention? The answer is that beyond an incisive analysis of why masses of poor people in Third World countries remain poor or become poorer, Gran tells us *how* this process can be reversed. The result is a volume that reinforces its advocacy for human development — where *people* and their active participation matter — with specific prescriptions for bringing it about.

Is this yet another condemnation of the capitalist system and praise for a more economically redistributive socialist system — a common theme of reformers and revolutionaries? Hardly. "A pox on both your houses!" says the author in effect. Different though the two systems are, they converge in glorifying the unlimited acquisition of power by elites — in the capitalist case made up of individuals, and in the socialist one, the state. In either camp it is the masses of people who lose out as both ideologies "transform the formal will of the majority into the actual will of the minority."

This situation of limited access of the poor to power and decision-making is supported by the outlooks, structures, and procedures of international donor agencies, multilateral and bilateral. Gran focuses his critical attention on the largest among them, The World Bank (IBRD), the International Monetary Fund (IMF), and the United States Agency for International Development (USAID). Other United Nations agencies are largely spared his critique, in part because some of them — he specifies the United Nations International Children's Fund (UNICEF), the International Labour Organization (ILO), and the United Nations Research Institute for Social Development (UNRISD) — have fostered successful people-oriented approaches at the grassroots or community level.

Since neither the capitalist nor socialist systems have been capable of reformulating the nature of the relationships between institutions and people, does another viable alternative exist? It does, and its name is *participatory development*. This concept embodies a view of the world in which current injustices, inequality, exploitation, fragmentation, and marginalization of the poor are eliminated in favour of societies in which power differences between groups and individuals are reduced and basic human needs fulfilled for all. Through participatory development the currently marginalized poor become aware of the range of value choices open to them, and their social and political implications. Heightened consciousness makes disadvantaged groups more keenly and continuously aware of the reality about them and of their own capacity to transform it. They acquire a broader comprehension of the full range of human potential possible within socially defined limits. Particularly deprived sets of the poor, for example, women, the elderly, the handicapped, ethnic minorities and children, gain greater access to power and resources. Work and technology weave into patterns of human satisfaction.

A utopian dream? Not at all. For it is attainable. Experiments in participation have demonstrated time and again how much force and vitality people can unleash when they feel they have a stake in the direction of their lives. We cannot afford to dismiss too easily the knowledge that motivated citizens will initiate and sustain capital and labour investments in ways they perceive to be productive for them. The failure of antiparticipatory development strategies and the resulting global poverty and political chaos suggest that we really have no choice but to opt for a new people-based participatory development.

But how to translate aims and aspirations into operational programmes? Key strategies involve the promotion of self-reliance, local capacity building, mass empowerment, and scale or equitable use of resources. Since millions of the Third World poor have, over the past decades and centuries, accommodated distorted socio-economic hierarchies, the passive attitudes and the culture of silence have to be broken. Initially this may call for small groups of outsiders acting as catalysts for change in rural and urban slum communities. They will make up a network of intermediate organizations composed of persons dedicated to serving and empowering the poor through a process of conscientization, group decision-making on viable courses of action, implementation, monitoring, and evaluating their own progress. Intermediate organizations also serve as a buffer between still relatively powerless people, on the one hand, and bureaucratic imperatives or elite economic interests, on the other. From the still common "top down" service-delivery model of interaction between bureaucrats and people, they help reverse the direction of the thrust to a "bottom up" response-demanding model.

This model people themselves will formulate by learning to assess their situation from a holistic and historical perspective. Further, development catalysts or organizers can show them where and how to obtain needed scientific, legal, and technical information, much of it made available by other intermediate organizations at district or provincial levels, as well as how to gather data from the community itself and identify the most critical problem areas and monitor progress toward solving them. Political skills to protect their gains from predatory interest groups and new ways of achieving community-based conflict resolution, drawing upon appropriate cultural norms, also fall into the repertory of development catalyst-people interaction.

So also do techniques for obtaining seed funds and other resources where needed from the outside to bolster people's self-help initiatives. As this populist movement gains momentum and strength, and villages start to teach other villages, the need for intermediate organizations to advocate, expedite, refer, inform, educate, organize, keep records, and evaluate should diminish as local residents take on these functions and evolve into an enlightened national citizenry.

The role of the central government in this participatory age shifts to that of coordinator, responsive to community desires and mediating equality among groups and communities. With governments accountable to their people rather than to international donors or trade partners, they can lessen their dependence on these outside entities. The new revenues coming from the increased productivity of creative, informed, and involved masses of people will allow reforms, such as assured market prices for farmers, rebalanced rural-urban terms of trade, local industries producing what peasants need, nonexploitative trading networks, physical infrastructure, social services, nonelite-controlled legal systems, and local autonomy, among other measures. With increased faith in the capacity of their citizenry and in response to pressures from them, governments will more likely reorient their political will in this direction.

And what of international donor agencies? Do they have a role to play in any part of this process? Not in their present form. Gran calls for significant reforms, such as the need to change the project design process and the planning of programming activities. Measures include involving (or creating where necessary) intermediate organizations and nationals who understand local situations and cultures and who are sympathetic to participatory development; consultations or negotiations with community residents; technical staff with an interdisciplinary, nonelitist type of professionalism that is open to social and political learning; the integration of planners and implementors; and evaluation schemes in which community residents establish their criteria for success and gather data for their own use, as well as outside evaluations, that emphasize the issue of equity, or "who benefits" from the project, in qualitative as well as quantitative terms.

Beyond dramatic shifts in operational procedures must also come a recognition on the part of donor agencies that their efforts can too readily sustain repressive governments, exploitative economic systems, and self-perpetuating, antiparticipatory bureaucracies. Whenever appropriate, donor agencies need to distinguish between serving elite-controlled governments that sustain an inequitable status quo and serving people.

Whether the reader is a development analyst or practitioner working out of an international donor agency, a government or private sector bureaucrat, a university professor or student, a community organizer or social development catalyst, a community leader or resident, he or she will find in this book a wealth of information and insight. Its thrust is clear and its synthesis of an enormous body of development literature impressive. In whichever part of the development system one is located, there is at least a chapter or two that specifically addresses immediate issues and pressing questions. Those readers searching for a better understanding of how

x

mal-development comes about and for constructive antipoverty models that supersede recalcitrant structures and counterproductive processes, the formidable and selective bibliography of items comprising more than 2000 current titles will serve as an invaluable guide. The exhaustive listing has something for everyone, whether a specialist or generalist.

For myself, whose involvements over the last 20 years have spanned participatory research with rural and urban slum groups, active membership in intermediate groups of community organizers, consultancies with government agencies interested in instituting participatory modes of development planning and programming, and most recently community participation adviser for UNICEF programmes of cooperation, *Development by People* has affirmed my own convictions about the validity and viability of participatory development. To be sure, the many organized groups of men and women whom I have met in every continent of the world, struggling to control their destinies in the face of countervailing forces, had already taught me this lesson first-hand. But it is Guy Gran who placed my observations within a systematic framework of analysis and understanding. He shows us that from the ashes of disintegrating world systems can emerge the phoenix of a just and satisfying world for all — if we are perceptive enough to recognize it, brave enough to formulate it, and concerned enough about people to make it happen.

Preface

I propose that we construct a different and more voluntary future. A study of human development in the recent past demonstrates that the processes that perpetuate relative or absolute poverty for more than a billion people in the Third World and for many millions elsewhere are logical products of a world-system at work. Following conventional ideas of economics and politics will not change this reality. A paradigm shift for all of human development is therefore in order. The necessary educational, institutional, and cultural changes are described in operational detail. Each citizen in the North or South should as a result have a clear idea what to do next and how to proceed.

The idea of citizen is the heart of the solution. For a humane, just, productive, and survivable twenty-first century, the world has to have far more and far better citizens. The common dimension of all aspects of the human dilemma — the arms race, the Cold War, global poverty, monopoly capitalism, totalitarianism, global bureaucratization, the commodification of life, ecological destruction, and overpopulation — is the concentration of power. The only way to dissolve concentrated power is to democratize it. This book is about creating more and better citizens and their empowerment. Without such empowerment none of the other problems can be effectively solved.

In particular, poor regions and poor countries need greater productivity, yet they cannot expect vast new external investments. The only logical answer is to get more productivity from the factor of production that is in great abundance — human labor. People will invest more labor only when they control the activity and are assured of keeping the fruits of their labor. The answer is thus to democratize the economy by participatory development. Horvat (1982) shows how and why this could happen in the First and

Second Worlds; this book shows how and why it could be accomplished in the Third World.

Democratic habits are strange to some political cultures, but that does not mean they should or will remain so. In a world of continuous and rampant cultural imperialism in many ideological forms, I seek open and honest communication about the real nature of human beings and their needs. Man does not live by bread alone, if he has enough bread. All human needs cannot be met by market forces or by planning. You cannot go to a store and buy two dollars or two rupees worth of love. The ways the world discusses human needs must change, as well as the ways it discusses politics, economics, and the just society.

Those who try to redesign the human future and their own must face three kinds of exclusionary forces. The first is the concentrated political and economic power in states and corporations that crush, exploit, and marginalize individuals in many ways. Cultural stratification is a second major blockage to human development. As long as an elite can enforce cultural norms, patterns of exclusion will persist; how can a Zairian woman develop when a Zairian man is brought up to define his identity and self-esteem by his ability to exploit women? The modern social form of organization adds the third form of exclusion. The bureaucratic imperatives of security, control, and growth are fundamentally opposed to the human liberation inherent in authentic development.

Capitalist, state socialist, and subsistence economies have not and will not produce the quantity and quality of citizens to overcome these three dominant trends. Creating such citizens starts instead by consciousness raising through a specific curriculum. The development catalyst who begins such a process of education also helps in the formation of base organizations. Both are supported and defended by a network of intermediate institutions. In turn, diverse local groups all over the North can assist in the funding and defense of such institutions and in their growth. States, multinational corporations, and major donor agencies, after generations of deliberately confusing growth and development, are thus rendered essentially passé.* As

---

*As new local democratic institutions evolve, citizens will find relatively few justifiable functions for large organizations of any sort.

the central actors in the growth and evolution of the world-system that created the present mass poverty, such organizations could scarcely be viewed as basic parts of the solution. That would defy basic systems logic.

There are many inherent difficulties in trying to propose and put in operation such a paradigm shift. The Third World people I would most like to communicate with will have a hard time coming up with ten dollars or more for a book, obtaining something published so far away, and reading such a long volume in a foreign language. Energetic students and practitioners in these countries will be rightfully appalled at the cost of most of the works suggested in the bibliographical guide to development studies at the end of the book. Writing to people in different parts of the world-system at the same time is inherently difficult. Those in donor aid agencies, those in community change work in the Third World or the West, and those in schools and universities will each find some topics more immediately relevant than others. This work of synthesis will be justified, however, if it helps each kind of reader realize that he or she is part of the world-system. It is a system designed and built by human beings. It can be changed by other human beings. It will not take vast new sums and giant technological strides, but it will take far more, and more competent, citizens. The challenge to the reader is to become one of those citizens.

A book of synthesis naturally rests on the results of numerous other inquiries both theoretical and practical. I was assisted by many in the data-rich world of Washington, D.C., and by research groups and UN agencies around the world. As the citations suggest, great intellectual debts are owed to many who have written about issues of organizations, political economy, and culture in different parts and on different levels of the world-system. Funding was provided in part by grants from UNICEF and from the Institute for World Order in New York. Views expressed in the book are, however, solely my own. Funding also came in part from madcap development consulting adventures, themselves highly educational; I owe special thanks to my friend Galen Hull for facilitating many of them. What mattered ultimately more than money and access to new material was the psychological support and encouragement from my network of family and friends over two and a half years of struggle. In particular, for rescuing my spirits so many times, I offer *ancienne* peace warrior Eleanor Garst so very many thanks. All such endeavors demand much typing and editing labor; in these efforts yeoman assistance of the highest quality and in continued good cheer was rendered by Naomi Howe.

A final word to many kinds of skeptics who may feel that any real change is impossible. It seems unlikely that the world can survive very much longer a nuclear balance of terror, the spread of nuclear weapons to more and more nondemocratic governments, a world monetary system prey to speculators, ever more severe debt crises for both public and private institutions, the inability of capitalism or state socialism to meet mass needs, and the destruction of the natural habitat for individual short-term profit. The costs of a democratic revolution are tiny in comparison with the costs of anything like the present efforts to sustain the status quo.

Contents

List of Acronyms

ADB	Asian Development Bank
ADF	African Development Foundation (forthcoming)
AID	Agency for International Development
ARTEP	Asian Regional Team for Employment Promotion
BIS	Bank of International Settlements
CIA	Central Intelligence Agency
CNRS	Centre Nationale de Recherches Scientifiques
DAI	Development Alternatives Inc. (Washington)
DC	Development catalyst
DCC	Development Coordinating Committee
D-GAP	Development Group for Alternative Policies (Washington)
ED	Executive director
FAO/ROAP	Food and Agricultural Organization/Rural Organizations Action Program
FY	Fiscal year
FNSP	Fondation Nationale des Sciences Politiques
GOZ	Government of Zaire
GAO	General Accounting Office (of the U.S. Congress)
IADB	Inter American Development Bank
IAF	Inter-American Foundation (Rosslyn, Virginia)
IBRD	International Bank for Reconstruction and Development — World Bank
ICLD	International Center for Law and Development
IDA	International Development Association
IDCA	International Development Cooperation Agency
IFDA	International Foundation for Development Alternatives
IGGI	Inter-Government Group on Indonesia
ILO/WEP	International Labor Office/World Employment Program

IMF	International Monetary Fund
ISHI	Institute for the Study of Human Issues
LDC	Less Developed Country
NAC	National Advisory Council
NLB	New Left Books
NSC	National Security Council
OECD	Organization for Economic Cooperation and Development
OMB	Office of Management and Budget
OPEC	Organization of Petroleum Exporting Countries
ORSTOM	Office de la Recherche Scientifique et Technique Outre-Mer
PUF	Presses Universitaires de France
SIAS	Scandinavian Institute of African Studies
SSA	Security Supporting Assistance
UNCTAD	UN Conference on Trade and Development
UNDP	UN Development Program
UNICEF	UN Children's Fund
UNRISD	UN Research Institute for Social Development

1

Development, the World-System, and Human Potential

Under capitalism, man exploits man; under socialism, it is the other way around.

Anonymous Pole

The world is tightly in the grip of elitism. . . . It cannot be the task of world bureaucracy and elitism alone to transform rural societies of the world unless the rural masses are represented.

Lesotho Agriculture Minister Lerotholi at the
1979 Agrarian Reform Conference in Rome

As the 1980s progress, development remains more a dream than a reality for most people in the Third World. Indeed, more than 30 years of rhetoric and money-pushing have diminished expectations and left more than a billion people still deprived of most basic human needs. This is neither satisfactory nor necessary. There is an alternate to the official future. It is time to brave the furor from supposed experts and global elites. It is time to define the operational and practical means of this alternative to advance human welfare, not just in the Third World but in the Soviet bloc and the West as well.

BEGINNING THE PARADIGM SHIFT

The principal problems for human development are large concentrations of power (governments and corporations), the ideologies or economic doctrines they proclaim, and the processes of exclusion they practice. Any solution for mass development must overcome all three. The issues of political power and bureaucratic imperatives are well known and will be exhaustively treated in the following pages. But the issue of ideology must be clearly stated at the start. For this ideology, the prevailing wisdom known as the discipline of economics, is largely propaganda. It is neither a science nor a solution, but rather it is part of the problem.

Such an assertion is not heresy but common sense. As a methodology for understanding and changing reality, economics, as normally presented in the West, fails at least five basic tests. It accounts human goals as material, largely ignoring what it cannot quantify. It denies the implications of historical evolution and context. Activities are treated in isolation or in pseudo-systems, not in the true world-system context that historians of the 1970s have demonstrated. The economic dimensions are artificially separated from the social, the political, and the ecological; this distorts the multifaceted nature of reality. And last, capitalist economics preaches a myth of harmony in a world of obvious conflict; Marxist economics asserts the importance of class conflict and ignores in practice the more important dilemmas created by the generic conflict between organization and people.

It is an illusion to think that one can work through the economic ideology or the organizational forms of the global elite, the governments and major corporations of the world, to accomplish any rapid improvement in mass human welfare. Any elite and any organization, whatever its mandate, will seek to survive, to grow, and to control. Development, in its broadest meaning, is the liberation of human potential. To best develop and best use finite resources, humans need the maximum practical control that is socially feasible over all aspects of development, most particularly over those goods and processes necessary for meeting basic human needs and security. The poor must participate effectively in political and economic terms. Without this empowerment, significant economic advance is impossible. (So are global demilitarization and an end to the Cold War.) This alternative strategy for human development is called participatory development. This book demonstrates how elites, through organizations, ideology, and the world-system, work to exclude and impoverish people. Then it shows what people can do with participatory development to reconstruct the global development process in the interests of long-term mass welfare, the poor, and the fulfillment of a full range of real human needs.

The hope that we can end the hierarchical modernization of global poverty by a strategy of participatory development has its utopian side. I write, however, in a spirit of hope backed by experience, that some people in every part of the global development system from Washington to the most remote Third World villages do care about and will fight for a better world. To reach and put into operation a solution that will produce both equity and growth means changes in systems, processes, institutions, and values. It is not beyond human capability or desire to do this. For it is in large part a matter of the analysis and change of a human system. Feedback provides the incentives for the ways any system works and the ends toward which it works. Change the feedback by getting poor people effectively involved, and you will get more equitable, resource-efficient results. If the poorest Zairian peasants in Shaba province ever sat down before a U.S. congressional committee in Washington and told it exactly how and why AID (Agency for International Development) project funds for maize development were being spent, it might be the dawn of a new era in foreign assistance. This scene can not take place, of course, at present. But something more than the current minimal (elite-dominated) feedback and evaluation process is imperative in any human-centered solution for global development.

That this is a hard-nosed utopian book in the tradition of E. F. Schumacher, Johan Galtung, and Ivan Illich should already be *out* apparent. To understand my desire for change, I think the reader must first be made aware of the normative assumptions I am advancing about human and developmental potential. Communicating comfortably to readers in many cultural and organizational locations would be difficult without this. Indeed a normative stance is essential for grappling with the three central elements of this first chapter: the human development problem in the contemporary world-system; the further dilemmas posed by organizational imperatives; and the fundamental operational dimensions of participatory development.

The articulation and implementation of a new global development policy — alternative development, as some call it — should not be stymied at the outset by the obvious chasm between what is ideal and what is politically feasible. What is feasible is largely a function of a historic moment and the individuals involved. Moments pass quickly in the contemporary world. The broad lines of strategy must rest on enduring ideals. From the historic and global commonality of ethical traditions embodied in the major faiths and from the 1948 UN Declaration on Human Rights signed by most nations, a set of common ideals has crystallized. It is not a facet of cultural imperialism to talk about them or explicitly base a strategy on them.

The long-term interests of both the North (or core) and the South (or periphery) are a just and sustainable world order. Most, but not all, people want a world of peace, social and economic well-being, social and political justice, and ecological quality. Human civilization can accomplish the consciousness raising, mobilization, and transformations necessary to have such a world. We can reject the prevailing neo-Darwinian ethic of the current set of winners in the present world-system. Indeed global society as a whole does not have the resources to permit the luxury of individuals monopolizing billions or even millions of dollars of the planet's scarce resources. It is a form of ill health that people become so fixated on material needs in lieu of growing to meet their own social and moral (or self-actualization) needs. Different orders of human needs will be explored shortly. Here I wish simply to introduce the point that development requires a different kind of human being from the one required by mere growth. One goal of participatory development is to create a more socially responsible human being without either the hunger and deprivation historically associated with market economies or the terror and totalitarianism often associated with command economies.

Given the general antagonism of the prevailing world-system to mass human welfare in the Third World, thanks to inevitably self-interested concentrations of public and private wealth in nondemocratic societies, I am not sanguine that too many people will be much persuaded by idealism alone. What I propose to add are three further compelling reasons, beyond moral ones, for the global adoption of participatory development: the larger financial environment impels it; it is the most productive strategy per unit of resources involved; and it is, despite its own set of practical problems, significantly more practical than the large-scale, top-down social engineering development model inherent in the project cycle of major donor agencies like the World Bank (International Bank for Reconstruction and Development).

Despite the Brandt Commission report (Brandt, 1980) and kindred pleas, a realistic view of the political climate in the 1980s and 1990s does not find hope for massive increases in conventional aid from North to South. The real value of resource transfers will likely decline. If properly accounted to include items like debt repayments, transfer pricing, profit repatriation, and unequal exchange, the real nature of resource transfers would indeed be seen as a continuous drain on the South. Poor countries, regions, and communities have to work to diminish these financial hemorrhages (see *Development Dialogue*, 80, 2, for instance), but they must work even harder on using the scarce resources at hand in a far more productive and equitable fashion. With current approaches, external resources will never bridge the gap between perceived needs and perceived realities. This book seeks to show how needs, realities, and strategies can all be brought into far closer harmony.

Small amounts of external aid through appropriate channels are part of a participatory solution. But resource flows, aid or investment, will continue to go to countries and sectors of interest to the aid givers. The existence of these flows discourages, if not blocks, the implementation of alternative methods of resource use and the social changes they require. Neither the nature of such aid nor its potential as an obstacle should obscure the simpler reality that such flows will never be enough to deal with the basic needs of billions of people over the next century. The present system presages growing mass misery and political instability. Adoption of a new, more resource-efficient development strategy will become more and more of a political necessity for elites, not only in the Third World but in resource-poor regions and communities in the developed countries.

Research over the last decade has indicated, and I think proved, that in agriculture and in the manufacturing or industrial sectors a more participatory workplace and structure lead to higher productivity. Corporate elites have been reluctant to accept this because they see power falsely as a purely zero-sum game. In reality the value, meaning, and magnitude of power are highly situational in nature, as the many contemporary European experiments in worker management demonstrate. Conventional class conflicts may be recast in diminished form. If the workers (who enjoy the quality of life improvements), the owners of capital (who also benefit from the higher productivity), and the government and society (which need and benefit from the higher productivity) would crystallize their understanding of the alternatives, the administrator/manager class could not perpetuate the unnecessary degree of coercive power now typical of the modern industrial organization.

In like manner, comparative studies of family farming and large-scale agribusiness of many, but not all crops (see Lappé, 1979, or Perelman, 1977, e.g.) in both the United States and the Third World have usually indicated a higher yield per hectare or acre by the more labor-intensive small-scale producer than by the capital-intensive procedure. If a coalition of landless, *minifundistas*, and government revenue collectors was made aware of their common interests, land reform would face far smaller political obstacles in many countries. Given the budgetary squeezes on poor states, there would be sound political reasons for such reforms; governments weary of massive food imports might have reason to move in similar directions if food aid shipments were not so easy to come by. In sum, there are good political reasons for moving toward more productive forms of economic activity.

The exclusionary dimensions of the generic aid project process in the Third World is central to the discussions of Chapters 9, 10, and 11. The conventional project cycle, it will be argued, serves bureaucratic interests, but it cannot locate or implement the most scale-effective and productive use of resources. Outsiders simply cannot know enough about the project environment and the desires and abilities of local inhabitants to do quality social engineering, even if they had the right to. In an ever more resource-scarce world, the case for participatory development is overwhelming.

Aspects of the four arguments for participatory development (the moral, the financial, the productive, and the practical) are expanded on many times in this book. Before the operational nature of this alternative development strategy is explained, the real contours of the development problem must be clarified. New intellectual tools must be created, borrowing only where necessary from the current ruin of capitalist and Marxist economics.

THE CREATION AND PERPETUATION OF MASS POVERTY

The current global distribution of wealth and poverty is not the result of historical accidents. Villagers can usually see rather clearly how local landlords, merchants, moneylenders, and notables cooperate among themselves and with regional and national elites to maintain power and privilege. Not so visible at the village level is the cooperation of national capital, the state, and international capital in a triple alliance (Evans, 1979); this alliance provides overall direction and control of development in most Third World societies. But, as I shall argue in many ways, villagers are very often more perceptive about the intent and abilities of corporations, aid agencies, and national governments than are most of the "modernized" inhabitants of these institutions themselves or those other Westerners who write about development. This is not too surprising; villagers must live with or endure the results. Thus much of what follows must effectively demystify development for the "modernized" developer more than for the villager. Both will change in a true development process. That in turn will transform the conventional hierarchical and authoritarian relationship between official and peasant, organization and society.

The process begins with destroying the myths of the benevolence of organization, the neutrality of economics and the market, and the nature and meaning of history. Human beings in all societies live, more or less comfortably, by myths. Myths define most important aspects of the good, the beautiful, and the possible. To adopt and implement the basic elements of participatory development does not imply the debunking of one set of myths and the creation of another. We have to deal with the real world. Hundreds of millions of starving or deprived people are obviously a reality from which the mind seeks to flee into convenient escapist myths. Yet we among the modern and literate of the world's elite are engaging in little more than sophistry to dismiss the world's poor as history's sad losers whose plight is not our fault. Sophistry works in the interest of the self-interested elites who engage in various combinations of "blame the victim" or "help the benighted savages." But the reality of processes connecting rich and poor and serving to perpetuate various kinds of impoverishment cannot be understood with the prevailing myths, the evasiveness of the mythmakers (no matter how noble their intentions), or the intellectual tools at hand.

To implement true development, one has to grasp these connective processes, anticipate their negative effects, and design development activities that overcome or preempt them. Neoclassical economics (the Keynesians and their successors) and classical organization studies are largely oblivious to the real implications of very imperfect markets and do not contain the tools to face them. Given that most resources in global development are now controlled by just such economic thinking by people working in just such organizations, it is small wonder that the world economy and its development serve the poor so badly. What is needed are new intellectual tools and a world model with empirical integrity, minimal mythology, and a degree of social responsibility. To be truly effective in development is to be the hard-nosed utopian, not the bleeding heart, the bureaucrat, or the businessman. A less self-interested and self-centered view of history is the place to start.

The world model underlying conventional global development policy and practice as the 1980s begin can be reduced to a series of historical and normative assertions that Wallerstein has synthesized as "developmentalism."

> This perspective assumed that all states were engaged in "developing" (which for many meant "becoming nations"), that their progress along this path could be measured quantitatively and synchronically, and that on the basis of knowledge derived from such measurements, governments could in fact hasten the process, which was a highly commendable thing to do. Since these states were proceeding down parallel paths, *all* states were intrinsically capable of achieving the desired results. The only serious intellectual question was why so many resisted doing so (Wallerstein, 1979: 153-4).

Unfortunately for the United States, Europe, and the Soviet Union, which all proceeded to develop parts of the Third World on these theoretical assumptions, the inaccuracies of the model have been well demonstrated by historical experience. The gap between rich and poor has grown wider; most societies prove incapable of the results expected or hoped for by national and international planners.

When an operational model fails, it is premature to offer new treatments for visible symptoms of the problem before one understands the theoretical flaws and institutional processes that cause the result. One manifest failure of developmentalism was to choose state or society as the unit of analysis, as though each nation-state were a relatively autonomous unit. But Zaire, Egypt, Israel, and many other states would not survive without their external links and support. Even more extreme cases exist; between 1970 and 1975 the United States paid 80 percent to 90 percent of the annual operating budget of the governments in Saigon, Phnom Penh, and Vientiane. It would seem inappropriate to base a theory aimed at economic results on analytical units that are basically sociopolitical in nature.

To replace developmentalism one needs ways of understanding people as they act and relate to each other economically. The term that encompasses these concerns best is "mode of production": this includes "the way in which decisions are made about dividing up productive tasks, about quantities of goods to be produced and labor-time to be invested, about quantities of goods to be consumed or accumulated and about the distribution of the goods produced" (Wallerstein, 1979: 155).

Individuals or families fit into different modes of production that can be defined by three degrees of self-sufficiency. All figure in contemporary Peru, one of several countries that this book explores in detail. Some Peruvian households, such as those of the highland villagers of Uchucmarca described by Brush (1977), are largely self-sufficient. Many households in both the highlands and lowlands now earn partial subsistence and maintenance within world-economy production but also earn part from their own (and kin) subsistence efforts. At the other end of the spectrum are sugar plantation workers and urban bureaucrats whose entire lifetime needs must be met by their role in the world economy. A development model must first explain where and how individuals fit within different modes of production at a particular time.

A development model must also entail an understanding of different modes of production — what they are and how they evolved. For it is these processes and links that are fundamental to creating and recreating what Wallerstein calls the world-system perspective and what I use as one basic theoretical element of this work.

The term "world-system" is fully understandable only when placed within a historical perspective. There are, to be sure, additional and subsidiary organizing forces that have worked in varying degrees of conflict and cooperation to give form and direction to historical change. One is the formation and disintegration of national states, of which much is known; a second is the evolution of cultural communities. Far more research is in order on these issues. But the broad outlines of basic changes in modes of production will show clearly how any social group has arrived at its current predicament.

The earliest form of human production, apparently common in much of the ancient world but with few vestiges today, was the reciprocal-lineage mode. Production and exchange were carried out by and among kin, normally in relatively small political and social units. Human labor was the principal production input. Economic needs helped to generate social sanctions on women and children to protect and ensure the source of new labor. Inequalities existed, but too much wealth destabilized overall social control. The incentive for maximizing production was thus absent.

What are commonly termed "civilizations" or "empires" inaugurated the second major mode of production: the tributary mode. It differed from the initial mode by having a sufficient technological base to produce enough surplus (production beyond the costs of recreating the labor) to support people who were not producers but bureaucrats or clerics. Weber and many others have described this tributary mode in detail. Wallerstein synthesizes this mode with the term "world empire" and points to its fundamental similarity to the earlier mode. Both need their subjects to survive. The same bureaucracy in the world empire that collected the tribute also distributed it; the more of it that reached the top, the greater the potential target and thus the incentive for self-enrichment for all intermediaries. Ch'u T'ung-tsu's *Local Government in China under the Ch'ing* (1962) is a famous exposition of this. If the rulers pressed too hard, producers would starve, flee, or revolt. At base the ruler's standard of living depended more on stability and continuity of production. New technology per se was not central unless to reverse decline. But as in the earlier mode, there *was* a profound integral incentive to insure a fixed income and thus assure that the producers, society's poor, not starve.

It is this minimal human rights component that *departs* from the third mode of production that began its sweep to world dominance around 1450 in Europe. What we have now is a world economy, defined by Wallerstein (1979: 159) as "a single division of labor within which are located multiple cultures. . . . but which has no overarching political structure." It is the market instead that distributes surplus according to whatever exchange is most profitable.

This opens up at least two fundamental potential abridgments of human rights, the rights that current international aid policies are supposedly trying to advance.

The "free" market embodies a basic ambivalence about freedom. Both the buyer and the seller naturally want maximum advantage and thus maximum freedom for themselves. At the same time each seeks maximum constraint on the other. Both compete for power through social and political channels. Historically it has been far easier to organize the few than the mass; several centuries of monopoly, shared monopoly, and highly disparate incomes have resulted. This dynamic is generic to all parts of the world-system today and must be addressed by any strategy promising development.

An even greater infringement of human needs comes with the impact of profit. In a market both the accumulators and producers (terms I deem more precise and appropriate than those common in capitalist or Marxist parlance) are struggling to control the surplus. Wallerstein compares the ultimate utility of the producer for the elite in the world empire and world economy in this fashion:

> In a redistributive system, the primary weapon of the powerful is the sword. Thus death of the political resistant, but minimal life for the acquiescent producer is the basic law of political life. But in a capitalist mode, with *economic* cycles, the life of the producer can be more unprofitable as consumer of surplus than profitable as producer of surplus. Thus the politico-military machinery can frequently best serve to maximize profit by permitting starvation, both literally and figuratively (Wallerstein, 1979: 160).

This does much to explain the protein deficiency and/or starvation in Peru, Brazil, Zaire, Namibia, and nearly every other country in the world. The rhetorical mandate of global development agencies runs precisely counter to processes that bring such results. Working in a historical era when it is not conventionally thought feasible to make 25-75 percent of any given society into significantly more profitable consumers or producers, development officials have found themselves stymied. Accumulators throughout most societies actively undermine efforts to improve the present production opportunities of the poor because such activities seem to threaten their own semi-monopoly on what surplus there is.

If the operating processes of the current world-system raise considerable obstacles to human rights and needs over time, so do they also over territorial space. In designing international development interventions, one must face not only the wide disparities in control of and access to constituent parts of the overall mode of production (patents, investment capital, etc.) but also disparities and conflicts born of the distribution of production and specialization among regions and countries. The terms now widely used for this spatial division are *core* and *periphery*. Peru, producing predominantly primary commodities for export with relatively low wages paid its producers, sits as one of many peripheral states interacting with the core societies of the United States, Europe, and Japan. Characteristic of core societies are high wages, high capital intensiveness, and more widespread use of state-of-the-art technology.

The peripheral status of Peru in the world-system and of various regions within Peru vis-à-vis its capital, Lima, and other urban centers are chronicled and documented in the country study in Chapter 8. What must be addressed here is the generic predicament of peripheral states and regions. Is it possible to accumulate capital and invest in productive opportunities under the control of and for the benefit of indigenous poor majorities and at the same time be part of the international flow of goods, capital, labor, and ideas? For the periphery confronts not simply the disinclination of international corporations and banks to invest in opportunities for the poor majority to any significant degree. There is also a process of perpetual impoverishment that works against a Third World society's ability to retain a substantial portion of its surplus and use it to effect.

The central issue is the commodity exchange relationship. Trade between societies at vastly different stages of modernization, wage levels, and technology is inherently disadvantageous to the less modern. A most readable synthesis of a complex argument is that by Amin (1976: 138-54). Classical economics promotes a theory of comparative advantage, inspired by a Renaissance trade example, that does not correspond to twentieth century reality. Cumulative Western investment, aid, and advice, combined with export-led growth models, serve to enlarge trade and the advantages of the core societies. For the poor state at the periphery, trade is in large measure composed of primary agricultural and mineral products, and (more recently) semiprocessed goods like electronic parts, in return for Western technology, machinery, food, and finished products. At each stage in the process, price is controlled and determined less by supply and demand than by the political and economic strength of the various market actors and also by the differential in wage levels. These are the elements of what is known as unequal exchange.

The debate has barely begun about how to conceive of equal trade between entities of greatly different power, wealth, wage levels, and technologies. Yet it is critical to understand the current process as the most elementary perpetuation of both Third World poverty and internal inequities in almost every society the world over. Calls for a new international economic order look less like hyperbole in this perspective.

The international dynamics of the world-system thus give birth or rebirth to, condition, and sustain a series of processes within and across national boundaries that underwrite poverty for the many and ever more efficient accumulation by the few. There are of course partial exceptions to this bleak assessment in specific regions or societies; later chapters try to weigh these various efforts to transform overall system behavior. But those involved in the design of international development programs, given reasonable agreement among serious development experts, must meet such blockages head on.

English sociologist-theologian Charles Elliott, in one of the best books on microdevelopment, shows how these impoverishing processes work. He calls them confidence mechanisms. They have the following characteristics:

> 1. Individual enrichment. 2. Intragroup competition for that enrichment. 3. Selective biases within that competition. 4. Selective biases that are not obvious to those who compete. 5. A system sufficiently "open" to retain competitors' confidence and/or bestow legitimacy on those who compete successfully. 6. Acquisition of direct and/or indirect benefit to those who control the mechanism (Elliott, 1975: 11).

Confidence mechanisms do not fully explain why the system evolves to a given form, but they do lay bare the psychological and social glue that keeps the system going. They permit the urban bureaucrat to place the new school near his own home, making it cheaper and easier for his own children to attend. They permit the rural moneylender to charge 200 or 300 percent on short-term loans so that the small farmer, as in western Sudan, produces two to three times what is necessary for adequate subsistence but lives at 60 to 80 percent of subsistence, dying in his 30s or 40s from accumulated ills brought on by long-term malnutrition. Three of his four children never make it to age five. But his labor helps make urban food cheaper and thus quell the political unrest of the urban poor.

Development assistance efforts, if they are going to improve tangibly the lives of the poor majorities in Third World societies of the periphery, have in sum deeply entrenched, multidimensional obstacles to overcome. The alternative analytic approach just sketched suggests that the task should begin by understanding where individual poor people fit in the prevailing mode of production and how and why specific confidence mechanisms work to keep them there. Resource and environmental limitations must also be placed in this framework. What emerges are varied patterns of accumulators and producers in unequal struggles for control of the productive process, the surplus that accrues, and the overarching sociopolitical institutions that assist in this control. To affect these struggles, development projects must go beyond surface aspects to the substantive processes, the multiple forms of unequal local, national, and international exchanges. Project designs must not gloss over surface harmony when the underlying reality is conflict, and they must not treat symptoms for causes. In an imperfect world where incremental change is often the only practical one, the human energy and resources devoted to the struggle for economic justice and human rights are obviously insufficient. But it is not utopian to try to use these limited resources to help the earth's poor devise better ways to survive in the world-system.

ORGANIZATIONS AS THE TOOLS OF ELITES

Political processes, unequal exchanges, and resource constraints are sadly not all that the poor and powerless must face in the contemporary world-system. Modernization has brought change not just in technology and material culture but in the nature and structure of human relationships. The world-system is replacing the kind of unequal social ordering based on individual surrender to the traditional authority of tribe, kinship group, religion, ideology. Elites have naturally not stood by idle. They have sought to harness new forms of technology to transform old forms of organizations, like the states and trading companies of the preindustrial era, into new, more effective control mechanisms — the modern state and the modern corporation. Hierarchical ties have been modernized and exclusionary incentives expanded. If the goal of development is human liberation and the fulfillment of needs broadly conceived, one cannot avoid raising awkward questions about the utility of the modern organization, public or private, and the structure of work it has propagated and legitimized.

This book searches for a practical solution to the following irony: while organization is a major weapon of the strong against the weak, it is also often the only weapon of the weak against the strong. Human society is not going to dismiss organizations out of hand. People need frameworks for social ordering. But those who care about human development must develop far more discriminating approaches to social forms if they seek to use scarce resources to optimal effect. For more than a generation, most interested participants in the West have been content to throw money into Third World development via large foreign aid organizations like the World Bank (IBRD) and the Agency for International Development (AID). The message was this: "You, large organization, go out there and help poor people." The problem is that large organizations cannot do that. Organizations and people have different languages and cultures; even if they learn how to communicate to an extent, they still have different and opposing agendas.

These are not new conflicts. Max Weber wrote about them decades ago. Social service practitioners in the United States and Western Europe have been struggling with these practical dilemmas for decades. Bureaucrats may have a mandate to do one thing, but it is in their organizational interest to do something else. Organizational inhabitants do not often talk about such bureaucratic imperatives; indeed, from inside an organization it is hard to see how resulting processes warp the good intentions of individuals. But the advocate of participatory development must clearly understand the aspects of the modern organization that, by their very nature, work against participation. For the development process is filled with exactly these obstacles.

The logical place to explore for answers is the field of organizational sociology. But the inward-looking view of mainstream modern texts like March and Simon (1958) is not helpful. They portray an unrealistically positive view of the organization and of the individual in it. Recent work by Swedish sociologist Bengt Abrahamsson has shown the predatory dimension of bureaucracy. He writes (1977: 11) that "organizations are deliberately designed social structures which have been established by a certain person, group, or class in order to implement certain goals." Thus an external force or forces, which he terms "mandators," shape fundamental aspects of the nature and procedures of each organization. Mandators are concerned with three goals: maintaining organizational efficiency, making the organization represent its interests, and insuring that the organizational inhabitants work toward those interests and not their own.

This dimension of organizational sociology is critical in the study of donor agency organizations. It is not simply because external forces bear on the nature of project procedures as well as on the overall institutional structure but also because donor agencies typically do not have a coherent, unified ruler. Many aspects of the conflicting mandates that donor agencies receive are treated in succeeding chapters. But such intrinsic initial conflicts are basic to an understanding of the nature and results of conventional project design and implementation procedures. The reader should thus not leap to a premature conclusion that a series of quick technical fixes in a mandate can do more than moderately improve some of the procedural constraints to be discussed.

There is one further and far more disturbing area of organizational analysis that is central to the study of participatory development. This is pursued in a work by Ralph Hummel (1977), who demonstrates that the internal workings of the modern bureaucracy are a basically alien world, quite distinct from either society or its predecessor, community. The imperative inside this new world is control. Its essential nature is rationally organized action. The gap between bureaucracy and the rest of society is quite wide.

Hummel portrays the conflicts that result between the two worlds by exposing five aspects of organizational behaviour. As a political entity, bureaucracy is an authoritarian, hierarchical control instrument. It replaces the needs of people with the needs of systems. It hires functionaries instead of citizens; they apply management instead of leadership. As a cultural entity, bureaucracy replaces social norms with operational codes and ethics with effectiveness. As a psychological instrument, bureaucracy creates new forms of dependency. Role and work identity replace person and personality, conditioning takes the place of socialization, and teamwork is more rewarded than skill. Bureaucracy also changes the way people think and the words they use. It replaces dialogue with command and causal reasoning with analogous (acausal) reasoning. It also develops specialized and secret language to help prevent external supervision. Finally, as a social entity, bureaucracy turns people into cases and social actions into functions. The result is dehumanization.

One should not conclude that such a black and white portrait resembles the exact internal workings of aid organizations like AID or IBRD. But there are enough similarities and tendencies in their processes of paper and money pushing, the quality of work life in them, and their paternalistic approach to aid "clients" or "targets" to make this model an analytic jumping-off point. Chapters 9 and 10 explore more than 30 specific ways in which organizational culture and its imperatives have discouraged participation by the poor in project procedures.

Such a thumbnail sketch does not do justice to the elegance of Hummel's synthesis of individual experiences in metropolitan U.S. bureaucracies with the insights of major classical theorists like Weber. But for the analyst of international development, aspiring to enhance human participation, Hummel pinpoints the irresolvable dilemma. If the essential nature of organizations in the modern industrial world is to seek to control, how can one use them as a tool for the liberation implicit in a participatory society and participatory development? This book lays out the concrete ways of humanizing organizational imperatives through smaller, more decentralized institutions with fundamentally new feedback mechanisms. For without such a transformation, what will continue? At each stage of the project cycle and within each procedure applied, one now finds an organization seeking to control human thought and action. At each point one must therefore ask if the administrators or the degree or kind of control designed exists as a function of productive efficiency and general social welfare or simply as a function of organizational need.

Hummel's model also has revolutionary implications for the supposed objects of international development, the clients or the poor. He puts it this way.

Without the initial institutional support given to recruits into bureaucracy, clients must learn a new language, tune in to new norms, bow properly to immense institutional power, understand and flatter the bureaucratic personality, and try to become a "case." Paradoxically, especially in welfare bureaucracies, only to the extent that clients surrender their humanity are they given the bare promise of material support by which to uphold that humanity (Hummel, 1977: 17).

It would thus appear that much of what is frequently described in development literature as the problem of cultural fit between Western bureaucratic culture and poor people in the Third World is a matter less of national cultural disparities than of the basic gulf between organization and human society.

Narrowing the gap and diminishing the basic antagonisms between organizations and people are essential parts of the agenda for participatory development. But that cannot be the whole agenda. The nature of organizational behavior reflects as well the nature of the mode of production that gave birth to it. The mode of production in the contemporary world-system seeks the expansion of profits and surplus value by trying to turn all human interactions into market commodities. Organizations, as one tool of system elites, naturally tend to seek to control and homogenize people in the most profitable ways. Needs are defined more and more as commodities. Autonomy is abhorred and undermined. As the servants of modernization so defined, organizations are profoundly hostile to the model of participatory development I advocate in this work. This suggests, following Illich (1977: 107), that part of the solution must depend "on the ability of a society to agree on fundamental, self-chosen antibureaucratic and antitechnocratic restraints."

This in turn implies altering the mode of production itself. There should be nothing untoward about such a suggestion. The world-system has been evolving under human direction for hundreds of years. Human beings continue to pursue power and profits at the expense of the needs and rights of others. The natural environment sustains ever greater abuse; humans have only partial understanding of potential catastrophes. More than 20 percent of the planet's citizens lack the most basic subsistence needs. There is no correlation on a global basis between the human need for productive and rewarding jobs and the ability of the world-system to provide them; indeed, the massive unemployment and underemployment in the periphery is a major reason that employment in the core is as high as it is. Most who do find jobs in the "modern" sector would admit that they are more or less alienating. Finally, much of the work humans need to have done society does not recognize as worth tangible reward. If this is the best way we can devise to produce goods and enhance human welfare, consider human education a failure. I do not do so. Upon a more socially responsible definition of development and new forms of social organization can be built a humane alternative. The key is the creation of citizens and their effective participation in the decisions that shape their lives.

PARTICIPATORY DEVELOPMENT AS THE OPERATIONAL RESPONSE

The world may be entering the so-called Third Development Decade, but the voluminous, official literature that looks toward the future (the Brandt Commission Report, the Global 2000 Report, and the World Development Report, 1980, to name three) offers no definition of development that links human needs and goals to an actual operational process. One gets enormous catalogs of problems but no solution. Anything proposed that looks like a practical solution would have tangible and measurable dimensions. It is not in the interest of any organization to put itself in a position to be evaluated (a dilemma addressed in Chapter 11). One cannot thus expect any organization to produce the necessary strategy. That too will have to be developed by people.

The most perceptive efforts to date have been the works of global humanist scholars Ivan Illich and Johan Galtung. Illich has laid bare the essential nature of the processes that the world-system has wrought. In this system, development

> implies the replacement of widespread, unquestioned competence at subsistence activities by the use and consumption of commodities; the monopoly of wage-labor over all other kinds of work; redefinition of needs in terms of goods and services mass-produced according to expert design; finally, the rearrangement of the environment in such fashion that space, time, materials, and design favor production and consumption while they degrade or paralyze use-value oriented activities that satisfy needs directly. And all such worldwide homogeneous changes and processes are valued as inevitable and good (Illich, 1981: 15).

It is clear that each of these changes serves to diminish the quantity and quality of human participation. An effective strategy in response must encompass the same holistic, interdisciplinary concerns. Most importantly, such a strategy must address the question of power, for without empowerment one cannot develop any secure way to meet physiological needs or any healthy way to meet social needs or moral needs. As has been often noted, man does not live by bread alone. Humans seek safety, affection, and self-esteem. They also need love, justice, and purpose. To relate economic activity to the fulfillment of such a breadth of needs is the purpose of a relatively new school of economics, humanistic economics.

This book is not a restatement of humanistic economics, but the basic text in that field (Lux and Lutz, 1979) would be a useful supplement to this chapter. Humanistic economics is a synthesis of moral, psychological, economic, and scientific concerns. It explicitly recognizes that development, unlike growth or modernization, is at base a moral activity. Quality participation is the essential affirmation of humanity. To the extent we become simply good little producers and consumers, we are little more than robots.

> To call for participation is to render "cognitive respect" to all those who cannot claim the status of experts. . . . such "cognitive respect" is not an arbitrary or even eccentric ideological decision. It is based on the understanding that every human being is *in possession* of a world of his own, and that nobody can interpret this world better (or more "expertly") than he can himself (Berger, 1974: 60).

Capitalist mythology reveres such individualism, but capitalism in practice seeks every means to diminish its positive sides and enhance its negative elements. These departicipatory processes are a natural result of unequal concentrations of power and the uneven nature of development in the long cycles of modern world history. What is central to this book is the implications of unequal power for development.

Galtung (1980) has approached this question most directly. He argues that power is based on negating the goals of development via inequality, injustice, exploitation, penetration, fragmentation, and marginalization. Such power, actively applied through institutional forms, he terms "structural imperialism." The intent of development must be the reduction of power differences, the creation of processes that reduce power over others and enhance power over the self. Power that is innate must be distinguished from power that stems from having resources or occupying a position.

Humans existing in a world of scarcity and insecurity are more prone to aggression; it is a long way from this reality to a socially responsible consensus on the nature and use of power in human development. We will never start this essential political process, however, by avoiding the issue of power, as neoclassical economists have done for so long.

In *The True Worlds*, Galtung is primarily concerned with the relationships among development, power, violence, and peace. One cannot avoid the linking of peace and development. He has explored strategies of demilitarization and correctly posits that peace and development are two sides of the same coin. A society cannot expend a large portion of its resources through hierarchical organizations for aggressive purposes without it having a negative impact on the society as a whole and its potential of human development. It is a harmful practice not just because it wastes resources but also because it promotes miseducation. The United States and the Soviet Union, for example, both permitted the growth of military-industrial complexes based on a mythological construct called "national security," which was invented and spread in good part by those who benefited most directly from the resulting increased share of social resources, the military itself. One cannot blame organizations for behaving like organizations. One can, however, rue the failure of people in both countries to be citizens. Galtung (1980: 62ff) ably summarizes what the world goals of development must be: personal and socioeconomic growth, equity, solidarity, diversity, equality, autonomy, social justice, and participation. But he is only marginally concerned (1980: 413) with history as *process*. It is the *process* of participation that is the key to attaining any of these goals.

It is unreasonable to expect poor villagers trying to assure subsistence needs to have much immediate or direct impact on military budget decisions in nations' capitals. But as the Kenyan *harambee* self-help program is demonstrating (see Chapter 6), participation in microdevelopment has the ability to ripple out in some positive ways through a society. I am not oblivious to the perils of nuclear arms and military spending, but, without far more and far more effective citizens, there seems little real hope of bringing the arms race to an end. Citizens are created by educational processes, broadly speaking. Participatory development is the single most effective way of spreading and internalizing this education.

The way to do this is to crystallize an overall model of what a participatory development project should look like, explore with the local inhabitants their ideas for feasible projects and the practical and political obstacles, and then encourage those involved to create the kinds of social organization and reorganization that could and would carry through the necessary implementation processes. Building on the work of the Development Group for Alternative Policies (in Washington), the Inter-American Foundation, the United Nations Research Institute for Social Development (UNRISD) and other UN agencies like the ILO, FAO, and UNICEF, I posit that the ideal participatory development project has at least these eight characteristics:

1. A significant percentage of the specified group must participate in and control as many elements of project initiation, design, operation, and evaluation as is possible.

2. The project design must include clearly defined and operational participatory mechanisms to guide administrative, productive, and distributive elements of the project.

 3. The institutional linkages of the project with the larger economic and political system must be functional for those at the bottom; the aid inflow and the productive gains must be protected. Thus the hostile development environment and prevailing confidence mechanisms (Elliott, 1975) must be explicitly dealt with in project design.

4. Technological and organizational aspects must be culturally feasible. If women are the farmers, it is counterproductive to train only male agricultural extension agents.

5. The project design must reach some reasonable standard of ecological soundness that reflects an empirically defensible analytical framework by the participants.

6. The project must show the potential for self-reliance; resources should serve a catalytic function, not a welfare function encouraging further dependency.

7. Comparable potential for self-sustainment must be evident; conventional aid activities often die when funding stops.

8. The project design must include enhancement of self-directed learning. Intellectual dependency, as much as political and economic dependency, saps creativity and productivity.

Such a model contains a good number of practical and political problems that must not be sidestepped. How much participation is enough or ideal in a specific part of a specific project process? The AID-funded Cornell research project on participation in rural development has produced a host of studies and literature reviews (summarized in Cohen and Uphoff, 1980) which have explored how to measure participation in various ways. These works and the many typologies they have developed for different kinds and degrees of participation are not, it seems to me, ultimately very useful to the practitioner. The development catalyst needs to keep in mind issues like levels of empowerment, but what matters more are the quality and nature of communication among catalysts, the local poor, and the local elite. This suggests that development agents need far more sophisticated area studies education than is now deemed appropriate, in particular the training to perceive quickly the local confidence mechanisms at work. Only when so equipped can a catalyst begin to judge how much it matters that one individual or group participates at one stage or another in a development process.

Pursuing this model of participatory development will naturally produce various kinds of political problems. Any development project is inherently political, for it is in essence a change exercise that affects in some way (not necessarily negatively) those who benefit from the status quo. Power does not have to be a zero-sum proposition. Much of what will decide the degree and nature of the political feasibility of a particular development initiative will be determined by local perceptions of what power is and how those perceptions can be changed. Beyond productivity, other positive results of self-reliant participatory development can be stressed: better use of local resources, more local creativity via applied learning, more compatibility with local conditions and ecology, more diversity, less alienation, and less outside manipulation and dependence (Galtung, 1980: 404ff). Elites cannot be avoided, but they can sometimes be coopted by visions of a larger pie. For both the poor and the elites, this must be part of the lure. Sometimes elites cannot be coopted but can be cut down to size; thus the critical importance of the defensive and offensive elements of social organization is inherent in the model of participatory development.

As with any human endeavor, this development model cannot end all inequalities or meet all the human needs of all people. But to the extent the participatory processes succeed in raising mass human consciousness, thousands or millions of people will gain the ability to work successfully to fill more and more of their own needs in a self-escalating process. A less materialistic, more humanistic person will begin to emerge, one more attuned to long-term survival in a real world environment of diverse material limits and immutable natural laws. It is difficult to see why most people would not find such a vision preferable to the prevailing possibilities of global bureaucratization, nuclear war, mass starvation, and an ecologically uninhabitable planet.

In Chapters 6 and 7 the operation of creating participatory development is presented in detail. With both theory and examples from various parts of the world, these chapters describe how development catalysts and intermediate institutions can enter into or interact with different types of local communities. In Chapter 8 the case of Peru is then explored to show the kinds of learning and classes of questions that such a development promoter must apply to locate and assist the poor in the typically hostile and stratified terrain on the fringes of the world-system. Because in the short term many readers may belong to or be affected by governments and aid agencies, Chapters 9, 10, and 11 study in detail those aspects of such organizations that work against participation and, where possible, suggest how individuals could seek change. But first the rhetoric of major donor agencies must be assessed against the real workings of the world-system of which they are so much a part. It is to the fundamental contradictions between the world-system and true human development that the next four chapters now turn.

2

Development:
The View from
Organizational Washington

To move from the abstract processes encompassed by the world-system framework and its participatory development alternative to the real world of people, commerce, wars, governments, and other weighty concerns is sobering. There is no small chasm between Wall Street or the International Monetary Fund (IMF) on the one hand and the slums of Calcutta and the villages of rural Zaire on the other. Some people in the former universe shift millions of dollars about on a routine basis. Most people in the latter situation could not conceive of such a sum; many of them cannot worry about much more than the next meal. The next four chapters try to lay bare the bridges and processes that make the Wall Street banker and Indian street beggar part of a system.

The word "system" is so abused now in so many disciplines that some concrete picture is in order. This book is centrally concerned with development in the capitalist world-system, comprised of different sizes of governments, corporations, parastatals, and multinational entities that act primarily through imperfect market mechanisms. The experiences of the Soviet, Chinese, East European, and Vietnamese models of command economies will become more germane as I begin to explore in Chapter 6 how participatory development interacts with different kinds of political and economic superstructures.

AID FLOWS IN THE LARGER CONTEXT

A concrete picture of the world-system is one of unequal and uneven growth in the jerky manner of long historical cycles. The short-term view is one of flows of money, trade, aid, and weapons. This chapter is about the larger organizational environment of aid flows, particularly American foreign aid flows. To put such flows in initial perspective one must first see how small they are in the total macroeconomic and institutional universe.

World monetary flows are now in aggregate unknowable and out of control. On top of a turbulent pyramid rests the Bank for International Settlements (BIS), the $50 billion central bank for the central banks of most developed countries. The BIS dates from 1930 and sits in Basel, Switzerland as a unique and secret quasi-private institution. It manages about 10 percent of the world's $340 billion (October 1980) in official reserves, serves to link East and West monetarily, makes short-term secret loans to central banks, and generally maintains the short-term monetary security of the world-system (*Wall Street Journal*, October 10, 1980). Beneath the BIS sit the national banks. Complementing the BIS is the post-World War II creation in Washington — the IMF. The IMF plays the more direct role of global economic policeman and medium-term government creditor. Its role is explored in detail in Chapter 5.

These institutions together create a remarkably laissez-faire atmosphere for the operations and expansion of private transnational banks. Unlimited freedom is often used irresponsibly. The best recent studies on the banks (Crough, 1979 and the UN Centre on Transnational Corporations, 1980) reveal how incomplete and outdated public knowledge remains. Several trends look most ominous for human development. Many Third World countries have borrowed more than they are likely to be able to repay. A number of multinational giants like Citibank and Chase Manhattan have made an increasing percentage of their profits in Third World operations and do not wish to lose their loans. Spurred by modern technology, lending in the Eurodollar market accelerated during the 1970s; at this writing total Eurodollar credits have crept over one trillion dollars. Even less regulated are offshore banking subsidiaries like those in the Cayman Islands and the Bahamas. It is quite clear, in sum, that the world's poor, indeed nearly all of the world's citizens, are structurally excluded from any voice in the use of a vast proportion of the world's liquid financial assets.

World trade flows in aggregate also dwarf the resources defined as directly developmental. In 1979, for example, the IMF chronicled total world exports of $1.564 trillion; of this total the oil exporting countries accounted for $213.4 billion, and the nonoil developing countries about $260.8 billion. International trade, by its inherent size and expense, is beyond the effective control of the world's poor.

Outlays for military expenditures are another element of a world-system that soaks up the world's resources while maintaining the relative or complete exclusion of most of its citizens. Military expenditures, as Galtung (1980) and others have shown so well, are particularly perverse. They crystallize power imbalances, are universally controlled and used by large power concentrations, spread inherently nonparticipatory and authoritarian education, and produce very little reinvestable social surplus. In 1978 national governments wasted about $480 billion in this fashion; by 1981, the figure was $550 billion (Sivard, 1981), and it continues to climb today.

In the same year of 1978, official bilateral and multilateral assistance to the developing countries on a concessional basis was about $30 billion. Organization for Economic Cooperation and Development (OECD) figures showed investments, loans, and other nonconcessional transfers totaled another $70 billion (Lewis, 1979: 66). It is therefore a tiny percentage of total international flows that are customarily viewed as development aid. Certainly the end use of some part of international trade is developmental in nature. Some proportion of Third World government budget outlays also represent actual development expenditure rather than personal consumption or bureaucratic corruption. Whatever the figures and the expressed intentions of those involved, 800-1,200 million people are rather completely excluded from development and deprived of basic human needs. It is therefore incumbent on those interested to see that the meager resources now available are used not simply with far greater efficiency but with far greater educational impact. It is not the resource transfer that will ultimately matter but the catalytic quality of the education involved in the development process.

How that education is molded then becomes the crucial question. If resources are inefficiently used, power maldistributed, and people starving, there must be educational and political forces creating and sustaining such results. It is easy to blame dictators, bureaucrats, and monopoly capitalists. That does not mean, however, that donor agencies are necessarily doing the best they can under adverse circumstances. For aid agencies, both public and private, have been very slow to recognize that they exist in the world-system as modern organizations, with all of the complexities that both of those concepts imply. The inhabitants of the World Bank, AID, and other agencies do not operate in an isolated universe populated only by poor people in the Third World. A collection of people with good intentions and even some relevant education, assembled into the social form called an organization, does not inevitably result in an entity that can actually fulfill a mandate calling for aiding the participatory development of poor and marginal people in alien cultures.

It is therefore appropriate to begin with the immediate organizational environment of donor agencies to see what incentives the organizations' sponsors or funders provide. The World Bank is commonly viewed as the principal teacher of economic development in the world today. The U.S. bilateral agency, AID, directly backed by the power of the United States, produces the second most powerful lesson in global development education. Separately and together they largely determine the ideology and operational model of a host of UN and regional agencies. By subcontracting they mold or control dozens of private groups and consulting firms. Thus to understand their overall behavior one must first study the organizational environment they share in Washington. Specifically what do the functioning of the executive and legislative branches of the U.S. government suggest for participatory development?

This discussion will focus on the nature of development politics in the 1970s and what it implies for the 1980s and beyond. Foreign aid as a Cold War weapon in the 1950s and as a growth tool in the 1960s has been the subject of several previous works. In a valuable 1973 study, Packenham showed the parallels between the United States' own exceptional development heritage and the assumptions it has applied overseas since World War II. Americans believed and still hold to four propositions: (1) change and development are easy; (2) all good things (capitalism and democracy) go together; (3) radicalism and revolution are bad; and (4) distributing power is more important than accumulating power. These ideas do not relate well to poor, new, and unstable states experimenting with political and economic models. The history of this struggle between U.S. political philosophy and practical reality overseas (see Packenham, 1973; White, 1974; Brookfield, 1975; and Wolfe, 1980), is beyond the scope of this work, but it will be seen that development spokesmen in the late 1970s have not adopted new philosophical and analytical approaches consistent with the participatory rhetoric that began to gain vogue after 1966 and flowered in the 1973 U.S. congressional mandate called New Directions. What is of most concern here is the real operational response to the new participatory rhetoric, first in Washington and then (in Chapter 3) in the field, and what this implies for the future of global development.

DONOR AGENCIES WITHIN THE U.S. EXECUTIVE: STRUCTURE, PROCESS, AND CULTURE

To understand how aid agencies are directed in Washington, it might be well to begin by examining the structural setting of AID in the U.S. government and the decision-making processes that determine AID loans and U.S. votes on World Bank loans. AID, despite some changes, remains a de facto part of the Department of State. Some AID matters are determined in a nonstructured fashion inside the State Department; AID, as one subsystem within State, deals with State's regional bureaus or country desks or other department officials. Other matters have become the concern of two interagency entities, the National Advisory Council (NAC) and the Development Coordinating Committee (DCC). This institutional structure was reshaped by the 1979 addition of the new umbrella International Development Cooperation Agency (IDCA), a subject to be returned to.

The oldest of these interagency committees is the NAC, which has been around in roughly the same form since 1945. In its own words it

is responsible for coordinating United States participation in the international financial institutions and the policies and practices of all agencies of the U.S. Government which make, or participate in making, foreign loans or which engage in foreign financial, exchange, or monetary transactions (NAC, 1978: 105).

The NAC is composed of the chief officials of the State, Treasury, and Commerce Departments, the Federal Reserve Board, and the Export-Import Bank. Designated alternates, U.S. representatives of the World Bank, IMF, and regional banks, and a staff committee also participate in the work of the NAC. Other government departments enter on specific issues.

Senior government officials cannot allocate time to regular meetings. NAC formal sessions are infrequent, as need arises — some five to ten times a year. A typical decision-making process, called an "action," is carried out by polling the agencies represented; that took place 816 times in fiscal year 1976 (FY76) and 726 times in FY77. The staff committee, lawyers and economists appointed by the agencies represented, does the routine research and writing and meets weekly.

With the advent of the DCC in the mid-1970s and now with the arrival of IDCA, the substantive responsibilities of NAC have diminished in some areas. A review of its annual report, a public document, specifies them. NAC is now concerned primarily with the largest monetary and policy questions: international financial institution (IFI) borrowing and capitalizations, annual budgets, and policy matters like potential IFI charter changes. The Treasury Department, whose secretary traditionally chairs the NAC, has not, however, lost significant power, as will be seen.

The Development Coordinating Committee (DCC) originated with the Foreign Assistance Act of 1973 and began to operate in earnest in the spring of 1975. Its first annual report, *Development Issues*, which went to the Congress in May 1975, was not subtle about why the DCC was needed.

> The U.S. Government policy-making process, almost inevitably, concentrates on developed countries. When it does focus on less-developed countries, there is a tendency to highlight relatively short-term political considerations or partial perceptions of national security interests. The economic development aspects of our decisions frequently are examined superficially, if at all (DCC, 1975: 3).

With the creation of an interagency unit chaired by the Administration of AID (now by the head of IDCA) it was thought that development needs might become more central to government policy.

A structure like that of NAC was set up. AID, State, Treasury, Commerce, Labor, Agriculture, OPIC (Overseas Private Investment Corporation), Action, Office of Management and Budget (OMB), and the Office of Special Trade Representatives take part. Full committee meetings involve assistant secretaries or above and occur 10-15 times a year. Typical issues considered are country strategy papers and food aid. Most of the DCC work is done by 6-8 subcommittees, of which 3 have been particularly active — those on food aid, health, and multilateral aid. They meet every two to four weeks, depending on the interests of the chair. The staff is supplied by the agencies involved. Treasury, which retains its major say over U.S. policy on the loans, is the only department that applies more than a handful of people to DCC activities apart from the annual report, *Development Issues*, prepared by AID for the Congress.

This brief sketch of the structure and processes of U.S. global economic planning inside the Executive branch during the mid and late 1970s is presented in order to raise some larger issues of systems analysis that bear on the nature and quality of a participatory development outcome. It is not enough to agree with a March 1979 House Committee staff report that "there is little evidence that creation of the DCC has added any cohesiveness or worldwide strategy planning to the U.S. approach to bilateral and multilateral assistance" (U.S. House of Reps. Appropriations Committee, 1981a: 87). Cohesion, coordination, and similar verbiage are bureaucratic words that obfuscate. The question is, can these members of the national managerial system, what Scott and Hart (1979) call the significant people and their professional supporting cast, sitting in comfortable Washington offices, relate to the issues of participatory development in any operational sense?

It would appear at first glance that even the best intentioned would not have the time. Too few people and too few hours are allocated to understanding how any World Bank or AID project actually fits into the local environment of a specific country. Such an analysis, to meet even the most minimal professional standards of a caring human being who is making decisions affecting other human beings, would require empathy, the equivalent of at least an M.A. training in area studies at a good university, and a couple of weeks exploring the cream of relevant multidiscipline material on the specific country and theme. Time does not permit field visits.

If, as is normal, several country strategy papers or country loan documents are scheduled for one meeting, it would be impossible for one individual in a week or two to provide an independent assessment of the developmental analysis in a World Bank or AID document. What can happen does. Papers glide through the system, and most of the time most of the data and assessments go unchallenged. This all presumes that the staff is composed of people capable of professional foreign area studies analysis. Sadly this is not usually the case. As Vietnam, Angola, Nicaragua, and Iran have demonstrated again and again, the average inhabitants of the U.S. foreign policy bureaucracies are lawyers and neoclassical economists. Neither training encourages one to realize fully that foreigners are different. Foreigners have different world models. Successful cross-cultural communication, participatory development, for example, implies a recognition and acceptance of this reality. There is little in the training of a lawyer or an economist, if not buttressed by very different life experiences or education, to overcome the ethnocentrism generic in mainstream Western education and values. Indeed, lawyers and economists have traditionally been principal culture bearers of that world model. It would be unlikely that, without great incentives, they would begin asking the kinds of questions originating in anthropology, political economy, world-systems studies, and organizational studies that are inherent to understanding the operational nature of participatory development.

These questions of professional education are endemic not just to the staffs of the NAC and the DCC but to the personnel of nearly every aid institution touched upon in this book. These people are, however, appointed and continued in employment by superiors. Obviously they are doing what the superiors, in this case department secretaries and their assistant secretaries, desire. Such GS (Government Service) 17 and 18 officials do not provide staff time and learning time either to produce or to read detailed, critical reports on the gap between what AID and the World Bank are doing and what authentic development calls for. Either these officials do not know what they are mandated to do, will not rock the boat, or do not care.

A more serious question is that the larger political system rewards this behavior. Specifically, it sanctions the appointment of managers, as opposed to leaders, to head large organizations such as State or Treasury. Most other important individuals and social forces, themselves part of the bureaucratic culture do not see the true implications of this choice. Certainly the Congress and the media do not make such distinctions when viewing or voting on nominees to these positions. Citizens rarely intrude on what is seen as a president's prerogative. The nominating process is rarely more than a ritual. The result has become the regular appointment of a managerial class. For the advancement of participatory development one must understand how managers view their own role, that of subordinates (the professionals) and that of insignificant people in the organization. The last matter will be a clear indication of how managers will think about the peripheral poor in the Third World who are supposed to take part in and benefit from foreign aid processes.

The overall nature of organizations and their basic imperatives of survival, control, and growth as centrally antagonistic to the autonomy and liberation of human development has been noted in Chapter 1. Managers, no matter how decent and well intentioned, are to a large extent imprisoned by these organizational imperatives. The organization needs managers to coordinate specializations, make grand strategy decisions, and deal with crises and threats. Organizations do not provide the climate or incentive for managerial creativity beyond that. For all the talk of an increasingly complex and interdependent world, management science in particular and social science in general have not come to grips with the mental or physical needs of managers to deal with such crises (Scott and Hart, 1979).

The search for superior performance is likely to take on not participatory but elitist and totalitarian dimensions. The U.S. government response has been to facilitate the identity of a managerial class of GS 16-18 appointees. Management schools and seminars reinforce this. No incentive exists for managers to communicate directly or frequently with the people the organization is supposed to be helping. Imagine what might happen if senior aid officials had to live in a Calcutta slum or Bas-Zaire village for a month each year without access to any but local amenities and institutions. The powerlessness of marginal groups and the imperative nature of participatory development would become clear. Instead managers are culturally and institutionally divorced from the products of their organizational efforts. This is particularly unfortunate in the foreign aid business, because there is rarely if ever any political feedback from the affected population in foreign aid as opposed to domestic programs. Now that organizational culture has prevailed in Washington to the extent that conventional wisdom routinely accepts the appointment of managers to posts where they have no substantive qualifications, the system has at the top no arbiter of output quality.

This might be thought too strong a generalization. Professionals working under managers still try to establish and maintain standards. What happens in most organizations, however, especially those with products hard to measure like foreign aid projects, is a process of homogenization and deprofessionalization. The result is that paper-pushing members of a Third Culture triumph; they are neither scientist nor humanist. This process has been best analyzed by Frances Moore in a highly provocative April 1979 *New York Times* op-ed. Another way of describing this is that professionals, in order to survive and prosper, absorb a sequence of beliefs of the managers' credo: the manager's intentions are decent; organizational welfare means the manager's control must grow; the job gives life meaning; the management process is universal; education must be made vocational for the social good; and management functions always take precedence over specialists (Scott and Hart, 1979: 141-60).

I have met and witnessed these conflicts for years and believe that many readers will recognize from their own life experiences specific episodes. I still remember the puzzled anguish of mid-level career CIA analyst Samuel Adams trying to explain in a mid-1974 House Foreign Affairs Committee hearing how he could not get his superiors to accept his conclusion that the Khmer Rouge army was twice as big as previously thought. Organizational culture determines in sum that, while it would be most improbable for new managers to enforce successfully substantive new standards of participatory project design and implementation, it would be comparably unlikely that mid-level professionals could get such a model widely accepted in the organization against managerial opposition. This same mutually defeating cultural conflict is duplicated in all the other institutions that affect the donor agencies in Washington.

It is worth repeating here that human welfare is diminished not only by the culture conflict between managers and professionals but also by the overall attitudes of both toward the powerless and insignificant people beneath them. It is difficult to imagine how a large organization can approach development in a participatory fashion when it is at the same time seeking in a paternalistic fashion to mold people into submission through what amounts to threats and bribes. If human beings are thought to be and treated as malleable to suit organizational imperatives, it quite naturally follows that, contrary to organizational rhetoric, there cannot be innate human rights and needs. A few policy statements from the top will not undo fundamental bureaucratic norms.

To bring this theoretical portrait of the culture of different actors in the larger organizational environment back to the specific work of the two interagency committees at hand, consider the discussion of what the DCC termed a participatory development strategy, which appears on pages 106 to 108 of its May 1979 *Development Issues*. As evidenced in these annuals the degree of analytic sophistication about development grew after 1975. There was much more awareness in 1979, for example, that basic human needs constitute a goal, but that goals and operational strategies are two different things. In many other areas, however, policy and practical progress trailed far behind intellectual advances in the independent literature. The May 1979 discussion of participatory development used phrases like "improved access" and "farmers to participate in decisions affecting them." It recognized that growth and equity were compatible. On the other hand, reading through the two pages one was left with an intellectual amalgam, a homogenization of growth with equity, integrated rural development, and participation concepts. As guidance to the Congress or to career professionals it was scarcely operational.

AID AS A PRISONER OF THE NATIONAL SECURITY STATE

Donor agencies face not only the constraints created by the modern social form, organization, but also the more specific goals of at least nine other departments and agencies in the United States Executive branch: the National Security Council (NSC), the CIA, State, Treasury, Defense, Commerce, Agriculture, Justice and the OMB. There is quite obviously nothing in the mandates of these institutions to indicate that the enhancement of participation by the marginal poor in Third World development should be an operational priority. Each has varied private interests and parochial concerns that create far different priorities. But one overriding credo dominates the world model and operational philosophy of the most important of these agencies and poses a constant and unavoidable impediment to participatory development and human welfare.

That theme is national security. It is central to the policy rhetoric and actions of the CIA, the NSC, State, and Defense and is frequently raised elsewhere. Yet it is impossible to get a substantive discussion in Washington on what it means. In May 1979 Robert Macnamara said again what all who care about human development must grapple with. Our definition of security is out of date (indeed was it ever up to date?). "We cannot build a secure world upon a foundation of human misery" (*New York Times*, May 5, 1979, Reston op ed). The discussion has to go further than pontification. Why, for instance, did the *Washington Post*, the *New York Times*, the World Bank, and others espousing humanist norms support the initiatives of Western states to coordinate military and economic aid to Zaire to maintain President Mobutu in 1977 and 1978, exchanging continued starvation and malnutrition of 60-80 percent of its people (20-24 million out of 26-27 million) for some supposed continuity of Western cobalt imports?

Never mind for a moment the specific contradictions: cobalt supplies were interrupted and the price went through the roof anyway; and the future looks no brighter (Gran, 1978 and 1979). The fact remains that the various U.S. Executive Branch agencies including AID, along with the World Bank and the global financial community, were and remain willing to throw scarce development resources at one of the world's worst-run and most nonparticipatory economies. This they call development in Western security interests. The precedents set are appalling. Since it is quite obvious most decision makers have little idea what the world of Zaire is like, it must be some notion of national security that is at stake in their minds. What then does such a policy choice really mean?

At base such policy decisions are shadow plays in a war. It is not a war between the United States and others, but between two major world views in the United States contesting for alternative futures. One is the view that led the United States and the West into and through the Vietnam War. It now clings to an ideological past of an essentially bipolar, permanently antagonistic universe. It bitterly seeks to replay all of global policy in a mythical psychohistorical matrix to deny and overturn the historical verdict symbolized by Vietnam. The resulting contradictions between rhetorical ideals and actual policies in such a world model remain too painful to face in open intellectual debate. Such debate has thus been avoided.

A second view, rarely represented clearly in the media or in policy-making circles, is that of a humanist vision of a just world order of relatively egalitarian, participatory societies with no unbalanced concentrations of political or economic power. It was representatives of this view who "won" the actual Vietnam debate momentarily in Washington and in Vietnam. But, as was so ably painted by Roger Morris in the October 1977 *Harper's*, those of this view have since largely lost the symbolic debate in Washington (and the policy debate in Vietnam). The key to understanding these results – the war itself, as well as the slow philosophical and practical advance of participatory development – is the misnamed globalist world model based on the ideology of national security.

What national security spokesmen have been asserting for nearly 40 years in episodes like Vietnam and Zaire is that there is an empirical and operational meaning to the phrase "national security"; upon this one can, with intellectual, constitutional, and moral integrity, base political and economic policies. It is not so. Beneath a thin layer of rhetoric there is an intellectual vacuum. The rhetoric is made up of ideological platitudes and myths that are a skillful means of preserving and expanding the world-system. They are also a very severe threat to real human needs.

It should be obvious at the start that there must be one or more reasons why national security is not seriously defined. It is certainly difficult to do so in this age of scientific advance. No superficial statement would cover all cases. There is no easy verification except in extremity. But are these really the core reasons? It would appear more correct to conclude that the groups, forces, and institutions that most frequently use the rhetoric for their own ends want an amorphous concept precisely in order to have the flexibility to expand its application whenever it is ideologically, bureaucratically, or politically convenient to do so.

It is less understandable why the media, the political process, the courts, academia, and average citizens have accepted this charade for so long. Certainly it helps one's short-term career and personal needs to go along with the status quo and defend the past. But it does not help the country. Given the present ecological decay, the effect of monopoly power on human welfare, the inappropriateness of the global structure of production for human needs, the totalitarian potential of the triumph of organizational imperatives, and an escalating threat of nuclear destruction, one would think that most Americans should be involved in formulating an ever more creative and intelligent definition of national security. That the processes of departicipation in this society are not even a subject of discussion here does not bode well for enhancing participation by the poor in other societies.

True national security demands accepting the fundamental nature of history as it is, one of change. By developing a shared consensus of historical reality our society could begin the process of defining and developing security in a changing world. Unhappily, many people who went to school in the 1930s, 1940s, 1950s, and even the 1960s still think history is a narrative of names and dates. The state of the art in this discipline is, however, now very different. It is the paradigm of world-system analyses, history as processes evolving in a definable series of interrelationships as suggested in Chapter 1. As the rest of the country ought well to know, Washington bureaucracies do not structure activities to allow much reading of anything but their own paperwork. Would you, the reader, go to a doctor who had not looked at medical advances since 1940 or 1950 to define and prescribe for your security of health?

Given a reestablishment of an analytic consensus of where we are in history, the following issues, if professionally explored, would begin to yield the outlines of an operational definition of national security:

1. Granted the hostile potential of any major or nuclear power, what specific technical areas of weapons knowledge, production, and deployment can and should be classified and by what criteria?

2. What specific classes of data does world-system analysis require for an optimal understanding of historic change and our maximum security? Is the U.S. allocating resources and collecting data on peripheral or irrelevant concerns; does one need to know the personal habits and foibles of foreign leaders if one is not going to interfere in or manipulate the affairs of others? If the last answer is no, do we need case officers, moles, and the resulting human corruption that mocks our stated ideals?

3. Are short-term (5 years) or long-term (25 years) definitions of national security synonymous and, if not, how does one defend

the priority of either?

4. Given the political and intellectual abilities of the consumers of intelligence, is the system not misbalanced with too much data collection and not enough quality analysis? On what criteria can such judgments be based? Can a large bureaucracy muster or allow the creativity we need for survival in an ever more complex world? (There is much reason for pessimism.)

5. Does any definition of national security and any analysis matter if the people at the top do not get the product or do not have the time or education to understand it when they do?

6. Against what criteria can one measure to what degree the balancing or oversight activities of the legislative branch are sufficient or effective?

7. On what logical grounds does personal or institutional embarrassment constitute a threat to national as opposed to individual security?

What this easily expandable list suggests is that no public or private group of citizens has done the kind or degree of analysis necessary to give operational meaning to the term national security. Shue (1980), Johansen (1980), and Lovins and Lovins (1982) have made a start. But at this time it would be at best premature and at worst inane to assert, for example, that cable traffic stamped confidential by some bureaucrat following a hoary ritual represents, if leaked, a de facto and de jure threat to national security. That is not to argue that a few specific kinds of material ought not to be kept classified. But the 20-24 million starving or malnourished Zairians, subject of such policy documents as the classified January 1979 country development strategy statement by the State Department and, simultaneously, trapped at the bottom of one of the most exploitative and corrupt segments of the world-system, are but one of many real world situations demanding a paradigm shift in national security ideology.

ADDITIONAL CONSTRAINTS POSED BY SPECIFIC EXECUTIVE AGENCIES

Each agency brings to DCC, NAC, and other aid-related meetings its own additional limitations and desires. The National Security Council, with 20 to 30 eager-beaver workaholics trying to cover the whole world, wants to have a say on almost all aid packages. It would be too simplistic to say the only NSC concern is security. What is frightening about its staff's frenetic paper pushing is that they read too much of what the government produces and not enough of other, more independent and important research. Consider the cumulative impact. One NSC staff member was quoted in 1978: "In these jobs, we work off our intellectual capital. We don't have the time to think new thoughts." Brzezinski admitted bouncing from issue to issue: "You don't have enough time to reflect on long-term issues" (Elizabeth Drew in the *New Yorker*, May 1, 1978.) The kind of mind and the kind of work style that is involved in endless crisis management creates as a result a world that is coping super-ficially with ephemera. It is not a world that is planning processes of human development for real human security. That such an agency is at the apex of the foreign policy apparatus and has the president's ear every morning says much about U.S. society and its potential.

One does not normally associate CIA activities with development policy making. Yet such activities should be for the incentives they create. As a citizen never privy to the span of CIA research and analysis, I can make only deductions. These seem warranted. Concern with who holds political power at the national level of a foreign society, their "friendliness" toward us, and thus our supposed security, leads the CIA to comparatively elitist and primar-ily political emphases. Much less attention goes to understanding who holds economic and social power at various levels of society and how stratification is maintained. It is clear that aspects of the cultural conflicts of modernization bearing on economics and politics are quite alien in Washington, as the official response to the Iranian crises so well documented.

The CIA does not use a great deal of its resources in finding out whether common people are participating very effectively in the economy. U.S. leaders and average citizens have only the odd news-paper story, such as "Millions of Peruvians Starving — Hunger Kills a Child Every Eight Minutes" (*Los Angeles Times*, October 18, 1979), to tell them where human misery might ignite historic change. As the appendix of this book illustrates, there are ways to be better informed than the president's NSC or CIA aide who reads an IMF report on an ongoing "stabilization" program. But senior govern-ment officials, deluged with political reporting, simply perpetuate their passé assumptions about the significance of the state structure in comparison to changes in the mode of production. Kissinger's incredible economic myopia and his continued legitimization as a coherent policy spokesman on any issue is merely the most obvious example. In sum, beyond the questions of what matters are classified and what national security means, participatory development is hindered by the dependence of top policy makers on so much data and analysis from large organizations with very alien and in many ways antagonistic research agendas.

The impact of the particular institutional imperatives of the State Department on development cannot be reduced to any short set of general theses. For the day-to-day relations involve the interplay of several different subsystems often with different and conflicting policy goals: the regional bureaus, policy planning, human rights, politico-military affairs, and economic and business affairs. Paper-pushing rituals in most bureaus prevent much new learning time of any sort. Modern organizational culture has triumphed. Not surprisingly dissent is not rewarded. Yet while some bureaus in State could be expectedly hostile to the peripheral poor and some might work with more neutral preconceptions, there is at least one bureau that has the policy mandate to become an effective advocate of participatory development.

Contrary to the most ethnocentric interests inherent in representing the United States abroad that are common to most bureaus, the Bureau of Human Rights and Humanitarian Affairs has the formal humanist mandate to advance participation in U.S.-funded programs. The April 1977 speech by Secretary of State Vance defined economic as well as political rights. Thanks to the work of Amnesty International and others, policy makers are quite conscious of the latter. State Department concern for powerless, marginal, exploited, and starving people, deliberately denied access to development possibilities by corrupt and self-centered elites, would be a major stride forward for global human welfare. If the United States proclaims principles, it should stand for them on a consistent basis.

Such a heretical thesis must of course bring to mind the reality that, food aid aside, at least half of U.S. bilateral assistance program each year goes not to programs of development assistance under the New Directions mandate but to programs under the rubric of Security Supporting Assistance (SSA) with the most meaningless legislative instructions imaginable. For FY78 AID spent $1.15 billion on economic aid programs, $242 million on operating expenses,

$441 million in international organization programs (not counting the multilateral banks), and $2.22 billion in Security Supporting Assistance. For FY80 about $2 billion was proposed for SSA and another $2 billion for these other programs of development aid.

The vast bulk of SSA funding since FY75 has gone to Israel, Egypt, and adjacent countries in an effort to buy peace. To question it is to appear to attack both peace and Israel, not a viable posture in Washington. Leaving aside the internal validity of the policy to produce a durable peace, consider the external precedents set. Secretary Kissinger vastly expanded a funding channel over which Congress allowed itself little or no oversight. Great pressure to expend funds leads to large capital projects of a technocratic rather than participatory nature.

The scale and nature of such programs make it impossible for the State Department or the Congress to allocate money to countries on the basis of defensible developmental principles as opposed to political whimsy and expediency. Virtually every country below a certain per capita income seems to merit some support. Socially responsible developmental behavior is often no more rewarded than outright thievery. Without more political will and intellectual creativity than that by the donor, Third World elites are being given little external incentive to use resources for the welfare of the poor. Standards have to be set. What can the people of Mozambique, more closely meeting the humanist development norms of New Directions than probably any other government in the Third World, think of U.S. foreign aid in light of U.S. ethical and constitutional heritage?

More serious investigation needs to be done on the State Department's role in development on a bureau-by-bureau basis using extensive interviewing. Such an exploration should also include the Defense and Treasury Departments. In its annual congressional presentation books, Defense discusses various programs of military sales, training, and grants within a consistent national security model. The need for "stability" and good relations along with assertions of "strategic importance" fill its discussions. There is never any thought given to the equivalence of "stability" with the status quo, the perpetuation of elites by the exclusion of the poor, a process I call structural aggression and one that is the antithesis of participatory development. It does not speak well of the Congress, the media, or the American people that they do not possess the degree of citizenship necessary to see and face this fundamental contradiction.

The impact of the Treasury Department on development is to emphasize neoclassical economic concerns, banking principles, and U.S. commercial interests. Its major role in and superficial handling of the U.S. judgment of multilateral aid projects, assessed previously and detailed by the Senate Governmental Affairs Committee (1979: 48-51 esp.), does not hold out hope for participatory development. Treasury is concerned with issues like rate of return. Mainstream economics, as an ideology not a science, does not incorporate most elements of the social relations of production. Treasury, replete with classical economists, has not yet understood the correlation between worker participation and worker productivity or the question of scale of resource application to the scale of human need. It would not be reasonable for one adjunct of an essentially domestically focussed department to develop or muster the cross-cultural, historical, and multidisciplined perspectives necessary to advance participatory development overseas. The gap between the macroeconomic concerns of most of Treasury's work and the microeconomic processes of participatory development is quite wide. In the coming age of scarcity the two paths may well merge, as some of the theoretical goals like higher productivity per unit of resources, are similar. But moving from theory to practice may well take a decade, as education now progresses.

Much more could be detailed about the specific goals of other Executive Branch departments and how they impinge on participatory development. Commerce seeks to advance U.S. trade and investment, which often, if not inevitably, run counter to self-reliant development models. It typically fosters quite inappropriate technological transfer and quite unequal exchanges. Those corporate interests most able to benefit from aid activities may not be those that a Third World society could most benefit from interacting with. Few people try to distinguish the difference. The Agriculture Department still dumps surpluses through the Food for Peace program into Third World countries with all the corruption and disincentives that entails. The literature on this is massive; see Lappé and Collins (1979), Ball (1981), and Cadett (1981) for bibliography. Even the Justice Department, through its support of police forces under Drug Enforcement Agency aegis, adds to the forces of stability and security; getting people out of drug growing would imply giving them more productive and rewarding alternatives, treating the causes, not the symptoms, of the problem.

One more part of the Executive Branch could have major impact on development policy. That is the Office of Management and Budget. Each year a small group of OMB officials judges the funding levels appropriate for what the departments propose. The same contradictions are repeated in miniature. Funding is provided for widely varied and antithetical development, growth, political and ideological goals. No principles are apparent. The Inter-American Foundation, an independent, long-time successful practitioner of participatory development, is regularly funded. But budgetary constraints in the late 70s stymied proposals for a parallel African Development Foundation or for research on participatory development by a small UN agency. OMB is a small agency that could escape many organizational imperatives, if its leadership or the White House were willing. Part of the problem for OMB is the difficulty of moving from a defensive to a creative posture, but another part of it is a testament to the strength of bureaucratic culture even in relatively small decentralized organizations.

THE LIMITS OF INTERNAL REFORM: IDCA IN 1979

Some of the problems just chronicled, along with a number of other technical and practical constraints to development assistance became the focus of a congressional reform effort in 1977-78. This resulted ultimately in the passage in summer 1979 of an Executive Branch proposal for an International Development Cooperation Agency which came officially into being in October 1979. It is not the first such reform or new name in the history of foreign assistance. Without a detailed chronology of various congressional committee actions, best explored in work of the U.S. Senate Governmental Affairs Committee (1979a and b), it is still worth seeing if the issues raised and the structural changes resulting will lower any of the barriers to participatory development.

The Executive Branch analysis by Henry Owen to the Senate of April 27, 1979 raised these problems. No single U.S. official coordinated an overall government policy on development. Other economic decisions were often made with no consideration of aid issues. Executive Branch officials before Congress on aid matters were not in an authoritative position. Science, technology, and long-term development research were being given short shrift.

The critique of the General Accounting Office (GAO), given by its comptroller Elmer Staats on May 1, 1979, centered on these issues. AID, chairing and staffing the DCC, has not been viewed as a neutral "honest broker" by other agencies involved in the DCC; AID has instead been seen as pursuing its own agenda. GAO also saw the AID Administrator lacking the stature to exercise this coordinating responsibility well. Focus of activity has been to review projects and policies within programs rather than to consider relative merits of different programs. GAO found the IDCA proposal a marginal improvement in some areas; but the reform did not well define the distribution of control over multilateral aid or provide the number of personnel to do the job.

It was this question of jurisdiction that occupied the most attention in the April 1979 Senate staff report *U.S. Participation in the Multilateral Development Banks* and in congressional debates over IDCA. The Senate Governmental Affairs Committee report argued inter alia that Treasury was the wrong agency to oversee the multilaterals, that 15 professionals were far too few for serious oversight, and that the time allotted was too little. Different interest groups then joined the congressional debate as Treasury, Agriculture, and others sought to preserve turf.

Questions of turf remained central through the remainder of the legislative process. Unsurprisingly IDCA was born as a series of political compromises. Jurisdiction over the multilaterals was divided, with Treasury overseeing monetary and macroeconomic project issues and IDCA reviewing development project issues. A new technology institute and the Overseas Private Investment Corporation joined AID under the IDCA umbrella. But food aid programs, IMF issues, and other matters did not. The initial staff of IDCA was quite small, some 30-40 people drawn primarily from AID. They were lawyers and economists with broad, amorphous policy and budget mandates. There was nothing to indicate that IDCA would not be a slightly larger and more efficient version of the DCC.

Looked at from the vantage point of participatory development, the situation offers no initial reason for optimism. Neither branch of government involved in the reform gave any thought to the appropriateness of the organizational form and content in relation to development quality. It is more than questionable that lawyers or economists are relevant to participatory development. It is difficult to imagine how any handful of people with such traditional educations could even raise the appropriate questions, never mind gain any sense of the answers in the time allowed. The failure to give IDCA the personnel and mandate for real, as opposed to paper, evaluation of development projects represents a major lost opportunity. Nowhere now in the U.S. system is there the capacity to establish standards of development quality — how to measure it and how to enhance it. Until there is such a feedback system, participatory development in large donor agencies can be little more than the dream of isolated individuals and their own small attempts.

Finally it must be said of this attempt at system reform, as of almost any other, that it is hard to see how people inside the system can alone challenge its basic operating assumptions. An organization does not encourage its inhabitants to challenge its appropriateness as a social form for the task at hand. That would defy the prime organizational imperative of survival. Is it any wonder that public organizations cling so fiercely to the national security ideology and that people in organizations have such a hard time moving participatory development beyond the stage of rhetoric?

One might well dream that a set of individuals in an ideal organizational island like IDCA and possessing a fresh mandate could move other system actors toward behavior more suitable to participatory development. History suggests otherwise. Part of the reason is that there are even more cooks and ingredients in the development broth working against participatory development. The next part of this chapter turns to these actors, the ones outside the Executive Branch who provide additional disincentives and constraints for the global development system.

AID AND THE CONTRADICTIONS
OF ITS LEGISLATIVE MANDATE

The world of aid agencies in Washington outside the Executive Branch is more culturally, politically, and institutionally complicated. The activities of many groups and individuals bear on the global development process through legislative and educational efforts and through activity within the aid agency project cycle as consultant, contractor, or corporate supplier. Both private and humanitarian interests dilute the organizational imperatives and national security ideology prevalent in the Executive Branch. On the basis of events during the 1970s there is not great reason for optimism that these various, often conflicting, efforts will create the incentives for AID and the World Bank to adopt and implement participatory development. For what is needed is more than good intentions, a policy statement, an institution, and money.

The sections that follow attempt to illustrate this thesis by exploring some of the relevant contradictions of conventional Washington political and organizational culture. A first section explores the incentives created for AID and the World Bank by the amalgam that is congressional aid legislation. The additional limits of congressional culture and oversight rituals are then addressed. With more space one might explore the institutional adjuncts to Congress. A few comments would be in order on the overall development industry as it now supports the status quo or advances peripheral, nonprescriptive criticism; this industry includes public institutes, consulting firms, universities, the media, corporate suppliers, and critics. Here I shall focus on just the U.S. Congress to suggest the limits of any political oversight in Washington for real development quality in the Third World.

Matters of policy, procedures, ideology, and culture all affect the cumulative message that the U.S. Congress sends to AID every year. It would not be well founded to argue that changing foreign aid legislation would, in and of itself, bring more than marginal improvement in the climate for participatory development. But aid legislation, misconceived or contradictory, has created myriad opportunities for donor agency officials to pursue whatever policy is convenient. A reasonable place to start an analysis of the congressional contribution to foreign assistance would thus be *Legislation on Foreign Relations Through 1978* which presents (pp. 1-187) the Foreign Assistance Act as amended up to December 1978. Aid legislation in subsequent years did not modify the sections to be discussed here.

Part I, Chapter I of the act begins with Section 101, "General Policy," and Section 102, "Development Assistance Policy." Together they reveal the humanitarian spirit of the U.S. Congress and people. These two sections also reflect their utter confusion over how the world-system works, how poverty is created and sustained, and what would have to be done if poverty were to be ended or greatly diminished. The most important contradiction, as detailed in Chapter 1 is the prime congressional directive: you, large Executive Branch organization, go forth to alien lands and cultures and enhance the ability of the marginalized poor to participate in development. Generations of social programs run by large organizations at home have failed to do that for a significant number of our poor in the United States. Such a historical reality should create far more contemplation about the inherent appropriateness of large organizations overseas.

The second basic contradiction that multiple interests in Congress, as in the society as a whole, continue to espouse is that there is "an open and equitable international economic system" that our development policy should encourage poor countries to join. These countries know quite well that the world economy is not equitable. Large concentrations of public and private power, largely from core countries and now from OPEC as well, do not provide an environment where poor countries and poor people fare well. If the Congress really wants to achieve the first three policy goals of Section 101 – alleviate absolute poverty, promote conditions for self-sustained growth with equity, and enhance fulfillment of human rights – then sober reconsideration of many premises about this fourth policy goal (the international economic system) is in order.

One cannot elegantly reduce such an agenda to a few words, but central to such a discussion must be these issues. Despite the fact that more U.S. exports are usually beneficial to at least part of the U.S. economy, an export-led growth model is not an effective way to meet mass needs in a poor country. Most Third World nations may be better off to selectively delink themselves for a time from the more advanced economies. Despite the clear benefit to private banks and corporations of their presence in Third World countries, they do not normally create a cumulative economic, political, and sociocultural impact conducive to structuring production or using resources in ways conducive to the results the U.S. foreign aid legislators proclaim they seek. A third congressional premise is an assumption that Third World officials share humanitarian and participatory development goals rather than antagonistic bureaucratic, cultural, economic, and political motives of a more personal nature. Should donor agencies have to work with national, regional, or local governments that are hostile to the interests of the poor?

That these topics and other comparable matters are outside the bounds of permissible congressional discussion is both surprising and not surprising. Given that Congress represents the interests of people in a core society and reflects most consistently the short-term goals of the most powerful, it is not surprising. But if one actually reads the rhetoric of Sections 101 and 102, the several paragraphs of what "Congress finds" contain many themes supportive of the participatory development principles proposed in this book. In Section 102 one finds, for example: "Activities shall be emphasized that effectively involve the poor in development by expanding their access to the economy through services and institutions at the local level, increasing their participation in the making of decisions that affect their lives. . . ." If this is indeed the goal, Congress must raise questions of world-system analysis as suggested above.

Following the paragraphs of participatory rhetoric in Section 102, there are 12 principles enumerated which are supposed to be applied to achieve the development objectives of the preceding paragraphs. It is no wonder the Executive Branch is confused. Some of the principles do not logically relate to the goals and, in fact, would contribute to antithetical goals. In addition many of the principles are mutually conflicting. An Executive Branch official can find any policy guidance desired if he or she reads long enough. It will quickly be clear to such an official that Congress also does not insist upon the consistent application of a number of the principles. Nor does it say how to apply them. All this calls into question the utility of having such principles. Some specific examples are in order.

Principle 1, a series of participatory and democratic premises, includes this clause: aid "shall be concentrated in those countries that take positive steps to help themselves." If this were implemented, aid would have to go to places like Mozambique and Grenada. This would doubtless outrage some of the ilk of Senator Helms. But it would also put the world on notice that we really did intend to have aid help poor people in a participatory fashion. The power of example and real resource flows, combined with a comparable and active posture from the U.S. Executive Director of the World Bank, would, more than any other elite reform, advance participatory development. But nothing of the sort happens. State and AID divide up bilateral assistance according to friends, enemies, intrabureau politics, natural calamities, and arbitrary statistical choices. Congress with rare exception has ignored the issue or sought to alter allocations for the same reasons. The world can understand such a performance only as hypocrisy. It is one of the reasons why historical antagonisms of the Third World toward the West endure.

Principle 2 says development planning must be the responsibility of each sovereign country. The activities of the world-system actors, especially World Bank project papers and IMF stabilization packages, render such an assertion naive. Large organizations like AID, guided by control imperatives, are quite likely to move from collaborative to manipulative interactions. Principle 3 says support projects helping the poorest while helping the government enhance its ability to carry out such projects. It is not recognized that the interest of a government in reaching the poor is in order to tax them, not help them. Principle 4 tries to create the criteria for assessing a country's progress. AID's response over the years has been several papers saying: "It is too hard to do; we're working on it; and here are the criteria" (so many as to make none of them operational). AID judged correctly that congressional attention would wane, and it did. Congress must realize that no organization will create effective means of judging its own performance. That goes against nature. But absence of any real standards of evaluation puts all the rhetoric about helping people in the realm of sophistry.

Principle 5 continues the functional division of labor into problem areas, as does the main text of the Foreign Assistance Act as a whole. This greatly discourages a coherent systems attack on poverty by dividing social reality into artificial categories and focussing the mind on amorphous goals rather than concrete processes. Principle 6, promoting the inclusion of women in development, is redundant if participatory development is properly understood. Principle 7 calls for a strategy of efficient energy use without defining it. Soft energy paths is the participatory strategy and should have been mentioned if the subject had to be raised at all. Principles 8 and 9 restate U.S. cultural biases for private sector activities and its own private economic interests. The question for human development is not capitalism or socialism but the nature of the relationship between organizations and people.

One could continue such an exegesis of this text and the 150-200 pages of legislation following, but the central theses are, one hopes, clear. Congress has produced a moderately coherent policy statement promoting participatory development. It has provided little real guidance on designing, implementing, or evaluating such projects and has not sought or been able to judge AID's efforts constructively. Simultaneously Congress has added an amalgam of other foreign assistance language, some illogical and some contradictory, which provides sufficient cumulative flexibility for Executive Branch officials to continue to repackage and get funded many more traditional projects of a more technocratic and elitist nature. The question then becomes what else Congress does and does not do that helps to diminish the participatory potential of its core legislative mandate.

AID AND THE LIMITS OF CONGRESSIONAL OVERSIGHT

The literature on the congressional process in general and on Congress and foreign policy in particular is not very helpful to problems of participatory development. Work by people inside the system, such as articles in *Washington Monthly*, provide cultural slices without a larger understanding of systemic and historical forces. Efforts to date from outside viewers, most recently Franck and Weisband (1979), skim along the narrative surface, without any semblance of world-system analysis. What needs to be explored here is the interplay of cultural, legal, and institutional interests among Congress, its staff, and the Executive Branch that do so much to guide the annual ritual wherein foreign assistance funds are authorized and appropriated.

Some readers might wish a guide to the process first. The Executive Branch presents the Congress with a series of requests in February or March for funding for the fiscal year ending 18 months later, September 30. Until 1977 it had been June 30. The request is in the form of notebooks totalling several thousand pages. General policy and program statements, topical discussions, country situations, one-page discussions of new and ongoing projects, and statistical tables fill these notebooks. Physically they were about three to four times longer in FY80 than in FY75. Additional presentations come from Defense, via State, covering military and security supporting assistance and from Treasury on multilateral aid. These documents are far shorter and more quantitative in nature.

In the House the Foreign Affairs Committee treats the bilateral aid authorization and the Banking Committee, the multilateral.

The Foreign Affairs Committee allows regional and topical subcommittees to hold hearings and have a first mark-up (decision-making) session on the parts of the whole under its jurisdiction. The full committee then marks up a final draft, pieces together a bill report and sends it to the House floor. Many members and many staff thus play at least some role. The multilateral requests are treated in less detail by a banking subcommittee and rather pro forma by the full Banking Committee. In the Senate all of the aid bills are handled by the full Foreign Relations Committee backed by a few staff. When authorization bills have been reconciled between the two chambers, appropriations bills commence in the Foreign Operations subcommittees. Hearings and discussions are important at this point. Full appropriations committee consideration is pro forma most of the time. The sum of produced paper in all of these exercises — that is, published hearings — has grown since 1974-75 and some areas of sophistication have developed. But some very real constraints to participatory development endure even as the cast of characters slowly changes.

The most basic problems have to do with the nature of the congressional inhabitant and how the system structures work and produces behavior incentives. In essence the goal of enhancing participatory development starts with enormous obstacles. In the present media age it takes one kind of person to run successfully for office. It takes quite another kind of mind and psyche to deal with substantive, complex issues in a brief period, go into detail enough to make responsible choices, and be comfortable admitting ignorance so that sufficient learning is possible. Few people like that get elected. Those with good intentions and even some substantive ability face the following dilemmas. To survive, work time must be allocated not just to committees but to issues on the floor and to constituency and case work. At least one-third of staff time goes to the last category. A member must divide committee time among several assignments. Even were one to come to office with enormous professional training, a truly professional oversight of very much of foreign assistance is simply impossible.

Foreign relations issues have the additional constraints of being poorly thought of by constituents. Many senators and representatives cannot politically afford to choose such an assignment or spend much time on it thereafter. The results show in a mutually reinforcing vicious circle of ignorance between the people and their representatives. That the average citizen does not understand world-system analysis and does not see most relationships between his or her own welfare and foreign events does not encourage Congress to act. Notice, despite OPEC, how slowly and naively conventional wisdom has begun to add any substantive understanding to the word "interdependence."

Despite these handicaps some do take on foreign relations committee assignments, even with interest. Special interests like Israel or anticommunism occupy inordinate attention. It's fun and a power trip to "show boat" to grab headlines, especially when few constituents really care and there is no ultimate responsibility for carrying out policy initiatives. In foreign as well as domestic affairs little thought goes to whether implementation can or will happen.

Deducting these constraints from substantive understanding of and oversight over development, one must then understand the ritual of the congressional hearing process as a very poor and deceptive way of transmitting information or developing consensus. Aid bills come every year. It is difficult for the veteran not to view the process as a ritual to be endured; this is not an attitude of spirited investigation. But the more sobering reality is that the member of Congress is, on average, intellectually and culturally unprepared to challenge the content of what the Executive Branch presents.

In practice members do not read much material in advance. They rely on aural learning, as do most members of the managerial class, especially in Washington. Thus members do not have the substantive or theoretical understanding to know the value and integrity of what they hear. They realize that the Executive Branch spokesman will always, as a good organization man should, put the best foot forward and downplay the warts. When staff suggests questions that show contradictions, the members do not know how to follow up. One wonders often if they want to. Executive Branch witnesses are members of the same managerial culture, and it would be most unseemly for either to embarrass the other. Most of the time it's a game of slow pitch softball, although exceptions exist.

The most recent and vigorous effort of congressional oversight, relating mildly to participatory development, has been the work of Congressman Clarence Long of Maryland, Chairman of the House Appropriations Subcommittee on Foreign Operations. Congressman Long has been trying to show that conventional aid programs, particularly those of the World Bank, do not effectively help the poor and may in fact be harmful. He offers appropriate technology and other alternatives. The ambitious reader will find in Volume 6 of the FY80 hearings from this House subcommittee nearly 1,000 pages of this conflict between Congressman Long on the one hand and Fred Bergsten and other U.S. Treasury Department officials defending the multilaterals on the other.

This debate is instructive on many levels. Treasury, defending its left flank, appeals many times to the right by showing how much the U.S. profits from and controls the multilaterals. One will rarely see the world-system so clearly described as a system by its rulers. Herewith, from the volume cited above, a few samples from Treasury spokesmen.

> This level of lending gives the banks important influence in recipient countries. Because of their apolitical [!] character, and the fact that they operate on the basis of economic and financial criteria, the banks are able to encourage the adoption of appropriate economic policies. They finance programs of technical assistance, to strengthen local institutions and provide training for local officials. They encourage coordination of the resource flow to developing countries and promote cooperation among official lenders by chairing aid coordination groups for particular countries. . . . (p. 43).
>
> The record is clear over 35 years: these institutions have successfully advanced U.S. policy objectives in the developing nations while the burden of financing has been met increasingly by other donors. . . . (p. 461).
>
> The development banks are looked to by private lenders around the world as an indicator of whether a particular developing country has sound development policies and sound projects. And . . . the development banks are increasingly able to cofinance, get private banks to join in their projects and even more than that, their view is kind of a good housekeeping seal of approval. . . . (p. 486).

Lenin never had it so easy. But Congressman Long was much more interested in another level of Treasury analysis that was repeatedly summarized by this series of thoughts: the poor are there; the project is there; the project therefore helps the poor.

Congressman Long has the unusual congressional background of a Ph.D. in labor economics and demonstrates a gut feeling that the rhetoric of the aid agency spokesmen is simply rhetoric. He does not appear to know how to raise and carry through the social science and historical questions of processes at work that would show who benefits in specific situations. The World Bank tube-well project in Bangladesh was talked to death in these hearings, as Congress learned more about one project than has probably ever been presented in a hearing. Congress needed an anthropologist. Endless details from Treasury wore down the critics present. Treasury made admissions, omissions, and assertions. When cornered it claimed lack of sufficient data and incomplete results. One should not say it lied. Reality in organizations does not contain lies, only operative or existential truths of the moment. Treasury spokesmen were being good organization men, whereas Congressman Long was forgetting his class obligations and actually trying to be a professional. It is little wonder that the interaction and the results were dissatisfying to both sides.

This quite unusual performance by Congress is worth contemplating for what it implies about the potential for the kind of substantive foreign aid oversight required by participatory development. Neither of the core actors in a hearing, as it is now structured, can go beyond the surface of the issues. One and usually both lack the professional grasp of processes at work necessary to see what is really happening on the ground. The Executive Branch witness is the comparative specialist and controls the flow more often than not, skillfully pulling the discussion away from threatening topics or implications. The whole process is guided by elaborate courtesies, not by compunction. I witnessed hundreds of organizational lies on Vietnam by Kissinger, Schlesinger, and others to the Congress that went unchallenged and unpunished. Whatever the Congress believes, the Executive knows that in foreign affairs it can still lie forever until, and sometimes even after, its funding gets cut off.

Those of good will and good intention on both sides of this conflict face further obstacles created by additional undercurrents of antagonism. Because so many AID spokespersons have come to Congress as good managers saying, "Yes, we know what we are doing and it's successful," it is very difficult for other, more professional agency people to tell Congress the truth: "No, we're not sure how to do what you ask; the work is experimental so do not expect predictable results. But give us more personnel, allow us to fire outdated people, and give us the flexibility that the tasks of participatory development imply." Neither side seems capable of this dialogue, and personalities are only a part of the problem.

In several chapters of this book I will return to the questions of the political culture and institutions of Washington and how specific structural change might affect global development policy. Here, however, it seemed important to dwell at length on the national security state, the managerial culture of modern organizations, and the limitations of system oversight (the U.S. Congress) to drive home a central reality about the world-system to those in the development business. The real impetus for participatory development will not come from Washington. No matter what the rhetoric is, ignore it and get on with the business of using the resources at hand in a more constructive and humane fashion.

Romantic and liberal political battles may be fought and won at the heart of the world-system, but there is little or no possibility of significant change in the mode of production from the top alone. There is no shared consensus on the nature of modern history and thus little real communication between the core and periphery, the North and South, capital and labor, and rich and poor. That consensus must be built up from the bottom by participatory development. Large organizations are usually part of the problem and rarely and marginally part of any solution. The national security state, like centralized power systems, private international banks and their unbridled avarice, and any other large concentration of public or private power, stands in the way of humane alternatives. The participatory answer must address systems, institutions, values, and myths simultaneously.

CHAPTER BIBLIOGRAPHY*

Sivard, Ruth (1981). *World Military and Social Expenditures 1981*. Leesburg, Va.: World Priorities.

National Advisory Council (1978). *National Advisory Council Annual Report for 1977*. Washington: Department of the Treasury.

---

*In this and some succeeding chapters some sources are relevant only to the technical issues raised. The bibliography at the end of the book contains the other works mentioned. That listing is designed as a more general introduction to all of global development studies.

U.S. Congress. House of Representatives. Appropriations Committee (1979a). *Foreign Assistance and Related Programs Appropriations for 1980 – Part 2*. Washington, D.C.: Government Printing Office.

—— (1979b). *Foreign Assistance and Related Programs Appropriations for 1980 – Part 6*. Washington, D.C.: Government Printing Office.

U.S. Congress. Senate. Committee on Governmental Affairs (1979a). *U.S. Participation in the Multilateral Development Banks*. Washington, D.C.: Government Printing Office.

—— (1979b). *Reorganization Plan No. 2 of 1979*. Washington, D.C.: Government Printing Office.

3

The Project Process
and Conflicting Reality:
AID in Zaire

The journey from the top of the world-system to the bottom is more than the geographical distance from core country capitals like Washington to the most remote and impoverished villages of peripheral nations of the Third World. There are considerable cultural distances to be bridged. These are not simply differences in language, social custom, and speed of activity. They are also the conflicts between the capitalist or exchange mode of production and the subsistence or peasant mode and between needs of organizations and those of people. International development agencies like the World Bank and the U.S. Agency for International Development have not been comfortable with conflict. Cognitive respect for the position of others is hard for the products of most cultures. Westerners and their aid organizations are no different in this respect.

Instead these and almost all other donor agencies begin to face the Third World and its poverty with their own, most elementary, organizational imperatives. Accepting the mandate of citizens and politicians of noble intentions, AID and the World Bank have claimed that they can help and are helping the world's poor. They assert that large organizations can send forth material and human resources and improve human welfare. Such a process is called a project. In the 1950s and 1960s project goals were basically material ones like road building; goals in the 1970s have been broader and included a truer definition of development as enhanced human participation. This chapter is about the project and its efforts to pursue its goals in the real world. It is the story of one project struggling in a sea of adversity, the AID-sponsored North Shaba Maize Production Project in rural Zaire between 1976 and 1980.

I state at the outset that I have not visited or taken part in this project. What makes possible the following discussion is an unusually enormous volume of literature about the project generated by AID, by its implementing contractors, Development Alternatives Inc. (DAI) of Washington, D.C., and by other evaluation missions. In addition some of the participants have been available for discussion. The rarity of this situation is attested to by the lack of really detailed micro project discussions in the published literature; Emmerson (1976), de Silva et al. (1979), Adams (1977) and but few others come to mind. The North Shaba project provides, however, not just an educational example. It is one of a set of test cases by which AID is judging the viability of its basic strategy for rural development — integrated rural development. Furthermore some in AID view DAI as the leader in making participatory development operational. In several ways North Shaba can thus be seen as an important development indicator for African and for world food prospects in the 1980s.

THE PROJECT AND ITS LARGER SETTING: ZAIRE IN THE 1970S

Zaire today is not a hospitable place for enhancing human welfare, the expansion of food production, or the implementation of rhetorical goals of international agencies like participatory development. Zaire, the former Belgian Congo, is a Central African country of about 27 million spread over 2,345,000 square kilometers. Although it is a major mineral exporter (world leader in cobalt and industrial diamonds and significant in copper), Zaire has become a classic case of development disaster. Under the tutelage of President Joseph Mobutu Sese Seko, the country has not used its export taxes for productive purposes and balanced development. Instead the government budget expanded during the 1970s, the oil crisis was ill met, and the government borrowed far beyond its means. It became in the late 1970s a ward of the international economic system. These macroeconomic issues and the world-system response will be returned to in Chapter 5 and are treated at length in Gran, ed. (1979).

To understand the particular setting of AID's North Shaba Maize Production Project, one must first see the overall nature of Zaire's rural world and its food production problem. About three-quarters of the population are farmers producing varying mixes of subsistence and cash crops. Estimates of GNP per capita ($150-$200) are not meaningful. Daily protein and caloric intakes in many rural areas are well below internationally recognized minimums. Natural disasters and invasions exacerbated specific conditions in 1977 and 1978. But deep systemic contradictions and long-term processes account for the two-decade decline in rural welfare and food production per capita.

Mobutu, like his predecessors in the civil war period (1960-65), has controlled the prices the producers receive in order to keep down the cost of food to civil servants, the army, the copper workers, and the general urban population. Mobutu has deep political interests in pacifying these groups. Rural interests, however, have no effective representation in the political balance. Spread over an enormous territory and hindered by disintegrating and insufficient transportation, rural Zairians have not to date been able to mount an effective political challenge. As the terms of trade turned against food producers, they stopped producing for market. Mobutu has been pressured by international donors to produce several generations of agricultural development plans in the 1970s. But the Zairian government has not had the political necessity to implement a more productive rural development strategy.

Instead the Zairian government has been able to manipulate the world-system to receive ever more financial aid. Mobutu has kept the wages of cooper miners relatively low; both the state and foreign interests have profited handsomely. Stability, however, has been consistently threatened because the ruling class lacks any deep sense of national responsibility. The colonial heritage of the state as parasite endures. Wild swings in available resources have added to a process of long-term stagnation and disintegration. The Zairian elite do not follow Mobutu's advice, offered at mass rally in November 1976, to "steal cleverly." Instead they follow his example and steal immoderately. Schatzberg (in Gran, ed., 1979, and his own 1980 work) and others have chronicled how this example ripples down to produce similar corruption at the bottom of the Zairian political system, the *collectivité* or village leadership. But the lure of minerals and the exposure of private banks and corporations has embroiled the U.S., Belgian, and French governments, the World Bank and the IMF in trying to perpetuate this "stability" despite its awesome human cost.

Neither the world-system nor the Zairian elite can survive an indefinite decline in national maize production, for that crop has been the most important staple after manioc in most regions. In the mineral-rich areas of southeastern Zaire, Shaba and Kasai provinces, maize is the staple. Most of the maize goes into meal porridge. Some goes into local beer production. Production estimates vary; for example for 1975 the government figure was 495,000 tons. More certain is that Zaire was a modest maize exporter late in the colonial era, was down to self-sufficiency in 1960, and has imported a growing volume in the 1970s. The import figure exceeded 100,000 tons in 1975 and reached 175,000 tons in 1978, about one quarter of national consumption. By 1985 imports could rise to 45 percent of national needs (IBRD, 1980a: 4). The drain on foreign exchange for a country with frequent budget deficits and debt arrears has been obvious to all.

International agencies have pressed the government for years to raise the price incentives for local maize production. The government has maintained inequitable prices over the last decade. It decrees a minimum price to the farmer and permits regional elites and private traders to inflict oligopolistic prices on small farmers. Insufficient investment in road and rail maintenance has led to the disintegration of rural links. So has the cost of fuel. The Zairian government did respond to international urgings to create a National Maize Program to breed and field-test new varieties. Farmers have not taken kindly, however, to the bureaucratic approach of the program's extension agents.

The Government of Zaire (GOZ) has been open as well to foreign donor agency proposals and been willing, on paper more than in fact, to commit resources to them. AID's project in North Shaba, the subject of what follows, was not the only major initiative in maize production of the late 1970s. Elsewhere in Shaba Province at Kaniama Kasese is a Belgian-funded project. In Western Kasai is the French- and European-funded Mweka project. Both are large-scale, mechanized, agribusiness efforts stumbling along against the practical obstacles of rural Zaire. The World Bank agreed to a project in Eastern Kasai in 1980 that had been under discussion since late 1976. It commits $38.5 million, including $19.7 million in international funds, to a six-year effort to raise production from 80,000 to 120,000 tons by supplying inputs, services, and market channels to some 53,000 farmers in an area with a population of about one million (IBRD, 1980b: ii, 11-12). The French, Belgian, and World Bank projects appear to be the common top-down, production-centered processes typical of international efforts. AID's North Shaba venture promises much more. That is part of what makes it a good vehicle for study.

THE POLITICS OF PROJECT DESIGN

Neither AID nor the GOZ approached the problem of designing the North Shaba maize project devoid of ulterior motives or a hidden political agenda. AID, as a part of and under the control of the U.S. Department of State, started from its conception of U.S. interests in Zaire, bluntly revealed in a 1975 Development Assistance Program document to be the following:

(1) To maintain U.S accessibility to raw materials which are in abundant supply in Zaire;
(2) To foster U.S. investment in Zaire so that we will have access to the Zaire market; and
(3) To sustain our political interests in Central Africa, bearing in mind that Zaire is the "bellwether" for political stability in this part of the world (Gran, ed., 1979: 310).

AID in 1975 had to contend as well with its other major mandator, the U.S. Congress. The Congress had just legislated a New Directions aid policy, aid to the poorest people in the Third World. AID had to appear competent before Congress, was obligated to pursue development work in Zaire, and yet was in some quarters acutely aware that it did not know how to fulfill this new mandate.

More precisely AID in the mid 1970s, as it usually is, was internally divided by conflicting approaches to development. Some involved with Zaire were veteran technocratic supporters of the Green Revolution and content to work with the rural elite and the central government. Others were willing to reject trickle-down approaches, admit ignorance, and seek outside assistance. It was through their efforts that the young but growing Washington consulting firm, Development Alternatives Inc. (DAI) became involved, both as project designers and as implementers. DAI staff were disaffected veterans of the project process, particularly interested in new approaches to enhancing popular participation in development. They were also liberals, sensitive to the reality of poverty but less conscious of the processes creating it: the world-system, the triple alliance, and confidence mechanisms. DAI, funded by AID, had in any case to accept political limits enforced by its sponsors.

The Zairian officials also entered project design discussions with hidden items on the agenda. Ostensibly they were seeking to lessen the large maize deficit in South Shaba affecting the city of Lubumbashi and the mining areas nearby. The mining parastatal GECAMINES ran a flour mill, but its mechanized farm could meet only a small portion of the need. The price for most consumers in South Shaba had been and remains highly subsidized. As long as government decrees deflected market prices and banned most inter-province trade, a variety of officials and traders at the regional and provincial level could profit even more in the ongoing parallel markets by enlarging North Shaba's production. Thus most Zairian officials did not have immediate political reasons to oppose a technical approach to maize development in this region.

AID and the DAI consultants produced, however, a far more complex multidimensional project than was customary. The project paper itself ran to some 400 pages, four to five times the average length. It began by identifying what it saw as the major constraints to maize production: the lack of improved technical packages and an effective system to deliver them; an insufficient transport network for trade; and the lack of a reliable marketing system. The designers proposed a $19 million six-year effort, with AID supplying $9.8 million. The first goal was national maize self-sufficiency; this project would raise the regional yield from an estimated 22,000 MT in 1977 to 66,000 MT in 1986 (AID, 1976: 240). Another, central goal was to start a self-sustaining rural development process by increasing small farmer production and the farmers' role in the process and the benefits. It was to address all of the major constraints to production and represent the state of the art in integrated rural development. It was also to become the model to be duplicated elsewhere in Zaire (AID, 1976: 64).

To meet these varied goals the project designers started with a project steering committee, representing the interested government agencies and the Office of the President. Beneath that came a liaison committee for day-to-day assistance to the project director, who would have overall authority. Zonal-level authorities would have an advisory committee to help coordinate local activities (AID, 1976: 67-69).

The project itself was designed with six components to span the broad range of development constraints noted. It is worth noting the precise language defining the goals of each subsystem, for they promise interactions between organizations and people in a world highly unlike the real world of rural Zaire.

1. A subsystem of research and extension to "insure close communication between farmers, researchers, agricultural assistants and trainers."

2. A subsystem to develop "farmer groups/pre-cooperatives which will help insure that project benefits reach small farmers."

3. A subsystem for small farmer marketing and credit "to facilitate the improvement of the private sector marketing activities in the project area by fostering competition."

4. A subsystem for intermediate technology "to alleviate peak labor constraints."

5. A subsystem for "road rehabilitation and maintenance."

6. A subsystem for "planning, monitoring, and evaluating all project activities." (AID, 1976: 65)

Inherent at the start are an assumed potential harmony between a small farmer and a market and between the technocratic constraint-bandaid approach and real participatory development.

The 1976 project paper does contain a number of references to participation as "a more collaborative approach with small farmers" (AID, 1976: 64). Farmer groups "will be encouraged on the basis of popularly defined needs and opportunities," and will operate in ways "compatible with existing local decision-making processes." Yet in the same section the authors realize that "within each locality, there are subtle differences in organization and decision-making, as well as not so subtle conflicts or competing interests among groups" (AID, 1976: 87, 89).

Ignoring for a moment whether these are *really* aspects of participatory development, it is still worth noting that the project paper there and elsewhere contains an unusual degree of cross-cultural sophistication. This is because two U.S. anthropologists had just been working in the region and, despite intrateam controversy, contributed heavily to the sections on social soundness analysis and because project paper authors talked to farmers and merchants to elicit grievances. Annex K provides a good grasp of the local political economy and the reasons the poor are stymied. But many of these issues are not well reflected in the body of the project design and remain to impede the project to this day.

The project implementers received, in sum, a voluminous blueprint far from the norm, specific and highly optimistic goals, and, upon reflection, considerable inkling that this was a mission impossible. It does not appear, however, that many decision makers in Kinshasa and Washington read Annex K or thought through some of its implications. As is the norm in international development, dealing with the real world fell to those who would implement the project, the team of consultants created by DAI.

PROJECT IMPLEMENTATION: NORTH SHABA 1977-80

Making any project work is hard. Making a project work in a multicultural, highly stratified environment is exquisitely difficult. Project designers added many further complications and contradictions, rendering the effort essentially unrealistic. Central was the assertion that there existed such an entity as a "small farmer" who could be aided by adding to but not changing existing local organizations. By misunderstanding or mystifying the meaning of power and its relationship to human development, the designers could also claim that working through the local political and economic institutions that helped create the poverty could lead to ending the poverty. The hostile, unstable macroeconomic climate would not irreparably damage such an effort. People, money, and a few quantitative targets would be enough to produce and define success.

Four years later all involved were much more realistic. A most somber judgment came in a November 1980 internal report by DAI itself. It found that Zaire's "economic problems are so serious and deep-seated that even with the most determined efforts, few desirable improvements at the level of individual projects can be expected in the short run" (Barclay et al., 1980: 21). Yet DAI and AID agreed that year to extend the project from 1982 to 1983 and add $3.7 million in U.S. grant aid. The project goal was in AID's eyes "unchanged . . . to contribute to the achievement of maize self-sufficiency"; the production goal was, however reduced from a 300 percent increase to a 75 percent increase (27,000 MT in 1978 to 49,000 MT in 1983) (AID, 1980: 1-3). There remained little talk of a model integrated development project suitable for duplication elsewhere. How all this could come about is now the subject of an analysis treating one project subsystem at a time. In the concluding section the central contradictions of the project as a whole will be explored in more detail.

The project director and his management unit faced the immediate difficulties of recruiting the technically and linguistically qualified people the project design called for and of molding them into a team. Efficient channels had to be set up to get supplies to this remote region of Zaire. Working relations had to be created with AID officials, several levels of GOZ officials, and the Zairians who joined the project staff. Communication, accounting, and evaluation procedures had to be set up. It is little wonder that the project director was soon overextended and that project communication and quality began to suffer.

DAI discovered before long that the staff design and schedule was impractical. Many of the first-generation crew were not in place and functioning until the beginning of 1978. Technicians fluent in both Swahili and French proved hard to find. The role of the agronomist was critical. It was filled briefly and poorly from mid 1978 to late 1979 and vacant until 1981, leaving a Zairian staff, which had grown to 5 technicians and 40 extension agents by mid 1980, untrained and undirected for the adaptive research program called for (AID, 1980: 11). Despite the strong plea in the project paper to engage a woman rural development specialist, key to the effective engagement of half the work force in project activities and benefits, the project manager was unable to get one that was mutually agreeable. Four women were used between 1977 and 1979; because of the general chauvinism of the environment and for varied other reasons each found the task unpalatable or beyond her (Bukaka Bonani, 1979: 4). There were significant staffing holes in other subsystems as well. DAI in November 1980 recognized far more than in 1976 the complexities of this kind of recruiting. But it has not budged from its institutional optimism to rethink the basic practicality of such a large-scale project and its inherent reliance on quality performance by expensive foreigners.

Project leaders would have not only to recruit the expatriates but also to mold them into a team. DAI was quite candid in how this failed to take place between 1977 and 1980.

> . . . conflicting personal styles and agendas interfered with communication. The team in its entirety never met, except on social occasions. Few had any interest in discussing broad developmental issues which the project was designed to address, and many were sceptical of each other's competence, motivation and usefulness to the project . . . information flows and decisionmaking became inconsistent and unpredictable. . . . (Barclay et al., 1980: 56).

Americans set their own priorities, and subsystems began to operate in competition and even at cross-purposes. Given the conflicting philosophies in the project design itself, it is hard to see how new personnel who are better team players can entirely overcome this disharmony.

Unsurprisingly the Zairian staff was confused and disheartened by this staff conflict. Their own bureaucratic needs were encouraged. That the first Zairian project director did not share the idea of participatory decision making or participatory development made the period from September 1977 to April 1978 even harder. This Zairian wanted total control of *all* project personnel and saw the project was essentially one of corn production. Accusations flew back and forth, paralyzing work. New personnel and management relationships ultimately eased some aspects of the conflicts (DIMPEX, 1979: 135). But the Zairians on the project staff have even more serious complaints which project evaluators have not downplayed. The funding from central government authorities has been scanty and irregular in the extreme. A cadre will not work indefinitely for nothing. Worse, Zairian staff feel they have not received the kind of "specific, structured, on-the-job training" they anticipated and feel is necessary. DAI recognizes that this has happened and that the educator role "is the only real justification for sustaining a large American team in the project" (Barclay et al., 1980: 55-56). But there was no evidence at the end of 1980 that verifiable and appropriate training programs were underway or that any kind of regular feedback mechanism yet existed so that such grievances would not go unremedied for another three years.

Difficulties inside the project staff were compounded by the larger political environment in which it existed. Problems were legion, and a small sample suffices. The *Commissaire de Zone*, the most important local official, struggling with minimal resources to hold onto his turf, sought to control the project and its resources. He fought for the use of vehicles, the expulsion of certain Zairian project staff, and the inclusion of government extension agents and agricultural monitors in project activities. Project managers fended him off but apparently succumbed to another political threat, Commissaire Politique Nyembo from Kongolo. This man has national political ties and used them to help the project more than once; project managers have reciprocated in small ways. One evaluation team dared this gentle rebuke.

> The Commissaire himself represents the entrenched commercial/political oligopoly that controls the zone. For Project Nord Shaba (PNS) to give special consideration to the Commissaire in anticipation of favors in return certainly compromises its proclaimed mandate to aid the poor majority. If the present political/social conditions continue until the end of the American presence in PNS, it is possible that the project purpose and outputs will be very seriously compromised.
>
> By aiding small merchants and farmer groups in marketing of their produce, PNS will almost certainly come into conflict with the Commissaire's own interests. He is presently unhappy about the project's intention to help small farmers sell their maize directly to Tarica Freres at a price higher than he (and his agents) is offering (DIMPEX, 1979: B 11-13).

It is doubtful that the Zairian poor are unobservant, and it is difficult to see how the project could maintain or enhance its legitimacy among the poor under such circumstances.

The project managers must also face the political and economic dimensions of national and international conditions. The relationship with AID has been uneven. Varied Kinshasa embassy staff brought different interests to bear. Some fought to get reform pressures put on the Zairian government, only to be overruled by embassy political officers citing security and political reasons. With criticisms voiced by DAI staff, the U.S. Congress, and U.S. Zaire specialists, AID personnel became quite defensive in some instances. Losing sight of the need for critical learning, they sought to shape the evaluation efforts made during 1979 and 1980. The DIMPEX team found its agenda sharply defined by AID to omit macroeconomic concerns, for example. Some discussions are careful studies in optimism (Resseguie, 1979, in several places) or simply at odds with logic. In February 1980 an AID committee said "no evidence has been presented which precludes proceeding with the project" (AID, 1980: Ann. 8). The next two pages are a sad catalog of exactly such evidence, the larger macroeconomic environment.

It is that situation that gave to the management unit its most intractable dilemmas. It could not get supplies in; even through largely U.S. channels, delay and thievery were the rule. War and floods were of some matter. But AID and project authorities in the middle of a system of extreme oppression seem to see only the symptoms: inflation, depression, imbalance, collapsing transport, skyrocketing fuel cost, price quotas, etc. They appear unable to understand this chaos as a deliberate system perpetuated by an elite and the world-system for an elite and for the world-system. To the project officials involved it was simply a system of shortages and disincentives to production and marketing. In sum, multiple environmental thorns plagued the project management unit. They could scarcely avoid affecting as well the performance of each project subsystem.

DILEMMAS WITH SPECIFIC PROJECT SUBSYSTEMS

The research and extension subsystem was viewed by many as the most important one. For without a new "technical package" they felt no production increase could result. Yet little was accomplished between 1977 and 1980. People, politics, and organizational factors all played a part. DAI could fill the chief agronomist slot only briefly, during 1978-79, and the consensus in hindsight was that the choice was poor. His written work suggests that he was a narrow technician. Two excerpts from one of his papers (Thies, n.d.) suffice. "It would be evident to any student of agriculture that the addition of chemical fertilizer would have an immediate beneficial effect"; to any organic farmer or anyone else at peace with nature, this is the epitome of the world food system's ignorance of ecology and of energy efficiency. "Manioc, the next important staple in the area, is possibly the most neglected" and its production should become more important; this is economics as if people matter not at all, contravening AID's own research that manioc, even when "properly" prepared, retains trace elements of poisons (see Gran, ed., 1979: 313-14) and has minimal protein value.

With this expatriate and without him the subsystem had to face the Zairian Naitonal Maize Program (PNM), its local officials, and their priorities. The PNM inherited the traditional disgust of villagers who had been visited since colonial times by such agricultural monitors seeking to enforce obligatory cultivation and collect taxes. PNM cadre approached farmers in an authoritarian fashion with a predetermined technical package that they asserted to be superior. The farmers were not impressed. PNM cadre began some research trials in these years. But no one tried very hard to understand the variety and complexity of existing farm systems. Insufficient field trials took place. Little participatory learning happened so that, while some farmers accepted new seeds, the attendant crop techniques were largely ignored (Barclay et al., 1980: 74).

What had seemed a sufficient amount of agricultural research in 1976 to start the project eventually became obviously inadequate. For reasons to be returned to, no baseline survey of existing practices was taken. One could scarcely measure incremental gains from fertilizer, for example. By 1980 DAI (Barclay et al., 1980) was ready to admit amazing levels of ignorance:

> It is not known at this time how maize production compares with production of palm oil, rice, peanuts and other economic activities nor how much competition there is between them for labor. . . . (p. 11).
> Although the nature of potential risks to farmers in adopting this package is known, no effort has been made to assess the tradeoffs between increased benefits and increased risks. It is known that the variety Kasai I is vulnerable to yellow streak virus, but that early planting minimizes this risk. In promoting pure stand cropping, the project may be upsetting the traditional system for maintaining soil fertility. To recommend a shallow-rooted crop (maize) in savannah areas can potentially accelerate erosion. . . . (p. 40).

These few glimpses reveal the rush of organizations and technology, trampling autonomy and threatening human livelihood in multiple ways to try to fulfill larger system needs.

DAI recognized by 1980 that a more systematic and adaptive approach under the leadership of a more sensitive agronomist was imperative. More than maize would have to be involved. But thought has yet to go to the magnitude of bureaucratic difficulties involved in actually implementing any drastically better strategy. If extension agents are paid by the GOZ now, or will be not later than 1984, why should they threaten their own careers and financial security by ignoring GOZ imperatives and pursuing new project approaches? Beyond the politics of implementation is a more serious philosophical issue for DAI and AID. If a DAI evaluator can write that there is "almost no indigenous capacity in Zaire to carry out integrated small farmer production projects" (Barclay, et al., 1980: 76), it is clear that the project does not grant Zaire's millions of farmers the true measure of cognitive respect that is essential for real participatory development.

The farmer group development subsystem got off to a fair start toward some of the goals the project set: 165 small farmer groups and 75 farmer councils as the basic means of reaching 15,000 farmers. By June 1980 extension workers had been placed in 37 farm centers and subsystem cadre were working toward creation of groups and councils (AID, 1980: 15). To put this in initial perspective, these efforts were reaching only men and were lumping together rich and poor as though all households were two-hectare farming entities. Failure to retain in place a woman expatriate meant severe limits in encouraging any organization among half the work force. Total population in the project area is about 130,000 so that women were not the only marginalized subset.

The project's attitude toward the sensitive matter of women in development has been a good barometer of the limits of its participatory rhetoric. Failure to place a woman expatriate as rural development catalyst permitted an easy assertion that nothing could be done, repeated in several documents. It is not true that "little is known about women's social and economic roles" (DIMPEX, 1979: E1), though much more needs to be explored. In the zones of Kongolo and Nyunzu, women are in a delicate position, isolated and viewed ambivalently by men. A woman is sacred, a source of goodness, especially if she works in the fields. A man can marry up to ten. Violence and jealousy are not uncommon. In public the women sit silently behind men. It is, in sum, a particularly exploitative situation and one where the development of women would seem to be directly threatening to the way men define their own identity, self-worth, and social esteem (Bukaka Bonani, 1979: 5). It would be possible to start enlarging women's consciousness in the few areas where there is now a small degree of cooperative effort. Zaire, like the rest of the human race, can ill afford to stifle and underutilize half its social and productive resources. It is a mockery of human rights that cannot be attacked by female efforts alone. AID, DAI, and GOZ officials should not sit on their hands.

It is not fair to characterize all farmer groups and councils as skillful confidence mechanisms. There were reports that some particularly poor or parasitic government agents were forced to transfer or resign in the face of local action. But the cumulative impression from several evaluations is that through 1980 these groups were viewed by both GOZ and project officials as a vehicle from which to elicit farmer preferences. Little or no legitimacy was given to farmer demands that strayed outside the production goals of the project. Extension agents were not rewarded or paid by the farmers. AID claims (1980: Ann. 3) that much study and discussion have gone into the creation of farmer councils and that the sub-system's abilities have improved markedly over time. The same paragraph begins, however: "The organization of Farmer Councils has been largely done within the context of the existing village systems." Clearly the village elite run most of these councils, and an extension worker, rewarded for raising production, is unlikely to seek out other than these, the richest and most productive farmers. Stratification is sustained and enhanced. This is not participatory development.

The marketing and credit subsystem was originally designed with the contradiction of working through the marketing parastatal ONACER "to promote a strong competitive market system by increasing the number of viable grain merchants" (AID, 1980: 17). ONACER was soon disbanded. Its replacement was slow to function, and a supplementary AID project loan was slow to materialize. Some appropriate activities are on the drawing board, but early efforts seem to have had marginal impact on the local oligopoly. There is much reason to believe that project aid for fuel, sacks, and truck rentals in the late 1970s served the elite much more than it did fledgling merchants and cooperatives. One merchant-politician was particularly active in preserving his turf. Even if this politician is harnessed, the other proposed changes can only partially overcome the combination of micro and macroeconomic conflicts.

Many aspects of the villagers' marketing dilemma are well portrayed in a letter from Kongolo farmers to the *Commissaire Politique* in Lubumbashi in the first part of 1979. The terms of trade between city and country have worked to pauperize the farmers. Pathetic comparisons are offered. But the plague of parasitic policemen erecting tax barriers at every step outrages them even more. How can a woman with 5 Z in goods to sell pay a 10 Z fine or a tax for a market place? How can a farmer prepay for hospital admission out of harvest season? DAI's own research showed farmers refusing to sell to monopolists and being tricked by merchants when sacks of maize were weighed. Indeed both sides tried to trick each other. Then the merchants sought to avoid the milling monopoly of Tarica Frères by moving the maize clandestinely to markets in the Kasai Provinces (Roth, 1978a and b). Most of these matters were also raised in one annex of the original project paper (AID, 1976: Ann. K), but the project was not designed to meet them in operational terms.

The macroeconomic dilemmas for marketing were and remain even farther from the project's grasp. By overvaluing its currency, the GOZ hindered merchants in three ways: rationing cut the purchase of oil, vehicles, and spare parts so traders could neither reach farmers nor sell in the market (these conditions drove poorer merchants out of the market, enhancing monopoly); undervaluing the cost of imports encouraged the GOZ to import maize from Rhodesia instead of offering a fair price to North Shaba farmers to produce more (Roth, 1978a: 15-16). In every evaluation the officially established farm gate price was seen as the biggest disincentive to more production. DAI and AID officials fought this issue with State Department and GOZ officials for four fruitless years; they left the IMF to pressure for currency devaluation (to some cumulative avail 1976-80). The best AID and DAI could manage was a covenant with the GOZ in the 1980 project revision agreement. The latter would "review actively its agricultural marketing policies in the North Shaba region, giving particular attention to" narrowing the price gap between the official and black markets, removing interprovince and interregional trade barriers, and ending "unnecessary and unessential taxes" on trade (AID, 1980: 6). This and the other eight conditions laid down are as likely to be fulfilled as any human effort to legislate morality. Such charades do, however, fulfill internal bureaucratic needs on both sides. Prices were raised in early 1981, enough to look good but not enough really to threaten elite interests.

The intermediate technology subsystem seems by all accounts to have had the most auspicious start of any part of the project. A highly regarded young Peace Corps volunteer guided the effort. Former railroad and shipyard workshops were available so that some tools and much metal (old barges, etc.) could be salvaged. In the first three years 15,000-20,000 hand tools and more than 100 processing machines were turned out. About 50 villagers were trained as blacksmiths and provided with new tools. Raw material and markets appeared to be sufficient to justify official optimism that the subsystem would be self-sufficient if not profit making by 1981 or 1982. But the Peace Corps volunteer departed in 1981. The hand tool market changed, and local producers lost out to Kinshasa producers. Pessimism replaced optimism by 1982.

No available evaluation thought it worthwhile to seek to analyze why this intermediate technology subsystem was initially more successful in meeting its mandate than any other subsystem. Success needs to be understood even more than failure. Scattered impressions suggest that several critical factors played a part. The Peace Corps volunteer (and later DAI employee) apparently knew what he was doing both technically and organizationally. He did not have to relate to the macroeconomy or the GOZ; his contact with much of the local regime did not have to be great. Raw materials were free. Customers were interested, the producers' jobs appealing, and the new market not easy to monopolize in traditional ways. Perhaps some new blacksmiths became village monopolists, but otherwise this subproject, by showing many of the aspects of participatory development, suggests that even in an unutterably hostile climate, small flowers of human development can occur.

The infrastructure subsystem receives the lion's share of project resources, so much so that one evaluation termed this project a "modified version of the capital projects undertaken in former decades by AID instead of a truly integrated rural development project" (DIMPEX, 1979: 9-2). AID did not like this, nor did it like the further comment that small farmer income seemed secondary to road construction and other efforts to help the grain merchants. Yet the initial work done was on housing in Kongolo, Mbulula, and Ngaba for the project staff. After recovering from a 1979 flood and endless procurement delays (Resseguie, 1979), DAI's contractors were able to begin road and bridge rehabilitation in the summer of 1979. An elaborate work schedule was revised several times.

Targets remain as originally proposed: 724 kilometers of roads and 55 bridges rehabilitated. Perhaps they will be approached. As with so many Third World road projects, there is little indication that sufficient incentives exist to maintain them after the project ends. Twenty years of Zairian rural history leaves no room for optimism.

The monitoring and evaluation subsystem had considerable difficulties getting very much done between 1977 and 1980. Official evaluators pointed to the absence of full-time staff and the subsystem's equal relationship to units it was supposed to evaluate. Such analysts were less prone to suggest the organizational disinterest in being monitored at all or in producing materials that would allow negative judgments higher up. Project management did not have time for thorough surveys, just for inquiries necessary for its own decision making. This is part of the reason why an original assessment – "too politically sensitive" to do the thorough baseline surveys necessary for real evaluation – held sway for so long.

The practical result of all this is that the quality of data and the procedures for getting it remained primitive. The DAI consultant who worked on sporadic temporary duty was candid about the limits of the *fiche du village* (village questionnaire) and the Zairians trying to carry out the data collection. In early 1979 he commented that at the moment he did not even have "a basis for guessing at the proportions of maize output that are consumed, lost in storage, or sold locally." He was not unaware that "the accuracy of data gathered may vary widely from one village to another, and also from one question to another of the *fiche* itself" (Resseguie, 1979: Ann. IB). Over four years the project did become more sensitive to the human rights of farmers as well as to their precarious political and subsistence situation. In some ways farmers are taking control of their own data collection; participating farmers are said to be keeping their own journals, for instance (AID, 1980: Ann. 3). It will probably be several years before it is clear whether the government agents or the peasants capture control of the information system. In this as in the other project subsystems, modest gains will remain threatened by Zairian political realities for the foreseeable future.

NORTH SHABA AS AN EXTENSION OF THE WORLD-SYSTEM

This troubled saga of one development project by a major donor agency working at the very fringes of the world-system has been pursued not primarily to make a case that the project does not meet the goals it set for itself. What matters more are the generic issues this project raises about the basic nature and core validity of this scale and organization of cross-cultural engineering we term development.

Despite some participatory rhetoric and a few tangible aspects of participatory development, this project represents at base a production-centered growth effort in the eyes of most involved. A small number of the "more progressive" (entrepreneurial, politically connected, etc.) are getting new seeds and extension advice encouraging them to grow a little more maize. Merchants are finding the parallel markets profitable enough to encourage them to continue. The local elite and their minions continue to prey on the system. The national and urban elite maintain the overall parasitic price system. In basic dimensions the project reifies and expands the status quo, allowing a few more villagers and merchants slightly better access to the world-system and its spoils. Despite farmer councils, women's literacy classes, an ephemerally successful intermediate technology subsystem, and well-meaning project personnel, the North Shaba maize project, like most other donor projects in most countries, is not a satisfactory answer to the nature and magnitude of world poverty.

This is why. First is the matter of scale. Project North Shaba will spend a total of $23 million in AID and GOZ resources hopefully to raise production by 22,000 tons. The 1980 World Bank maize project in Kasai Oriental will spend a total of $38.5 million to try to raise production by about 40,000 tons. The Bank estimates projected the 1985 deficit to be between 270,000 and 401,000 tons. To reach maize self-sufficiency by means of such donor agency projects and comparable GOZ efforts would thus require 10 to 15 times the amount of food development resources being applied. This is absurdly unrealistic; public and private investors do not have any incentive to oblige. Such donor agency projects cannot therefore be viewed as significant strides toward self-sufficiency.

Development, properly conceived, is centrally a human rather than productive activity. If the goal is to meet human needs, the starting point must be those needs. The North Shaba project claims that it will positively affect a total of 15,000 farmers by 1983, providing at least seeds, extension advice, and opportunities to have other needs voiced. Even if one grants such claims, the project area has about 130,000 people in it; this implies job needs of 50,000-70,000. The project is thus exclusionary in its basic design. What happens to the other 30,000-50,000 underemployed adults for whom the world-system has no need? Has not betting on the strong revealed its inequitable and unproductive nature long enough? Zaire cannot afford not to invest in its own human resources.

By the same token one must question the scale of average project investment in foreign consultants. DAI has budgeted $110,000 a year to meet the costs of fielding one agronomist. Similar sums go for other long-term personnel. Short-term consultants can be even more expensive. It takes no imagination to see that somewhat more than half of project expenses go to foreigners. Much of this money will not enter the Zairian economy. But the essential point is that poor countries cannot afford such expertise and, with some creativity, can usually find less expensive substitutes who can accomplish far more per unit of resources. Even if DAI staff is sensitive to life-style issues, they cannot help but teach inappropriate dreams to Zairian project staff and others they come in contact with. This sensitive question and the whole topic of efficiency of resource use will be returned to in later chapters. One should note in closing that North Shaba can scarcely be termed a model for the rest of Zaire to duplicate on the matter of expatriate costs alone.

The question of standards and evaluation has been touched on several times and needs to be crystallized. The failure to do the initial baseline survey* or to heed very carefully some of the work of project anthropologists* permitted a crucial and fuzzy simplification to creep into a central role in project thinking. That idea was that there really was a universe of small farmers out there. Using a log frame (see Chapter 11) helped such mystification along by insisting on body count targets of "small farmer participants." The social processes of stratification and the reality of inequality conveniently disappeared. Rich and poor, men and women, young and old, would develop in harmony. From this intellectual process it is easy to assume that women's subcouncils alone could become an effective means of enhancing the welfare of Zairian women.

---

*or even the work of agricultural economist Terry Hardt, who did the first real baseline survey in March 1980. She found that only 22 percent in a village in the suburbs of Kongolo had even heard of the new variety!

Absence of standards also precludes intelligent discussion of what matters most to participatory development, the quality of human participation. To claim "frequent contact at the village level" (AID, 1980: Ann. 3) by project personnel does not indicate whether these are courtesy calls to village leaders or some more substantive discussion with poor villagers. One is prepared to believe that greater informal contact is taking place. But effective participatory development involves much more. That AID, the GOZ, and the project management "are in firm agreement that resources must be concentrated on the production and marketing activities for which the project was designed" (AID, 1980: 15), suggests very clearly the bureaucratic and political imperatives that control the project. Farmers expressing social needs, for medicine in particular, would have to wait. Those involved do not appear to realize how perfectly this approach refutes any claim that the project is a model of either participatory development or integrated rural development.

Absence of evaluation and research standards also worked to devalue the claims that could be made about the more narrowly conceived economic goal of improving farmers' income. This concept remained quite fuzzy in the project documents, because no one wanted to try to design project operations to diminish all the non-economic (that is, political) ways that farmer livelihood was harmed. Gross sale of kilograms of maize does not equal equivalent improvement in welfare. Project officials did raise issues like terms of trade and political oppression; these matters did find their way into the conditions precedents set in the 1980 project revision. Words on paper, however, do not translate automatically into solutions implemented. By skimming the surface of mass empowerment, through the farmer council mechanism, the project obscures the deeper and more complete participation necessary for true human development. By avoiding discussion of or concrete strategy for change in political institutions, the project helps assure that these changes will be partial, insufficient, and evolutionary in nature. This ideological bias of U.S. social science and its sponsors is of little comfort to the villager who needs protein and health care now.

Beyond raising farmer incomes and enhancing maize self-sufficiency, North Shaba was intended by AID and DAI to be or to evolve into a model integrated rural development project. Several points have already been made about the incompleteness of its overall design. But its theoretical vacuum must be made explicit as well. Integrated development is not the sum of x times the sum of constraint plus bandaid. That does not necessarily result in either integration or development. What is necessary is the perception of development as processes unfolding to define a system in operation. To change processes means not just adding some material inputs; it means understanding and modifying all the incentives in the system as a whole.

The issues of scale and of the efficiency of resource use in relation to need, as well as the issues of the theoretical flaws and willful myopia of conventional social science, on which projects rest, will be relatively easy to resolve. The issues of standards and evaluation will not. The generic need to avoid measurement prevents the establishment of the means to do it. This has tragically wasteful results where organizational and world-system imperatives merge to reinforce each other. The macroeconomic climate in Zaire, as widely admitted by AID and DAI, renders development inhospitable in the extreme. Conditions if anything deteriorated between 1976 and 1980. Project expectations were drastically lowered in important ways. Yet no effort was made to define a situation so bad that the project would be halted as pointless. Neither AID nor DAI could afford to establish such benchmarks because, as with Vietnam in the early 1970s, AID could not tell the State Department that development was impossible in the middle of a war. In concrete ways rural Zaire is a political war zone between rich and poor.

By staying in a project and a project environment as bad as North Shaba, the donor agency is not simply wasting scarce resources, raising false hopes, and preempting more effective development elsewhere. AID is sending a message to the GOZ and governments nearly as antihuman elsewhere that its policy of human needs and human development is really only rhetoric. Any government that fulfills larger world-system needs can ask for and receive aid.

The depth to which this deprofessionalizes and dehumanizes those involved is caught in the language and procedure by which AID and DAI argued to continue the project during 1980. DAI suggested that "the agricultural potential of the area and the needs of the rural population justify some type of development activity" (Barclay et al., 1980: 72); perhaps so, but that is true of dozens of other regions as well. DAI sought a more modest program and felt it might be a positive model for the rest of Zaire; is it on balance a positive model? AID argued with far less embarrassment for the project continuance on four assertions that amounted to little more than saying that it was important to prove that development can take place at all (AID, 1980: Ann. 8). If it could not, that would threaten AID's organizational legitimacy and the validity of its other Zaire projects. That, in turn, would threaten the legitimacy of the Western presence in Zaire and was politically unacceptable. To avoid individual responsibility, at least 13 AID officials signed off before the action memorandum reached the AID Administrator for Africa. Sadly one concludes that donor organizations and the world-system are well served. The organizations at least continue. The world-system may get more cheap maize. Most Zairians, however, are still poor and hungry. We can do better.

CHAPTER BIBLIOGRAPHY

AID (1980). *Zaire North Shaba Maize Production Project (660-0059)*. Action Memorandum and Project Paper Revision with Annexes, August 27.

—— (1976). *North Shaba Maize Production*. Project Paper for 660-11-199-059.

AID, Auditor General (1979). *Review of the AID Program in Zaire*. Report 3-660-80-1, November 28.

Barclay, A. H. (1979). "Anthropological Contributions to the North Shaba Rural Development Project." Paper presented at the annual Society for Applied Anthropology Conference, Philadelphia, March 17.

Barclay, Albert H., et al. (1980). *Development Alternatives, Inc. (DAI) Internal Evaluation of Project North Shaba*. Washington, D.C.: DAI.

Bukaka Bonani (1979). "Une première approche des structures d'intégration de la femme du milieu rural de l'aire du Projet Nord-Shaba au processus du développement." Kongolo, Document de Base No. 8.

Cultivateurs de Kongolo (1979). Letter No. 206/KL/79. on farmers' grievances to Political Commissioner Mulongo Misha K., Lubumbashi.

DIMPEX (1979). *Evaluation of the North Shaba Integrated Rural Development Project Zaire*. July.

Gran, Guy, ed. (1979). *Zaire: The Political Economy of Underdevelopment*. New York: Praeger.

Hardt, Terry Lee (1981). "Decision Making Roles in the Rural Household and the Adoption and Diffusion of an Improved Maize Variety in Northern Shaba Province, Zaire." Unpublished Ph.D. dissertation, Iowa State University.

Hull, Galen (1980). "Is AID Meeting the New Directions Mandate?: A Look at Projects in Zaire and Upper Volta." Paper presented at the 6th Annual Third World Conference, Chicago, March 26-29.

IBRD (1980a). *Zaire Smallholder Maize Project – Staff Appraisal Report.* 2194-ZR, May 2.

____ (1980b). *Report and Recommendation of the President of the International Development Association to the Executive Directors on a Proposed Credit to the Republic of Zaire for a Smallholder Maize Project.* P-2817-ZR, May 16.

Resseguie, Robert W. (1979). "Project North Shaba Internal Project Review – January 26-February 4, 1979." Kinshasa: USAID.

Roth, Alan (1978a). "Maize Marketing Study for Shaba Province, Zaire." DAI, February.

____ (1978b). "Ag Marketing Loan Marketing Survey: Survey of Tanganyika Sub-region, The Role of PMU/PNS." DAI, December.

Thies, S. A. (n.d.) (c1978). "Research/Extension – Mbulula" (8p). Unpublished.

U.S. Congress. House of Representatives. Committee on Foreign Affairs (1980). *Foreign Assistance Legislation for Fiscal Year 1981 – Part 7.* Washington, D.C.: Government Printing Office.

4

Development vs. the World-System: The World Bank in Indonesia and Thailand, 1960–80

AN INTRODUCTION TO THE TRIPLE ALLIANCE
AND THE WORLD BANK

> The review concludes that, despite deficiencies in some projects, the Bank's portfolio in Indonesian agriculture is of overall good quality and likely to contribute substantially to increased production. One of the deficiencies noted is the Bank's inadequate knowledge of prevailing socio-economic conditions in Indonesia.
>
> IBRD,OED (2166, 1978: v)

In sum, the projects are good, production is going up, and yet we don't know what is going on. Here, juxtaposed in a 1978 synopsis of an internal review of 32 World Bank projects begun in Indonesia between FY69 and FY77, are the generic optimism and stunning myopia of the major institution in global development. How can an aid project be good if one does not know what is going on? And is a production rise the equivalent of either quality or development? This chapter will explore how the ideology and the institutional imperatives of the World Bank, mixed with both greed and good intentions, combine to shape the basic processes of national development. Specifically it will explore the impact of the World Bank on two average Third World countries, Thailand and Indonesia, as they struggled with the conflicts between development and the world-system over the last two decades.

To work toward participatory development, it is not sufficient to understand the project process in operation and how the local, regional, and national interests work against the accumulation of surplus by the poor. It is necessary to explore how such interests, through the organizational forms of governments and corporations, interact with international capital to create even more sobering dilemmas for the participation of the poor in the improvement of their livelihood. Peter Evans (1979) in an important study of Brazil has synthesized the matter elegantly with the term "triple alliance."

The triple alliance — local capital, the state, and international capital — produces a form of dependent growth, but it is inherently unable to meet the basic needs of most people. Inherently unable is a disturbing assessment. One must focus not on the conflictive dimensions of this alliance but on its collaborative aspects. A number of studies, especially of Latin American cases, have laid bare the clashes between the global rationality of the multinational corporation and the nationalist needs for local accumulation by the state and by local entrepreneurs. This conflict is often described in terms of core versus periphery. Against this tension, however, areas of common interests and needs merge — merge into a triple alliance.

Most Third World states face a deep and growing gap between citizen aspirations and needs on the one hand and the productivity and equity of economic development on the other. A government, like any organization, wants first and foremost to survive. That means stability and revenue. Poor people, especially alienated ones, are not good citizens or taxpayers. Politics and organizational limits encourage states to look elsewhere for resources. Exporting a taxable primary commodity, foreign investment, and foreign aid have been the attractive solutions provided by the world-system. Both the state and local capital have in most situations found it more alluring and profitable (and far less politically threatening) to share national production with international capital than with local citizens en masse.

Accepting international capital means accepting a wide range of unequal relationships. States are encouraged to provide modern infrastructure, organizational skills, political stability, cheap labor (and thus cheap food and/or malnutrition) and low-priced commodity exports. These interests of international capital in particular and core nations in general set parameters of and condition the development strategies of Third World states. To the extent such a state seeks to encourage the participation of private capital of any sort, it is enticed toward a development strategy of production for profit, not for human need.

The real world is not so neatly organized. Governments also face a domestic agenda including food and energy needs. Some world-system actors, most notably international development agencies, despite their wants-based methods, proclaim more humanistic, needs-based goals. People in both kinds of organizations assert that they are using resources and working successfully to help the poor. Neither analytically nor operationally can government officials or aid agency employees be reduced to simply ideologically guided puppets imprisoned by the overall world model of the triple alliance. Many such officials mean well. The result is ambivalence. They want to help poor people and yet meet institutional or corporate needs at the same time. This chapter will explore how this ambivalence has been acted out as two governments and one aid agency, the World Bank, have tried to go about development, especially agricultural development.

Thailand and Indonesia have both been facing a particular set of basic problems in food production and, with World Bank assistance, have pursued comparable Green Revolution paths. Each country discovered during the 1960s that to stay in one piece and feed itself, it had to raise food productivity. Development had to include small farmers. How to control the process was the central dilemma for the state. How to gain maximum profit was the fundamental motive of international agribusiness. Both proclaimed nobler intentions as well. The Green Revolution solution, however, became "the ideal way to attempt the *rapid* integration of the entire peasant community into both the national and international frameworks, socially and economically" (De Koninck, 1979: 266). The questions for development designers of the 1980s are "ideal" for whom and for what? Ignorance of "socio-economic conditions" that have resulted is no replacement for good intentions.

This particular primary solution for agricultural development in these two Southeast Asian nations will be explored here within the context of how the two countries have adapted to the world-system and its needs during the 1960s and 1970s. For it is only in relation to the balance of forces in the triple alliance at any point that major development decisions and resource allocations make sense. The impact of the World Bank as development guide, bank, analyst, and teacher in world-system processes will be reflected throughout by an examination of the country memoranda and project reports on these countries.

It is important to understand the Bank's impact on nominally independent states from at least three theoretical perspectives. First is the Bank's own view of itself. Given its charter as a bank and beholden to host governments, the Bank has long held that it is most proper and efficient to give its money to the government as the organization that can most effectively reach the most people. The Bank's objectives, as it sees them, are three in number: resource transfers; direct attacks on poverty, unemployment and basic needs; and building development institutions. The mix varies over time and by country. In its sober moments the Bank will even admit that for countries like Indonesia "in the present circumstances . . . a 6 or even 7% per annum growth rate of GNP will not generate sufficient employment opportunities and cannot ensure a significant increase in living standards of the poor" (Hasan, 1978: 21).

Analysts more skeptical of the good intentions of governments and aid donors have tended to assess the role of the Bank by where it puts its money. The needs of the world-system are readily apparent. Money has gone to infrastructure investments facilitating private investment, to productive activities for export (not for capital goods), and to agricultural and urban development that diminished mass discontent. Project financing has maximized corporate supplier profits of core countries and speeded private bank penetration. As for energy, the Bank is supposed to assist the development of fossil fuels for export to the core, while nonfossil fuel (and nonexportable) and high technology (nuclear) sources are to meet Third World needs (Caldwell, in Elliott, 1978: 20-21). The Bank is in an early stage of energy analysis, but its first publications give no attention to solar or soft energy paths.

Neither of these perspectives is very useful in moving the real world toward the effective, as opposed to verbal, involvement of people in development. One must understand how the Bank can create internal work incentives so that after 10 years and 32 projects, it can know, for example, so little about village Java. The world of internal organizational issues occupies several subsequent chapters. But external work incentives are also at work. Such an absence of quality must have been satisfactory to the host government, which cooperated. Examining this relationship as one between two organizations, as well as between members of the triple alliance, sheds a great deal of light on the practical contradictions of using large organizations in the world-system to promote human welfare. It will also begin to suggest practical means to surmount them.

This chapter will pursue three tasks: describing how two average Third World countries, Thailand and Indonesia, have become ever more enmeshed in the world-system between 1960 and 1980; chronicling the World Bank in this process, more directly in Indonesia since 1966 and more subtly in Thailand throughout the period; and weighing concrete Bank projects both before and after the 1973 Bank policy changes toward helping the poor. The goal is to understand the processes of mass exclusion and what, in practical terms, would have to be changed to bring about participatory development.

INDONESIA IN THE CONTEMPORARY WORLD-SYSTEM

Indonesia gained political sovereignty from the Netherlands in 1949. Its population, then about 77 million, grew to 97 million in 1961 and 119 million in 1971; birth control measures had some impact in the 1970s and the 1976 estimate is 130 million. Although the territory contains thousands of islands, about 82 million people live on Java alone, more than 600 per square kilometer. Nearly 80 percent of the population live in rural areas and are primarily involved in rice agriculture. Countrywide per capita income in 1976 was about $280, but more than 50 million people were below $90 per capita. East and Central Java contained 45 percent of the urban and 55 percent of the rural poor (IBRD, 2093: iv). The country has made progress in erasing illiteracy, but more than 100 million do not have safe drinking water. The development problems for any government would not be small. Such figures indicate that no government yet has effectively involved the great mass of people in development.

The colonial heritage was not auspicious. Infrastructure and investment had gone to export crops like rubber, tea, tobacco, palm oil, and copra. The modern sector was dominated by Europeans and Chinese. The colonial state did not have the incentive or the ability to be much more than a night watchman. Some Indonesians got involved in nationalist politics, but most did not escape local concerns. The arrival of political independence did not overcome this fragmentation or the kind of patron-client social ties that insured that unequal participation in political and economic affairs would continue.

Under the leadership of President Sukarno, Indonesia struggled with the world-system through early rehabilitation plans and a first Five Year Plan (1955-60). Despite much socialist rhetoric and a spirited anti-Western line in international forums, Dutch enterprises were not nationalized on any scale until 1958 and others not until 1964-65. Sukarno's efforts to develop indigenous small industry in rural and semirural areas did not appeal to agents of the world-system like the World Bank. Indonesia joined the Bank in 1954 only to be told by a Bank mission the next year that "problems of inflation, continuing budget deficits, and compensation issues for former Dutch property" precluded lending until "the stabilization of political and economic conditions" (IBRD, OED, 2166: vii). International capital, public and private, remained unenthusiastic.

Sukarno, leaning on a power base of the army, the students, and the Muslims, struggled in vain to deal with adverse world trade terms, inflation, and mounting debts. Elite consumerism, military outlays, disdain for family planning, and failure to carry through land reform laws all worked against human development (Palmer, 1978: 14-15). Indeed the communist party, the PKI, was comparatively the most effective force mobilizing for political and economic development by the early 1960s. International antagonism, internal conflicts, and financial bankruptcy led to a violent political transformation in 1965-66. There followed a new military leadership under Suharto, an abject surrender to the world-system and its export-led growth model, and massive capital inflows spearheaded by the World Bank.

The working of the Bank, under the aegis of an Inter-Government Group on Indonesia (IGGI), in economic stabilization and rehabilitation in the late 1960s has been well chronicled (Palmer, 1978: chapter 3 for instance) and will be returned to later as part of the long-term systems maintenance process central to this chapter. But foreign aid deeply affected other political and economic processes in Indonesia, creating for the state both chains and freedom. What is often termed the New Order was a return to the triple alliance Sukarno had tried to undermine. The new military government looked to the army, the planners, the bureaucrats, and urban intellectuals as core components of the state. Although the military built stronger links with the Chinese business community, overall development served the export sectors and international interests to the detriment of local concerns. It is worth exploring how such mass exclusion was maintained.

After squashing the communists, student groups, and Islamic political parties, the government created its own party GOLKAR, less as a means of mobilization than of occupying space. The generic patron-client relationships, which worked against participation, perpetuated a society described (Jackson and Pye, 1978: 34-55) as a multitude of complex molecules with weak linkages. The government penetrated the country by appointing more and more army officials to regional and local positions. Communication flowed down through local elites. The mass at the bottom remained isolated. The physical means of communication are not there. A steady concentration of power has produced an ever more bureaucratic state and reinforced cultural perceptions that power is a zero-sum game.

Because there are cultural justifications of inequality does not mean that Indonesians accept them gladly. Violence is common. As the old social values of sharing decay and class conflicts sharpen, there remain limited legal and effective channels to seek change. Occasional outbursts against corruption can have effect but in no measure represent effective participation or a means of ending corruption. As long as revenues and aid do not cover administrative costs, corruption will be widespread. Indeed, participation comes largely by opposing concentration of power and spreading corruption to maintain stability.

This corporatist approach between organizations and people extends throughout the economic sphere as well. The military has worked cooperatively with foreign interests and the Chinese in various components of export-led growth. Investments have been unbalanced among sectors and regions. They have overpromoted rice against other foods, worked against indigenous and small-scale entrepreneurs, been scaled with little thought to capital limits or job needs, and in general reflected the priorities of international interests (Palmer, 1978: 152-53). It was in the promotion of rice development that the state most typified its fundamentally elitist and authoritarian attitudes and showed most clearly how the triple alliance works to exclude most from significant benefit.

From the mid 1960s, the government has sought to raise rice yields and production by irrigation rehabilitation and by the technology of the Green Revolution through evolving generations of programs called BIMAS and INMAS. By working through regional and local elites and by introducing a technology requiring substantial amounts of capital and labor, it was assured that only the rural elite would profit. An improved BIMAS credit program at its height during 1974-75 reached a little over 20 percent of the Indonesian farmers and about 33 percent of the rice-growing area (IBRD, 2060: 4-5). Elites were able to coopt efforts at building cooperatives and to avoid repaying government loans. One could chronicle the international interests, the endemic practical problems of getting appropriate amounts of inputs delivered, the weaknesses of government marketing and much else (see Hüsken, 1979; Palmer, 1977; Hinkson, 1975; Franke, 1972 et al.), but the interplay of social forces is what is crucial for world-system concerns.

De Koninck (1979) is the best brief synthesis of the issues; Gibbons et al. (1980) is the basic work. The new technology, by demanding more labor and capital, sets off a process of concentrating control in the hands of the large farmers who can afford to increase productive inputs. While these farmers become ever more dependent on and vulnerable to world market forces, they in turn lure the marginal producers into becoming the reserve army of labor needed. Three rural classes have been evolving on Java in the last decade: the integrated merchant producers; the marginal (0.3 hectare or less) producers who sell more and more labor; and the middle peasants who create enough surplus to survive but not to accumulate and, more importantly, play the intermediary role that cushions conflicts. Dependency grows unevenly for each class as control over land and livelihood diminishes. It is a pristine case of nonparticipatory development and the basic process by which the needs of the world-system and state are being met. The World Bank's most recent thesis (IBRD, 2093: 30) is that this production process did permit benefits to continue to reach the bottom 40 percent over the 1970-76 period; seven pages later it chronicled a decline in caloric intake for the same group and period. In its inimitably understated way the Bank summed up Indonesia's development dilemma far better than it understood; the theme of this 1979 report is the "need for a truly comprehensive, long-term, employment-oriented development strategy." (IBRD, 2093: 16), a thesis that sits incongruously with many of its growth-oriented prescriptions to be analyzed.

THAILAND IN THE CONTEMPORARY WORLD-SYSTEM

Thailand's entrance into the world-system in the nineteenth century, moving from subsistence rice agriculture to export production, was far gentler and more subtle than kindred Third World experiences. The country did not have Indonesia's ethnic diversity, geographical fragmentation, population density, colonial heritage, or political turmoil. Western observers relate that Thailand's 42 million people (1976) enjoyed minimal unemployment with an average 7.6 percent Gross Domestic Product (GDP) – 4.4 percent per capita – growth rate between 1960 and 1977, largely by expanding the area under cultivation and broadening its export base (IBRD, 2059). Gross National Product (GNP) per capita in 1977 was $410. Yet, even from a world model of harmony, limits appear. Thailand is running out of land, pursues an industrialization strategy not related to future job needs, and distributes government services in ways that maintain major areas of poverty outside the Central Plain. International authorities, working from surveys from 1962/3 and 1975/6, concluded, however, that growth benefits spread enough so that the population deemed in absolute poverty fell from 52 percent to 25 percent over this period.

Economists tend to ignore social processes and social costs. Urban Bangkok, whose population rose above 5 million in 1978, has at least 500,000 living in 300 slums. A report to the 1979 Rome Food Conference (IASG, 1979, II: 13-14) noted one of the world's highest homicide rates, 300,000 prostitutes by a 1973 national estimate, 600,000 drug addicts by a 1979 report, and a deplorable record of child malnutrition and abuse. Child labor is common both in the countryside and, mostly unrecorded, in urban homes, shops, and factories. The Bangkok Post (December 3, 1978) reported a raid on a toffee factory in Thonburi finding 56 girls, age 8 to 15, working as forced labor; most were malnourished.

It is important not to draw too many detailed generalizations about either strengths or weaknesses in the Thai developmental experiences without first sketching some of the enormous regional variations. Of 7.82 million households counted in 1976, 82 percent were in rural areas; most people are self-employed, and by the 1973/4 survey only 12 percent of the land is rented, mostly in provinces of the Central Region. Regional differences in income are considerable, with the Central Region households outearning those of the Northern, Northeastern, and Southern regions by a 5/3 margin in 1975-76 (IBRD, 2059: 34-36).

Keys to the regional inequalities have been skewed national investments, access to markets, and particular crop production. The 20 percent of the population in the Central Plain have excellent rice lands. Improvements in water control have now reached more than 60 percent of the area, but only 35 percent of the farmers are double-cropping. New seeds, fertilizer, tractors, and a much higher quantity and quality of government services help them. Specialized fruit and vegetable farms enjoy the access to Bangkok's market. East and west of the Central Plain, farmers are now producing maize, cassava, sugar, and rubber for commercial sale. The 40 percent of the population in the Northeast Region, in contrast, pursue rain-fed agriculture against uncertain weather. There and in the Northern Region the organization of labor and capital and the absence of rural roads serve to limit commercial possibilities and even the production of surplus. Here too the rapid expansion of holdings, combined with cumbersome entitlement processes, has left widespread insecurity and poor access to credit. Nationwide in 1976 40 percent of the holdings lacked formal title. The other major region, the Southern, has an additional set of problems. Rubber is the major commercial crop. Smallholders face market uncertainties and stagnant yields amidst growing land scarcities; farmers devote primary attention to subsistence rice plots. Moslem provinces in the lower Southern Region get even less national investment (IBRD, 2059: 12, 34-52).

These enormous regional disparities, resulting in far greater average wealth for that 32.5 percent (1976) of the population in Bangkok and the Central Region, are not a historical accident. They are the logical result of the uneven development characteristic of the world-system, as the agents of the state, local capital, and international capital interact over time. Some brief historical points are in order. There were many parallels between the behavior of the Thai monarchy and that of the neighboring colonial governments. Both excluded the mass from effective political participation while using force to extract as much economic surplus as feasible. The Thai military, like the rest of the bureaucracy, was modernized mainly as a means of internal royalist consolidation in the face of far more instability than is conventionally recognized (Anderson, 1978: 16). The state could not extract enough revenue from Thais in the nineteenth century and so imported Chinese. Taxation on their opium, gambling, and spirit farms garnered 40-50 percent of state revenue between 1850 and 1900; Chinese were also found necessary for public works activities early in this century. A central precedent was thus laid. The Thai state could modernize and expand its revenue base by international links. It did not have to involve the Thai people in development activities, only growth activities, in order to enlarge a surplus and thus a revenue base.

Neither the advent of the military in 1932, the uncertainties of World War II, nor Thailand's subsequent strategic value to the Western powers opposing communism in Indochina altered this basic reality. The 1932 coup changed the class basis of the government (Elliott, 1978: 78 ff), sharpening the struggle between those trying to centralize economic control for local and state interests and those serving international needs. The balance of forces shifted several times (most clearly laid out by Bell, in Turton, ed., 1978: 51-79). The central international link with the United States was formed in the 1950s. U.S. training of military officials and U.S. bilateral aid programs of nation building in the 1950s and counterinsurgency in the 1960s (Caldwell, 1974), combined with the efforts of the World Bank and international investors, provided ideological and political continuity. This was only briefly interrupted by a civilian interregnum between 1973 and 1976 when the balance of power among the triple alliance swung toward a state-local capital axis.

More central to the World Bank's role in the triple alliance than details of these world-system conflicts are the aspects of system collaboration over the last generation. As in Indonesia, a highly centralized bureaucratic polity perpetuated cultural and political means to maintain inequalities and exclude the mass of Thais. State capitalism grew spectacularly in the 1950s, and military officials supplemented earnings by joining the boards of directors of many new banks and firms. By 1957 at least 141 direct state enterprises existed with the development corporation, NEDCOL, probably the most egregious drain on the treasury (Elliott, 1978: 116-17).

The Vietnam War brought this elite not only great wealth but also severe political problems and lessons. A portion of the elite learned some lessons. Some with good intentions and some in a defensive spirit tried, with varying degrees of success, to push agricultural development and social programs. In the Central Plains, Green Revolution technologies were introduced with the same degree of obliviousness to local social relations as in Indonesia. The

World Bank, which assembled much data on land tenancy and average incomes (IBRD, 2059 and its Annexes 1 and 4), relates little about processes like rural indebtedness. One recent independent investigation of villages in the lower Northeastern Region described these conditions in one locale.

> Practically every household is hopelessly indebted to one person, Chusak. Chusak holds all their land titles as collateral. Most villagers sell *kao kieu* ("green rice"), a practice fairly common in many parts of the country whereby the peasant presells his entire crop, either in advance of planting or harvest below one-quarter, even up to one-half, of the eventual market price to Chusak. . . . To survive, peasants have to take out rice loans (or cash loans), both at the charge of over 100% interest rate per month. The legal rate is 15%. Several families owe Chusak more than ฿10,000 ($500) of debt each for initial loans of only ฿1,000. Chusak himself owns several Japanese pick-up trucks, two small-scale rice mills, some 100 *rai* (= 16 h.) of rice land, and is also the village's fertilizer distributer. Workers in the rice mills are paid in kind about 100 kgs. of poor grade milled rice (worth about ฿450-460 or $22.50 or -.60) per month. Two other members of Chusak's family have almost similar control over two nearby villages. Small rural capitalists are numerous throughout the province, and in other regions of the country. . . . They are likely to have considerable power over local politics, . . . sometimes virtual control, over the poorly paid government officials. It is not uncommon that they take the law into their own hands with hired thugs and gunmen (IASG, 1979: 16-17).

Conditions like this have led to violent peasant reactions to central authorities in all regions of Thailand. Surveys over recent years have found anywhere from 60 to 90 percent of the peasants significantly in debt. It is thus not obvious that growth in per capita income, so pleasing to the World Bank, has resulted in improvement of life quality. The Thai government recognizes this in some measure as the 1975 land reform and 1977 *tambon* project suggest. But cursory investigation of either demonstrates their cosmetic effect in reality. The budgetary allocations in 1979 (the proclaimed year of the farmer), the rapid transformation of small peasant production of pineapples into international agribusiness plantations, and many other trends suggest that as the decade ended the long-term syndrome of counterinsurgency and increasing productivity held sway. Given thus the broad outlines of the reign of the triple alliance in these processes, it is now time to address head on the role of the World Bank — on its terms and those of its critics — in its contradictory roles as adjunct of international capital (i.e., a growth agency) and as a humanitarian development agency, its post-1973 claim.

THE WORLD BANK: ADVICE PLUS MONEY EQUALS DEVELOPMENT?

There is no analytically perfect way to focus on one element of an organic or human system and measure the impact of that element alone on the quality of the system as a whole. As Tables 4.1 and 4.2

TABLE 4.1 World Bank in Thailand and Indonesia: Projects and Commitments

((#) $ mil.)

	Thailand		Indonesia		East Asia & Pacific Total	
FY50-60	(6)	106.80	—		—	
FY61-65	(8)	104.10	—		—	
FY66	(1)	36.00	—		—	
FY67	(1)	5.00	—		—	
FY68	(2)	55.00	—		(12)	167.5
FY69	(1)	23.00	(4)	51.0	(19)	307.3
FY70	(1)	46.50	(4)	80.5	(17)	364.0
FY71	(1)	12.50	(8)	95.9	(22)	398.0
FY72	(2)	42.40	(8)	105.5	(21)	316.3
FY73	(5)	105.60	(8)	144.9	(26)	546.5
FY74	(4)	149.00	(7)	132.0	(27)	703.9
FY75		—	(7)	332.0	(24)	976.4
FY76	(6)	228.00	(9)	517.0	(35)	1,458.5
FY77	(5)	162.80	(11)	440.0	(36)	1,475.0
FY78	(7)	231.45	(7)	435.0	(37)	1,726.2
FY79	(9)	325.10	(11)	830.0	(40)	2,130.0
Totals	(60)	1,590.47	(86)	3,163.8	( )	12,681.1

Sources: Hasan, 1978: 77; World Bank Annual Reports; IBRD *Statement of Loans,* December 31, 1979. Discrepancies exist between sources because a few loans change value over time.

TABLE 4.2 World Bank in Thailand and Indonesia: Project Distribution by Sector

((#) $ mil.)

	Agriculture Food, Img.		Pop., Educ., Social		Power, Infrastructure		Industry DFC		Tech., Other	
Thailand										
FY50-60	(1)	18		–	(5)	88.45		–		–
FY61-65	(3)	25.11		–	(4)	48.91	(1)	1.04		–
FY66-70			(1)	5.9	(6)	148.02		–		–
FY71-75	(2)	12.49	(2)	34.9	(7)	248.6	(1)	11.7		–
FY76-77	(5)	204	(1)	31	(2)	76	(3)	79.8		–
FY78-79	(3)	82.5	(4)	76.7	(8)	392.6	(1)	4.75		–
Total	(14)	342.1	(8)	148.5	(32)	1,002.58	(6)	97.29		
Indonesia										
FY66-70	(5)	86.5		–	(2)	43		–	(1)	2
FY71-75	(16)	373.4	(4)	37.6	(9)	258.8	(5)	111.5	(4)	29
FY76-77	(8)	334	(4)	133	(5)	422	(2)	55	(1)	13
FY78-79	(8)	627	(3)	118	(5)	460	(1)	50	(1)	10
Total	(39)	1,420.9	(11)	388.6	(21)	1,183.8	(8)	116.5	(7)	54

Sources: IBRD, 1973, P-1251: Annex II; IBRD, 1979, P-2549 IND; IBRD *Annual Reports*; IBRD, *Statement of Loans*, December 31, 1979; IBRD, 1979, P-2410-TH: 28; earlier loans listed as of December 31, 1979 value.

suggest, the World Bank has transferred large amounts of capital to Thailand and Indonesia, most of it during the 1970s. Specific problems in food production and infrastructure needs have been favored. National debts have risen appreciably. The Bank has inflicted its organizational culture on its own projects and on the departments it deals with, especially the national planning agencies. But the sum of its direct influence would seem to have varied widely over the last two decades, and it is the Bank's indirect role as long-term system stabilizer and guide that is most crucial to the triple alliance. Critics would argue that the Bank has consistently sought to defuse the contradictions, weaken the struggles of the mass for a greater share of the productive surplus, and alert the triple alliance to threats and the means of overcoming them. Those in the Bank who recognize conflict in the world might argue in return that, especially since its new policy mandate in 1973 to help directly the poorest of the poor, it is attempting to surmount or diminish such conflicts. It is little wonder then that the particular country papers reveal so many inconsistencies, omissions, and ambivalences.

What follows is based primarily on internal project papers and country reports. One despairs of trying to relate quantitatively total Bank flows to total national expenditure on development. No consistent benchmark or definitions appeared. It seems unlikely that, before the late 1970s, Bank disbursements alone could have disrupted national finances in Thailand or Indonesia. During FY73-77 Bank flows were 13 percent of new Indonesian and 15 percent of new Thai long-term capital; but during FY78-80 a Bank estimate put the figures at 50 percent for Indonesia and 19 percent for Thailand (Hasan, 1978: 32). Indonesia thus faces a new loss of de facto autonomy that must concern all contemporary analysts. The task here, however, is to see the more historical and multidimensional implications of resource and idea flows.

Table 4.1 indicates that Thailand and Indonesia are two of the major recipients in a very rapidly growing Bank program for East Asia. If the Bank itself receives the funding it aspires to, Indonesia will maintain and increase its growing lead as the major regional borrower; the Bank sees Indonesia having enormous capital needs in the early 1980s, finds itself playing the major role, and projects lending more than a billion a year by the mid-1980s (Hasan, 1978: 39, 77). As will be noted, such a progression would represent historical continuity. Funding cuts for the World Bank in the early 1980s have, however, served to temper actual outlays.

In large measure the level of funding to each country has reflected current needs and fears of the world-system. Thailand was under the U.S. umbrella in the 1950s and 1960s and received bilateral funding. The denouement in Vietnam created political conditions whereby both countries desired a larger, more indirect aid flow. The Bank cooperated. International capital did not like the new civilian government that arrived. The 1973-74 strikes by students, workers, and peasants were viewed ominously. Foreign investment stopped, growth slowed, and the Bank essentially stopped preparing new projects. Only American military aid flows increased. (Bell, in Turton, 1978: 68-69). It was not an original strategy (witness Chile under Allende), and it worked again. In the late 1970s Bank flows grew rapidly as a new Thai military government reaffirmed its international linkages. Indonesia's interface with the Bank has represented the world-system's antipathy for Sukarno and pleasure with his successors. The major constraints in the 1970s appear to have been the ability of each party to process money more quickly. Notice how the average project size grew.

Even the very general sectoral breakdowns provided in Table 4.2 indicate that the rhetoric of the Bank of new policy directions is not consistently supported by its monetary allocations. If aid is to help the poorest directly, it is not apparent in this portrait. Infrastructure needs still dominate both country portfolios. If agricultural irrigation projects were also so defined, the distribution would be even more slanted. A closer examination is in order (see the next section) to see whether agriculture or social programs in the late 1970s embrace any of the elements of participatory development. First it is necessary to sample the prescriptive advice and overall development guidance the Bank offered Indonesia, from a uniquely intimate relationship since 1966, and Thailand from a more orthodox, distant and yet comparably successful link. In both cases — Thailand since the mid 1950s and Indonesia since the mid 1960s — the broad lines of Bank advice have accorded with the needs of international capital and have, in general terms, been followed by the Indonesian and Thai states to the overall advantage of the triple alliance. In neither case was this surprising. Indonesia's ties will be explored first.

Given the global educational threat for the world-system posed by Sukarno, it was logical for international capital and its surrogates to solidify ideological control on the government of his successor Suharto. Under the consortium umbrella of creditor nations (IGGI), the World Bank and the IMF did more than renegotiate Indonesia's debts and lay down the overall outlines of stabilization in 1966 and 1967. The Bank sent a large mission in the fall of 1967 and quickly approved (March 1968) a small project as a sign of good intentions. A resident Bank mission (the RSI) set up shop in September 1968, and its first director had an extraordinarily close and influential relationship to Indonesian planners in the years that followed.

Difference in Bank/Government strategies would hardly have been likely to emerge in the early years of RSI. The central planning agency, Bappenas, shared the same building till 1973 with the Harvard Advisory Development Service team, the Netherlands Economic Institute team and RSI. Contacts between all these groups of economists were so close as to ensure a unified strategy (IBRD, OED, 2166: 24).

Add that many of the BAPPENAS economists were University of California, Berkeley, Ph.D.s, and one can understand why the triple alliance marches on.

It is important to suggest limiting factors at the outset. Notwithstanding biannual, and more recently annual, IGGI meetings advised and educated by the Bank, donor coordination has had many practical and procedural problems. The IGGI ignored development quality and could not even prevent project overlapping by donors. Despite close Bank supervision, the Bank's own early 1970s projects (and later ones) were exercises in ignorance of implementation theory; of the first 15 agricultural projects, 60 percent ran two or more years behind (compared with 27 percent worldwide Bank experience) and there was an average 76 percent cost overrun, well above Bank norms (IBRD, OED, 2166: 19).

A more serious hindrance for these Bank technocrats was, however, the ambivalent and sometimes hostile reaction of Indonesian officials and people to their new-found dependency on the world-system and its aid. In the early 1970s Franklin Weinstein (1976) interviewed a spectrum of these leaders and found a high distaste for aid dependency. It made Indonesia look weak and undignified. Defining success on IMF terms was demeaning, undermining national sovereignty and portending corruption. Most interviewed felt foreign influence excessive. Japan was particularly noted as using its aid for its own gain. While some of the Indonesian economists ruefully admitted to being aware of these sentiments, they felt too weak on the whole to oppose foreign intrusions. The Indonesian elite as a whole saw the world as a hostile place and "80% were convinced that the industrialized countries assisted Indonesia only to serve their own interests" (Weinstein, 1976: 264 and 228-85 in general). This is one reason that technocratic development strategies flowing from foreign advisors did not move easily from paper to practice.

These caveats notwithstanding, the Bank has produced an enormous volume of documentation and advice on Indonesia in the last dozen years. The most important overall treatments or basic reports were completed in 1970 (EAP 19a), 1972 (25-IND), 1975 (708-IND), and 1979 (2093-IND with seven associated sector studies). A number of other country and sector papers, the mass of reports involved in 86 projects (FY68-FY79), and diverse thematic, evaluation, and research papers add to the literary universe. How much is read very widely in Indonesia is open to question. The Bank was quite proud of the 1974 agricultural sector survey as the state of the art but could find no major result from it except the revival of transmigration projects. It is less in specific advice than in the general world model and its reification that the Bank succeeds in perpetuating and deepening the export-led growth model and thus the domination of the triple alliance. Two reports on Indonesia and three comparable reports on Thailand demonstrate the fundamental tenets of Bank advice and analysis.

The three-volume November 1970 basic report on Indonesia lays bare the Bank theses. A fair synthesis of its own synthesis could be reduced to these eight points, which reflect the Bank's euphoria over Indonesia's progress between 1966 and 1969.

1. Progress equals growing investment, output, and exports.
2. Imports also grew.
3. The government is firmly committed to the operation of market forces and will only use indirect influence on them; it will work toward the financial independence of state-owned enterprises.
4. New projects march forward and administrative problems are recognized.
5. The government is aware it needs more revenue for projects and must resolve the resulting problems.
6. Debts have been rescheduled and the situations stabilized.
7. The beginning of the process of economic development, made possible by stability and new capital, was seen in 1970.
8. More important in the long run than new resources will be improvements in managerial capacity and organization.

(IBRD, EAP, 19a, I: i-iii)

One might hope that point 8 hinted at some real understanding of development, but it did not. The Bank was thinking of technical bureaucratic changes. Indeed much of the Bank advice is that of one bureaucracy encouraging another one to improve, that is, to be more like it. There are also clear ideological choices. These eight points in sum crystallize neoclassical capitalist ideology, its technocratic and elitist basis, its oblivion to the effective relationship of people and economic process, and its mystification of empirical reality and the English language. Inside the three volumes one finds a few human concerns; the new health plan created at international urging has some participatory aspects. But volume 2, a discussion of the 98 projects to be funded by international capital during 1971-72, is a sobering compendium of the contradictions between development and the world-system. The Bank's portfolio at that point looked quite small in comparison to the sum of international interests.

The less proprietary and more subtle way the Bank acts toward more sovereign countries is reflected in two basic country reports on Thailand during the same intellectual and policy generation. One, dating from work during 1957-58, was published in 1959 in book form. The other, a mission of mid-1971, emerged as EAP-28, a six-volume internal report of January 1972. The 1959 report can be summarized by these eight conclusions and prescriptions.

1. The rising government role has contributed much to the considerable post-World War II economic progress and the high growth of export volume.

2. Central attention should go to expanding primary production; double-crop rice on the Central Plain; expand rubber production in the south; develop fishing potential; give priority to agriculture in the Northeast.

3. Encourage private sector activity in light manufacturing.

4. Face the shortcomings of haphazard planning, uncertain financing, shortage of trained manpower, influence of political considerations, institutional limits, and ignorance of physical resources.

5. Create a central planning agency, improve attitudes on providing information, upgrade budgeting forms, procedures, and accounting.

6. Withdraw the government from industrial activity where its record is for the most part poor.

7. Plan much larger capital expenditures, enhancing irrigation and agriculture extension; IBRD chronicled levels.

8. Public development priorities should be power, roads, transport, communications, social programs, and local urban development.

These prescriptions reveal the multiple ways the Bank works to open a country to the world-system, encourages public capital to set the stage for private gain, and prepares the state to play a more efficient role in the process.

The Bank's perceptions and advice 13 years later reflect the progress it has made, the continuation of long-term systemic needs, the new tactics necessary, and Thailand as a good partner. Report EAP-28 contains these basic points:

1. The last two years have been spent adjusting to the unusually favorable GDP growth of 1966-69 caused by the Vietnam War and high rubber and rice prices.
2. Development has concentrated in Bangkok, and large regional income disparities have resulted.
3. The Bank supports the objectives of the third Five-Year Plan, 1972-76, which calls for 7 percent growth in GDP, stability, more exports, fewer imports, major capital inflows (especially official credits), and a stress on agriculture.
4. Long-term needs exist to build exports faster than the plan envisages.
5. Agriculture yields have to rise and fertilizer prices have to come down to permit the introduction of HYV (High Yield Variety) seed technology.
6. Shift the emphasis in manufacturing from domestic orientations toward exports, and give it financial incentives.
7. The family planning program is progressing well, but education will need more than the planned budget increases.
8. A general need exists for more urban and regional planning to supplement the USAID-assisted Northeastern Region plan and for improvements in project planning and implementation capacities.

One would not know that inequitable rural conditions had sustained both poverty and revolution in a neighboring rice agriculture economy for 25 years and that some of the same issues in political economy might be germane to Thai development needs. Development was instead seen as more money, new seeds, and the trimmings. Given the wide disparities in economic and cultural realities between Indonesia and Thailand at the beginning of the 1970s, one cannot, in sum, account for the similarities of Bank prescriptions without adducing the machinations of both an institutional cookbook and a world-system for which the Bank prepares its clients for assimilation.

In 1973 the World Bank rhetorically recognized that trickle-down development was not reaching poor people. By the mid-1970s the preface of its annual reports read in part that "present developmental strategy places a greatly increased emphasis on investments which can directly affect the well-being of the masses of poor people of developing countries by making them more productive and by including them as active participants in the development process." One could reasonably expect that such ideas would play a great part in subsequent country reports and project papers. However, while such rhetoric has had some success in encouraging further financial support from industrial countries, it has rather less if not minimal impact on the operational aspects of the Bank. The contradictions grew sharper for those in large organizations like the Bank actually *trying* to help people, rather than just asserting that growth per se must help people. It is important to see how the world-system development guide tried to come to grips with this dilemma.

In February 1979 the Bank issued a major country report on Indonesia (IBRD, 2093-IND) which, with its associated sector papers, provides one with a clear idea of intellectual advances over the decade, their limitations, and the operational conflicts that result. The report sketches its own conclusions and prescriptions right at the start. Indonesia's current situation, it argued, includes these elements: a good track record through the crises of the 1970s; material progress at all levels despite wide income disparities; a tightening resource position demanding major additional public resource mobilization efforts; and, despite difficult structural adjustments in the 1980s, the expectation that the severe poverty and food security problems could be resolved as soon as the year 2000. The Bank prescribed these remedies:

1. Enhance public sector job-creating investments and avoid capital-intensive ones.

2. Improve the incentives and remove bottlenecks for foreign investment, especially outside Jakarta.

3. Reduce budgetary and nonbudgetary subsidies.

4. Give special emphasis to promoting labor-intensive export-oriented industries.

5. Maintain a positive real lending rate — avoid subsidizing the use of capital at the expense of labor.

6. Improve food security by work on price policies, research, extension, irrigation, and large-scale settlement.

7. Strengthen institutional support for rehabilitation of labor-intensive export crops like rubber, oil palm, and coconut.

Pause and contemplate this catalog from the point of view of the needs of the triple alliance. While much of it represents export-led growth and business as usual, there has been a growing appreciation of how mass poverty and food insecurity threaten local capital and the state. Thus the triple alliance needs to incorporate a larger proportion of the mass into "development," raise the quality and quantity of employment, and raise food production. It is not clear that the Bank fully understands the motives of the players. Consider for instance this assertion: "Government programs in the smallholder sector, more by default than by design, have tended to favor rice farmers at the expense of non-rice farmers, and the landowners over the landless" (IBRD, 2093-IND: 14). One could conclude charitably that the Bank really believes its conclusion: in Indonesia there is "no lack of political commitment to development," (88) just a relatively weak administrative framework. But good intentions do not feed hungry people.

Given the global literature that distinguishes growth from development, there is no honest reason for continuing such mystifications. Nor can one countenance simply oblique references to politics every 30-40 pages (the potential dangers of land sales and concentration that need urgent study, for instance, on page 46). Assembling the raw data of human poverty and exhorting change are no substitutes for an analytic methodology. Authentically developmental analysis would consistently link politics and economics, explain how and why the processes of stratification work as they do, and create practical relations between people and productive activities through participatory processes. If the thesis of the report is really the "need for a truly comprehensive, long-term, employment development strategy" (IBRD, 2093-IND: 16) as noted before, the methodology for such a needs-based economics is not in evidence.

One starts the September 1978 Bank report on Thailand (IBRD, 2059-TH) with some hope. Both its title (*Thailand: Toward a Development Strategy of Full Participation*) and its structure are far from Bank norms. Much of the 131 pages of text is devoted to profiling the regional desparities in income, economic activity, and potential. Long-term development problems are recognized. There is even some occasional understanding of the triple alliance. The Thai government (v) is described as caught between the rhetoric of social objectives and priorities and both a "growth process and operating decisions that seem to appeal particularly to higher income groups as well as foreign investors." Local government control over development is encouraged and decentralization endorsed. In what must be unique among Bank reports, there is even a suggestion that diminishing some enticements to foreign investment would be apropos. The report concludes with this prescriptive synthesis.

> The key elements of a strategy of full participation would be special programs to help low-income farmers better utilize their land holdings; research to develop varieties and cropping patterns suitable for the poorer areas of the North and Northeast; a public works program over the next decade to build roads, schools, health centers, etc., in the poorer provinces with the dual objectives of redressing the considerable disparity that now exists in access to public services and of creating income and employment opportunities at a time when population pressure on land is intensifying; immediate extension of universal education to six years and improvement of the quality of education in rural areas; and shifting the priority in industrial development from promotion of heavy industry and high protection of consumer goods industries to increased promotion of industries producing for export as well as capital equipment needed for the country's own industries and agriculture (IBRD, 2059-TH: 131).

It is clear that the Bank's concept of participation is quite narrow and not at all in keeping with its own rhetoric. With humanist technocratic accretions, capital inflows, and exhortation, the Bank is trying to get more of the poor to be more efficient producers with an assumption that their incomes will also rise. The goals are food security and agricultural export growth. No conflict is seen, no matter how jarring the intellectual juxtapositions are. The reader is expected, for example, to absorb an enormous table of inequities with this conclusion: "Income disparity also appears to be growing as income in the poorer provinces is growing more slowly than in the rich" (IBRD, 2059-TH: 26). On the very next page the reader is then greeted with this assessment: "Measured against its limited objectives as set out in its First Development Plan. . . , the performance of the Thai Government over the past two decades has certainly been commendable. It has provided an environment for the private sector to operate efficiently and effectively."

This report and its eight annexes betray an enormous effort at retrieving data and trying to measure changes in income. A number of its goals and prescriptions are humanitarian. But by not integrating politics with economics, the prescriptions have little rational value. The Bank occasionally recognizes this. It admits, for example, that after 25 years of counseling and coaxing a national planning agency, it is evident the national plans do not guide or govern Thai government actions on a day-to-day basis. Given the Bank's cognizance of indigenous pride and historical patterns, one might imagine that it could recognize that Thailand has always presented the outside world with whatever cultural and institutional veneer would satisfy it. Creating a planning agency is thus a largely meaningless gesture that helps assure the ongoing security of local capital and the Bangkok elite.

Deep operational contradictions in Bank analysis such as these are not openly admitted. Instead they are sometimes pointed to as areas of ignorance that need to be remedied. In an October 1978 review of irrigation in Indonesia (IBRD 2027a-IND), the Bank authors commented several times (8, 50, 76, 92-93) on how little they knew of the impact of irrigation projects and HYV technology on the village world. This suggests several conclusions. The Bank has been involved in Indonesian agriculture for 10 years and 39 projects (through FY79), and yet will put forth such an excuse? The Bank staff is so incapable of retrieving the mass of independent scholarly literature that it literally does not know it exists? The Bank staff find it preferable, easier, and acceptable to push controversial topics and analysis into the future to avoid having to take the responsibility of a position now? The Bank management finds any or all of these behaviors acceptable? It must have, for this report and a legion of comparable ones found institutional acceptability. One contemplates in sum how human development fares with the kind of oversight that two large organizations (the Bank and the State) are inclined to offer each other.

WORLD BANK PROJECTS – PARTICIPATION BY WHOM?

Overall development advice in country and sector papers is ultimately but words on paper. Bank projects start as paper flows between organizations but result in resource transfers, changes in productive processes, and rebalancings of social forces. They affect people's lives, people far away and beyond the sight of the bureaucrats who create and approve these projects. Given the rhetorical goals of the Bank, particularly the post-1973 goals, it is not unreasonable to examine a few sample projects to see to what extent the Bank has developed any operational meaning for participation. As was suggested by the 1978 Thai report, the Bank is now defining the term as participation with greater efficiency in the productive process. The unstated and unproven assumption is that this leads to improvements in the individual income and then to improved livelihood. While some would agree, many other poor villagers in Thailand and Indonesia would attest otherwise.

As earlier chapters in this book argued, participatory development is, in ideal form, a process that creates economic citizens, people able and willing to enhance their own livelihood by controlling the basic decisions that affect their lives. It is not measured simply by gains in material welfare, for such are only symptoms. Development is the process for getting people involved. A participatory development project should include all of these elements: popular participation in project initiation, design, implementation, and evaluation; participatory mechanisms for distributing surpluses created and for defense of such surplus by the beneficiary; cultural feasibility and ecological soundness; processes enhancing self-reliance, self-sustaining progress, and self-directed learning; and a scale of resource use and job creation appropriate to social need.

The Bank portfolios in Indonesia and Thailand, a total of some 149 projects through FY79, are far too large to do any reasonable survey of, even were complete project files available. Having only a percentage of the appraisal reports means raising only a few elementary questions about the way projects were designed, not the way they have been modified in the field in the course of implementation. If, however, a project was not designed around the issues raised in the preceding paragraph, it will, almost inevitably, become a growth project, not a development project. What neoclassical economics deliberately mystifies is that a project process does not enter a neutral universe, a world of equal economic men. The concept of economic man indeed is invalid, as Chapter 1 pointed out. The worlds of rural Thailand and Indonesia are typically quite stratified, with a confluence of political and economic power. The most technically perfect road or irrigation project, implanted in such a universe, will benefit disproportionately those who have the most resources to use this new production factor. The rich get richer. This, as will be shown, is not the only practical approach to human development.

Bank projects that predate 1973 accept this imperfect universe as beyond their concern. A cursory survey of infrastructure project papers — the Thai highway projects of May 1963 and November 1972 and the Thai power projects of August 1957 and December 1969, for example — reveals that the basic project issues for study and design are those that directly affect the production goals of the triple alliance and the organizational needs of the donor. Thus technical feasibility and the abilities of the implementing agency of the government are assessed. A hypothetical use rate is fashioned to help create on paper a bankable rate of return.

The generic agriculture projects of this generation — the Petchburi Project of December 1962 and Chao Phya Project of the same date in Thailand, and the Indonesian Irrigation Rehabilitation Project of August 1968 — are not significantly different in their concerns. A few paragraphs deal with farmers and potential benefits in a mythical world of small independent producers in a freely competitive market with an efficiently functioning extension service (like BIMAS in Indonesia). The vast majority of the report is a technical exercise. One does need to know technical details. But would it have been too much, even under institutional time pressures in the 1968 Indonesian case, for example, for the project designers to have explored the collection of studies on village Indonesia published by Cornell just the year before? It was indeed to be 1979 before the Bank hired an anthropologist full-time for its work on Indonesia.

Bank projects of the 1950s and 1960s do not in sum make any pretension of considering the issues of participatory development. But policy supposedly changed in 1973. Projects in the pipeline then, given internal institutional imperatives to be discussed, were most unlikely to be reworked. But those emerging in the late 1970s are open to different evaluation, especially given the enormous claims of "benefitting the poor" made by U.S. Treasury officials in 1978 and 1979 while defending Bank appropriation proposals before the U.S. Congress. What one finds in these more recent Bank projects, unsurprisingly, is an occasional effort to graft a few dimensions of greater participation onto what remain essentially growth exercises. Whether the interaction of large organizations (states and donor agencies), which control all major aspects of a project, has even the theoretical possibility of producing anything like real participatory development is a fundamental concern of later chapters. But the Bank has made many claims that projects help poor people. On average the claim rests on little more than this assertion: the project takes place in an area where x poor people live; therefore, x poor people were helped.

Such a claim raises a host of theoretical problems. Words are not defined. Gross statistical averages are compiled. The difference between helping people, with its connotation of elitism and patronage, is not distinguished from the creation of processes by which and in which people help themselves. It is more than the difference between a focus on ends and a focus on process. Given the generic nature of a large (or any) organization, how can one imagine that it can grant the freedom implied by authentic participatory development? It cannot. Nor can it assure that the increased wealth produced will actually accrue to the most needy unless local social institutions are hospitable to the long-term defense of those needy. The question for development in the 1980s is quite clearly to seek practical alternatives to such process and to the organization limits created by the triple alliance and its needs.

Concrete projects show how the Bank has dealt operationally with these issues. The May 1979 Northern Agricultural Development Project in Thailand (IBRD, 2269-TH) provides one specific example. The project paper is thematically organized much like those of a decade before although it is longer and more detailed. The $25 million effort seeks to facilitate development of upland agriculture in a 50,000 h. area (gross) of the upper Northern Region. Some 21,500 Thai, mostly families in neighboring lowlands, about 50 percent of whom have legal tenure to half the project area, are the prospective project beneficiaries.

Tha Bank has targeted a very poor region and two problems: growing shortage of arable land and "lack of full participation of low income families in the benefits of development." What the Bank means by this phrase is spelled out early on (pp. 3-4); it is technical in nature, devoid of social, political, or local dimensions. Institutional change means more effective state penetration of the locale, not local mobilization for locally conceived goals. On pages 8-9 the eight project objectives are stated; the one that does not deal with production or national security reads in part "raise the standard of living of the rural poor by increasing and stabilizing farmer income." The project paper talks a bit about the technical and financial world of an "average" farmer and the production inputs that would raise incomes. It says nothing about the social relations in the 200 villages in the project site. The role of Thai government agencies in extension service is laid out. A few times the importance of people in the process is implied: "LDD also would assist in the formation of farmer groups to increase the efficiency of land development. . . ." (p. 13). Village woodlot associations are envisaged. The project component dealing with 6,500 hill tribe families calls for issuing land use permits. Perhaps the families will have some say as well in where small-scale irrigation happens; but no discussion of their local politics is visible. A project component also calls for 80 schools and 32 health posts. The role of women receives one paragraph.

In sum this sample agricultural project and kindred others in food production, urban sites and services, and social issues suggest that the political and policy changes of the 1970s have had at least an incremental impact on aspects of Bank project design. Such projects are more often rhetorically targeted at a country's poorest regions. That the poor "participate in benefits" is a consideration. Some kinds of social needs are recognized. Occasional internal papers even focus on job creation per dollar outlay and per social need (Hasan, 1978: 55-59), but such comments have not led to the intellectual and operational revolution in development they imply. The Bank project designers have not accepted the validity of authentic, autonomous human participation in development as either appropriate or operationally feasible. Whether individuals in a large organization can reach such a philosophical perspective, practical matters aside, is indeed questionable. It refutes the fundamental institutional need to control.

A CONCLUDING NOTE ON PEOPLE
AND THE TRIPLE ALLIANCE

The evolution of international development thinking in the 1970s has put the triple alliance in a somewhat defensive position, intellectually if not politically. The concepts of basic needs and participation run counter to a wants-based economics geared to profits and to the immediate gratification of organizational imperatives like those of the state. The triple alliance is simply too myopic to see the long-term potential of participation for a far more productive, humane, and secure world. All three members of the alliance think in relatively short terms. This has left its adjuncts like the World Bank in an exposed and ambivalent position. It is supposed to help poor people, but help them through structures, systems, and processes that created and sustained this poverty and still profit by it.

The major actors of the world-system are not standing still. The triple alliance is trying to put a human face on its operations and continues to mystify the world's citizenry by use of its near monopoly on most means of mass education. One particularly distressing example focussed in part on both Thailand and Indonesia was the recent publication of an AID-funded international agribusiness textbook, which gained wide dissemination in parts of AID. A product of Harvard's multinational enterprise project, Goldberg and McGinty (1979) try to define a world corn system as a subset of a food system that involves producers of all sizes. By claiming to be seeking ways to provide "more equitable treatment" for subsistence farmers seeking to enter the market (p. xxiii), they are prescribing a kind of social conscience that flies in the face of history and logic. By lumping together producers of all sizes, they are deforming the meaning of the term agribusiness. The claim (p. 415) that the agribusiness system exists to fill the needs of consumers is a form of altruism that the hundreds of millions of global citizens too poor to pay for food would not find comforting. Most disturbing of all is the hubris of the claim (p. 16) of international agribusiness to be the ones who upgrade the producers and workers on the world's 100 million small farms.

In some of the most recent work on the Green Revolution in Southeast Asia, focussing on rice rather than corn production, De Koninck provides a compelling rebuttal of why this vision is the antithesis of participatory development.

> Firstly, it very rapidly *specializes* peasant farmers in the production of rice, their staple food, and thus makes them clients of industry. Such peasants do not change let alone diversify their type of production; on the contrary they only intensify their labour and expand their output of rice. The position of the peasant rice producer thus becomes fixed: he is captured in the process of producing his staple food, over which he has less and less control. Secondly, since it is accompanied by a sharp rise in overall productivity and production, this specialization becomes increasingly irreversible: the chain reaction of dependency ties the peasants to interests that extend far beyond the geographical boundaries of the nation (the international fertilizer market being but one example) (De Koninck, 1979: 293).

This suggests that, if the corporatist approach to human development and participation practiced by states like Indonesia and Thailand did not bode well for participatory development, the attack by international agribusiness represents a far more profound and perhaps permanent cancer.

The World Bank, as a large organization, cannot see the first problem, and, as a capitalist organization, is similarly oblivious to the second. While the center of its intellectual universe is still entranced by growth with equity and the few cases where particular historical conditions permitted its application to produce improvements in mass welfare, individuals in the Bank are less sanguine. A few points in the Hasan (1978) paper have already been cited. A short-lived Bank policy planning paper series (1977-78) on participation contained a few kernels. But the fate of this paper series is yet another indication that neither the Bank management nor the Bank as a whole has any real grasp of participatory development and its implications.

Good intentions are simply not enough in the face of organizational imperatives and the triple alliance. As an organization the Bank is handicapped in multiple ways to be explored in later chapters: its top-down approach, its front-end bias (faith in rational planning), its own quality of work life, perception of resource use scale, the size of its projects, and much else. As a part of the world-system and triple alliance, the Bank is imprisoned by the ideology and politics of its funders. Thus Zaire continues to receive Bank aid while the Bank, at this writing, continues a long-term conspiracy with western powers to deny aid to Vietnam. Many authors, such as Payer (1982) and Stryker (1979), have commented on this political dimension of bank lending.

Participatory development implies, in sum, not just the fundamental reconsideration of the project process, but an operational systems response to those dimensions of the world-system and its triple alliance that work against participation. Eliminating one of its adjuncts, defunding the World Bank for instance, is not by itself a coherent systems answer, for it leaves the triple alliance essentially unscathed. The alliance would then reinvent a comparable entity. To undertake appropriately profound changes in the Bank's charter, structure, administrative class, ideology, and operating processes would mean to surmount the powerful vested interests of the international development industry both inside the Bank and out. The triple alliance would scarcely be pleased either. But Chapter 1 did not suggest that participatory development would be easy.

CHAPTER BIBLIOGRAPHY

Anderson, Benedict (1978). "Studies of the Thai State." Paper presented at the Conference on the State of Thai Studies, March 30, and reprinted in Ayal, Eliezer B., ed. (1978). *The Study of Thailand*. Athens, Ohio: Ohio University, Center for International Studies.

Asian Development Bank (1978). *Rural Asia: Challenge and Opportunity*. New York: Praeger.

Caldwell, J. Alexander (1974). *American Economic Aid to Thailand*. Lexington, Massachusetts: Lexington Books.

De Koninck, Rodolphe (1979). "The Integration of the Peasantry: Examples from Malaysia and Indonesia." *Pacific Affairs*, 52,2:265-91.

Elliott, David (1978). *Thailand: Origins of Military Rule*. London: Zed Press.

Evans, Peter (1979). *Dependent Development: The Alliance of Multinational, State, and Local Capital in Brazil*. Princeton, N.J.: Princeton University Press.

Franke, Richard W. (1972). "The Green Revolution in a Javanese Village." Unpublished doctoral dissertation, Harvard University.

Gibbons, David S., et al. (1980). *Agricultural Modernization, Poverty, and Inequality*. London: Saxon House.

Golay, Frank H., et al. (1969). *Underdevelopment and Economic Nationalism in Southeast Asia*. Ithaca, N.Y.: Cornell University Press.

Goldberg, Ray A., and McGinty, Richard C. eds. (1979). *Agribusiness Management for Developing Countries – Southeast Asian Corn System and American and Japanese Trends Affecting It*. Cambridge, Mass.: Ballinger.

Hasan, Parves (1978). "Economic Perspectives on Southeast Asia and East Asia." Unpublished IBRD discussion paper, April.

Hayami, Yujiro, and Hafid, Anwar (1979). "Rice Harvesting and Welfare in Rural Java." *Bulletin of Indonesian Economic Studies*, XV,1:94-112.

Hinkson, Jim (1975). "Rural Development and Class Contradictions on Java." *Journal of Contemporary Asia*, 5,3:327-36.

Hüsken, Frans (1979). "Landlords, Sharecroppers, and Agricultural Labourers: Changing Labour Relations in Rural Java." *Journal of Contemporary Asia*, 9,2:140-51.

Indochina Resource Center (1980). "Thailand Plays the Great Power Game." *Southeast Asia Chronicle*, 69:1-32.

International Agrarian Studies Group — Asia (IASG) (1979). "Report on Thailand." Rome: World Food Conference.

Jackson, Karl D., and Pye, Lucian W., eds. (1978). *Political Power and Communication in Indonesia*. Berkeley: University of California Press.

Meesook, Oey Astra (1979). "Income, Consumption and Poverty in Thailand, 1962/3 to 1975/6." Washington, D.C.: World Bank Staff Working Paper 364.

Palmer, Ingrid (1978). *The Indonesian Economy since 1965*. London: Frank Cass.

_____ (1977). *The New Rice in Indonesia*. Geneva: UNRISD.

_____ (1976). *The New Rice in Asia*. Geneva: UNRISD.

Rudner, Martin (1976). "The Indonesian Military and Economic Policy." *Modern Asian Studies*, 10,2:249-84.

Short, Kate (1979). "Foreign Capital and the State in Indonesia: Some Aspects of Contemporary Imperialism." *Journal of Contemporary Asia*, 9,2:152-74.

Stryker, Richard E. (1979). "The World Bank and Agricultural Development: Food Production and Rural Poverty." *World Development*, 7,3:325-36.

Turton, Andrew, et al. (1978). *Thailand: Roots of Conflict*. London: Spokesman Books.

Weinstein, Franklin B. (1976). *Indonesian Foreign Policy and the Dilemma of Dependence*. Ithaca, N.Y.: Cornell University Press.

Wihtol, Robert (1979). "The Asian Development Bank: Development Financing or Capitalist Export Production." *Journal of Contemporary Asia*, 9,3: 288-309.

World Bank (IBRD). Washington, D.C. *Annual Report*, various years

_____ *A Public Development Program for Thailand*. Baltimore: Johns Hopkins University Press, 1959.

_____ *Statement of Development Credits*, 12/31/79.

_____ *Statement of Loans*, 12/31/79.

World Bank. (IBRD). Unpublished.*

_____ EAP-19a (11/1970) *The Indonesian Economy: Development Trends and Foreign Aid Requirements, 1970-1972.* 3 volumes.

_____ EAP-28 (1/1972) *Current Economic Position and Prospects of Thailand.* 6 volumes.

_____ 25-IND (12/1972) *Development Issues for Indonesia.*

_____ 82a-TH (3/1973) *Current Economic Position and Prospects of Thailand,* 2 volumes.

_____ 708-IND (4/1975) *Indonesia: Development Prospects and Needs – Basic Economic Report.* 2 volumes.

_____ 924-TH (11/1975) *Thailand: Current Economic Prospects and Selected Development Issues,* 2 volumes.

_____ 2027a-IND (10/1978) *Indonesia Irrigation Program Review.*

_____ 2059-TH (9/1978) *Thailand: Toward a Development Strategy of Full Participation: A Basic Report,* 8 volumes of Annexes (November).

_____ 2060a-IND (12/1978) *Indonesia: A Review of the Support Services for Food Crop Production.*

_____ 2093-IND (2/1979) *Indonesia: Growth Patterns, Social Progress and Development Prospects.*

---

*Citations for project papers available on request.

____ 2374-IND (3/1979) *Indonesia Supply Prospects for Major Food Crops*.

____ 2378-IND (2/1979) *Employment and Income Distribution in Indonesia*.

____ 2379-IND (2/1979) *Indonesia Health Sector Overview*.

____ OED, 2166 (8/1978) *Sector Operation Review: The Agricultural Program in Indonesia*.

5

The Sociology of
World-System Stabilization:
The IMF in Zaire, 1978–80

The world-system is not a stable entity, as our growing knowledge of long cycles in modern history has begun to clarify. The system managers, the financial and political elite of the core powers, have long recognized this. Their principal institutional response for system stabilization since World War II has been the International Monetary Fund. The IMF was founded and is still supposed to promote monetary cooperation, facilitate trade expansion, promote exchange stability, and provide assistance to surmount short-term balance of payments problems. Its nucleus of neoclassical economists grew over the years, occupying ever larger quarters in official Washington. The IMF talks to and answers to governments, not to people. That, in sum, is the problem.

To those who seek true human development, especially those engaged in trying to use small amounts of resources on participatory development, the IMF is remote. It is far away physically, organizationally, politically, and intellectually. It is not an accident that the organization with the all-encompassing mandate for global economic health is one of the most nonparticipatory public organizations in the world. As was done with the U.S. Federal Reserve Board early in this century, the organizations that really matter to international capital are placed as far from popular reach as possible. How else could elites expect to survive over time?

For real human welfare the first task is to bridge this gap and lay bare the hidden agenda mandated to the IMF by its sponsors.

The IMF plays political and intellectual as well as economic roles. All are crucial to the welfare of core powers, their private banks, and the governments of the Third World. But by 1980 even the system sponsors were beginning to see that the IMF was not up to the tasks of a new historical era: long-term balance of payment stabilization, far more detailed and effective system policing and early surveillance, and a recycling of much greater amounts of capital. Reformers in the North (Shapiro, 1980, for a summary) began to call for much greater resources, power, and bureaucratic courage in the IMF; reformers from the South (*Development Dialogue*, 1980, 2, for the key discussions) opted for rewriting the IMF charter to diminish the prevailing ideological bias for market forces and the overall domination by the North.

True reform, however, demands understanding of issues besides bureaucratic economy. These are the issues of political imperatives. The IMF exists as an organization, in an environment of other organizations. The IMF has governments (large organizations) as its de jure mandators and banks (large organizations) as its de facto mandators. No reform proposal to date would fundamentally change these realities.

The matter of bureaucratic imperatives has been effectively marginalized in most work on international politics and economics. Given the elitist and organizational origin of most of those involved in writing about the IMF, this is not surprising. This chapter, like this book, is concerned with all aspects of structural aggression (structural imperialism in Galtung's [1980] sense) and unequal exchange. For human welfare, no reform based solely on conventional views of politics and economics can ultimately succeed. That is why this chapter looks beyond the political economy of the IMF to its organizational sociology. If a just new alternative process for global development can be envisioned, as later chapters will attempt, it will do no good if it cannot be implemented.

This chapter will thus explore both agendas, the first as the means to understanding the second. The initial section will focus on the nature of the IMF as a political and economic entity, a world-system mystifier and legitimizer, and how it is used by different system actors. The second part will explore how the IMF mandates are translated into bureaucratic imperatives; a case study of system stabilization in Zaire will be laid out. The third part will describe how bureaucratic imperatives make the system run amok, divorcing the IMF ever farther from empirical reality for the quintessential need and convenience of its bureaucrats who must defend themselves against utterly unfulfillable mandates. Zaire is again the case study. The chapter will end with a reassessment of the current rhetoric of reform and suggest how to start creating the basis for what a just world economy really requires.

THE IMF AS A POLITICAL AND ECONOMIC ENTITY

Analyzing the IMF in theoretical terms means departing from the vast establishment literature generated by IMF economists and their academic and journalistic supporters (see Salda, 1980, for a recent bibliography) and striking out directly against more than a generation of some of the most sophisticated intellectual mystification of modern times. One cannot avoid this task. Neoclassical capitalist economics is not a human science but an elitist ideology, an ideology that justifies and sustains a particular distribution of wealth between haves and have-nots. It is the unspoken role of the IMF to maintain and enforce the intellectual purity of this ideology. Any discussion of the political economy of the IMF in the modern world-system begins with its notions of organizational truth and how they originated in the initial IMF mandate.

For the sake of brevity only one of the six parts of the IMF statement of purposes, Article 1 of the 1944 Bretton Woods Agreement, will be examined. It reflects a good sample of the mythology the IMF was saddled with. Part ii reads as follows:

> To facilitate the expansion and balanced growth of international trade, and to contribute thereby to the promotion and maintenance of high levels of employment and real income and to the development of the productive resources of all members as primary objectives of economic policy (quoted from Abdalla, 1980: 35).

The post-World War II economy was marked by significantly unequal development proceeding by means of colonial rule and unequal exchange. The political trappings of colonialism have passed, but the expansion of structural aggression and unequal exchange over 35 years has not abated. They cannot produce "high levels of employment and real income." The world-system does not work that way;

labor is expensive and unreliable, so capital-intensive development has been the choice of most elites. The IMF is clearly mandated to pretend that unequal exchange does not exist, that trade in all circumstances produces high levels of employment, and that developing a society's productive (i.e., material) resources equals mass human welfare. One should not expect a very different piece of mythology from the elites of that era, but it is little wonder that some progressive voices in the Third World today seek alternatives.

Part ii of Article 1 thus mandates the continuation of unequal relationships and value transfers to the perpetual advantage of the core countries of the world-system. In the age of decolonization and national liberation, the 1950-75 period, the world-system could not hope to promote monetary cooperation and a "stable" world economy by means of an institution that appeared other than apolitical, neutral, and professional. To create the needed imagery four tactics were devised: classification, acculturation (guild behavior), mystification, and legitimization.

The easiest way for any organization to maintain the image it wishes to propagandize is to prevent any examination of its real actions. The IMF publishes four sets of relatively harmless global economic data and some self-serving pamphlets and institutional autobiographies. Its more important work, annual or biennial country assessments and consultations, remain as confidential as possible; these reports circulate outside the Fund only to select parts of member governments. Thus the reports are purely products of bureaucratic convenience and compromise. Since the government being assessed sees the initial draft, it also has a significant damper effect on any intellectually critical spirit. Outside of my own work on Zaire (Gran, 1978, 1979a and b), and the papers at the 1980 Arusha conference on the IMF (in *Development Dialogue*, 1980, 2), there appear to be few other independent studies of the IMF to date that have evaluated internal documentation in any detail.

This stunning success at obfuscation for 35 years, only recently tarnished as the IMF appears more and more obsolete and impotent in the present historical moment, could not have happened just by keeping documentation secret. The actual participants had to be motivated. The IMF has managed amazing internal conformity in classic style. Reports for countries all over the world ask the same questions about the same macroeconomic abstracts, manufacture endless statistical tables, and studiously ignore human beings and welfare. The IMF professional staff has come largely from the most orthodox economics Ph.D. factories in the West. IMF non-Western professionals, if not Western schooled, have traveled through banking and governmental ministries wherein they have been properly socialized by IMF staff or their kin. Promotion is done from within. The key intellectual leadership has remained unchanged for decades. I spoke on the phone once briefly with its noted architect, J. Polak, to ask whether the overall IMF model of economic stabilization was sufficient for Zaire's recovery. He assured me it was. It did not matter to him that three-quarters of Zaire's population are malnourished or starving as a result. His organization did not need to know.

This overall combination of secrecy and acculturation has laid much of the basis for the IMF to seize significant de facto political power over poor countries when its mandate and resources did not suggest any such abilities. But the IMF needed external recognition of authority beyond its simple creation and the endorsement of its early members, largely core country governments. This authority grew by acts of legitimization and acts of mystification.

The primary tool of legitimization the IMF has used is the one of recognition. It has recognized governments that agreed to submit to its rules and not recognized others. This process has done much to crystallize and expand the political superstructure of the world-system. When a Third World government that has lived far beyond its means seeks out the IMF for a stabilization package and accepts it, that government exchanges a measure of its economic sovereignty for a new veneer of legitimacy it can use to cow domestic critics and lure further foreign capital. How this works is the subject of section two.

Beyond legitimization is mystification. Elites have been shaping words as political weapons since the days of ancient Greece, if not before. The IMF mandators accept and personally prosper in a capitalist universe. The IMF has done its best to propel market forces and deny the existence of any other social ordering. Marxist alternatives are not part of the intellectual possibilities; that is the "other" and unmentioned school. One doubts that anyone at the IMF has even heard of humanistic economics. Instead IMF economists have created a universe of issues called "economic." They have decreed that the determining cause of balance of payments problems is the amount of money in supply, wrapped their analyses and prescriptions in ever more mathematical and econometric garb, and, like the modern scientist, asserted this behavior to be "professional," "neutral," and "scientific." Unfortunately this is not a joke.

From the vantage point of participatory development and human welfare, not to mention empirical reality, such a vision of economics is not satisfactory. The IMF has not only denied that the world-system is one of structural aggression and unequal exchange, but it has also denied any link between welfare and economic analysis. This was explained to the U.S. Congress by Treasury Under Secretary Anthony Solomon in February 1980:

> To the degree that the IMF is still pursuing its stabilization and monetary function, there may be flexibility for consideration of basic human needs, but any criteria which diverts the IMF from considering the economic criteria to meeting purely social criteria would basically be a distortion of the IMF's function and would make it ineffective.
> Chairman Neal. From an IMF function to an aid function essentially?
> Mr. Solomon. Right, or to a humanitarian function.
> (U.S. House of Reps. Committee on Banking, 1980: 24-25)

It is a tribute to capitalist education that this exchange could take place in a hearing of the House of Representatives of the United States.

Spokesmen for the IMF deny not only the validity of economics as if people mattered but also the merit of other basic tools for understanding reality. There is no visible grasp of systems and process. Such tools would be admittedly inconvenient to their mythology. The Fund also denies any intellectual or operational link between politics and economics. As Maryknoll priest Thomas Burns demonstrated in his testimony on Peru (U.S. House of Reps. Committee on Banking, 1980: 247), this is quite hard to do in real world situations. In Washington, however, the IMF and its spokesmen, such as the Treasury Department in the U.S. government, insist that the IMF is not and cannot be, legally or operationally, a political institution.

The magnitude of the political use of the IMF has been independently chronicled for many years, most recently in the 1980 conference at Arusha. Such analyses, no matter how sober or grounded, have not to date had impact on the operational behavior of the IMF. The Fund does not even get embarrassed at such imbroglios as the May 1979 "stabilization" package for the Somoza government in Nicaragua.

> In the confidential staff recommendation accompanying the stand-by arrangement the Fund staff noted that the program carried "substantial risks," yet considered the details of the program "technically sound." The program was approved on May 14 and on July 19 the Somoza regime was overthrown. The question is not whether the Fund should permit shaky governments to enter into stabilization programs, but how a competent staff could consider a program "technically sound" which fails to take account of the economic effects of a civil war (Michael Moffitt in U.S. House of Reps. Committee on Banking, 1980: 197).

What has confused this and other outside observers is their assumption that the organizational definition of competence bears any relationship to its societal definition. It does not. The chasm between the culture of society and that of organizations will be explored in later parts of this chapter; here one should note that U.S. congressional hearings (to the extent a member represents social interests) provide at best a marginal way to communicate across this cultural gap to the IMF.

It is difficult for world-system managers to maintain such a complicated intellectual charade over an indefinite period. Careful readings of U.S. congressional hearings yield multiple slips and contradictions. In the February 1980 hearing, for instance, the U.S. Treasury official (Solomon) argued for several pages that the IMF did not and could not add politics to such an economic and technical issue; but then he let loose that "you are absolutely right, that these interact, the economic and the political and the social decisions" (U.S. House of Reps. Committee on Banking, 1980: 30).

These system managers provide not just contradictions but also flat refutations of the apolitical nature of the IMF. One of the Fund's original mandates was "to promote exchange stability." It was satisfactory to the dominant world power, the United States, to have fixed exchange rates and the dollar convertible to gold up until the Vietnam War. When the United States began to export its war costs via inflation in the late 1960s, other countries sought to convert excess dollars to gold. This threatened the depletion of U.S. gold reserves. In 1971 President Nixon suspended convertibility of the dollar, notifying the IMF just before he publicly announced it. As Treasury Secretary Miller told Congress in 1980, the situation had become "both unsustainable and intolerable in terms of U.S. economic interests" (U.S. Senate Foreign Relations Committee, 1980: 11). Clearly the mandator's interest overrode the organizational interest in this instance; the organization was simply ignored when it was inconvenient.

To focus just on the contradictions and political basis of the Fund's four tactics of image making does not provide a full picture of the Fund's larger environment in the world-system, the political economy of its raison d'être. One must also examine the particular interests of different groups among the mandators, for they sometimes conflict. Much of the ensuing organizational sociology of the Fund is an effort to accommodate these conflicts with its own organizational will to survive. Brief note must be taken of what core powers, private multinational banks, and Third World governments seek beyond the image of an apolitical, neutral, and professional world-system stabilization mechanism.

For the core powers the Fund is first and foremost the policeman of international capitalism. It is the indirect means of political control that maintains the "free" trade necessary for accumulation. For many years control took place by secret economic report cards and private negotiations. Fund policies were, however, so intrusive and harsh that Third World governments began to avoid its aid until an extreme situation arose; thus in 1978 the Fund was given more explicit "surveillance" powers to try to provide the world-system with more of an early warning system (Shapiro, 1980).

The core powers have additional needs. Their own social irresponsibility must be sanctioned; so long-term trade deficits by the United States and surpluses by Japan and West Germany are filtered through the system despite the grumbling of other core powers. Core powers also need protection from Third World exports. One major means is to facilitate and enlarge less developed country (LDC) financing to keep up the value (likely to overvalue) of LDC currency and thus of their exports. The Fund imprimatur on a Third World economy helps it get private bank loans. More trade means more chance for one core power in particular, the United States, to export not just commodities but the reality of its own balance of payments deficits to the Third World. Trade deficits with OPEC can be somewhat eased by building a trade surplus with the

Third World (Hulbert, in U.S. House of Reps. Committee on Banking, 1980: 492). Too many imports can, of course, lead specific LDCs to disaster, and the IMF then counsels currency devaluation and other palliative measures. But these are the extreme cases, not the average system performance.

Core powers also use the IMF as a political weapon. The many cases of its legitimization of Third World governments that have too clearly prostituted themselves to the interests of the world-system are on record. The matter of Zaire in the late 1970s is to be explored herein. The IMF is also used as a tool to discredit a government that too closely identifies with the interests of its own citizens; failing a country on performance against its stabilization program targets or simply creating unattainable targets are not difficult (Girvan, 1980: 67).

International private banks have interests not entirely congruent with core country governments. The banks find the Fund advantageous, if not essential, as financial insurance. The Fund provides the economic discipline that allows the banks to be far more daring, rapacious, and irresponsible than would otherwise be possible. During the 1960s and 1970s banks like Citicorp made numerous loans to Third World governments for essentially nonproductive purposes: recycling existing loans, sustaining parasitic governmental units, and increasing the personal consumption of elites. Banks expect their money back. It's not just that the IMF will help bail them out indirectly with stabilization loans to impoverished governments. The IMF will keep the semblance of order in LDC government finances and add to the various political pressures that assure at least minimal loan repayment performance. While some actual communication takes place between the Fund and the private banks, it is the banks' de facto political control over finance ministries or treasury departments of core countries (which in turn dictate the policies of Fund Executive Directors) that assures an appropriate environment. Sometimes this can result in more support for a Third World government than liberal core governments would approve.

Third World governments use the IMF for varied political purposes. They postpone necessary, but politically unpalatable, economic reforms because the Fund exists as a final safety net. The lower tranche Fund credits (the ones with minimal conditionality), like foreign aid and commercial loans, allow the government to endure, if not thrive, without taxing its citizens. This is especially useful for governments that do not have the legitimacy to tax or the ability to live within their means. The Fund stabilization program and the inescapable adjustments it implies can then be used as a scapegoat; the government can blame the Fund for the human suffering that results. The exact nature and implementation of a Fund stabilization then provides weapons to Third World elites for interor intraclass struggles. In sum, for all three groups of mandators the Fund is a remarkably useful political, economic, and ideological weapon.

AN IMF STABILIZATION PROGRAM
AND ITS ZAIRE APPLICATION

The IMF stabilization programs in recent years have been based on the theory that governments in balance of payment troubles have committed two classes of economic mistakes. On one level they spent beyond their means; this allowed too much money into circulation, overvalued exchange rates, and often hampered imports. On a more theoretical level the Fund finds fault with the entire historical import-substituting industrialization strategy of the Third World. A strategy that might lead to more self-reliant development would mean less profit to the core countries, the Fund's principal mandators.

Until recently the typical, demand-oriented, IMF package of policy responses, analyzed in some detail by Feinberg (1980a: 8-15), may be here crudely summarized to include these elements: devalue currency to encourage exports; relax exchange controls, tighten private credit, and remove interest rate ceilings, all to make the most efficient use of scarce capital; release price controls to encourage investment; put a ceiling on wage increases in the public sector and seek other measures of budget restraint; and transfer parastatals to the private sector, reducing taxation and raising productivity.

The political and ideological content of this generic prescription clearly derives from the free market premises of the IMF mandate. It cannot be said to be neutral or scientific. What the IMF does not recognize in theoretical or programmatic terms is that, to achieve either the kind or the quality of economic results intended, the policies would have to be applied in a relatively pure market economy. Zaire, the case to be considered here, contains nothing of the sort. Neither does any other country that applies to the IMF for help. Few other economies may be as assymetrical, extroverted, parasitic, monopolistic, and corrupt as that of Zaire, but they share significant degrees of structural inequality. IMF solutions, translated through such structures by people with many motives beyond or in addition to market motives, cannot be expected to succeed. The IMF (Johnson and Salop, 1980) is finally beginning to recognize these negative results, if not the reasons why.

The IMF staff has not persisted with such a model for a generation solely because its mandators gave general instructions to protect and enhance the capitalist world-system. The staff developed these particular policies in part because they were also the most organizationally convenient. There is no sense in the IMF proposing policies over which it cannot have significant control. Thus the policy prescriptions devised were ones that were theoretically under the jurisdiction of national leaders, finance ministers, Central Bank officials, and others with whom the IMF staff could deal directly. It is easy to press one or two officials to devalue currency or limit the money supply; it is impossible to oversee and improve domestic tax collection on internal production or trade. In sum the intellectual and programmatic universe was one of rarefied macroeconomic indicators to be juggled by senior host country officials. Unfortunately for such officials and for the IMF, economies are not econometric models but human systems. Nowhere is that clearer than in Zaire and the world of Joseph Mobutu Sese Seko.

As Chapter 3 suggested, the Mobutu government has plundered rather than developed Zaire since the middle 1960s. The long, sad history of this process has been chronicled elsewhere (Gran, 1978, 1979b), and so a brief introduction will serve to set the stage for exploring recent IMF stabilization programs. Zaire has a highly stratified society of about 27 million spread over an enormous 2.3 million square kilometers of mineral-rich land in Central Africa. The estimated GNP per capita in 1978 was $210 by World Bank figures (IBRD, 1980b: 110). Such a figure suggests little of real life quality. Political independence did not bring economic independence or development for most Zairians.

Coming to power with Western assistance in the mid 1960s, President Mobutu inherited a potentially rich country. With the guidance of European mining interests, the World Bank, and the IMF, Mobutu proceeded to lock Zaire into an export-led growth model. The Mobutu government has allied itself with international capital, accepted the central teachings of the world-system agencies, and significantly inhibited local capital. The result is, in sum, a misshapen triple alliance. Export taxes permit the governing class to thrive while ignoring mass welfare. The colonial legacy of pillage and order lives on. Mobutu's kleptocracy surmounts one crisis after another thanks to world-system rescue missions. The lure of minerals has blinded even rhetorical supporters of human rights in the West to the real causes of the permanent development crisis of Zaire and to the ongoing malnourishment and starvation of three-quarters of the population. A brief look at different sectors in the economy will permit a greater appreciation of the surrealistic way the IMF tried to approach Zaire in recent years.

The modern sector is dominated by the mining of copper. Production reached a high of 471,000 tons in 1974; it fell for the rest of the 1970s to a 1979 low of 372,000 tons (IMF, 1980: 3). The average real price Zaire received per ton of copper for 1975-79 was a little more than half of the 1970-74 average price (IBRD, 1980a: 310). Production of cobalt, of which Zaire is the principal world producer, rose to 14,800 tons in 1979, but all other output from Gecamines (the mining parastatal) fell. World-system managers point to staffing, organizational, technical, maintenance, infrastructure, and myriad other problems. But even if all these problems were solved, market corruption ended, and prices returned to the real value of the 1965-69 modern high and the West were not in a recession, Zaire would still be trapped in relative poverty. The West can buy minerals only at the rate it grows itself, and Zaire can thus never export its way out of the world-system periphery (Gran, 1979).

According to conventional economic theory, Zaire is supposed to spend its export receipts on development in other sectors to diversify the economy and meet social needs. The world-system, however, provides incentives and opportunities for Zaire's elite to put its mineral profits elsewhere — back into mineral expansion, into the expansion of the government payroll and urban services for political purposes, and into their own Swiss bank accounts. All of the diamond trade and much of the coffee trade, for example, avoid official accounting. Most of the population is needed neither as producers nor as consumers. The vast majority of the 70 percent who live in the countryside and try to subsist by farming are not even needed as food suppliers to urban elites. Foreign capital permits food to be imported, largely by air from South Africa, at the level of $300-350 million a year; the estimate for 1980 was $340 million so allocated (U.S. Dept. Commerce, 1980: 4). Artificial exchange rates spur such trade.

The long-term agricultural stagnation in Zaire is symptomatic of the real motives of both the Zairian government and its international partners. Agriculture made no overall gain in the 1970s. Marketed output fell 10 percent in 1978 and a further 18 percent in 1979 (IMF, 1980: 3). The government has not put any significant investment in rural development in modern times and lacks the organizational and political will to keep even main regional routes in passable condition. Mid-1970s Zairianization measures severely damaged the network of expatriate rural traders. Facing them and their comparably parasitic and monopolistic replacements, producers have been overwhelmed. Local political authorities side with the traders and mimic their national leaders in the use of force and corruption. Could a producer retain much of his earnings, there is little to buy at a remotely equitable price. Producers have exercised the moral economy of peasants in many societies and turned back to subsistence.

The government response to this and to international prodding has been two major policy papers: in January 1978 came *Programme de Relance Agricole* and during 1979 came multiple editions of *Plan Mobutu: Programme de Relance Economique 1979-1981*. In these and other recent documents, more aspects of the rural realities appear than in prior efforts, but there is no sense of the operational nature of development in the countryside or how to do it. These plans are little more than shopping lists aimed at foreign donors. How such projects will involve the producers in participatory development, given the obstacles at every level of the world-system, is not evident. Yet if average social productivity per unit of resources does not rise, the best that can be expected is more years of starvation, parasitism, and food imports.

Conditions in urban Zaire are not significantly more productive. The manufacturing sector operates at about half capacity, with spare parts and price freezes particular blocks to further effort. Unemployment figures are meaningless, as the informal sector and black market are basic to most aspects of existence. Inflation may have eased a little in the early 1980s (around 50 percent in 1980 and 1981), but for the latter 1970s it averaged 80-100 percent a year. Wages did not keep pace. Student strikes in the spring of 1979 were a typical sign of the mammoth, but highly fragmented, popular resentment at the economic anarchy, favoritism, and corruption of daily life. Every four to six months Western journalists (*Wall Street Journal*, June 25, 1980; *Now*, July 11, 1980, for example) chronicle the saga of wealth, poverty, and anger: the nationwide growth of lawlessness of "Zaire: Creaking On" (*Africa Confidential*, September 3, 1980).

Encouraged by irresponsible international banks and high copper prices in the early 1970s, Zaire had borrowed heavily. Its external public debt rose from $1.75 billion at the end of 1973 to $3.54 billion at the end of 1977. The market value of its major export, copper, collapsed in 1974 at the same time that global energy and food prices went up dramatically. The Zairian elite had neither the will nor the ability to do the necessary retrenchment. The rest of the decade was one of declining outputs, drastic drops in real imports, sharp reduction in (official) net transfers from abroad, and a long-term series of rhetorical and statistical mystifications. Mobutu sought to stay in power, the West sought debt repayments and secure supplies of cheap minerals, and the IMF sought to paper over the enormous resource gaps and conflicts.

Zaire fell into arrears slightly by the end of 1975, and a stabilization agreement was reached with the IMF in March 1976. In return for a one-year IMF loan of SDR*40.96 (and its good housekeeping seal to allay the fears of international banks), Zaire's government agreed to reach certain macroeconomic targets by the end of 1976. It did not come close. The overall budget deficit, supposed to be SDR60 million, reached SDR313 million. Debt payments arrears, supposed to fall by $70 million during 1976, rose by more than that. Inflation ran rampant. But because some denationalization measures were announced and the currency was devalued, IMF authorities released the money (Gran, 1978: 21).

The continued growth of debt arrears led to further discussions and a new agreement with the IMF in April, 1977. End 1977 targets were set for the overall budget deficit, the trade balance, the level of debt arrears, money supply, and rate of inflation. In return Zaire was offered a further loan of SDR45 million, paid in installments. Zaire's continued failure even to approach the agreed targets

---

*Special Drawing Rights. SDR1 = U.S. $1.15 at that time.

discouraged IMF authorities. Part way through, in early 1978, IMF loan installments were cut off. Debt arrears continued to grow, reaching an incredible $1.76 billion by mid-1979 (Rep. of Zaire, 1979b: 2).

By 1977 it had become apparent to major Western governments that the IMF could not handle Mobutu alone. While both official debt rescheduling meetings (under the Paris Club) and commercial bank rescheduling meetings (termed the London Agreements) were set up, an overall coordinating mechanism was needed. The solution was the reestablishment of a general Consultative Group involving the United States, Belgium, France, Britain, Zaire, and other interested governments under the general aegis of the World Bank. The Consultative Group met in June 1977, June and November 1978, November 1979, and May 1980 (and June 1981 and . . .) to review and negotiate an overall development strategy whereby Zaire could supposedly work its way back toward solvency. Mobutu heard many different reforms proposed and proposed many himself, both in these meetings and in annual addresses to the nation. For Mobutu it is a rhetorical game that keeps the kleptocracy going. Western officials keep sanctioning a solution calling for "substantial and increasing assistance from abroad." Enough aid continues to arrive to keep Mobutu afloat and keep him seeking more. It is not in reality an environment suitable to attain even the neoclassical economic goals of the IMF, never mind any real stability or development.

One is therefore impelled to explore, as a case study, why and how the IMF would justify the task of yet a third stabilization package, sign it in August 1979 (to run to December 1980), and attempt to implement it. In its major April 1979, August 1979, and May 1980 internal reports, the staff does not explore at all why their previous programs failed. No one in their official literary universe wants or needs to know. This is an awesome commentary on organizational product quality. The only recent document to touch, however briefly, on such a topic was not even the November 1979 consultative meeting papers (prepared for GOZ presentation by a New York investment bank) but the IBRD-authored paper for the May 1980 consultative meeting. This World Bank paper says very, very little in bland bureaucratic style:

> The failure of these two stabilization attempts is attributable to both internal and external factors such as expansionary fiscal and credit

policies, lower world metal prices than assumed in the programs, the failure to fully repatriate and properly allocate export earnings, and a decrease in net transfers of external resources (IBRD, 1980c: 9).

Zaire is reported to have spent 1978 and early 1979 on diverse reforms, most concretely a five-stage 62.5 percent currency devaluation.

Against this background the IMF in mid-1979 commenced another effort at redirecting the Zairian economy. It was not enough to have a small team of expatriates at the helm of the Central Bank; during 1978-79 the Zairian system of corruption had basically stymied reform efforts by these IMF-sponsored officials. Apparently Erwin Blumenthal, the principal person involved, did not or could not convey the systematic depth of corruption to Washington. For the IMF sent out in the fall of 1979 a milder-mannered replacement and commissioned as well a team of Belgians to revamp the customs bureau.

The IMF also set seven specific economic targets, the performance on which, summarized below, suggests the overall lack of standards, integrity and human welfare acceptable to those involved. The budget deficit was to be reduced. Instead it rose Z113* million over the end-79 target to Z558 million; overspending on education and defense were cited along with less than anticipated revenue (IMF, 1980: 5-8). Zaire was to begin an "orderly process" of reducing debt arrears. That was not hard, given the willingness of international lenders; agreements were signed in late 1979 with both public and private lenders, rescheduling about SDR818 million ($1.06 billion) of the debts in arrears. Zaire was to limit new foreign borrowing; this was not a real constraint since no one would be likely to lend. Zaire was to reduce real wages in the public and private sectors, a goal inflation continued to accomplish handily. Zaire was to continue a "flexible" exchange rate, which meant further feasible devaluation. Zaire was to "improve foreign exchange management"; food and oil scandals in the early 1980s joined the ongoing coffee and diamond trade corruption.

Seventh and last, Zaire was to limit domestic currency in circulation to an end-79 figure of Z2.916 billion, up from an end-78 figure of Z2.286 billion. At the end of November 1979 Zaire was at Z3.471 billion, well over the target. Facing failure on budgetary

---

*Z1 = U.S. $0.64 (1/2/79-8/23/79) and U.S. $0.49 (8/24/79-2/22/80).

(not to mention overall inflation and balance of payments) targets, Mobutu knew that IMF officials might cancel the program in early 1980 and jeopardize his political situation if he did not move to meet one substantive goal squarely. He could reduce the currency in supply by introducing new currency, and in late December he took this option. Banks were suddenly ordered to change all the Z5 and Z10 bills (the two largest) in circulation for new currency in a space of three days. Individuals were limited to Z3000, bank accounts blocked, and the border closed. At the end of three days of anarchy and unbelievably creative new forms of corruption, Mobutu had extracted almost Z700 million from circulation and reduced the money supply to Z2.783 billion, Z133 million below the IMF ceiling (IMF, 1980: 8-14).

The portrayals of this awesome economic dislocation by different system actors are an illuminating commentary on the political economy of the currency reform. The IMF denied (IMF, 1980: 8) any part in the currency change and avoided more than quantitative review and brief comments on implementation. In a March 1980 letter to the IMF, Mobutu argued the currency scheme was needed to curb the "excess liquidity in the economy, a large proportion of which was in the form of currency in circulation that fueled illicit trade and foreign exchange transactions" (IMF, 1980: 27). The view from the bottom was quite different. The financial loss to lower and middle classes was considerable. As an exercise in trickle-up development and class war, it was quite a coup.

What this 1979-80 stabilization package accomplished toward its stated goals — curbing inflation, lowering trade deficits, and establishing the basis for development — was limited at best. The IMF, in a subsequent (August 1980) discussion, began to admit to itself the degree of chicanery involved in most of the data it was using. On a more basic level, however, neither false data nor unmet targets really matter to the Fund staff. By providing so many different criteria for Zaire to aim for and by changing the rules so often, they can always deem Zairian performance to be in some way marginally acceptable. At worst the dialogue can be broken off for a bit, a more complex negotiation can ensue, and new conditions open another round. Mobutu profits by every delay. Private banks maintain their global credibility. Belgium still gets its copper and the U.S. its cobalt. The Zairian people still starve. These are the real purposes of IMF action. To do something about this overall reality requires more than the recognition of the political needs of particular world-system actors and the way the IMF implements them. It requires an understanding of how an organization will literally redefine reality, legitimacy, and propriety to bridge the gap between its mandators' current needs and its traditional organizational purposes and imperatives. In the process, organizational inhabitants adopt situational ethics that further and further undermine the organization's credibility and effectiveness.

THE SOCIOLOGY OF THE IMF AND
WORLD-SYSTEM TRANSFORMATION

Unless a great many people in a society are active citizens, there is little likelihood its government will use resources on behalf of mass welfare. Public and corporate elites have long been at pains to hide or mystify this reality with rhetoric about human needs and rights. The combination of long historical cycles and the generically uneven nature of monopoly-capitalist development makes both the rhetorical and the practical job of system stabilization quite difficult. Cases like Zaire, which may represent the world's leading model of antidevelopment, put the system stabilizers in an impossible position. The IMF has to accommodate simultaneously at least five different interests: its own internal organizational ones; its original mandate; the empirical reality it is trying to affect; the political interests of the most affected mandators at a given moment; and the dominant personalities in the process. The resulting contradictions are impossible. The IMF must, to survive, lie to its mandators. To lie here involves the creation of an organizationally convenient reality. This process, by which the IMF accommodates the contradictions and produces a mystification the world-system mandators will accept, is the central topic of its organizational sociology. It is this process that clearly reveals the bankruptcy of the organization from the perspective *both* of the mandators and of mass human welfare.

The original Bretton Woods Agreement ordered the IMF to try to deal with international economic disorder with the same capitalist approaches that were creating the disorders. The global problems the IMF faced were long-term and structural in nature, but its mandate was to deal with the short-term monetary symptoms of these problems. The IMF was not given resources to lend for long-term productive investment, even if a deficit country had the political will to use such resources to grow out of its problem. Left with short-term monetary responsibilities, the Fund pursued interventions to balance accounts. This was inevitably deflationary. As Brett (1978: 3) has noted, many such interventions slow the growth of the system as a whole. This is not the desire of international capital, but it is not clear that system mandators grasp all such system links.

The immediate task for the IMF has become to paper over such contradictions in a way that pleases its immediate supervisors, the Fund Executive Directors. These are appointed by government finance or treasury ministries or Central Banks to represent one or a group of nations. Their likely pedigree has been in economics or finance and their support staff comes from the appointing ministry. Meetings cover several topics and swiftly bounce around the world. The literary universe is not much more than Fund documents and Fund-sponsored daily-newspaper synthesis. Tenure in office is rarely more than a few years. In sum, for all practical purposes organizational culture has triumphed. It subtly controls the parameters of perceived reality and the possible policy choices for the mandators' representatives. It is an exceptional executive director who will challenge much of what the Fund staff proposes. Much activity is instead little more than paper pushing involving countries of peripheral interest. This decision-making system is not an accident.

To gain and maintain control of the process, thus insuring their own security and potential growth, the Fund staff have to package a reality that will suit the world-system managers and their representatives, the executive directors. Only one reality is possible: the world-system is in control. There may be short-term problems, but no country of monetary or strategic value like Zaire can be other than remediable. The Fund managers have designed a paper format and a process of work so that the product going to the board meeting provides the apparent remedy.

The process begins, as noted before, by hiring malleable young neoclassical economists from elite establishment schools and placing them in small country or regional teams. The documents they study in Washington are largely those produced by the government they are reviewing or by quasi-official agencies. Only rarely is it evident that independent scholarly or journalistic analysis has been consulted; such research occurs usually not in the country papers but for the separate DM series of topical reports. The average country paper has no footnotes; only such institutional voices with no accountability have such intellectual arrogance. The IMF has a mediocre mainstream library. Staff are shifted from one assignment to another every 2-4 years and thus have little incentive to build area expertise; one can imagine that paper flow and mission trip requirements are scheduled so that staff do not have the time for real area studies. The system does not want any kind of professionalism, for substantive knowledge threatens the status quo.

Work in the field is similarly sheltered. Missions are very brief, often not more than one or two weeks. The IMF staff stays in the nation's capital and meets host government officials. Its task is largely updating statistical tables. Questions of substantive policy are left to senior staff in sessions where the rhetoric of national sovereignty smoothes over awkward conflicts. There is no investigation of the human or developmental results. One does not see the starving people in the local Hilton Hotel.

These investigations then result in papers to the board on recent economic developments, requests for or reviews of standby (loan) arrangements, and reports on periodic consultations. Economic surveys are rarely more than 80-100 pages and other papers much shorter. I find them some of the most turgid, unreadable prose imaginable, surely a bureaucratic ploy to discourage close scrutiny by executive directors. My own worldwide survey (papers on several countries read carefully, and those on several dozen others skimmed over the years) indicates a remarkable uniformity of content and tone. Writers carefully avoid as many aspects of potential conflict as possible. As much as half of many reports is statistical tables. They give a patina of authority and are useful for all kinds of mystifications; one of the commonest is interyear comparsion that neglects to notice the rapidly shifting real value of the currency or commodity in question. While some tables do give important historical depth, the text is usually confined to general quantifications involving not more than a year or two. Common to all organizations is the need to avoid its own history and thus any means of judging its accountability. Central to human welfare is accountability.

From this sheltered work process thus flows analysis of macroeconomic realities that conform to the kind of universe that a finite and narrowly educated audience wants to read about, and that the government under discussion will admit to. Until the mid 1970s and OPEC, such a facile operation in cultural and intellectual imperialism conformed well enough to the observable universe to permit the systemic contradictions to be successfully ignored. This is no longer the case, and again the issues of recent IMF handling of Zaire will be used to demonstrate this.

During the late 1970s the IMF has had the difficult task of transforming Mobutu's kleptocracy into a mythical entity capable of using resources in ways resembling a government engaged in a responsible process of reform. It was easy for the IMF staff to assert to its non-African executive directors that the mess came in large measure from factors beyond Mobutu's control (terms of trade shift, transport decline, external invasions in 1977 and 1978) while obliquely and impersonally sliding around the essential issues: "expansionary fiscal and credit policies, coupled with weaknesses in the management of domestic and foreign exchange resources, contributed importantly" (IMF, 1980: 2). The crux of the problem for the IMF is to make the reforms *appear* creditable enough to convince foreign donors to come up with massive new aid. Whether anyone involved really believes Mobutu's survival, governmental stability, or human welfare can be so purchased is debatable; but by pushing the decision into the future with other people's money and with lies no one will be penalized for, no one now involved will have a damaged reputation. In many ways it is just a game and one step on a career ladder.

The particular topics that need to be reshaped are corruption, invalid statistics, illusionary budgets, and the politically unrealistic size and indefinite need for aid to maintain even a veneer of status quo. To many aspects of these problems IMF reports reveal an awesome ability to project oblivion. Reforms at the top of the national government will be carried out if announced. They will have meaning. They will lead to improvements at regional and local levels. These are topics that the IMF, as an organization, needs not to know about. So they do not exist.

Other aspects are too obvious to ignore and so must be transformed. The word "corruption" is never used. "Mismanagement" is a favorite euphemism, but there are a number of others. General market speculation and rip-offs suggest the need for "more realistic cost-price relationships" (IMF, 1979b: 11). Coffee export taxes were lost by "underinvoicing and quality downgrading" (IMF, 1979a: 48). Diamond exports are talked about in terms of projected revenue and then as revenue shortfalls; one never understands that the trade is the private domain of Mobutu and his family. The question of Mobutu's direct slice of the annual national budget, the presidential *dotation*, is a very delicate topic the Fund cannot avoid. It was about 12 percent of the total as late as 1977 (IMF, 1979a: 80). In each report *dotations* are noted as a category of budgetary overrun, and reforms are promised. In August 1979 the Fund staff declared, "It has been decided to discontinue the practice of the Presidency making expenditures on behalf of departments, which had been a cause of overruns" (IMF, 1979b: 13). A new chief controller would monitor *dotations*. In May 1980 the Fund, commenting on massive budget overruns in 1979, found "certain categories of expenditure expanded more rapidly in the second half of the year than had been foreseen, particularly *dotations*. . . ." (IMF, 1980: 8). Mobutu, second or third richest man in the world, is probably the greatest thief in the annals of crime. You would never know it from 15 years of Fund studies of his economy. When there is no accountability, there are no limits to what an organization (or a person) will do or say.

Budgetary overruns consistently plagued the Fund staff because budget ceilings were one of the most precise targets in stabilization packages. One is treated to endless no-fault-here-comes-remedy explanations. Reviewing 1978 performance on spending for wages, the IMF staff slipped this sentence in at the end of a paragraph: "Moreover, widespread irregular practices played a major role in the rapid increase in the wage bill in recent years." Three pages later it is an obvious lead sentence of a paragraph that promises reform: "In October 1978 various measures were taken to improve budgetary control over expenditure" (IMF, 1979a: 25-8). The reforms are simply unbelievable as a remedy for the problems evident from a careful reading of the previous pages. Did anyone ever read it carefully? The IMF staff certainly needs to give credence to gestures of reform to build the image of positive change, but it is quite a system commentary that such intellectual sleight of hand suffices. Sometimes the Fund can take an active hand in the actual process; the Fund will criticize illusionary budget targets and press for lower ones, for example (IMF, 1979b: 6).

All of these discussions are based on the premise that the statistical base has some validity. Global economic data are far less accurate or uniform than is conventionally thought. The Fund staff is uncomfortably aware that it is being asked for kinds and quality of analyses for Zaire that are well beyond what is intellectually honest, given Zaire's statistics. Indeed there are probably very few numbers on Zaire that could be viewed as empirically accurate. This is mentioned from time to time: "analysis of developments in Zaire's external sector is hampered by statistical problems, which seem to have become even greater in recent years" (IMF, 1979a: 37); "as a result, balance of payments data in this report are subject to a wide margin of error" (IMF, 1979a: 38); and "given the paucity and other deficiencies in available data. . . . key parameters in Zaire are subject to a much wider margin of error than normal" (IMF, 1979b: 19). There is, however, no discussion of why the data are so bad or what kind of society could produce reasonably valid data, or, for citizen welfare, whether such data should be produced. The IMF simply plugs numbers into formulas, further legitimizing the illusion that Zaire has a government rather than a parasite.

The bottom line for the IMF in each report is to sustain and enhance this illusion and put the best possible face on the future. Carried to extremes, this led to paragraphs that begin "In 1979 Zaire's performance under the current stand-by arrangement was mixed." The more energetic reader was then treated to a string of negative assessments concluding with this: "More important, only limited progress was made toward reducing the acute internal and external imbalances, while the economy stagnated. . . ." (IMF, 1980: 21). Then the IMF turned to a few minor positive signs, pointed to a few recent reforms, asserted that this put stabilization back on track, proposed more aid, and proclaimed it all "a significant step toward internal balance" and "a sound basis for a resumption of economic growth" (IMF, 1980: 23-24).

It would not be fair to suggest in closing that this long exercise in mystification in world-system stabilization is unique to the IMF or to Zaire. The document produced by the World Bank for the May 1980 consultative group meeting on Zaire faced most of the same issues the IMF did in the same way. In some ways it was more candid about the problems. Without pursuing the details, suffice it to say that it proposed desirable foreign aid commitments to Zaire to average $1.05 billion a year from 1981-85 (IBRD, 1980c: 26). Mobutu's Swiss bankers would be pleased.

For those seeking real human development there is a pleasant irony in the way the IMF's efforts to enhance Mobutu's Zaire as a legitimate and supportable development model have rebounded to corrupt the IMF and reduce its own legitimacy throughout the world. By accepting Zaire's data as sufficiently valid to work from, the IMF staff corroded its own professionalism and made it that much harder to get valid data from other countries. A second kind of precedent was set vis-à-vis stabilization programs. Zaire did not come close to most of its targets in three straight stabilization efforts. Yet the IMF continued to sanction its overall performance with only mild delays; Peru, Turkey, Jamaica, and other countries must have found this educational. The case of Zaire has demonstrated one final element of the IMF's ethical bankruptcy. If the core system stabilizers, under pressure from a major mandator like the United States government, approach a situation like Zaire with only one possible outcome, such an organization has refuted its charter and lost its integrity.

It is sadly apparent that the Zairian people will not eat well in the present circumstances. But constructive lessons for global alternatives are evident in their plight. Reading much IMF documentation corrupts one's language with bureaucratic jargon, confines the mind to the wrong set of issues, and perpetuates false assumptions about the scale use of resources. One cannot ever expect an organization with such an antihumanistic mandate to contemplate participatory development. But changing its mandate, as suggested by Rweyemamu (1980), can be only part of the solution. As long as a world-system organization works in an environment of mandators composed of governments, it is being conditioned to behave like an organization. That bodes ill for participation. Any new organization must be designed with the representation of authentic citizen interests in the key positions. Relocating authority for naming Executive Directors, Managing Director, and senior staff would be one element. Independent citizen evaluation mechanisms would be another. Publication of all documentation would be a third; how else can one end the global phenomenon of socially irresponsible organizations masquerading as governments? But this line of reform itself can generate undue optimism, for without effective citizen participation in local and regional development, there is little reason to believe that national or international organizations can be directed from elite to mass welfare. To move beyond the contradiction between development and the world-system, this book now turns to the practical issues of creating more and better citizens.

CHAPTER BIBLIOGRAPHY

Abdalla, Ismail-Sabra (1980). "The Inadequacy and Loss of Legitimacy of the International Monetary Fund." *Development Dialogue*, 2:25-53.

Abrahamsson, Bengt (1977). *Bureaucracy of Participation: The Logic of Organization*. Beverly Hills, Calif.: Sage.

Brett, E. A. (1978). "Development Theory, the IMF, and the Periphery: Towards an Alternative Strategy." Geneva; IFDA.

Feinberg, Richard (1980a). "The Stand-By Arrangements of the International Monetary Fund and Basic Needs." Paper presented at a Woodstock Theological Center Conference, Washington, D.C., April.

——— (1980b). "The International Monetary Fund and U.S.-Latin American Relations." Paper presented at the CIDE Conference, Guanajuato, Mexico, July.

Girvan, Norman (1980). "Swallowing the IMF Medicine in the Seventies." *Development Dialogue*, 2:55-74.

Girvan, Norman, et al. (1980). "The IMF and the Third World: The Case of Jamaica, 1974-1980." *Development Dialogue*, 2:113-55.

Gran, Guy (1979a). "Zaire 1979: The IMF at Waterloo," pp. 406-17 in U.S. House of Representatives. Committee on Foreign Affairs, *Foreign Assistance Legislation for FY1980-81 – Part 6*.

——— ed. (1979b). *Zaire: The Political Economy of Underdevelopment*. New York: Praeger.

——— (1978). "Zaire 1978: The Ethical and Intellectual Bankruptcy of the World System." *Africa Today*, 25,4:5-24.

IBRD (1980a). *Price Prospects for Major Primary Commodities*. Rpt. No. 814/80, January, unpublished.

——— (1980b). *World Development Report, 1980*. New York: Oxford University Press.

——— (1980c). *From Economic Stabilization to Recovery: An Appraisal of the Mobutu Plan*, Rpt. ZA 80-2, May 15, unpublished.

____ (1979). *Zaire – Economic Memorandum*. Rpt. No. 2518-Zr, October 19 (published May 1980).

International Monetary Fund (IMF) (1979a). *Zaire – Recent Economic Developments*. SM/79/85, April 4. Unpublished.

____ (1979b). *Zaire – Request for Stand-By Arrangement*. EBS/79/497, August 15. Unpublished.

____ (1980). *Zaire – Review and Consultation Under Stand-By Arrangement*. EBS/80/100, May 5. Unpublished.

Johnson, Omotunde, and Salop, Joanne (1980). "Distributional Aspects of Stabilization Programs in Developing Countries." *IMF Staff Papers*, 27,1 (March):1-23.

Republic of Zaire (1979a). "Balance of Payments Projections for 1980-1985 and Analysis of External Resource Gap." October.

____ (1979b). "Information Memorandum." October.

____ (1979c). "Request for Emergency Assistance in the Context of a Recovery Plan for Zaire."

____ (1979d). *Plan Mobutu – Programme de Relance Economique 1979-81*. 5 volumes. November.

Rweyemamu, Justinian F. (1980). "Restructuring the International Monetary System." *Development Dialogue*, 2:75-91.

Salda, Anne (1980). "The International Monetary Fund, 1978-9: A Selected Bibliography." *IMF Staff Papers*, 27,2 (June):380-436.

Shapiro, Harvey (1980). "The IMF's Identity Crisis." *Institutional Investor*, September:96-120.

U.S. Congress. House of Representatives (1980). "International Monetary Fund Quota Increase." *Congressional Record*, H9027-H9050 and H9130-H9143, September 17-18.

U.S. Congress. House of Representatives. Committee on Banking, Finance, and Urban Affairs (1980). *To Amend the Bretton Woods Agreement Act. . . .* Hearings, February-April.

U.S. Congress. Senate. Committee on Banking, Housing, and Urban Affairs (1980). *International Monetary Fund and Related Legislation*. Hearings, March-April.

U.S. Congress. Senate. Foreign Relations Committee (1980). *The Bretton Woods Agreements Act*. Hearings, March.

U.S. Department of Commerce (1980). "Zaire", *Foreign Economic Trends*. 80-074, August.

6

Empowering People to Develop

+ subordinate peasant
↗
Elites central ← Prob 1
Understand Problem, small   ← means 2
group organizing
Conscien . .
(Participatory Dev't 3
↘ form dev't curricula (plan of
action)
dev't can't be externally
managed 4

The first five chapters have chronicled major activities of elites in the contemporary world. Elites use ideology and mask it as science and law. Their structural aggression is packaged by organizations commonly called aid agencies, businesses, and governments. Processes, termed projects, investment, and markets serve to perpetuate and enhance the relative poverty and marginalization of billions of poor people all over the world. That such a state of human affairs has gone on for decades does not make it inevitable. The same technological and organizational "advances" that made possible military dictatorships, totalitarianism, the Cold War, the arms race, monopoly capitalism, and the global spread of the bureaucratic culture of the twentieth century also provide other kinds of education. The world-system is spreading the consumer mentality to billions of people who cannot attain great material wealth with the prevailing exclusionary social orders and scale use of resources. It is in the inherent long-term interests of most such citizens to pursue an alternative vision. Given the possibility of attaining both material security and social *and* moral needs, it is my hypothesis that most citizens will not permanently sanction or put up with the ecological ruin, balance of terror, and individual resource monopolization now prevalent.

THE DEVELOPMENT PROBLEM AND THE
EMPOWERMENT SOLUTION IN BRIEF

(to material dev't complex)

The alternative is to advance by means of education in the broadest sense a process through which individuals carry out three tasks. The individual must move from a position as subject to one as an actor who defines the goals, controls the resources, and directs the processes affecting his or her life. An individual is in an unequal contest against large organizations. Thus individuals must also create small groups to enhance their power and ability to deal with external change agents. But against most such agents, small sub-village groups would still be overmatched. A network of supportive intermediate institutions must be built to buffer the bureaucratic imperatives and elite economic interests. Above them should emerge a cooperative set of government and nongovernmental actors and institutuions (see Chapter 12) committed to this overall process of authentic participatory development and working on all levels of the world-system to dissolve any opposing power concentrations.

It will be a long, unequal struggle. But to the extent such a democratic vision more accurately crystallizes and works toward the breadth of real human concerns, it will attract adherents from the sterile materialism of capitalism, the unrealistic utopianism of state socialism, and the oppressive bureaucracies of both. Small social fragments working through a systems approach can enormously magnify their impact even against great political forces. Despite their limits, the processes of the U.S. antiwar movement from 1972-75 and the work of Amnesty International with local groups give one some sense that it will be practical in overall terms.

It should be clear at the outset that, despite the synergetic advantages of such a development system, the essence of the effort by base organizations must be one of relative self-reliance. Intermediate organizations are not to conceive of their role as long-term conduits of external resources to mobilized villagers. Such organizations have many essential functions: defenders against assaults by elites; idea brokers and catalysts on matters of social mobilization; trainers of local group organizers; and advisors on the social implications of technology choices, market information, legal and political empowerment, and credit mechanisms. To the extent that any supravillage entity supplies resources on a steady basis, it creates a dependent bureaucratic relationship with the local citizen group. This leads to clients, not creative citizens, as Gittell (1980) demonstrates.

The theoretical basis for self-reliance has been presented many times, perhaps most coherently by Galtung (1980: 404-13). Self- reliance implies selective resistance to specialization of production in order to use local resources more efficiently. It demands mass participation. Basic needs receive greater priority. Creativity is stimulated; the economic history of regions or countries entirely cut off from the world-system by war or other disaster clearly shows this. The results will be more attuned to local conditions, producing diversity rather than homogenization and alienation. Ecological balances will more likely be observed. Psychological solidarity can be built among mature socially conscious citizens. The lessons of social irresponsibility from the outside world may then be less dominant, and socioeconomic inequalities at the local level will have less and less justification. Human beings are imperfect, and local conditions vary widely. Some inequality will remain, some needs unmet. What matters are overall tendencies, the power of positive example, and the definition of citizen that emerges. If *both* values *and* objective conditions impel it, participatory development is more than possible.

It will not, of course, be so neat and easy to produce participatory development as this précis suggests. Profound obstacles must be clearly in view of the practitioner at all times. By obstacles I do not mean the pseudo-question raised by Western social scientists about such matters as how much participation is enough or how authentic is a specific process or act. In a series of papers (notably Uphoff et al., 1979; Knight, Peter T., ed., 1980; Cohen and Uphoff, 1980) members of the Cornell Rural Development Committee have treated AID and the World Bank to endless social science typologies about participation in development. The results have not been very practical.

Devoid of a precise organizational, political, and social context, it is essentially pointless to try to quantify levels and types of participation in development design, implementation, or evaluation. Small group relations in the non-western world are not well portrayed with the primitive methods and ethnocentric biases of conventional social science. It should be reasonably clear from the actors themselves how much participation is appropriate and practical at a specific point in a specific process.

Instead obstacles must be sought in the activities of specific actors in the modern world-system. For it is crucial to know in the clearest terms how and why system elites will try to oppose, squash, preempt, and manipulate new development initiatives. Participatory development must encompass every facet of this system and devise both offensive and defensive strategies in response. The problems are many:

1. System elites seek rising levels of profit and security within a short-term (2-10 years) perspective. These elites propel a process of the commodification of goods and services to extract wealth via the market mechanism and its unequal exchange. The result is uneven and exclusionary.

2. Diminishing the cost of labor raises profits, so efforts at proletarianization are inherent. Given capital's goals, labor is inevitably in a situation of conflict.

3. The result, aptly put by Robertson (1978: 90-91), is not enough jobs, meaningless jobs, and much important work not done at all.

4. Elites work through power concentrations to create exclusionary political structures, termed structural aggression or structural violence. Processes of partial mass empowerment are manipulated via confidence mechanisms to sustain prevailing political balances.

5. Elites control the value, supply, and distribution of money and scarce resources. One result is enormous waste on security outlays and conspicuous consumption. Another is scale inappropriate investment and technology.

6. All aspects of culture and language at the national level come to serve elite purposes. It is not easy to use a legal system and culture that created injustice and sustained inequitable property rights to work for the empowerment of the rural poor.

7. Creation of the modern organization has added new system imperatives of security, control, and growth. They tend to work in ways contrary to either elite interests or those of supposed clients. Bureaucratic imperatives work on human behavior in the organization, on the structure of its internal work, and on all aspects of its result.

8. Critical for a participatory society is the way bureaucracy transforms humans. Street-level bureaucrats face multiple constrictions. The poor and their organizations become targets or clients, not citizens.

9. Underlying self-sustaining choices of law, social organization and technology, elites perpetuate an illusionary view of human nature, the origin and meaning of poverty, and human inequality. As a result the poor are subhumans, not deserving of authentic cognitive respect. Indeed, as Adams (1979) describes it, the outsider or the elite cannot really even see the peasant.

10. The results are violence, inequality, ecological harm, overpopulation, alienation, and profound structural instabilities that encourage elites to devise newer and more efficient exclusionary and extractive processes at each historic stage.

It is a somber view of the modern world. People at all levels in all societies do seek to avoid conforming to these overall system tendencies and to work in small ways toward a more humane and participatory world. Important too is Wertheim's (1964: 23-39) portrait of society as a composite of conflicting value systems; local traditions and culture continue their war against the twentieth century version of the great culture, the world-system. The solution that follows inherently depends on those "improperly" socialized human splinters who reject the addictions and dependancies of our time that leave "autonomy undermined, satisfaction dulled, experience flattened out, and needs frustrated" (Illich, 1977: xiii). Illich is correct in his analysis of the radical nature of the attack by the industrial mode of production on subsistence values. That one can build an SST or a neutron bomb does not make it a developmentally responsible choice. That a small number of people monopolize millions (or billions) of dollars of resources does not mean that it can be socially defended in a world of scarcity and deprivation. Socially defined, situationally appropriate limits must be crystallized in a wide-ranging participatory process of public education.

The solution that follows begins with the individual. In this chapter the nature of the marginalized human is explored and the content of the necessary transforming education is detailed. Then the creation by development catalysts of small groups as authentic participatory organizations is treated, with all the complexities of decision making, implementation, and distribution in a world of scarcity. In Chapter 7 relations with the outside world come into focus: the nature and functioning of intermediate organizations and the multiple roles of the development catalysts; the relationship of this microdevelopment system to different types of village governments; some potential strategies against predictable actions by regional or provincial authorities; strategies toward national governments; and suggestions on acclimatizing international aid agencies and linking with specific types of private voluntary organizations. Together these two chapters are intended to provide a practical guide to participatory development for all who will work within or with intermediate institutions at the local level.

CREATING CITIZENS: UNDERDEVELOPMENT IS A STATE OF MIND

Citizenship demands education, values, and motivation. This section will begin by exploring how the essential actors in Third World development define their needs and seek their fulfillment in the conflicting and diverse educational environments of the world-system: peasants in different social situations; elites at different political, economic, and organizational places; forces in the larger culture espousing capitalist norms; other forces teaching etatist or state socialist goals; and diverse theocratic or sectarian visions. None of these educational paths is resulting in thinking, autonomous, creative, critical, optimally productive, or even happy individuals in very large numbers. A different education system must therefore be designed, based on generic universal needs. This system requires fairly specific goals, a practical implementation process, and some clear ideas of curriculum content.

History's winners have traditionally been the ones to define historical truth, including the nature of the poor and the inevitability of poverty. The poor in general and peasants in particular have only recently begun to fare better in Western social science, as students of Tilly, Hobsbawm, E. P. Thompson, and Barrington Moore began to apply new frameworks in the last twenty years to the study of non-western peasantry. Traditional, primitive, and irrational man has, hopefully, been replaced by some idea of a rational man whose conservative response to outside forces is logically grounded. Any understanding of development must begin with the perception that the peasant does not face the outside world as either a tabula rasa or a passive, uncritical sponge.

Understanding peasants begins with appreciating their particular roles in the contemporary world-system. Variations in both the macroeconomic and microeconomic relations of the peasant to the larger system matter enormously to the peasant's perceptions of security and subsistence. No one definition covers all situations, but Klein has distilled the following useful synthesis from African writers.

PEASENT V. SYSTEM

(1) Peasants are agriculturalists who control the land they work either as tenants or smallholders. Landless laborers are not peasants.

(2) They are organized largely in household units which meet most of their subsistence needs.

(3) They are ruled by other classes, who extract a surplus either directly (rent) or through control of state power (taxes).

(4) Peasant culture is distinct from, but related to, the larger culture of the dominated group.

(Klein, 1980:11)

In most contemporary situations there are not just peasants but also small commodity producers, petty entrepreneurs, landless laborers, and people playing multiple roles.

Despite the relative imperfection of any model, one must note correctly the operational premises of peasant logic in subsistence situations. Much cultural ethnocentrism still pervades Western debates on this issue. Popkin (1979), opposing Scott's (1976) vision of the moral economy of the peasant, would, for example, apply not just Western political norms but capitalist economic norms to precolonial Vietnamese peasants. One can agree that peasants of all ages have always been remarkably enterprising and creative in their day-to-day adaptations to the vicissitudes of nature. This does not make the premodern peasant an entrepreneur in the capitalist sense that Popkin applies to the Vietnamese in the Nguyen Dynasty.

Peasants like these, as Berger (1978) shows, were part of a tributary mode, not a capitalist mode, of production. They embraced a culture of survival, not a culture of progress. An entrepreneur builds toward an improved life, accepting risk toward a more knowable and controllable future. The subsistence peasant has less a linear than a cyclical view of history. The future is not necessarily more knowable. Limits to knowledge are not going to be greatly reduced. Thus the best one could do is to guard against threats to subsistence, many appearing like ambushes, and to follow paths that have worked before. It is quite rational, but it is not the sort of cost-benefit calculus neoclassical economists preach. Nathan Wachtel has captured these dichotomies in his provocative study *Vision of the Vanquished: The Spanish Conquest of Peru through Indian Eyes* (Eng, ed., 1977).

Western elites have not to this day accepted the possible validity of this alternative human accommodation to nature. Peasant dreams of a millenarian past have always been the object of utopian taunts because no rulers have wanted to recognize that such dreams could preface a future when the road to subsistence was not rendered impassable by the exactions of elites. Instead over the centuries Western elites have defined the marginal and poor in terms most useful to the ideological, economic, or psychological needs of the moment. Ivan Illich, in his recent work (1981), has looked back through history at this process.

For the Greeks and Romans aliens were deemed barbarians, and the indigenous poor were serfs and slaves. It was the medieval Church of the West that termed the alien someone to be incorporated or brought in; it has been elemental to western values ever since. The Church transformed barbarians into pagans needing baptism. Eventually most were baptized if not converted. With the appearance of the Moors, who needed both subjection and conversion, the alien was now an infidel. By the sixteenth century the Spanish had driven back the infidels and found a new alien threat across the seas in the wild man as noble savage. The noble savage did not correspond to the needs of an incipient world-system.

> This independence made him noble, but a threat to the designs of colonialism and mercantilism. To impute needs to the wild man, one had to make him over into the native, the fifth stage. Spanish courts, after long deliberation, decided that at least the native of the New World had a soul and was, therefore, human. In opposition to the wild man, the native has needs, but needs unlike those of civilized man. His needs are fixed by climate, race, religion and providence. Adam Smith still reflects on the elasticity of native needs. As Gunnar Myrdal has observed, the construct of distinctly native needs was necessary both to justify colonialism and to administer colonies. The provision of government, education and commerce for the natives was for four hundred years the white man's assumed burden (Illich, 1981: 19).

As the world-system evolved, it needed natives to play greater and more complicated roles.

In the post-World War II era peasants earned a new linguistic designation. The needs of the core for material markets and investment sites as well as for cheap labor and commodities helped transform natives into underdeveloped peoples. It was not enough to inflict economic man on the Third World. System imperatives suggested the incorporation into the market of one region or sector of activity after another. Planners and educators would conquer through a process of institutionalization and bureaucratization in the Third World. Unsurprisingly the World Bank, leader of this process, has slowly begun to discover opposition. The Bank terms it "mismanagement" and the lack of management skills. The Bank, as a part of the system, cannot see the basic cultural conflict.

> More than skills, then, management demands a reservoir of a particular type of person, people who are willing to subordinate their ambitions and idiosyncrasies to the needs of the corporation (or government agency), people with self control and that old Puritan ability to postpone personal gratification on the short term in the hopes of long-term dividends — in other words, people who are capable of fitting the rational mold foisted on behavior in a consumer society (Linden, 1976: 254).

This is nothing less than a radical cultural assault by Western societies on the normative reality of subsistence people in the Third World.

The capitalist world-system is certainly not the only external force seeking to redefine human needs for the marginal poor of the Third World. Two other agents deserve attention: organized religion and the state socialist or etatist alternative. Both are more overtly authoritarian in their restructuring of human needs. In practice they usually demand a more explicit true believer, one who will not respond critically to ultimatums from above. The impossibility of creating participatory development from the top down has been demonstrated by many clerical and ideological leaderships, even the most nobly intentioned. One well-studied case should suffice to suggest why.

The Nyerere government in Tanzania came to power with a fuzzy state socialist vision and few resources. To extend many social or economic opportunities to scattered villagers was too expensive. Tanzania's socialist and communal approach led in 1967 to a policy of scale-efficient socialist villages termed *ujamaa*. Calls for voluntary participation soon gave way to a combination of sticks and carrots. These were not sufficient. The practical obstacles to the resettling of large numbers of people were underestimated. The political cadre assigned to the task had neither the community development skills for authentic popular mobilization nor the technical skills to merit local respect. Villagers began to reject the assignment of outsiders and seek the training of local people. As criticisms mounted, the government cadre behaved like normal officials and sought to avoid threats; the bureaucracy grew and so did the size of the average village. Beyond a relatively small number of 90-150 families it proved impossible to engender great cooperative spirit. No policy was ever developed to alter the self-interested political behavior of local elites. The peasants saw through the paternalism and utopianism to the de facto alliance of the state with local elite and foreign interests. One can add technical and financial disincentives, but the peasants' central reason for noncooperation and nonproductivity in the 1970s was the inevitable cultural imperialism of a central bureaucratic authority that was incapable of granting the peasant authentic cognitive respect (among many, Freyhold, 1979 and Coulson, 1982).

It should be quite clear by now that millions of marginalized people will not be able to alter their status to any appreciable extent by letting external agents define their needs and goals. Such agents continue to appeal to narrowly conceived aspects of the human personality. Defining all social relations and endeavors by their degree of profitability, the way they support an ideological state system, or the purity of allegiance to a religious creed is seriously limiting and distorting human potential. It is the height of arrogance for those of one culture, religion, nation, class, region, or group to seek to inflict normative choices on those of another. A number of authors have made this point in the predominantly European debate over basic human needs. One cannot expect elites to stop using culture, language, and even word definitions (see Chorover, 1979, for instance) as tools for stratification. In a world of scarcities and limited visions, it is not surprising that many humans find it comfortable and sustaining to define their self-esteem in terms of differences in material wealth and the sociopolitical domination of others. This occurs worldwide from Washington, D.C. to the remote villages of Zaire.

THE HIERARCHY OF NEEDS AND THE
CURRICULUM FOR CONSCIENTIZATION

Only by enlarging vision and raising consciousness can the motives for mass exclusion and pauperization begin to be undermined. The first step is the widespread understanding of true human needs. Humanistic economists have begun this pursuit by seeking to synthesize universal physical and psychological drives. Two University of Maine professors have produced an initial elementary text (Lutz and Lux, 1979). Central to their work is the writing of psychologist Abraham Maslow and his belief that humans grow through meeting a progression of needs. The ideal life is a process of maturing toward higher levels of self-realization, realizing ever more of one's potential. There is no universal ordering, no ordained path to maturing. Human beings are unique, and material and ecological conditions vary widely. Yet there is an irreducible essence that Maslow has arranged in a classic hierarchy. (See Figure 6.1.) Others (Horvat,

FIGURE 6.1. Maslow's Hierarchy of Needs

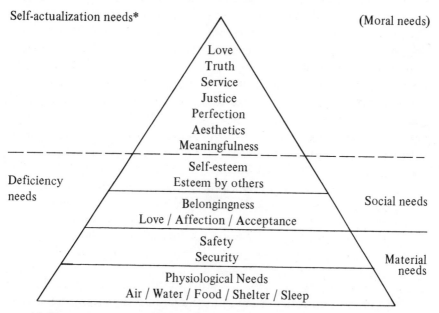

Self-actualization needs*   (Moral needs)

Love
Truth
Service
Justice
Perfection
Aesthetics
Meaningfulness

Deficiency needs

Self-esteem
Esteem by others

Belongingness
Love / Affection / Acceptance   Social needs

Safety
Security   Material needs

Physiological Needs
Air / Water / Food / Shelter / Sleep

*Self-actualization needs are of equal importance (not hierarchical).

Source: Lutz and Lux, 1979:11.

1982: 416ff) have found a simpler ranking more empirically sustainable, but Maslow's pioneer effort merits primary attention to illustrate some basic points.

What Maslow is saying, in his own words, is that "man does not live by bread alone – *if* he has enough bread." In the face of this triangle I think both the human needs debate and the question of its potential cultural bias are rendered marginal to the development practitioner. Clearly it is necessary to fill lower needs to an acceptable level to be physically able to aspire to higher ones. Beyond that, two other issues are more important. The hierarchy is posed in this manner because reaching and fulfilling a higher need tends to render a lower one less important. Distressing or incomprehensible as it may be to many elites, there are things more fulfilling than great political power or material wealth. That so many people cannot see beyond these relatively infantile needs suggests widespread and common blockages to human development. Psychologists call them materialism and egotism. Any successful development model will have to have a process for overcoming them.

The world-system and its state socialist alternatives in the Soviet Union and elsewhere have clearly failed to do any such thing. As Lutz and Lux suggest, a major reason is that neoclassical economics has preferred to discuss wants rather than needs, as though all human desires could be reduced to marketable commodities. "An economics that has no theoretical way of making a distinction between the importance of supplying water and the importance of supplying tobacco hardly seems relevant to a living organism, let alone a human development" (Lutz and Lux, 1979: 18). They go on to define the humanistic solution in terms not of class struggle but of the more basic conflict in values.

> Humanistic economics is a scientific framework for the theoretical understanding, as well as design of appropriate institutional arrangements pertaining to, the processes of production, distribution, and consumption that will enable optimal satisfaction of the hierarchy of human needs (Lutz and Lux, 1979: 23).

Their text is largely concerned with the fallacies of economic man and the broad theoretical themes of the humanistic alternative. What international development needs is a practical process through which the marginalized poor, indeed all people, become aware of this range of value choices and their social and personal implications.

Such an educational process cannot be a didactic intrusion from the outside world. Nor can it be an arbitrary, predetermining one. Human responses to different needs will clearly vary with cultural, ecological, and material limits. Humans will sometimes desire a greater measure of autonomy than a greater amount of material wealth, defining security in ways the outsider cannot easily see; Wallman (1977) contains a number of such cases. The most logical and efficient way for humans to make conscious value choices and create processes balancing social and personal goals is the method called *conscientization*.

Conscientization is the term given by its creator Brazilian educator Paolo Freire to the process

> in which men, not as recipients but as knowing subjects, achieve a deepening awareness of the sociological reality which shapes their lives and of their capacity to transform that reality (from de Silva et al., 1979: 56).

One of the most illuminating examples in current development literature is the struggle of the deeply marginalized group, the *adivasis*, maintaining ethnic traditions against the onslaughts of caste and capitalism in an Indian village two-hours' drive from Bombay. Their movement is called Bhoomi Sena. The *adivasis* had faced centuries of brutality, especially at the hands of the landowning caste, the *sawkars*. An uprising in 1945-47 made some gains, but political consciousness was demobilized by various state tactics. A new series of efforts began with an August 1970 land grab, part of a national effort. Thereafter struggle and learning evolved slowly into an organized effort. Organization was not built upon abstract principles, but on people's will and initiative (de Silva et al., 1979).

The process and pitfalls of small group mobilization in consciousness raising are the subject of the next section. Here the effort is to deduce from the Bhoomi Sena and other comparable experiments the main elements of the content of this participatory and dialogic educational process. By a somewhat arbitrary listing I would include at least the following topics: conflict; process and relationship; nuclear social relations; community relations; and the hierarchy of needs as they relate to work, technology, and human satisfaction.

Marginalized people, as do most people, live in an environment of conflict. An education that begins with the premise of harmony, as does neoclassical economics, will be refuted by the everyday behaviour of authority figures and others in the local environment. Small group discussions, initiated at first by a development catalyst, in which each member recounts specific incidents of conflict will begin to create a collective consciousness. Participants will see that individual experiences are not isolated accidents but elements of consistent patterns of oppression. By illuminating groups of winners and losers in local conflict, it will become clear who at least some of the oppressors are. Types of conflict, arenas of conflict, uneven access to resources, the legal basis of oppression, and kindred topics should all be part of this discussion.

Inherent in these discussions will be processes and relationships. They need to be crystallized as such by putting pieces together and talking about the motives and needs of each person involved. Three basic relationships should be explored in detail: "between the individual and the structure; between the individual and all oppressed; between all oppressed and the structure" (de Silva et al., 1979: 43). It might well be possible at this early point to clarify the whole idea of a confidence mechanism: how, as Chapter 1 suggested, elites maintain stratification by setting up psychological lures for ill-rewarded mass participation.

A participatory process forbids the exclusion of any set of disadvantages for any reason, be it of age, sex, race, or creed. Yet virtually all societies routinely practice all kinds of discrimination. These early small discussions must explore why people threaten other people, how scarcity encourages selfishness, and how people build up false and limited perceptions of identity and security through the domination of others. These are deeply rooted habits reinforced by specific cultural norms in specific settings. They will not disappear in a few discussions. But they can be linked to a specific mode of production that the mass have already found unsatisfactory. It should not be overly threatening to suggest that the role of women that sustains the present situation will *have* to be quite different to create the changed and improved situation desired. An exploration of woman's role around the world would be a liberating session for all involved.

The idea now prevailing in international development is that women develop either as an adjunct to a male dominated project or by means of a separate activity. Such approaches reinforce the prevailing discrimination. Poor groups and poor societies have only one resource in any abundance — their own labor. To perpetuate a system of under- and misemployment is stupid and counterproductive as well as immoral. Without initial wide-ranging discussion of why and how men and women can interact in an egalitarian and cooperative fashion, one cannot expect this to happen after small groups are mobilized and begin to envision a development activity. At that point the outside force is likely to enter as an agent of the status quo, even in a potentially revolutionary situation. AID is involved for example in a rice agriculture project in a Muslim area of Guinea-Bissau. AID's social anthropologist did recognize the exclusion and illiteracy of women despite their key role in the work process itself. But after assessing the relative strength of the traditional leadership, which dominated the new local producer associations, vis-à-vis the new government development cadre, AID opted to build its project on the local elite and graft on top a palliative literacy program for women. Efforts of PAIGC cadre will be undercut. In sum, the project started too soon. If the proper community education and group organizing had been done first, the boundaries of political possibility would have been very different. Then the project design choices would have been far better.

An egalitarian participatory dialogue between men and women does not do much to prevent continued discrimination against the old and the young. Traditional societies may venerate the elderly, and modern ones may discard them. Clearly some elderly wish to continue their education and social contributions and have much to give, while others represent exclusionary traditions of the past and are not open to new ideas. The early period of group education should include the old in an open discussion of the roles they would like to play in a changing world. The relationship of age and respect in such a world will create philosophical conflict that every society must ponder anew.

The role of children in modern history is all but invisible. With Mozart as an exception they do not usually leave enduring legacies. The modern world still uses them as cheap labor or trains them in authoritarianism in warehouses called schools. As Aries's classic on the history of children shows, however, before the industrial revolution, children were young citizens participating and learning in the group economy and society. Any excluded group of adults should devise ways to have the active involvement of children in the development process. Children often have a compelling ability to discuss social responsibility and ethical choices. They have enormous imaginations. It is their future. It is indefensible that they not be permitted the fullest possible role in its creation. The first step is the affirmation of their abilities as citizens. Any development practitioner who thinks that this would be utopian, impractical, or of limited value would do well to explore the 1978-79 project in Naples and Oxford called Children's Participation in Futures (Nicholson and Lorenzo, 1981).

The broad choices of community relations are a fourth essential part of the educational content at every stage. Capitalist ideology glorifies an assumed right of any individual to pursue unlimited material or financial resources for personal satisfaction. Socialist ideology, as now practiced, glorifies an essentially unlimited contribution by the individual to the social whole, usually the state. Neither ideal is an accurate or healthy goal for the human creature and its needs. The neurosis of materialist drives unforgivably overlooks or mystifies the reality that an individual on earth must exist in relation to others. The existence of others creates limits for each individual. If one person monopolizes most of the small resources of a village, it has multiple bad effects for both labor productivity and the fulfillment of needs. Thus the philosophical and practical issues of justice, equity, and ownership are essential parts of conscientization. It is improbable that without a consensus on relatively egalitarian limits to the use of resources, a very participatory society will result. It is similarly illogical to think that a productive and participatory citizen will result if the social body chooses to ignore the essentially personal dimensions of human needs at each level. The heart of the discussion must be the need for balance and the nature of the balance most socially appropriate in that particular material setting.

Galtung (1980: esp. 61-72) has developed a very clear position on the necessity of balanced social relations and reduced power differentials for development. Differences in innate human abilities are to be expected. Such diversity can help or hinder development. Differentials in structural and resource power work against the central goal of development, power over oneself or autonomy, by creating and sustaining opposite results: inequality, injustice, exploitation, penetration, fragmentation, and marginalization. Development inherently *implies reduction of power differentials.* Similar logic links peace and development. The development education process must join this discussion to concrete human results in the immediate location. It should not be hard to link inequality, structural power, and protein-deficient, brain-damaged children.

The marginalized poor must face a fifth and final area in their basic development curriculum: the relationships of technology, work, and human satisfaction. It is a long road from backbreaking labor for subsistence survival to activities pursued for reasons of self-actualization. Yet beginning to expose such a range of choices to marginalized people will evoke a ready response. In subsistence economies resources are renewable, and production is judged on its use value rather than its market value. Illich (1981) has broadened our understanding of the choices between hard and soft technology. Small groups embarking on development must consider more than just the choice of renewable energy versus fossil fuel or nuclear power. How much health care should be centralized or institutionalized? One cannot develop personal definitions of need satisfaction without taking personal responsibility for what you teach and learn. This means denying ritualized professional status. It means struggling against the centralized, institutionalized, and homogenized educational process the world-system uses to create its profitable little consumers and producers. Peasants are professionals in a number of survival tasks. They are quite capable of undertaking education in other topics. Instead of luring them into new dependencies, the development catalyst needs to be reinforcing instincts and strategies for self-reliance.

Such a far-reaching development curricula may seem a bit impractical and utopian at the onset of a development process. To the extent, however, that any small group of marginal people do not begin such reflections, they will begin a project with their preexistent culture as peripheral subjects of the world-system. One cannot build anything without proper foundations. Conventional aid activities for decades have ignored such elementary logic and made at best marginal use of scarce resources. The participatory alternative instead produces, through conscientization, an education in the full range of human needs and in the habits and aspirations of socially responsible citizenship. This will not happen, of course, in an organizational vacuum. It is to the practical problems of small group organization for participatory development that this chapter now turns.

SMALL GROUP ORGANIZATION:
BEGINNING ACTIVE CITIZENSHIP

The general theory behind organizing the poor should be easily acceptable to most development practitioners except the most insecure and rapacious elite. Most poor, unskilled individuals acting alone cannot deal effectively with large power concentrations, their bureaucratic culture, and their exclusionary and exploitative processes. A small group of 8-15 households acting together, however, can build group skills to gain greater access to and control over resources, productive activities, and their rewards. With tangible and secured gain, the individual will have incentive to invest scarce resources and more labor. Political skills must advance to protect the gain from public and private predators. The results should turn poor marginal subjects into prospering citizens making optimum use of scarce but growing material resources and meeting more and more of their needs in a self-sustaining process.

If this sounds like a lot of slow difficult work, that is a correct appreciation. That both elites and aid organizations perceive (or have) imperatives to produce quick results is one reason why the requisite education and social reorganization does not take place. As Chapter 7 will show, elites have other reasons to oppose this development approach; here we are concerned with building a base so firm that eventual opposition would be overmatched or held at bay. To do this means understanding the spontaneous and planned approaches, the premises of community organizing as opposed to community development, the complexities of the catalyst role, basic characteristics of participatory (as opposed to standard) organizations, and the generic limits of democracy in small group behaviour.

There would seem to be two general routes to the creation of effective small groups. One is based predominantly on planning and presumes relative harmony; the other seeks to build through "sequences in the dialectical development of spontaneity and its opposite." The first would apply greater use of a catalyst, a culture broker from the outside, who organizes these stages: an initial mobilization; the first action; extension of activities; further division of labor; and stabilization (Buijs, 1979: 24 ff.). The second crystallizes the growth of consciousness and skill through continual struggle as schematically represented below.

Spontaneity	Unites with, and opposes
1. Primordial (eruption)	Mobilization
2. Mobilized, unconscious	Conscientization
3. Mobilized, conscious	Organization
4. Mobilized, conscious and organized (self-management)	Centralization

Source: de Silva et al., 1979: 61.

Real world applications are rather likely to be mixtures of these approaches. One cannot wait endlessly for a spontaneous event to start from, nor can one analytically plan in entirety an activity involving multiple, independent decision makers.

The community organizing catalyst entering a specific micro-environment must have both the theoretical grounding in several disciplines and the interdisciplinary analytical skills and local language capabilities to communicate in that location. Very few foreigners qualify on even two of these grounds, a subject to be returned to. The generic principles of community organizing are widely known. Nowhere are they better summarized and applied than in the work of Mary Hollnsteiner on the Philippines.

1. People generally act on the basis of their self interest
2. People move *from* simple, concrete, short-term personal issues *to* more complex, abstract, long-term and systemic issues overtime
3. The Establishment reacts in ways that give people the opportunity to become angry and militant
4. Tactics against the powerful should be within the experience of the powerless and outside the experience of the powerful
5. Through the organizing process, people make their own decisions.

(Hollnsteiner, 1979: 408-9)

Note that unlike the emphasis in traditional community development, the intent here is less on transferring skills than on self-development. One member of the Bhoomi Sena cadre in an August 1977 discussion made this distinction with great clarity:

> An outsider who comes with readymade solutions and advice is worse
> than useless. He must first understand from us what our questions are,
> and help us articulate the questions better, and then help us find solu-
> tions. Outsiders also have to change. He alone is a friend who helps us
> to think about our problems on our own (de Silva et al., 1979: 45).

The degree of maturity and training necessary for the outside catalyst may seem to be considerable until one starts to consider the full
range of practical and political problems that must be overcome to
unleash the untapped talent in the local arena.

Local organizations of some sort already exist in most poor communities. A voluminous literature by North American aid agencies
(see Gow et al., 1979, for one sample) has pointed out many times
that they are not very effective vehicles for helping the poor. This
is true but not illuminating. One needs to know precisely what it is
about the origin, growth, objectives, legal status, organizational
setup, membership, leadership, management, services, activities, and
external links that will appeal to or repel poor people (Van Heck,
1979: 58-61). In such matters FAO and other UN and European
groups forged ahead in the late 1970s; much of what follows draws
on their work, for example, that of the Rural Organizations Action
Program of FAO in Asia.

FAO studies defined a quick and clear way to determine if an
organization would promote participation by the poor or be a tool
of elites. Most traditional organizations had a common set of characteristics termed standard; participatory groups developed a reverse
set. Detailed discussion of this is so critical, and so well defined in
Hollnsteiner (1978) that, following Van Heck (1979), a two-page
comparison is excerpted as an appendix to this chapter. A brief
synopsis follows.

Poor people might join a participatory organization if it grew
informally out of their own needs and designs to work under their
own control toward goals they were specifically interested in. Organization flowing from conflict situations and a collective sense of
injustice can generate significant commitment. Democratic decision
making and relatively small and homogeneous membership maintain
optimum communication; putting rich and poor in the same group
without transformative education tends to perpetuate inequalities.
Outside forces may play an early catalytic role and an intermediate
organization continues to play supportive roles (Chapter 7), but

there should be no significant enduring control. A look at the local organization of most major donor agency projects and Third World government efforts in the last generation shows a very, very different pattern. Productive goals set by elites have led to blueprint, top-down, social engineering that draws the local elite and "progressive" (a misnomer in the extreme) farmers into a technical exercise built on the prevailing inequalities and values that sustain them. Not unsurprisingly the poor are not greatly attracted or assisted.

TRAINING AND SELECTION OF
THE DEVELOPMENT CATALYST

Since many forces and values oppose the spontaneous conflict route to participatory organization, a catalytic agent is usually called for. Different investigations have applied many terms.* For convenience I shall stay with development catalyst (hereafter, DC). The DC has multiple roles (see Chapter 7) but most crucial for the success of later roles are the initial training and the cultural fit between the village and the DC. Two schools of thought are common: select one or two villagers for perhaps 3-6 months of training by an intermediate organization and then return them to the cultural and human setting they know best; or train an educated young couple as DCs over some appropriate period and then assign them to a village for a long-term tour. There are practical complications with either choice.

To seek local villagers for brief outside training has been my consistent preference. Much sophistication must go into the selection of people who can gain and retain the respect of varied local actors. Will relatively young people (possibly better educated in formal terms) have the respect of middle-aged peasants and will such young people be likely to stay in the village over an extended period? A recent survey (Esman et al., 1980: 24 ff) found on balance that it was middle-aged people, especially women, who had more attributes of reliability. Given the general global oppression of women, this

*For instance: community organizer (Hollnsteiner, 1978 and 1979); group organizers (GO/ARF) in the FAO work (Van Heck, 1979); culture broker or mediator (Buijs, 1979); *animateur* (Gellar et al., 1980); paraprofessional (Esman et al., 1980); development systems manager (DSM) (Korten, 1979b).

strongly suggests that a multiperson team be trained including at least one middle-aged woman. As these Cornell researchers found in Guatemala and Senegal, a bit of training does not generate automatic respect; outside links and resources and personal charisma are important. Clearly any intermediate organization involved in training must weigh not just the economics of numbers trained and villages covered but the tangible and intangible elements generating personal respect in the local culture.

Particularly sensitive will be the actual selection of the villagers to be trained. If the choice is made from the outside, it is a clear statement to villagers that their voice does not really count. Yet a choice made solely by villagers risks being made through nonparticipatory, elite-dominated processes. It would not be very wise to train DCs who are under the thumb of the village chief. Conversely it would not be particularly wise to choose only young Turks by whom the village leadership would feel immediately threatened. This all suggests an unavoidably difficult political process that involves slow, well-planned and sophisticated discussions that reach toward consensus decision making. One scenario would be nomination by the poor through their own selection and discussions and a final selection made by the training agency after an initial series of exchanges. Some villages will have great difficulty, given extremely stratified internal realities and concomitant tensions, in presenting any appropriate candidate. Training agencies should refuse to accept candidates with no empathy for or commitment to the poor, no interpersonal skills, or no capacity for and love of education. A village meeting explaining this refusal, pointing to reasons why candidates were accepted from neighboring villages, and inviting the villagers' reconsideration of what constitutes an appropriate potential DC should have a salutory educational effect.

Finances present additional thorny problems. Local citizens who are to serve as full-time DCs in the nurturing of however many village groups seem called for have to be paid or have to have other jobs or income. Someone well enough off to donate time to DC activities may be some social and economic distance from the poor villagers he or she must deal with. It is unreasonable that a group of poor peasants pay someone a salary at the start, but it may be quite reasonable to envision a period of growth during which several different small groups could plan to take on the salary of the DC to permit more and more activity. Given the present leadership and ideology of international donor agencies, it would be naive and probably dangerous for most intermediate organizations to seek money directly from them for the training and maintenance of DCs. Yet there are private voluntary agencies and other indirect channels for resources, if one has sufficient creativity to seek them out.

Training of local villagers in community organizing skills ideally implants among the poorest precisely those social resources that hold the key to their empowerment. If local people are used, those skills stay in the community and can be built on through a combination of practice, further training, and discussions with members of the intermediate organization. Sometimes, however, local politics in an entire region may be so hostile and manipulated that no suitable candidates for DCs emerge. In its Asian activities the FAO is now experimenting with the alternative choice for DCs (GO/ARFs in their terms). In the FAO projects young couples and individuals with rural roots are being trained to work short tours in selected villages. FAO's Rural Organizations Action Program (ROAP) has done two dozen country studies (summarized by Van Heck, 1979a) and diverse field surveys to help make its DCs sensitive to the diversity of local possibilities.

Without prejudging ultimate success it is worth noting some of the practical problems of this approach, most of which are visible to FAO itself. Given a DC who can stay put for only a finite period, the village runs the risk of losing the social investment of other villagers who have not fully absorbed organizing and catalytic skills. Intergroup links and the intermediate organization may or may not successfully compensate. FAO has considered the issue of scale and decided that it will take quite a while to train people in the 64,000 villages of Bangladesh. It seems to me that one should not try to settle this basic quantity versus quality issue without trying rough cost estimates of potential needed human investment per province. The problems of an outsider penetrating the internal communication channels, normative reality, and historical context of a village to implement successful social engineering seem consistently underestimated in the development literature. A U.S. specialist with years of experience in Thai villages described to me, for example, the stunning chasm between the reality collected by Thai census takers and the real world conditions in the village. Finally, one must consider the defensible unwillingness of poor villagers to let loose sensitive economic data to any outside agent;

one can more reasonably expect such a villager to begin to trust fellow villagers at his or her own level. The general DC activities and group formations should certainly not produce any centralized data base that the state or regional elites could seize upon. For these reasons and others, it would seem inherently more practical and defensible to spend the extra time and energy to invest in improving the skills of selected villagers to lead in the redesign of their own future.

The DC beginning work in an average peripheral environment needs a deep understanding of a wide range of practical and theoretical issues in small group behaviour. Some issues are contingent on the particular type of local political structure, a topic for Chapter 7. Others are generic and will be treated now as elements of the ideal organization and of predictable problems of human cooperation.

It is worth stressing why base organizations need to be fairly small, in the range of eight to twenty households. Rahman (in Galtung et al., eds., 1980: 80-97) suggests that there is an optimal center of gravity in a development effort that balances economic resources with emotional resources. Emotional resources are to a large extent a function of the growth of self-respect through self-reliance, a process of awakening inner needs and finding emotional satisfaction in social efforts. But the unit of self-reliance must be kept small enough to return a high degree of tangible commitment. Tangible rewards build commitment and consciousness allowing larger-scale organization; a group will soon need many leaders to take on tasks of growing complexity within and between base organizations. Keeping the initial size small lessens the corrosive, timewasting political conflicts possible with many actors. It also gives the space and encouragement to all members to gain the political experiences necessary for understanding and defending group interests (Mansbridge, 1980: 278 ff.). Yet the base organization cannot be so small as to lose all scale efficiency in resource use or not to appear able to defend itself in political conflict; for example, irrigation systems in rice agriculture villages might put a premium on a social form of a larger initial size.

In addition to substantive knowledge of some technical development issues and a comfortable grasp of the essential supplementary learning available from the intermediate organization, the DC must approach organizing with operational premises far different from those his mentors might have learned from elite education in international agencies. The conventional development process is based on a project cycle and the analytical assumption that obstacles can be planned for. As Korten (1979b, 1980, etc.) has clearly shown, the analytical paradigm and the hierarchical, centralized approach are singularly inappropriate. Organizations inherently seek routinization and control; participatory development is permanent change and ever growing individual freedom. The DC must begin with a method that incorporates many decision makers, many unknown elements, and continual interchange and learning. Korten calls this the cybernetic model. The DC works in an indeterminate and not ultimately controllable situation where powers of persuasion are critical. He or she cannot begin with a detailed blueprint of issues that can only be seen from the inside. Essays by Adams (1977 and 1979) and Emmerson (1976) are brilliant sobering demonstrations of this. Without a clear vision of many kinds of learning as goals of the process and without measures of achievement for both the DC and the peasant, participatory development will not take place.

DECISION MAKING IN SMALL GROUPS: ON NOT MANAGING DEVELOPMENT

Decision making is another element easily susceptible to inappropriate Western norms. Those who begin thinking about this issue from social science and elite perspectives may be tempted by something like the "humanistic-democratic participative management" philosophy (Jedlicka, 1977: 35-36) based on such elements as these: free communication; consensus decision making; influence of an idea by its merit; an atmosphere also permitting feelings; and an expectation of conflict to be met by rational mediation. This represents a giant liberal stride from the authoritarian norm of capitalist and communist societies. Participatory development, however, requires further giant strides.

It should be clear by now that, despite many available texts to the contrary,* development cannot and should not be externally managed. More properly, development should be but lightly guided,

---

*Waterston (1965); Honadle and Klauss (1979); Gant (1979); Goodman and Love (1979 and 1980); Bryant and White (1980 and 1981); Lindenberg and Crosby (1981); Mickelwait et al. (1979), etc.

usually only when elites create insuperable distortions or obstacles. Certainly coordinating activities by intermediate organizations (and national and international entities above) will need managing in certain ways. But the essence of participatory development is self-management. One of the harder tasks of the DC in the village will be to move from fountain of wisdom and respect to a collegial helper and thence to a semiemployee of some cooperative and representative organization of a group of base organizations. Ultimately the representatives of base organizations should supplant and phase out the original intermediate organization. No organization or individual will, to be sure, find it easy to work itself out of existence. But it is crucial that most kinds of external dependencies (especially of resources) be as brief as possible. Material aid does not build a self-reliant model, and the selfishness of the North precludes much greater resource transfers anyway for the foreseeable future.

The DC must also leave behind Western habits of decision making. It is not obvious that consensus building or adversary (winner take all) procedures are optimal ways to protect human needs in Third World villages. Mansbridge (1980) has explored these questions in U.S. settings with great effect. Adversary procedures such as a voting democracy are an all-or-nothing proposition generating and crystallizing conflict. They leave an unsatisfied, if not embittered, noncooperative minority in their wake. Villagers who have to live and work together the next day cannot afford to settle disputes this way. The need to maintain a veneer of friendship and harmony is one of many reasons making consensus building the commonest approach to decision making in small groups.

Decision by consensus is not, however, the panacea it might seem, as Mansbridge (1980: 165 ff.) discovered. Consensus creation benefits specific people: those who are pro status quo; those who can make things happen in alternative ways; those who can stand up to group pressures; those with resources to act on their own; and those who control the tone and content of the discussion. Consensus building is not without positive aspects. More communication happens, and less immediate conflict results. But the very nature of a consensus leaves most or all participants partially dissatisfied, yet having to cooperate to implement something.

Trainers for DCs would therefore do well to pursue Mansbridge's concluding suggestion that an alternative European model — consociational decision making — be explored. This method divides benefits in proportion to the expressed positions of the participants. Not all situations can be handled in this manner, but it would certainly be appropriate for the DC to explore in base organization meetings all aspects of each alternative and be open to flexible adaptations and new possibilities.

Overcoming Western cultural biases will still not leave the DC with a remotely easy task in small group mobilizing. The process of group selection, however arranged, will inevitably leave some villagers excluded and others dissatisfied. Periods of trial membership could be considered. Those who deliberately choose to remain aloof can watch the growth of psychological maturity and, hopefully, material benefits of group members. Discussions with these social fragments can be reopened from time to time. Even in a self-selected group of peasants of relatively equal status, however, the DC must face subtle realities working to generate exclusion and inequality.

Human beings are not born with nor do they develop equal abilities in verbal and social interactions. Some are more extraverted and more comfortable expressing opinions than others. To the extent that the group develops subunits by reason of operational needs or charismatic personalities, those in charge of or closest to communication channels have an advantage. Older group members may tend to marginalize new ones. Michel's classic discussion of the emergence of elitist rule (summarized in Abrahamsson, 1977: 67 ff.) also needs consideration. Expertise, perceived need for quick decisions, or a desirable continuity in leadership may all solidify inequality. So can the melding of ego and power. The DC must meet all these tendencies with the vision, perhaps best articulated in Mozambique, of the leader as the *responsavel*, the one responsible rather than the boss (see Lappé and Beccar-Varela, 1980: 65-80, for example). Yet people do begin their growth processes at different places and proceed at different rates. The essential issue is that individuals develop as quickly as they need to or are comfortable doing. This raises further complexities. Previous experiences or disadvantages affect one's ability to learn; the DC must consciously develop processes that avoid the capitalist extreme of betting on the strong, yet not conversely be limited by the current vision and abilities of the weakest. By keeping groups small, the DC can help individuals tailor their own special learning paths; the role of intermediate organizations as learning resource centers will make this practical, as the growth of village libraries in Tanzania and India have suggested.

The most skilled and perceptive DC will still not be able to prevent conservative and status quo tendencies from appearing in the base organization. To the extent the educational agenda, outlined earlier in this chapter, is not thoroughly absorbed, peasants may proceed with much participation toward consensus decision making along previously trodden paths; Hopkins (in Nash et al., eds., 1976: 99-112) describes this happening in rural Mali. In like fashion one will also meet the free rider who has so delighted Western critics (Popkin, 1979, for instance) of any group effort. The consociational approach, rewards in proportion to labor invested, along with group discussions less brutal than the Chinese *fan-shen* (Hinton, 1966) method, should diminish, but not totally eliminate, this problem.

There should be no illusion that the sum of global experiments has produced a foolproof defense against all human limits and all aspects of bureaucratization. Abrahamsson (1977: 50), one of the most enlightening students of these issues, has summed up some residual conundrums this way. New socioeconomic organization of production may make administration more, not less, complex. Equal pay regardless of work is a major disincentive, especially to technical specialists; yet at what point does unequal pay become "unacceptably privileged position." Rotating tasks provides experience at some cost in continuity and efficiency; yet not to do so risks professionalizing political positions and recreating political inequalities. Even before creating and implementing strategies to deal with the larger village and the world beyond, the development catalyst must pursue through many sessions of conscientization a very wide agenda of issues. Subsistence economic needs may force the base organization to focus much early effort on material pursuits. But the liberation and empowerment of people, that is, the essence of participatory development, will come only by people investing in the raising of consciousness to imagine the full range of human potential.

APPENDIX: Standard Versus Participatory Organization

A comparison of reasons why the rural poor:

Join C-O* style rural organizations	Do not join standard rural organizations
1. Members make the major decisions and carry them out with the assistance of their leaders. Incentives to join are high when participation is real.	1. Elite leaders make most of the decisions and the members carry them out. There is thus little incentive for active participation.
2. The members together with their leaders have *a personal stake* in the successful outcome of an activity because they have been involved in its conceptualization, decisions on action, implementation and evaluation. Continuity is virtually assured.	2. The members play *a passive role* or are not involved at all in conceptualizing, deciding upon, or evaluating organizational activities; expected merely to implement the organizations' aims, the members have only a limited stake in the success of the activity and therefore provide limited cooperation. Continuity becomes a problem as any initial enthusiasm wanes.
3. Leaders are of the same socio-economic background as the members, and therefore represent the same kinds of interests. This enhances the solidarity of the group. It also encourages the membership to exercise surveillance over its leaders lest they be tempted to favour personal interests over group ones.	3. Leaders are mostly of a higher socio-economic background than are the members. The differing interests can lead to tension and suspicion within the organization or between the organization and other poor residents, and prove harmful to it. Nonetheless, because of the leaders' higher status, the rank and file are reluctant or do not dare question their leadership even if the latters' actions call for it.
4. Leaders emerge in the context of informal group activities and mobilizing efforts. They are formally elected only some time after the group efforts have begun. Thus they command the support of their members because they have proven themselves worthy of the designation.	4. Leaders are chosen when the organization is first formed; hence, they only prove themselves later on. Should their performance turn out to be inadequate, they win little support from the members or some groups of members.
5. Members and leaders organize around issues in which they feel an emotional involvement, partly because their levels of conscious-	5. Leaders and members are asked to respond to ready-made projects or to new, unfamiliar tasks usually by outside entities. They feel little

ness have been raised by organizers, and they believe they can do something to change or improve the situation.

6. Mobilizations of large numbers of people to confront an appropriate authority figure as target and negotiate the settlement of an issue with him or her gives the members and leaders a sense of power. The mass action helps balance out power differentials and reduce fear and feelings of inferiority among the poor. The experience of power enhances their self-image as persons having dignity and rights.

7. Community organizers give considerable attention to both leadership and membership training. This entails issue awareness, understanding the details of organizational activities and projects, and confrontation tactics. Leaders get special training on the job, learning to run meetings, keeping the issues focused, handling confrontations and negotiations, and remaining accountable to the members.

8. Participation occurs across a broad spectrum of the local poor populace — old and young, men and women, small owner-farmers, share tenants, landless workers, and housewives — because the organization focuses on issues that command near universal concern, as opposed to projects of more limited scope. Moreover, the holistic presentation of issues conforms more closely to the perspectives of rural people, and their categories of thought.

if any emotional involvement in the project. If any emotions exist, these are either loyalty to the proponents or leaders, or fear of negative consequences if they do not participate.

6. Activities center around meetings in which the members are lectured to by leaders or outside resource persons. Being always the passive recipients of information and instructions, the members rarely gain the exhilarating experience of active and meaningful participation associated with real power. Instead, they are bored. The growth of self-confidence in the management of their own affairs is correspondingly stifled.

7. Outside sponsoring entities give heavy attention to leadership training assuming, usually erroneously, that the leaders will communicate their knowledge to the members. Hence, members may become alienated from their leaders in terms of awareness of what is going on in the organization, and lose interest in it.

8. Because the focus of attention of standard organizations is on some particular set of aims or projects, the types of community residents who would be attracted to participate are already specified, e.g. owner-farmers for compact farming, women with children for nutrition or family planning programs, landless workers for skills training. Hence, not all the poor can join. Moreover, projects come in artificially compartmentalized categories that are often alien to more holistically oriented people.

9. From an informal group of people with a common issue interest, informal leaders, and ad hoc committees to run things, the organization after some time decides to shift into the status of a formal organization complete with elected officers, a constitution and bylaws. Through their experience with the growing informal organization, members and leaders have obtained firsthand experience in organizational matters and are therefore ready to assume the obligations of formal membership and leadership.

9. Members enter a full-blown formal association even before they understand what it entails. The ready-made complexity of its activities or aims may alienate them from continued active participation. Not knowing how to play an active member role, they drop out or participate only passively.

10. In fostering through role-playing, confrontation, and reflection, the concepts of equal worth, rights, and dignity of people regardless of socio-economic status, community organization gives concrete evidence of attempting to shift the local power structure to a more egalitarian one. It thus presents the poor with a new vision of society in which they can command greater access to power and resources. The peasant is thus more willing to risk an alternative mode of behaviour besides the traditional patron-client dependency ties.

10. In maintaining a membership that largely implements plans instead of also formulating them, the standard rural organization does not attempt to change the local power structure. Under the circumstances, the vertical hierarchy of patron-client dependency still offers the most efficacious means for the rural poor to survive or improve his life.

---

*Community organization.

Source: Van Heck, 1979: 35-37, synthesized from Hollnsteiner, 1978.

7

Defending and Enhancing Development

The education and organization for empowerment described in Chapter 6 lays the basis for participatory development, but it is only the beginning. Quite clearly the moment a group of poor people seeks to use its labor, with or without new resources, for new productive or social purposes, the group disturbs the status quo. It is quite likely that individuals and groups among the local elite will see either a threat or a new source of potential profit. The stage is set for conflict.

The task in the following pages is to build new layers of organizations and define new approaches to conflict resolution. The goal is to overcome or neutralize every obstacle that can be anticipated from the political interests of the world-system and its bureaucratic imperatives. Among the many topics this involves, in order of treatment, are: the development catalyst (DC) needs an assured base of support and thus one must define the multifaceted roles of the intermediate organization; village ecology varies widely, and different strategies are necessary for organizing in diverse, uncertain environment; regional and provincial authorities are subject to conflicting pressures that open them to appeal by sensitive local groups; generic bureaucratic and political norms do not make national governments uniformly hostile, and within specific agencies short-term alliances are sometimes possible; no international actor at present comes devoid of self-interests and cultural norms, and general strategies must be devised for each.

What is intended is the ultimate creation of a development system designed and run from the bottom up by citizens. It will borrow from both capitalist and socialist methods and seek to develop new and better ones. The state will wither but not wither away. There will remain necessary coordinating roles for a central authority; in most countries resources are unevenly spread, and the poor region should not be condemned to permanent relative poverty. National dialogues will be necessary on the use of local mineral resources, for example. This requires citizens with a larger view than the village, something that will best be created by a series of experiences over time. Chapter 12 will take up these issues.

HEY NOW!

AN INITIAL SKETCH OF THE OVERALL DEVELOPMENT SYSTEM

An overview of the model solution would be helpful. It begins with sober recapitulation of the handicaps base organizations and their poor members must overcome. Marilyn Gittell, studying the plight of local groups trying to affect public school systems in urban areas of the United States, has summed up many issues very clearly in this part of her conclusion:

> It is unfortunate but true that the demand we are placing on lower-class organizations is one which they are, as a population, least in a position to meet. We are asking those with the most limited resources to be the most resourceful; to eschew individual needs and incentives for the good of the group; to maintain allegiance to broader social issues and goals and limit their efforts to build large and stable organizations; to broaden the base of their own participation and internal democracy and become more independent and self-reliant; and to reduce direct external dependency. We encourage them to sustain advocacy as a primary strategy, although this requires the greatest investment of time and energy, and they are the least able to make this investment. In fact, we are asking them to be the source for reform of the very system that has denied them any means of access (Gittell, 1980: 250).

Clearly the poor cannot do all this alone. External organizations sensitive to and guided by the precepts of participatory development must be created to fill many roles. A brief organizational overview comes first. To make the discussion more concrete a picture next emerges of who might create, staff, pay for, and sustain these new organizations over time. The stage is then set for a detailed look at the work they should do and the necessary styles of management and social learning this implies.

In most situations it would seem necessary to have two levels of intermediate organizations. One is geared to day-to-day support and encouragement of the DC and is responsible for perhaps 8 to 15 different DCs and their base organizations. With a full-time staff of three to six, it cannot handle either really technical issues or the bureaucratic imperatives (like paperwork) created by national and international development agencies. Thus, depending upon the population size and breadth of terrain, there needs to be one or more district or provincial organizations to take on the complicated political and cultural conflicts with outside forces. This unit will be larger, contain technically and legally skilled people, and be prepared to be effective advocates for the poor at the provincial and national level. This overall organization pattern is not, in sum, unlike that developed by several countries for primary health care to use minimum resources for maximum social impact.

The money and the personnel for these two kinds of intermediate organizations will at the start have to come from the outside in great measure. The human abilities exist at the local level to play most of or all the necessary roles, but people need various kinds of training. In almost all settings, however, there will be some people who have gained a reasonable degree of literacy and some appreciation of the positive and negative lures of the urban Western culture. It is important that even at the start some of the personnel at both levels come from the immediate locale. Many kinds of detailed social learning inherent to any successful project activity depend upon people making others involved sensitive to local realities.

Other personnel for intermediate organizations could and should come from varied cultural sources. A foreign private voluntary agency could provide resources and personnel to begin work in a region. Young, educated, urban citizens with rural roots and paper-pushing jobs might be lured back to their home areas by a socially meaningful challenge. Staffing organizations for the urban poor may be easier on this account. The U.S. Peace Corps might be considered if the individual displayed appropriate values, skills, and sensitivities. Independent universities, institutes, and church agencies could be approached. In some situations members of government agencies could in theory fit as technical specialists; in practice they would usually need a lot of resocialization (see Chapter 9). Local elites should normally be avoided for actual staff jobs.

Money for staff salaries and operating expenses will often be hard to generate. This should be no surprise. It is hard even for central governments to fund local activities on any scale. One advantage with these organizations is that, with salaries pegged to local conditions, not elite standards, the cost will be far less than the government activities. At a rough estimate, one local network totalling about 103 positions (8-10 organizations, each assisting multiple DCs, and one central resource base) might cost $50,000-$60,000 a year while providing divers< development assistance to 5,000 to 8,000 people. Capital and start-up costs must also be met. Ultimately the cost of these positions should be borne by the base organizations from new revenue locally generated, because the people in these jobs are working for and responsible to the base organizations and such leadership committees as they evolve.

Start-up resources, for a period of as much as eight to ten years, will have to come from outside. Local, regional, and national elites will not provide funds without unacceptable strings. International donor agencies, with rare exceptions like ILO/WEP, UNRISD, UNICEF, and FAO/ROAP, so misperceive the human purposes of authentic development that they should not be approached at this historical moment. The risk of political and bureaucratic subversion is a considerable and hopefully unnecessary price to pay. There is instead a realistic alternative, one that has been used only sporadically in times past. This is the concept of sister-city linkage. One town, city college, civic group, church, high school, labor union or even local corporation anywhere in the core countries could be approached with the needs for a specific development campaign in a specific far-off corner of Senegal, Bolivia, or India. For the cost of two average Western salaries per year, the funding of one network for participatory development could be met. No longer would the appeal be simply to send money and food into a void, supposedly to provide momentary but ultimately futile aid to the needy. Under the guidance of returned Peace Corps volunteers, professional foreign area specialists, Public Interest Research Groups, and dozens of other local civic groups, there should be the reservoir of social and ethical consciousness to set this in motion.

Local communities in core countries will gain more than the sense of enormous emotional satisfaction. By exploring deeply the social and organizational evolution of authentic participatory development overseas, they will discover its many advantages for creating a better world where they are. Studying another culture enlarges the human capacity for empathy, which is everywhere in short supply. In some situations it may be feasible to arrange visits or student exchanges; appropriately skilled local citizens might go overseas to join intermediate organizations for periods of time if the need were merited. New crafts, recipes, and low-cost technologies could flow both ways. Best of all, the resource transfer could go without substantive strings attached; the world-system and global bureaucracies would be essentially avoided. One cannot underestimate the necessary mobilization to create perhaps 200,000 links. It will not happen in a day, but it could happen over a few years.

The initial momentum to begin the organizing and education to divide tasks and start building linkages could come from a global network created in the late 1970s. This network, the International Foundation for Development Alternatives (IFDA) is a Swiss-based global effort to present an "alternative development" strategy to the UN system as the basis of its efforts for the 1980s. The UN system, as a large organization, is generically ill disposed toward a paradigm shift; its member governments, as large organizations, are similarly incapable of the necessary degree of change. There is no reason that IFDA and other global citizens cannot act outside the major institutional framework of the world-system.

INTERMEDIATE ORGANIZATIONS AND THEIR BASIC TASKS

Intermediate organizations face extremely difficult jobs in the average situation at the periphery of the world-system. Members must pursue relatively unmeasurable tasks in an inherently political situation. The paradoxes are severe. Korten (in Korten and Alfonso, ed. 1981: 220) finds this one central: "the need to exert influence over people for the purpose of building their capacity to control their own lives." At what point does facilitation become manipulation? Change is the routine. Can organization, the means of elite dominance, become the route to mass empowerment, yet not create new elites? Amidst the paradoxes, people must accomplish certain tasks, and the system must provide sufficient incentives to foster and reward the creative, risk-taking behaviour needed to overcome the many ambiguities and obstacles. This section focusses first on the concrete tasks, then on issues of organizational style, incentives, and philosophy.

In much development literature members of intermediate organizations are termed paraprofessionals or professionals. In the West the term professional has lost its proper meaning and come to refer to an accumulation of pedigrees and positions held that supposedly accord the person validated superiority as teacher or decider. In Washington the word *professional* has now been bureaucratized; a professional is one who, like a lawyer, ably marshalls just the evidence that supports the organizational interest. It takes no imagination to see how inappropriate this is for human development. In days gone by I was taught that a professional was a broadly educated person continually reconsidering new data and accepted truth to rebuild the optimum new reality. It is the learning process approach that must be the hallmark of the development professional in the 1980s and beyond.

The professional and paraprofessional members of the two levels of intermediate organizations sketched in the last section have a wide range of tasks. Esman et al. (1980) have treated many of these tasks under these eight headings: service delivery; education; community organization; advocating or expediting; referral; record keeping; data collection and analysis; and demonstrating and testing. As Chapter 6 suggested, community organizing is the essence of the overall change process. Without empowerment the rhetoric of participation becomes little more than the provision of services. Thus the above list needs reordering, expansion, and refinement.

Community organizing as a process of conscientization and mobilization through meetings, dialogues, group discussions, demonstrations, and political action is the central task of the DCs and thus of the supportive workers in the intermediate organizations. Aside from assuring a predictable flow of capital and material resources, many of the most important jobs fall under the general category of education. This involves far more than a moderately formalized initial training period for the DC.

Both levels of intermediate organizations must be ongoing learning laboratories in every sense of the word. Every individual involved must believe that development is first and foremost a permanent learning experience; if this attitude is not developed, the outsider will approach the peasant with the illusion that development equals the transmission of some piece of specific technical knowledge to an ignorant person. Each local center must develop a basic library of practical titles likely to be most useful to the DC and moderately literate villagers; each regional center should create over time a major collection of several thousand items covering all aspects of the human development experience. Many books and magazines now available are too advanced or in foreign languages; specific titles can be translated or simplified for people with moderate skills in reading. This can be part of the refocussing of the colonial education system still plaguing much of the Third World. A vast number of titles are little more than world-system apologias or ideological propaganda. Representative samples of each ought to be available but the selection bias for the moment should be on things people will find practical, uplifting, and entertaining. Darrow et al. (1981) is the way to begin.

The essential part of the learning process for any human is love of reading. This can be created at any age, but it is ideal to begin with the very young. The DC should consider every conceivable way to offer literacy courses to every age group at any feasible hour of the day or season of the year. Without literacy citizens can develop only so far. It is worth training one or several of the most literate to offer beginning classes if they are willing.

Beyond literate, citizens must be healthy. The DC and the intermediate organizations can and should be instrumental in setting up the primary health care system. Each base organization can select an individual for training in village primary health care. This may prove too expensive; three to five base organizations may need to select one candidate jointly. The intermediate organizations can take on these tasks: securing the funding for the training and supplies; agitating with the national health system and any other potential donor for the creation of clinics and public health stations and the training of staff; and educating both politicians and donors on the necessity of the preventive approach to medical care and the technological inappropriateness of much of Western medicine. Although the Chinese model is the one conventionally discussed, it is the Vietnamese model, especially from 1954-78 in the North, that will be most educational (Gran, 1979b: 266-67). International specialists have prepared several suitable teaching anthologies on the social and political aspects of a participatory medical system; Rifkin (ed., 1980) is a good place to start.

Literate and healthy citizens contemplating new productive possibilities, improving market conditions, or seeking alternative credit mechanisms face in almost all situations a major series of obstacles in the legal environment. Elites at all levels have always molded the legal system to be a tool for the exclusion of the poor. Without challenge they will use the laws to forestall mobilization efforts, limit access to official decision makers, and impoverish local group enterprise. The New York-based International Center for Law and Development has explored case studies in detail to create some overall guiding principles by which the poor can counterattack. Villagers in Kagawasan in the Philippines mobilized to confront a government land official to force him to do his job. Realizing the bias and impracticality of continuing to work with government surveyors, they created a local people's court to solve land boundary disputes. A small alternative legal resource center provided legal education, enlarging local vision about the positive use of law. What this and kindred cases showed were specific obstacles to asserting legal claims even with organizational strength and just outrage: people were ignorant and suspicious of the law; they feared reprisals; they faced multiple biases in the application of law as, in the Philippine case government officials sided with agribusiness banana plantation owners; and legal resources were not easily at hand (ICLD, 1979; Paul and Dias, 1980a and 1980b).

This New York center has sketched out a range of research and clinics that would get paralegal resources into the hands of base organizations. National centers would seem to be obvious targets for the concentrated power of national elites. A series of regional networks might be the first organizational effort; with their sponsorship and the solicitation of political allies in other arenas, a national center might then have a better chance to survive. Intermediate organizations can help build this network and send at least one staff member for paralegal training. Local mobilizing will uncover new legal concerns that will force intermediate organizations to become local legal resource centers along with their many other tasks.

When laws are used as a means of oppression, they will have to be eliminated or changed. This cannot always be done peacefully, and those involved in international development must think through the practical and philosophical issues involved. Most of Western education is ill suited for this task. Capitalist ideology, based on the preservation of private property at all costs, displays a singularly ambivalent view of violence. Used to protect or extend property rights of the rich, it is defensible; used for similar goals by the poor, it is deemed indefensible, indeed revolutionary. Modern historians, especially Barrington Moore (1966), have posed the essential rejoinder: sometimes the cost of the change is less than the cost of the status quo. It is not up to any outsider, including the intermediate organization, to apply its normative judgments as the basis for counseling on such a political choice by a base organization. The poor themselves must weigh the pain of the status quo against the potential of bloodshed and reprisal. Intermediate organizations can help in crystallizing choices and costs. Much more often than is customarily discussed, there are more choices than inaction and physical violence. In each situation paralegals and DCs should seek to create appropriate alternative and intermediate strategies such as civil disobedience and other Gandhian tactics.

At the heart of any such analysis must be a clear understanding of the moral economy of the peasant (Scott, 1977) and how elite culture is violating its precepts. Solutions with which the poor will be comfortable and effective must be built on both normative principles and activities the poor can actually implement. Looking back to traditional conflict mechanisms in that culture is one possibility. Looking at solutions tried elsewhere will be educational. Thousands of base organizations struggling with generic conflicts can certainly be expected to come up with new lines of attack. They can also be expected to create larger-scale political movements, whether or not smaller change efforts meet success. Intermediate organizations for development should not abandon their primary purpose but rather quietly encourage the creation of regional and national political organizations when the time comes. Whatever political choices base organizations and their representatives make, whether reformist or revolutionary, they will still need legal resources for the next stage of development.

The professionals and paraprofessionals in intermediary organizations must naturally provide more technical kinds of aid to DCs and base organizations. One could predict the utility of building up knowledge of global experiments in appropriate technology. Another task will be to monitor consistently a wide range of economic conditions and possibilities at the regional and national level. Local situations vary widely, however. So do relations with national governments and their ministries. The presence of donor agency projects, internationally linked enclaves, or other factors all argue that the precise skill base of a specific intermediate organization should evolve slowly out of an open-ended dialogue primarily with base organizations.

Other roles besides educator and organizer would include the following: advocate; expediter; provider of referral service; supervisor of service delivery; record keeper; data collector; tester; and evaluator (from Esman et al., 1980: 8-10). The role of advocate will be discussed later in this chapter. Ambivalences in some of the other roles might be raised here.

Data collection and record keeping have political and social as well as technical and economic implications. Peasants have been historically justified in refusing to cooperate with central authorities and aid agencies whose interests were clearly taxes and production for export. Peasants mobilized in base organizations, dealing with intermediate organizations they control and personnel whose absolute discretion they trust, may be willing to let sensitive production data be accurately collected. It will take a while to create such bonds of trust even after the logic of scale-efficient activity becomes clear. A great deal of dialogue must take place to build the trust, surmount ideologies, and locate the particular mix of public and private incentives that best balances efficiency and equity at that place and time. It is inconceivable that national or international authorities could or should contribute much to this process or make these decisions.

Yet the operational premise of such authorities remains, after years of counterproductive and imperfect efforts, to do precisely that. International aid agencies are, to be sure, becoming more aware of how little local data they have and how hard it is to get. Two conferences were held on such issues at the Institute for Development Studies at Sussex in 1979. Chambers (1980) sums up their findings. "Quick and dirty" surveys suffer severe antipoverty biases; rural tourists tend to stay on roads, visit projects, not marginal areas, meet the more active, male, and less poor citizens, travel in dry season, and pursue protocols excluding the poor. In lieu of long and clean surveys, Chambers suggests an intermediate synthesis termed rapid rural appraisal. While it marks a considerable improvement over previous methods, it harbors the same operational flaw.

Until a certain degree of social development and mobilization has taken place, a particular locale is not ready for a development project conceived as materially productive activity. Indeed it is the obligation of intermediate organizations to forestall such foreign intrusions until base organizations are ready to use external resources in an effective way. This issue will come up again in Chapter 9.

Intermediate organizations should not carry out evaluations of base organizations in the sense of creating an annual report card. Evaluation must be built into the daily and weekly work as part of many dialogues with the DC and base organization members. Evaluation should be a tool for teaching and learning within and between base organizations. As Chapter 11 will explore, this is no easy task to promote. Much of it will depend on the DC and paraprofessionals above being comfortable with admitting ignorance and mistakes. That takes a special human being and a supportive environment uncommon in both the Soviet Bloc and the West.

Intermediate organizations and the DCs face more than a set of tasks vis-à-vis base organizations. There are intangible and psychological aspects in their relationship. Some provoke contradictions that must be squarely faced and planned for. Constantino-David (1981), in one of the many creative pieces of learning based on Philippine experiences, has explored nine potential contradictions in a very useful fashion: self-reliance versus dependence; evocative versus provocative organizing; facilitation versus manipulation; felt needs versus objective needs; consciousness raising versus dole-outs; immediate economic impact versus long-term political development; issue based versus non-issue based organizing; democratic participation versus creating new elites; lawful versus subversive acts. Most, if not all, of these potential problems would be minimized in a situation where community organization was based on the process of conscientization and its curricula as discussed in Chapter 6. Most development efforts are going to be less than ideal. Thus it is important to think through the operational strategy in order to respond when one of these contradictions appears.

It would be quite human for the base organization and its members to seek out the DC to solve difficult crises in the process of group formation and development. If the DC is not a village native there will be a further tendency in this direction, one argument for the training of indigenous DCs. Yet for the DC to make many decisions is to slow the development of other citizens. It should be made clear that the DC, whether or not a native, will retire in a finite time period and that the base organization must develop its own means of group problem solving and momentum. The network of intermediate organizations can be viewed as a reassuring and permanent support framework. This does not mean a permanent crutch but instead, as in the Mozambican theory, a group of *responsavel* following the expressed preferences of multiple base organizations.

The DC and intermediate organization start organizing with a collective consciousness and an analytical method quite different from those of the poor peasants beginning conscientization. It is more commonly argued that the DC should adapt to the frameworks prevailing and seek to evoke greater awareness rather than provoke reaction to a reality not yet perceived. Still, as Constantino-David concludes, balance must be sought between the approaches; deep seated illusions cannot be quickly erased and sometimes cannot even be raised directly. The generic problem of any teacher is still whether to pitch the lesson at a level that most understand or at a more challenging level that provokes greater individual growth. The choice of facilitation or manipulation raises the same quandary. Whose objectivity measures the desirable goal? A lot of dialogue is called for before the DC should provoke the destruction of the psychological props that, for instance, make patron-client ties a preferable way to create security in the face of poverty.

Constantino-David explores several other kindred dilemmas. Does the DC accept the felt needs of the moment or insist on his or her idea of more objective needs? Does the DC ever respond to specific material need or focus strictly on consciousness raising? More insidious is the choice of quick economic result or more long-term political growth. Small projects may meet immediate needs.

> At the same time, however, these types of projects which bring superficial improvements to their lives also carry with them the potential of developing, too readily, a sense of satisfaction. These projects also serve as palliatives in the sense that they prolong the illusion that the system has a self-correcting mechanism. The people content themselves with small concessions and minor welfare gains which may retard their political development (Constantino-David, 1981: 15).

In these and other issues this article raises many of the difficulties community organizing faces by failing to generate in the base organization a larger social vision. Such a failure is the inevitable result of failure to begin with the topics of basic social consciousness as sketched in Chapter 6. Building on poor foundations is not the way to produce an optimal social process and a responsible result.

INTERMEDIATE ORGANIZATIONS AND LOCAL GOVERNMENT

As any practitioner knows, the mobilization of marginalized peasants or slum dwellers will not be taking place in an organizational and political vacuum. It is imperative that the DC move into a particular location with a very clear understanding of the real power relationships as well as the surface ones. Unless the DC has an overall framework for understanding the type of village, as defined by both its organizational structure and its degree of incorporation into the larger world-system, it will be very difficult to form operational base organizations, never mind proceed with participatory development.

One cannot hope to create an exact strategy for each location without knowing both the specific political ecology and the personalities involved. Our general wisdom has, I think, moved beyond the earlier notion that forming a village association or working through preexisting village leaders was a very effective way of involving the poor in development. Van Heck (1979a) has clearly shown the difference between community development and development for the poor. Different types of villages must be distinguished and a strategic orientation prepared for each possibility. The University of Leiden project, Access and Participation, has begun work along these lines by creating a tentative village typology. Boer (1980: 5 ff.) has worked out seven categories, several with subvarieties: the isolated, relatively closed community; the precapitalist, relatively stable community; the immigration village; the stratified "smallholders" village; the emigration village; the plantation village; and the new settlement.

The isolated hierarchical village is still fairly common in most parts of the Third World. Power rests with an oligarchy that controls the land and most other productive resources, directly or indirectly. Patron-client ties, caste, or religion provides the social glue and the cultural context for inequality. Living conditions of the poor majority are generally called subsistence level, a phrase that poorly communicates high infant mortality, brain damage from protein deficiency, and a short, unhealthy life. Such people may be so limited in their horizons as to view this as a happy existence. To disturb such a world model might strike some as cultural imperialism. That would not, however, take into account the real choices soon to be presented by the world-system: extermination, as in Paraguay, or proletarianization and "coca-cola-ization."

The DC enters such an environment with a low-key learning process in mind. The elite are likely to be quickly antagonized by ideas that smell of political organization. The DC must explore existing local organizations among the poor to see if any could become a nucleus of a forum for conscientization. If nothing looks particularly feasible, contemplate the particular issues that reappear as grievances. If they all look explosive as subjects of community organization, look for cultural, athletic, or religious activities where groups may learn to work cooperatively. Few societies lack such social outlets, and, as Reilly (1980) has shown, they can be used as surrogates for beginning participatory activities. Elites, facing a united group pursuing a marginally threatening activity, are not likely to respond with violence. A small wedge can grow. The DC can approach lesser elites and the younger members of the oligarchy with indirect comments about the village needs for health, productivity, education, and preparing for a different future. The DC can also work with the intermediate organization to create communication links to district and regional elites. When a conflict arises and the local elite scream for aid to put down an "uprising," the network will then be in place to bring an alternative explanation to district or provincial elites of people organizing for concrete, logical, and finite purposes. Political contests will be lost or short-term retreats made. But the lessons of successes in neighboring villages or districts will percolate through the countryside.

There are also relatively egalitarian isolated villages. They are characterized by shared poverty, not stratification; communal mechanisms still work to assure some basic social security for all. The DC has here a far easier task. People are likely to be used to cooperative efforts for specific purposes. The obstacles are likely to be more technical and ecological than social in nature. Better water and sanitation systems along with primary health and literacy campaigns would lay the basis for more conscious choices on how to begin to respond to and defend themselves from a fast encroaching world-system. The DC should be very cautious about evoking suggestions to diminish local self-reliance and autonomy without a clear understanding of the full costs.

The recent history (1977-80) of one AID-sponsored intrusion into such an environment in the Eastern Region of Upper Volta reflects precisely the kind of process of social engineering to be avoided. Into this area of small farmers, traders, and craftsmen AID sent the private voluntary agency Partners for Productivity in an effort at small enterprise development. The staff provided credit and technical advice to fledgling entrepreneurs too poor to deal with established lending institutions. The project is enhancing capitalist motivations among the fraction of the local population it interacts with, accelerating the growth of their links with the larger market. Visions of selling food to urban markets is on the horizon. AID applauds itself for building "self-reliance" but cannot see that, while the income of some rises, others are excluded and inequalities are building. Those involved did not see this process of marginalization and had no answer for it (data from Hull, 1980). Participatory development is quite something else.

The precapitalist, relatively stable community maintains a subsistence exchange economy in the village and carries on some cash-earning activities outside. Kinship and reciprocity networks endure but are under attack by external forces; Poewe's description (1981) of a matrilineal society in Luapula, Zambia captures the resulting conflicts well. In the early stages the preexistent levelling mechanisms have probably prevented extreme inequality. The political variable for the DC is whether the traditional leadership is united in general orientation toward innovation or status quo, or divided in its attitude toward change. Strategies of organizing would have to be carefully fine tuned. Local elite are likely to be on better terms with regional elite and more easily able to seek assistance. Physical distances may be less and transport and communication infrastructure better. On the other hand, more villagers will have experience with economic and political alternatives elsewhere. Some may be migrating for seasonal work on a regular basis. Their sum of political skills will be greater.

Immigration villages are those in economic flux or transition where employment possibilities lure in new settlers. Typical possibilities include those on an economic frontier, those new settlements ringing major cities, and those at the apex of a new transport link or economic enterprise. The DC should avoid trying to create base organizations solely from either original inhabitants or newcomers. Deliberate social bridge building is in order. Otherwise newcomers may be marginalized or uncooperative, and competition may develop between different base organizations.

In the stratified smallholder village, whose economic activity is geared to the external market, the DC will have a particularly difficult challenge. Capitalist values are now predominant. Social position and identity may well be defined in small increments of wealth that divide middle and small peasants. A multiclass situation has developed with enough political consciousness that major land-holders would certainly notice and oppose efforts to organize landless laborers and tenants. As with the Green Revolution villages of Indonesia described in Chapter 4, the multiple external links with outsiders for fertilizer, seeds, credit, and other items make a cozy relationship likely with regional elite. Labor surplus and lack of mobility work against the interests of the poor. In debt or lacking food-producing resources, they must hire out their labor most disadvantageously. The DC may well face a growing class conflict and the expectation of direct violent response. The suggestion that land should go for local food production rather than exports will not sit well with elites. Subtlety, timing, backup defenders, and tight intervillage strategic moves will be important. Alliance might be developed with those most directly affected at the national level by low food productivity and the financial drain of importing and thus of borrowing. The stratified export-led village or region requires much more preorganizing systems preparation. Identifying the true costs to each part of the system of the prevailing use of productive resources is a good place to start. Gibbons et al. (1980) and Franke and Chasen (1980) have insights, but the true global food systems portrait, suggested by Cleaver's (1977) discussion of elite use of food as a weapon, has just begun to emerge (see de Janvry, 1981, for example).

Communities exist where the resource base is so poor that male members emigrate for extended periods leaving women the predominant local food producers. There are many such villages in Southern Africa as the logical result of apartheid's land policies seeking to create cheap labor. While change in the larger system would be desirable at once, a more realistic and operational path is to begin to create better citizens of the migrant laborers and their families. They first must eat. Initial efforts by DCs should combine mobilization and medical programs with an energetic search among underexploited tropical plants (several volumes from the U.S. National Academy of Science) to raise energy and nutrition levels. This may appear a liberal palliative, but the history of Southern Africa (Palmer and Parsons, eds., 1977, for instance) is not one to inspire hope that outside agents will do anything but make the situation worse.

In other areas of the world are communities facing extreme ecological limitations that are not amenable to political change. The world-system cares little as there is no profit to be easily made. There is unlikely to be much stratification. Here mobilization may not be difficult and the challenge will be to tap the global resource network for new appropriate technological solutions. Gontard (in Galtung et al., eds., 1980: 330-36) drives home with a brief case study what incredible advances can be made in life quality and production by the simplest applications in new appropriate technology. Villagers in many parts of Niger in the mid-1970s were losing much of their harvest to rodents and exhausting themselves chasing rats with sticks. But north of Maradi, in the remote village of Kornaka, they were using something else: the Kornaka trap. A clay urn at least two feet high was buried to the rim, half filled with water and a powdered plant substance (*ceratotheca*) creating a sticky liquid. Around the rim a trail of millet or sorghum grains was carefully laid. The rat goes for the grain, falls in the urn, and drowns. The results are awesomely efficient. At the same time as I read this item, I saw in the newspapers reports of yet another plague of rats destroying the Egyptian harvest. Should citizens wait for governments, corporations, or aid agencies to do the obvious?

A sixth type of local community is the plantation village where the structure of the production is centrally controlled by one corporate or parastatal entity. Such villages are common in the Caribbean, Central and South America, and parts of Southeast Asia. Here the absence of owners on the scene may or may not help the DC; sometimes the hired overseer can be a more vigorous opponent than the actual absentee owner. It should prove easy to focus peasant discontent and crystallize the concrete advantages of change. The many degrees of worker management can be explored and the basis for successful cooperative operations (Oakeshott, 1981) can be laid. This type of village may, of course, have multinational enterprise owners who will use the world-system to pressure the host government to quell disturbances. At that point the intermediate organization might present to the appropriate government agency a chronicle of the poor productivity and low national tax receipt of the present arrangement and the several advantages of an alternative. At the same time core country allies could work to diminish the interest of world-system agencies in supporting corporate propaganda against human welfare, productivity, and rhetorical ideals in this specific case. Keeping targets finite and vocabulary nonideological will create a far less threatening image to the world-system.

One further category of small community deserves mention: new settlements. Wars and famines in Africa have created hundreds of thousands of refugees; most are rural people who are now building de facto new settlements. Other refugee flows are creating similar results. A few governments have attacked overpopulation by planned transmigration to new villages. Building cooperative links among people with little or no common heritage will be difficult. Absence of stratification will be a help. The conscientization process will have to explore basic questions of security with great sophistication. There is no intrinsic reason why a skilled DC could not use the change momentum provided by physical movement to evoke thoughts of alternative social organization, technological application, and productive possibilities.

This very general sketch of community typology raises some of the questions that the DC and intermediate organization need to consider to begin a mobilization strategy. There are other kinds of questions. Some have to do with the political economy of the relationships among groups, villages, regions, and nations; these will be explored through a series of Peruvian case studies in Chapter 8. Others have to do with the particular ecological, technical, and cultural variables of the micro setting, suggesting the necessity of broad interdisciplinary training, a topic in Chapter 9. With all these abilities and perceptions, however, the DC will still fail without an intuitive ability to grasp how communication is really happening in the village.

Unfortunately, with the exception of a very few essays like Emmerson (1978) and Adams (1977), one is not left with much guidance on this question in contemporary development studies. Fuglesang (in Rifkin, ed., 1980: 79-89) is one of the few to have raised a number of these issues very well. People in villages do not communicate freely and randomly. There are definite patterns indicating an internal system at work. Some people have more credibility than others, and their opinions are sought out. Individual decision making is conditioned by this system and one's role in it. The credibility of information coming from outside the system is normally far less. The average historical experience of a village with outsiders has not been positive, and there is little reason to accept a new intrusion. The DC must recognize and react to these handicaps to the extent he or she is an alien or, by external training, is perceived as alienated. Essential to entering the internal communication system successfully is not just identifying opinion leaders but overcoming through genuine empathy this initial antagonism. For villagers are more than tired of seeing their "capacity, including their emotional capacity, . . . grossly underestimated. It hurts to be 'underdeveloped.' Communication cannot succeed unless there is a sincere feeling of equality in the system." (Fugelsang, in Rifkin, ed., 1980: 82). Combining these human capacities with organizational, educational, and technical skills will be no small feat. But then these are some of the most important and challenging jobs in the world; there will be intrinsic reward and satisfaction in building such skills.

INTERMEDIATE ORGANIZATIONS AND PROVINCIAL AND NATIONAL GOVERNMENT

It takes no imagination to realize that a network of people geared to mobilize the poor for participatory development will not be kindly received by the triple alliance. Yet the alliance is not immutable or impermeable. Intermediate organizations cannot avoid the reality and existence of each member of this alliance and can neither assume that nor act as though corporations or governments will sit by passively. The best defense is always a good offense. The ultimate goal is to make really democratic whatever smaller "national" entities citizens will deem necessary. The immediate effort is to disengage government from the control of a small number of large concentrations of capital. The reason for thinking this is theoretically possible is that the governments of peripheral countries are now in an impossible financial bind.

Virtually all governments in the Third World face the same revolutionary pressures: desperate poverty and mass consciousness of the injustice of economic inequality. Both the parasitic ruling classes and the have-nots struggle for the same insufficient surplus. The revolution of rising expectations pushes each contestant on. Bureaucratic growth imperatives continue to add to bloated government payrolls. These pressures for development outlays, government salaries, and personal perquisites combine to overwhelm the fiscal base of most states. Urban and elite bias has stifled food production, leading to ever more expensive food imports. Importing oil has added appreciably to the cost of living. Terms of trade for commodity exports have been disastrous in the latter 1970s as every issue of *South* chronicles. This is not a new problem. Exporting such commodities, as the Zairian case (Gran, 1979a) so painfully shows, is in any case nothing but a prescription for permanent underdevelopment. The core can buy the commodities only at the rate it grows itself, and the periphery can thus never overcome its historical handicap.

Lacking the legitimacy to tax those with resources, governments of the periphery have turned to international lenders to cover all these enormous needs. The result has been the debt trap; the poor country surrendering autonomy to the world-system agencies as Chapter 5 described. Significant further borrowing is no longer possible for many states, and their number will grow. Repayment of current obligations by many looks hypothetical. Governments are told to tighten their belts by world-system agencies. Beyond a point this becomes political suicide. New revenue and greater productivity are thus imperative.

Intermediate organizations in the 1980s thus face Third World governments that have a powerful incentive to listen to anyone who can deliver more productivity from the minimal available resources. Intermediate organizations can approach governments at all levels with precisely this message: decentralize, get off the peasant's back in legal and fiscal ways by specific reforms as we suggest, and productivity will soar. The issues are, of course, more complex. The incentive system for more production must be complete and secure; input prices and market prices must be assured; urban-rural terms of trade need to be rebalanced with great speed; small local industry must be providing the things peasants desire; cooperative and nonexploitative trading networks must be in place; the physical infrastructure must be maintained and improved; and elites cannot use force or the legal system to attack productive gains. Such a list is suggestive, not exhaustive.

Even if the low-key approach to financially beleagured government officials is found acceptable, relative local autonomy for peasants and local reorganization in return for greater agricultural productivity, intermediate organizations must be aware that governments are large organizations poorly designed for such reforms. Red tape, centralization, duplication, and waste are logical results of generic internal incentive systems and bureaucratic need. Heaver (1980) explored four sets of motivations that affect most regional bureaucrats: personal priorities, official and unofficial pressures from superiors, and local pressures. To the extent that a project or a reform challenge does not create more than minimum conflict among the four types of pressures, it may have some chance of implementation. The reforms suggested above have implications for all four kinds of bureaucratic incentives; for each there need to be plans. One way to align or realign incentives is by internal organizational reform; this is beyond the direct ability of staff of intermediate organizations and is the central issue in Chapters 9, 10, and 11. Another, more indirect route to change is within reach. That is metamanagement or the strategy of influencing the problem-solving process itself rather than trying to locate the proper solution to a problem and propel it to bureaucratic victory.

Metamanagement is a slowly developing field in development administration most associated with David Korten and his work to decentralize the National Irrigation Agency in the Philippines. It intends to propel bureaucratic self-transformation toward development as a learning process. Social development is quite a different task from setting up a factory. Organizations and their work processes have to be redesigned to fit their new tasks. Decentralization is a critical aspect of the change, because, for success, much greater knowledge of local needs, preferences, and realities is necessary.

Work in Philippine irrigation development demonstrated the many local considerations that could not be uncovered without a participatory dialogue with the farmers involved. When engineers worked on their own, they overlooked the social context.

For example, whereas the engineers generally lay out distribution canals so as to minimize their length in the interests of saving costs, the farmers in the pilot project expressed a strong preference that these follow field boundaries in order to avoid traversing the middle of a single farmer's field so that each farmer would lose as little land as possible. While the engineers preferred to apply the NIA's standard of one turn-out for every 40 to 50 hectares, the farmers wanted to have one turn-out per field so that each farmer would have direct access to water. For reasons of economy the engineers suggested a dam built with either gabion or interlinked wire filled with rocks and other materials. The farmers, who had long since tired of reconstructing diversion structures destroyed by floods, argued strongly that they needed a concrete dam. Engineers normally scheduled construction activities around the availability of materials, equipment, and NIA supervisory personnel. The farmers insisted that the schedule also take into consideration standing crops that might be damaged during construction and competing demands on time of farmer laborers to meet planting and harvesting schedules.

(Alfonso, in Korten and Alfonso, eds., 1980: 46-47)

Predictable problems of trying to mobilize unorganized farmers for volunteer labor were also chronicled. The obvious point is that in such ever so common situations there is a cultural and organizational chasm between the government agency and the local inhabitants. Ideally, intermediate organizations should begin to play a mediating role. In cases where major infrastructure development is agreed upon and government resources and personnel are necessary, intermediate organizations need to be guiding the creation of new, appropriate organizations combining social and technical specialists and local citizens. In most other cases government agencies at all levels should be encouraged to work through the intermediate organizations to advance educational, health, and productive facilities in the locale.

Such an evolution directly threatens the raison d'être of local and regional government. In the transitional period intermediate organizations must use great tact and diplomacy. Some officials will appreciate a less expensive, more efficient and effective way of getting things done. Others will see threats to stature and perquisites. They need to be isolated and replaced as quickly as feasible. This will require skillful intervention at several levels at the same time. Ideally base organizations will start electing local and regional officials at some point, but the transition may well cause conflict. There is no escaping the political essence of development, and it is up to intermediate organizations to learn how to use the strength of numbers to maximum effect. If not, their staff will have neither legal force nor great material resources with which to prevail.

The work of local and regional officials and of ministry extension agents is in most situations quite difficult. They must deal with contending interest groups, uncertain tenure, insufficient resources, ambiguous tasks, unclear feedback, and unruly clients. Intermediate organization staff, not unfamiliar with these pressures, must approach these officials with initial empathy and understanding. Lipsky (1980) in a prize-winning study, *Street-Level Bureaucracy*, has analyzed cogently how these pressures will result in predictable bureaucratic strategies to overcome the indeterminate reality. Bureaucrats will try to limit demands, modify their jobs, and modify their clients; they will do this by structuring work routines toward these ends, by rationing services, controlling clients, reducing uncertainties and husbanding resources (Lipsky, 1980: 81ff). It is Lipsky's overall thesis that the routines established to reduce these uncertainties and pressures effectively become the public policies implemented.

By understanding these natural motivations of local and regional officials, intermediate organization staff can define strategies that offer officials reduced uncertainties and less need to control clients. It may seem that mobilizing the poor in base organizations will create far greater and more complex demands on government. But intermediate organizations can explain and demonstrate the practical and productive nature of authentic self-reliant development. Base organizations can offer their support to officials who cooperate with autonomous local development; intermediate organizations can help define practical steps that local officials may undertake.

There is always the threat that local officials, especially when they are also the local economic elite, will go around intermediate organizations to pressure or manipulate base organizations. It would be surprising if this did not happen. To the extent the conscientization process is incompletely or poorly done, the poor peasants will be vulnerable to various lures. If, however, the mobilization process was done with care and thoroughness, such attempts would be quickly reported to the intermediate organization and a group counterstrategy prepared. There is rarely reason to let conflict degenerate into something local elites might use to justify seeking military assistance. It is the role of the intermediate organization to step into what look on the surface to be irreconcilable class conflicts and transfer them onto terrain in which *either* the conflict loses importance and subsides *or* the poor have an excellent chance of winning. A handful of outraged peasants fighting it out with better-armed provincial militia in military terms would suggest a considerable series of failures by the staff of the intermediate organizations.

The sum of all these difficult tasks for intermediate organizations, some will argue, requires an extraordinary set of skills beyond the abilities of most humans. Certainly the DC and the staff above have to be very socially responsible and competent people. Every society has them and invariably uses them badly or not at all. There are certainly not enough for the task, but the conscientization process is going to create an entire new generation of leaders. Progress will be slow and uneven. Individuals will fail, weaken, tire, and sicken. But the power of example, the success of a fully mobilized district or region and its impact on life quality and spirit, will have a ripple effect invigorating efforts in neighboring areas.

The presence of international donor projects presents special additional challenges in maintaining cultural integrity (see Chapters 9 and 10) in specific locations. But such projects are ephemeral and their capitalist cultural heritage should not be insuperable. Intermediate organizations can build on the rare good projects and work to redesign those that perpetuate and enhance inequality. The power of better alternatives nearby will attract donor agency personnel, and some of them will see the advantages and pursue their normative (as opposed to bureaucratic) motives to become allies. Indeed what look on the surface to be large, authoritarian organizations almost always harbor an internal counterculture. Allies should be sought on all occasions.

Looking at the awesome human tragedies wrought upon the children of Zaire, Namibia, South Africa, and so many other areas, one cannot be overly optimistic that the true believers, ideologues, materialists, and totalitarians will quickly yield. Yet the lessons of the struggles of peasants in Kagawasan and Bhoomi Sena, in Mozambique and Grenada, reported in *IFDA Dossier* and *Assignment Children* and in many less recorded spots, combine to suggest that betting on the peasant as the professional is the practical long-term strategy for a more just world order. It is up to the DCs and the intermediate organization to see that by conscientization peasant professionalism in subsistence matters grows. Peasants must control and redesign the processes of commodification, incorporation, and technological change by which the world-system is now dehumanizing its opposition. Given the basic behavior and goals of the world-system, peasants should not find it too difficult to devise a saner, more peaceful, and more rewarding alternative. By participating in this process, local communities in the core may develop some of the skills to become part of the solution themselves.

8

Putting the Poor in Context:
Some Samples from Peru

SOCIAL SCIENCE, LANGUAGE, AND
THE RURAL POOR IN PERU

Individual groups of base and intermediate organizations do not each face totally individual development problems. Groups in the same ecological zone, geographical region, crop production, socioeconomic class, or productive structure share similarities that suggest cooperation could be advantageous. What sounds logical in theory may well be difficult in practice. Third World communication links run from major cities to more remote areas, not between different remote regions. Physical impracticalities are only one block. Ethnic, caste, and religious cleavages prevent effective communication among different groups. Regional and national elites will see linkages among different groups of mobilized poor as threatening. Yet the step beyond developing intermediate organizations is the development of this larger consciousness in an institutional and operational way.

The first step is to develop a method of social analysis that clarifies the general patterns of stratification and marginalizations common to multiple groups of the poor. Each base organization needs, in other words, a practical model of its larger world. Confidence mechanisms, discussed abstractly in Chapter 1, need to be put into the particular national and regional context. This chapter proposes to provide a sample of such analysis by looking at some common patterns of impoverishment in the rural areas of the Latin American country of Peru.

It may strike some readers and practitioners that such a task is not necessary. Governments issue five-year plans, the World Bank writes country and sector papers, and AID produces Country Development Strategy Statements. All proclaim that there are poor people out there and discuss them with various abstract and quantitative generalities. But such institutional documents, products of the bureaucratic needs discussed in previous chapters, do not locate or analyze the poor in a way useful to development. The poor are just static units to be manipulated, not humans caught in systems and processes and in need of liberation and empowerment. With but rare exception the planning documents of aid agencies and governments are devoid of the social context, cultural nuance, political conflict, parasitism, and corruption that are the real world of the supposed beneficiaries of their efforts.

The major official documents produced on Peru during the last decade are not exceptions. An available recent sample is a public version of an IBRD country paper, *Peru: Major Development Policy Issues and Recommendations*, dated June, 1981. It will give the reader much aggregate data on all parts of the modern sector and on government budgetary actions. The Bank is not unaware of many serious problems in the Peruvian economy: inflation, urban unemployment, agricultural stagnation, and a "deteriorated pattern of income distribution," to name a few. But from this and kindred reports one does not really find most of the 17 million Peruvians.

Space does not permit here much of the detailed background on the varied ecological settings of Peru's three major regions: the Coastal region running from desert to irrigated agriculture the length of the country and containing most of the tangible wealth and modern sector activity; the Sierra region of three ranges of the Andes; and the underpopulated Selva region, the forested eastern slope of the Andes and the tropical lowland beyond. The historical evolution of the mode of production, from the tributary Incan Empire to the contemporary capitalist export-led growth model based on minerals, fishing, livestock, and agriculture, must also rest underexplored. What does it mean for most Peruvians to be on the periphery of the world-system? The major system actors and classes must first be defined. Their drives should then be assessed by the actions of state ministries in the way Cleaves and Scurrah (1980) have treated some themes from the Velasco period (1968-74).

Intermediate institutions and those in outsider roles truly concerned with development need to do such interdisciplinary macroanalysis. This chapter will provide illustrations. It will also be concerned with a more finite task. How can groups of what bureaucrats call "development targets," once the control of the local development system is assured, move to develop the analytical tools, vocabulary, and policy framework to redirect provincial and regional development onto a participatory path.

First, perhaps, is to challenge the use of terms like *client*, *target*, or *beneficiary*. Targets as a term connotes aggression and ethnocentrism, but to call the subjects of development beneficiaries implies paternalism. Language does not glorify poor people. It is a tool of historical winners, not losers. This analysis begins with semantics because most Peruvians and students of Peru have until recently referred to the poor, certainly the rural poor, as Indians. Indians speak Spanish badly or not at all, follow relatively powerless subsistence economic pursuits, wear certain kinds of clothes, etc. The term, however, has a racist basis that reveals its raison d'être. Piel put it most succinctly in his definition:

> "Indian": a concept created by the dominant classes in Peru to cover in one word the rural and partially autochthonous mass of the population, which was dominated by a "white," creole or *mestizo* elite under a system of social, fiscal, and juridical values of a racist and colonial type, inherited from the time of Spanish rule. In no circumstances is the word of any use for describing a racial or ethnic identity; it does not exist and has never existed at any time in the history of Peru (Piel, 1970: 108).

As soon as the Indian goes after a modicum of socioeconomic power, succeeds in defeating some of the confidence mechanism at work keeping most people comparatively poor, and achieves a measure of social and economic mobility, then he or she is no longer an Indian but a *mestizo* (or at least a *cholo*). The empirical reality is that the terms have no racial meaning. Essentially all Peruvians, except the ethnic minorities of the Selva, are quite racially and culturally mixed. It is a rare Europeanized member of a Lima's elite who under scrutiny does not reveal "Indian" cultural patterns.

Development, however, is a historical process. It is the entrenchment of cultural belief over time within a prevailing mode of production that matters here. How do feelings modify or guide action? The *mestizo* townsmen described by a premier anthropologist (Stein, 1972: 24) "appear to be firmly convinced that Indians are biologically inferior and consequently deserving of a foul condition and contrary, hostile treatment." How a government whose personnel cannot be immune to widespread social norms can carry out development programs in such an environment is not a problem unique to Peru.

It is, however, critical to development efforts and their designers to incorporate into design structures an understanding of the fundamental motives of each actor in the process. If *mestizos* at the bottom of government bureaucracies, for example, are called upon to do things contrary to what they have normally found or defined as rewarding, government mandates are sure to be warped.

Understanding underlying normative elements does not imply placing them into a sociological model like the plural society. This form of cultural explanation is handy for a "developmentalist" school which treats poverty as inevitable and the solution as cultural adaption. But it is not analytically valid. Both rich and poor can see that the relative disparities of wealth, education, and opportunity are a function of mobility per se, not some innate ability of cultural adaption. What affects mobility is not poverty or illiteracy; these are but external symptoms. It is instead mechanisms of domination or, as Elliot (1975) calls them, confidence mechanisms. Stein draws the conclusion exactly.

> Therefore to the extent that "Indian-ness" is an instrument of mestizo domination in the Peruvian social system, and to the extent that traditional Indian culture is nothing more than the result of mestizo action which forces "patterns of Indian behaviour," the system itself as a mestizo creation is part of mestizo culture and there is no separate "Indian culture." It is inappropriate to view Indians as "responding" or "reacting" to outside cultural influences with their "own" cultural creations; rather, Indians are to be viewed as part of the system and lacking both alternatives and the autonomy to make a choice (Stein, 1972: 46-47).

The job for development promoters in Peru is to identify the mechanisms at work maintaining domination and to devise ways of changing or destroying them. If that proves politically impossible, then the mission would certainly be to mitigate to some degree the mechanism while simultaneously working to make the optimum structural change a politically possible one. At the very least, specific projects should mobilize poor people to work toward specific economic goals at the local level.

The basic paradigm widely used in Peruvian studies to begin an analysis of the mechanisms of domination is the baseless triangle. A recent and satisfactory discussion is by Whyte (of *Street Corner Society* fame) and Alberti (1976: 206-10). One individual with some land or other productive base employs indigenous workers and monopolizes their access to much or all of their material, informational, social, and financial needs. By keeping the level of socioeconomic awareness extremely low, the landlord could prevent the political consciousness of peasants leading to political mobilization against him and thus a change in the degree of exploitation. The model is most applicable to pre-1960s haciendas in the Sierra; it endures in modified form through various kinds of patron-client relationships and through institutional, policy, and cultural biases. The model is less applicable in the most remote highland world where reciprocal ties still predominate.

The following sections will pursue this model, subsidiary confidence mechanisms, ecological constraints, and any other relevant blocks to development to try to present the kind of material that is necessary for the design of development activities promoting participation. Some of the groups in rural Peru that would seem to merit attention are these: relatively autonomous villages in the highlands, workers now in cooperatives, and other highland and lowland smallholder communities. With unlimited space, the problems of the urban *barriadas*, the Amazon ethnic minorities, fishermen, and miners would also be addressed.

HIGHLAND VILLAGES: THE CASE OF UCHUCMARCA

It is impossible to do real justice to the considerable variety of village experiences in highland Peru. Each region and area has its unique ecological and resource base that modifies how and to what extent a given village interacts with the world-system. Thus the parting critique by Orlove (1977: 204) of both modernization and dependancy theories about the inevitable nature of the world-system and its penetration is not entirely out of line. People do act creatively where given relative freedom and motivation to do so. What Stein and others argue persuasively in return is that to the extent a village enters into trading relationships with the larger system, its field of choices is constricted. The control of the dynamic and the preponderant advantage lie with the greater in a relationship of unequals. This section will explore through one case study the essentially inwardly controlled highland village to try to suggest what outside development assistance might be called for either by the villagers or by the long-term weaknesses in the delicate balances with nature that permit reasonable subsistence.

The villagers high in the Andes have had to adapt to a degree of ecological complexity with few if any parallels in the world. In one valley in north central Peru is the village of Uchucmarca with a population of about 1,000. It was visited by anthropologist Stephen Brush (of William and Mary College) in 1970-71 and 1974, and his book appeared in late 1977. Many, many aspects of his research effort could serve as a model for the depth and sophistication necessary for development designs worldwide. Here a few elements must do.

Uchucmarca sits in awesome and rugged terrain whose very nature imposes a degree of isolation from the world that makes impractical great reliance on the outside for any economic need. Indeed within the valley, transport by foot, horse, or truck is usually arduous and time-consuming; one can see places it takes twenty hours to walk to. In such a habitat these Peruvians developed one or more ways to reap economic rewards from each of seven different microclimates and biological communities that correspond to seven altitude ranges between 800 meters and 4,300 meters. Nearly all families cultivate crops at several of these levels while following a complex yearly agricultural cycle. The pattern for Uchucmarca is thus a bit more elaborate than the common four crop zones described elsewhere in the Andes: 1) a lowland tropical zone for sugar cane, fruit, and cocoa; 2) a temperate grain-producing zone; 3) a cooler potato and tuber zone; and 4) a highland grass zone suitable for herd animals.

Uchucmarca's economic activities, from the bottom up, begin at the *temple* zone (800-1,500 meters) where irrigated agriculture is practiced. Competition for plots is considerable in the areas where cash crops are possible. Such plots are few in number and the most remunerative. Fruits, maize, cocoa, manioc, plantains, and peppers are grown, but by far the most important crop in terms of labor and reward is sugar cane. If no flooding intervenes, a cycle of 3-5 years is followed allowing 2-3 years of harvesting. Cane is cut by hand, hauled to one of four mills, and processed into ten-pound cones of crude sugar to be sold outside the village. It appeared to be the only crop of which more than 10 percent was sold outside the village. Not very many villagers seem to have been involved; the economy of Uchucmarca functions basically by exchange relationships.

The next zone (1,500-1,900 meters) suffers drought often enough to discourage cultivation. It serves instead as a basic source of firewood, the only fuel. Pursuit of firewood occupies every family member and roughly 10 percent of the time used in subsistence activities. The third zone, *kichwa*, (1,900-2,450 meters) has, in contrast, predictable and reasonable rainfall and temperatures. This is the basic grain-producing area; wheat and maize are staples, with wheat the largest single protein source. Beans, fruits, squash, and even chickens and pigs thrive at this level. But grains are central. More than half the plots are being sharecropped, but despite land pressures production is still basically noncommercial and within the subsistence mode. There are as well some cash transactions with outsiders.

Above the *kichwa* sits the *templado* zone (2,450-3,100 meters) and the village of Uchucmarca itself. It is a transitional region between the dry forest above and the warmer moist one below. Some crops from both are present; the field pea is the only important one exclusively at this level.

The fifth zone is the *jalka* (3,100-3,500 meters) and the area of potato production. Villagers have more land here and spend more time in this activity than that at any other level. Only about a fourth of the crop is produced by sharecropping. Just under half of all households own at least one plot at this level and 77 percent are involved in some form of production; these are the highest degrees of ownership and participation of any crop.

The last two distinct zones are basically communally used. One is the *jalka fuerte* (3,500-4,300 meters) which has frequent frosts and much rain. Here are the grasslands that provide pasture for cattle and sheep. More than half of the households maintain at least some cattle as a form of living bank account that is easily convertible.

The last of the seven zones sits to the east of Uchucmarca Valley, stretching away from communal lands at an initial height of about 2,500 meters. It is a very thick forest, good for hunting and for wood.

The sum of these seven zones is a quantity of resources allowing perhaps an unusual degree of independence from outside market activity for a highland village. This has led to a very highly developed and successful subsistence economy; Brush saw income and wealth disparities based largely on historical and demographic settlement patterns, but he found no visible evidence of malnutrition or diet deficiency. No family owns more than 10 hectares of land. The inheritance system tends to fragment holdings, leaving a *minifundio* pattern and an average of 1.58 hectares per household. This does not promise long-term stability. A few families have no land, and the holdings per crop zone vary.

To maintain such an economy requires a considerable social harmony and the mechanisms to insure it. Key to Uchucmarca, as in any basically reciprocal lineage mode of production, is a web of exchange relationships with the kinship system as the foundation. "As if it were the nature of the universe," the kinship system embraces all human actions from birth to death. The nuclear family is the heart, but the "general kin universe" (Brush, 133-34) extends to about 10 percent of the village for any individual. For most it represents a considerable pool of human resources. At least six major types of exchanges are distinguished. Principal is the *sociedad* or sharecropping exchange of land and labor; the owner provides the capital inputs, and the yield is divided equally. About 70 percent of the households are involved in this form alone. Other forms include labor exchange, labor for food or cash, ritual harvest exchanges, exchanges of goods, etc. The result for each household is a strategically designed network, and the sum of the networks is the economy.

To be sure, individual strategies sometimes fail. Many mechanisms come to bear to lessen failure and inequality. Brush summarizes them in this fashion.

> Redistribution of resources occurs throughout the period of production: land is made available to those who do not have it through the system of *sociedad*; seed and oxen are obtainable through rental or exchange of services; labor is offered and utilized through reciprocal labor exchange and through systems of payment involving the use of cash and crops (Brush, 1977: 91).

The system was indubitably imperfect since some did not have land. Laziness was not reported. A further avenue for those deprived was emigration. Brush enumerated 178 adults who had emigrated permanently; in 31 percent of the households at least one member had done so temporarily (in their most productive years). It is this process that makes villages like Uchucmarca outposts of the world-system. This village and others like it pay the initial social cost of producing a vast quantity of labor whose production benefits another region — largely the Coast. It is only partially compensated by immigrants and by wealth brought or sent back.

A development designer looking at a village of this nature is faced with several areas of possibilities. Initially one should be concerned that the potentially destructive forces of monetization be clearly and publicly articulated in group meetings; aspirations to trade have become more and more obvious. How will accumulations of wealth be stored and used in socially responsible ways? Nonmonetary exchanges are now veiled in great secrecy. Conflicts are normally solved within kinship norms. Taxes are paid through ritual labor obligations. Much new education is called for, as the villagers themselves see. Brush (p. 119) discovered among their perceived needs secondary education. The Peruvian government has done an excellent job in many areas establishing primary schools in easy walking distance for 6 to 9 year olds (personal communication). At the central location in each school district an education service center is planned; part of this complex will be the regional secondary school. As they become operational, one of the basic confidence mechanisms, unequal access to education, may diminish appreciably. An absence of secondary roads and school buses will continue the hardship for some villages. At some point people may wish to move to where social services can be offered, given visible financial limits.

One could in addition look closely at how the villagers spend the hours of the day. For the neoclassical economic analysis of underemployment (that the marginal productivity of such workers is zero) collapses before anthropological evidence. Brush calls it (pp. 117-32) the myth of the idle peasant. Peasants are *not* full-time agriculturalists; Brush makes the case thus:

> The fact that they do not specialize means that regular portions of their time must be set aside for doing tasks which in industrial or market economies people are employed full time to do. One finds little

evidence that the hours spent on nonagricultural activities such as house construction, braiding rope, making roof tiles, gathering firewood, fence building, tending a few head of livestock, and so forth have been counted in the formal economic estimates of underemployment. Moreover, many such estimates tend to overlook labor inputs that the people themselves may consider as an essential part of agriculture (Brush, 1977: 119).

It is manifest that aspects of subsistence employment are not easy to measure. A more appropriate task for participatory development is to see how specific villagers allocate time and try to suggest ways to complement ongoing efforts to improve its productive use. Uchucmarcans spend much time looking for firewood, a basic but vanishing resource. Here is one more village on this globe needing the appropriate technology for solar power. In the meantime someone might explore with the villagers the use of the coal frequently available. Investment is called for in low-cost mountain transport as well. Even Uchucmarca, relatively more fortunate than most, is running up against ecological limits that cannot all be avoided by emigration. As these villagers seek to enter the world-system more fully, they must develop the capacity to see that they can defend themselves well enough to benefit. It will not be easy.

HACIENDAS TO COOPERATIVES IN
THE HIGHLANDS AND LOWLANDS

Between 1968 and 1976 Peru carried out one of the statistically most impressive land reforms in modern world history. Yet in 1977 the *Latin American Political Report* summed up the result in this depressing fashion.

The enormous problems facing the reformed rural sector are only too obvious and are not confined to political identification of the main *campesino* organization, the Confederacion Nacional Agraria (CNA), with the opposition Partido Socialista Revolucionario (PSR), embarrassing though this is. Paradoxically, after years of spectacular land ownership transfers, Peruvian agriculture is still beset by the structural problem inherent in excessively large farms with distorted linkages to the rest of the economy. Most of the large units are now nominally cooperatives rather than private estates. There are some 1,450 of them, the majority extremely poor, lacking in technical help and administratively unwieldy. These problems apply particularly to the highland area (*Latin American Political Report*, July 1, 1977).

Fitzgerald (1976: 31-32) captured the heart of the paradox. Reform changed the pattern of ownership for some 25 percent of the rural workers, but the overall structure of production or the use of labor and land remained the same for nearly all. To help undo the long-term agricultural stagnation that has resulted, one must explore deeply what other factors are involved. One cannot assume that the current stage of reform is sufficient, that only new inputs of technology and capital are called for.

Several frames of reference should be kept in mind. There are wide income gaps between the richest sugar cooperatives on the Coast and most highland cooperatives. Similar gaps exist among members of a single cooperative, especially on the Coast. Finally there are wide income disparities between cooperatives and small-holders. These remain. So do severe conflicts in the processes of interaction between cooperatives and the larger world-system. Ecological constraints endure as well. Peru has the lowest ratio of cropland to population in South America. Long-term land scarcity, adverse price movements, and, until recently, insecure* land tenure all reflected the basically ill-designed and conflict-ridden nature of the domestic economy and its political and cultural expressions. To affect any of these conditions, one must know something of the prereform situation, the underlying goals of the reform, its nature, its magnitude, and the limiting factors.

The traditional haciendas of the Sierra, as well as the plantations of the Coast, were born and existed as part of the world-system. The internal structure of the hacienda, however, contained a number of noneconomic elements amidst the vast web of relationships between *patron* and *colonos*. The basic tie was an open-ended, quasi-permanent allocation of land by the *patron* in return for labor and goods. The breadth of ties included all aspects of juridical,

---

*Changes in the national Plan Inca in the late 1970s have destroyed such security as there was; land is now to be tied not to the cultivator but to the person's registered production record. Without such registration smallholders can be denied the following: (1) water, (2) technical assistance, (3) state monopolized fertilizer, hybrid seeds, etc. and (4) sale at the guaranteed prices at the state food wholesaler/retailer (EPSA).

economic, and social life for the *colonos*. The *patron* made additional profit by selling his peon labor outside the hacienda. Field bosses and overseers also used their positions to appropriate labor and goods so that a degree of corruption was deeply institutionalized. The peon's social recourse was to seek a socioeconomic benefactor or protector, usually by the ritual *compadrazgo* tie.

The abuse of the *colonos* by the *hacendado* has been widely chronicled and need not be repeated. The degree of interaction with townsmen that left the poor prey to more than one *patron* opened up a far wider field of abuse, abuses that are not necessarily harnessed merely by land reform.

> An hacendado can at the same time be judge or governor; a mestizo merchant can be town boss and civil authority. The Indians themselves can at the same time be dependent on a church, a boss, the neighboring hancendado, and the authorities. This diffuseness of the boundaries between the several cases. . . . is reflected in the extensive terminology relating to the institutions and the obligations which are joined to them. Out of this come the permanent confusion and ambiguity regarding what some owe others. What is designed to take care of the *campesino* is order to lighten his load is what in the last analysis especially benefits the masters of local society, those notoriously deceitful and avaricious *mistis* who derive advantage from the situation (Piel from Stein, 1974: 22-23).

It is confidence mechanisms such as these that lead one to call Peru today an aborted revolution.

Useful to understand as well about traditional hacienda relationships are the factors that accounted for the survival and continuity of the system. Paige (1975: 170-74) summarized them well. The highland *patron* was content with a labor supply of subsistence-level serfs because any surplus could not easily be reinvested for greater profit. Technology and a dearth of reachable markets encouraged the *patron*, particularly of a larger estate, to spend on his own life-style instead. A limited output thus created a balance of coercion and subsistence; any significant gain by peasant or *patron* endangered the other. Seasonal and legal insecurities made the peasant very chary of challenging the system anyway. For the same reasons, peasants would not invest in capital improvements. Within a given hacienda there was enough social and economic ranking and therefore potential mobility to provide the basis of other confidence mechanisms to sustain the status quo. Limited resources and their skewed distribution precluded large-scale political action; smaller actions left peons open to considerable retaliation.

Obviously these limiting factors were not operative in the few highland and in most lowland estates where the introduction of cash crops gave both lord and peasant new economic possibilities and resources. The export economy made pastoralism economically profitable, created the commercial plantation as its rival, and provided both with the resources for consumer goods and modernizing technology. The stage was set for conflict, and peasant land invasions in the 1950s and 1960s were a large precipitating factor for the reforms that came after 1968. Others (from Whyte and Alberti, 1976: 200-6) included declines in return for labor or land, worsening of market conditions, and threats to recently achieved gains.

Many narrative elements of the history of the last decade's land reforms are not particularly apropos to development designers. But it is important to understand the reform's key goals as something more than idealistic and humanistic help for some of Peru's most downtrodden. Specifically it was national entrepreneurs who were trying to expand their own internal markets for consumer goods and agricultural inputs. An optimal discussion is that of Wilson (1975: 223-31). To a large extent such goals were realized indirectly by several kinds of government policies. For one, the government left unchanged the patterns of unequal exchange between urban goods and rural food commodities.

> Even the government take-over of the marketing of basic food items (through EPSA) has resulted in continued price policies favoring the urban consumers (which in turn cheapens the cost of reproducing the urban-industrial labor force) . . . The market mechanism, reinforced by government price policies, continues to make it impossible for more and more low productivity peasants to make a living from the land. Agrarian Reform does not detain the process of rural marginalization . . . that forces more and more peasants to migrate to the cities, where they became part of the urban marginalized sector (Wilson, 1975: 227-28).

It is in all a not uncommon demonstration of economics as if people do not matter.

How neatly then the overall political goals mesh with these fundamental economic motives. Peruvian scholar Julio Cotler (in a

1971 essay excerpted by Wilson) summarized them in this manner:

> The law of agrarian reform . . . seeks to pacify the peasant masses and eliminate the possible operational basis for another guerrilla attempt; likewise it attempts to undermine the Aprista bases and the rural political mobilization of that party generally; . . . it provokes a state of confusion among the fragmented left; it eliminates the rural sector of the bourgeoisie, which had been the most important obstacle for the development of the country and for social homogeneity. . . . The President recognized the injustice and exploitation to which the peasant was subjected and the urgent need to eliminate peasant marginality which would in turn allow for the industrial development of the country (Wilson, 1975: 224-25).

Against this background the many limits to the reform become much more explicable as do the difficulties faced by any development designers in rural programs. First, however, a quantitative and structural portrait of the problem is in order.

The Velasco government began the accelerating of land reform in Peru with a 1969 law that took three major steps. It created a new specialized branch of the judiciary to deal with the legal issues involved. It forbade all forms of land rental; all landowners were to live on and work their own properties. Lastly it insisted that all agricultural workers take part in the management and profits of the plantations or enterprises where they worked (Horton, 1975a: 52, inter alia). Many reforms in the Ministry of Agriculture made more resources and personnel available. A rational methodology of nine steps, with its acronym PIAR standing for Integrated Rural Settlement Project, was laid out as the operational guide to land reform by region. All agrarian zones were divided into a manageable number of PIARs with the intention of restructuring all unproductive agricultural activities, not just the large estates. The process in action, however, attacked *latifundio* and has yet to arrive at a theoretical or operational approach to *minifundio*.

The principles governing the cooperative and quasi-cooperative productive forms that resulted from the seizure of sugar, cotton, and coffee plantations and highland haciendas were summarized (Horton, 1975a: 61) in this way. The government wanted to retain the integrity of the unit and its infrastructure yet use available resources with optimal rationality and economy of scale. It sought as well social goals — more jobs, better living conditions, and less isolation. But it did not come to grips with the contradictions implied. Attention went to forms, not content. The two major forms that emerged were the Agrarian Production Cooperatives (CAPs) and the Agrarian Social Interest Societies (SAIS).

CAPs were intended to be truly collective operations without individual production. In practice in most cases a professional manager was hired and in the largest sugar cooperatives some technicians as well. The CAPs were permitted, and did hire, nonmembers who partook of neither profits nor control. CAP members have no incentive to enlarge their rolls by allowing marginal workers on; everyone's profit share would diminish. The SAIS form (Horton, 1975a: 65-68) resulted when the government found it impossible to allocate a hacienda to one community of workers. The SAIS groups haciendas with *campesino* villages and shares control, labor, and rewards with both workers and surrounding communities; legal ownership is vested in a service cooperative.

Above the SAIS, CAPs, and other smallholder groups, the Peruvian government erected central cooperatives to promote larger-scale social and economic ties beneficial to them. These are called CECOAAP and provide "marketing, credit, processing, accounting, technical, and managerial assistance." (Horton, 1975a: 69). Ministry of Agriculture officials and those of SINAMOS (a separate activist bureaucracy created by the Phase I military leaders) made some progress in most PIARs to implement overall reform goals. But in small communities they struck out, a topic dealt with in the next section.

Table 8.1, drawn from the most analytically important work on the reform (McClintock, 1981: 93), gives the best available approximations of the overall accomplishments of the Peruvian land reform. It is apparent that only about 25 percent of the peasant families can be said to have benefited in any appreciable way. The remaining skewed patterns of holdings reflect the ongoing disparities of access to resources and thus of wealth. Families in CAPs average 24.4 hectares and those in SAIS, about 47.3 hectares; the rural elite, including former *hacendados* and their choice retained holdings, average a comparable 40 hectares. But at least 400,000 families, one-third of the total, have too little land or none at all. The overall goal of productivity rather than human rights is clear.

TABLE 8.1 Estimated Distribution of Peruvian Peasants by Type of Agricultural Work, 1977

	N	Thousands of hectares	Total farm families	Families benefiting from reform	Percentage of total rural farm families
CAPs	578	2,225	107,137	107,137	7
Peasant Groups	798	1,586	43,945	43,945	3
SAIS	60	2,802	60,930	60,930	4
Peasant Communities	4,000	8,191	500,000	110,971	31
Private Farms	N.A.	8,000	600,000[a]	31,918	37
Eventuales	—	—	250,000	—	16
Total	—	23,500	1,600,000	356,276[b]	

[a]Approximately 20 percent of these farms are over 20 hectares, but under 100 hectares, and 75 percent under 20 hectares.
[b]Figures include 1,375 peasants in Social Property enterprises.

Source: McClintock, 1981: 93.

The limits of the reform are far more than quantitative. They involve basic contradictions in the government approach and in the workers' and peasants' responses. Who controls the key decisions? In recent years the bureaucracy has been criticized from both ends of the spectrum. If it is passive, participatory inequality would persist; action by central authorities, however, could appear as cooptation and would certainly undermine authentic participation. Government held onto overall wage and production decisions and at times intruded even more. Peasants, fearful of "easy come, easy go" and the talk of more change embodied in the concept of Social Property, did not give the government great support. McClintock concluded that the result was a vicious circle:

> Skeptical of government action, cooperative members were inclined to perceive officials as even more intrusive than they were, and to try to block these policies. Observing peasant resistance, officials at times pushed their advice vehemently, and reinforced peasants' image of the official as intrusive (McClintock, 1976: 411).

Beneath this communication conflict is the fundamental problem of modern Peru, a corporatist mainstream political culture of a

defensive elite that litera᠎ ᠎es not accept the democratic, participatory vision implici᠎ ᠎n rights.

Further confu᠎ ᠎ absence of answers to several obvious
policy question᠎ ᠎AIS (and CAPs) in cooperation or in
conflict with᠎ ᠎or government resources, and how is
or should ᠎? The various cooperatives of the early
1970s w᠎ ᠎n wealth, yet there was no visible strategy
to wo᠎ ᠎responsible balancing. Indeed the govern-
men᠎ ᠎ce on the profit motive skewed choices the
ot᠎ ᠎nd remains, despite the IBRD's reports, no
vis᠎ ᠎long-range farm policy. Thus, as McClintock
co᠎ ᠎6-59), the government is trapped by political
pre᠎ ᠎emeal programs and inequitable resource alloca-
tion᠎ ᠎rary conclusion argued by some was that under the
surfa᠎ ᠎a very sophisticated system of controlling all phases of
agricultural production, marketing, and research was being built
up. One proof of the latter's viability would be when agriculture
imports begin to diminish. Figures from 1975 to 1979 showed little
overall change (IBRD, 1981: 190).

The problems as seen from the bottom begin with the fact that
the Velasco government and its successors since 1974 have usually
installed the changes from the top down instead of beginning with
social mobilization for self-directed action. Peasants held on to their
fear of dependence on the new reform enterprises for several reasons.
Failure meant suffering. The past history of dependence on outsiders
and outside markets, as Horton (1975a: 129) found, was a very negative memory. Instead peasants developed a collective spirit toward
each other, a situation McClintock (1976: i-ii) termed group egoism.
Self-management fed this inward perspective so that the conditions
of women (in larger cooperatives, particularly), of disadvantaged
outsiders, and indeed of the nation received little or no concern.

Symptomatic of the entire range of unresolved conflicts from
either perspective was the way in which Peru's announced philosophy of the early 1970s, "neither capitalist nor communist," translated into confusion in the matter of work compensation. Wages
went up in cooperatives, but disparities remained and so therefore
did competition for higher posts. Most surveys (McClintock, 1976:
288-96) indicated workers did not prefer income equality more than
getting ahead. But neither wages nor profit remittances were strictly
tied to work performance or hours put in. Nor were promotions and

advances predictably related to open criteria; personal ties remained important. All these disincentives apparently drove down productivity and diminished solidarity. Workers could not be fired; logically many spent as much time as feasible in private pursuits. Clearly it was not an auspicious start.

To be fair to the workers, one critic reminded me that there were other substantive reasons why reform may have created production declines. Intrusions by Ministry of Agriculture technicians forced ill-accustomed and sometimes ill-advised changes in crop choices. Initial marketing changes were handled unskillfully, resulting in losses. Less production being marketed could also have been a sign of workers eating better. Finally one should not expect to eliminate overnight centuries-old patterns of dependency and risk aversion.

With all of these limits and constraints, the government was slow to begin rethinking philosophic assumptions. It instead made predictable technocratic responses: training managers and peasants in practical and administrative issues and enlarging the credit, technical assistance, market, and distribution systems. Horton (1975a: 180-81) saw the practical results. Choices made for practical political reasons and profit motives led both to productivity over participation and to investment choices that widened the gap between rich and poor. The somewhat more coherent systems-based approach of a private Peruvian development group, DESCO, was also seemingly (Horton, 1975c: II.4) trapped by a dependence on collectivization rather than participation. At the end of the 1970s this, the most productive and wealthiest quarter of the agriculture sector, was still prevented by philosophical and psychosocial contradictions from creating the overall socioeconomic organization and motivations to undo the long-term stagnation.

THE POLITICAL ECONOMY OF RURAL MARGINALIZATION

The 900,000 or more families constituting the fringe of the world-system within the national and regional subsystems in Peru contain, of course, both commonalities and differences. No entirely universal solution exists for their development needs. Some provide cheap food or labor to the system. Others provide a commodity or product made cheap on a world scale by the subsistence return to the producer. Many or most of these families are not significant consumers of modern goods. Indeed the larger system, having no effective way to make them more profitable either as producers or as consumers, sees them as a drain on scarce resources and thus opposes significant public investment in them. This is the most basic underlying systemic contradiction that should encourage development catalysts toward participatory development.

This section will show what the varied subsidiary obstacles are to political and economic participation to a degree that might engender sustained development and meet basic human rights. That implies a multidisciplinary inquiry into how the political and social systems use confidence mechanisms and other means to skew the allocation of the rewards of labor and how peasants in various settings attempt to fight back and create alternatives. Given the variety of ecological and economic settings, only a few samples are feasible. Such a variety, however, does not entirely support the analytical approach termed the sectorial model and its critique of the theories of modernization and dependency as advanced by Orlove. He argues that

> the sectorial model, by viewing individuals as actors, shows history as something they construct. People are faced with forces not of their own making, but they respond actively to these forces rather than receiving them passively. Their reactions are based on their particular circumstances as well as their common position in export economics and nation-states. The variety of local conditions thus generates a variety of responses to these global forces, so the interlocking of alliance and conflict, of internal and external dynamics, proceeds differently in different cases. The sectorial model shows that what is universal about the people of the Sicuani region is their uniqueness. . . . It allows us to comprehend our world is: unitary but not uniform (Orlove, 1977: 204).

Orlove's wool exporting region had the financial base to be more creative than many. But the sectorial model is most flawed by focussing on the uniqueness of the case and on symptoms rather than the commonalities of impoverishing *processes* and the way in which the larger system conditions and guides development choices and the sociocultural matrix.

The cases drawn upon are not quite as varied in locale as would be desired. Dew (1969) wrote about Aymara speakers on Lake Titicaca in the Altiplano; Handleman (1975), Whyte and Alberti (1976),

Van den Berghe and Primov (1977), and Orlove (1977) all wrote about communities in the department of Cuzco. Some touched also on adjacent departments. Stein's various essays on Vicos, however, and Brush (1977) both center on northern highland communities. A number of other ethnographic works are also drawn on for these works, so, with Orlove's caveats in mind, most marginal communities face these problems.

Peruvian municipal governments, whose town councils have a long heritage of *mestizo* domination, saw much of their power taken away in the early 1970s by the newly implanted military bureaucrats from SINAMOS during its heyday as the national agency for social mobilization. Duties left to town councils were the most mundane: upkeep of markets, sewers, streets, and registries. Budgets are vastly insufficient, requiring subsidy from above and thus dependency. Order is provided by units of the paramilitary Guardia Civil in most towns of any size. By education they "quickly identify with the little local mestizo oligarchy of teachers, shopkeepers, and medium-scale landowners" (Van den Berghe and Primov, 1977: 73). Guardias live largely off the land, helping themselves in the market place and elsewhere. A secret police serves one kind of judicial back up. SINAMOS played additional roles (diminished by the mid 1970s) as government propagandist, patronage agent, and facilitator of services. At least in Cuzco, and likely elsewhere, it was perceived as the most powerful government presence and thus the scapegoat for assorted ills.

The smallest and more remote communities are much more likely to be run by some variation of the *varayoc* system and consensus of village elders. The *varayoc* are persons serving in ranked civil authority or ritual positions. Lower-rank positions are refilled annually in a prescribed fashion. Service in these positions is quasi-obligatory for most males. Rank in large measure determines ceremonial duties and obligations. The degree of community political autonomy depends naturally on how near it is to a larger political or economic force. Most such communities not only do not have a sufficient bureaucratic structure to face the outside world, they also do not have the legal status or ingenuity to protect their lands. A 1958 survey (Handelman, 1975: 32-33) showed 75 percent of the nearly 6,000 peasant communities were vulnerable to land encroachment; financially ruinous legal fights, draining as much as 50 percent of a village budget, went on for years against encroaching haciendas, plantations, or neighboring communities. A 1970 Peasant Community statute tightened up the rules, requiring all individual *comuneros* in petition to be resident farmers. Growing need of boundary security impelled "open" farm communities to apply for legal status as territorially inviolable *communidades campesinas*, but with mixed results.

Villages appear to be often divided in a number of ways that can serve to warp or destroy the best-planned development activity in a specific locale. Whyte and Alberti (1976: 238-39) put them in a useful typology. Factionalism can emerge between age groups, economic activities, indigenous-*mestizo* conflicts, neighborhoods, religious observances, or political belief. In one Whyte and Alberti case, 30 young men were expelled from a community. A village with two predominant economic activities might see competition for resources lead to a polarization. Some communities were split by more than one variant of the indigenous-*mestizo* culture conflict. Sometimes neighborhoods marked severe political and economic barriers; a long study of one village dominating another nearby appears elsewhere (127-28) in their work. Religion can divide communities into factions in the rare community where Protestants made headway. Similarly when political party activity grew more complex, as it certainly did in the 1970s, further divisions arose.

A more sophisticated way of viewing community factionalism has been provided in an unpublished work of Brownrigg (n.d.). She looked first at the basic cultural conflict between traditional and modern psychological outlooks as they were translated into community organizational change. The more modern villagers sought new education and technology; in so doing they were often absent for extended periods from community labor duties, which eroded traditional authority and work patterns. This provoked particularly visible conflicts between youth and elders, especially in communities with limited resources and no annual distribution of land. Close examination of many other conflicts revealed a second basic thesis. There were competitions between kin groups being carried on under the cover of multiple cultural, political, and economic organizations. Such complexities suggest that development catalysts must apply a lot of anthropology and that villagers must be the central actors in the design process.

The economic predicaments of most of the highland and lowland residents who are not members of cooperatives or of the urban *criollo* world are severe. The world-system works effectively to take their labor cheaply while allowing individual advances of some to maintain the illusion for nearly all. Most at a disadvantage are those landless families and individuals who can count on nothing more than labor and social ties for survival. Slightly better off are the small farmers and village entrepreneurs who need to engage in wage labor only part of the time. Best off are those with a relatively full-time pursuit, like wool producing, that provides some degree of autonomy and security, albeit dependence upon and loss to a market system.

There is no proper way to generalize on the specific issues of particular productive forms in particular regions as so much depends on the spatial and historical setting of a given location. Van den Berghe and Primov (1977: 93) argued, for example, that Cuzco's overall stagnation represents the aftermath of exploitation in the colonial era and relative marginalization thereafter as resources, investment, and growth elsewhere made much of this region a backwater. What their analysis slights is that such a backwater, via migration, produced cheap labor, even if it produced relatively few commodities. Even one such microcosm suggests the variety possible.

What appears more universal is the considerable degree of antagonism in nearly every account of productive activity and exchange. The worst elements of hacienda conflicts have been mitigated within cooperatives, but there is little to suggest that in other areas the remaining landholders treat or are treated by hired labor very much better than Bourricaud found in the early 1960s.

> What is very remarkable — if not very surprising — is that the two parties have the sentiment of being exploited. The Indian complains that the lands he has received are of mediocre yield, that their (*colono*) neighbors have been treated better, and that the *patron* has excessively reserved the best land for his own use. In short he has the sentiment that his work is worth more than the remuneration he receives. The *patron* stresses the poor quality of the Indian labor, the negligence of the shepherds who let the sheep die, and the spirit of theft by which he alleges the Indian profitably substitutes the animals of his own flock for those of the hacienda (Bourricaud, quoted by Dew, 1969: 76-77).

Bits and pieces of evidence suggest that this distrust runs the gamut of economic activities. Trading relationships were cause for deep unhappiness. Handleman (1975: 201) found in interviews that merchants were perceived as buying for unduly low prices and selling manufactured products at top prices. Villagers, prey to many forms of labor and commodity tithes, cannot clearly articulate such a basic form of unequal exchange. But they could see how the superior transport abilities of local merchants hurt their own ability to retain the fruits of their labor.

The most detailed recent discussion of rural trade is that of Orlove (1977: 57-61) on the Sicuani regional economy's export of wool in the southern highlands. He found the direct vertical marketing ties the most important: one middleman with several suppliers and one purchaser among the export houses in the province capital of Arequipa. Personal ties are critical to maintaining these links. Orlove advances a thesis of "a high degree of competition among middlemen" but then shows multiple ways in which the producers' ability to benefit is limited. Personal ties often lead to advances of credit, the obverse of which is debt entrapment; this cuts down the major natural advantage to producers of being able to store wool when the price seems low. A buyer in a more remote area often has a de facto monopoly as the only one traveling through the area; there is then no incentive for higher prices. In areas where an established market exists, its surface competitiveness may be destroyed by informally dividing the routes that approach the market; the result is a somewhat more subtle monopoly.

Most apparent, however, is the impossibility that producers know as much about changing market conditions as do the buyers. The higher the level in the system the easier it is to find out and to shift costs. Orlove described the view from the bottom in this manner.

> On occasion, publications have appeared stating market prices for wool, but these are infrequent, irregular, and do not account for short term fluctuations or the considerable price variation in the Sierra. They often reach the potential wool seller several weeks late. At best they serve to inform some *hacendados* and large-scale wool wholesalers of general trends and, on rare occasions, of specific prices.
>
> Less formal mechanisms also fail to communicate full information on prices. Wool prices are a common topic of conversation, but information travels slowly outside an area larger than a province. Stories tend to be exaggerated, and information spread by word of mouth is most inaccurate when prices are changing rapidly. Even within small areas, information about price rises may be kept secret. One buyer may give his suppliers an increase of 5 to 10 percent without the others knowing for several weeks (Orlove, 1977: 57).

Given such an informational imbalance, combined with the power imbalance in specific dialogues over the exact weight, color, and quality of the wool, the average producer cannot be said to be in a position of strength. Wool producing, parenthetically, appears to be one of the most remunerative activities among marginal highland communities.

Other confidence mechanisms could be elaborated which skew allocation of resources and rewards in local economic activity. Agricultural extension officers exist in some towns and offer short-term loans to peasants, those few peasants who appear to have the ability to repay. Officials thus have a few model individual peasants to show superiors how well the program is going. A large middle group of peasants sees such credit models as not hopelessly out of reach. They continue to try, though over time few succeed. But the system retains its legitimacy and survival through the cumulative false hopes, despite its failures.

A similar confidence mechanism is at work in the village upkeep of roads and irrigation canals, alluded to before as a community ritual. All families are supposed to contribute an equal share of labor for equal benefits. The reality is rather regressive. Wealthier peasants and *mestizos* have the resources to pay to avoid such labor. More importantly they gain a disproportionate amount of the water and the road use since they have more resources to apply to the productive activities that use these inputs. The poor are on balance paying to make the rich richer but do not perceive it. It is not surprising; poor people in this and every other country cannot see most of the confidence mechanisms they are trapped in.

AVENUES OF PERSONAL MOBILITY
AS CONFIDENCE MECHANISMS

The world-system offers two principal avenues of escape for marginal peasants at this point in history. These are education and migration. Education provides an opportunity for personal change and mobility on a one-at-a-time basis. Looking beyond the promises of the Peruvian Educational Reform Law, one can see several reasons why bureaucrats in that country will continue to be retitled and reshuffled but many poor people may gain but little functional education.

Van den Berghe and Primov surveyed the situation in Cuzco and came up with a biting critique with four basic points. Most teachers in the Sierra know the local language and use it orally; but they invariably teach reading and writing in Spanish, despite visibly negative effects on learning speed. Worse are the more subtle culture conflicts going on.

> Teachers are by definition mestizos. Though many are of Indian origin, when they learn Spanish — a necessary condition to become teachers — they become mestizos. As such they generally share all the prevalent stereotypes about the Indian's supposed backwardness, slowness of wit, sluggishness, laziness, stupidity, ignorance, stubborn conservatism, and so on. Many teachers have low expectations of their rural pupils; indeed, some firmly believe that their educational task is doomed to failure. This belief, in turn, is almost certain to become a self-fulfilling prophecy (Van den Berghe and Primov, 1977: 78-81).

Absenteeism by teachers assigned to rural areas remains, one observer told me, as critical a problem today as it was in the 1960s. Rural teaching assignments are much resented; the least qualified and experienced are assigned the posts. Distance from supervision has meant phenomenal absentee rates. Finally and inevitably, rural education has been starved for funds; the farther from major towns, the worse the situation. Teachers might live off the country, but that did not provide books and paper for children.

Education must be seen as well as an elaborate confidence mechanism. As Elliott (1975) painted it so well for African and Asian societies, education raises the hopes and vision of many families to dream far beyond reality. Most children are entranced to enter the race, and a tiny number make it all the way through to high status jobs. Many make it some part of the way and do improve their life conditions. But all who participate are validating yet another institutional skewing of resources and rewards that serves to perpetuate the relative poverty of most, albeit at a higher absolute level. In Peru, the educational system legitimizes the entire socio-economic, cultural-linguistic prestige structure (*indigene-cholo-mestizo-criollo*) as not only *a* positive achievement structure (and normative reality) but as the *only* one. Given the alternative models of Freire and others, development designers are up against yet another basic conflict in the pursuit of human rights for the world's poor.

The conventional developmentalist school has long regarded rural-to-urban migration as a relatively positive process. According to this rationale, peasants get better-paid jobs and greater possible access to needed social services; by leaving unproductive rural settings, they supposedly leave more land and productivity to be shared by those who stay behind. The latter is not usually the case, but this is not the basic issue at stake. What is happening is that rural society is losing its most adventurous and often best trained human resources; it is these people who might have forced change if they had to stay home under open-ended impoverishment. Andre Frank has shown aptly how such a force for change becomes, through migration a force of status quo.

> Those persons in underdeveloped countries who have migrated from country to city or moved from a lower economic and social status to a higher one often say in one way or another that they have made their own individual reform or revolution. In so doing they express not only the conservatism which reflects their desire to maintain their newly gained position but also a fundamental social scientific truth which seems to escape the attention of diffusionists and others: "social" mobility is really individual mobility and does not transform social structure: rather, a change in the social structure may render possible *social* mobility and economic development (quoted in Stein, 1974: 48).

Migration does in sum nothing about the fragmentation and distrust, the vertical patron-client ties, and the way both distort the peasant's perceptions of possible change. Migrants may send money back to rural families. They even return to villages and apply enhanced skills to promote change. But the cumulative impact of all of these related processes is on balance one of perpetuating relative poverty for many.

What one comes to from this bleak assessment is a considerable respect for the world-system's ability to maintain the prevailing distribution of wealth and power. Confidence mechanisms with their elegantly flexible nature give enough substance to the illusion of realizable progress that most people are fooled into passive acquiescence if not active support most of the time. But any mandate to create development activities to support the poor majority cannot be deterred by such sociopolitical and psychological complexities. The task is to design ways of encouraging the cooperative spirit and social mobilization that are inherent to the participatory strategy and structural change without which the poor will be permanent losers.

THOUGHTS ON THE RESEARCH AGENDA
FOR PARTICIPATORY DEVELOPMENT

Such a whirlwind tour of some of the disadvantaged groups in Peru and the mechanisms of their marginalization is really little more than a few tastes of the kinds of interdisciplinary analysis necessary for participatory development. The unique elements of local ecology, personalities, and conflicts must be operationally linked to the regional and national realities. That means not just statistical portraits of the surface symptoms of an evolving mode of production. It demands explanations of processes and the motives behind them. This implies synthesizing issues of political economy with issues of cultural marginalization and bureaucratic imperatives. One must know not only what economic interests a particular agency or group is pursuing but also what additional imperatives condition the behavior of a bureaucrat in his or her institutional role.

Without the clear presentation of the process of marginalization and the actors in it, one cannot begin to design a change process to reverse departicipation. Large donor agencies, both as products and as prisoners of the world-system, cannot be expected to produce such analysis with any consistency. Few of their thousands of reports over 30 years have done so. Nondemocratic governments do no better. Intermediate organizations and allied social scientists will have to do most of this work. Some UN agencies have taken on parts of the task; work by UNRISD, FAO/ROAP, and ILO/WEP on rural development suggest how local and international analysts can join forces. A great deal more needs to be done. For if people cannot define the real problems of development, there is no reason to expect them to arrive at coherent solutions that promote human welfare.

CHAPTER BIBLIOGRAPHY

Abusada-Salah, Roberto (1977). "Industrialization Policies in Peru 1970-1976." Paper presented at the LASA Meeting, Houston, November, 1977.

Bodley, John W. (1972). "Tribal Survival in the Amazon: Campa Case." Copenhagen: International Work Group on Indigenous Affairs, IWGIA Document No. 5.

Bourricaud, Francois (1970). *Power and Society in Contemporary Peru*. New York: Praeger.

Brownrigg, Leslie Ann (1974). "The Role of Secondary Cities in Andean Urbanism: A Bibliographic Essay Exploring Urban Process." Chicago: Northwestern University, Center for Urban Affairs.

____ (n.d.). "Ethnocentrism: An Applied Anthropological Test of Theories in the Peruvian Sierra," unpublished.

Brush, Stephen B. (1977). *Mountain, Field, and Family: The Economy and Human Ecology of an Andean Valley*. Philadelphia: University of Pennsylvania Press.

Chaplin, David, ed. (1975). *Peruvian Nationalism – A Corporatist Revolution*. New Brunswick, N.J.: Transaction Books.

Dew, Edward (1969). *Politics in the Altiplano*. Austin: University of Texas Press.

Dietz, Henry A. (1980). *Poverty and Problem-Solving Under Military Rule: The Urban Poor in Lima, Peru*. Austin: University of Texas Press.

____ (1977). "Political Participation by the Urban Poor in an Authoritarian Context: The Case of Lima, Peru." *Journal of Political and Military Sociology*, 5, 1:63-77.

Fitzgerald, E. V. K. (1979). *The Political Economy of Peru: Economic Development and the Restructuring of Capital*. Cambridge: Cambridge University Press.

____ (1976). *The State and Economic Development: Peru since 1968*. Cambridge: Cambridge University Press.

Handelman, Howard (1975). *Struggle in the Andes*. Austin: University of Texas Press.

Horna, Hernan (1976). "South America's Marginal Highway." *The Journal of Developing Areas*, 10, 4:409-24.

Horton, Douglas, E. (1975a). "Land Reform and Group Farming in Peru." IBRD, Department of Development Economics, Studies in Employment and Rural Development No. 23.

—— (1975b). "Land Reform and Reform Enterprises in Peru." IBRD, Department of Development Economics, Studies in Employment and Rural Development No. 24.

—— (1975c). "Peru Case Study Volume." IBRD, Department of Development Economics, Studies in Employment and Rural Development No. 22.

IBRD (1981). *Peru: Major Development Policy Issues and Recommendations.* Washington, D.C.: IBRD.

Leeds, Anthony (1973). "Political, economic, and social effects of producer and consumer orientations toward housing in Brazil and Peru: a systems analysis," pp. 181-215 in Rabinowitz, Francine F., and Trueblood, Felicity M., eds. *National-Local Linkages: The Interrelationships of Urban and National Policies in Latin America.* Beverly Hills, Calif.: Sage.

Lowenthal, Abraham F. (1975). *The Peruvian Experiment.* Princeton, N.J.: Princeton University Press.

McClintock, Cynthia (1981). *Peasant Cooperatives and Political Change in Peru.* Princeton, N.J.: Princeton University Press.

—— (1976). "Structural Change and Political Culture in Rural Peru: The Impact of Self-Managed Cooperatives on Peasant Clientalism, 1969-1975." Unpublished doctoral dissertation, Massachusetts Institute of Technology (revised).

Orlove, Benjamin S. (1977). *Alpacas, Sheep, and Men: The Wool Export Economy and Regional Society in Southern Peru.* New York: Academic Press.

Stein, William W. (1975). "The Peon Who Wouldn't: A Study of the Hacienda System at Vicos." *Papers in Anthropology* (Univ. of Oklahoma, Dept. of Anthropology), 16, 2:78-135.

—— (1972). "Race, Culture, and Social Structure in the Peruvian Andes." Buffalo: State University of New York at Buffalo, Dept. of Anthropology.

—— (1974). "Countrymen and Townsmen in the Callejon de Huaylas, Peru: Two Views of Andean Social Structure." Buffalo: State University of New York at Buffalo, Council on International Studies, Special Studies No. 51.

Thomas, Vinod (1978). "The Measurement of Spatial Differences in Poverty: The Case of Peru." World Bank Staff Working Paper No. 273.

van den Berghe, Pierre L., and Primov, George P. (1977). *Inequality in the Peruvian Andes: Class and Ethnicity in Cuzco*. Columbia: University of Missouri Press.

Varese, Stefano (1972). "The Forest Indians in the Present Political Situation of Peru." Copenhagen: International Work Group for Indigenous Affairs, IWGIA Doc. 8.

Webb, Richard C. (1977). *Government and the Distribution of Income in Peru, 1963-1973*. Cambridge, Mass.: Harvard University Press.

Whyte, William F., and Alberti, Georgio (1976). *Power, Politics and Progress: Social Change in Rural Peru*. New York: Elsevier Scientific.

Wilson, Patricia Ann (1975). "From Mode of Production to Spatial Formation: The Regional Consequences of Dependent Industrialization in Peru." Unpublished doctoral dissertation, Cornell University.

9

Working from the Inside: Enhancing Participation in Project Design

Up to this point I have pursued the operational means of promoting authentic human development through the optimal organizational process, empowerment through individual growth and small group activities. The logical necessity of this path derives both from the individual need for self-directed learning and from the antagonism of the world-system to any process not feeding its desire for control and profit. Organizations like governments and aid agencies are the tools of system elites, as Chapters 2-5 demonstrated. Organizations also have their own internal agenda of security, control, and growth. That agenda also runs counter to promoting the participation of human beings in their own growth, self-enhancement, and liberation.

This is not a practical overall analysis for many readers currently making their livings as inhabitants of just such bureaucracies. Realistic concerns like money impede resignation for the alternative life of community organizer or cadre in an intermediate organization. In an imperfect world and in this period of transition as large aid organizations become more and more anachronistic, is it possible to work inside aid agencies to improve the quality of beneficiary participation in the aid project process? It depends. Certainly the top-down, blueprint project process with its elitist front-end biases can be improved. The question is whether the improvements work to create a project process that adds to the empowerment of the poor or conversely improves a coopting process wherein elites more smoothly incorporate into their fold previously marginalized individuals or groups. As it now stands, far more of the latter than the former transpires in most projects. All the incentives, from both the capitalist or state socialist environment and from the bureaucracies they employ, are for the corporatist approach to uncaptured peasants and slum dwellers and for the expansion of the status quo.

These next two chapters are for those institutional readers who, recognizing these constraints, still intend to work in specific places and on specific projects to overcome them. It has been done. In many projects relatively small changes in design and implementation procedures could offer major possibilities for transformative education, if not material advance, for the poor. Those implementing projects in rural areas in particular have a great deal of de facto freedom to consider the prescriptive changes suggested in the following pages. The donor organization and larger system has far more control over the design stage of the project, before resources are transferred, than after implementation has begun. Aggressive implementers can simply state, "This won't work as planned because. . . ." and foster a more participatory alternative. Many cases will not be so simple. But there is nothing in most project papers to preclude the creation of base and intermediate organizations as natural project adjuncts.

This chapter will focus on the activities that take place in donor agencies, particularly the World Bank and AID, during the design stage of a project cycle. Most national governments follow a similar work process. So do private voluntary agencies. A project idea must be conceived. An original sketch of it is prepared and approved. A design team is formed that does the detailed research. Then comes operational planning: writing the project paper, negotiating with host nationals, and pushing the project over funding hurdles to its official approval. Many individuals have a chance to affect the process. Once it is started, however, few try. The potential beneficiaries become more and more remote. Understanding the internal organizational reality of this work process is the first step to prescribing changes in procedures and work incentives.

THE PREPROGRAMMING ACTIVITIES

The initial idea for a development project requiring external resources can in theory come from anyone within a beneficiary group, a local institution, a regional or national agency, or the foreign donor itself. It is usually hard to track down the true originator. Development students have not thought it worth surveying this topic. Yet a reasonable sample from any country portfolio would reveal some basic aspects of how the project cycle customarily begins in an exclusionary fashion. Projects appear almost always to have originated to fulfill purposes of regional or national elites and the bureaucratic imperatives that result. A donor agency forced to push vast sums because of political pressures, AID in Egypt in since the middle 1970s, for example, is likely to initiate project ideas wherever feasible. In either case the mass of people affected have not been consulted on whether the project should exist or be a priority. Project officers in field missions and national agencies could, however, work around the natural imperatives of the political economy of development by carrying out initial field surveys. Capacities of local organizations could be examined, and their decision-making processes as well as expressed needs evaluated.

Indeed the tendency toward large donor projects could be preempted at the start by unilaterally seeking out intermediate institutions already engaged in local mobilization. AID has been doing this in a number of countries. Small seed grants could help the mobilization process along until a particular microdevelopment system is *organizationally prepared* to handle larger funding for projects of a more specifically productive sort that capitalist donors would support. As it is now, most projects enter unprepared local environments. Local people are overwhelmed by the financial and organizational capacities of the outsiders. It is little wonder that projects work poorer and more slowly than planned. Mission officials will find the work of development surveyers and catalysts to be more time-consuming than is personally feasible. Expensive foreign consultants do not have to be hired. Educated but underemployed young host nationals could work in teams for a fraction of the cost. Over time the mission could develop a universe of local organizations with projects ready to go, which could then compete on quality grounds with the more elitist choices of a typical line agency or national politician. Sometimes the better project would get funded.

More typically the design officer in the mission or government agency is informed from on high that project X should be prepared for preliminary discussion. If no area evaluation and human mobilization work has been done, the design officer starts with handicaps that can be partially overcome by the appointment of an appropriate design team. This means thinking about the kinds of skills and attitudes that would be conducive to beneficiary participation in the initial learning phases, never mind the actual design and implementation.

This has historically been a mundane issue. An agriculture project is said to need an agricultural economist and so on. Mickelwait et al. (1978b: 141-43) has begun to raise the level of discussion by recognizing the utility of shared developmental perspectives on the design team, the application of human social sciences, and the use of women professionals if one expected to communicate with half of the beneficiary group. More importantly these authors argued for the breadth of skills necessary to do projects sensitive to the particular social and cultural milieu and to negotiate with host country officials. But participatory projects are not processes inflicted on people. They are exercises in, at best, equal communication, dialogues across cultural chasms built on mutual cognitive respect. Design officers choosing people to do even initial survey work, never mind detailed research, should be looking above all for people with the empathy and learning capacity that could lead to effective communication with the poor.

This is not to say that technical competence is not also required. But the team designer needs to have both a general understanding of the social origins of knowledge and of the specific interdisciplinary training necessary to grasp development issues. Hobbes wrote several centuries ago that "the most powerful instrument of political authority is the power to give names and enforce definitions."

The creator of design teams thus faces a serious quandary. Using the intellectual models and vocabulary prevailing in the West in the hope of empowering the poor in the Third World is clearly contradictory. One way to start changing the situation is to challenge the job categories created by the personnel departments of aid agencies. The World Bank list for its consultant roster is the apogee of technocratic education. Personnel officers want a neat and static universe of defined specialists. Development demands interdisciplinary generalists who see education as a permanent activity. Changing personnel listings will be slow. But rewriting specific job descriptions for specific design teams can be swift. The way to get people comfortable with political economy, systems thinking, human ecology, social learning, and appropriate technology is to demand such education explicitly.

Surmounting the elitist biases of conventional social science is only one part of the task. To promote development by people one must counteract the bureaucratization of knowledge, particularly its dehumanization. Organizations do not see people; they see clients. If we are to use knowledge to help people, starting by denying their humanity is perverse. It is very much like bombing a village to save it. In the bureaucratization of knowledge lurks an even more sobering process. An organizational inhabitant needs the bureaucratically convenient reality, not the empirically defensible one. Moore described the results as a Third Culture whose members are neither scientists nor humanists:

> For them it is never a question of thought or research or discovering the truth and *then* telling it, but rather the expedient, the transient, trying to adopt the most praiseworthy stance, making the most acceptable temporary statement, and then hoping against hope that it might all turn out to be correct (Moore, *New York Times*, April 17, 1979).

In development agencies it is the norm to avoid controversies and unpleasantness because they hold up paper flows and money pushing. Consultants adapt to these norms in order to get rehired. Quality of work suffers. Mission design officers are under pressure to produce bureaucratically saleable projects. Unless they can change this series of incentives in substantive ways, mass welfare will not prosper. Preparing the development environment is one possibility. Reeducation of fellow officials is another.

In the latter process it would be good to develop practical examples of how bureaucratic norms defeat stated project objectives. One of the clearest is the use of Western scientists in Third World agricultural development. It is still common to see agriculture discussed as a purely technical subject. Planners consciously or unconsciously start from technocratic premises and reach technocratic goals. More recently some of AID's work has reflected a "farming systems" approach with some participatory learning; but the current state of the art (Gilbert et al., 1980) reveals a narrowly drawn system with the political variables treated as exogenous. The bias toward individual entrepreneurs in that discussion is clear.

Most IBRD projects are still reflecting Chambers's (1974: 131) findings in East Africa. Misfocussed research aimed to raise yields per unit of land instead of per unit of labor. Agencies and governments prodded peasants to plant cash crops in a timely manner regardless of how that jeopardized local food security. If the project goal is to contribute to national food self-sufficiency, why would anyone expect farmers to participate at the expense of their own self-sufficiency?

It is common in development literature to criticize prevailing models of technical assistance and prescribe refinements. Mission design officers can easily fall into this cycle if they talk only to technicians and lose sight of the real goals of participatory development: empowerment and building local capacities. That means considering not just the substance of technology transfer but also its style. Is the Western perception of expert appropriate? Participatory development implies open-ended egalitarian learning, not hierarchical authoritarian learning. How technical specialists can maintain both traditional self-esteem and the requisite humility and flexibility in development learning situations is a question that needs to be talked through before a specialist is contracted. Paying technical specialists hundreds of dollars a day, as major donor agencies often do, sharpens this contradiction by enlarging the culture gap and creating irresponsible desires among those local officials and citizens affected by their presence. Appropriate technology ought to generate appropriate pay scales.

Mission design officers also have a hard time adapting the work habits of the Western social scientists, habits that are not conducive to either participatory processes or bureaucratic needs. Part of the problem is the conflict Hummel (1977) describes of organization versus society. Marson put it this way:

> . . . the administrator and the anthropologist are members of rather distinct subcultures with very different values and goals. . . . While the social scientist typically sees knowledge as the highest work-related value, and seeks to develop theories from this knowledge, the administrator is a problem solver who seeks knowledge as a useful tool to achieve administrative and program goals (Marson, 1971: 612).

Another critic saw social scientists as tending to talk to each other rather than pursuing policy related research, typically unable to produce in a cost-effective manner, and no more able to talk to physical scientists than were others in the development system (Stevens, 1978). Social scientists have also been accused of naiveté about the complexity of development and their stance of either neutrality or activism (Spain, 1978: 26). Conversely social scientists will not respond well to the bureaucratization and dehumanization of their work.

Academia is imprisoned by guilds and the tenure system. Few social or natural scientists, traditionally trained, will have the incentive or vision to surmount these dilemmas and create the multidisciplinary, human-centered theories upon which to base the policy research needed for systemic change and participatory development. Administrators, technicians, and social scientists in development clearly need to create a common language and a common perception of work.

By this I do not mean that school of thought busy reducing social science to an applied technology. Contractors have done this often. Cochrane (1979), for example, sifted out of anthropology six criteria for the social mapping of a national inventory of cultural resources and ten criteria to consider during project design. There is general mention of participation. But the stunning denial of any operationally useful theory of social change, combined with a clear production-centered bias, leads to a mechanistic, manipulative methodology.

In contrast, those seeking to build an underlying normative consensus on the organization of knowledge for development must look to the holistic approaches provided only in properly conceived historical or literary studies. History viewed as processes unfolding, classes producing, and mechanisms impoverishing is central to the work of any development design team. The implications of examining past failures are threatening both to elites and to organizations. Thus there are energetic forces trying to diminish its availability so as to limit potential social learning. But designers who fight to put history into the center of the project research will force all of those involved into multidisciplinary thinking about why and how the status quo maintains itself, who benefits and who is excluded, and how mechanisms of stratification are being enhanced or dissolved. For a sample of how history raises consciousness and propels participatory development, consider how central the articulation of village history, individual human struggles over time, was to the change process of *fanshen* in village China in the latter 1940s (Hinton, 1966). It is little wonder that no contemporary historian has ever been recruited for a project design team by any major donor agency.

The sum of these sobering strands suggests that designing jobs and creating a team of any mix of technical, organizational, and social science skills is far from a trivial activity. Many people who put themselves forward for such work are not ready. Their technical learning has not been matched by their political and social learning. Skilled mission design officers and others involved can contemplate what kinds of education in what kinds of formats could compensate in some measure for the biases inflicted by the social origins of knowledge, the lack of historical training, and the pernicious Western schisms between politics and economics and between the physical and human sciences. A lot of discussions with poor peasants would be a good place to start.

Once a design team is assembled, preprogramming activities normally begin with some compilation and processing of secondary data on the country or region. This is usually a topic beneath discussion. One is supposed to have developed a research ability in school. What happens in the real world of major donor agencies? Neither time nor incentives encourage a professional review of the literature. Despite the availability of computers and libraries, many critically important items are not readily accessible. They are published far away, often obscurely. It is a rare donor agency official who has much of a professional library in the office. Yet a simple fiat from on high plus a short course in research methodology could start the creation of permanent minilibraries in the field missions and at the country and project desks.

Instead development designers typically read World Bank reports, relevant contract and project papers, and perhaps a smattering of published items close at hand. Rarely are theoretical works considered. Data gathering is the main goal. For AID employees, the Daines (1977) report conditions the mind in this manner. Designers rightly feel that prevailing work pressures do not allow a fully professional review of the literature. Yet it does not take much time if the research collection has been built up and regularly renewed. Clearly neither the organization nor its inhabitants are being rewarded for state-of-the-art work or the improvements in project quality and beneficiary participation that might ensue. Tendler

(1975), Carmichael (1976-77), and others have commented on the factory nature of work, the money and paper processing, in donor agencies. These incentives clearly work against intellectual inquiry. This is a good example of the deeper, unresolvable issue that development is essentially a long-term process of growth and change, while bureaucracies are essentially driven by the short-term need to routinize and control.

The bureaucratic inhabitant must consciously struggle against routinization every day on a personal level; try designing free learning space into a daily or weekly routine.

Practical as well as intellectual limitations bear on a design team at this early stage. As at all project stages, time is money. A premium is thus put on ability to identify material, physically lay hands on it, and decide what is worth reading and what is not. It is an art. It is discouraging how poorly it is done on average. The practical constraints of assembling the human material are also immense either in the field or in a core capital like Washington. Some firms in the development industry maintain a corps of consultants and develop shared perceptions and competence. Other firms maintain paper rosters and recruit with little thought of the final product. All firms face contracting and scheduling snafus. Sending one cable and receiving an answer can take weeks. So can payments. It is hard to retain quality people or the enthusiasm to do professional work in such circumstances. Contracting procedures, designed by one organization for its own convenience in dealing with another, thus work to exclude the independent and creative individual who might have much more to offer the aid process. Such an alienating process is one of many reasons to seek local contractors whenever possible.

Another practical problem begins to work to exclude the poor at this point. Not only are they relegated to subjects of the project design process as opposed to cooperative designers of their own empowerment, but the poor face an organizational process so slow and routinized as to be inherently useless for real mobilization purposes. Is this an accident? AID contractors, Booz, Allen & Hamilton, found in a 1978 survey that the average AID project took 19.7 months from inception to approval. It is hard to see how poor villagers facing immediate subsistence dilemmas could sustain interest, resource commitments, and cooperative attitudes over such a time span. This argues strongly for much smaller, less complex projects.

AID does some of these under the heading "special activities"; often they are close to authentic participation, responding to small local initiatives like a group of poor urban women needing capital for a few sewing machines. By contracting through private voluntary agencies, some AID missions have been able to expand this style of resource flow.

One further issue should surface before a design team moves into the field for preliminary programming. What thought has gone into how likely the various project designers are to understand the motives of one another? Of course, most of this learning will occur during field research. To some extent such learning is colored by the personal ties that develop. It is important, however, to look beyond ideological and monetary motives. Each actor now on the team is part of a development system imprisoned in part by culture and in part by larger organizational needs. What additional motives will planners bring to the process?

Caiden and Wildavsky (1974) explored this question in some detail, arriving at a critique of planning as part of the problem rather than the solution. Warwick (1977: 23) neatly sums up their conclusions that planning, as done by aid agencies or local officials, often produces these negative results: (1) planning can be used as a substitute for action; (2) planning drains scarce human capital; (3) planners, for many reasons, seek the larger, more complex and thus more expensive possibility; (4) "planners create problems to gain influence; . . . (5) planners generate false hopes which lead to disillusionment; . . . (6) planners are an interest group with their own biases." In sum planners are thus no more neutral actors than anyone else in the system. Conscious recognition of such tendencies would be helpful. But to get poor people effectively involved, this entire up-front blueprint approach to social engineering will have to be drastically modified in the direction of process planning. Part of development must be the empowerment of people to do their own planning. If they are not ready to plan, they are not ready for a complicated interaction with an outside agency. By deliberately planning to learn and to replan all the way through the project, participants will suffer minimally from institutionalized elitist planning. Such a learning process will provide the maximum feasible practical education for the poor.

PRELIMINARY PROGRAMMING: DIAGNOSES
AND BUILDING COLLECTIVE THINKING

A design team or any other donor agency component arriving in a Third World country to help identify a project has a difficult task. Data bases, research aides, Xerox machines, and transportation are limited. Language and culture are usually alien. Political and economic forces look upon the potential project as something threatening to be opposed or as possible spoils to be preempted. Internal bureaucratic norms of the aid agency impel the collection and packaging of certain data in a certain format, or a plausible facsimile thereof. A very short period of time is allocated, usually a few weeks and often less. It is impossible that even a well-meaning design team could hope to create a relationship of mutual trust, confidence, and shared learning to have a truly participatory project. The structure of the procedures involved prevents such a result.

Project designers feel they need information because they are taught that it is imperative to reduce uncertainties as far as practical as quickly as possible. Collecting information means creating communication. What happens in fact is usually what Chambers (1980) calls "rural development tourism"; in Chapter 11 (on evaluation) this activity will be discussed in detail. What ought to happen instead is a process of information gathering that finds, evolves, enlivens, or even creates the institutions and forums suitable for consensus building and participatory development. Without generating commitments to action by all involved, the project design will be just a paper exercise. There must be time for serious contemplation as well as give and take. Initial priorities must be selected. Without the mobilization described in Chapters 6 and 7, area visitors are likely to be communicating with standard organizations, eliciting elite preferences, and designing a continuation of the status quo.

A design team can try to overcome these handicaps in the following ways. It can hire host country assistants for research surveys and observation. A mixed group of local and nonlocal people, male and female, young and old would be ideal. Give them relative freedom to wander off the obvious paths, seek out the hidden agendas, and talk to the poorest citizens. The team can avoid elite-staged mass meetings. It can carefully chronicle the personal and bureaucratic agendas of each potential project actor. Any argument that the aims of the government and the needs of the poor are synonymous should be politely sidestepped. Look instead for the degree of social conscience in specific local officials and their potential longevity in office. Information is power. Peasants are not going to surrender such power to strangers or to anyone seen cooperating with local elite.

One of the best current planning discussions (Warwick, 1977: 103) concludes that some formal planning may be worse than none, smaller planning efforts are better than large ones, and too much data can be worse than too little. As suggested before, a number of others, analysts at the Washington consultant firm Development Alternatives, Inc., for example, have been arguing for a process approach rather than the creation of a project blueprint. Not only is it impossible to really grasp many critical aspects quickly, but too much planning prevents many kinds of participation down the line that are in turn imperative for implementation success. Here, as at so many other places in the project cycle, the basic conflict is clear. Donor organizations want data to reduce uncertainty and gain control; the human growth of participatory development needs space and time. One or the other gives way in current practice.

Expatriate donor agency staff do not frequently exchange views or data with the urban or rural poor of the Third World. Bryant (1979a) describes how social and culture pressure within what she terms the mission tribe work against such contacts. It is quite difficult even to maintain contacts with host country officials of comparable rank. Paper-pushing duties and practical obstacles also stand in the way of the most determined. Thus, when a design team arrives for its brief period of research, the local mission is often not even in the position to locate the kind of public or private intermediaries who could open up communication channels. Some, like the Washington-based consultants, the Development Group for Alternative Policies (D-GAP, 1978a, for instance), do offer examples of such alternatives.

David Korten in his recent work (1980, 1981a, 1981b) has been trying to develop practical steps to innovative learning to break down the chasm between organizations and their clients. He argues that managers should seek to become facilitators, tolerant of ambiguity, encouraging of local initiatives for self-control and feedback. His specific prescriptions will be part of the discussion of alternative project implementation in Chapter 10. Here it is worth noting that it is a rare bureaucratic and political environment that is conducive to experimenting with alternative management styles. One thinks of the *responsavel* in Mozambique, described by Lappé et al. (1980), as one of the few types of government official worldwide who are explicitly forced by the political culture to be the ones responsible to the wishes of the people they serve.

Even if a more flexible organization develops some aspects of innovative learning, the culture gap described by Hummel (1977) remains. Thomas and Brinkerhoff put it this way:

> The capability of an administrative system does not depend solely upon the abilities of its administrators; it also depends heavily upon the capacity of its clients to use the system effectively. If the administrative system operates such that only those who share the values and norms inherent in its dynamic are able to participate in the benefits it has to offer, then there is little possibility for marginal client groups to link successfully with that system (Thomas and Brinkerhoff, 1978: 7).

To the extent that Third World government agencies adapt to the culture of modern bureaucracy, which donors like the World Bank consistently seek to implant, they demonstrate the same problem servicing clients. Leonard (1977) has described such issues in detail in his work on the agricultural extension service in Kenya. This dilemma continues throughout the project cycle.

Designers need organizations as well as data. What present or potential groups can serve as intermediaries for designing and implementing participatory projects, if one starts with no previous mobilization effort? Organizational as well as political imperatives urge donor agencies toward the host government. Upon occasion corporate entities are favored. The independent evidence is overwhelming that neither organizational type is very effective at engaging the marginal or assetless poor to the latter's benefit. One can cite Rene Dumont's lifetime work, multiple volumes by Keith Griffin, many studies by the UNRISD on the Green Revolution, and much recent work on Africa like Heyer et al. (1981).

Less than coherent understanding of local realities of all sorts — organizational, political, cultural, social, economic, and ecological — also serves other bureaucratic needs. It is far easier to try to overcome contradictions and conflicts by ignoring them. When they are out of sight, the poor can be neatly homogenized. Then they can be neatly categorized as, for example, all poor farmers in need of land reform. Designers seeking alternatives must slow the process down, break it into smaller pieces, stretch it out over time, push more elements into the implementation phase, and try to incorporate dialogues with the beneficiaries as the central learning process. Frame for daily view the credo devised by James Yen in the 1920s to guide the Rural Reconstruction Movement in China.

> Go to the people
> Live among the people
> Learn from the people
> Plan with the people
> Work with the people
> Start with what the people know
> Build on what the people have
> Teach by showing; learn by doing
> Not a showcase but a pattern
> Not odds and ends but a system
> Not piecemeal but integrated approach
> Not to conform but to transform
> Not relief but release
>
> (from Korten et al., 1981: 210)

Working in modern office buildings in capital cities is not the way to implement such a philosophy.

Pursuing the trickle-down approach to learning and organization building, development designers have historically found it hard to generate deep commitment from local officials and, more particularly, from potential beneficiaries. Many if not most areas have a collective memory of years of failed projects sponsored by outsiders for outsiders since the colonial era. Just because each new generation of bureaucrats wishes to ignore history does not mean that peasants can or will. Ritual meetings in the project area often happen during the design stage. Very few studies of development actually go into enough detail about such interactions to show whether such consultations are the veneer or the substance of participation. One notable exception is a Senegal example, presented in a memorable discussion by Adrian Adams. She witnessed varied encounters between the national development authority SAED and the villagers, and describes the confrontational dialogues in detail wherein peasants rejected capital-intensive and large-scale irrigation schemes for cash crop production.

For the leaders of the peasant association, on the other hand, there were two kinds of development, two ways of bringing agricultural change to the area; the choice was not between innovation and stagnation, but between change evolved from within, and change imposed from without. They had organized on their own, and had shown themselves capable of adapting to new crops and new techniques: that was *développement paysan*. The SAED takeover, they felt, could not be justified in objective terms; its purpose was to deprive them of the freedom to control their own productive activity and its fruits, and make them work for outside interests rather than for the good of their own community. That was *développement de fonctionnaires*. The SAED officials often spoke in terms of national interest, one and undivided; but the peasants saw no necessary fit between their interests and those of officialdom (Adams, 1977: 50).

Some samples of meetings building commitment through participatory development are revealed in Latin American credit programs sponsored by the Inter-American Foundation (D-GAP, 1979b), in the work of Mary Hollnsteiner (1978, 1979) on the Philippines, and in articles in *IFDA Dossier* and *Development Dialogue*.

The nonparticipatory nature of donor organizations also works against building necessary commitments by constricting what can and cannot be said at meetings. If poor villagers are afraid to speak to donor agency officials when local officials are present so also organization members fear to take risks or participate when procedures or goals are not crystal clear. Carmichael describes the inability of the World Bank to face the political context of its work.

Other goals, such as what the Bank must do to survive and maintain its integrity as an institution, are not made explicit. It is usually said that to do so would be self-defeating since by drawing attention to them it politicizes the atmosphere. This factor has a profound effect on work. It leads to a fear of error, fear of leaks, and worst fear that comes from staff not being sure of what can and what cannot be talked about *to each other*. The work consequently often hides realities rather than clarifying them (Carmichael, 1976-77).

Other donor agencies are not immune. I have for years studied aid programs wherein national security mythologies warped empirical reality and developmental concerns. In the case of AID, its current Zaire program demonstrates that the Vietnam program was not such an aberration.

Given data, intermediary organizations, and communication leading to commitment, the design team needs a further and rare commodity: time to reflect. At this point and at several subsequent ones in the project cycle, there should be space for contemplation and for the give and take that permits informed decision making on all sides. Organizational imperatives work against this. Even if designers are part of in-country missions, too many other duties intrude to permit deep consideration of serious and complex issues.

Tendler (1975: 10-11) commented on this need for learning space as hard for a culture that "does not contain concepts for simultaneously thinking about rationality and indeterminateness"; all other reforms are limited unless "the organization is set up in a way that requires learning as an output." No donor organization to my knowledge has faced this, even the Inter-American Foundation. In a 1979 paper the Catholic Relief Service showed some understanding, but the proof will be five years after it has transformed its task, not during the ferment of transition. Relfection would require, of course, the meaningful discussion of goals and criteria; rarely is this evident. Disturbing contradictions must remain hidden for general organizational health. Heaven forbid someone should say "Is all growth good?" rather than "Was the lending target met?"

Participatory development implies not just facing the political and normative questions of for whom and why, but it also requires the free flow of the appropriate data whereby all interested parties can get involved and make reasoned judgments. Mickelwait et al. (1978a) began to investigate information requirements for rural development; but they quickly showed their bias for the technical needs of donor agencies as opposed to the needs of others, like the beneficiaries. Uma Lele (1975: 53) demonstrates how such elitist perspectives are confounded by the real ecological variability of rural Africa; she argues that regional and local research are essential. Gruhn (1978: 550) shows how many of the prefeasibility studies produced by UN agencies, generated not by local, felt needs but by donor needs, have little impact or circulation.

Thus most project designers get only some of the data they need. Donor organizations treat information as power, not as a freely available commodity. This contravenes both rhetorical goals and the basic democratic principles for whose realization aid organizations are supposed to work. But it serves larger organizational purposes of preventing informed evaluation and oversight that might threaten organizational interests. The Senegalese peasants with whom Adams (1977) worked and lived were, by dint of watching the development experiences of neighboring villages, informed enough for participatory decision making. Most fringe populations are not so fortunate. Third World governments and donor agencies are a good part of the reason why. Officials in either arena can, however, work on their own to bypass regular channels to keep local inhabitants informed. Providing knowledge of larger political purposes in advance may provoke or permit villagers to organize and defend themselves or to offer alternative proposals.

After the initial investigation of mission personnel or a design team comes the decision making that turns a proposal into a candidate for full-fledged project investigation. This is not a very participatory stage. Agency and host government officials reach general areas of agreement. But the primary work is done within the donor organization. In AID, for example, this project identification document legitimizes the project within the Agency by passing through reviews in regional and central bureau offices in Washington. The supposed beneficiaries do not see the document before it leaves the field. Input they may have had earlier can easily be dropped by mission personnel seeking smooth sailing through bureaucratic channels. Here, in sum, is the first of many points in the process where control is totally within an organization far removed from poor peasants.

OPERATIONAL PLANNING AND DESIGN

The creation of what is customarily termed a project paper or appraisal report follows roughly the same path as did the feasibility study. The need for data, effective communication, and appropriate analytical methods is now far more intense. Problems sketched in the last section reappear. Several other enduring issues are thrown into sharper perspective at this project stage and so will be discussed here. In particular, if the poor are to participate to anything like the degree that is theoretically, as opposed to conventionally, practical, much more attention must go to the implications of the unequal bargaining relationships that exist among donor agencies, local institutions, and poor people.

The unequal nature of relationships begins with the obvious. The donor agency has the finance capital. This is not, however, a normal banking situation wherein real value is repaid within a finite time. Foreign aid is usually grants or very long-term, low-interest loans. Once money is paid out, aid agencies have relatively little practical control over its actual use. Thus donors seek to gain as much control as possible by planning. Simultaneously, recipients try to push as many of the details into the implementation stage wherein they will have greater leverage in negotiating details (Strachan, 1978: 473).

The many aspects of over-planning deserve and will get their own summary (in the conclusion of Chapter 10). Here it is important to understand how the political and psychological imbalances create a sense of "powerlessness, passivity, and subterfuge" (Strachan, 1978: 472) which allows and facilitates a degree of technical and substantive control by the donor agency that the apparent situation would not suggest. Situations do vary widely. Many host country institutions have at least some highly competent officials. Most of them know more about local development issues than do donor agency officials. The latter are often poorly trained in area studies. Because of frequent transfers and other disincentives, they do not tend to build substantive capabilities beyond the purely technical. It is not surprising that organizations seeking control over aid processes try to make development more an issue of routinized procedures than of unruly substantive concerns.

Because local officials want the money and are not conversant with certain forms of donor agency paperwork, they tend to let the donor agency do as much of the paperwork as they seem prone to do. The best of local officials see that foreign donors have their own priorities, strategies, and packaging techniques and that, if they follow them, money flows (Strachan, 1978: 472). This nonparticipatory process is duplicated at the lower levels. It is staffs and consultants of aid agencies who shape most of the structure and strategy of most of the projects funded, appearances aside.

Third World officials must also work within their own bureaucratic culture and its resource constraints. Moris (in Black et al., 1977: 78-80) and Grindle (ed. 1980) have shown in general terms and Gould (1980) and Schatzberg (1980) in the specific case of Zaire that this administrative culture is quite different from that in the West. Patron-client links, greasing the wheel, and other forms of flexibility serve to redistribute resources and preserve privilege. As Chapter 10 will pursue, these practices mock Western implementation plans and perpetuate stratification.

In all but a few Third World countries the larger political environ-ment encourages a symbiotic link with foreign donor agencies and, quite clearly, the continued nonparticipation of the poor. Neither foreign nor local control systems are likely to face or encourage the degree of public pressure that might lead to (or evolve from) effective mass participation. In such circumstances variations in the balances of control may not have too great an impact on popular involvement in development. One or more of the actors must change to give participatory development a chance. Donor agencies, for one, have the possibility of offering a different methodological and procedural approach. One place to start would be a reconsideration of the conventional social science methods now being used for project appraisal, as suggested in Chapters 6, 7, and 8. One cannot expect to use the historical and economic approaches of the lords to empower the peasants.

It is not surprising thus that the marginal poor are all but invisible in donor agency project papers. A focus on productivity, misconceived as most efficiently resulting from large-scale capital-intensive productive units, is not a focus conducive to seeing human beings as individuals, never mind as potentially effective participants in development. A strategy with that focus will never overcome its elitist impact no matter how many accretions of other social science are grafted on.

A design team, charged with the detailed research and preparation of a project paper (what becomes the guide for project implementation), must work through this institutional environment of conflicting bureaucratic cultures, development philosophies, and policy mandates. Clearly it is easy to be blocked or sidetracked from getting necessary cultural, political, and technical data. When given a technocratic production-centered mandate and a topical outline that focusses on generating data for rate-of-return analysis or for filling in boxes on a legislative checklist, it is very hard to focus on human welfare, conflictual reality, and participatory development. The long-term goal, abolishing the blueprint project process and its replication of the status quo, may be beyond immediate reach of those working on specific projects. It is not impossible, however, to start proposing substantive revisions of project paper guidelines that would work to bring the poor into the process.

To improve the ability of marginal peoples to get more control over and reward from daily activities, the team has to know what they do every day in every season. Donor agencies, forced by their environment to claim competency they lack, usually believe their own rhetoric: they know what to do and the questions are solved. But a few inquiries of local elite do not produce real microeconomic detail. Even knowing a little about how progressive farmers work does not tell one anything about the contributions of tenants, the assetless poor, women, children, or the elderly. Setting up a research network of intermediaries to do such learning cannot be done quickly.

Collecting data on microeconomic and social reality is one task in a series. Interested reformers have found it very hard to get issues like social and cultural conflict effectively integrated into project papers. The World Bank continues to act as though such matters are irrelevant to its work. Its few social scientists have a marginal impact and, from a wide reading of project papers, there is little to suggest that occasional mention of culture and political conflict in external working papers has real operational significance. AID, conversely, began in the late 1970s a "social soundness analysis." Its early efforts to use sociologists and anthropologists were largely defensive in nature. Since conventional methodology does not recognize the multidimensional explanatory power of mode of production, culture and economics were not effectively linked. Instead, traditional culture was said to inhibit "development," and effort went into trying to understand how to change the peasants' perception of risk. Given the wealth of helpful literature, some of it available for quite some time (Marson, 1971, for example), this lack of sophistication must be credited to deeper overall organizational need, the need for ignorance. Some project officers and social scientists in AID persisted, especially in the Near East Bureau. Ingersoll et al. (1981) reviewed the mixed progress to date; this report also proposed significant reforms in the project paper guidelines. Despite disinterest from on high, project officers can explore these ideas as well as topics raised here in preceding chapters.

Beyond data and the relationship of disciplines through systems thinking, project designers seeking participatory development with a top-down project approach (in contrast with the bottom-up mobilization model) have a severe communication problem with potential project beneficiaries. Participatory development would imply a process within which people at different stages of modernization communicate with each other in a nonexploitative manner and in such a way that each accepts the needs and values of the other. This rarely happens. Hummel's (1977) portrait of organization in search of control displays one hindrance. The entrepreneurial excesses of modern capitalism suggest another. Modernization is, as many authors have noted, a very cruel process. Participatory development intends to humanize and soften the cultural and economic conflicts. There is a practical and pragmatic as well as humanitarian dimension to this. Emmerson in his brilliant analysis of developmental conflict in an Indonesian village, summed it up this way:

> More broadly, the irony of the modernization of rural life on Java, and in other comparable regions of the poor nations of the world, is that this process, partly spontaneous and partly inflicted in the name of an elite ideology of development, is undermining the structures of vertical trust and reciprocity without which it cannot be acculturated, at least not without a simultaneous revolutionary transformation of class and power relationships (Emmerson, 1976: 15).

This is certainly true of Vietnam and Zaire, societies I have studied for years, and it appears true for much of Africa. Failure of farmers to produce worldwide seems quite clearly a result of the elites' transformation of structures of reciprocity (Cleaver, 1977 and Heyer et al., 1981, for example).

In Southeast Asia studies, this issue has received probably the most attention thanks to James Scott's *The Moral Economy of the Peasant* (1977). It has been touched upon in other books and articles that relate examples from all over the Third World. What it challenges for development practitioners is their overall reliance on an analytic paradigm. Can development obstacles be planned for? Korten (1977: 12 and his more recent work), for one, argues persuasively that they often cannot. He argues for a different model of analysis, a cybernetic paradigm, to satisfy cultural and technical information needs. His model is as participatory as a donor project process can become, for it is based on multiple decision makers at, or close to, the scene making decisions on the basis of continuous feedback. Without this kind of adaptive problem solving, it is difficult to see how the fundamental culture conflicts of modernization can be resolved in any human-centered way.

Designing to enhance equitable communication, reciprocity, and trust means designing against stratification. Some social scientists working with AID have been struggling with this issue with diverse vocabulary. Leonard's study of agricultural extension in rural western Kenya shows it to be a confidence mechanism with inequitable results.

> There is a substantial bias in the distribution of agricultural extension services in Western Kenya in favor of the wealthier and more progressive farmers. This favoritism accentuates rural inequality and probably prevents the maximum possible acceptance of agricultural innovations (Leonard, 1977: 193).

Leonard attributes this bias to the progressive farmer strategy Kenya pursues (a form of trickle-down development), to the squawk factor — the ability of rural elites to be more vocal — and to class factors at several levels of administration.

Blair, in one of the most sophisticated development case studies in recent years, reviewed the Comilla experience in Bangladesh. He quantified and described the large farmer bias at both the macro and micro level.

> What had happened in Kotwali Thana was that the larger farmers had taken over control of the credit societies in the rapid expansion of the programme during the later 1960's. The Comilla cooperative then began to resemble those elsewhere in South Asia, in that these larger farmers were able to steer the loans to themselves and were able to get away with defaulting on those loans. That they were able to do this was a function of their position in the rural economy as surplus farmers, as moneylenders, and as patrons in the patron-client system (Blair, 1978: 69).

The history of Third World development, indeed of all world development, is littered with discussions of this sort. Politely it is termed the talents effect, less politely, structural aggression and unequal exchange.

A practical design response is not to work to enhance an individual farmer's ability to deal slightly better with an inequitable system. Nor is it to work through elite-dominated preexisting organizations that have created and sustained present levels of poverty and exclusion. It is instead to seek out or create intermediate institutions that will train development catalysts to organize groups of the poor. Only through organization can the poor gain the skills and power to interact effectively with the hostile larger economy. Until their terms of trade are balanced, it is pointless to expect them to have the incentive to invest labor in further production. A project designed to transfer only technical skills or material inputs will not accomplish this.

A brief comparative look at Mozambique and Tanzania in the late 1970s illustrates this clearly. As Lappé et al. (1979: 37ff) suggest, the *responsavel* is not the boss in rural Mozambique but the one responsible for carrying out decision making that happens at all levels. Development plans are here a melding of need assessments and operational methodology from the grass roots, with advice and vision from the national level planners. This can be contrasted to the Tanzania "village manager," who is supposed to empower villagers by granting technical knowledge and material inputs. Mozambique seems to have understood and is trying to make operationally self-reliant development. Tanzania continues to struggle, according to many independent discussions: von Freyhold (1979), Coulson (1982), and Resnick (1981) in particular. All governments have great trouble in recognizing their own inabilities as large organizations. This should not stop development designers in aid agencies from proceeding with a more human-centered agenda.

It would not be helpful to ignore the real political threats that such an approach would pose to the job security of consultants or agency officials. Humanitarian approaches do not appeal to the administrator class or elites in general. But the argument for human welfare is inextricably linked to the practical means to enhanced productivity. This appeals. One way to attack is to argue for change on simply informational grounds: to do the job, the process needs more and better information. Present methods and time allocations will not suffice. This has led a number of analysts to argue that the way to get the more sophisticated data base is to pursue a process approach rather than the current planning/implementation sequence now used. This is, however, not the crux of the problem.

There is a more seriously contradictory and disfunctional element in the prevailing discussions and practices of data gathering. All of the light, or intensive, survey and sampling techniques now in use and discussed in these works are inherently elitist in nature, not participatory. They are conceived and carried out from a top-down perspective. It is a matter of degree, not ultimate nature, whether no villagers, a handful of elite, a sample of its most vocal, every household, or even every village is polled, if the polling is done by an international agent entering the village and leaving it afterwards. This generic form robs the village of the basic formative experience of learning that they can do it themselves and of developing the ability. Major donor agencies now use little or no village-originated data in projects and strategies fashioned by the agency. Without a development process that begins with the training of development promoters or catalysts from the village, one cannot get either a participatory development process or enough local data to design any project that would attract the commitments of many area citizens in a productive way.

Once the various forms of data deemed necessary are collected, the project designers are often, as in integrated rural development projects, required to select specific project localities. This is obviously a basic choice — who gets aid, who does not, and what it means. This stage in project analysis goes unstudied as a theoretical problem. Conventional wisdom of donor agencies and governments is that such choices belong to them. On one level it is clear that most governments allocate development funds as a result of intraelite bargaining within the bureaucracy with inputs from donor agencies and foreign corporations. No research is required to show this.

> The Birla Institute of Technology and Science stands out in this desolate township, situated 120 miles southwest of New Delhi and surrounded by sand dunes and scattered villages populated by illiterate peasants who ride camels and till their land with the crudest implements. But inside the 1,000 acre complex, more than 2,000 students from all over India study engineering and science and learn advanced technical skills with the use of models of factories or rockets. They walk about with the nonchalance of people whose future is assured (*New York Times*, July 29, 1979).

The institute is modeled on the Massachusetts Institute of Technology and has been funded in part by MIT and the Ford Foundation. To get a different result contemplate not intraelite politics or rhetoric about sequential approaches but instead a mixture of equity (comparative degree of regional poverty) and publicized standards of sociopolitical integrity, competence, and responsibility. How has one specific region used its own resources as opposed to another? Investment in the truly developmental and not the reverse will, at every level of the world-system, set a critically important educational lesson by the power of positive example. How, for example, can one take humanistic rhetoric from AID or the World Bank seriously, given their continued investment in classic anti-developmental models like Zaire?

FROM PROJECT PAPER TO PROJECT APPROVAL

The next step in the project planning process is writing the project paper. This step and all those succeeding it (as modeled in Rondinelli, 1976a and b, and Booz, Allen and Hamilton, 1978) form the heart of the process by which donor agency officials control and define Third World development. The poor do not write project papers, negotiate with senior host country officials, attend bureaucratic meetings in Washington, or play a role in the last negotiations prior to the start-up of implementation. A first-order problem is thus posed. If the donor agency organization insists upon this structural form and procedure, it is difficult to see how the last part of the cycle can become in any degree participatory or how gains of the poor earlier in the cycle will be preserved and protected.

Further contradictions abound. Project papers are written by agency officials and consultants. English is the principal language. Spanish is also used in the IDB, OAS, and IAF. Style is reasonably technical and very dry. A variety of statistical mystifications are used in place of causal reasoning. The writers' goal is not project quality, participatory or otherwise. It is a successful project, successful in that it surmounts all bureaucratic obstacles without undue challenge or delay. Carmichael (1976: 7) describes many aspects of this as a factory process.

He also points out many of the results. The assembly line precludes serious attempts to resolve basic problems, for that takes too much time. Good projects require real innovations, but that is too risky. They also require horizontal discussions that threaten the hierarchical, authoritarian work culture and substantive discussions that threaten project and program assumptions. The organization inflicts quantitative targets because, when forced to have goals at all, it can control these and profit from them. Donor agency managers can articulate such numerical goals and judge their attainment. Process goals, like the enhancement of participation, threaten donor organizations as less measurable and controllable. Thus project papers are inherently a social product of an organization, used as a tool to solve its bureaucratic ends. People are not very relevant. It is not surprising that they are rarely visible in the actual content. To all of these general tendencies there are exceptions; particularly noteworthy to explore for alternative models are papers from the Inter-American Foundation and private agencies like Oxfam and American Friends Service Committee.

Many other factors bear on the nonparticipatory contents and processing of project papers. Some, like the organizational economy of large projects, are among the most generic contradictions of donor agency procedures; they will be treated in the conclusion of Chapter 10. Many others are reflections of external influences on internal organizational behavior. Tendler shows how, for example, the implanted motive to increase exports from the country of the donor agency enhances dependency, not self-reliance. One tool is foreign exchange.

> . . . the result is that the availability of project financing for only foreign exchange costs causes the priorities of recipient countries to almost invisibly rearrange themselves around foreign exchange-intensive projects and encourages maximization of the foreign exchange component for any desired project. Thus although development financing at concessional terms is supposed to help recipient countries overcome their foreign exchange scarcity, the form of the financing nevertheless creates an incentive to increase unnecessarily the demand for that scarce exchange (Tendler, 1975: 74).

This process ripples through the project cycle with multiple effects on donors and recipients. One result is that the poor become even poorer because more of the economic production, surplus, and opportunity stays in the First World exporting country. Participatory development will in contrast build primarily on local resources and design productive processes geared to optimum scale use of any resource, not to the profit of any segment of the triple alliance.

Draft appraisal reports are usually cleared by host country officials. Virtually no analytical discussion of this stage has appeared. It is hard to see how the poor and illiterate far from a nation's capital could have any impact on a typical situation. The unequal bargaining relationship previously analyzed (Strachan 1978: 472) would become more severe. The supplicant bows to the paper fantasies of organizational need, realizing that it, the recipient, will have more control at the implementation stage.

The project paper is then sent off to the bureaucratic wars of the donor organization headquarters. It is reasonable to suppose that in this process the generic norms and culture of Western management, as well as the work structure and the operational procedures of the donor agency, would all obey the larger organizational will to control, survive, and grow. It is not surprising to find that the few written discussions and one's own experience indicate that project papers serve several organizational needs, depending upon the moment or individuals involved. DAI (1978: 211) termed them "essentially advocacy documents written to persuade doubters." It was even more critical of cost-benefit projections. These have no long-term value but only "serve the short-term function of recurring approval within the AID bureaucracy." These projections have ideological purposes as well, as Chapter 11 will explore.

The cast of those who might be involved at a project paper review would include one or more senior managers. Their motives might include the need for self-justification, which could lead to a control demonstration (Bryant et al., 1979) called preemptive planning. This can happen because of incumbency, data decaying on its upward journey, the overall poor quality of data and vagueness of goals, timidity of subordinates, ideology, or happenstance.

Others present may include project technical specialists and regional desk officers. They need to demonstrate a raison d'être as well. The project paper may threaten turf, quota, or professional preference. Conversely, it may enlist new supporters who like a procedural or substantive approach. That requirements of project reviews are not well specified or consistent and management responsibilities are not clearly delegated (Booz, Allen, and Hamilton, 1978: VI:2) would suggest considerable room for maneuver. What also appears inevitable is that few if any of the potential participants would have a very deep professional understanding of the specific country issues being judged. For most it is one meeting among many, one project among many, one ritual among many. The institutional pressures are toward consensus, conformity, and pushing the paper along.

This picture of bureaucratic needs and motives is drawn as the basis for a central dilemma of participatory development, one no source appears to have commented upon. There is no one in this organizational universe who has an institutional incentive to defend or enhance participation of the poor in development. It is enough of an obstacle that the officials present have no operational criteria or model of participatory development by which to judge project papers. Such officials are likely not to have absorbed policy rhetoric from the top and may view participation as alien, irrelevant, or counterproductive. What is central here is that no one present, by reason of his or her institutional imperatives, needs to raise the awkward question that such and such project paper has not really shown how the poor will participate, benefit, or retain those benefits. The few meeting summaries I have looked at suggest such a question would be most out of place even in the most egregious situations. For the multilateral agencies one might propose that Executive Directors from Third World countries should raise issues of project quality in general and participation by the poor in particular. But the EDs are usually products of Third World finance ministries. They are appointed by large organizations (governments), not by poor people.

This is not to say that human questions are never raised during project approval. Individuals, as individuals, do raise them. No study of this has ever been done. My impression is that constructive critical comments are received as unwanted delay factors and attacks upon professional credibility. Such remarks are seen as absences of teamwork and severely threatening to both the organization and its members. Thus, unless an ombudsman of participatory development, institutionally independent of the regional and project bureaucracies, were installed as an organized component of these review/decision-making sessions, it is difficult to see how aspects of participatory development can survive, grow, or prosper in such an environment. The end of the formal project planning process, however, is not likely to be the most productive place to introduce or even protect participatory development. Should there even be a world wherein people make decisions vitally affecting the lives of other people thousands of miles away?

10

Working from the Inside: Enhancing Participation in Project Implementation

IMPLEMENTATION THEORY AND SOCIAL PROGRAMS

Project implementation remains amazingly understudied despite the efforts of some institutional and consultant analysts like Ingle (1979) and Crawford (1981). Should one encourage more study? The results could be development projects that actually empower people or they could be projects that are more effective expressions of elite and organizational needs. The more modest goals often proposed by aid agencies — increased productivity or more efficient use of resources — would become more attainable if organizational inhabitants had a much clearer understanding of the inherent dynamics of project evolution. But discussions to date have only begun to show some recognition that, in Perrow's terms (1980), organizations do not have goals; they have usages. Actors inside and outside the project system bring their own agendas to bear. Elites use projects for political or economic advantage. Bureaucrats use them to advance careers or stake out new turf. Poor communities use them as a means to attract external resources. Understanding project implementation is, however, more than defending against competing interests and building consensus for specific sequential actions.

Development is in simple terms a change process. It is essential to understand a project as an organism existing over time both as an entity unto itself and as part of larger systems. Successful

261

implementation must be based on a framework that simultaneously adapts and relates to several kinds of change. It will be quickly obvious that the project design paper had an imperfect grasp of local realities; this will require changes in response. Local conditions will change because of the project. The larger environment may shift considerably. It may have been misconceived at the start; it is customary to find unwarranted assumptions of harmony in project papers. The project's internal behaviour will also evolve as personnel changes, resource constraints appear, and project beneficiaries present new challenges.

These are some of the specific manifestations of the generic laws of program evolution. It is analysts in computer science, centrally concerned with systems change, that have led the way in this inquiry. They demonstrate the theoretical necessity for the process approach to development over a blueprint model. Lehman has synthesized a great deal of research into five laws of program evolution. They are presented below:

LAWS OF PROGRAM EVOLUTION

I. *Continuing Change*

A program that is used and that as an implementation of its specification reflects some other reality, undergoes continual change or becomes progressively less useful. The change or decay process continues until it is judged more cost effective to replace the system with a recreated version.

II. *Increasing Complexity*

As an evolving program is continually changed, its complexity, reflecting deteriorating structure, increases unless work is done to maintain or reduce it.

III. *The Fundamental Law of Program Evolution*

Program evolution is subject to a dynamics which makes the programming process, and hence measures of global project and system attributes, self-regulating with statistically determinable trends and invariances.

IV. *Conservation of Organizational Stability (Invariant Work Rate)*

During the active life of a program the global activity rate in a programming project is statistically invariant.

V. *Conservation of Familiarity (Perceived Complexity)*

During the active life of a program the release content (changes, additions, deletions) of the successive releases of an evolving program is statistically invariant.

(Lehman, 1980: 1068)

A brief discussion of their application to the process of social development is in order.

The first law, continuing change, expresses more theoretically the central thesis above: the combination of imperfect initial knowledge and continuous change in all parts of the system impel consistent attention to redesigning the structure and process of work and modifying incentive systems. The second law, increasing complexity, states the practical implications of the second law of thermodynamics; without feedback systems, far better conceived and implemented than is now the case in a typical aid project, the chances of project success will remain small. The third law states what is supposed to happen in the ideal rational world that bureaucrats and administrators prefer to believe in. In a bounded system such as a computer program in a mechanical device, one has some hope for statistically regular behavior. In an unbounded system involving the unpredictabilities of people, weather, and technological advance, project goals are treated with far more plausibility than they merit.

The fourth law, conservation of organizational stability, reflects basic bureaucratic imperatives. Administrators seeking stability will try to avoid drastic shifts and discontinuous growth. Human and material resources will be applied to produce predictable patterns. The real world of long cycles, uneven growth, bad weather, and human excesses bodes badly for such dreams. It is difficult to see how the empowerment of people, particularly their self-reliance and thus the end of donor agency activity, can be accommodated against the expressed need for stability. A more common result is that the project may generate growing attention over time as political and organizational turfs are established. Pressure for success leads to investment of energy and resources of the kinds within the donor's control; success of the project may well require instead more energy and resources from the project beneficiaries, and further external inputs are wasted or counterproductive. Organizational imperatives work against developing this sensitivity. In like manner, as the fifth law suggests, individuals in all parts of the development system will display the human characteristic of clinging to the familiar far more comfortably than welcoming the new. Changes will happen more and more quickly than they can be understood; human nature, time allocation, and institutional inflexibility all work against developing a matching learning curve. In a microcosm a development project reflects the societal dilemma as a whole: the complexity of our problems continues to escalate in the late twentieth century while the large bureaucratic form demonstrates less and less ability to address complex problems creatively.

It is not surprising that many in the development business are now willing to admit privately that even ordinary things are extremely hard to do. Predictions and expectations created by the professionals for the administrator class and their political sponsors are far too optimistic and exact. Given the control mechanisms and political incentives in Washington, for example, this is not surprising. The costs are severe. Deprofessionalization comes in many forms. Common is the kind of intellectual and linguistic degradation revealed in this 1978 World Bank evaluation of a set of its rural development projects begun between FY67 and FY73:

> The performance of the rural development projects reviewed here was mixed. They did well as a group: individual performance varied from excellent to poor. When compared to original expectations, actual performances tended to be disappointing. Moreover, actual results were governed by factors which were different from those anticipated to have the major impact at appraisal (IBRD, 1978a: 4).

This chapter is not designed as a critique of past practices of project implementation and the ways they have been organizationally defended. It intends rather to move from limitations in present practice to concrete reform possibilities.

Reform in this context means specifically attacking those procedural elements that prevent or diminish participation in development by the poorest and most marginal groups. Five groups of issues will be treated in the following order: appropriate implementation technology; risk aversion of project managers; slow adjustment to problems and the need to redesign; use of foreign technology and contractors; and implementation process incentives. A concluding section will distill from Chapters 9 and 10 a half-dozen major issues that symbolize the irresolvable dilemmas of the conventional, nonparticipatory model. Readers may test the practicality of each proposed change by whether it meets the challenges of elite and organizational interests and pays also proper heed to systems behaviour and biases built into our analytical tools — questions of the sociology of knowledge.

ISSUES OF APPROPRIATE IMPLEMENTATION TECHNOLOGY

Several authors (Korten, 1979b; Ingle, 1978, etc.) have recently argued that if one is to adopt the perspective of the assetless or peripheral poor, the rules, procedures and institutions that donor agencies bring to the field are not very suitable for the communication that leads to participatory development. The practical obstacles in a project environment require considerable flexibility and cultural adaptation from donors, governments, and peasants. None of the three enter the process devoid of cultural and organizational habits. Donors in particular display their preconceptions about social process and organization by means of the project paper, which specifies agents of implementation and the nature and schedule of the activities. Real people and real development environments, however, add new needs and interests to any change process. The implementer is immediately faced with what the planner often neglects to do, finding out what those affected are willing to do and what forces stand in the way. Style can be as critical as substance in this communication.

There are several ways to begin to judge the participatory efficiency of donor agency rules and procedures. One can analyze social change as a social scientist, define participatory goals, define discrete principles conducive to social change, and survey the participants to see if the implementing procedures are perceived to violate the principles. Zaltman and Duncan (1976) started along this line by surveying several hundred sources and defining 178 principles. A more practical approach would involve far fewer. A commonsense application of the participatory development model, the eight principles outlined at the end of Chapter 1, could result in 10-15 indices appropriate to a specific locale, type of project, and historical moment.

A second analytical approach might be to break down the sum total of rules and procedures a donor agency inflicts on a project environment into categories revealing varying degrees of flexibility that are hypothetically possible. Abrahamsson (1977: 30) defined four kinds of rules governing an administrative system: goal formulations; procedural rules; rules indicating what cannot be done; and formalizations of rules inflicted from external power centers. Such an investigation would uncover a number of procedures that potential participants could challenge as based on nothing more than internal bureaucratic convenience or control imperatives, not efficacy in reaching goals. Agricultural credit projects routinely discriminate against the poor by applying capitalist norms of creditworthiness; mobilized peasants could argue for a low maximum individual loan ceiling instead of the typical high minimum ceiling. Each class of traditional projects contains similar exclusionary premises.

The strategic response from the bottom would focus initially less on goal creation and more on the way the implementing agency will actually behave. Any tactic not specifically excluded can certainly be considered. No project paper ever says *do not* mobilize poor peasants into base organizations. Naturally, then, the content of such a process could be up to the local initiator to whatever extent he or she gained local support. Another arena is the gap between prevailing legislation and its enforcement by regional and local authorities; major advances in empowerment can be attained by the application of legal resources at points never before challenged.

The importance of timing and context cannot be overemphasized in planning alternatives or additions to a project. Implementation takes place not just as an interaction between a donor agency and poor people. The surrounding environment impinges, and the project entity takes on a life of its own. Particularly important are the relevant bureaucracies of the host government and their attitudes toward rules and procedures. Moris developed a long list of attributes of African field administration. One sample is enough to suggest how permeable the process really is:

> There is a flexible attitude toward plans which are viewed as paper commitments mirroring a certain situation in power relationships at one point in time. Power relationships and circumstances change; as they do, so will the urgency of carrying our mutually agreed actions. If there is any uncertainty about the authority relationships, implementation will be held in abeyance (Moris, in Black et al., 1977: 79).

This suggests much about the potential efficacy of donor agencies' planning and even more about the participation of the poor. To participate the poor must have impact on those in power. But poverty and powerlessness breed each other in a vicious circle. In many development settings, in sum, if donor agency plans and procedures are not conducive to participation, the catalyst is not otherwise present to break that circle.

There is a further, and I believe more elegant, way to see the participatory appropriateness of donor agency procedures and the institutional arrangements that become the framework of the project environment. For poor people to participate, as for any aspect of the project to advance, procedures have to be simple. The fewer the decision makers and decision points, the faster and smoother anything goes.

This commonsense conclusion is best documented in the classic study of a U.S. federally funded development project in downtown Oakland (California) in the late 1960s. In studying the actual decision making, Pressman and Wildavsky found that it was far from enough that participants agreed on project ends. There were many reasons why individuals might oppose, delay, or cause to fail by omission any particular action necessary to attain the agreed goals. Quantifying the potential for success in such a situation of relative agreement and goodwill led to the results in Table 10.1.

The central point for participatory development is that complexity of procedures and project organizational structure adds more decision points. That means more chances of delay or failure when or if processes that might enhance participation are up for consideration. Given the overall hostility of other project actors and the high probability of conflicting rather than harmonious perceptions of what the project is or could be doing, as shown by Blair (1978), Adams (1977), Emmerson (1976), and many others, there is little reason to hope that participatory development can flourish by trying to run any significant magnitude of procedural hurdles. Local level

TABLE 10.1 Program Completion Doubtful Unless Level of Agreement among Participants Is Terribly High

Probability of Agreement on Each Clearance Point (in percent)	Probability of Success after 70 Clearances	No. of Agreements That Reduce Probability below 50 Percent
80	.000000125	4
90	.000644	7
95	.00395	14
99	.489	68

Source: Pressman and Wildavsky, 1973: 107.

projects designed by foreigners to be implemented through national agencies cannot avoid this quandary.

Three other issues, aside from complexity of rules and procedures, are important for participation in project implementation and could be considered as issues of appropriate implementation procedures. One is the physical and institutional separation of those who plan from those who implement in major donor agencies. On the surface this appears a relatively inevitable cost in efficiency and practicality. Projects take many years to complete. It is unusual for an official to be assigned to one country more than three or four years. Often it is less. Consultants work a few weeks or months on one segment, unlikely to be associated again. No one in the donor agency thus develops any institutional need to assure any aspect of project success or excellence. That includes effective participation by the poor (Siffin, 1979; Korten, 1979b; Mickelwait et al., 1978b).

Some argue that this division of work is inevitable. So it is, as long as the sharp division between large organization and people is maintained. This division serves elite interests and those of the administrator class who seek control over professionals. One can begin an operational response by decentralizing work and building local capacity. But this is at best a partial solution. Can one plan a logical series of steps to move from point A to point B in a development situation? There is much to suggest that what was developed for a static productive environment and workers of a single culture will not work neatly, if at all, in a situation of a change or multiple cultures. Consider now more specifically what the Pressman and Wildavsky study found could discourage implementation from moving ahead:

(1) Direct incompatibility with other commitments
(2) No direct incompatibility but a preference for other programs
(3) Simultaneous commitments to other projects
(4) Dependence on others who lack a sense of urgency in the project
(5) Differences of opinion on leadership and proper organizational roles
(6) Legal and procedural differences
(7) Agreement coupled with lack of power

(Pressman and Wildavsky, 1973: 99-102)

In other words, an organizational process designed for the regularity and continuity of factory production does not meet well the different needs of human development. It is illogical to think that the optimum quality of development could result. Part of the answer must be to reduce the number of cultures, power blocks, and organizational entities involved. Small-scale, decentralized, participatory projects do this best.

To continue present project models suggests a sobering underlying conclusion. Quality of the development product matters only to the extent it enhances linkages to the world-system. The impact on people is largely irrelevant to organizational welfare. Control is what matters. By dividing planners from implementers, the administrators have made both more dependent on managers. The organization wants clients considered as cases on an assembly line, not as human beings with dreams and rights. A bureaucracy seeks to rationalize social relations. Bureaucrats who become deeply involved in the life of a client are considered either undependable or corrupt (Hummel, 1977: 34 ff). Face-to-face relationships, the foundation of social life, are thus discouraged; in the development world very few donor agency officials actually spend very many, if any, days per year talking to the poor. Thus separation of planners and implementers discourages participation at many levels.

One line of practical response could be to reallocate use of time by donor agency mission personnel. How could the paperwork, now gluing individuals to desks in capital cities, be reduced? Quarterly and monthly reports could be diminished. They could also be redesigned to force people to do field inspections and talk to peasants. The literature on devolutionary administration (Brinkerhoff and Thomas, 1978) and metamanagement (Korten and Alfonso, eds., 1981) contains a number of such practical suggestions. What needs more thought by mid-level bureaucrats is how to convince superiors that better results could be obtained by less top-down control efforts. This leads right back to building local capacity. Only through local empowerment can centralized control really be diminished. Officials in the middle, being paid and promoted from above, face a delicate task. By linking participation to greater productivity it may become, however, a realistic task.

Pressures for comprehensive up-front planning by foreign donors work to exclude peasants in indirect as well as direct ways. Data standards are imposed that are beyond the means of host country officials. Rondinelli terms this the "imperious rationality of international procedures" and argues that Third World governments, with limited administrative abilities often

> delegate some of their most critical administrative functions — the identification, preparation, analysis, selection, execution and evaluation of major development projects — to expatriate experts and consultants. In many cases they conform superficially to imposed requirements without fundamentally changing indigenous behavior or planning and management procedures, or, more often, subvert externally imposed rules to meet [the] indigenous constraints. And perhaps, most importantly, the prescriptions have profound effects on the types of projects developing nations choose and the way they analyze them, which, in the long run may be adverse to their own welfare (Rondinelli, 1976a: 575).

There would seem to be further indirect results. To the extent donor agency procedures organize and soak up the time and creative energy of implementers, there is less of both commodities available for the interplay with beneficiaries that will create institutions and commitments to get the job done.

This is not to argue that implementers do not need continued data inputs, especially upon potential conflicts. But the energies spent in accumulating or concocting what become tables in World Bank appraisal reports do not produce the kind of data necessary for participatory development. This, on occasion, has been admitted. Reviewing its own rural development projects in Africa, the World Bank concluded, inter alia: the data on farmer income was sparse, missing, unreliable, and obviously fabricated; no data existed on the distribution of project effects; all families were assumed to be equally poor; and project reports did not clearly define target groups (IBRD, Report no. 2242, 1978a: 12-13). Participatory development begins only by asking the right questions.

The Bank did revise its project design instructions in August 1978. It has since claimed (IBRD, Report no. 2946, 1980a: xii) that in these revisions "the knowledge of intended beneficiaries, local involvement in the process and the need to ensure country commitment to project objectives were stressed." In 1980 and 1981 project appraisal reports, however, there is no significant improvement in social, political, or institutional analysis. It is still argued, sometimes even directly, that if the project is located in a place containing poor people, the poor people are being helped. In Chapters 6, 7, and 8, alternative analytical approaches for real empowerment are demonstrated.

Comprehensive up-front planning contains as well a bias toward political and economic stability. It is inherently a prescription for planned, orderly, controlled change — a not illogical organizational desire. Development happens, however, on both macro and micro levels, at a very uneven pace that is discomfiting to those few who evaluate its rate and nature. Planning in major donor agencies thus preserves a greater status quo through guiding change that does not disturb power relationships. This theoretical tension with development has never been resolved or faced squarely by donor agencies, although one can point to occasional exceptions.

Several authors (Blair, 1978; Ingle, 1979; Honadle, 1979; and Leonard, 1977, for example) have noted that implementation technology has one other significant weakness. Planners underestimate the political nature of data use and resource allocations. What looks good on paper will often result in the field in further subsidy to a local power group or individual. Given a methodology that does not recognize conflicts, inequities, and the processes by which they are maintained, this is not surprising.

Posit that a donor agency had a typical small farmer credit program in Western Kenya and its implementing agency in turn chose local banks to play the intermediary role. One way authority patterns could get disrupted and resources rerouted could be ethnic ties.

> The bank's sixteen Luhya employees were divided into two neat cliques, both reaching from the managerial level right down to the messengers. The line of division between the two could be accounted for perfectly by lineage alliances. The formation of these two cliques seemed to have been initiated by the manager and accountant, who were engaged in a power struggle. The manager had gained his allies by promoting those in his ethnic group, while the accountant was promising protection and future promotion to those in his (Leonard, 1977: 235).

It would be highly likely that customers for credit would be treated as they related to this power struggle. Myopia by major donor agencies to most of the levels of most of these conflicts and how they are represented in local institutions has been noted. Implementers should begin to create alternatives by examining local conditions with much greater sophistication, rethinking the differences between standard and participatory organizations in that setting, and developing the local contacts suitable for beginning the process of mobilizing base organizations capable of pressuring for reconstitution of development initiatives like this Kenyan effort.

These are in sum the major procedural implications for participatory development of applying the technology of Western planning and public administration to alien tasks in alien environments. Implementers were equipped to deal with political stability and the improvement of existing organizations in a harmonious, equitable society. These conditions did not exist. They then tried to use their tools to redefine or paper over the problems of development. Not surprisingly, it has not worked well in terms of human participation. The situation called for new institutions, new outputs, new behavior on all sides, and enthusiasm for open-ended innovation. Organizations generically do not do such things. Planning in the dark and establishing no responsible link between planners and implementers are not conducive to a quality product. That donor agencies are rewarded for their behaviour suggests a chasm between participatory rhetoric and real intentions or abilities of their sponsors.

ISSUES OF RISK AVERSION OF PROJECT MANAGERS

The logical way that a project manager could or should determine how any aspect, including participatory aspects, of a project are progressing would be to take targets, an appropriate time framework, and some rational criteria out into the field and talk to a reasonable sample of intermediaries and beneficiaries. To assure project quality and uncover problems quickly, one would suppose such an activity would occupy a project manager quite regularly, and often. It does not occupy a project manager. Instead of continued process evaluations, there appear to be several other, more episodic efforts. One cannot investigate very far. Virtually no public discussions are available. Progress reports and most evaluations are closely held. No organization will give external agents the means of judging its competence and legitimacy without profoundly compelling motives. The world-system does not provide them.

Could current forms of evaluations overcome the project manager's natural desire to appear successful and uncover problems that could lead to the realization of more elements of a participatory project? In some donor agencies the only evaluations are those written by the project manager on an annual or biannual basis to fill larger organizational needs. The organization wants a report showing compliance to its project planning, an affirmation that it is still in control. The manager departing from this format very far is in a risky position. Often preordained forms constrict him or her even further by defining specific assumptions, questions, and topics. One of the negative aspects of AID's log frame is its use in this process. The project manager is thus strongly conditioned not to present a picture of his real world uncertainties and why the project is the largely or entirely new animal that it becomes. A project manager, mission officer, or consulting firm seeking a more partici-patory result must seek different and better questions, as Chapter 11 will explore.

A second common model, pursued by some agencies regularly and by others in time of crisis, is an evaluation mission of home office staff and consultants. Such a mission rarely goes in the spirit of an investigative reporter. Its members want to avert risks them-selves. Consultants are concerned with future livelihood. A white-wash does not necessarily result, but overall organizational needs define implicitly or explicitly the boundaries of possible truth. It is difficult for field personnel not to react defensively to such intrusions no matter what spirit the outside evaluators bring to the task. Often political and ideological issues are at stake. Even in the most placid situations, there is no institutional imperative that participatory elements be closely examined unless, and even if, the project paper so mandates.

This points up a central dilemma, noted by Ingle (1979: 75). Between the planning and the realization of participatory develop-ment there must be specific practical procedures of empowerment. Until the organization is guided by an overall set of people-centered principles, built on flexibility and on rewarding managers for taking the risks inherent in the reality of development as permanent experi-ment, managers will act according to the present prevailing norms, avoid risks, and try to provide the larger organization with the data it wants. The result is that continual process evaluations do not happen and project quality suffers. If the larger political environ-ment provides management with the wrong incentives, it is up to mid-level professionals to provide the administrator class with better alternatives. The World Bank Staff Association, for example, made a few strides on quality of work life issues in the late 1970s. Scott and Hart (1979) conclude their study of *Organizational America* with a direct plea to the professional for heroic action: "The professionals must not only rebel against their individual absorption into organizational anonymity, they must also assume the burden of leadership in fundamentally reforming modern organizations" (Scott and Hart, 1979: 228). When political appointees bring less and less knowledge to donor agencies, do professionals have any other alternative?

There are more than the obvious costs with such a status quo. There are frequent occasions where risk aversion does not have a neutral impact on all potential beneficiaries but works instead to facilitate allocation to the wealthier and to ensure the continued powerlessness of the poor. Blair has demonstrated this very clearly in several ways in an essay on the Comilla project in Bangladesh:

> Since all these developments took an immense amount of time and energy, the care devoted to any one aspect of the operation necessarily diminished: the criteria for loans became less stringent; the farmers were allowed to take out new loans without repaying old ones; administrative officers were given quotas for loan issue to be disbursed; cooperative managers were promoted to inspector in spite of poor personal repayment records. Villagers found amid the slack supervision that they could start up new societies with bogus memberships so that a few men could get all the loan money. . . . (Blair, 1978: 74).

Blair concludes pessimistically that beyond a certain size, a program will almost necessarily be perverted by local elites. I would argue here, as in previous chapters, that the basis for an alternative is a matter of anticipating potential aggrandizement by local elites and designing into the project the scale and quality of institutions that will prevent it. This also implies that project managers and their subordinates have the vision, motive, freedom, and ability to see such issues and continue to redesign the project to meet further challenges of this nature.

ISSUES OF SLOW ADJUSTMENT TO PROBLEMS AND THE NEED TO REDESIGN

It has been noted by several general surveys, but not in as many published case studies as one might wish, that the donor organization tends not to grant various levels and kinds of decision making to project managers, to the detriment of project quality and efficiency. Here is one of the most fundamental dilemmas of sending the social form known as an organization off to deal in the matter of human development. The organization seeks control. But it cannot control what it does not know. It cannot know until it learns. It cannot learn unless it gives members the freedom to learn. It cannot give freedom without having its control threatened. Donor agencies tend to underestimate how much the project manager has to learn, how difficult it is when so many people have to learn together, and how the one-directionality of bureaucratic language works against the give and take that is necessary for learning.

The problems that can accrue when a manager lacks authority to act in specific situations are considerable and diverse. Honadle (in Honadle and Klauss, eds., 1979: 99-110) suggests some samples: delays to project activities lead to losses by beneficiaries who gambled on inputs arriving; delays to needed remedial action to the point when the action is no longer the appropriate one; and lack of direction to the field, creating confusion, allowing benefits to be siphoned off. He argues that there is no generic project organization, that "appropriate project organizations are situational." The paper that follows is an exploration of how to anticipate particular road-blocks. How funds will flow can be explored by examining the number of decision points and the presence and nature of incentive for cooperation, for instance. Given the kinds of data necessary for participatory development, as outlined previously, many kinds of anticipations are possible. Conversely the less empowerment and dialogue, the less project managers will know about potential problems and how to deal with them.

A further and more direct implication for participatory development (also one concerning the internal institutional quality of life) is how distribution of authority can alter the project manager's basic orientation to the job and the people in it. A traditional bureaucracy grants the manager low power and opportunity, producing a top-down orientation in his self-perception. A participatory bureaucracy that grants the manager high power and high opportunities will produce a bottom-up orientation in his self-perception. Brinkerhoff (1978 and 1980) has begun to explore how managerial style relates to empowerment. In the conventional organization the project manager is an administrator coping with change. He sees clients as targets, particularly as inexpert intruders, and human needs as a collection of categories. Conversely the participatory bureaucrat views himself as a champion of projects and an advocate who influences change. He sees clients as individuals with choices and legitimate participants with human needs requiring comprehensive integrated analysis.

Devolution of authority bears directly on productivity as well as participation. A number of Western corporations have recognized this and have turned toward more decentralized alternatives. Kollmorgen Corp., an electronics firm based in Stamford, Connecticut, has developed broad segmentation that keeps management out of day-to-day problems. As Thames (1981) reports, Kollmorgen runs each of ten divisions and two subsidiaries like a small company; when one grows too big (beyond $15 million annual sales), it is split. "Each division contains manufacturing groups of about 75 employees. Each group's manager is responsible for profit and loss, and for such policy matters as setting price and delivery times, and collecting receivables." The company is doing very well both by its own standards and by those of industry analysts. It helps to be in a growth industry like electronics, but it helps even more to have real decision makers so close to those actually testing the market (the sales force) that its signals can produce quick policy changes. Although not all aspects are parallel, this corporate experience is a compelling argument for a decentralized and smaller-scale organization of development.

The structural implications of a manager's relationship to the larger organization thus have considerable impact on his ability to adapt to change, redesign the project, and get people more effectively involved. The way information flows within the project and between entities in the overall project environment has similar impacts. Mickelwait et al. (1978a and b), has analyzed this in the greatest detail with a number of prescriptions. Cochrane (1979: 71) recapitulates the critical need of information systems showing many reasons why implementation must be as much a learning process as was planning. Tendler (1975: 38-51) describes some of the drawbacks of information systems that do not know how to sort inputs in relation to project goals. She argues that AID institutionalizes criticism by coming to identify with the very interests of the bureaucratic entities it was trying to fend off. Goal displacement is not limited to AID. Even critique and prescription by knowledgeable professionals, however, is not going to the heart of the matter.

Donor agencies spend a disproportionate amount of time and energy dealing with host governments. They spend little or no time talking with poor peasants or even intermediate institutions. It is impossible in such an educational structure to oppose effectively the double nexus of the triple alliance and the comfort organizational inhabitants find in dealing with their own culture. The idea that donor agencies have to act only through governments must be dispelled. Contrary to popular wisdom there is no legal mandate to do so; governments may be members of the World Bank in terms of its management (via the Executive Directors), but there is no reason why the Bank cannot lend to nongovernmental entities. It has lent to corporations, for example. One way professionals can break up the larger political symbiosis at work is to seek out appropriate intermediate institutions and generate projects that will be demonstrably superior. Failure to do this simply tightens the links of the triple alliance, thus insuring the continued marginalization of the poor.

The larger political and educational environment is not the only component of a project manager's incentive structure. Individual education matters also. Uphoff (et al., 1979: 80-82) among others shows the paternalism among development administrators is not limited to any region or ethnic group. The implications of elitism for participation, noted previously in the discussion on planning, continue to affect project quality and human elements. One ripple out effect can be the judgment of priorities. Large World Bank projects set ambitious, short-run production goals to get an internal rate of return sufficiently high to get Bank funding. Elitist perceptions of local abilities then lead to the creation of an alternative project structure. This short-changes the kind of investment in local human capital that would help make the project a long-term success. The implications of this are severe.

> The greater administrative flexibility and financial resources of the autonomous project authorities and the higher salaries and administrative incentives that they may offer to the local staff may also become a source of annoyance and envy to the indigenous administration. An elitist project administration may develop that is not capable of establishing rapport with the normal administrative structure (Lele, 1975: 129).

This is a two-edged sword. Indigenous administration may be equally or more elitist and anti-participatory in nature. Clearly it would be more conducive to participatory development to start by seeking to develop local and regional institutional intermediaries capable of participatory development rather than trying to inflict goals of material production on a particular region. Heyer et al. (1981) contains particularly good African examples of how counterproductive it has been for aid agencies and governments to try to tame peasants by such means.

One is left with a sobering overall conclusion. The donor agency lacks the ability to internalize the idea that change is inevitable and healthy in development designs and projects. It is not apparent that managers get any reward for efforts to redesign projects. The larger system seems to view such efforts as factory slowdowns, threatening the attainment of statistical targets. Thus incentives built into the project cycle at the beginning continue to diminish project quality at this stage. The problems of appropriate human beings for field assignments and the practical issues in recruitment are even more severe than those outlined at the planning stage. Participatory projects clearly demand someone who had not been bureaucratized to manage them. Project managers, as consultants, are poorly positioned to lead a reform to overcome these deeper contradictions between organizational and human welfare.

ISSUES OF IMPLEMENTATION INCENTIVES

How the donor agency defines its goals should have a lot to do with how and why its officials work toward one end product and not another. In development, however, it does not appear to work that way. The implementer is not rewarded or penalized because the road is not built or the production target quota not met. He or she is rewarded by the internal needs of the organization. There are several ways this can be understood. Hummel succinctly abstracts from the decline of one organization, the U.S. Postal Service, this thesis:

> Bureaucracy is concerned with means, society with ends. Here lies the essential difference in the cultural norms associated with each. It is essentially a conflict between control and service. Service, as its name implies, is the outer imperative for which public-service bureaucracy

is established. Control is the inner imperative of any bureaucracy, public or private. The tendency of any bureaucracy is to substitute inner control for outward service (Hummel, 1977: 62).

This represents an initial series of considerations why insuring high levels of participation, even when a rhetorical centerpiece of a project paper, may not be very central to the behaviour of the project implementer.

Donor agencies faced with this generic contradiction have not chosen the direct and straightforward answer: goals and procedures are mutually conflicting so that even marginal success is a problem. Change basic goals or change structures and procedures. If it is not clear or certain what will work, do not create elaborate linear programs and schedules as though a specific path is valid. Instead donor agency bureaucrats in the 1970s have chosen in part to redefine stated goals, pretend they know what will work as they define it, ignore elements that do not fit, and avoid any detailed or substantive evaluation, particularly one that might allow effective participation of project beneficiaries. Implementers, as the street-level bureaucrats (Lipsky, 1980), are caught in the middle of this charade. Simultaneously they are on the cutting edge in the field, having to deal with the real world as opposed to the paper world, and trying to contrive actions that will work or appear to work toward project goals. No one set of universal criteria can sort out how or why one kind of pressure as opposed to another will determine behavior in a given situation.

Planners, however, set quantitative targets that have at least an indirect impact on implementation. It is not a direct impact because individuals are almost never held responsible for failing to meet stated goals. For those goals everyone, the whole team, is responsible; in practice that means no one is responsible. Rarely is one person in charge of a project throughout its duration. Many aspects change over time. It is ultimately considered impractical to judge an individual on qualitative targets, even on whether a segment of a plan is met within an allotted time. No external force, as Chapter 2 described, provides more than superficial financial or human rights incentives except in rare instances. So there is nothing to prevent the application of purely internal organizational norms: lending and disbursement targets, paper pushing, and demonstrations of subordination to authority.

There is not, in sum, any institutionalized incentive to enhance the participation of project beneficiaries in any of the ways suggested in previous chapters. The implementer has to decide that the participation of the poor is a good thing in and of itself. The obstacles to moving from thought to action are immense, like "swimming upstream" as one analyst (Bryant, 1979a) puts it. Dozens have been commented on already. Unless one designed an implementation team with a shared world model, as a few contractors have urged, it is difficult to see how a single individual could have great impact on any but the smallest projects. This suggests that professionals need to create new action committees inside donor agencies, build links with interested public voices and political actors, and work to raise the general level of sophistication up to a point where coherent reform proposals could even be understood by the political systems that would have to embrace them. Such liberal suggestions are contradicted every day by a public media and a political process that effectively excludes voices of change.

Beyond the absence of positive incentives for project implementers are the distracting and negative ones created by needs inside the organization and the forces that sponsor it. Many of the issues have been talked about for some time and been part of aid organizational task force discussions for years. It is widely agreed (Warwick, 1977: 47; Tendler, 1975: 87-88; Mickelwait, et al., 1978a: 216) that the existence of a funding or budgetary cycle, combined with the shapeless, unquantified nature or real (as opposed to paper) development goals, hurts development and the people in it.

If an organization does not spend or commit funds at the rate its funders or management allocates them, it perceives that future funding will be threatened. This leads to pressure at each point in the project cycle to meet disbursement goals internally set. Donor agencies must then generate enough projects per unit time to soak up the allotted funds. This pushes officials toward more capital-intensive approaches and even greater control over host country development administration to ensure their project quality meets donor agency standards. Sometimes an agency will get ahead; a good supply of projects on the shelf ready to go reduces these incentives. Sometimes the regional or country office falls behind; quality takes a beating. In extreme cases, as politics takes over, money just flows under rubrics like commodity import programs.

What the implementer has to work with and its potential impact on people and participation is not hard to imagine.

Given the seriousness of this issue for participatory development or any goal of development professionals, it is curious and worth querying why the situation goes on year after year. One thought is to judge the purpose of the system by what it really does. If foreign aid opens markets, facilitates exports, helps keep "friendly" governments in power, and generally helps smooth troubled waters, then that is why it exists. Rhetoric involving poor people is simply frosting to get liberal support. Aid bureaucrats have not effectively sought change. Donor agency administrators must find something positive about a funding cycle not to challenge its necessity. It would appear that they do. Obligations and spending goals are tools to control the behaviour of subordinates just as project papers are. Unless or until other and better tools for control are granted them, or a new form of social organization is devised that does not have control as its basic imperative, it is unreasonable to think donor agency administrators will view funding cycles as other than a necessary evil with positive uses.

Another central donor agency reality impinging on the entire project cycle and especially the implementer's reality is the widespread use of consultants. Neither donor agencies nor their funding entities have faced the staffing implications of participatory development. But even modest strides in that direction have been recognized as being more people-intensive. Additionally, rises in total funds moved have not been matched by further direct hire staffs. More and more work is thus being done by consultants, leaving donor agency personnel to read contract bids and try to judge if the work produced is anywhere near an unknown potential. It is a very cost-inefficient way to proceed with development that considerably diminishes the resources that could go to the poor. At the same time it creates a self-interested and vigorously self-perpetuating development support industry as the Senate Foreign Relations Committee discovered in a 1978 attempt to diminish the flow of AID resources now funding the U.S. land grant colleges to pursue dozens of identifiably dubious activities.

Hypothetically, the rise of consultants implies the use of more highly qualified personnel for a specific job than might otherwise be available within a donor agency. There are many reasons why very often this does not come to pass. Many agency officials, bouncing from one job to the next, are not capable of distinguishing quality work; development consultants know this and produce mediocre results, knowing they will be rewarded for unchallenging and uncreative activity. A relatively small number of firms have established market preeminence by getting to know the right people and the appealing packaging techniques. For many of them, development is a business of technical rituals; it is difficult to imagine how the participation of poor people would matter to such a world model. Perhaps most disturbing are the body shops that bid on indefinite quantity contracts and put together design or evaluation teams from a collection of résumés on file after they get a contract.

More straightforward corruption is very common. Intellectual corruption, in particular, is endemic. A veritable "alphabet soup of management innovation" flourishes from CPM to ZBB; the many games played and palliatives offered, surveyed by Kline and Buntz (1979) are guided by entrepreneurial instincts far removed from development concerns. Fudged statistics, fancy jargon, and slipshod scholarship are common in both proposals and work products. I have seen papers from major Washington consulting firms that, as a former university teacher, I would not have found acceptable as undergraduate research.

Financial corruption is apparently standard throughout the process. Salaries, expenses, and institutional overhead are routinely padded. There is no obvious way to judge the monetary value of most products. Organizations seem to feel that paying more insures higher quality work, which is demonstrably false more often than not. More blatant activities go on. Preference to minority-owned small business is misused by both parties. Consultants design projects and then seek and win the contract to implement.

What hurts participatory development the most, however, is intellectual timidity. If donor agency officials have many motives not to be creative (Carmichael, 1976: 7), consultants seem to have a compelling set of their own. Rocking the boat is not the usual way of getting rehired. The crux of participatory development is change in power relationships. It is hard to talk about such politically, culturally, ideologically, or institutionally sensitive topics and get a receptive audience. Empirical integrity and highest analytical standards can also be very threatening to basic organizational norms that are more focussed on efficiency. There are, in sum, a number of direct and indirect reasons why widespread use of consultants is not conducive to long-term solution of enhancing participation in development.

It would be unfair, however, to leave the reader with the impression that all consultants behave according to these patterns. As with any human group, development consultants come with diverse skills and motivations. Many of the best deliberately take remote field assignments where they can have major impact on a specific project and minimal contact with bureaucratic authority. With few exceptions they are doers, not writers; much valuable experience is thus accumulated but not widely circulated. Consultants are sometimes successful in using, or being used by, donor officials to produce analysis and advocacy pieces that the political climate in the bureaucracy would not support as an in-house product. Two discouraging results are frequent: the report goes on the shelf unread because officials read little that is not essential to the never ending paper flow; and the consultant has made reemployment difficult.

Several reforms in the use of consultants are called for. The contracting and payment procedures are medieval; "hanging twisting in the wind" is normal, and quality people are deeply alienated by such bureaucratic arrogance. Consultants and agency professionals must combine efforts to force the creation of regular learning spaces in a weekly routine; lip service is paid to development as a learning activity but most people in the field have neither time nor inclination to read. The results for quality of development are appalling; virtually no one involved has read works in either theory or area studies. I have actually had contracts intended to synthesize new literature for agency officials. Implementers in the field need to receive relevant new material on a timely basis; it does not happen now. Major donor agencies have in-house development studies programs; they reach only a portion of the necessary audience. Better would be regular colloquia and seminars within regional and functional bureaus with attendance and performance essential for career promotion and raises. No official should be exempted. Potential appointees to any administrator role should have to pass a basic competency examination. Lawyers, doctors, and other professionals do. I do not wish to advocate the creation of another guild, but the endless string of often well-meaning but typically incompetent ideologues appointed by politicians in Washington is most unlikely to produce participatory development.

The current sponsors, structures, and processes of major donor agencies thus leave little room for more than mild unthreatening reforms. Development officials caught between local elites and national elites or donor agency interests, typically opt for the latter, which pay their salaries and facilitate their careers. Serving as the link between local and national concerns encourages the personalization of communication, not the institutionalization of communication. The latter is what the poor and powerless need to begin down the road of participating in their own future. There are few, if any, donor agency incentives for building such an intermediate institution as a tangible development product in most situations. It is not surprising. This goes back to a very basic premise: for participatory development to prosper and the poor to get any meaningful access to productive assets, the creation and improvement of organizations is more critical than technical or material inputs. Without the former, the latter is largely wasted. Implementers who realize this are not faced with an easy job. The absence of a coherent organizational mandate on this point supporting the multiple kinds of creative activities possible (see D-GAP, 1978 or 1979a and b, for example) is one of the most critical disincentives for participatory development in the entire project cycle.

CONCLUSION – SIX GENERIC DIFFICULTIES FOR PARTICIPATORY DEVELOPMENT

Chapters 9 and 10 have treated the abstract contradictions between organizational needs and the human needs implicit in participatory development. How these abstract contradictions have been translated into practical obstacles has been discussed at each step of project planning and implementation. In between the abstract and the most specific contradictions there are an additional half-dozen or more generic difficulties that are a function of the overall structure of work in donor agencies. These issues are the most critical, for it is difficult to see how participatory development could flourish if any are left unaddressed.

In brief, they are the following. Either too much or too little project management works against participation; both are endemic. Far too much effort of the wrong sort is spent at the front end of the project cycle and almost none trying to find out what the results were or meant. Faith in rational planning is significantly overemphasized. The needs of the project manager are significantly slighted. The cost effectiveness of the use of project resources and personnel time is very poorly considered. Most disturbing of all, the size of the average project of major donor agencies is unrelated to the scale of the immediate needs and abilities of most poor people.

The question of degree of project management has long been caught up in the larger debate over decentralization and government control in the economy. State socialists opt for government control at the top and, in theory, much participation at the bottom. Capitalists proclaim that minimal governmental control at the top results in human freedom at the bottom. The organizations both produce tend, for different reasons, to seek control of human endeavors, including development. Loveman (1976: 617-18), for one, has described how Soviet state administration and the prevailing academic ideology of U.S. development administrators of the 1960s shared basic authoritarian assumptions and in practice "have . . . progressively increased state and bureaucratic control over human beings." In the twentieth century, neither the left nor the right has solved the apparent contradiction between complex organizations and personal autonomy. Without the latter, participatory development becomes at best partial or artificial.

Before Horvat (1982), few development analysts ventured far into this thicket. It has been noted (Bryant, 1976: 47) that decentralization is not a panacea where local elites stand ready to preempt any productive gains. Yet for participation local-level decision making is essential. The analysis must be developed far beyond this contradiction. Two episodes, one from the external work environment of aid organizations and one from the internal work environment, suggest avenues of attack.

Blair demonstrated in rural Bangladesh how bureaucratic focus on default meant that loans went to bigger farmers. It did not matter that they defaulted more often.

> . . . this is irrelevant. What is relevant is that the bureaucracy be able to defend itself against a charge of fiscal irresponsibility in its distribution policy by showing that it lends only to the "best" credit risks. . . . The wise bureaucracy as a whole, in seeking to show objective measures of progress, tries to minimize default, but in so doing forces officials to pursue policies that in fact tend to maximize default. Too much

supervision, just like too little supervision, results in the benefits going to the local rich (Blair, 1978: 73-74).

A similarly counterproductive paradox emerges inside the donor organization in an equally nonparticipatory work structure. Innovation from below to solve problems is not unreasonable as a goal of management. But management's own failure to participate stifles the possibility, as this analysis of World Bank culture suggests:

> What all this means in practice is that the Vice Presidents cannot expect their staff to solve any of the major problems unless they themselves will be committed and involved in every step of the change process. In their absence all other managers are continually trying to outguess the VP who in turn will pick and choose what meets his limited understanding at the time results are presented to him. . . . nor will he understand the depth of how and why the staff had gotten to where they have. The process remains essentially an uncooperative one bound to frustrate everyone (Carmichael, 1976: 7).

How to determine the appropriate level of supervision for participatory development thus involves an awesomely complex inquiry into the interplay of the internal and external work environments of donor organizations. Such an inquiry has barely begun.

Beyond the structure of work is the focus of work. Dozens of the constraints to participatory development raised in previous pages are tied directly or indirectly to the front-end bias in the donor agency's handling of the project cycle. Biting criticism of the illogicality of this is found in several recent studies.

> . . . any system which promotes detailed planning years in advance, by people who are neither going to be responsible for implementation nor even likely to be involved in the implementation of the project, is almost surely going to be ineffectual (Strachan, 1978: 473).

To which, with a modicum of diplomacy, DAI has added:

> To place the emphasis on upfront planning and justification of the design, when the state of the art in development assistance is such that there are no certain paths to follow, is a clear instance of misplaced priorities and incentives (Mickelwait et al., 1978: 214).

How people can be expected to participate in any authentic fashion when bureaucrats far away have already made most of the basic decisions shaping a forthcoming development process must be an interesting exercise in intellectual gymnastics.

Beyond the focus of work is the ideology of work. This chapter and others have commented on the faith in rational planning within donor organizations as a prime means of gaining control. Long lead times, high financial costs for the organization, implementation obstacles, and diverse counterproductive behavior from other actors in the project environment have been acceptable costs for the larger organization to maintain this faith in the rationality of planning. All of these costs lessen project quality. They work against participation of the poor. The poor do not have time for pointless meetings and paper pushing. They cannot play political and bureaucratic games from their village to Washington and back. This book has already shown that it is the peasants who are rational, not the planners.

Beyond the ideology of work is its human cost for the developing society. It has occurred to very few Western authors (Chambers, 1977: 10-12; Strachan, 1978: 475) that the application of large numbers of the host country's administrators to the needs of relatively few donor agency projects may not be a very cost-effective use of human capital by a developing country. The enforced preparation of project documents, the collection of statistics, and the implementation of large projects are all people-intensive. Like inappropriate material technology, such a use of human capital produces a smaller, more elitist and more capital-intensive nucleus of administrative cadre than is appropriate for the optimum development progress of poor countries. It teaches these administrators many habits unsuited for participatory development. Large-scale, capital-intensive projects are scarcely what poor countries can afford to try on their own. That so many try anyway is a clear commentary on many national and international forces. That there is apparently no detailed investigation of this contradiction, no development of analytical criteria by which developing countries can measure comparative costs, and little visible consciousness of this as an issue in the West is yet a further series of obstacles to a development path wherein the poor have much of a chance.

Beyond the human costs of misstructured work are the impracticalities and failures that result by not equipping the implementer of the work properly. Donor organizations treat the project manager, like the project itself, as a function of its needs. It is not surprising that implementers do not receive the resources and do not have the motives necessary for creative adaptation to changing possibilities in a project environment. A development system built on the top-down infusion of technology and resources as the development solution for poor people would not easily focus on any human component. Its basic nature thus precludes an initial concern with encouraging the resourcefulness of people, both project managers and participants. It is a question of the initial premise: is development more fundamentally a matter of proper organization or of additional resources? Support of the former implies that poor countries and poor people cannot afford those organizations like donor aid organizations that pursue the latter premise. This suggests that if development strategies are to change, processes by which societies make development-related decisions must be studied and changed (Korten, 1979b: 33).

One further generic point remains. Donor agency projects are typically too big for people to participate in effectively. No other thesis in the literature is so consistently endorsed. Tendler (1975: 85 ff) and Chambers (1974: 150-55) discuss in some detail the organizational economy of large projects. The issue of size has intruded on many issues raised already. Organizational need for control generates a great deal of paperwork; the more money flowing per unit of paperwork the more economical and effective both the bureaucrat and the organization as a whole are perceived to be by outsiders and sponsors. Not surprisingly, the organization is sympathetic to a development strategy that meshes with its needs. As a large organization it needs large, homogenized products if central control is to have even a superficial method to use for evaluation. There are thus compelling reasons not to think about small and diverse projects. Organizational sponsors certainly agree.

Rhetoric aside, major donor agencies have not come to grips with the basic contradiction between large projects and helping very poor people. Large projects violate every premise of participatory development. Top-down blueprints preempt most basic decision making in initiation and design. Powerless people cannot suddenly act effectively and with wisdom in institutions and on issues far beyond the scale of their previous concerns. Even when large projects design participatory mechanisms, it is inherently a top-down exercise in social engineering; this denies the poor the possibility of developing their own creative skills, which is the process of development with the greatest long-term potential for human welfare.

Size has many more implications. Large amounts of resources flowing into an environment ensure efforts by local elites to siphon them off; the larger the project the less likely it is that the poor will be protected in practice by the institutional linkages designed for that purpose. Large projects are prone to supply inappropriately large-scale technology, creating new dependencies and reproducing further social and economic inequalities. Large projects are many people's responsibility, so they are no one's; issues like ecological quality are slighted. Large projects imply quantities and quality of paperwork beyond the abilities of poor regions and their administrative cadre, further undermining self-reliance. Large infusions of resources raise expectations, but it is questionable if what they do can be sustained over time without participation mechanisms. The Third World is filled with roads built by donor agencies but never maintained thereafter. If people matter, in sum, small is indeed beautiful.

It would not be honest to conclude that the sum of reforms suggested in Chapters 9 and 10 constitute more than palliatives. They will not produce mass empowerment. Procedures at every step of project design and implementation work against participatory development. These procedures come from the fundamental imperative of the organization, the need to control. Organizations are, in turn, reflections of the larger political and economic forces that sponsor them as useful tools. It is illogical to think that donor agencies alone could surmount the contradiction. Individuals inside and outside aid agencies can seek to capture some agency resources for processes of authentic empowerment. This is, however, no real solution for the world's poor. The large organizational form and authoritarian style are inappropriate to human development, some kinds of infrastructure projects aside. The question for those who choose to continue the struggle from within is this: Can any combination of internal and external pressures force changes in both organizational reward systems and feedback mechanisms enough to change fundamentally the scale and processes of development to begin real empowerment? The most practical approach to building local capacity is going to be the creation of better mechanisms and measures of evaluation. It is to this topic that Chapter 11 now turns.

11

Evaluation As If Development Quality Mattered

Evaluation in development, as in most human activities, is neither a neutral nor a popular pastime. Those who plan and implement development projects do not want to see critical information surface that could hurt careers or paychecks. Those who benefit most from project activities do not want this noticed in a way that would threaten their gains. Benefits are often concentrated among a small elite who have used the project as a confidence mechanism, a process of maintaining and enhancing their economic and political advantage. Open discussion would not be profitable. It is little wonder that development evaluation, as historically practiced by major donor agencies, does not provide the systems feedback that would result in major systemic change or improvement.

The thesis of this chapter is that without mass empowerment in the evaluation process, the interests of the majority will not be served. The more removed evaluation is from the people and the processes involved in design and implementation, the more likely the evaluation product will reflect external bureaucratic and political needs. The only way to counter elite interests is to build a constituency that will support and carry out such an alternative approach. The essence of such an approach is better citizenship. Individuals need to mature by *conscientization* to develop their own critical faculties, their own abilities to be knowledgeable and constructive critics. The growth of an evaluative personality is opposed by all cultural and political processes of the status quo. Elitist societies, both capitalist and state socialist, typically do not reward critics. Yet without developing the degree of psychological security and social trust to be able to give and receive constructive criticism, an individual remains the object of manipulation and exploitation by others. Humans are capable of more.

Chapter 6 set forth the educational process to generate the self-transformation from subject to citizen. The task for this chapter is to begin to fashion appropriate evaluation tools for the citizen in base and intermediate organizations. Readers now inside donor agencies may also wish to explore ways of making evaluation more participatory, more honest, and more effective. Suggestions for systems engineering and metapolitical reform within donor agencies will be offered. In many ways they will parallel those made for peasants and base organizations. The political and bureaucratic obstacles to overcome are largely similar in the two arenas. Human frailties and insecurities are universal conditions.

Without clearing away the prevailing methodological dogma of cost-benefit analysis and related approaches, however, new suggestions are not likely to be well received. Education can be imprisoning as well as liberating. The familiar is the comfortable. The familiar will be shown to be part of the problem, part of an economic ideology masquerading as a scientific method. Thus the initial section of this chapter will uncover the enormous range of problems hidden beneath the simple query about any part of any evaluation – the question of who benefits. Sections that follow will then investigate small samples of evaluation material from two institutional sources – the World Bank and AID; space does not really permit merited coverage of the UN agencies and the PVO (private voluntary organization) community. To what extent have their evaluations recognized any of these philosophical and practical contradictions and to what extent could any evaluation have more than a marginal impact on present or future projects? Alternative solutions then form the last part of the chapter.

THE THEORETICAL TRAPS IN THE EVALUATION OF SOCIAL PROCESS

No form of social inquiry or analysis can be unbiased. No writer or analyst can completely escape the impact of being part of a particular moment in history and having lived through preceding periods. My own particular career was profoundly shaped by the death of Kennedy, the Vietnam War, the work of specific scholars, a dissertation on the world of Vietnamese peasants in the colonial era, and much else. In like manner no one can totally leave behind one's cultural conditioning. One is part of a mode of production, prey to the process of commodification, the imperatives of organizations, and the ambitions of individual and collective political forces. The means of communication and the language itself are the products of that social reality. Thus no evaluation of human development can be a neutral exercise. The critical first step is to develop a defensible situational context.

To create any sense of context one begins with the questions, Development for whom and for what? Context can be broken down in two ways. The evaluation process itself can be divided into at least these six parts: funding; choice of questions; methodological design; implementation; distribution and readership; and use. The potential actors at any stage are quite numerous. In Figure 11.1, I have arranged an illustrative list against the different steps in any evaluation to give a visual image of the enormous potential variety. No effort seems merited to eliminate a few of the blocks that at this moment look improbable. Poor village women are not going to fund and design an evaluation to which World Bank administrators will pay any attention. But after conscientization and the formation of base organizations, they will certainly have both the ability and the desire. Obbo (1980), for example, chronicles the sophisticated strategies for survival of poor Ugandan women; it takes more than a little evaluative capacity to escape male domination. Spirit possession, hard work, migration, and the manipulation of motherhood and respectability are all applied.

A brief perusal of some of the commonest patterns of evaluation sponsorship, implementation, and use in international development will suggest why tools and approaches to evaluation now in vogue should be considered suspect. The largest quantities of evaluation are, not surprisingly, produced by the World Bank and AID. The Bank prepares two types of evaluations. Mid-level professionals from the project and country departments do regular but quite brief field evaluations during the project implementation phase. Such reports are never publicly released. They are intended to alert Bank managers and host governments to current problems and possible

FIGURE 11.1 Evaluation Processes: Participatory and Conventional

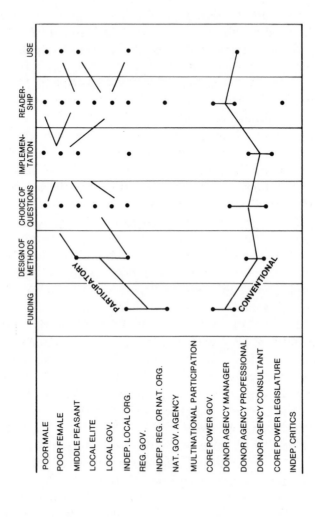

solutions. Upon completion every project is subject to a performance audit report (PPAR) by a separate Operations Evaluation Department. Between March 1972 and June 30, 1981 there were 564 such reports (IBRD, 1981a: preface). They were done by the staff of that department for the Bank management. As audit reports they studied a standard set of technical, insitutional, financial, and scheduling issues. Aggregates are quantified and humans are invisible. Cost-benefit analysis is always applied. One learns little or nothing of actual project impact.

AID is a much less rigid bureaucracy, and most of its evaluations are in the public domain. In recent years there have been three kinds of internal assessments. AID missions enlist AID personnel and contract others to study problem projects or perform mid-term and end-of-project evaluations for the mission's use. Upon completion every project gets a brief ritual look as the project evaluation summary is completed. A central Office of Evaluation selects a certain number of projects for more detailed impact evaluations. These reports, 35 as of June 1982, are more critical and sometimes more sophisticated. They are prepared by interdisciplinary teams of AID and (independent) host country specialists. The primary audience is top AID managers, for whom, one suspects, they are too substantive. Key secondary audiences include the U.S. Congress and AID professionals.

Leaving aside for the moment the issue of quality, consider the cast of characters. All of these reports are funded, implemented, and read almost entirely by representatives and agencies of the core powers in the world-system. A few local actors may have been sought out as sources of data, thus having some impact on some of the topics in AID's impact evaluations. But most of these reports are written for donor agency managers. What does the larger system want of these managers? As Chapter 4 specified in two case studies, projects are the tangible expressions of systemic desires for ordered growth, more cheap food and labor on the one hand and (contradictorily) more consumers on the other. AID managers are to implement such projects within the constraints of funding cycles, financial accountability, and a satisfactory rate of return. Exceptions do, of course, exist.

Larger system incentives are partially and sometimes largely displaced by internal organizational goals, particularly that of pushing money and paper through the system at the approved pace.

Evaluation at any point in the project cycle is viewed like any other system input as either helpful advocacy (an educational tool toward some bureaucratic goal) or as threatening static to be ignored. More likely is the latter response. Critical evaluation implies the need for change. This slows down the paper and money flow. There are regions in the World Bank so bureaucratically programmed that nowhere in the entire project cycle — from initial project identification to final evaluation — is there any receptivity to critique, no matter how constructive.

A micro organizational situation will illuminate this built-in resistance to evaluation of project quality. Anthropologist Alan Hoben has developed from his AID experience a cultural model of what an AID mission director will focus on to decide whether to send a project to Washington for approval. The project's acceptability hinges, in short, on nine aspects of organizational fit: its mesh with effective AID approval process in Washington; with mission ideas on how to relate to the country; with host country national politics; with the line agency responsible; with AID's present project mix in that country; with the mission budget; with mission staff needs; with potential objections from the U.S. ambassador or U.S. congressional elements; and with AID's history on similar projects (Hoben in Barlett, ed., 1980: 352-53). In sum, the factors in decision making are organizationally and politically derived.

In terms of both macro political and micro organizational processes, the development system has effectively excluded anyone, be they supposed project beneficiaries, independent critics, or internal reformers, from enforcing visions of project quality based on optimum scale use of resources and mass welfare. Incremental reforms are possible in favorable political or bureaucratic moments. But the overall environment of project evaluation, and country assessment as Chapter 4 chronicled, is one of meshing larger world-system needs with internal bureaucratic imperatives. Specific development evaluations of the major donor agencies must be approached from this basic framework.

When one looks then at the ubiquitous exercise termed cost-benefit analysis, the most widely known and applied tool of a priori project assessment, one must first understand why the world-system and its agents find it so suitable. There have been many renditions of this theory in World Bank and other literature; most well known are probably Little and Mirrlees (1974) and Squire and van der Tak

(1975). The critical literature is, in contrast, tiny; years of searching turned up only Franco (in Amin et al., 1975) and Barnett (in Heyer et al., eds., 1981). Evaluation of foreign aid is both underdeveloped and badly developed.

Cost-benefit analysis asserts that one can measure any activity as one would the profits of a private firm: income less expenses equals profits. Social development, despite often vaguely defined objectives, can be measured in the same manner. The basic logic has been expressed in this classic statement.

> The essence of a cost benefit analysis is that it does *not* accept that actual receipts adequately measure social benefits and actual expenditures, social costs. But it does accept that actual receipts and expenditures can be suitably adjusted so that the difference between them, which is therefore very closely analogous to ordinary profit, will properly reflect the social gain. The prices used, after such adjustments have been made, will be called 'social accounting prices', or for short 'accounting prices'. The difference between receipts and costs measured at accounting prices is, therefore, most appropriately called 'social profit' (Little and Mirrlees, 1974: 19).
> (quoted by Barnett, in Heyer et al., eds., 1981: 307)

As hundreds of World Bank documents have shown, one can assign ever more shadowy prices to whatever needs to be priced. One can also account goods, services, costs, and any other factor in enough different ways to come out virtually every time within the organizationally acceptable range of rate of return.

What matters more than internal inconsistencies in application are the implicit biases in the method as a whole: benefit for whom; system expansion and status quo; and the mystification of social conflict and process. Barnett (1981) gathers these ideas neatly into the phrase "black-box fallacy." A few aspects of each element suffice.

Benefit for whom is obviously the crux of development. Figure 11.1 suggested the outline of a system of unequal players. Representatives of the state or of the donor agency are not neutral actors in a mathematical exercise. They measure costs and benefits as they perceive them. The cognitive reality of a peasant is necessarily different. To the extent that the state sees development as the subjugation or capture of the peasant (Adams, in Heyer et al., eds., 1981), measurement of costs and benefits are particularly disparate. In like manner the efficient use of resources is a social and situational judgment. Projects are put in motion by state authorities; states in most societies represent the interests of economic elites. Projects implanted in normally stratified societies and devoid of processes of empowerment, the typical World Bank project, serve to reinforce imperfect markets through unequal decisions. Social results cannot be optimal. (Franco, in Amin et al., 1975: 116). It is one thing to manage a firm as a unit and calculate its profit as a unit. But society cannot be managed as a firm; as has been analyzed, a project contains many actors with varying degrees of control over parts of the system. Even if some statistical game shows society as a whole benefiting, that says nothing about how the benefits are shared (Barnett, in Heyer et al., eds., 1981: 309).

The degree to which the concept of the project and its evaluation serve to expand and deepen the status quo, amidst much rhetoric of change, has been skillfully mystified. If, for example, one calculates a rate of return over 20 years, one must suppose that rates of interest, market behavior, and much else will remain structurally intact. The present system, capitalist or etatist, each with its open-ended exclusionary processes, will be reinforced and expanded. It may result in growth, but not in development. Working through existing political structures toward production goals by the corporatist strategies of defensive or offensive modernization will not empower people. The propaganda dimension of social science is useful for politicians and bureaucrats who want to hide the normative basis of elitist decision making. It is a shortsighted approach, however, because unempowered people will not have the incentive to invest capital and labor in ways that will reverse stagnating national food systems and deteriorating fiscal situations.

The artificiality of cost-benefit analysis reaches its height when one gets down to its practical implementation. One has to assign quantitative values for human health, preservation of the commons, and other social realities the project affects. That cannot be done apolitically, as one is standing somewhere in the political context when one makes the judgment. Measurement is limited to tangible inputs and outputs. Surface economic trends alone can be deceiving; AID reviewed (Steinberg et al., 1980a) a Philippine irrigation project in which the yields went up but the costs of inputs went up further and faster, progressively impoverishing the trapped peasants. The cost-benefit model has no way to explore the process of implementation because it is ahistorical and has no notion of the idea of a process. The project, by definition is a process, a process of change.

One of the clearest summations of the resulting real world contradictions comes in Barnett's evaluation of the Sudanese irrigation project known as the Gezira Scheme, a long-term effort that dates from 1925. His most recent paper concludes with a synopsis that shows precisely how the *nas tayyibin* (rich people) permanently entrap and impoverish the poor.

(i) An account of the history of the establishment of the Scheme shows how the original land owners, at least largely coterminous with the *nas tayyibin*, were able, through provision of credit and involvement in trade, to increase their participation in circulation and the state. At the same time they maintain their dominant position in the local communities.

(ii) There was a failure to recognise that the domestic development cycle of tenant families would make the tenants dependent on informal sources of credit, and thus on the *nas tayyibin*. This ensured that they were trapped as price takers in relation to the labour they had to employ in order to meet the terms of their contract.

(iii) Together, these two processes produce a situation where distribution of the benefits of the Scheme is unequal and the Scheme can promise no reversal of this state of affairs.

(iv) The tenants' consciousness of their situation effectively lowers the level of cotton production, as they decide that labour expended on millet has a higher return than labour expended on cotton.

(v) The form of the organisation makes it unresponsive to new information from the field level. This results in wasteful water use. The novel system of water economy which the tenants have developed is actually illegal in terms of the organisation's rules.

(vi) The organisation, operating on an assumption that tenants do not change, becomes inappropriate to the operation of the Scheme. The organisation is designed to cope with a stable situation, but in its very nature a rural development project is dynamic and changing.

(Barnett, in Heyer et al., eds., 1981: 323)

A March 1982 evaluation of the AID-supported Rahad Irrigation Project (Benedict et al., 1982) shows comparable corporatist and exclusionary structures. During 1980-81 the World Bank embarked on several similar projects (White Nile, Blue Nile, New Halfa) in Sudan, proving once more the bureaucratic imperative for self-perpetuation: failure of a policy means not enough resources applied, so spend more.

COMMON BIASES IN DATA COLLECTION AND SYNTHESIS

The social context of bureaucracy and elite politics has dictated not just an inappropriate theory of evaluation but also limited and biased means of data collection and synthesis. Aid agencies have focussed on a broad range of technical issues; the 10 working papers from the 1980 World Bank project, the Living Standards Measurement Study (LSMS), provide a good sample. Symptomatic is this definition of the "basic problems of measurement": "operational and readily comprehensible concepts" cost and relevance "to the needs of policymakers" (Saunders and Grootaert, 1980: 46). The propriety of collecting personal data goes unaddressed in most situations. Bureaucrats and political elites share what Senator William Fulbright called the arrogance of power. They do not ask whether it is right or proper to have such personal data. Instead they define their own needs and act. This contrasts sharply with domestic U.S. practices.

The serious analysts in the World Bank and elsewhere (Freeman, et al., 1979; Dupriez, 1979; Chambers, 1980; etc.) are aware that people in all countries lie to census takers and surveyors, especially about financial issues. Why do people lie? That issue is rarely raised because, if carried any distance, it calls into question the legitimacy not just of the research but of the sponsoring organizations. If governments really represented mass interests, the mass would understand and respond with integrity to tangible legitimacy. The poor in the Third World lie because they have long experience with outside agents. That experience is negative. Governments are parasites. One of the central purposes of participatory development is to build base and intermediate organizations that are perceived by local inhabitants as so legitimate that sensitive socioeconomic data can be collected for local use for popularly defined social purposes. Without rebuilding local institutions in a truly democratic way, no amount of cajolery and coercion from the outside will suffice. Sober study of Western data on OECD (Organization for Economic Cooperation and Development) countries suggests similar problems, rendering suspect, for example, legions of tables pretending that income data is comparable (McGranahan, 1979).

Poverty has perceptual and social aspects as well as quantitative dimensions. The limitations of the outsider are many. The bias of professional training works against understanding the holistic view of the peasant and his experiencing of five aspects of what Chambers (1980: 5) calls integrated rural poverty: assetlessness; physical weaknesses; vulnerability to contingencies; powerlessness; and spatial, social, and intellectual isolation. To the extent observers take their own professional pedigrees seriously, they cannot really learn effectively from or with others. It is not just a matter of elitism in financial and technical dimensions. The way people perceive is conditioned by both social and historical context. A child in the United States now grows up with computers as a norm; the parents must make a conscious effort to accept what they did not grow up with. It is a different way of perceiving. Take away the common culture and language, the situation between Western observer and Third World peasant, and there is a much broader cognitive gap. The outsider may count certain tangible items but cannot fully grasp the villager's view of relative poverty. The villager may not even see himself as poor, but rather may see the rich outsider as bankrupt.

The typical visitor to a Third World village from aid agencies enlarges this perceptual gap by the style of visiting, what Chambers has called rural development tourism. The investigation is done in a manner suited to the practical convenience of the visitor. The observer stays on the road, missing the spatial distribution of poverty. He visits the project site, ignoring other areas. He tends to talk to the elite, the men, the participants, those active enough to be there, and those still alive; this avoids the most disadvantaged at every turn. He talks to the most verbal, frequently in polite dialogues orchestrated by local elites. Visits take place in the dry season* (Chambers, 1980: 6ff). This critique, published as a World Bank working paper, may provoke some reforms, but given constraints of time, money, and culture, where would incentive come from to actually implement drastic procedural change?

Even with the most impeccable style of approach, the project visitor cannot expect to find data on most crucial topics easily available. Time does not exist to build personal relations to overcome distrust of outsiders. Baseline data are invariably lacking; project-generated data tend to be on the subject of the project, not the microeconomy as a whole. Given average turnover in project staff, it is often hard to find individuals with long historical memories; this ought to lead to even more, and more varied, discussions

---

*See recent research on seasonality in Chambers et al., eds. (1981).

with project participants, but few reports indicate such thoroughness. To the extent project goals or processes were ill defined at the outset, post facto evaluation is in the eye of the evaluator. Biases in arbitrary judgments are very difficult to weed out; can any indicator of minimum food intake distinguish variation for physical activities, season, age, sex, health, etc.? Many specific assessments are so conditioned by individual circumstances that one wonders at most Third World aggregates on unemployment, income, and the like. Is the urban pedicab driver, on the street for 14 hours to get two hours' worth of rides, underemployed or not?

Partial solutions are offered by several authors. As noted before, the Sussex colloquium (see Chambers, 1980) coined the phrase "rapid rural appraisal" for a method to upgrade rural development tourism. More coherent would be month-long visits by indigenous observers who passively measure all aspects of daily activity. A particularly thoughtful review (Fergany, 1981) suggests several improvements in ways to measure poverty: replace money indicators with goods; devise direct measurements of need fulfillment, not indirect indicators like children enrolled per thousand of population; develop ways of treating poverty as a continuum so that distribution becomes central; construct sets of concrete indicators allowing multivariate analysis. Ultimately, however, one cannot escape the central political questions: Knowledge for whom and for what? Most international discussions prescribe methods too complex for semiliterate Third World peasants. No methods are suggested to describe links between the state of poverty and the processes that create it. Until development is designed and implemented by the poor themselves, evaluation and data collecting will reflect the kinds of selective ignorance and political needs of those who control the process. Some representative samples are now in order.

DEVELOPMENT EVALUATION AS NOW PRACTICED BY THE WORLD BANK

As I have noted before (Gran, 1979a: 296), the amount of serious evaluation literature on international development is neither large nor satisfactory. If one excludes studies produced under quasi-official auspices or as part of the normal workings of the development industry, the amount is far smaller. However, several works in the early 1980s (Heyer et al., eds., 1981; parts of Galli, ed., 1981; and de Janvry, 1981) have significantly advanced both theory and practice, creating a partial basis against which to judge the efforts of aid agencies and previous generations of external critics like Feder, Payer, van der Laar, and Lappé and Collins. All of these recent works have, of course, their own normative positions, critical of the exploitation of the poor. But they also contain a critique based on a foundation of logic that should gain the cognitive respect of any of the actors enumerated in Figure 11.1.

An average project in rural development, a product of efforts by an aid agency and a host government, typically accomplishes at best only a portion of its productive and social goals. Often, even on its own terms, it is a waste of money. The inherent logic of systems analysis explains why. Projects posit multiple goals that are mutually incompatible, such as helping the poor and helping the rich. Projects also pursue goals and means that are essentially antagonistic. This is especially clear in trying to work through central governments, which view peasants as the source of cheap labor and food, devoid of both history and human need. As Heyer and her colleagues put it, to gain maximum benefit,

> governments and foreign companies need to control the conditions under which peasants sell, or even produce their crops. The problem is, however, that they do not control directly the land or labor-power of the peasants. . . . Rural development projects provide one means of soliciting or forcing peasants to conform to the requirements of outsiders (Heyer et al., eds., 1981: 7).

It is not surprising that peasants do not cooperate and do not benefit.

Beyond these essential issues of logic, I shall also consider the quality of donor agency evaluations on their understanding of four central issues of participatory development: self-reliance, local capacity building, mass empowerment, and scale use of resources. To the degree institutional evaluations fail to address these topics, whatever else they attempt, they remain simply system expressions of self-perpetuation and enhancement.

World Bank evaluations focus on the degree to which productive targets and implementation schedules have been met. Time permits only the enumeration of a few simple variables such as number of loans to "small farmers" or number of wells dug. Little or no investigation takes place that would lay bare the quality of the activity. If a road is built, the entire community is assumed to benefit. No thought goes to building up the capacity and legitimacy of local organizations so that regular repairs on the road would take place. If the production does rise, the project gets the credit, as though simple direct links can be proven. If there are minimal production gains, local conditions or limited extension systems are to blame. Blaming the victim avoids system contradictions and dangerous political issues.

A November 1981 World Bank *Handbook on Monitoring and Evaluation of Agriculture and Rural Development Projects* is a sample public guide to the way in which the Bank would have evaluation take place. On page one it accepts the project structure as a given and breaks evaluation down into segments to mystify the idea of a system at work. On the next page the technocratic language of manipulation is introduced; target, impact, beneficiary, inputs, outputs, etc. The author does note the subjectiveness of project assumptions. Evaluation is not a matter of rigor but of what is plausible (p. 21). What is plausible are indicators with hidden assumptions of harmony (pp. 30-46) and data sources (pp. 48-51) that will reinforce elite biases. The advice to field investigators is, in contrast, coherently aware of elite bias, stratification, and the difficulties of outsiders talking to the less vocal. This does not prevent the presentation of several intrusive sample questionnaires in the next sections.

The introduction to the internal literary universe of past World Bank evaluations is the annual concordance or subject guide. A look at the September 1981 report (IBRD, 1981a) reveals in some detail what topics the Bank authors deem important and some overall patterns of project success and failure. The bulk of the projects surveyed were begun in the late 1960s and early 1970s and reflect the norms of the Bank at that time (see Chapter 4). But even brief notations under specific topics suggest that cumulative Bank learning in the Operations Evaluation Department contains sobering overall limits. Very few of the approximately 210 topical headings relate to project participants. Under one agriculture topic (IBRD, 1981a: 145-46) there are several cases of large and middle farmer bias. Only one case (in India) suggests small farmers did well; but one does not know if small is validly defined. Several other cases talk of "socio-economic constraints." One additional topic (IBRD, 1981a: 79-81) is given to "socio-cultural considerations"; issues are mentioned from about 40 projects. The vast majority of comments suggest judgments that were negative. One noted "Bank's insufficient socio-economic knowledge especially in regard to women's role in the project becomes apparent" (in Senegal). But browsing through this reference work as a whole clearly shows that technical, financial, macro institutional issues predominate. Self-reliance, local capacity building, and mass empowerment are not topics; scale use of resources ("cost per beneficiary" on p. 26) is noted in but five evaluations. The cumulative feedback message will not greatly advance authentic development.

Looking at specific reports is one further way to get a sense of the actual Bank process. Two mid-1981 Ghana agricultural evaluations serve for this purpose. One project sought to rehabilitate cocoa production in the Eastern Region. Cocoa production fell over the 1970s, and the Bank blamed a broad range of macroeconomic policies. Project-specific targets (rehabilitation and replanting) were met, but at an 80 percent time overrun and a 148 percent cost overrun. Yields fell, as did income. Loans were not repaid. Low producer prices and labor shortages were bemoaned in detail. The report conclusion is apt: "The project addressed the problems but not the causes; it mopped the floor with the tap running" (IBRD, 1981c: 6). The auditor wondered why, given frequent reports that prices were so poor and farmers so alienated, the Bank did not shift its efforts from a poor project to an attempt to alter poor sectoral policies. The most important lesson was deemed to be that any further lending in the cocoa sector "must be based on a full comprehension of the farmer participation problem" (IBRD, 1981c: 43). Participation is the solution, not the problem. The Bank investigations of Ghana, here and elsewhere, do not go into the interdisciplinary micro issues of participation but recognize only a few of the market topics. No competent macroanalysis was constructed (see Beckman, in Heyer et al., eds., 1981, for such an example) to turn lists of symptoms into a system understanding. The Bank could not face the political implications. Loans to the cocoa sector ceased after the 1975 Ashanti Region project; other loans continued despite the systemic corruption and parasitism of regional and national elite.

The second Ghana project evaluated in mid-1981 was a 1973 sugar rehabilitation effort. It failed at every stage, with production reaching a low of 18 percent of the appraisal target in 1978. The audit apportioned blame in many directions, citing as decisive "political and economic problems, and the resulting bureaucratic indifference and apathy" (IBRD, 1981d: 4). While Bank staff were faulted for not doing a thorough early review on suspending efforts entirely, major attention in the audit was allocated to counter-productive government policies. "This was a technically marginal project from the outset, requiring the timely combination of very specific conditions for its success" (IBRD, 1981d: 41). Given the marginal or failing results of other Ghana projects at the time, it does not appear too much to wonder why more thorough oversight and more hard-nosed politics were not pursued. It is not just a matter of insufficient staff. It is a matter of the politics of avoiding issues like political economy, corruption, and the world-system.

These two samples of Bank failures in a particularly hostile development climate were not selected to suggest that the Bank considers its average project a failure (on the Bank's terms). But it is illuminating that in these situations where projects have clearly failed from all perspectives and face-saving is not possible, analysis centers on symptoms of macroeconomic disease and how they stymied practical implementation. There is little grasp of the range of socioeconomic constraints at the local level; this makes it impos-sible to judge the compatibility of different project goals based on farmer behavior. By ignoring corruption and the real workings of politics and bureaucracy, the fatal mystification of incompatible means and goals was permitted. Finally, if self-reliance, local capacity building, and mass empowerment had been central to the project (or the audit report), they might well have forced significant changes in the macro as well as the micro environment. In sum the two reports are critical, but they are critical of failed growth, not of failed development.

In 1980 two internal reflections on the Bank's project imple-mentation history added some further insights on the Bank's percep-tion of its own efforts. A study of project delays (IBRD, 1980a) found that the 250 projects audited from 1975 through 1978 exceeded their projected schedule by an average 40 percent. Besides issues of contracting, staffing, and design, the author pointed to general ignorance of local areas. This was being remedied, he claimed, by April 1979 revisions of the Project Brief System, in which "knowledge of intended beneficiaries, local involvement in the process, and the need to ensure country commitment to project objectives were stressed" (IBRD, 1980a: xii). I have looked at many post-April 1979 appraisal reports and seen none to date that really reflect those instructions. A review of Bank supervision of its projects (IBRD, 1980b) was even more sanguine that internal reforms were satisfactory: "with few exceptions, the [supervision] mission terms of reference addressed relevant issues" (IBRD, 1980b: iv). Yet that optimism about the value of supervision and evaluation of projects is ultimately refuted in the same report.

> There is, however, a widespread view among Bank staff that these mechanisms do not provide the feedback needed to ensure that relevant experience is generally available. As many as 40% of those interviewed believed that feedback and lessons learned on current projects (other than experience personal to the staff immediately involved) are not used in the design of subsequent projects; another 30% believed that feedback from others' supervision experience only occasionally influenced project design. Even among the remainder, concern was expressed over a perceived lack of cross-Regional lessons. . . . (IBRD, 1980b: 80-81).

Learning is not systematically shared even within a division. It is not clear that supervision or evaluation reports are widely read; the time is not there to do so, even if there is the desire.

It is little wonder, if internal criticism has so little impact on either the Bank professionals or the Executive Directors, that external attack has little chance for constructive change. As a system of money and ideas flowing around the world, the World Bank is in many ways remarkably insular. It is not accountable to national legislatures or to the public. In his efforts to woo the U.S. Congress the most recent Bank President, A. W. Clausen, is making a mild and probably short-lived exception. The vast majority of Bank reports, including all project-related work and most country papers remain internal documents theoretically in perpetuity; in research for Chapter 4, I was unable to get the Bank to admit even to having a policy about historical inquiry. In January 1982 the Bank began charging for the reams of relatively marginal published material, like working papers ($3-5) and public versions of country papers (at $20), that heretofore had been free. Though understandable for certain reasons, this decision will have the effect of making the Bank more remote; most potential critics and most Third World peasants are poor. Third World governments have many reasons not to publicize their projects or to permit independent field evaluations by potential critics. The sum of these efforts is a relatively closed system neither needing nor accepting alternatives.

The system, is, however, breached in two ways. The Bank contracts out a certain amount of basic research and project work. Virtually all research contracts go to fellow adherents of the modernization school and neoclassical economists. Consultants on project appraisal teams are rigidly socialized and their work drastically sanitized; for an illuminating personal memoir of such an experience with a Rwanda agriculture project, see Lemarchand (1982). Despite overall organizational efforts a few new ideas creep in, so that over the last decade the Bank as a whole has managed to stay only three to four intellectual generations out of date.

The second way new ideas occasionally enter is from the work of independent critics. The Bank has found organizational critics (like Tendler, 1975; van der Laar, 1980; and Chambers, 1980) mildly interesting and even noted some of their work in various reports; such efforts have had no impact, however, on the Bank's top-down, blueprint project process. Other critics (notably Galli, ed., 1981; Payer, 1982; de Janvry, 1981; Lappé and Collins, 1977, 1979, and 1980; Gran 1978 and 1979a; and Heyer et al., eds., 1981) have pursued various lines of the political economy thesis: in a stratified society aid channeled through governments helps the rich and hurts the poor. Whether the analysis is based on field research or internal documentation or both makes no difference. The Bank, as part of the elite, cannot afford to grant this argument cognitive respect, so it is simply wished out of view. Occasional media attacks based on leaked documents provoke only a momentary bunker mentality. Neither approach has had any impact on the way projects are processed; at most such attacks have weakened the liberal side of the middle-of-the-road aid lobby in the United States, making it harder to get U.S. funding for one part of the Bank activities, the International Development Association (IDA), the loan window for poorest countries. Without mass mobilization in many countries, it is thus improbable that the Bank will move very far toward authentic development.

This brief review of efforts by the Bank and others to evaluate its work should not end with the assumption that the Bank has never heard of, thought about, or practiced participatory development. The Bank has anomalies among its personnel and activities.

Its former head of policy planning, Mahbub ul Haq, published a book in 1976 refuting export-led growth and arguing for self-reliant development; he stayed around until early 1982, but the book had no policy impact. There was a 1977-78 series of papers from the Policy Planning Division on participation and worker management; they were swallowed by bureaucratic forces. There was at least one urban project in the 1970s that used intermediate institutions in a participatory way. The PIDER Rural Development Project in Mexico also has partially participatory dimensions and local evaluation; weigh the material in Cernea (1979) against the model in Chapters 6 and 7. In 1980 the Bank's Development Economics Department put out a compendium (Knight, ed., 1980) by consultants on implementing programs of human development; with the exception of the essay by Everett Rogers, which is usually quite coherent (see pp. 263, 271ff, 296), this is a particularly disturbing volume. It pretends sophistication and balance in treating different aspects of participation in local organizations. Some perceptive comments emerge, but one gets a general feeling of damning with faint praise; myriad difficulties and limitations are suggested within an overall belief that participation "may well be taken as one measure of human development. . . . [Thus] some kind and degree of beneficiary organization and participation are essential" (Uphoff, in Knight, ed., 1980: 70, 82). But it is to be guided change with the poor playing useful subsidiary roles. One cannot be surprised, for guiding change on behalf of system's elites has been the Bank's task for 35 years.

The World Bank's approach to development evaluation is not the only one among international donors. Certain multilaterals, the Asian Development Bank in particular, have copied the World Bank model. Most other donors have not. They tend to ignore detailed cost-benefit analysis. A more loosely run and decentralized bureaucracy is common. The projects are smaller. Organizational contexts vary, but on average most other agencies seem marginally more open to new ideas and experiments. Some samples should be explored.

AID'S RECENT EVALUATION EFFORTS

AID's environment, as suggested before, impels evaluators to try to please the U.S. Congress and AID administrators. Professionals also see some need for information that will appease AID auditors and a more sceptical U.S. public. Most AID administrators and most people on Capitol Hill (both members of Congress and staff) are not knowledgeable about the fine points of the project process or country situations (see Chapter 2). Evaluations do also go to the internal agency budget office and occasionally to the overall Office of Management and Budget. Most projects get little external scrutiny. Routine postproject summaries follow a standard form and mix descriptive, quantitative, and subjective judgments. Rarely has baseline data been there that would permit really rigorous measurement. The system does not reward brilliance or thoroughness, so few of these reports are noteworthy or much used thereafter. Unlike the World Bank, where the Operations Evaluation Department is structurally separate, AID performs regular evaluations with an assortment of agency personnel versed in the region or the project types. On average they cannot afford to be too critical; the players have to continue working together. The system is, however, far more open, so that provocative, critical work appears irregularly throughout the project cycle.

In the fall of 1979, AID's Office of Evaluation (in the Bureau for Program and Policy Coordination) embarked on a more serious effort to find out what development evaluations have yielded. The AID Administrator wanted a basis for discussions of how to build new standards. Some of the professionals involved were interested in ways to improve future projects or better meet New Directions criteria that aid efforts really do benefit the poor. The result has been several publicly available series of reports: program evaluation discussion papers; program evaluations; project impact evaluations; and special studies. In the marshalling of data and in overall sophistication, these papers are as good as, and sometimes better than, any evaluation work done by any official source in recent years. The studies contain numerous reflections on issues of political economy, bureaucracy, and participation. The relative freedom of AID's bureaucratic operation in Washington, the academic skills of some of those involved, and the interdisciplinary and cross cultural team approach all contributed such understanding.

Yet these reports are also quite limited in certain crucial ways. It is not just that they focus largely on donor agency needs, slightly on host country needs, and very little on needs of project participants. There is a consistent pattern of bureaucratic timidity about concluding policy recommendations, an unwillingness to go where much of the evidence pointed. As an occasional consultant, I understand reasonably well the pressures to bureaucratize language and substance in order to be found acceptable. Yet the result robs the effort of value. It is a neat circular pattern by which new ideas and the interests of the poor remain excluded or poorly represented. A brief look at two impact evaluation studies shows how this works in practice.

The Philippine Small-Scale Irrigation Project, treated in the report of Steinberg et al., contains much hard analysis of how national agencies and the world market work perpetually to disadvantage small farmers. Consider for example the problems of selling the crop.

> One of the major difficulties for many farmers is their inability to sell the product at a price that covers the cost of production, earns them a profit, or provides sufficient income to cover their debts. The governmental institution for buying and selling rice, the National Grain Authority (NGA), offers the fixed price of P.1.30 a kilogram — the highest in the country. Even though most farmers think this amount is too low, they are forced to sell their product at even lower prices to private traders because they are unable to meet the technical standards of NGA. Palay (unhusked rice) presented to the Authority must be 95% pure and have a moisture content of no more than 14%. In most parts of the Philippines, mechanical threshers and driers, which farmers cannot afford, are needed to meet NGA standards, which are geared to quality rice for export or elite internal consumption. The standards are necessary for international marketing and competition, but limit the farmers' ability to raise their income. Furthermore, if farmers sell to NGA, they often do not receive the funds for their produce for up to one month after sale and few are economically able to afford this or even a shorter wait (Steinberg et al., 1980: 4).

In other sections the issues of tenancy and debt are treated in detail. Study of the overall economics of the Irrigators Service Association (ISA) demonstrated that costs rose faster than income. In one appendix there is even a fairly clear assertion that without local level analysis and mass participation, affording a true picture of perceived needs, even purely economic goals will be difficult to reach.

Yet when one reaches the conclusions in the body of the text (Steinberg et al., 1980a: 9-11), several of the major points are quite at odds with evidence already presented (and with other points).

Number six reads: "The Irrigators Service Association is valid and effective because it is built on existing local leadership and is focused on a specific and immediate goal that is important to the farmer." This study, as well as countless others (McCoy, ed., 1982, for example), has shown that it is precisely the local elite, combined with their external links as shown above, that has created and maintained the stratified local society. That local leadership has controlled the new ISA institution and guided the villagers into believing that it has no role beyond agricultural production is another elegant example of elite maintenance. In theory an alternatively designed ISA could have served as a vehicle for smaller, subvillage groups to challenge the status quo. Point seven claimed: "Those farmers being assisted under the FSDC program are the appropriate beneficiaries of A.I.D. assistance under the New Directions." A strategy that reaches some of the moderately poor but not any of the truly poorest can be politely termed a poor man progressive farmer strategy. Indeed, among this set of poor, they may be most able to use the particular kind of world-system lure being offered. The result is not broadly based, participatory development but the creation of new dependencies and social differentiation at the local level. In sum the writers are not afraid to catalog enormous economic and technical contradiction, but such issues are not linked to sociopolitical structure in any operational way.

The Rahad Irrigation Project in Sudan, subject of a report by Benedict et al., is in many ways a stunning indictment of Sudan's corporatist strategy toward agricultural development. Many types of conflicts "between the goals of productivity and equity and between corporate and individual aspirations" are explored. Rahad is a corporation that hires tenants for fully mechanized production. A taste of the overall totalitarianism is in order.

> From recruiting and settling tenants to their possible eviction due to failure to meet contract conditions, the Corporation maintains strict authority. It provides all agricultural inputs and markets and processes the cotton production. More than this, through controlled monitoring and sanctions it supervises what decision-making is to occur on each tenancy and assesses all costs against profits.
>
> The tenancy is a non-mortgagable, non-transferable, 22 fed* farming unit registered in the name of a single responsible individual. Full

---

*Fed = feddan = 1.04 acres or 0.42 hectares.

100 percent intensive rotation of cotton (11 fed), groundnuts (8 fed) and fodder (3 fed) constitute the basis of the farming system. In addition to approximately 12,800 such tenancies, a second category of tenancy is a five fed vegetable/fruit tenancy. The number of these tenancies is uncertain. Livestock tenancies of 12 fed each amounting to a total of 1,296 fed are being created for meat and milk production. Provision was also made for a non-tenant resident laboring population. Theoretically 1/2 of the Rahad population would eventually fall in this category and constitute a labor pool for tenants. The production system is administered and supervised by a hierarchy of inspectors from village to group level. Distribution of Corporation income is based upon the "individual account system" wherein the tenant is assessed the full amount of imputed costs of production inputs, services, and partial water charges. The tenant receives as profits what remains when costs are deducted from gross product receipts.

(Benedict et al., 1982: 5-6)

It is hard to imagine how this productive process could be organized in a less participatory fashion. Yet it is essentially typical of large-scale irrigation in Sudan and what foreign donors have been funding for many years.

The enumeration of lessons learned (Benedict et al., 1982: 17-19) contains two kinds of policy recommendations. Most of the 13 suggestions are palliative in nature. They note technical and organizational reforms that might help this model run with fewer conflicts and more productivity. The model itself is not inherently challenged in any fundamental way. It is apparently satisfactory that one-half of the local population simply sit on the sidelines as a labor pool. Two of the 13 points do, however, argue for more participation by the tenant farmer, whose minimal role in decision making contributes to low productivity. A statement of the obvious does not tell AID managers what to do about it. The writers know that top-down farm management is alienating and that local institutional change can have little impact against continued centralization of power. AID, like the World Bank, has no operational answer to problems that are beyond the scope of a specific project and systemic in nature. Few serious problems are other than systemic. Neither the project nor the proposed changes fall within New Directions guidelines. Nor does this project meet the more specific mandate for AID programs in the Sudan that was legislated (H. RPT. 95-240, pp. 21-22) by the U.S. House of Representatives in the spring of 1977.

AID's best evaluations, in sum, are far more cognizant than efforts by the World Bank that there may be some contradictions among different project goals and between means and goals. In the Sudan it was clear that the project structure impeded gains in productivity. These AID papers showed much less awareness of basic operational dimensions of participatory development like self-reliance, mass empowerment, and scale use of resources. There was much attention to building local capacity, but it was in terms of productivity as opposed to political and social abilities. Healthy human beings cannot grow from such a division.

Space does not permit a proper exploration of varied evaluations of UN and multilateral programs (see UNDP, 1979; Miller, 1979; Kirsch et al., 1980; Dupriez, 1979; and Ledesma, 1980), of the private voluntary agencies (see Barclay, 1979; Schmidt et al., 1981; O'Regan and Hellinger, 1980; Linden, 1976; Lissner, 1977; and Coombs, 1980), and of the most explicitly participatory development agency, the Washington-based Inter-American Foundation (see IAF, 1977; Meehan, 1978; and Tendler, 1981). But it is from primarily these reports that one can begin to get some of the pieces that can be shaped into a model for implanting truly participatory evaluation into social process. It is to this task that the final section of this chapter now turns.

IMPLANTING PARTICIPATORY EVALUATION

Participatory evaluation means that those involved in project design, implementation, and benefits also play the major roles in regular and continuous evaluation of the activity. Ideally the same people, mobilized in base organizations and assisted by intermediate organizations, play all three roles. In this setting the optimum form of process evaluation will result. Most settings are now far from ideal. External funders, working through inappropriate and often counterproductive local organizations, control not just evaluation but the rest of the project process as well. External funders clearly must play some role in evaluation. There must be reasonable accountability for all transfers of resources. It will be one task of this section to provide and justify operational definitions of the key terms in the preceding sentences. The place to start is to meet head-on the theoretical contradictions suggested in preceding pages and, where possible, work through them to participatory strategies. From there this chapter will conclude with some further practical ideas for working within a mobilized society and, less satisfactorily, for efforts from within the present generation of donor agencies.

Since evaluation cannot escape bias, one must start by stating explicitly what the biases are and why they are the defensible ones for a given inquiry. Aid projects, by the rhetoric of the donors and the real needs of the poorest, ought to assist the poor. Thus the solutions that follow are concerned with tools and methods that will accomplish that goal. One is faced then with a division of tasks in the evaluation process: funder, method designer, question designer, implementer, and end user. Different actors from different institutional and political locations cannot help but bring different biases to bear, creating an environment of conflict in which the most powerful prevail and overall product quality reflects it. The poor are not the most powerful. For them to be assured of optimum evaluation in their interest, they must occupy all of the roles in the process. In practical terms the poor may need help with funding and methodological design. But an evaluation in which they do not decide what questions really matter, do not agree to a range of acceptable answers, and do not actually learn the results is not an evaluation of very much practical use. In that case why should they participate?

Evaluations praise the status quo or, with criticism, promote change. Elite actors benefit from the status quo and from change they control. They seek to avoid what might threaten them; little wonder that their evaluations do not talk about power relationships, do not link symptoms to processes, and do not suggest social limits to private property. The essence of development is empowering change. The poor must have such topics addressed in an operational fashion; few outside their ranks can or will do so. As examples in the last section showed, the interest of external agents is to deepen the status quo, guiding a process of growth that does not greatly disturb overall power relationships. Only the poor have the real incentive to pursue their own political interests. Evaluation is a critical tool, not to be preempted by elites. Indeed such preemption robs the poor of both capacity building and political effect.

The poor need an evaluation product that requires a quantity and quality of data quite beyond the abilities of typical elite approaches. The logical alternative is for a mobilized group of poor to collect their own data by recording their own use of time and resources. The process itself can help further mobilization, build functional literacy skills, and develop critical faculties and self-reliance. Collecting and sharing data for authentic developmental purposes is impossible in a typically stratified environment. Quality results require a degree of psychological security and social trust improbable without a mobilized, relatively egalitarian society of true citizens. In sheer practical terms who but the poor themselves can get the detail of household data, labor time use, and situational health needs that real development demands? Elites naturally desire ignorance and a homogenized poor for maximum manipulation. No wonder they are satisfied with the kind and quality of data now customarily accepted by national governments and donor agencies.

Elites are not only motivated to seek the wrong kind of data and not enough data, they are also inclined to research methods and indices suitable to Western social science. Such tools are too complex for partially literate societies. The FAO/ROAP program for one has sought simpler alternatives through field workshops; Ledesma (1980) provides a good introduction to its papers. As suggested earlier, indirect poverty indices are also inappropriate to measure specific aspects of human welfare. Increasing the number of physicians per 100,000 of the population does not guarantee improvement of health and health care. That goal requires broad health education of preventive medicine and a primary health care system with universal access.

Understanding the combination of political and practical necessities of mass participation in development evaluation is not itself an operational answer. Such an answer involves a way to define direct indices and specific organizational processes that are sensitive to general systems analysis and particular institutional settings. These are the final tasks pursued in the following pages.

Developing indices appropriate to mass welfare first means asking questions about scale and cost-effectiveness, not cost-benefit. These questions in turn imply setting social goals as bench marks for progress over finite periods. Elites have generally resisted setting such goals in every society. Setting relatively high goals invites politically threatening disappointment down the road. Setting low goals, more in line with the development models and magnitude of resources now available, invites political unrest now. It is expedient not to set concrete goals or talk about the topic in public. Indeed the world-system endures in part by never admitting that some regions and classes should be permanently impoverished so that other regions and classes can prosper.

A truly democratic society will in contrast wish to set social and economic goals. Many Third World societies have gone through the rhetoric of national planning for periods of one to five years; in few instances have plans represented authentic democratic expressions, mobilized the constituency for implementation, or harnessed and applied the resources called for. But posit here that goals are set for meeting food, job, education, or health levels by a specific future point. A particular route to a given goal implies investment of specific amounts of labor and capital. The next problem comes when, as is all too often the case, needs cannot be met by conceivable resources. Contemporary elites now customarily forge ahead with traditional approaches and try to mystify the gap or to seek to deflate expectations. Neither capitalist nor etatist authorities are exempt. Consider the potential human results in a specific, albeit dated, example, that combines capitalists and etatists, the Dau Tieng Irrigation Project in Vietnam begun in July 1978 with World Bank and other international assistance.

> The entire investment of $110 million will, after five years, produce an incremental 100,000 tons of milled rice annually. This is, by Bank estimate, a tiny fraction of what will be needed in the near future. "With population growing at 2.5-3.0 percent per year and a target consumption of 180 kg per capita, the domestic demand for rice in 1990 would be between 12.2 and 13 million tons, or about double 1977 production" (IBRD, 1978a: 3b). In sum, an investment of $6.5 to $7 billion in international resources would be needed in the next ten years for domestic food expansion alone. This is unlikely in the extreme. Even with a severe decrease in birthrate, the gap looks unbridgeable; the next few projected Bank projects are not in food production, for example (Gran, 1979b: 279).

Clearly labor will have to be far more effectively mobilized through different social forms. Different crops and technical proposals are called for. Vietnam and other societies, by admitting the validity of mass needs, must face its revolutionary consequences on the definition and practice of development.

Appropriate indices are based on overall knowledge of what it ought to cost to do something most efficiently. Very rarely are such real examples tabulated and averaged in a useful way. In an internal World Bank seminar paper (Hasan, 1978: Ann. 9), most of the Bank-sponsored agricultural projects in East Asia (FY73-FY77) were arranged for a statistical portrait. In this set of 48 projects, the dollar cost per job created ranged from $1,290 to about $37,000 (discounting two cases of $57,000 and $405,000). The bulk of the projects showed figures in a range from $4,000 to $8,000. If one took an average in that range and multiplied by the actual number of people needing a job, one would find an investment figure far removed from financial possibility. Looking at a nearby column, the rather mythical "farm families benefited," one can find costs per family from $3.40 to $16,900. Multiply the total number of families in the region who might hypothetically pursue agricultural activities by an average of figures in this column, and again the result would be resource needs far beyond reason.

A democratic political and economic process could, however, proceed along the following lines. If, as in most cases, human beings are poorly rewarded for labor, do not base a strategy on just trying to get more from an investment of scarce capital. Focus instead on the poor person getting more from the investment of his or her labor. Develop a measurement of average return on labor in terms of subsistence rather than on average productivity in terms of abstract market values. Real world cases suggest that, for example, a shift to commercial crops may not be as advantageous to most farmers as elites and aid agencies proclaim. Table 11.1 for example "compares the quantities of food that Togolese farmers could earn in 1975 or thereabouts either by growing food crops themselves or by growing cotton. Productivity per unit of labor in this situation suggests subsistence food production is a much better investment. Focus on this indicator as opposed to overall market figures, and one gets a more valid picture of individual gain or loss.

The practical implications of pursuing this kind of measurement of individual welfare, especially for issues like health or life quality that are not material in nature, are severe. Individuals are the most, in many ways the only, valid judge of their own welfare. A specific list would be presumptuous, although Mazlow's hierarchy (see Chapter 6) could provide suitable topics to start with. What matters, and therefore what should be evaluated, is a function of consciousness level and culture as well as material well-being. An appropriate indicator thus becomes one easy for the individual and small group

TABLE 11.1 Labor Productivity and Food Production in Togo 1975

Food crops	CFAF/kg	Food productivity of one day's work in subsistence farming		Food productivity of one day's work in cotton-growing	
		kg per day	%	kg per day	%
Rice	30	11.5 to 16.6	100	8.8 to 10.8	53 to 108
Beans	60	9.2	100	4.4 to 5.4	48 to 59
Groundnuts	50	8.7	100	5.3 to 6.5	61 to 74
Sorghum	30	17.1	100	8.8 to 10.8	51 to 63
Maize	25	20.8	100	10.6 to 13.0	51 to 62

Note: As this table shows, the farmer who grows cotton and buys his food with the proceeds needs to work approximately 50% longer for a unit of food-stuffs. This loss of productivity in terms of food purchasing power increases sharply if the food has to be bought between seasons or during a shortage.

Source: Dupriez, 1979: 146.

to apply, indicative of social gain or loss, and offering comparability over time and space.

The most critical issue for evaluation then becomes not the development of socially appropriate specific indicators for evaluation but the degree of social development of the individual or group trying to do the evaluation. A base organization whose members had thoroughly studied and absorbed the curriculum outlined in Chapter 6 would have relatively small problems developing a consensus on specific indicators, processes, goals, and uses of an evaluation. A well-run, worker-managed productive entity, Mondragon in Spain, for example (see Thomas and Logan, 1982), has encouraged the growth of an evaluative person capable of judgments about, for instance, why one position merits more reward than another in a workplace. A nonmobilized, fragmented, and hierarchical society must devote enormously greater energies building workable compromises on many issues before evaluation even begins.

Generally, it appears that for the evaluation to be relevant, agreement on several prior issues is essential: 1) the goals of the programme, 2) the nature of programme service (and any variants thereof), 3) measures that indicate the effectiveness of the programme in meeting its goals, 4) methods of selection of participants and controls, 5) allocation of responsibilities for participant selection, data collection, descriptions of programme input, etc., 6) procedures for resolving disagreements between programme and evaluation personnel, and above all, 7) the decisional purposes that evaluation is expected to serve (Hoole, 1978: 165).

Clearly a nonmobilized society is likely to accomplish far less evaluation of a far lower quality. This follows naturally since it would be a less democratic society with poorer overall feedback mechanisms.

Such an analysis suggests varied problems in trying to make evaluation significantly more participatory working through major donor agencies. Korten (1979, 1980) has written extensively about the need for bureaucratic self-transformation into authentic social development managers. In some discussions such a figure begins to resemble what Chapter 7 described as an intermediate organization. In specific favorable settings it indeed may be possible to build coalitions to make significant reforms from within. An AID administrator or mission director is in a position to improve evaluations in many ways: by institutionalizing regular learning time each week and development competency exams that affected one's chance of promotion and assignments; by building a truly separate evaluation component whose inhabitants dare prescribe from the data they find; by sending mid-project evaluations to the internal budget office so that decisions to continue bad projects are not based entirely on the paper traffic of self-interested bureaucrats; by mandating all officials to live at least one full month a year in a remote village as the poorest peasants do; by mandating that every desk and project officer in Washington and every field mission build and maintain state-of-the-art research collections on all aspects of their assigned country; by assigning personal responsibility for a specific project to a small number of relevant individuals so that people's careers depend on quality results as judged by independent evaluation; by rewriting the evaluation handbook to meet the standards of an authentic participatory project; by appointing to positions in the evaluation unit the most broadly and deeply trained development analysts money can buy; and by building a constituency in the U.S. Congress to support legislative changes to facilitate diverse other reforms. Those just mentioned do not need congressional approval.

Move now from that illusion to the more plausible reality that an AID administrator will represent the political and ideological norms of the Department of State. Mid-level donor agency officials still have considerable opportunity, working with consultants and intermediate institutions in host countries, to bring the poor and their perspectives into development evaluation. The heart of any project can be building local capacity. Work to make essential information public or available prior to critical decisions. Raise the issues and value of participatory development throughout the aid process. Fight for time and materials to improve professional skills (the bibliography at the end of this volume is designed to assist). Recognize the futility and harm in trying to work through governments, ministries, or local organizations that have antidevelopment agendas. Find alternative aid channels. If none exist, try to create some. If that is impossible, terminate programs and flows and make public the reasons. Establishing the concept of quality in international development will come only when mid- and upper-level aid professionals behave like professionals and refuse to propose or implement projects to institutions, like the government of Mobutu Sese Seko in Zaire, revealed by repeated evaluation as inappropriate to human development.

In the forthcoming world of local and intermediary organizations, development evaluation will avoid a great majority of the problems chronicled in this chapter. But as with any human activity there will still be difficulties. Building consensus in a base organization may work to impede innovation. Disorganization may be used as a strategy of resistance by one part of a local system against the decisions or evaluations of another. Imperfect consciousness raising can lead to diverse blockages, as Roca and colleagues (1980) have neatly reviewed in the recent Peruvian experiment. The world-system will offer endless lures to create new dependencies and ways of impoverishment. A good citizen is, however, a permanently learning person. An intermediate organization of good citizens, backed by a good library and good citizens in local organizations, will be facing the future knowing that people can design and control their own future. It is to the broad outlines of the larger elements of the task, the transformation and democratization of the world-system, that the final chapter now turns.

CHAPTER BIBLIOGRAPHY

Amin, Samir, et al. (1975). *La planification du sous-développement: critique de l'analyse de projets*. Paris: Anthropos.

Barclay, A. H. (1979). *The Development Impact of Private Voluntary Organizations*. Washington, D.C.: Development Alternatives, Inc.

Benedict, Peter, et al. (1982). *Sudan: The Rahad Irrigation Project*. Washington, D.C.: AID, Project Impact Evaluation Report No. 31.

Berry, Leonard, et al. (1980). *The Impact of Irrigation on Development: Issues for a Comprehensive Evaluation Study*. Washington, D.C.: AID, Program Evaluation Discussion Paper No. 9.

Cernea, Michael M. (1979). *Measuring Project Impact: Monitoring and Evaluation in the PIDER Rural Development Project – Mexico*. Washington: World Bank, WP332.

Chambers, Robert (1980). *Rural Poverty Unperceived: Problems and Remedies*. Washington: World Bank, WP400.

Coombs, Philip H., ed. (1980). *Meeting the Basic Needs of the Rural Poor: The Integrated Community-Based Approach*. New York: Pergamon Press.

Dupriez, Hughes (1979). *Integrated Rural Development Projects Carried Out in Black Africa with EDF Aid: Evaluation and Outlook for the Future*. Brussels: Commission of the European Communities.

Fergany, Nader (1981). "Monitoring the Condition of the Poor in the Third World: Some Aspects of Measurement." Geneva: ILO, WEP 10-6/WP52.

Freeman, Howard, et al. (1979). *Evaluating Social Projects in Developing Countries*. Paris: OECD.

Galli, Rosemary, ed. (1981). *The Political Economy of Rural Development: Peasants, International Capital, and the State*. Albany: State University of New York Press.

Gran, Guy, ed. (1979a). *Zaire: The Political Economy of Underdevelopment*. New York: Praeger.

_____ (1979b). "Vietnam in Pursuit of Development: Socialist Promise, Natural Calamities, and Permanent Learning." *Cultures et développement*, XI, 2:261-81.

Hasan, Parves (1978). "Economic Perspectives on Southeast Asia and Asia." Washington, D.C.: IBRD, seminar discussion paper, unpublished.

Heyer, Judith, et al., eds. (1981). *Rural Development in Tropical Africa*. New York: St. Martin's Press.

IBRD (1981a). *Concordance to Project Performance Audit Reports Issued by the Operations Evaluation Department March 1972 to June 30, 1981*. Washington: IBRD, September 30, Report 3625, unpublished.

——— (1981b). *Handbook on Monitoring and Evaluation of Agriculture and Rural Development Projects*. Washington: World Bank.

——— (1981c). *PPAR – Ghana Eastern Region Cocoa Project (Credit 205-GH)*. Washington: IBRD, June, Sec. M81-571, OED 3526, unpublished.

——— (1981d). *PPAR – Ghana Sugar Rehabilitation Project (Credit 354-GH)*. Washington: IBRD, July, Sec. M81-591, OED 3525, unpublished.

——— (1980a). *Operational Policy Review: Delays in Project Implementation*. Washington: IBRD, April 11, Report 2946, unpublished.

——— (1980b). *Operational Policy Review: The Supervision of Bank Projects*. Washington: IBRD, February 22, Report 2858, unpublished.

Inter-American Foundation (1977). *They Know How*. Washington, D.C.: Government Printing Office.

de Janvry, Alain (1981). *The Agrarian Question and Reformism in Latin America*. Baltimore, Md.: Johns Hopkins University Press.

Kirsch, Ottfried C., et al. (1980). *The Role of Self-Help Groups in Rural Development Projects*. Heidelberg: Research Center for International Agrarian Development; and Saarbrucken: Verlag Breitenbach.

Knight, Peter T., ed. (1980). *Implementing Programs of Human Development*. Washington, D.C.: World Bank, WP403.

Korten, David, ed. (1980). "Community Organization and Rural Development: A Learning Process Approach." *Public Administration Review*, 40,5:480-511.

——— (1979). *Population and Social Development Management: A Challenge for Management Schools*. Caracas: IESA.

Ledesma, Antonio J. (1980). *350 Million Rural Poor – Where Do We Start? (A Review and Evaluation of Three United Nations Initiatives in Asia)*. Bankok: UN/ESCAP (ST/ESCAP/125).

Lemarchand, René (1982). *The World Bank in Rwanda – The Case of the Office de Valorisation Agricole et Pastorale du Mutara*. Bloomington: University of Indiana, International Development Institute.

Linden, Eugene (1976). *The Alms Race: The Impact of American Voluntary Aid Abroad*. New York: Random House.

Lissner, Jørgen (1977). *The Politics of Altruism: A Study of the Political Behaviour of Voluntary Development Agencies*. Geneva: Lutheran World Federation.

Little, I. M. D., and Mirrlees, J. A. M. (1974). *Project Appraisal and Planning for Developing Countries*. London: Heinemann Educational Books.

McGranahan, Donald (1979). "International Comparability of Statistics on Income Distribution." Geneva: UNRISD, 79/C.23.

Meehan, Eugene J. (1978). *In Partnership With People: An Alternative Development Strategy*. Washington, D.C.: Inter-American Foundation.

Miller, Duncan (1979). *Self-Help and Popular Participation in Rural Water Systems*. Paris: OECD.

O'Regan, Fred, and Hellinger, Douglas (1980). *Assisting the Smallest Economic Activities of the Urban Poor: Part II – Case Studies Africa*. Cambridge, Mass.: Accion International/AITEC.

Roca, Santiago, et al. (1980). "Participatory Processes and Action of the Rural Poor in Anta: Peru." Geneva: ILO, WEP 10/WP.12.

Saunders, Christopher, and Grootaert, Christiaan (1980). "Reflections on the LSMS Group Meeting." Washington: IBRD, LSMS Working Paper No. 10.

Schmidt, Elizabeth, et al. (1981). *Religious Private Voluntary Organizations and the Question of Government Funding*. Maryknoll, N.Y.: Orbis.

Squire, Lyn, and van der Tak, Herman G. (1975). *Economic Analysis of Projects*. Baltimore, Md.: Johns Hopkins University Press.

Steinberg, David, et al. (1980a). *Philippine Small Scale Irrigation*. Washington: AID, Project Impact Eval. Report No. 4.

——(1980b). *Korean Irrigation*. Washington: AID, Project Impact Eval. Study No. 12.

Tendler, Judith (1981). *Fitting the Foundation Style: The Case of Rural Credit*. Washington, D.C.: Inter-American Foundation.

Thomas, Henk, and Logan, Chris (1982). *Mondragon: An Economic Analysis*. London: George Allen & Unwin.

UNDP (1979). *Rural Development: Issues and Approaches for Technical Cooperation*. New York: UNDP, Evaluation Study No. 2.

12

Beyond Local Empowerment: The Construction of National and International Processes for Participatory Development

> The more fully lower level needs are satisfied, the less important pecuniary incentives become, and the greater becomes the emphasis on things that "money cannot buy." But the danger exists, and it is certainly not a good policy to wait passively until the force of material incentives is fully exhausted. Nor is it good to deal with it so as to replace material incentives by "moral" incentives. What should be done is to begin replacing incentives by self-determination, competition by cooperation, exchange by solidarity, accumulation of things by personal development, having by being. Socialism will not develop automatically. Conscious social action is required. In particular, education for domestication, appropriate for a class society, must be replaced by education for freedom, appropriate for a classless society. A free man is not likely to waste his life accumulating gadgets, despairing about a few additional dinars, or begging for the favors of superiors.
>
> (Horvat, 1982, 503-4)

Participatory development is the self-sustaining process to engage free men and women in activities that meet their basic human needs and, beyond that, realize individually defined human potential within socially defined limits. Poor people in the Third World (and elsewhere), having undergone the educational transformation and social mobilization set forth in Chapters 6 and 7, will very likely find their path of progress blocked by the larger system. Concentrations of political and economic power in this world-system are not now, with rare exceptions, the result of authentic democratic processes. Indeed one could describe most contemporary democratic experiments as systems cleverly run to "transform the formal will of the majority into the actual will of the minority." Little else can be expected from a capitalist culture which legitimizes, encourages, and even glorifies the unlimited acquisition of wealth by an individual. Comparable results inevitably come from a misnamed socialist culture that legitimates, encourages, and glorifies the unlimited acquisition of power by the state. Mass human development has not prospered and will not prosper under either set of circumstances. Thus this chapter will be concerned with the processes to break up or make more democratic all concentrations of power, especially those at the national and international levels.

The capitalist world-system has shown a remarkable creativity over the last few centuries in producing uneven growth and surmounting diverse crises by war, technological change, the incorporation of new areas, and the further commodification of social and economic activity. Nothing short of a systems attack will change such patterns. This means thinking and acting locally, nationally, and globally at the same time. Such an idea is not new to readers of *IFDA Dossier*. To many others, however, systems thinking remains difficult. People with Western education in social science or law are not trained in such all-embracing terms. They have instead been taught to divide problems into small pieces and offer partial solutions; the committee structure of the U.S. Congress is one example of this in operation. Common sense suggests, however, that we live in a world of interacting systems. If one wants an organization, nation, or individual to behave in a certain way, all of the important incentives affecting its behavior have to be addressed.

Systems analysis alone is not enough of a methodology to overcome the triple set of exclusionary processes created and sustained by the present world-system: stratification by elite dominance, bureaucratic imperatives of organizations, and the further structural aggressions of culture — like male-female dynamics. One must deal with more than questions of substance. An operational strategy for political change is not simply a catalog of preferred goals but a guide to what to do to reach such goals. As suggested in previous chapters, one cannot use capitalist values and capitalist processes to reach humanist participatory results. The essence of the strategy for world-system transformation must therefore be metapolitical. It must combine questions of substance with questions of process, values, and epistemology. If one controls the meaning of words, the means of expressing and spreading ideas, and the processes by which issues are discussed and decisions made, then one has an excellent chance of prevailing on substantive matters and of implementing decisions thereafter.

What follows is thus an exercise in world-system engineering by and for mass welfare, as opposed to an exercise in conventional politics with conventional results. The first step is to create education tools suitable to specific historical circumstances. These are the means to build a popular consensus on the nature of history, on human nature and human need, on the use and limits of the organization as a social form, and on the rights and responsibilities of citizens. Next is the meaning and operation of a planned market economy. The second step is therefore to establish the institutions and processes of a participatory, self-governing economy at the national level and show how peripheral states in the world-system, typical poor Third World countries, can carry out such a transformation of political, economic, and social reality. The third step is the reconstitution of global economic links that becomes possible when Third World governments develop authentic mass bases and thus mass aspirations. The book concludes with thoughts on catalytic forces and the deeper moral responsibilities of citizens at this moment in human history.

BUILDING A NATIONAL CONSENSUS ON CITIZENSHIP

Despite much rhetoric and discussion over many centuries, democracy remains more an ideal than a reality in those cultures in which it is at least marginally valued. Many Third World states have no democratic tradition at all. They moved from a tributary mode of production to a colonial status and thence to a modern form of authoritarian rule. Such states now rely on twentieth century technology and international capital rather than the consent and tax contribution of informed citizens. Most contemporary rulers are actively proceeding to perpetuate this situation by mystifying the meaning of citizenship and the real developmental choices of the society. Halpern (in Kitchen, ed., 1976) has described this process by African rulers as a strategy of incoherence that blocks psychological modernization, so that the transformation of human relations is not liberating but leads to new forms of old hierarchies. Leaders seek time to pursue power and profit by patterns of bargaining, manipulation, and deceit. This does not build local capacity or national purpose. Waiting for elite-sponsored educational efforts to produce authentic education in citizenship in any contemporary social context would be illogical. Elites have a vested interest in forestalling exactly such learning. The United States in the early 1980s is an illuminating example of the results of such elitist education; millions of Americans think that citizen responsibilities are to throw the rascals out every four years, and in 1980 about 45 percent did not even have the incentive for that effort or, more precisely, deemed such an effort of no personal value. The results of such depoliticization favored those seeking further aggrandizement. Their well-packaged spokesman, Ronald Reagan, easily prevailed.

Participatory development needs far more active and competent citizens. The educational process of consciousness raising, sketched in Chapter 6, is the imperative initial step. Mobilization through base and intermediate organizations is the only route to building local democratic capacities that will endure over time. Ephemeral single-issue efforts are often useful teaching exercises, but they do not tend to create lifetime commitments to being a broadly competent citizen. Building optimal local capacity does not of itself generate effective regional, national, and international abilities. A number of concrete steps are in order to transform aspects of contemporary elitist educational content and processes in established schools, especially by creating diverse nonformal learning possibilities. Much has been written of the technical and social content of this alternative education (see *Development Dialogue*, 1978, 2; Wesseler, ed., 1981; Kindervatter, 1979; Ribes, ed., 1981; and Searle, 1981 for recent discussions). Less has been said about some explicitly political and ethical imperatives.

The observant reader is now fashioning two objections. How can prescriptive thought escape the cultural norms of the writer? Of course, such analysis can never be normatively neutral. Participatory development — the fulfillment of needs and the realization of human potential — are not more neutral than the present processes of mass exclusion and alienation. But a goal of participation implies a process of empowerment and thus effective citizens. A civics course on voting will not accomplish that. People need an education that develops the individual's ability to make political choices within a socially defensible context. A second objection can be posed that political and ethical values can be deduced only from specific historical and cultural situations. On the contrary, values and forms of social process are universals. It is only the specific operational steps that are determined by the specific social forces and individuals of a given location and historical moment. Whatever additional factors are called for to develop a shared consciousness for regional, national, and international action, certain topics are part of a universal citizen curriculum.

The first of these is history. Despite various platitudes and ritual observances, the study of history has not been popular with elites. When U.S. industrialist Henry Ford said, "history is bunk," he was summing up two natural prejudices of the ruling class. Behind every fortune is a crime (usually more than one); historical investigation threatens the legitimacy of history's winners. Knowledge of the past also creates the possibility of negative comparison and evaluation of the present; this is particularly threatening to organizations with their well-developed imperative for survival. Yet developing a consensus of recent history from a mass perspective is as important to participatory development at the regional level and above as it is at the local level and the household. The average citizen needs to develop abilities for historical research and analysis. A specific operational example will show why.

In 1978 Sven Lindquist published, in Swedish, *Dig Where You Stand: How to Research a Job.* The book grew out of Lindquist's experiences working in China and the difficulties he faced at home trying to research the life of his grandfather, a cement worker. The book is a manual on researching the history of an occupation that any moderately literate worker could pick up and use. In Sweden there are now about 1,500 workplace groups exploring labor and industrial history to get ideas for contemporary reforms. Compensation for job-related injuries was one issue that the workers prevailed on at an asbesto factory in Lomma (Sweden). Lindquist has more than reformist intentions. "The book makes an explicit comparison between workers and shareholders. It asks the question: What did the worker leave when he died, and how does this compare with the estate of a major stockholder?" (*The Nation*, November 21, 1981). Translations and adaptions are in process for workers in Denmark, Norway, and Germany. Here is one valuable tool in the creation of political skills to attain a democratic economy. Many

Third World workers in urban industry or on plantations come from cultures where oral history is still an accepted activity. Expanding the range of questions asked would not be hard. Such educational tools should be prepared by every society.

A second topic of the universal citizenship curriculum is the issue posed by the endless further commodification of life by the advance of untrammeled capitalism. To turn every aspect of life into a commodity for the exploitation of the greedy would leave humans highly alienated and vulnerable, devoid of all competence at subsistence. Base organizations alone cannot fashion alternatives to large-scale systemic processes. Regional and national consensus have to be built on the value of maintaining local abilities for reasons not just related to security but to the meaningfulness of life. Just because one can buy a product on the market does not make it preferable to something one can grow or craft at home. Aspects of this issue will be settled in national-level debates on questions of technology and resource availability. But a citizen needs to be able to think about the relationship of commodities, work, and welfare in ways that capitalism tries to prevent. Capitalism thrives on malformed or misinformed mass consumption.

This topic has been recently explored by Ivan Illich in his treatment of shadow work. Shadow work is "the unpaid work which industrial society demands as a necessary complement to the production of goods and services" (Illich, 1981: 100). It includes housework, shopping, and commuting; add to these the mental wear of forced consumption — created wants, for example, or obedience to the fiats of professionals and bureaucrats. In modern industrial society shadow work is not subsistence labor but a form of bondage. Looking back at the history of work since the Middle Ages, as Illich, Braudel, and others have done, one can trace the evolution of the concept of work as a weapon elites used to transform the activities of the masses at different stages of industrialization. In the eighteenth and nineteenth centuries the poor, especially women, consistently rebelled against the British government's ideas of work and workhouses; the system, working through the state, won by enclosing women into housework in an economically redefined family. "In and through the family the two complementary forms of industrial work were now fixed: wage work and shadow work. Man and woman, both effectively estranged from subsistence activities, became the motive of the other's exploitation for the profit of employers and investments in capital goods" (Illich, 1981: 108).

Illich goes on to show how contemporary Western society seeks largely successfully, to mystify shadow work to obscure overall systemic advantage. Four tactics are used. Biology is touted as reason for defining "what women do as non-work." The value of social reproduction is lauded. Economists seek to quantify shadow work with shadow prices and fancy models. Feminists try to get payment for housework. But the overall alienation of the modern age is not removed. Instead we have created a modern class of professionals to supervise shadow work and treat the symptoms of the illnesses wrought by such alienation. Illich is pointing to the crucial cultural contradiction in modernization: it practices ever new forms of oppression as the means of reaching a future proclaimed to be without oppression.

More than anyone else writing today, Illich is provoking the needed rethinking of the concepts of human nature and human need. His insights on the ripple effects of the commodification of life perpetrated by capitalist modernization are the beginning of the development of the larger social curriculum for citizens building a participatory society. His book *Shadow Work* contains an annotated bibliography with many leads to aspects of the study of these topics, especially in the context of European history. Other guides include Borremans (1979 and 1981), work of the Annales school, Darrow et al. (1981), and Lipnack and Stamp (1982).

Many of these efforts are primarily focussed on the experiences of the First World. By perusing the bibliography of this volume one can find a vast variety of studies for the Third World on the role of women, the changing household, the attack on subsistence existence and local culture, scarcity, unemployment, and the meaning of poverty. From some of the best, like Obbo (1981) and Head (1981), one can appreciate that antagonism toward hierarchically and authoritarianly structured wage labor is a nearly universal phenomenon. Subsistence peoples do not want to give up all aspects of self-reliance. Women have rarely chosen (except via a cultural process of created want) to be type-cast into the few roles a prevailing mode of production finds profitable in a given era. It is more satisfying to do many, if not most, things for yourself. Studying human experiments across cultures and times is the essential prerequisite for seeking to define a more creative, productive, and humane future.

Each society, probably in some combination of regional and national forum, will debate these issues over and over as cumulative citizen consciousness grows. It is a bit presumptuous to go beyond suggesting some of the background reading national and regional analysts might profitably examine. But Illich has outlined an overall framework for the national debate that most social activists are likely to find useful. To get beyond left-right politics and expand citizen responsibilities and rights, try recasting sociopolitical choices into three dimensions. In one, place traditional topics about who gets what: social and political hierarchy, use of resources, and the ownership of the means of production. In a second, consider the questions of hard and soft as they relate to all kinds of technologies and the services they affect. In the third, raise the issues of human satisfaction, of organizing society to enhance satisfaction in having, on the one hand, or in doing, on the other. (Illich, 1981: 11ff.). By organizing curriculum, handbooks, conferences, and forum to reflect all three sets of topics, social education activists can help direct the creation of truly competent citizens and thus of a participatory society.

In essence this is a plea for all progressive educational activities to broaden and deepen their scope. Specific efforts now in progress encompass major segments of these topics; Shane and Tabler (1982) in their *Educating for a New Millennium* culled insights from 132 international scholars on what constitutes an anticipatory curriculum. They found cumulative awareness of the need for a conserving society, one that understands systems and examines its values. The Institute for World Order creates a periodically updated catalog reproducing syllabi of courses in peace and world order studies in U.S. colleges; the most recent edition is Schwenninger et al., 1981. Venezuela has a minister of State for the Development of Intelligence. Minister Luis Alberto Machado is leading an effort to teach people to think critically. In one program fourth graders are beginning Learning to Think courses; a handful of specialists taught 142 selected teachers who in turn trained 42,000 primary school teachers. While there are imperfections in such top-down methods here and in other adult and child education activities, Machado has in mind producing students who can "think in a critical, dialectical and systematic way." Machado does not shy away from the political implications. He wants fuller participation of citizens in political life to "institutionalize a democracy of participation" (*Science*, November 6, 1981).

Exploring the reference works alluded to in the preceding pages would uncover a rich mixture in experiments with alternative education for citizen building at the local level and a few more at the regional and national level. Education for empowerment must have more consistent structure, funding, and catalytic force to create the collective democratic consciousness necessary for social transformation on any scale. This means not just a systems understanding of historic change and how elites modify culture and human need to assist the profitable evolution of a mode of production. The political and economic organizations that sustain capitalism and etatism are not likely to be appropriate for a participatory and democratic arrangement of politics and economics. As new forms and strategies were needed for new activities at the local level, so they will also be necessary for regional and national change. It is to the interplay of organization, politics, and economics at those levels that this chapter now turns.

THE PLANNED-MARKET ECONOMY
IN THE THIRD WORLD CONTEXT

This book has suggested that human development should not be the further accumulation and concentration of wealth with the simultaneous destruction of all competence at subsistence. Development should rather be participatory because that is the most equitable and the most productive approach. The phrase *planned-market economy* suggests the essence of the institutional arrangement. It is not an evasion trying to appeal semantically to both capitalists and state socialists. It is the logical way of describing what accurately reflects the inclinations of humanistic man. As Chapters 1 and 6 described, man is naturally impelled by a mixture of social and individual motives depending on his particular circumstances and degree of maturity. The larger economic and political framework needs to reflect this. It is improbable that one can have an optimal market without social planning or implement a social plan without market signals at some levels. Thus the utility and meaning of a planned-market economy.

To be of use the following pages must describe the constituent parts of such a political and economic arrangement. They must also provide a practical strategy for base and intermediate organizations in the Third World to capture and institutionalize control over regional and national entities. A consensus must be developed on the specific economic and political functions to be performed at each level, how active citizens can maintain equality of producers, consumers, and citizens through processes like worker management. The Yugoslav economist Branco Horvat, in an awesome and seminal work in early 1982, has devoted several hundred pages to such topics. *The Political Economy of Socialism*, which ought to be one of the most important books of the twentieth century, is aimed primarily at the transformation of the First and Second Worlds. Horvat writes from incredible command of the experiences of Eastern and Western Europe, the United States, and Russia. His institutional solutions appear to be fairly universally applicable, as experiments indicate in Third World societies such as Mozambique and Grenada. The partial synopsis in the following pages is no excuse for avoiding spending the time and money on Horvat's work; it is indispensable for anyone trying to play a major role in building a viable twenty-first century society.

The national debate should begin with a brief recapitulation of the inefficiencies of capitalist and etatist organization in order to understand the logic of the proposed alternative. Capitalism produces class conflict affecting motivation, supervision, innovation, sanctions, and bargaining procedures. Horvat (1982: 192 ff) identifies these results: talent is wasted; income is irrationally distributed; social control is essentially impossible; oligopoly and monopoly result; social planning is hindered; high-pressure advertising leads to created want; and the state wastes its resources on expensive reconciliation efforts. The state socialist or command economies do not do any better.

The solution to these problems, what Horvat terms self-governing socialism* and what I term participatory development, rests on a moderately complex set of institutions and processes providing interlocking checks and balances to maintain authentic democratic control over all levels of political and economic activity. A few of the essential elements are presented here along with a tabular picture of the overall framework; the reader is urged to secure Horvat's text for more details.

---

*A word Horvat has rescued from its twentieth century abuse by Lenin, Stalin, and their followers by returning to nineteenth century ideas of a democratic and decentralized society.

Equality of producers (Horvat, 1982: 235-62) will be gained through social property and workers' management. It would not be possible to have a democratic or optimally productive economy where one individual or collective can command the labor of others or appropriate nonlabor income. The legal, social, and economic aspects of property rights have to be redefined. Autonomous collectives, for example, would have the right to use, sell, or change commodities and to reap the benefits; they would have the obligation not to diminish the value of productive assets. Each member of society has the right to work, the right to compete for any job, and the right to equal participation in management. Economic benefits are to come from collective or individual social property, not from command over the labor of others. Such a system implants social boundaries that limit capitalist claims of the social and economic rights of property.

Workers' management is the strategy to link democracy with efficiency and the market with planning. It has six organizing principles. The basic entity is a work unit; such units are grouped into work communities for sociopolitical purposes and into enterprises for economic relations. Decisions in one unit that affect another must gain the sanction of a workers' council. The rights of decision making have corresponding obligations or sanctions. Implementing decisions is a matter of professional ability, not democracy. Activities are thus divided into an interest sphere, decided by democratic political authority, and a professional sphere, in which appropriate ability is recognized. Complexities and the potential for abuse demand safeguards and adjudicators such as mixed commissions. Horvat then addresses with elegance many of the practical problems of individual and group egotism and of small group decision making that were covered in this book in Chapter 6. Table 12.1, for example, shows an operational way to link experts and laymen in a process of strategic decision making.

Equality of consumers (Horvat, 1982: 263-82) begins with reconstructing price theory to measure both direct work and entrepreneurship. The latter involves human relations, organization of work, and creativity. Practical definitions are developed for different elements of labor and nonlabor (rents) income. Determining first the labor income for the collective or work unit as a whole creates a basis for setting individual income levels. Overall social planning maintains relatively equal labor incomes across industries, but the

TABLE 12.1 The Process of Strategic Decision Making

Stages of decision making	Decision participants							
	Work community	Work unit	Workers council	Executive committee	General manager	Professional staff	Advisory commissions	Individual members
I. Initiative (definition of the problem)	X	X	X	X	X	X	X	X
II. Preparation of decision (elaboration of variants)		X		X	X	X	X	X
III. Taking of decision (selection of a variant)	X	X	X					
IV. Implementation of decision				X	X	X		X
V. Control of implementation (and possible corrections)	X	X	X	X	X	X	X	X

Source: Horvat, 1982: 253.

firm is an autonomous competitor within its industry. What is just is what people think is just: have the actors themselves engage in interpersonal welfare comparisons and make the relevant decisions. Any item, like health care or education, that greatly affects human development needs to be exempted from exchange links and distributed by needs criteria. The rest of social product (public consumption aside) should be organized on the basis of work contribution. How else can stratification and exploitation be avoided? In the real world of poor societies there will not be enough social goods and services; a limited market in these will have to be socially monitored during a period of development.

Equality of citizens (Horvat, 1982: 283-327) is produced by a combination of consistent citizen behavior and the decentralization and balancing of power. Society does need a central authority, but it needs effective institutional control over that authority. Such a premise leads to specifying six functions of self-government; legislative, judiciary, executive, administrative, control, and recruitment. Several kinds of courts, commissions, and ombudsmen help overcome unequal power conflicts. The Swiss model suggests that political parties are unnecessary as is much else from bourgeois and collectivist political cultures. Operational principles for democratic participation guide overall system activity; these five principles are those of importance, affected interests, exception, majority, and minority safeguard. Rights of personal integrity and social intercourse follow the philosophical traditions dating from the 1776 Declaration of Independence, the 1948 Universal Declaration on Human Rights, and similar documents: life, liberty, and security of person; freedom of thought and conscience; freedom of opinion and expression; freedom of peaceful assembly and association; and the right to information.

The institutionalization of planning with the market and the necessary macroeconomic organizations complete this brief synopsis of Horvat's vision (Horvat, 1982: 328-67). Without social guidance the market fails because producers and consumers may both be misled, markets are unstable, money prices do not always apply, and diverse externalities abound. Social decisions alone, pure central planning, also fails, as the planners can never have enough timely information. A mixture of regulatory mechanisms is suggested and a general investment theory developed for the worker-managed firm. At the national level four basic institutions are called for: a planning bureau; a national bank to handle short-term adjustment; a development fund for long-term investment; and an arbitration board for incomes and prices. Overall linkages are built between national, state, and communal levels for administrative, regulative, market, informational, and arbitration purposes. The economic tasks of the commune, for example, include getting failed enterprises and unemployed citizens back on their feet. Horvat does not address this, but society must also allow the nonjoiner to prosper to the extent he or she does not exert a net drain on social resources.

To get a better and more visual portrait of the organizational edifice Horvat builds over several chapters, I have also excerpted two figures (Figures 12.1 and 12.2) showing how the federal and state institutions might interact between and among themselves. It is worth mentioning again that my few pages of synthesis are no substitute for sustained attention to Horvat's text. But such a synthesis is crucially useful here to take the idea of a democratic and participatory economy on a national scale out of the realm of utopia and place it in the realm of concrete possibility and feasibility. Political architects transforming Third World (not to mention First and Second World) societies do not have to cast about in the polemical thickets of capitalism and etatism, solutions that have produced an endless string of partial or total failures except in the most unusual historical circumstances like those of the United States. Such architects can instead explore both the historical and the practical evidence that suggests the unimpeachable logic of the claim that the optimal route to equity and growth is the democratic or participatory economy.

Sitting in an armchair in Washington offering visions is one thing. Making them operational, given the typical political realities of the Third World in the 1980s is quite something else. The would-be political engineer is looking at a fragile, elitist, typically one-party state with most or all of these characteristics: the world-system has it effectively locked into a triple alliance; domestic opposition is deemed illegitimate; individual rights are not secure; democratic culture is scorned, alien, or unknown; stratification mechanisms built on politics, organizations, and culture are well entrenched; and the poor are fragmented by religion, ethnic ties, geography, and illiteracy. Strategy must grow out of context and out of deep understanding of how systems, particularly the world-system, work over time. If a strategy for political and economic change does not encompass all parts of the system, it will not work or work well. In a typical episode of revolutionary change in the Third World, great attention is paid to the marshalling of political and military strength for the seizure of power. Little thought goes into the practical steps to institutionalize legitimate, i.e., mass-based democratic, power for long-term human development.

The very first practical step to any change process, then, is to do your homework. It sounds simple, even insulting. But no one in any leadership position in any society in the world today is allocating learning time in relation to the real needs of the job. Popular in Washington is the absurd phrase "living off your intellectual capital." People there accept a harried existence with minimal learning space as though this was inevitable. Then they wonder why programs and policies fail. As in Western politics so in Third World politics, it takes one kind of person to run well for office or lead a revolution, but it takes quite another kind to help in the design, monitoring, and conflict resolution that are the day-to-day stuff of development. In sum, think about your own skills, drives, and limitations and those of others in any change process. Leadership should not be an exercise in self-indulgence, let alone aggrandizement.

Education for leadership in development at the state or national level is largely comparable to what Chapters 6 and 7 outlined for local operations. National leaders do need to be far more conscious of the ways in which the world-system tries to stifle unprofitable change. Financial attacks by limiting credit and aid are now receiving more sustained analysis thanks to events in Chile, Jamaica, Tanzania, and Vietnam. Yet there remains a great deal of naiveté in the Third World about how actions are perceived and responded to at the heart of the two major imperiums, Washington and Moscow. In early 1982, for example, Rawlings retook the leading role in Ghana's politics. He publicly stated his intentions to make progressive changes, nothing particularly avant-garde. Press headlines in the United States were consistently hostile, hinting at barbarism and chaos. A few of the stories themselves were more coherent. But the average Third World state depends in fact on episodic, unsophisticated coverage by Western media to generate a coherent picture of developmental reality. This does not happen, for the media are part of the larger culture sharing the biases of the world-system. This is no way to build cross-cultural communication.

FIGURE 12.1 Federal Institutions

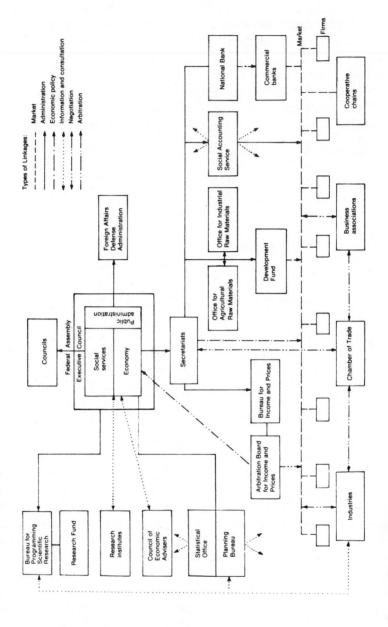

Source: Horvat, 1982: 356.

FIGURE 12.2 State Institutions

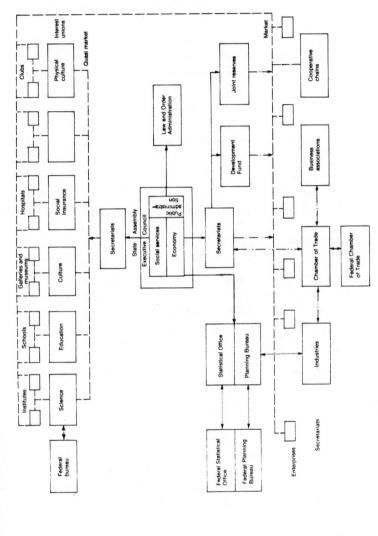

Source: Horvat, 1982: 363.

343

Considerations of the breadth and depth of education necessary for leadership help to define the overall outlines of the change strategy. The would-be political engineer must design interlocking strategies at the international, national, and local levels that address simultaneously questions of semantics, culture, politics, economics, and organizations. This means exercises in politics and metapolitics at the same time. In most situations power balances will be unequal. Those seeking change will have less military and economic power. One does not attack the opposition where it is strongest. Nor does one uncritically adopt the processes the opposition controls nor the vocabulary it tries to enforce. Metapolitics is the art or science of affecting political vocabulary and processes as means of changing the substance and thus the results of political action. In most societies, the real questions of development, the topics of this book or of analysts like Horvat or Illich, are not even legitimate topics for discussion in mainstream media. One cannot simply propose new ideas and expect them to be discussed on their merits. One thus needs to be as conscious of the strategy by which ideas are generated and spread as of the actual content of the ideas themselves.

With this brief synthesis of the specific institutional and operational goals and of the breadth of a systems framework for political and metapolitical change, attention can now be focussed on concrete strategy. Comments will first be addressed to the political engineer working toward the democratization of national institutions. Then analysis will turn briefly to practical considerations during the relatively long period of transition.

Political change at any level is a matter of people, organizations, and ideas. The greatest and least utilized resource of any Third World society is its people. Yet most instances of change involve a small number of people doing most of the work and reaping most of the gain or profit. Thanks to the vast majority of elitist theorists and to the psychological disposition of most would-be rulers, masses are seen and used as an object or recipient of change. From that perspective one is led inevitably to elitist party politics or coups and then an elitist government seeking to build bonds with greater numbers of people. The result is virtually never mass empowerment but rather forms of corporatism that suit the political and economic needs of elites. This will not produce participatory development. Nor is it the only choice.

People can lead their own change processes. They can be the actors, not merely the subjects of change. Not everyone, to be sure, can act at the national level; it would not be efficient. Democratic national politics begins by building up mass-based local government, one that evolves from base/intermediate organizations to councils, that represents citizens and work units. Such local governments would not be looking to improve local social services by handouts from national authorities. Instead the goal would be relative self-reliance by the more creative mobilization of local citizen initiatives. A reasonably participatory local society will be ready to project alternative visions of state or regional development and work to create the democratic institutions to carry it out. Several democratically based regional entities can then collaborate on an alternative vision of national development and on the means of its implementation.

This is not a very exciting route to mass empowerment. It certainly requires a lot more time, work, and trouble than collecting some disgruntled mid-level army officers and shooting up the president's palace. These are some of the reasons the latter course has been more popular. One can certainly argue that military coups or even revolutionary movements may be more efficient routes to power, less able to be preempted by the present rulers. But if one's goal is not power per se but a democratic society and economy, one cannot expect to get there in any foreseeable time frame (say 15 to 30 years) without laying the groundwork wherein the mass of people develop democratic culture, abilities, and aspirations and the habits of continuous citizenship. Conversely, one cannot expect people reaching national office by other routes to have deep and enduring motives to facilitate a democratic economy. Power corrupts. Without democratic checks and balances it is a rare individual who will not succumb sooner or later to the material or psychological lures that national office and the world-system provide.

To suggest what amounts to a peaceful route to structural change in a violent and lawless world may strike some as naive or impractical. Every situation is different; violence may be the only answer at a specific historical moment. But contemplate the question of long-term legitimacy. Using law and order for social reconstruction is the process one will wish to apply over the long haul. Using violence because it is expedient raises questions of legitimacy in the eyes of others; read a bit of Columbia's history, for example in the 1940s and 1950s, when the only legitimate political communication was through violence. Violence wastes resources and blocks development. Geurrilla war is not the only way to mass mobilization for political action. Using law creatively as a tool for empowerment, as opposed to a tool for exclusion, oppression, and the status quo, is a strategy slowly gaining credence. Useful practical examples have accumulated all over the world; for guidance, look at some of the activities of the U.S. Legal Services Program and case studies from the Philippines from the New York based International Center for Law and Development.

Activities for change at the regional and national level need more than a mass base. They need skilled people and appropriate organization. A few points may be added to the relevant material in Chapter 7. Cooperative behavior in work units requires people with skills in mobilizing and institutionalizing such cooperatives. A training institute is essential at a regional or state level; the literature on this is best explored through a study of Mondragon (Henk and Thomas, 1982). Information must spread efficiently; one or more publishing ventures and a local radio station are essential. Political efforts must be linked across economic activities and between levels. Institutes, credit facilities, resource centers, ad hoc coalitions, and similar efforts need to be designed into a system wherein three things happen consistently: issues are kept in view through continuous public education; a sensitized public develops channels to and is alerted for timely intercessions in the public process; and substantively skilled professionals reformulate data and theory from primary sources, academe, and any other appropriate sources into option papers and legislative initiatives that the public process can work with.

It was just such a systems approach to national political change in Washington that defunded and effectively ended the Vietnam War between 1973 and 1975. It was the failure to apply such a systems approach that doomed other U.S. social change efforts, like the Equal Rights Amendment, in the years thereafter. Specific application in the Third World suggests building support networks involving local, regional, national, and international actors not just to fund networks of base and intermediate organizations but to provide political and economic support across the board. The strategy of building alliances within state and national bureaucracies can be expanded to all kinds of international agencies for all kinds of developmental goals. Idea people and action people will also have to learn to work together and to value the contributions of the others in order to make such systems engineering work. Many years of personal experience suggest that, even for well-intentioned people, this is not easy. People in political and policy roles disdain academics and vice versa; neither see the poor as more than a mass of unruly amateurs. It is going to take conscious effort, education, and organization to bridge these gaps; elites and professionals will have to develop other intrinsic rewards as power over others diminishes.

Effective, operational strategy requires context and catalysts as well as human and organizational resources. The contradictions inherent in capitalism, etatism, and long cycles in the world-system provide ample reasons why people will support and work for change. Much of the overall analytic synthesis will be the task of scholar-activists at the state and national level; the bibliography of this book has been designed in part for such inquiries and the course syllabi in global micropolitics shows how to start preparatory education.

A brief synopsis of potential national crises in Third World states during the 1980s suggests the kinds of historical opportunities available to the creative political architect. Without pretensions of completeness, these issues are likely to be educational. Elites try to justify unwarranted privileges, salaries, and perquisites by routinely lying to their fellow citizens about the potential for development and the use of resources. Unmask such mystification by simple historical research to show an accumulation of false promises. Do comparative productivity studies over time, region, and industry to show how and why different work units contribute so little to job production and human need. Do extrapolations on past and present trends to show that some groups and classes are permanently impoverished within the status quo while people in other classes or regions could wait 50, 75, or 100 years to gain access to basic social services. Demonstrate publicly how alternative institutions and technology could be far more cost-effective and use specific work units, villages, or firms as models. Account resources wasted on military outlays, elite salaries, conspicuous consumption, and subsidies to international capital on a yearly basis and translate into lost development opportunities. Chronicle tax avoidance, government deficits, international debt and all other drains on social resources to be able to use recurrent debt and budget crises to optimum political advantage.

The cumulative effect of education for empowerment, the failure of Third World governments to secure resources for current or development outlays, the revolution of rising expectations, and the deeper structural contradictions between classes of producers and consumers will together create a situation ready for change. The public availability of alternative institutional forms and processes will diminish natural fear of the unknown. The most competent political architect will have designed a process of systems reconstruction so elegant and natural that violence will be minimized; history does suggest, however, that even the best ideas usually need a little help from the sword to prevail. A propitious historic moment will arrive, and a new democratic experiment will be born.

Fledgling progressive states in a hostile world-system need many kinds of educational and financial assistance. To the extent new first citizens recognize that quality leadership demands permanently learning people, they will organize processes and select people to ensure that this happens. A democratic state, based on continuous authentic dialogue between citizens and political units, will not be successfully tempted by the world-system. Neither the state nor local capital need be long dominated by external dependencies. This is not as utopian as it might first appear.

An effective process of defense against the world-system must be conscious of style as well as substance. By ideological rhetoric and diplomatic gesturing progressive Third World experiments have consistently abraded the nerves of leaders of the North. Western media have found it easy to paint alarmist pictures, which in turn provided anticommunist ideologues sufficient pretext to counterattack. It is easy to study this process as it happens in the United States in the pages of the *New York Times, Washington Post, Wall Street Journal, Congressional Record* and congressional hearings. There is no excuse for being caught in such a swamp. I am not urging that a new government hire a public relations firm and a Washington lobbyist; far too many of both already exist. But the study and practice of metapolitics is essential. Sufficient historical examples have accumulated and some case studies have been prepared; see Mittleman (1981) on aspects of recent Mozambique and Tanzania experience, EPICA (1982) on Grenada, and Collins (1982) on Nicaragua.

This book cannot be an extended text on this stage of historical transition; a book of this sort for societies on the periphery is quite overdue. But much can be learned from Horvat's extensive discussion of the potential transition in First and Second World societies. Here, for example, is how he would orchestrate the difficult movement from multiple kinds of ownership in an average mixed economy to an optimally productive worker-managed economy.

> The dynamics of the system ought to be clear by now. The resources of the national investment fund will be used primarily to develop old and create new state firms. Co-determination will be introduced into these firms and will help to check etatist tendencies. Co-determination will be generally extended and develop toward full-fledged worker management. The general manager will be appointed by the government and he may be given restricted veto power, but the rest of the organization will be based on labor management. The private sector will also develop and new firms may be established. But the faster the corporate firms grow, the faster they will be socialized. Co-determination will also be extended and will follow, with a lag, the developments in the state sector. Finally, the labor-managed sector will expand, will be supported technically and financially, and will increase its relative efficiency. The three sectors will be oriented to converge institutionally toward one single labor-managed economy. In a generation or so, the task may be achieved (Horvat, 1982: 484).

Horvat does devote some attention to the overall politics of transition in Third World societies. He imagines that there will be a typically undemocratic transition yielding an initial period of etatism with all the attendant dangers that state socialism produces. I do not see much beyond false expediency to recommend vanguard parties or an initial centralized phase; nineteenth and twentieth century history argues strongly that democratic results can come only from effective and continuous mass involvement by competent citizens. It is clear why the world has only a few, partially successful experiments somewhat akin to what this book envisions as possible. Healthy people produce a healthy society. If we invest far more attention in producing healthy people, cognizant of their humanistic nature and educated for freedom, we are far more likely to create and sustain a participatory society.

THE PARTICIPATORY SOCIETY AND THE GLOBAL AGENDA

It may have struck some readers as curious from time to time that this book has not addressed that familiar series of international problems that are the grist of most conventional discussions of the future of international development: multinational corporations; the banking system and the global debt situation; the arms race and the Cold War; the population issue; environmental destruction; the global trade and commodity issues; the World Bank and IMF; and the limits of the UN system. Chapters 4 and 5 aside, I did not focus attention on these macro issues not simply because of an overall microeconomic and institutional orientation but because the world is simply organizationally and politically unprepared to deal with these problems in any substantive fashion.

All of these problems are logical results of the world-system at work and represent expectable symptoms of social illness when citizens fail to be citizens and permit concentrations of uncontrolled political or economic power to form and expand. The natural tendency of capitalism is to centralize and accumulate wealth; the logical result is IBM, Chase Manhattan, and similar objects. The natural tendency of any large organization, government or corporation, is to pursue security, and thus control and growth. In this basic sense General Motors and the Soviet government are quite similar.

The size, longevity, and systemic nature of each of these problems argues against quick or painless remedies, if one seeks humanistic, developmental solutions rather than rhetorical or politically expedient maneuvers. Most Western readers are aware, for example, of a growing literature showing that intergovernmental arms control talks since the 1950s have not controlled arms but instead served to legitimize the expansion of conventional and nuclear arms production and deployment. That should be no surprise. Concentrations of military, industrial, and political power in the Soviet Union and in the United States wanted this expansion. Citizens in neither country created institutions for multilevel and multidimensional education in opposition or for effective political action to stop it. Instead small groups pushed at the edge of the system for liberal, incremental reform.

It is surely obvious that liberal reform is not a sufficient answer for a world dominated by a nuclear balance of terror and monopoly capitalism. The real answer, not satisfying to some I am sure, is to do the educational and organizational work to create the authentically democratic national level institutions outlined in the last section. Such institutions, controlled by active, competent citizens, would quickly see the military-industrial complex as a sheer waste of material resources, loss of social productivity, misdirection of research efforts – in sum, the negative political results of concentrated power. With great political pressure for the authentically developmental use of social resources would come applied creativity for ending the Cold War.

What every imperial system fears most are successful examples of real democratic development. Both the United States and the Soviet Union have sought to stifle and transform every fledgling experiment in socialist or participatory development in the Third World that threatened to exhibit the least bit of independence. The Vietnam War was the largest example by the United States; the bibliography of this book leads one into a large literature on many comparable cases. The Soviet behavior toward Poland and Afghanistan in the last three years is little different. The Soviet Union has been similarly repressive toward participatory experiments within its own borders. At Akchi between 1968 and 1970 local farmers attempted to move from the "juridical" socialization of property to a "real" change in relations of production, to the "collective management" of socialized property. This threatened the raison d'être of professional managers (endemic in etatist societies and hierarchical corporations) who moved to smash the experiment (discussed in Horvat, 1982: 471). Etatist Third World societies behave the same way; Coulson (1982) has recounted the history of the Ruvuma Development Association in the 1960s and why the Tanzanian government stifled it.

The Cold War is the most important tool of both imperiums to stifle democratic developments that could threaten the profits and power of imperial managers. The arms race justifies continuous and ever larger procurements of weapons that are used to maintain spheres of influence, market domination, and neocolonial control. This will go on as long as citizens fail to behave like citizens, or until one unstable nuclear power (or nuclear terrorist) sets off a holocaust. Barring the latter, contemplate an operational systems engineering exercise to end the Cold War.

To eliminate nuclear arsenals and drastically diminish conventional arms implies sustained activity by a fairly large number of citizens competently organized for interlevel systems change activity. The Cold War is a large, antidevelopment activity; an appropriate scale and complexity of organization is called for. If citizens in the West and in the Third World proceed to fulfill a major portion of the social change sketched in the preceding section, they will have the political and organizational resources to confront the crux of the problem of ending the Cold War. It is far more feasible to propel ideas of demobilization and development in the moderately tolerant and democratic political cultures of the West. It is quite a different matter to raise citizens' abilities in a totalitarian society shut off from the outside and devoid of any past democratic heritage.

This will be a supreme test of the power of ideas over the power of the sword. Contemplate a sustained global education program that spreads these ideas simultaneously. The U.S. could cut defense outlays by 50-60 percent, retain a sufficient nuclear shield, and reallocate funds to social and participatory development at home and abroad. Outlays to *organizationally prepared* Third World societies, not to typical elitist governments now ruling, would rapidly accelerate productive participatory development. The Soviet citizen will first be visited by news of diminished external military threat and by concrete successful examples of alternative development that is clearly neither capitalist nor etatist. Citizens can then be barraged with historically grounded analysis of specific failures and limits of modern Soviet development, the coming ecological disasters, and specific operational ways to attack the crevasses of the Soviet system to enlarge citizens' rights and control. The Soviet state will not be transformed quickly. But state socialist rhetoric, embodied in party documents and legal codes, contains many contradictions with everyday life. These contradictions can be used. Insist that laws be obeyed. Demand real worker management. Soviet citizens will certainly opt for butter when the outlay on weapons has no visible or theoretical utility. In sum I am talking about redirecting and redesigning the global revolution of rising expectations and then accelerating it in the Soviet Union.

Ending the Cold War does not, per se, alter or diminish the stranglehold of global financial institutions over the use of most investment capital, commodity trade, and development resources. Multinational corporations and private banks can be expected to resist vigorously suggestions of structural change. Yet worker-managed, participatory societies could not prosper in a global structure designed for inequality and the perpetual parasitism of the rich on the poor. As I have argued in Chapter 4 (and elsewhere, Gran, 1979a), peripheral societies cannot overcome historical handicaps by export-led growth, because the consumer countries will buy commodities only at the rate they can use them, the rate their own economies are growing. Most of the consumption of tropical agricultural and mineral products is still by countries in the North. These industrial countries are in the middle of a long-term recession/ depression; this means growth rates will stay rather low.

Third World exporters face further structurally insurmountable problems. The First World control over credit facilities, shipping, communication, and other dimensions of the international market make trade unequal. Long-term price trends look ominous; one typical study concluded that the real purchasing power of LDC exports in the 1990s is likely to be much lower than in the 1970s (Stewart and Sengupta, 1982: 108, based on *World Development Report*, 1981). The debt situation of most Third World countries has grown progressively more bleak over the last decade. There are a growing number of basket cases depending on stop-gap IMF funding and debt rollovers; there are fewer countries that can attract further private lending. Expanding these trends over the next 50 years would reveal the essentially permanent poverty and exclusion of most people in most countries. There is a clear and pressing need to make the international economy democratic.

Unfortunately this is not the historical moment for most of the work that needs to be done. We have not yet produced the citizens and institutions that can implement the solution. When a sufficient number of economic and political democracies have come into being, a series of initiatives like the following will look feasible. A democratic authority has to control the creation and expansion of currency in international as well as national trade. Unlimited expansion of Eurodollars by private concerns, in no relation to social productivity as a whole, is but one of the many speculative activities to be stopped. Offshore banking is another. One global currency should be used for all international trade. Its value should be determined by a basket of national currency values. Issuance of such an international currency should be restricted to a single international authority and distribution based on tangible demonstration of national productivity, not political muscle. These are significant departures from the current system and will be vigorously resisted by private banks. But if major progress has been made in making national economies more democratic, private banks will not exist in their present form or size. The groundwork for such a global transformation has to be laid by an accumulation of educational efforts and organizational activities to mobilize mass consciousness. Such an emphasis on bottom-up preparation is not, of course, meant to discourage the presentation of structural change proposals in the near future. But the political will is not there to carry them out. The world has witnessed some 30 years of liberal rhetoric and incremental reform in international arenas. The peasants of Zaire and of many other countries are not any better off. The present forum, the prevailing processes of debate and decision making in Washington, New York, Geneva, Rome, and elsewhere are not part of the solution. They are part of the problem.

A similar systems logic suggests that, if the World Bank has been the principal guide and manager of Third World development for the last 30 years, it should have no role in a democratic and participatory world economy of the future. Its policies, its work processes, and the training of its staff are all inappropriate to development properly understood. It was designed by capitalist governments to perpetuate and expand global commodification, and it is doing so. Chapter 4 explained that export-led growth and top-down, blueprint, elitist exercises in social engineering are the antithesis of participatory development. Chapters 1, 6, and 7 suggested the obsolete and inappropriate nature of Western social science and technical educations typical of the staffs of the World Bank and other multilateral and bilateral aid agencies. Efforts of these agencies at internal changes and the occasional accidental project with participatory elements do not merit substantive long-term reform efforts to rewrite the Bank's charter, appoint new personnel, and reconstruct internal work processes. For if that is the best the world manages, we will still be dealing with billions of poor, structurally excluded people in the years 2025, 2050, and beyond.

These are not cheerful or acceptable thoughts to thousands of international civil servants who have been working with humanistic motives on world development issues for the last generation. Good intentions are not, unfortunately, the same thing as good results. Everyone recognizes this in his private life; some quiet meditation should show how similar results obtain in professional activities.

What I believe and hope is that there are many inside the UN community and the multilaterals who accept some or most of these painful conclusions and are willing to join the fight for a fundamentally new kind of World Development Authority, one mandated to facilitate participatory development, not capitalism or etatism.

For there is much important work for them to do to facilitate this transformation. Chapters 8 through 11 suggest many ways this generation of aid projects can be made more participatory. Particularly crucial would be any efforts to redirect funds away from nondemocratic central authorities to intermediate institutions that demonstrate the ability to build local capacities for participatory development. A few people in major donor agencies are already doing this, so one knows it is not implausible in most specific situations. A second group of activities could be aimed at developing allies in the administrator class by the reeducation of donor agency managers and people such as directors of the World Bank from Third World and Scandinavian countries. A third set of activities should focus on crystallizing a charter and a style of operations for a small, decentralized World Development Authority. Making the idea a full-fledged entity on paper is the first step to making it a legal and operational reality. As Chapter 7 indicated, small amounts of resource transfers for finite time periods will be needed after locally funded First World-Third World transfers generate microdevelopment systems of base and intermediate organizations. Most of the present set of UN and multilateral agencies could then be phased out; democratic governments are, however, likely to want to retain a few of the humanitarian and technical agencies of the UN and provide them with refined goals and research agendas.

One further arena of activities will occur to Third World political leaders and their fellow citizens. There are certainly a number of structural changes that might be promoted to enhance cooperation among Third World nations themselves. Analysts in *South* and other journals have quite cogently demonstrated in the early 1980s that the ability to propose reforms is not related to the political will to carry them out. Proposing solutions like a new Bretton Woods Agreement for Group 77 nations can be made to look good on paper. But very few Third World governments are really very democratic. Few of their international representatives show much awareness of issues of bureaucratic imperatives or participatory development. It is practical to seek more regional market integration because, to the extent trade between equals expands, less unequally valued imports may be necessary from the First World. But the dynamics of the triple alliance are likely to forestall any large-scale, long-term institutional cooperation among Third World states until their societies have been structurally transformed by mass citizen empowerment.

CONCLUSION

No task of learning and change is ever completed, but all books must come to an end. This book has synthesized the historical lessons of modern development and the practical steps toward mass empowerment and a more productive and democratic future. I hope social change agents all over the world will find this mixture of theory and practice to be operationally useful in the advancement of participatory development. Others too may have found that beyond capitalism and state socialism there can be a different, less alienating, more peaceful and productive twenty-first century world that is feasible to struggle for. I make no suggestion that it will be quick or easy. But the tools are here to move beyond the rhetoric of a just world order to its realization.

These last words are written on Memorial Day, 1982 in the peaceful greenery of rural New England. Yet the radio and the newspaper bring the daily reminders of war, poverty, and oppression against which to pose these dreams of peace, development, and human welfare. A president of the United States with an unblemished record of supporting war and exploitation over several decades is today talking of peace and arms reduction because millions of Americans and Europeans have begun to insist vocally that those are possible and preferred realities. Is this not the substance of all social change and human advance? I cannot write human poverty out of existence with this book. But you, as a permanent citizen, can help to put poverty and war into the trash can of history in your lifetime. Can you do anything more important with your life?

A Bibliographical Guide
to Development Studies

PREFATORY REMARKS

In the course of preparing this reinterpretation of contemporary Third World development, I was both impressed and depressed by the current state of the art. Work from certain schools, institutes, and scholars in the early 1980s is contributing much toward a more participatory, productive, and humane twenty-first century economy. A lot of trees, however, are still being sacrificed on other kinds of education, as Section 4 will indicate. Also depressing is the narrow and incomplete vision of the literary universe that most scholars and practitioners continue to demonstrate. The primary purpose of the bibliography that follows is to guide the reader to a broader, more interdisciplinary and systems-based appreciation of the knowledge appropriate for authentic development work. Organizational and political factors oppose such learning. But spending scarce resources and affecting the lives of others cannot and should not be done in ignorance.

Global development studies are fragmented in many hurtful ways. Bureaucratic constraints are severe. Most people writing about development (or growth) sit in one of three institutional universes: bilateral or multilateral agencies and their consulting firms; universities and other social science institutes and research centers; and the corporate and banking world. These worlds interact very poorly, often not at all. Material from one is greeted with little interest or respect in another; independent scholarly inquiry is particularly slighted. A second fragmentation occurs in the way modern education mystifies systems understanding by the divisions known as disciplines. People trained in technical, social science, and cultural fields do not in most cases incorporate much from the other two realms. In this book and in the bibliography, I succumb as well and slight the technical and cultural. People trained in one language are averse to bothering with material in other languages. Westerners, for example, have been especially disinclined to collect and consider indigenous Arabic language material on local development in Islamic countries. A fourth division is created by class origins. Most people who publish on development and get their work very widely spread are rich Westerners. Most who can afford books are also rich Westerners. It is difficult to see how such elite Westerners can represent very accurately the cognitive reality of the Third World poor.

Overcoming these four dilemmas, even partially, has been the most important principle in creating the listing that follows. A second premise is that the volume of material on development is so large that most people are drowning in it. Thus I have sought to limit this bibliography to the newest and best books. Some of the most enduring classics were also added: Within each section or subsection, the reader can find an average of 5 to 15 citations on a country or category of interest. The sections are classified, so that a very brief search through no more than 2 or 3 of them will uncover either the specific sources and/or the current bibliography of such sources. Necessary additional bibliographical tools, annuals, and quarterlies are discussed in the following pages. There are, of course, gaps. Some countries or topics have no recent coverage of any real developmental quality.

You should know how I define good and new. Good research is interdisciplinary, historically and empirically grounded, and explicit and defensible in its normative choices. Since participatory development is the empowerment of the poor, I have chosen far more titles on social change at the local and regional levels than at national and international levels. A second bias is that research done in an organizational or corporate setting suffers from the constraints of its environment. I have been more inclined toward academic work, cognizant, however, that scholars usually do not write to address directly the needs of practitioners. A third preference stems from my understanding of the world of the poor as one of conflict. To act in or upon such a world, one needs to know about realities, not the myths of harmony in elite social science. The latter class of works cannot be ignored (see Section 4) but must be viewed within their social origins and goals. I have inflicted a fourth bias on the listings, one that favors books and largely ignores articles. Writers seem to follow a common pattern of several articles and then a book that surpasses the previous work. Very few articles survive in value very many years; a handful that I judge of continuing worth are included in appropriate sections.

New research may here be defined as material published in the period 1980-82. Titles from the late 1970s and before were judged more critically. The bibliography itself was compiled in mid-1982. It contains English language listings to the end of 1982, as I was able to look at the fall 1982 catalogs of most of the 15-20 most important publishers. French language listings stop with May, 1982, the latest available issue of *Livres du Mois*. Coverage of unpublished dissertations is episodic through mid-1981. They are, however, increasingly important to development studies, as more and more Third World students critically examine local development issues from the relative freedom of Western universities. Consult *Dissertation Abstracts International*, a monthly, and the occasional cumulative regional catalogs by University Microfilm for United States dissertations.

A comment or two is also called for on my specific knowledge of the listed sources. I have read, had in hand, or perused some short discussion or review of more than 90 percent of the 2,000-2,200 citations presented. Very few titles are included solely on the basis of subject matter or recentness. Publishers' catalogs and discussions were used extensively for 1981-82 titles; reviews and comments from friends helped on older titles. Particularly useful were the contributions of my brother, Peter Gran, to Section 7 on the Islamic world. The overall results reflect the pros and cons of working in Washington and dealing with too much Western language material. Vernacular material from all regions is insufficiently represented. Too much top-down bias endures. Too little evidence from cultural sources is included; the few novels listed are the tip of an iceberg.

SPECIFIC ADDITIONAL GUIDES AND SOURCES

No listing of books, no matter how designed, can ever present more than a partial introduction to a topic as broad as human development. As already indicated, this bibliography is focussed more on the sociopolitical, economic, and institutional aspects of development and less on the technical. Many parts of scientific inquiry are well organized for even novice research. One does not have to be a doctor to use *Index Medicus*. The quickest way to start locating guides to fields of knowledge in general is Sheehy, 1976 and

1980. Section 10 herein adds more current guides to specific subjects relevant to global development. As with the rest of the bibliography, gaps mean that no recent work of value was uncovered and you must seek out journal literature, *Books in Print*, library card catalogs, and bibliographic tools that are now to be suggested.

I propose a dual strategy: monitor a relatively small number of essential journals on a regular basis and examine bibliographical quarterlies and annuals on regions and subjects. This complements primary research and networking of all sorts, through travel, conferences, and conversations. An admittedly imperfect listing of alternative development journals of varying degrees of practicality, consistency, and quality includes the following:

IFDA Dossier
Assignment Children
Development Dialogue
CEPAL Review
IDS Bulletin
Culture et Développement
New Internationalist
Revue Tiers Monde
South
Economic Analysis and Workers' Management
Autogestions
Alternatives
Review
Le Monde Diplomatique
Journal of Peace Research
Journal of Peasant Studies
Rural Development Participation Review
Renewal
Economic and Political Weekly
Archives Internationales de Sociologie de la Cooperation
Revue des Etudes Cooperatives

For others consult the listing in Gellar (1982). Much more likely to be in a local library in the West are journals of another sort. The modernization paradigm continues to serve global elites. Their journals are legion and the following are suggested as a means of surveying recent perceptions.

World Development
Journal of Development Studies
Third World Quarterly
Public Administration Review
Economic Development and Cultural Change
Population Review
Population and Development Review
Euromoney

Studies in Comparative International Development
Journal of Developing Areas
Journal of Development Economics
Forbes
The Economist
International Currency Review

Journal literature of the modernization school is regularly tracked by the *Journal of Economic Literature* (quarterly). There is no satisfactory bibliography of current journal literature on development properly conceived. The closest contender may become *International Development Abstracts* (1982-) six times a year, under the editorship of Charles Elliott. It will abstract about 3,000 articles a year from journals and book collections and publish several annual indices. It promises to broaden and deepen coverage over time to remove its initial European flavor.

Quite useful general bibliographies on development come from the Commonwealth Agricultural Bureau in England. It produces many specialized bibliographic journals of abstracts of books and articles. Most well known of those with broader coverage is the monthly *WAERSA, World Agricultural Economics and Rural Sociology Abstracts*. More manageable is *Rural Development Abstracts*, a quarterly covering more than 3,000 books, articles, and dissertations a year. It has a broad vision of development and covers a good range of Western language material. European dissertations are one important gap.

Many more specialized research tools exist to aid different kinds of learning. Those who prefer topical pursuits will be most assisted by Sections 1-3 and reference aides in Section 10. For the technical side of agriculture see Blanchard and Farrell (1982), WAERSA and AGRICOLA; the social side is better covered first by Sections 2A and 2B herein, then by Ball (1981) and Currey (1981). SALUS (see Bechtel, 1980) is the annual guide to new health development literature. Altbach (1982) and Paulston (1978) are guides to education for the use of the modernization paradigm; guides to education by and for the poor are contained in Section 2C and in Borremans (1979). The most efficient way to start studying appropriate technology is to get the two very inexpensive volumes by Darrow et al. (1981 and 1977). They are so good that it was superfluous to put much on technology in this bibliography. Section 10 contains other new topical bibliographies that were found. For older ones consult Sheehy, (1976 and 1980), the *Journal of Bibliographies*, the *Bulletin signalétique*, or the *Referativnyi Zhurnal*.

Some topical guides (*AGRICOLA* in agriculture, *ERIC* for education, *Index Medicus*) manage to stay fairly current by use of computers. Many readers will not have computer access. More to the point, such subject guides are not conducive to interdisciplinary and systems thinking. I find such topical resources comparatively less useful than those devoted to area studies. These also vary in quality and fail to list much material of Third World origin. But the best efforts on Africa and the Middle East are reasonably coherent ways of tracking Western writing and tasting Third World material.

Africa, the last region intellectually colonized by scholars of the core, has become the most thoroughly monitored. The *International African Bibliography* (quarterly) is very good. The reference sections in *Review of African Political Economy* are also essential. Consider as well these reference publications: *Africana Journal*, *Bibliotheek Documentatieblad* (from Leyden University African Studies Center), *African Studies Associations Newsletter*, and the *Sahel Bibliographic Bulletin*. More material of Washington origin shows up in the *Current Bibliography of African Affairs* and in *SADEX* (on Southern Africa). To sample contemporary events in Africa start with *Africa News* (weekly), *Africa Confidential* (biweekly), *West Africa* (weekly), *Marché tropicaux et méditerranéen* (weekly), and the biweekly news clipping service on Southern Africa from Amsterdam, *Facts and Reports*. To start exploring more academic writing try these journals: *Review of African Political Economy*, *Journal of Modern African Studies*, *Africa Today*, *African Studies Review*, *Revue francaise d'études politiques africaines*, *Africa Development* (Dakar), and *Politique Africaine*. Hans Zell Publishing Company in London produces varied reference tools to literature published in Africa. The weakest areas of coverage remain local and regional vernacular material and institute papers done irregularly. These limitations are even more pronounced in the reference tools on other areas.

Islamic studies is still divided between those who feel that Arabic language material is essential and those who have made successful careers ignoring it. Learning Arabic is not easy. There are two current and moderately good starting places for current material: *Index Islamicus*, now a quarterly, is slightly better on Western and historical material; *Turkologischer Anzeiger* (an annual from Vienna) covers Soviet and East European material better. Both have considerable but imperfect coverage of Arabic material. *Annuaire de l'Afrique du Nord* is basic for the area it covers. For the more specialized country and topical bibliographies consult Grimwood-Jones (1979). For Western language periodical works there are also *Current Contents of Periodicals on the Middle East* (monthly from Tel-Aviv) and *The Middle East: Abstracts and Index* (quarterly). To taste contemporary events and scholarly work, look at the *MESA Bulletin, Middle East Journal, MERIP Reports, Middle East Economic Digest, Middle East International*, and *Maghreb-Machrek*.

Latin America is covered by the *Interamerican Review of Bibliography* (quarterly), which treats articles and North American dissertations. The *Handbook of Latin American Studies* is an annotated annual listing books and articles; Number 43, to appear in spring 1983, covers social science material over the 1977-80 period. The *Hispanic American Periodical Index* is unannotated and comparably out of date. Easier to start with for older English language material is Delorme (1981). Also consult all recent issues of the *Latin American Research Review* and the *LASA Newsletter*. To start locating institutes and research centers see Sable (1981). To taste contemporary events see the *Latin American Newsletters*, the *Andean Report*, and *NACLA Report on the Americas*; and to begin to sample more academic work try the *Journal of Latin American Studies, CEPAL Review, Latin American Perspectives, Amérique Latine, Economia De America Latine, El Trimestre Economico, Nueva Sociedad, Estados Unidos: Perspective Latinamericana*, and *Estudos Centroamericanos*.

Asia is the most difficult region to monitor. The linguistic variety has discouraged all-encompassing bibliographic efforts. There is no quarterly bibliographical review, and the annual *Bibliography of Asian Studies* is 3-4 years behind. It seeks to cover Western language books and articles. More complete on India has been *BEPI — Bibliography of English Publication in India* (1976-); other periodical guides exist as well, such as *Index India*. Recent standard reference guides to material on Asia prior to the late 1970s include Saito et al. (1979) on Southeast Asia, Patterson (1981) on South Asia, and Nunn (1980) on the region as a whole. See also more specialized aids like Kirchbach (1980) on multinational corporations. For contemporary events the *Far Eastern Economic Review* has been for a generation the finest weekly on any Third World region. The

Economic and Political Weekly is also essential for South Asia. Important contemporary analysis is found in the *Southeast Asian Chronicle* and *Sudestasie*; data are available in the *Asian Research Bulletin*, the *Asian Wall Street Journal*, and more specialized business publications like the *China Report* or *Institutional Investor*. More academic inquiry can begin with the *Journal of Contemporary Asia*, *Bulletin of Concerned Asian Scholars*, *Journal of Asian Studies*, *Marga Quarterly*, *Journal of Southeast Asian Studies*, *Pacific Affairs*, and *Pacific Studies*.

Scholarly and public affairs reference tools do have finite limits. Some portions of two other bodies of literature can help with data gaps: institutional literature and that of the business community. Neither of these is well surveyed by the sources just mentioned. Those outside these universes tend to be deterred by claims of secrecy and bureaucratic tactics that bar researchers from hearing about or obtaining reports. The obstacles to long-distance pursuit are severe, but I have found most aid organizations in Washington reasonably permeable and quite often quite helpful. Responses to requests vary widely over time and space within any large organization. There are usually several ways of getting a study once you know it exists. Here is a rough guide to determine that a report or study is likely to exist.

Easiest to track is the work of the U.S. bilateral agency, AID. Contrary to conventional wisdom, the best of AID's written work is far better than the more bureaucratic products of the World Bank; specific samples of such AID contract work appear in the bibliography. AID produces an annual policy document *Development Issues*. To start studying projects and country strategies consult the annual *Congressional Presentation* volumes. A page is devoted to each new project. For every country to which aid flows there are frequent, sometimes annual, Country Strategy Statements of 70-120 pages. For every project there is a project paper and usually also background consultant reports. There are also episodic sector papers on countries of interest. Other parts of the agency, notably the Bureau for Policy Planning and the Development Support Bureau produce many reports. Much, but not all, of this material is also available in AID's public reference libraries; computer searches are possible. Many agency staff will be quite helpful with country research; as in all organizations quality of knowledge varies widely.

The World Bank produces an enormous volume of material, making up in quantity what it lacks in intellectual quality. Policy papers, a few reference annuals and country reports, and hundreds of working papers are now expensively available to the public. Consult the annual publications catalog, for a few are of value. Every country that gets aid is the subject of country and sector reports, most of which remain internal documents. Every project is the focus of appraisal and evaluation reports and background research. An internal guide to appraisal reports and much of the rest of the literary universe the Bank recognizes is the monthly and cumulative annual *Documentation Available to Staff*. This reference guide is helpful to keep track of some of the work of other UN agencies as well. Most internal Bank reports reach a grey cover stage; depending on the individual country and the specific Bank staff involved, grey covers can in practice be obtained for scholarly research or consulting work. More sensitive reports, the internal Country Paper (a strategy document for the Bank), and most of the country studies of the International Monetary Fund are not normally available; this makes important areas of world-system analysis difficult. The development practitioner is not, however, severely hampered. Look at a published version of a Bank country study to see how marginal they are for true development analysis and action.

The UN system as a whole is too big for anyone to monitor. I find the annual catalogs and more frequent announcements from the ILO, UNESCO, and OECD helpful. To discover which agencies are working in each country, obtain the annual UNDP *Compendium of Approved Projects*. Behind each project are research reports and project papers. There is also a human network. Some of the people in the ILO, UNICEF, UNCTAD, and UNRISD, as well as in parts of UNDP and FAO, are very important sources of local knowledge. Note the many citations of UNRISD and ILO books and papers in the bibliography. In sum do not settle for what appears in public catalogs and libraries but seek out the primary reports and the people doing the work.

A final literary universe deserves at least brief mention. Some idea of what appears in the *Wall Street Journal*, the *New York Times*, the *Economist*, the *Financial Times*, *Le Monde*, *Euromoney*, *Business Week*, *Institutional Investor*, and comparable German, Italian, and Spanish language journals is essential for world-system and growth analysis. Section 10 contains a number of recent guides to corporate research, like Brownstone and Gorton, 1982. Publications of the UN Center on Transnational Corporations, for one, suggest by their data gaps and limits how effectively concentrations of private economic power hide their intentions and activities. Beyond what is conventionally discussed, consider the pursuit of the expensive business newsletters, especially industry journals. They are very often crucial for industrial sector analysis.

Such a cavalier dash through the literature cannot do justice to many subfields. Careful attention to all of these reference tools will, however, turn up substantially all of the research conceivable for citizens to reach at this historic moment. Further intellectual empowerment is essential to human development and welfare, as Chapter 2 argues at length. I am aware that access to such a range of material implies time and resources beyond the ability of most. Many of the new books are unjustifiably expensive. Knowing what exists and of what value it is, is, however, the first step toward public pressure to build greater library resources at every level of every society. It will also provide impetus to those inside development organizations who know that professional work demands continuous learning and that the structure of work must be redesigned to incorporate this regular learning space. Toward such learning, I have included as an appendix my most recent syllabus for an introductory (graduate) reading course on developmental conflict and political change.

A CONCLUDING NOTE ON THE FUTURE

If readers all over the world find this first effort to be useful and desire its expansion, I would like to consider a team effort for a global bibliography in early 1985. We could convene groups of local scholars in each subregion and category for a few months' efforts to accumulate and annotate the best works appearing over the period 1980-85. In this way local and vernacular material should begin to get the emphasis it deserves and scholars far away could learn far more about varied local materials of all sorts. If all this work were collected in one volume, it would dramatically encourage far more valid development research and practice, not to mention cross-cultural communication. (I would be interested in thoughts on this project, addressed to 1731 Corcoran St., NW, Washington, D.C. 20009, U.S.A.)

A CURRICULUM TO BEGIN MICRODEVELOPMENT STUDIES

This course will explore the nature of local and regional politics in the Third World to lay bare the conflictual realities with which national and international development activities must contend. It begins with a brief review of the generic conflicts created by elite interests and organizational imperatives (the work of Marx, Weber et al.). The nature of politics in the precolonial world is also introduced. The basic conflicts in different paths of modernization then serve as preamble to a detailed look at the politics of rural development through these five topics: the typology of rural communities; politics in conventional agriculture; the Green Revolution; social services; and rural marketing. The political conflicts of urban development are then treated in three areas: the informal sector; housing; and social services. The course concludes with the agenda of unresolved problems in the capitalist and socialist models and what would be implied by a future of authentic participatory development.

REQUIRED AND SUGGESTED READINGS*

Conflict in the World-System: An Introduction

D. Chirot (1977) *Social Change in the 20th Century* (Harcourt Brace).
L. S. Stavrianos (1981) *The Global Rift: The Third World Comes of Age* (Morrow).
I. Wallerstein (1980) *The Capitalist World Economy* (Cambridge).
C. Elliott (1975) *Patterns of Poverty in the Third World* (Praeger) (out of print).
Journals: *Review, South, Development Dialogue, Tiers-Monde*.
B. Abrahamsson (1977) *Bureaucracy or Participation* (Sage).
R. Hummel (1977) *The Bureaucratic Experience* (St. Martins).
W. G. Scott and D. K. Hart (1979) *Organizational America* (Houghton Mifflin).
M. A. Lutz and K. Lux (1979) *The Challenge of Humanistic Economics* (Benjamin/Cummings).

---

*Note: These are the titles that were required as the course was taught in the spring of 1982. This means they are the ones that seemed most suitable and affordable in December 1981. In an ideal world, start with Stavrianos (1981), Elliott (1975), Heyer et al. (1981), Bromley and Gerry, eds. (1979), and Lutz and Lux (1979). Then contemplate Illich and Horvat.

Theories of Organization: Classical and Contemporary and Their Application to Local Politics (discussion of Abrahamsson)

Capitalist Modernization and Its Micro-conflicts

W. Hinton (1966) *Fanshen* (Vintage).

B. Moore (1966) *Social Origins of Dictatorship and Democracy* (Beacon).

E. Wolf (1970) *Peasant Wars in the 20th Century* (Harper).

M. Taussig (1980) *The Devil and Commodity Fetishism in South America* (Univ. of North Carolina).

A. Warman (1981) *We Come to Object* (Johns Hopkins).

R. Palmer and N. Parsons (1977) *The Roots of Rural Poverty in Central and Southern Africa* (Univ. of California).

Socialist Modernization and Its Micro-conflicts

J. G. Gurley (1976) *China's Economy and the Maoist Strategy* (Monthly Review).

A. D. Barnett (1981) *China's Economy in Global Perspective* (Brookings, parts I and III).

M. Lewin (1968) *Russian Peasants and Soviet Power* (Norton).

G. Gran (1979) "Vietnam in Pursuit of Development: Socialist Promise, Natural Calamities, and Permanent Learning," *Cultures et développement*, XI, 2:261-281.

Modernization Seen from Below

J. Scott (1977) *The Moral Economy of the Peasant* (Yale).

S. Popkin (1979) *The Rational Peasant* (Univ. of California).

J. Berger (1978) "Towards Understanding Peasant Experience," *Race and Class*, XIX, 4:345-359.

A. Adams (1977) "The Senegal River Valley: What Kind of Change," *Review of African Political Economy*, 10:33-59.

D. Emmerson (1976) "Biting the Helping Hand: Modernization and Violence in an Indonesian Fishing Community," *Land Tenure Center Newsletter* (Univ. of Wisconsin), 51:1-15.

H. Blair (1978) "Rural Development, Class Structure and Bureaucracy in Bangladesh," *World Development*, 6, 1:65-82.

A Political Typology of Rural Communities: Conflicts at the Bottom of the World Food System

R. Dumont and N. Cohen (1980) *The Growth of Hunger* (Marion Boyars).
J. Potter et al., eds. (1967) *Peasants – A Reader* (Little, Brown).
M. A. Klein, ed. (1980) *Peasants in Africa* (Sage).
C. Lassen (1980) *Landlessness and Rural Poverty in Latin America* (Cornell, Rural Dev. Comm.).

Export-Led Growth and the Politics of the Green Revolution in Africa

R. Galli, ed. (1981) *The Political Economy of Rural Development* (SUNY Press).
J. Heyer et al. (1981) *Rural Development in Tropical Africa* (St. Martins).
R. W. Franke and B. Chasen (1980) *Seeds of Famine* (Allanheld Osmun).
G. Gran, ed. (1979) *Zaire: The Political Economy of Underdevelopment* especially, Chaps. 9, 12, and 15 (Praeger).

Politics of the Green Revolution: Cases from Asia

A. Pearse (1980) *Seeds of Plenty, Seeds of Want* (Oxford).
D. S. Gibbons et al. (1980) *Agricultural Modernization, Poverty and Inequality* (Saxon House).
R. De Koninck (1979) "The Integration of the Peasantry: Examples from Malaysia and Indonesia," *Pacific Affairs*, 52, 2:265-293.
H. Cleaver (1977) "Food, Famine, and the International Crisis," *Zerowork* (New York), 2:7-69.

Rural Socialist Development: The Case of Tanzania

M. von Freyhold (1979) *Ujamaa Villages in Tanzania* (Monthly Review).
A. Coulson (1980) *African Socialism in Practice* (Spokesman Books, London).
G. Hyden (1979) *Beyond Ujamaa in Tanzania* (Univ. of California).
F. M. Lappe et al. (1980) *Mozambique and Tanzania: Asking the Big Questions* (Inst. Food and Dev. Policy).

Rural Participatory Development: Avoiding Micro-conflict or Creating a New Conflictual Agenda?

G. V. S. de Silva et al. (1979) "Bhoomi Sena: A Struggle for People's Power," *Development Dialogue*, 2:3-70.

M. R. Hollnsteiner (1979) "Mobilizing the Rural Poor Through Community Organization," *Philippine Studies*, 27, 3:387-411.

D. C. Korten (1980) "Community Organization and Rural Development: A Learning Process Approach," *Public Administration Review*, 40, 5:480-511.

B. van Heck (1979) *Participation of the Poor in Rural Organizations* (FAO, ROAP, Rome).

S. Gellar et al. (1980) *Animation Rurale and Rural Development: The Experience of Senegal* (Cornell, Rural Dev. Comm.).

D. C. Korten et al. (1981) *Bureaucracy and the Poor: Closing the Gap* (McGraw-Hill, Singapore).

An Introduction to Urban Micropolitics: Politics in the Informal Sector

J. Perlman (1976) *The Myth of Marginality* (Univ. of California).

R. Bromley and C. Gerry, eds. (1979) *Casual Work and Poverty in Third World Cities* (Wiley).

J. Abu-Lughod and R. Hay, eds. (1980) *Third World Urbanization* (Methuen).

J. Nelson (1979) *Access to Power* (Princeton).

The Politics of Urban Housing and Social Services

J. L. Pressman and A. Wildavsky (1979, 2nd ed.) *Implementation* (Univ. of California).

M. Lipsky (1980) *Street-Level Bureaucracy* (Basic).

Nairobi, Kenya: Role Playing in a World Bank Sites and Services Project

R. Bromley and C. Gerry, op. cit., Chaps. 10 and 14 (on reserve).

Unresolved Problems of Development in an Environment of Conflict Rethinking Organization versus People

I. Illich (1980) *Shadow Work* (Marion Boyars).

J. Galtung (1980) *The True Worlds* (Free Press).

B. Horvat (1981) *The Political Economy of Socialism* (M. E. Sharpe).

E. P. Thompson (1978) *The Poverty of Theory* (Monthly Review).

TABLE OF CONTENTS OF THE BIBLIOGRAPHY

BIBLIOGRAPHY

I. Theoretical, Philosophical, and Historical Issues of Development: National and International Levels

I.A. World-System and Historical Framework

Amin, Samir (1980, 1979 in Fr.). *Class and Nation, Historically and in the Current Crisis.* New York: Monthly Review Press.

—— (1977, 1976 in Fr.). *Imperialism and Unequal Development.* New York: Monthly Review Press.

—— (1976, 1973 in Fr.). *Unequal Development: An Essay on the Social Formations of Peripheral Capitalism.* New York: Monthly Review Press.

—— (1974). *Accumulation on a World Scale: A Critique of the Theory of Underdevelopment.* New York: Monthly Review Press.

Anderson, Perry (1974a). *Lineages of the Absolutist State.* London: NLB.

Arrighi, Giovanni (1979). "Peripheralization of Southern Africa, I: Changes in Production Processes," *Review,* III, 2:161-91.

—— (1978). *The Geometry of Imperialism: The Limits of Hobson's Paradigm.* London: New Left Books.

Aymard, Maurice, ed. (1982). *Dutch Capitalism and World Capitalism.* Cambridge: Cambridge University Press.

Bergesen, Albert, ed. (1980). *Studies of the Modern World-System.* New York: Academic Press.

Block, Fred L. (1977). *The Origins of International Economic Disorder: A Study of United States International Monetary Policy from World War II to the Present.* Berkeley: University of California Press.

Borrego, John (1981). "Metanational Capitalist Accumulation and the Emerging Paradigm of Revolutionist Accumulation," *Review,* IV, 4:713-77.

Braudel, Fernand (1979). *Les Structures du quotidien: Le possible et l'impossible.* Paris: Armand Colin. (English translation 1981. *The Structures of Everyday Life.* New York: Harper & Row.) (N.B. The first of three spectacular interdisciplinary volumes on European history 1500-1800.)

Caldwell, Malcolm (1977). *The Wealth of Some Nations.* London: Zed Press.

Chase-Dunn, Christopher, ed. (1982). *Socialist States in the World System.* Beverly Hills, Calif: Sage.

Chesneaux, Jean (1978). *Pasts and Futures: Or What Is History For?* London: Thames & Hudson.

Chirot, Daniel (1977). *Social Change in the Twentieth Century.* New York: Harcourt Brace.

Chorover, Stephan L. (1979). *From Genesis to Genocide: The Meaning of Human Nature and the Power of Behaviour Control.* Cambridge, Mass.: MIT Press.

Cleaver, Harry (1977). "Food Famine and the International Crisis," *Zerowork* (New York), 2:7-70.

Duverger, Maurice, ed. (1980). *Le concept d'empire.* Paris: Presses Universitaires de France (hereafter PUF).

Faire, Alexandre (1981). "The Strategies of Economic Redeployment in the West," *Review,* 5,2:139-204.

Frank, Andre Gunder (1980a). *Crisis: In the World Economy.* New York: Holmes & Meier.

――― (1980b). *Crisis: In the Third World.* New York: Holmes & Meier.

――― (1979). *Dependent Accumulation and Underdevelopment.* New York: Monthly Review Press.

Friedman, Edward, ed. (1982). *Ascent and Decline in the World-System.* Beverly Hills, Calif.: Sage.

Fröbel, Folker (1982). "The Current Development of the World-Economy: Reproduction of Labor and Accumulation of Capital on a World Scale," *Review,* V,4:507-55.

Fröbel, Folker, et al. (1981). *Krisen in der Kapitalistischen Weltokonomic.* Reinbek bei Hamburg: Rowohlt.

――― (1980). *The New International Division of Labor.* Cambridge: Cambridge University Press.

Goldfrank, Walter L., ed. (1979). *The World-System of Capitalism: Past and Present.* Beverly Hills, Calif.: Sage.

Gordon, D. M., et al. (1982). *Segmented Work, Divided Workers: The Historical Transformation of Labor in the United States.* Cambridge: Cambridge University Press.

Heller, Agnes (1982). *A Theory of History.* London: Routledge & Kegan Paul.

Hobsbawm, E. J., et al., eds. (1980). *Peasants in History: Essays in Honour of Daniel Thorner.* Delhi: Oxford University Press.

Hodgson, Marshall (1974). *The Venture of Islam.* 3 volumes. Chicago: University of Chicago Press.

Hollist, W. Ladd, and Rosenau, James N. (1981). *World-System Structure: Continuity and Change.* Beverly Hills, Calif.: Sage.

Hopkins, Terence K., et al., eds. (1982). *World-Systems Analysis: Theory and Methodology.* Beverly Hills, Calif.: Sage.

Hopkins, Terence K., and Wallerstein, Immanuel (1977). "Patterns of Development of the Modern World System," *Review,* I,2,Fall 1977:111-45.

Hopkins, Terence, and Wallerstein, Immanuel, eds. (1980). *Processes of the World-System.* Beverly Hills, Calif.: Sage.

Kaplan, Barbara H., ed. (1978). *Social Change in the Capitalist World Economy.* Beverly Hills, Calif.: Sage.

Kolm, Serge-Christophe (1981). "Liberal Transition to Socialism: Theory and Difficulties," *Review,* 5,2:205-18.

Kreidte, Peter, et al. (1981, 1977 in Ger.). *Industrialization Before Industrialization.* Cambridge: Cambridge University Press.

Kuhn, Thomas (1962). *The Structure of Scientific Revolutions*. Chicago: University of Chicago Press.

Lindblom, Charles E. (1977). *Politics and Markets: The World's Political-Economic System*. New York: Basic Books.

Mandel, Ernest (1978, 1977 in Ger.). *The Second Slump: A Marxist Analysis of Recession in the Seventies*. London: NLB.

McLennan, Gregor (1981). *Marxism & the Methodologies of History*. London: Verso.

Mannoni, O. (1964, 1950 in Fr.). *Prospero and Caliban: The Psychology of Colonization*. New York: Praeger.

Meyer, John W., and Hannan, Michael T., eds. (1979). *National Development and the World System: Educational, Economic, and Political Change, 1950-1970*. Chicago: University of Chicago Press.

Michalet, Charles-Albert (1976). *Le capitalisme mondial*. Paris: PUF.

Moore, Barrington (1978). *Injustice: The Social Bases of Obedience and Revolt*. White Plains, N.Y.: M. E. Sharpe.

_____ (1966). *Social Origins of Dictatorship and Democracy: Lord and Peasant in the Making of the Modern World*. Boston: Beacon Press.

Petras, James F. (1981). *Class, State, and Power in the Third World*. Montclair, N.J.: Allanheld, Osmun.

Petras, James (1980). *Class, State and Power in the Third World: With Case Studies on Class Conflict in Latin America*. Montclair, N.J.: Allanheld, Osmun.

_____ (1978). *Critical Perspectives on Imperialism and Social Class in the Third World*. New York: Monthly Review Press.

Polanyi, Karl (1977). *The Livelihood of Man*. New York: Academic Press.

_____ (1944). *The Great Transformation: The Political and Economic Origins of Our Time*. Boston: Beacon Press.

Pryor, Frederick (1977). *The Origins of the Economy: A Comparative Study of Distribution in Primitive and Peasant Economies*. New York: Academic Press.

Rubinson, Richard, ed. (1981). *Dynamics of World Development*. Beverly Hills, Calif.: Sage.

Senghaas-Knobloch, Eva (1979). *Reproduktion der Arbeitskraft in der Weltgesellschaft*. Frankfurt: Campus.

Skocpol, Theda (1979). *States & Social Revolutions: A Comparative Analysis of France, Russia & China*. Cambridge: Cambridge University Press.

Starnberger Studien 4 (1980). *Strukturveranderungen in der kapitalischen Weltwirtschaft*. Saarbrucken: Verlag Breitenbach.

Stavrianos, L. S. (1981). *Global Rift: The Third World Comes of Age*. New York: William Morrow.

_____ (1976). *The Promise of the Coming Dark Age*. San Francisco, Calif.: W. H. Freeman.

Tigar, Michael, and Levy, Madeleine R. (1977). *Law & the Rise of Capitalism*. New York: Monthly Review Press.

Wallerstein, Immanuel (1980). *The Modern World System II: Mercantilism and the Consolidation of the European World-Economy, 1600-1750*. New York:

Academic Press.

———(1979). *The Capitalist World-Economy*. Cambridge: Cambridge University Press.

———(1974). *The Modern World-System I: Capitalist Agriculture and the Origins of the European World-Economy in the Sixteenth Century*. New York: Academic Press.

Warren, Bill (1980). *Imperialism: Pioneer of Capitalism*. London: NLB.

Wisely, William (1977). *A Tool of Power: The Political History of Money*. New York: John Wiley & Sons.

Wolf, Eric (1982). *Europe and the People Without History*. Berkeley: University of California Press.

I.B. Strands of Contemporary Development Theory

Abel, Richard, ed. (1982). *The Politics of Informal Justice*. 2 volumes. New York: Academic Press.

Allaby, Michael, and Bunyard, Peter (1980). *The Politics of Self-Sufficiency*. Oxford: Oxford University Press.

Amin, Samir, et al., (1975). *La planification du sous-développement*. Paris: Anthropos-IDEP.

Amoa, Ga-Kwame, and Braun, Oscar (1974). *Échanges internationaux et sous-développement*. Paris: Anthropos-IDEP.

Atkinson, Alexander (1981). *Social Order and General Theory of Strategy*. London: Routledge & Kegan Paul.

Attir, Mustafa O., et al., eds. (1981). *Directions of Change: Modernization Theory, Research, and Realities*. Boulder, Colo.: Westview Press.

Aydalot, Philippe (1980). *Dynamique spatiale et développement inégal*. Paris: Economica.

Bagchi, Amiya Kumar (1982). *The Political Economy of Underdevelopment*. Cambridge: Cambridge University Press.

Baroudi, Abdallah (1981). *Idéologie, savoir, pouvoir dans l'institution capitaliste*. Paris: Diff. Alternatives.

Barraclough, Geoffrey (1980). "Worlds Apart: Untimely Thoughts on Development and Development Strategies." Sussex: University of Sussex: Institute of Development Studies (hereafter IDS), Discussion Paper No. 152. (N.B. This is an ongoing wide-ranging series of papers.)

Beji, Hélé (1982). *Désenchantement national: Essai sur la décolonisation*. Paris: Maspero.

Benitah, Marc (1980). *Besoins économiques et pouvoir: Un modèle psychanalytique du développement*. Paris: Anthropos.

Berger, Peter (1976). *Pyramids of Sacrifice: Political Ethics and Social Change*. Garden City, N.Y.: Doubleday.

Berger, Peter, et al. (1973). *The Homeless Mind: Modernization and Consciousness*. New York: Random House.

Berry, Leonard, and Kates, Robert W., eds. (1980). *Making the Most of the Least: Alternative Ways to Development*. New York: Holmes & Meier.

Blanchard, Francis, et al. (1977). *Employment, Growth and Basic Needs: A One-World Problem*. New York: Praeger for the ILO.

Bognar, J. (1980). *End-Century Crossroads of Development and Cooperation*. Budapest: Scientific Council for World Economy.

Bok, Sissela (1978). *Lying: Moral Choice in Public and Private Life*. New York: Random House.

Brett, E. A. (1978). "Development Theory, the IMF, and the Periphery: Towards an Alternative Strategy." Geneva: IFDA.

Brewer, Anthony (1980). *Marxist Theories of Imperialism: A Critical Survey*. London: Routledge & Kegan Paul.

Brookfield, Harold (1975). *Interdependent Development*. Pittsburgh: University of Pittsburgh.

Brown, Richard (1978). *The Theory of Unequal Exchange: The End of the Debate*. The Hague: Institute of Social Studies, ISS Occasional Paper No. 65. (NB: One of an important, ongoing, wide-ranging series on all aspects of development studies.)

Chaliand, Gérard (1976). *Mythes révolutionnaires du Tiers-Monde, guérillas et socialismes*. Paris: Seuil.

Chester, Ronald (1982). *Inheritance, Wealth, and Society*. Bloomington: Indiana University Press.

Craig, J. H. and M. (1979). *Synergic Power: Beyond Domination, Beyond Permissiveness*. Berkeley, Calif.: ProActive Press.

De Bandt, Jacques, et al., eds. (1980). *European Studies in Development*. New York: St. Martin's Press.

Domhoff, G. William, ed. (1980). *Power Structure Research*. Beverly Hills, Calif.: Sage.

Dorf, Richard C., and Hunter, Yvonne L., eds. (1978). *Appropriate Visions: Technology, the Environment, and the Individual*. San Francisco, Calif.: Boyd & Fraser.

Elliott, Charles (1975). *Patterns of Poverty in the Third World*. New York: Praeger.

Emmanuel, Arghiri (1977). "Gains and Losses from the International Division of Labor." *Review*, 1,2:87-108.

⸺ (1972). *Unequal Exchange*. New York: Monthly Review Press.

Ferguson, Thomas, and Rogers, Joel (1981). *The Hidden Election: Politics and Economics in the 1980 Presidential Campaign*. New York: Pantheon.

Feyerabend, Paul (1975). *Against Method: Outline of Anarchistic Theory of Knowledge*. London: NLB.

FGA-CFDT (1981). *Alternatives pour l'aujourd'hui: La biomasse*. Paris: Syros.

Gamer, Robert (1976). *The Developing Nations: A Comparative Perspective*. Boston: Allyn & Bacon.

Germani, Gino (1981). *The Sociology of Modernization*. New Brunswick, N.J.: Transaction Books.

Giddens, Anthony, and Held, David, eds. (1982). *Classes, Power, and Conflict: Classical and Contemporary Debates*. Berkeley: University of California Press.

Godelier, Maurice (1977, 1973 in Fr.). *Perspectives in Marxist Anthropology.* Cambridge: Cambridge University Press.

Goulet, Denis (1980). "Development Experts: The One-Eyed Giants." *World Development,* 8,7/8:481-89.

_____ (1977). *The Uncertain Promise: Value Conflicts in Technology Transfer.* New York: 1DOC/North America.

_____ (1971). *The Cruel Choice: A New Concept in the Theory of Development.* New York: Atheneum.

Granotier, Bernard (1980). *La planète des bidonvilles. Perspectives de l'explosion urbaine dans le tiers monde.* Paris: Seuil.

Grjebine, André (1980). *La nouvelle économie internationale: De la crise mondiale au développement autocentré.* Paris: PUF.

Gurvitch, Georges (1971, 1966 in Fr.). *The Social Frameworks of Knowledge.* New York: Harper.

Hanane, Larbi (1978). *Modèles de développement industriel dans le Tiers Monde.* Casablanca: Editions Maghrebines.

Haq, Mahbub ul (1976). *The Poverty Curtain: Choices for the Third World.* New York: Columbia University Press.

Harris, Marvin (1979). *Cultural Materialism: The Struggle for a Science of Culture.* New York: Random House.

Harris, Stephen (1977). *The Death of Capital.* New York: Pantheon.

Hill, Kim Q., ed. (1979). *Toward a New Strategy for Development.* Elmsford, N.Y.: Pergamon Press.

Himmelstrand, Ulf, et al. (1981). *Beyond Welfare Capitalism: Issues, Actors, and Forces in Societal Change.* London: Heinemann Educational Books.

Hirsch, Fred (1976). *Social Limits to Growth.* Cambridge, Mass.: Harvard University Press.

Hoffman, Erik P., and Laird, Robbin F. (1982). *The Politics of Economic Modernization in the Soviet Union.* Ithaca, N.Y.: Cornell University Press.

Holland, Stuart (1975). *The Socialist Challenge.* London: Quartet Books.

_____ , ed. (1978). *Beyond Capitalist Planning.* London: St. Martin's.

Hoogvelt, Ankie M. (1978, 2nd ed.). *The Sociology of Developing Societies.* London: Macmillan.

John Paul II (1981). *On Human Work.* Washington, D.C.: U.S. Catholic Conference.

Kadt, Emanuel de, and Williams, Gavin, eds. (1974). *Sociology and Development.* London: Tavistock.

Kay, Geoffrey (1975). *Development and Underdevelopment: A Marxist Analysis.* London: Macmillan.

Khan, Khushi M., ed. (1980). *Self-reliance als nationale und kollektive Entwicklungsstrategie.* Munich: Weltforum Verlag.

Kohlberg, Lawrence (1981). *The Philosophy of Moral Development: Essays in Moral Development.* New York: Harper & Row.

Lacoste, Yves (1980). *Unité et diversité du tiers monde.* 3 volumes. Paris: Maspero.

Lieber, Nancy, ed. (1982). *Eurosocialism and America: Political Economy for the 1980's.* Philadelphia: Temple University Press.

Lloyd, Peter (1982). *A Third World Proletariat*. London: George Allen & Unwin.

Lovins, Amory, and L. Hunter (1982). *Brittle Power: Energy Strategy for National Security*. Andover, Mass.: Brick House.

Löwy, Michael (1981). *The Politics of Combined and Uneven Development (The Theory of Permanent Revolution)*. London: Verso.

Lustig, Jeff (1981). "Community and Social Class." *Democracy*, April, 1,2: 96-111.

Mahler, Vincent A. (1980). *Dependency Approaches to International Political Economy: A Cross-National Study*. New York: Columbia University Press.

Makler, Harry, et al., eds. (1982). *The New International Economy*. Beverly Hills, Calif.: Sage.

Marcussen, Hanrik, and Torp, Jens (1981). *Blocked Development? – Prospects for the Third World: A Re-Examination of Dependency Theory*. London: Zed Press.

Marković, Mihailo (1974). *From Affluence to Praxis: Philosophy and Social Criticism*. Ann Arbor: University of Michigan Press.

Mignot, Gabriel, ed. (1981). *Les pays les plus pauvres: Quelle coopération pour leur développement?* Paris: Economica.

Munoz, Heraldo, ed. (1981). *From Dependency to Development: Strategies to Overcome Underdevelopment and Inequality*. Boulder, Colo.: Westview Press.

Nabudere, D. Wadada (1979). *Essays on the Theory and Practice of Imperialism*. London: Onyx Press.

November, Andras (1981). *Les médicaments et le tiers monde*. Lausanne: P. M. Favre.

Owen, Roger, and Sutcliffe, Robert, eds. (1972). *Studies in the Theory of Imperialism*. London: Longman.

Oxaal, Ivar, et al., eds. (1975). *Beyond the Sociology of Development*. London: Routledge & Kegan Paul.

Palloix, Christian (1971). *L'économie mondiale capitaliste*. 2 volumes. Paris: Maspero.

—— (1969). *Problèmes de la croissance en économie ouverte*. Paris: Maspero.

Perroux, François (1982). *Pour une philosophie du nouveau développement*. Paris: Aubier-Montaigne, Presses de l'UNESCO.

Portes, Alejandro, and Walton, John (1981). *Labor, Class, and the International System*. New York: Academic Press.

Poulantzas, Nicos (1978, 1978 in Fr.). *State, Power, Socialism*. London: NLB.

—— (1975, 1974 in Fr.). *Classes in Contemporary Capitalism*. London: NLB.

—— (1973, 1968 in Fr.). *Political Power and Social Classes*. London: NLB.

Preston, P. W. (1982). *Theories of Development*. London: Routledge & Kegan Paul.

Rawls, John (1971). *A Theory of Justice*. Cambridge, Mass.: Harvard University Press.

Rist, Gilbert (1980). "Alternative Strategies to Development." *International Development Review*, XXII, 2-3:102-15.

Rousseas, Stephen (1979). *Capitalism and Catastrophe: A Critical Appraisal of the Limits to Capitalism*. Cambridge: Cambridge University Press.

Roxborough, Ian (1979). *Theories of Underdevelopment*. Atlantic Highlands, N.J.: Humanities Press.

Sachs, Ignacy (1981). *Initiation à l'écodéveloppement*. Toulouse: Privat Editeur.

Salama, Pierre, and Tissier, Patrick (1982). *L'industrialization dans le sous-développement*. Paris: Maspero.

Sau, Ranjit (1978). *Unequal Exchange, Imperialism, and Underdevelopment*. Calcutta and Oxford: University Press.

Seers, Dudley, ed. (1981). *Dependency Theory: A Critical Reassessment*. London: Frances Pinter.

Shanin, Teodor, and Alavi, Hamza, eds. (1982). *Introduction to the Sociology of Developing Nations*. New York: Monthly Review Press.

Sik, Ota (1967). *Plan and Market Under Socialism*. White Plains, N.Y.: International Arts and Sciences Press.

Sine, Babakar (1975). *Impérialisme et théories sociologiques du développement*. Paris: Anthropos-IDEP.

Spitz, Pierre, ed. (1980). *Il faut manger pour vivre . . . : Controverses sur les besoins fondamentaux et le développement*. Paris: PUF; and Geneva: I.U.E.D.

Stephens, John D. (1979). *The Transition from Capitalism to Socialism*. London: Macmillan.

Straussman, Jeffrey D. (1978). *The Limits of Technocratic Politics*. New Brunswick, N.J.: Transaction Books.

Szymanski, Albert (1981). *The Logic of Imperialism*. New York: Praeger.

Taylor, John G. (1979). *From Modernization to Modes of Production: A Critique of the Sociologies of Development and Underdevelopment*. Atlantic Highlands, N.J.: Humanities Press.

Tevoedjre, Albert (1978). *La pauvrete, richesse des peuples*. Paris: Ed. Ourvières.

Therborn, Göran (1978). *What Does the Ruling Class Do When It Rules?* London: NLB.

Thomas, Clive (1974). *Dependence and Transformation: The Economics of the Transition to Socialism*. New York: Monthly Review Press.

Thompson, E. P. (1978). *The Poverty of Theory and Other Essays*. New York: Monthly Review Press.

Thompson, James C., and Vidmar, Richard F. (1982). *Administrative Science and Politics in the United States and the Soviet Union*. New York: J. F. Bergin.

Vanek, Jaroslav (1971). *The Participatory Economy*. Ithaca, N.Y.: Cornell University Press.

Willis, David (1982). *Klass: Social Class and Privilege in the Soviet Union*. New York: Empire Books.

Wolfe, Alan (1981). *America's Impasse: The Rise and Fall of the Politics of Growth*. New York: Pantheon.

_____ (1977). *The Limits of Legimacy: Political Contradictions of Contemporary Capitalism*. New York: Free Press.

Wolfe, Marshall (1981). *Elusive Development*. Geneva: UNRISD.

Zwerdling, Daniel (1978). *Democracy at Work*. Washington, D.C.: Association for Self-Management.

I.C. Core-Periphery Studies and Related North-South and East-West Topics

Abdalla, Ismail-Sabra (1980). "The Inadequacy and Loss of Legitimacy of the International Monetary Fund." *Development Dialogue*, 2:25-53.

Abdel Malek, Anouar, et al., eds. (1971). *Sociologie de l'impérialisme*. Paris: Anthropos.

Agee, Philip (1975). *CIA Diary: Inside the Company*. Harmondsworth, England: Penguin.

Albertini, J. M. (1981). *Mécanismes du sous-développement et développement*. Paris: Ed Ouvrières.

Amin, Samir, et al. (1982). *La crise, quelle crise?* Paris: Maspero.

Arnold, Steven (1982). *Implementing Development Assistance: European Approaches to Basic Needs*. Boulder, Colo.: Westview Press.

Barnet, Richard (1980). *The Lean Years: Politics in the Age of Scarcity*. New York: Simon and Schuster.

Barnet, Richard, and Muller, Ronald (1974). *Global Reach: The Power of the Multinational Corporations*. New York: Simon and Schuster.

Beaud, Michel, et al., eds. (1979). *La France et le Tiers Monde*. Grenoble: Presses de l'Université de Grenoble.

Beckford, George L. (1972). *Persistent Poverty: Underdevelopment in Plantation Economies of the Third World*. London: Oxford University Press.

Bedjaoui, Mohammed (1979). *Towards a New International Economic Order*. New York: Holmes & Meier.

Brawand, Antoine (1981). *Nord-sud: De la dépendence économique au développement endogène*. Geneva: Institut Universitaire d'Etudes du développement, Itinéraires No. 17.

Bretton, Henry (1980). *The Power of Money: A Political-Economic Analysis with Special Emphasis on the American Political System*. Albany, State University of New York Press.

Burstall, M. L., et al. (1981). *Multinational Enterprises, Governments and Technology: Pharmaceutical Industry*. Paris: OECD (N.B.: One of several industry studies.)

Caballero, J., et al. (1981). *International Monetary Fund Policies in the Third World: Case Studies of Turkey, Zaire and Peru*. Norwich: University of East Anglia, Development Studies Occ. Paper No. 8.

Calcagno, Alfredo E., and Jakobowicz, Jean-Michel (1982). *Le monologue nord-sud: Du mythe de l'aide à la realité du sous-développement*. Paris. Le Sycamore.

Calleo, David P. (1982). *The Imperious Economy*. Cambridge, Mass.: Harvard University Press.

Carrére D'Encausse, Hélène (1980a). *L'empire éclaté: La révolte des nations en U.R.S.S.* Paris: Librairie Générale Française.

_____ (1980b). *Le pouvoir confisqué: Gouvernants et gouvernés en U.R.S.S.* Paris: Flammarion.

CEDETIM (1980). *L'imperialisme francais*. Paris: Maspero.

Chambost, Edouard (1980). *Guide mondial des secrets bancaires.* Paris: Seuil.

Chilchilnisky, Graciela (1982). "Basic Needs and the North/South Debate." New York: Institute for World Order, Working Paper No. 21. (N.B.: This is part of a series on world order topics.)

Chilcote, Ronald H., ed. (1981). "Dependency and Marxism," special issue of *Latin American Perspectives,* 30-31;VII,3-4.

Chomsky, Noam, and Herman, Edward (1979a). *After the Cataclysm: Postwar Indochina and the Reconstruction of Imperial Ideology.* Boston: South End Press.

____ (1979b). *The Washington Connection and Third World Fascism.* Boston: South End Press.

Clairmonte, Frederick, and Cavanagh, John (1981). *The World in Their Web: The Dynamics of Textile Multinationals.* London: Zed Press.

Cohen, Stephen D. (1981, 2nd ed.). *The Making of United States International Economic Policy: Principles, Problems, and Proposals for Reform.* New York: Praeger.

Crough, G. J. (1979). *Transnational Banking and the World Economy.* Sydney: University of Sydney, TNC Research Project.

Dardel, Jean-Jacques de (1981). *La coopération au développement: Certitudes et interrogations.* Geneva: Institut Universitaire d'Etudes du Développement.

Dias, Clarence, et al., eds. (1981). *Lawyers in the Third World: Comparative and Developmental Perspectives.* Uppsala. Scandinavian Institute of African Studies (hereafter SIAS).

Dufourt, Daniel (1979). *L'économie mondiale comme système.* Lyon: Presses de l'Université de Lyon.

Emmanuel, Arghiri (1981). *Technologie appropriée ou technologie sous-développée?* Paris: PUF.

Esser, Klaus, and Wiemann, Jürgen (1981). *Key Countries in the Third World: Implications for Relations between FRG and the South.* Berlin: German Development Institute.

Eudes, Yves (1982). *La conquête des esprits: L'appareil d'exportation culturelle américaine vers le tiers monde.* Paris: Maspero.

Evans, Peter (1979). *Dependent Development: The Alliance of Multinational, State, and Local Capital in Brazil.* Princeton, N.J.: Princeton University Press.

Falk, Richard A., and Kim, Samuels, eds. (1980). *The War System.* Boulder, Colo.: Westview Press.

Feinberg, Richard (1981). *Subsidizing Success: The Export-Import Bank in the United States Economy.* Cambridge: Cambridge University Press.

Feinberg, Richard (1980a). "The Stand-By Arrangements of the International Monetary Fund and Basic Needs." Paper presented at a Woodstock Theological Center Conference, Washington, D.C., April.

____ (1980b). "The International Monetary Fund and U.S.-Latin American Relations." Paper presented at the CIDE conference, Guanajuato, Mexico, July.

Gilmore, Richard (1982). *A Poor Harvest: The Clash of Policies and Interests in the Grain Trade.* New York: Longman.

Girvan, Norman (1980). "Swallowing the IMF Medicine in the 'Seventies." *Development Dialogue,* 2:55-74.

——— (1976). *Corporate Imperialism: Conflict and Expropriation.* New York: M. E. Sharpe.

Girvan, Norman, et al. (1980). "The IMF and the Third World: The Case of Jamaica, 1974-1980." *Development Dialogue,* 2:113-55.

Gisselquist, David (1981). *The Political Economics of International Bank Lending.* New York: Praeger.

Goulbourne, Harry, ed. (1979). *Politics and State in the Third World.* London: Macmillan.

Griffin, K., and James, J. (1981). *The Transition to Egalitarian Development.* London: Macmillan.

Griffith-Jones, Stephany (1981). *The Role of Finance in the Transition to Socialism.* Montclair, N.J.: Allanheld, Osmun.

Hayter, Teresa (1981). *The Creation of World Poverty: An Alternative View to the Brandt Report.* London: Pluto.

——— (1971). *Aid as Imperialism.* Harmondsworth, England: Penguin.

Hart, Judith (1974). *Aid and Liberation: A Socialist Study of Aid Politics.* London: Gollancz.

Helleiner, Gerald (1981). *Intra-Firm Trade and the Developing Countries.* London: Macmillan.

Helleiner, Gerald K., ed. (1976). *A World Divided: The Less Developed Countries in the International Economy.* Cambridge: Cambridge University Press.

Herman, Edward (1982). *Terror and Propaganda.* Boston: South End Press.

Horowitz, Irving L. (1982). *Beyond Empire and Revolution: Militarization and Consolidation in the Third World.* London: Oxford University Press.

Hudson, Michael (1977). *Global Fracture: The New International Economic Order.* New York: Harper & Row.

——— (1972). *Super Imperialism: The Economic Strategy of American Empire.* New York: Holt, Rinehart & Winston.

Hymer, Stephen H. (1979). *The Multinational Corporation: A Radical Approach.* Cambridge: Cambridge University Press.

Johansen, Robert (1980). *The National Interest and the Human Interest.* Princeton, N.J.: Princeton University Press.

Joseph, Paul (1981). *Cracks in the Empire: State Politics in the Vietnam War.* Boston: South End Press.

Kaldor, Mary (1978). *The Disintegrating West.* New York: Hill and Wang.

Kastler, Alfred, et al. (1981). *Le grand massacre.* Paris: Fayard.

Kegley, Charles W., and McGowan, Pat, eds. (1981). *The Political Economy of Foreign Policy Behavior.* Beverly Hills, Calif.: Sage.

Klare, Michael, and Arnson, Cynthia (1981). *Supplying Repression: U.S. Support for Authoritarian Regimes Abroad.* Washington, D.C.: Institute for Policy Studies (IPS).

Kumar, Krishna, ed. (1980). *Transnational Enterprises: Their Impact on Third World Societies and Cultures*. Boulder, Colo.: Westview Press.

Lappé, Frances M., et al. (1980). *Aid as Obstacle*. San Francisco, Calif.: IFDP.

Libby, R. T. (1976). "The Ideology and Power of the World Bank." Unpublished Ph.D. dissertation, University of Washington.

Lichtensztejn, Samuel, and Baer, Monica (1982). *Politicas globales en el capitalismo: El Banco Mundial*. Mexico City: CIDE.

Linden, Eugene (1976). *The Alms Race: The Impact of American Voluntary Aid Abroad*. New York: Random House.

Lissner, Jorgen (1977). *The Politics of Altruism: A Study of the Political Behaviour of Voluntary Development Agencies*. Geneva: Lutheran World Federation.

Long, Frank (1981). *Restrictive Business Practices, Transnational Corporations and Development*. The Hague: Martinus Nijhoff.

Loup, Jacques (1981). *Le Tiers-Monde peut-il survivre?* Paris: Economica.

MacBride, Sean, ed. (1980). *Many Voices, One World: Communications and Society, Today and Tomorrow*. Paris: UNESCO.

Mattelart, Armand (1979). *Multinational Corporations and the Control of Culture*. Atlantic Highlands, N.J.: Humanities Press.

Medawar, Charles (1979). *Insult or Injury? An Enquiry into the Marketing and Advertising of British Food and Drug Products in the Third World*. London: Social Audit Ltd.

Mende, Tiber (1973, 1972 in Fr.). *From Aid to Recolonization: Lessons of a Failure*. New York: Pantheon.

Menon, B. P. (1980). *Bridges Across the South: Technological Cooperation Among Developing Countries*. New York: Pergamon Press.

Mercier, Christian (1977). *Les déracinés du capital: immigration et accumulation*. Lyon: Presses de l'Université de Lyon.

Mirow, Kurt R., and Maurer, Harry (1982). *Webs of Power: International Cartels and the World Economy*. Boston: Houghton Mifflin.

Morgan, Dan (1979). *Merchants of Grain*. New York: Viking.

Newfarmer, Richard, ed. (1983). *International Oligopoly and Development: Case Studies of Their Transnational Industries and Their Growth in Latin America*. forthcoming.

Nore, Petter, and Turner, Terisa (1980). *Oil and Class Struggle*. London: Zed Press.

Nusbaumer, Jacques (1981). *L'Enjeu du dialogue nord-sud: Portage des richesses ou guerre économique*. Paris: Economica.

Packenham, Robert (1973). *Liberal America and the Third World: Political Development Ideas in Foreign Aid and Social Science*. Princeton, N.J.: Princeton University Press.

Paddock, William and Elizabeth (1973). *We Don't Know How: An Independent Audit of What They Call Success in Foreign Aid*. Ames: Iowa State University Press.

Payer, Cheryl (1982). *The World Bank: A Critical History*. New York: Monthly Review Press.

_____, ed. (1975). *Commodity Trade of the Third World*. New York: John Wiley/Halsted.

_____(1974). *The Debt Trap: The International Monetary Fund and the Third World*. New York: Monthly Review Press.

Prouty, L. Fletcher (1973). *The Secret Team: The CIA and Its Allies in Control of the World*. Englewood Cliffs, N.J.: Prentice-Hall.

Radu, Michael, ed. (1981). *Eastern Europe and the Third World*. New York: Praeger.

Raulin, Henri, and Raynaud, Edgar (1980). *L'aide au sous-développement*. Paris: PUF.

Rensburg, W. C. J. Van, and Bambrick, S. (1978). *The Economics of the World's Mineral Industries*. Johannesburg: McGraw Hill.

Revel, Alain, and Riboud, Christophe (1981). *Les Etats-Unis et la stratégie alimentaire mondiale*. Paris: Calmann-Levy.

Rhodes, Robert I., ed. (1970). *Imperialism and Underdevelopment: A Reader*. New York: Monthly Review Press.

Rweyemamu, Justinian F. (1980). "Restructuring the International Monetary System." *Development Dialogue*, 2:75-91.

Sampson, Anthony (1981). *The Money Lenders: Bankers and World in Turmoil*. New York: Viking.

Seidman, Ann, ed. (1975). *Natural Resources and National Welfare: The Case of Copper*. New York: Praeger.

Seidman, Robert (1978). *The State, Law, and Development*. New York: St. Martin's Press.

Senghaas, Dieter (1977). *Welt Wirtschaftordnung und Entwicklungspolitik: Plädoyer für Dissoziation*. Frankfort am Main: Suhrkamp.

Shoup, Laurence H., and Minter, William (1977). *Imperial Brain Trust: The Council on Foreign Relations and United States Foreign Policy*. New York: Monthly Review Press.

Shue, Henry (1980). *Basic Rights: Subsistence, Affluence, and U.S. Foreign Policy*. Princeton, N.J.: Princeton University Press.

Sid-Ahmed, Abdelkader (1981). *Nord sud, les enjeux*. Paris: Publisud.

Sklar, Holly, ed. (1980). *Trilateralism: The Trilateral Commission and Elite Planning for World Management*. Boston: South End Press.

Tanzer, Michael (1980). *The Race for Resources: Continuing Struggles over Minerals and Fuels*. New York: Monthly Review Press.

_____(1969). *The Political Economy of International Oil and the Underdeveloped Countries*. Boston: Beacon Press.

Tiano, André (1981). *Transfert de technologie industrielle: Indépendance et développement*. Paris: Economica.

Tuomi, Helena, and Vayrynen, Raimo (1980). *Transnational Corporations, Armaments and Development*. Tampere, Finland. Tampere Peace Research Institute. (N.B.: There were 22 development related reports between 1972 and 1980 in this series.)

UNCTAD (1981). *Trade and Development Report for 1981*. Geneva: UNCTAD (N.B.: Supposed to become an annual counterpoint to the IBRD annual effort.)

United Nations, Centre on Transnational Corporation (1980a). *Transnational Banks: Operations, Strategies and Their Effects on Developing Countries*. New York: UN, ST/CTC/16.

＿＿ (1980b). *Transnational Corporations in Food and Beverage Processing*. New York: UN/CTC/19. (N.B.: Two of an important ongoing series.)

Vaitsos, Constantine (1974). *Intercountry Income and Transnational Enterprises*. London: Oxford University Press.

Villamil, Jose, ed. (1979). *Transnational Capitalism and National Development*. Atlantic Highlands, N.J.: Humanities Press.

Weinstein, Warren, and Henriksen, Thomas, eds. (1980). *Soviet and Chinese Aid to African Nations*. New York: Praeger.

Weir, David, and Schapiro, Mark (1981). *Circle of Poison: Pesticides and People in a Hungry World*. San Francisco, Calif.: Institute for Food and Development Policy.

White, John (1974). *The Politics of Foreign Aid*. New York: St. Martin's Press.

Williams, William A. (1980). *Empire as a Way of Life*. New York: Oxford University Press.

Wionczek, Miguel (1981). *Some Key Issues for the World Periphery*. Elmsford, N.Y.: Pergamon Press.

Worm, Kirsten, ed. (1978). *Industrialization, Development, and the Demands for a New International Economic Order*. Copenhagen: Samfundsvidenskabeligt Forlag.

I.D. Transformational and Future Studies

Black, G. Michael (1981). "Re-Calling the Homo Dei: Towards a Politics of Synecology." Unpublished Ph.D. dissertation, University of Oregon.

Bookchin, Murray (1982). *The Ecology of Freedom*. Palo Alto, Calif.: Cheshire Books.

Brunner, John (1975). *The Shockwave Rider*. New York: Ballantine Books.

Carnoy, Martin, and Shearer, Derck (1980). *Economic Democracy: The Challenge of the 1980's*. New York: Pantheon.

Daley, Herman E. (1980). *Economics, Ecology, Ethics: Essays Toward a Steady State Economy*. San Francisco, Calif.: W. H. Freeman.

＿＿ (1977). *Steady-State Economics*. San Francisco, Calif.: W. H. Freeman.

Dammann, Erik (1979). *The Future in Our Hands*. Oxford: Pergamon Press.

Dumas, André, et al. (1981). *L'autogestion, un système économique*. Paris: Dured.

Falk, Richard (1982). *The International Quest*. New York: Holmes & Meier.

＿＿ (1981). *Human Rights and State Sovereignty*. New York: Holmes & Meier.

＿＿ (1975). *A Study of Future Worlds*. New York: Free Press.

Falk, Richard, et al. (1982). *Toward a Just World Order, I*. Boulder, Colo.: Westview Press.

Faure, John (1981). *La démocratie à double voie: Autogestion ou participation*. Paris: Grounauer-Chaix.

Galtung, Johan (1981). *World Conflict Formation Processes in the 1980's: Prolegomenon III for a GPID World Model*. Tokyo: UN University, Project on Goals, Processes and Indicators of Development.

—— (1980). *The True Worlds*. New York: Free Press.

—— (1975-80). *Essays in Peace Research*. 5 volumes. Copenhagen: Christian Ejlers.

—— (1979). *Papers on Methodology*. 2 volumes. Copenhagen: Christian Ejlers. (N.B.: These four citations are only a sample of the ongoing work of this premier global citizen and peace researcher — see Gleditsch (1980) in section X herein.)

Georgescu-Roegen, Nicholas (1971). *The Entropy Law and the Economic Process*. Cambridge, Mass.: Harvard University Press.

Godard, O., et al. (1980). *Substitutions et économie sociale des ressources naturelles*. Paris: Maison des Sciences de l'Homme.

Guénon, René (1972, 1945 in Fr.). *The Reign of Quantity and the Signs of the Times*. Harmondsworth, England: Penguin.

Hawken, Paul, et al. (1982). *Seven Tomorrows: Toward a Voluntary History*. New York: Bantam.

Heinlein, Robert (1951-53). *The Foundation Trilogy*. New York: Doubleday.

Henderson, Hazel (1981). *The Politics of the Solar Age*. New York: Doubleday.

—— (1978). *Creating Alternative Futures: The End of Economics*. New York: Berkeley.

Horvat, Branco (1982). *The Political Economy of Socialism: A Marxist Social Theory*. New York: M. E. Sharpe.

Illich, Ivan (1983). *Gender*. New York: Pantheon.

—— (1981). *Shadow Work*. Boston: Marion Boyars.

—— (1978). *Toward a History of Needs*. New York: Pantheon.

—— (1976). *Medical Nemesis*. New York: Pantheon.

—— (1974). *Energy and Equity*. New York: Harper.

—— (1973). *Tools for Conviviality*. New York: Harper.

—— (1971). *Deschooling Society*. New York: Doubleday.

Illich, Ivan, et al. (1978). *Disabling Professions*. Boston: Marion Boyars.

Kohr, Leopold (1978). *The Overdeveloped Nations: The Diseconomies of Scale*. New York: Schocken Books.

—— (1973). *Development Without Aid: The Translucent Society*. New York: Schocken Books.

Leiss, William (1976). *The Limits of Satisfaction: An Essay on the Problem of Needs and Commodities*. Toronto: University of Toronto Press.

Lifton, Robert Jay (1971). *History and Human Survival*. New York: Random House. (N.B.: 10-15 other titles by this author over the last two decades.)

Lovins, Amory (1977). *Soft Energy Paths: Towards a Durable Peace*. San Francisco, Calif.: Friends of the Earth.

Lutz, Mark A., and Lux, Kenneth (1979). *The Challenge of Humanistic Economics*. Menlo Park, Calif.: Benjamin/Cummings.

Meister, Albert (1981). *L'autogestion en uniforme*. Paris: Ed Privat.

Mendlovitz, Saul, ed. (1981). "On the Creation of a Just World Order: An Agenda for a Program of Inquiry and Praxis," *Alternatives*, VII,3:355-73.

_____ ed. (1975). *On the Creation of a Just World Order*. New York: Free Press.

Mische, Gerald and Patricia (1977). *Toward a Human World Order: Beyond the National Security Straitjacket*. New York: Paulist Press.

Nerfin, Marc, ed. (1977). *Another Development: Approaches and Strategies*. Uppsala: Dag Hammarskjold Foundation.

Ogilvy, James (1977). *Many Dimensional Man: Decentralizing, Self, Society, and the Sacred*. Oxford: Oxford University Press.

Perelman, Lewis J. (1976). *The Global Mind: Beyond the Limits to Growth*. New York: Mason/Charter.

Riddell, Robert (1981). *Ecodevelopment*. London: Gower.

Rifkin, Jeremy (1980). *Entropy: A New World View*. New York: Viking Press.

Robertson, James (1979). *The Sane Alternative: A Choice of Futures*. St. Paul, Minn.: River Basin.

Roszak, Theodore (1978). *Person/Planet*. New York: Doubleday.

Satin, Mark (1979). *New Age Politics: Healing Self and Society*. New York: Delta Books.

Sale, Kirkpatrick (1980). *Human Scale*. New York: Coward McCann.

Stokes, Bruce (1981). *Helping Ourselves – Local Solutions to Global Problems*. New York: W. W. Norton.

Thompson, Kenneth, ed. (1980). *The Moral Imperatives of Human Rights: A World Survey*. Washington, D.C.: University Press of America.

Thompson, William I. (1981). *The Time Falling Bodies Take to Light*. New York: St. Martin's Press.

_____ (1978). *Darkness and Scattered Light*. New York: Doubleday.

_____ (1976). *Evil and World Order*. New York: Harper & Row.

_____ (1971). *At the Edge of History*. New York: Harper & Row.

Tuck, Richard (1982). *Natural Rights Theories: Their Origin and Development*. Cambridge: Cambridge University Press.

U.S. Congress. Office of Technology Assessment (1981). *Genetic Technology: A New Frontier*. Boulder, Colo.: Westview Press.

Valaskakis, Kimon, et al. (1979). *The Conserver Society*. New York: Harper & Row.

Wiener, A. (1978). *Magnificent Myth: Patterns of Control in Post-Industrial Society*. Oxford: Pergamon Press.

Wilson, Richard W., and Schochet, Gordon J., eds. (1980). *Moral Development and Politics*. New York: Praeger.

II. Human Development at the Local Level

II.A. Participatory Development: Theory and the Best Case Studies

Abatena, Hailu (1978). "A New Dimension in Development Strategy: The Role of Citizen Participation." Unpublished Ph.D. dissertation, Syracuse University.

Adams, Adrian (1979). "An Open Letter to a Young Researcher." *African Affairs*, 78,313:451-79.

___ (1977). "The Senegal River Valley: What Kind of Change?" *Review of African Political Economy*, 10:33-59.

Ahmad, Nigar (1980). *Peasant Struggles in a Feudal Setting: A Study of the Determinants of the Bargaining Power of Tenants and Small Farmers in Five Villages of District Attack, Pakistan, 1980*. Geneva: ILO, WEP 10/WP11.

Barkan, Joel D., et al. (1979). "Is Small Beautiful? The Organizational Conditions for Effective Small-Scale Self-Help Development Projects in Rural Kenya." Iowa City: University of Iowa, Comparative Legislative Research Center, Occasional Paper No. 15, December.

Bengtsson, Bo, ed. (1979). *Rural Development Research – the Role of Power Relations*. Stockholm: SAREC, R:4.

Berger, Peter L., and Neuhaus, Richard J. (1977). *To Empower People: The Role of Mediating Structures in Public Policy*. Washington, D.C.: American Enterprise Institute.

Bezold, Clement (1978). *Anticipatory Democracy: People in the Politics of the Future*. New York: Random House.

Bhaduri, Amit (1979). "Agricultural Co-operatives in North Viet Nam." ILO, World Employment Programme, WEP 10/WP6, March.

Bhaduri, Amit, and Rahman, Md. Anisur, eds. (1982). *Studies in Rural Participation*. New Delhi: Oxford University Press.

Blair, Harry (1982). *The Political Economy of Participation in Local Development Programs: Short Term Impasse and Long Term Change in South Asia and the United States from the 1950's to the 1970's*. Ithaca, N.Y.: Cornell University, Rural Development Committee.

___ (1978). "Rural Development, Class Structure and Bureaucracy in Bangladesh." *World Development*, 6,1:65-82.

___ (1974). *The Elusiveness of Equity: Institutional Approaches to Rural Development in Bangladesh*. Ithaca, N.Y.: Cornell University, Rural Development Committee.

Boer, Leen (1980). "A First Design of a Typology of Rural, Local Communities." Paper presented at the Fifth World Congress for Rural Sociology, Mexico City, August.

Booth, John A., and Seligson, Mitchell, A. (1979). "Peasants as Activists: A Reevaluation of Political Participation in the Countryside." *Comparative Political Studies*, 12:29-59.

Botkin, James W., et al. (1979). *No Limits to Learning: Bridging the Human Gap*. Oxford: Pergamon Press.

Boyte, Harry C. (1980). *The Backyard Revolution: Understanding the New Citizen Movement*. Philadelphia: Temple University Press.

Brinkerhoff, Derick W. (1980). "Participation and Rural Development Project Effectiveness: An Organizational Analysis of Four Cases." Unpublished Ph.D. dissertation, Harvard University.

Bryant, Coralie (1980). "Organizational Impediments to Making Participation a Reality: Swimming Upstream in AID." *Rural Development Participation Review*, 1,3:8-10 (longer version exists, unpublished).

_____ (1976). "Participation Planning and Administrative Development in Urban Development Programs." Washington, D.C.: AID, Technical Assistance Bureau, Office of Urban Development.

Bryant, Coralie, and White, Louise, C. (1980). *Managing Rural Development: Peasant Participation in Rural Development*. West Hartford, Conn.: Kumarian Press.

Buijs, H. Y. (1979). *Access and Participation: On the Access Problems of Poor People and Participation as a Solution — An Interim Report*. Leiden: Institute of Cultural and Social Studies, Report No. 33.

Callaway, Helen, ed. (1981). *Participation in Research: Case-Studies of Participatory Research in Adult Education*. Amersfoort: Netherlands Centre for Research and Development in Adult Education. (A 1980 Ljubljana, Yugoslavia conference.)

Casse, Pierre (1981). *Participation et développement*. Washington, D.C.: IBRD, Economic Development Institute.

Catholic Relief Service (1979). "CRS Program Management: A Response to the Role of Base Organizations in Development." (Report on the South America Regional Meeting, Cali, Colombia July 20-31, 1978.) New York.

Cernea, Michael M. (1979a). "A Participatory Strategy for Programming Rural Development — Summary of Methodology Guidelines for PIDER Programming as Applied by CIDER — Mexico." Washington, D.C.: IBRD, Rural Operations Review and Support Unit.

_____ (1979b). "Measuring Project Impact: Monitoring and Evaluation in the PIDER Rural Development Project — Mexico." Washington, D.C.: IBRD, Staff Working Paper 332, June.

Chambers, Robert (1980a). "Rapid Rural Appraisal: Rationale and Repertoire." Sussex: University of Sussex IDS, Discussion Paper No. 155, September.

_____ (1980b). *Rural Poverty Unperceived: Problems and Remedies*. Washington, D.C.: IBRD; SWP No. 400.

_____ (1978). "Approaches and Realities for Project Selection for Poverty Focused Rural Development: Simple Is Optimal." *World Development*, 6, 2:209-19.

_____ (1974). *Managing Rural Development: Ideas and Experiences from East Africa*. Uppsala: Scandinavian Institute of African Studies.

Charlick, Robert (1974). "Power and Participation in the Modernization of Rural Hausa Communities." Unpublished Ph.D. dissertation, University of California, at Berkeley.

Checkoway, Barry, ed. (1981). *Citizens and Health Care: Participation and Planning for Social Change*. New York: Pergamon Press.

Cohen, John, et al. (1977). *Rural Development Participation: Concepts for Measuring Participation for Project Design, Implementation and Evaluation*. Ithaca, N.Y.: Cornell University, Rural Development Committee.

Community Development Trust Fund of Tanzania (1977). *Appropriate Technology for Grain Storage*. New Haven, Conn.: Economic Development Bureau.

Constantino-David, Karina (1981). "Issues in Community Organization." *IFDA Dossier*, 23,May-June:5-20.

Coombs, Philip H., ed. (1980). *Meeting the Basic Needs of the Rural Poor.* New York: Pergamon Press.

Coover, Virginia, et al. (1978, 2nd ed.). *Resources Manual for a Living Revolution.* Philadelphia: New Society Press.

Curtis, Donald, et al. (1978). *Popular Participation in Decision-Making and the Basic Needs Approach to Development: Methods, Issues, and Experiences.* Geneva: ILO, WEP 2-32/WP12.

De, Nitish R. (1980). "Organizing and Mobilising: Some Building Blocks of Rural Work Organization." Paper presented at the UNITAR Conference on "Alternative Development Strategies and the Future of Asia," New Delhi, March 11-17.

Derman, William (1978). "Cooperatives, Initiative, Participation and Socio-economic Change in the Sahel." East Lansing: Michigan State University for AID/AFR/SFWA, August.

Desroche, Henri (1976). Le projet coopératif. Paris: Les Editions Ouvrières.

Development Group for Alternative Policies (D-GAP) (1979a). "Public Participation in Regional Planning: An Integration." Washington, D.C.: D-GAP.

_____ (1979b). "Alternative Programs of Credit and Integrated Services in Latin America." Washington, D.C.: GAP, Paper No. 2.

_____ (1978). "Eliciting Local Needs in Planning for Urban-Based Services for Rural Development." Washington, D.C.: D-GAP for AID,DSB, Office of Urban Development.

Dupriez, Hughes (1979). *Integrated Rural Development Projects Carried Out in Black Africa with EDF Aid.* Brussels: Commission of the European Communities.

Emmerson, Donald (1976). "Biting the Helping Hand: Modernization and Violence in an Indonesian Fishing Community." *Land Tenure Center Newsletter* (Madison), Jan-Mar., 51:1-15.

Esman, Milton, and Uphoff, Norman (1982). *Organizing Small Farmers: Local Institutions and Rural Development.* Ithaca, N.Y.: Cornell University, Rural Development Committee.

Esman, Milton J., et al. (1980). *Paraprofessionals in Rural Development.* Ithaca, N.Y.: Cornell University, Rural Development Committee.

Fagence, Michael (1977). *Citizen Participation in Planning.* Oxford: Pergamon Press.

Fresson, Sylviane (1978). "Public Participation on Village Level Irrigation Perimeters in the Matam Region of Senegal." Paris: OECD Development Center, Occasional Paper No. 4.

Galjart, Benno (1981a). "Counterdevelopment: A Position Paper." *Community Development Journal,* 16:88-96.

_____ (1981b). "Participatory Development Projects: Some Conclusions from Research." *Sociologia Ruralis,* 21,152-59.

Galjart, Benno, and Buijs, Dieke, eds. (1982). *Participation of the Poor in Development.* Leiden: University of Leiden, Institute of Cultural and Social Studies.

Galtung, Johan, et al., eds. (1980). *Self-Reliance: A New Development Strategy?* London: Bogle-L'Ouverture.

Gellar, Sheldon, et al. (1980). *Animation Rurale and Rural Development: The Experience of Senegal*. Ithaca, N.Y.: Cornell University, Rural Development Committee.

Goldsmith, Arthur, and Blustain, Harvey (1980). *Local Organization and Participation in Integrated Rural Development in Jamaica*. Ithaca, N.Y.: Cornell University, Rural Development Committee.

Gould, Jeremy, ed. (1981). *Needs, Participation, and Local Development*. Helsinki: Institute of Development Studies.

Goulet, Denis (1981). *Survival with Integrity: Sarvodaya at the Crossroads*. Colombo, Sri Lanka: Marga Institute.

Gow, David, and VanSant, Jerry (1981). "Beyond the Rhetoric of Rural Development Participation: How Can It Be Done?" Washington, D.C.: Development Alternatives, Inc.

Gunatilleke, Godfrey (1978). "Participatory Development and Dependence — The Case of Sri Lanka." *Marga Quarterly Journal*, 5,3:38-93.

Green, G. D. (1981). "Training for Self-Reliance in Rural Areas." *International Labor Review*, 120,4:411-23.

Hall, Budd L., and Kidd, J. Roby, eds. (1978). *Adult Learning: A Design for Action*. Oxford: Pergamon Press.

Haque, Wahidul, et al. (1977). "Towards a Theory of Rural Development." *Development Dialogue*, 2:9-137.

Heck, Bernard van (1979a). *Participation of the Poor in Rural Organizations*. Rome: FAO, ROAP.

_____ (1979b). *Research Guidelines for Field Action Projects to Promote Participation of the Poor in Rural Organizations*. Rome: FAO, ROAP.

_____ (1977). *The Involvement of the Poor in Development Through Rural Organizations*. Rome: FAO, ROAP.

Hollnsteiner, Mary R. (1979). "Mobilizing the Rural Poor Through Community Organization." *Philippine Studies*, 27,3:387-411.

_____ (1978). *Development from the Bottom Up: Mobilizing the Rural Poor for Self-Development*. Manila: FAO, WCARRD and ROAP.

Hossain, Mahabub, et al. (1979). " 'Participatory' Development Efforts in Rural Bangladesh — A Case Study of Experiences in Three Areas." ILO, World Employment Programme, WEP 10/WP5.

Illich, Ivan (1982). "The Delinking of Peace and Development." *Alternatives*, VII,4:409-16. (N.B.: See the listings in I.D.)

_____ (1980). "The New Frontier for Arrogance." *International Development Review*, XXII,2-3:96-101.

Institute of Philippine Culture (1979). "Kagawasan: A Case Study on the Role of Law in the Mobilization and Participatory Organization of the Rural Poor." New York: International Center for Law and Development.

Institut Panafricain pour le Développement (1982). *Comprendre une économie rurale*. Paris: L'Harmattan.

Janeway, Elizabeth (1981). *Powers of the Weak*. New York: William Morrow.

Kemal, Mustafa (1981). "Participatory Research Amongst Pastoral Peasants in Tanzania: The Experience of the Jipemoyo Project in Bagamoya District." Geneva: ILO, WEP 10-8-16.

Kindervatter, Suzanne (1979). *Nonformal Education as an Empowering Process.* Amherst: University of Mass., Center for International Education.

Korten, David C. (1981). "Management of Social Transformation," *Public Administration Review*, 41,6(November-December):609-18.

_____ (1980). "Community Organization and Rural Development: A Learning Process Approach." *Public Administration Review*, 40,5:480-511.

Korten, David C., and Alfonso, Felipe B., eds. (1981). *Bureaucracy and the Poor: Closing the Gap.* Singapore: McGraw Hill and (1982) West Hartford, Conn.: Kumarian Press.

Lappé, Frances M., and Beccar-Varela, Adele (1980). *Mozambique and Tanzania: Asking the Big Questions.* San Francisco, Calif.: Institute for Food and Development Policy.

Lassen, Cheryl (1980). *Landlessness and Rural Poverty in Latin America: Conditions, Trends, and Policies Affecting Income and Employment.* Ithaca, N.Y.: Cornell University, Rural Development Committee.

_____ (1979). *Reaching the Assetless Poor: An Assessment of Projects and Strategies for their Self-Reliant Development.* Ithaca, N.Y.: Cornell University, Rural Development Committee.

Lecomte, Bernard (1978). "Participation paysanne à l'aménagement et techniques des projets." *Revue Tiers-Monde*, XIX, 73:93-108.

Lévesque, Benoit, ed. (1980). *Animation sociale, entreprises communautaires et cooperatives.* Québec: Editions cooperatives Albert Saint-Martin.

Lewycky, Dennis, ed. (1977). *Tapestry – Report from Oodi Weavers.* Gaborone, Botswana: National Institute for Research in Development in African Studies, Working Paper No. 11.

Lim Teck Ghee, and Tan Phaik Leng (1982). *Grass Roots Self-Reliance Initiatives in Malaysia: A Case Study of Kampung Batu's Struggle for Land.* Geneva: ILO, WEP 10/WP25. (N.B.: This ongoing series on participatory development case studies is the highest average quality series being published in development studies in the early 1980s.)

Lipsky, Michael (1980). *Street-Level Bureaucracy: Dilemmas of the Individual in Public Services.* New York: Basic Books.

Lustig, Jeff (1981). "Community and Social Class." (Review of Boyte, 1980 and Piven and Cloward, 1979), *Democracy*, 1,2:96-111.

Lynch, Frank, et al. (1976). *Let My People Lead: Rationale and Outline of a People-Centered Assistance Program for the Bicol River Basin.* Quezon City: Institute of Philippine Culture, Social Survey Research Unit for AID.

MacCall, Brian (1981). "The Transition toward Self-reliance: Some Thoughts on the Role of People's Organizations." *IFDA Dossier*, 22, March/April: 37-46.

Maeda, Justin (1976). "Popular Participation, Control and Development: A Study of Popular Participation in Tanzania's Rural Development." Unpublished Ph.D. dissertation, Yale University.

Maguire, Robert (1979). *Bottom-Up Development in Haiti.* Rosslyn, Va.: Inter-American Foundation.

Mansbridge, Jane (1980). *Beyond Adversary Democracy*. New York: Basic Books.

Marga Institute (1978). "Patterns of Self-Reliant Development in Sri Lanka — Village Development Programme-Walgampaya." Colombo, Sri Lanka: Marga Institute, M/56 RES/51/1. (N.B.: A sample of the dozens of working papers on local and participatory development.)

M'Bow, Amadou-Mahtar, et al. (1979). *Learning and Working* (essays from *Prospects*). Paris: UNESCO.

Meehan, Eugene J. (1979). *In Partnership with People*. Washington, D.C.: IAF.

Meow, S. Chee, et al. (1978). *People's Participation at the Local Level*. Bangkok: Stiftung.

Montgomery, John D. (1980). "Administering to the Poor (Or If We Can't Help Rich Dictators, What Can We Do for the Poor?)." *Public Administration Review*, 40,5:421-25.

Moore, Cynthia (1981). *Paraprofessionals in Village-Level Development in Sri Lanka: The Sarvodaya Shamadana Movement*. Ithaca, N.Y.: Cornell University, Rural Development Committee.

Nash, June, et al., eds. (1976). *Popular Participation in Social Change*. The Hague: Mouton.

Nesman, Edgar (1981). *Peasant Mobilization and Rural Development*. Cambridge, Mass.: Schenkman.

Nicholson, Simon, and Lorenzo, Raymond (1981). "The Political Implications of Child Participation: Steps Toward a Participatory Society." *IFDA Dossier*, 22:66-69.

Oakeshott, Robert (1981). "Cooperative Lessons for the South." *South*, June: 22-24.

_____ (1978). *The Case for Workers Co-ops*. London: Routledge & Kegan Paul.

O'Sullivan-Ryan, Jeremiah, and Kaplun, Mario (1979). *Communication Methods to Promote Grass Roots Participation for an Endogenous Development Process*. Caracas, Venezuela: Conferencia Episcopal Venezolana.

Paakkanen, Liisa (1981). *Participation, Needs, and Village Level Development*. Helsinki: Finnish National Commission for UNESCO.

Paranjape, P. V., et al. (1981). *Grass Roots Self-Reliance in Shamrik Sanghatana, Dhulia District, India*. Geneva: ILO, WEP 10/WP22.

Parenti, Michael (1980, 3rd ed.). *Democracy for the Few*. New York: St. Martin's Press.

Pateman, Carole (1970). *Participation and Democratic Theory*. Cambridge: Cambridge University Press.

Paul, James C. N., and Dias, Clarence J. (1980a). "Law and Administration in Alternative Development." New York: International Center for Law and Development.

_____ (1980b). "Law and Legal Resources in the Mobilization of the Rural Poor for Self-reliant Development." New York: ICLD.

Pearse, Andrew, and Stiefel, Matthias (1979). "Inquiry into Participation — A Research Approach." Geneva: UNRISD, 79/C.14, May.

Pearse, Andrew, and Stiefel, Matthias, eds. (1980). *Debaters' Comments on "Inquiry into Participation: A Research Approach."* Geneva: UNRISD.

Perlman, Janice (1976). "Grassrooting the System," *Social Policy*, 7:4-20.

Phillips, Tony (1978). "Popular Participation in Development: Lessons from the Community Development Program in India." Washington: IBRD, PP&M7.

Piven, Frances F., and Cloward, Richard A. (1979). *Poor People's Movements: Why They Succeed, How They Fail.* New York: Vintage Books.

Rahman, Md. Anisur (1978). "Research on Participation of the Poor in Development." ILO, World Employment Programme, WEP 10/WP4.

Reilly, Charles A. (1980). "Cultural Movements as Surrogates for Political Participation in Contemporary Latin America." Paper presented at the APSA Annual Meeting, Washington, August.

Rensburg, Patrick van (1974). *Report from Swaneng Hill: Education and Employment in an African Country* (Botswana). Uppsala: Dag Hammarskjold Foundation.

Rifkin, Susan B., ed. (1980). *Health: The Human Factor – Readings in Health, Development and Community Participation.* Geneva: Christian Medical Commission of the World Council of Churches, Special Series, No. 3.

Robinson, David (1981). "Self-Help Groups in Primary Health Care." *World Health Forum*, 2,2:185-201.

Roca, Santiago, et al. (1980). "Participatory Processes and Action of the Rural Poor in Anta: Peru." ILO, World Employment Programme Research, WEP 10/WP-12.

Silva, G. V. S. de, et al. (1979). "Bhoomi Sena: A Struggle for People's Power." *Development Dialogue*, 2:3-70.

Simmons, John (1978). "Basic Needs and Popular Participation: A Research Proposal." Washington: IBRD, Policy Planning Division, Development Policy Staff. (N.B.: This is No. 11 of 14 papers during 1977-78, marking the closest the World Bank has ever gotten to the subject of participation aside from the 2-3 other odd papers listed.)

Small Farmers Development Team (1978). *Small Farmers Development Manual.* 2 volumes. Bangkok: FAO.

Smith, Leo, and Jones, David (1981). *Deprivation, Participation and Community Action.* London: Routledge & Kegan Paul.

Solomon, Darwin D. (1972). "Characteristics of Local Organizations and Service Agencies Conducive to Development." *Sociologia Ruralis*, XII, 3/4:334-60.

Srisang, Koson, et al. (1981). *People's Participation and People's Movements III.* Geneva: World Council of Churches, Commission on the Churches Participation in Development (N.B.: One collection of case studies in an ongoing series).

Staudt, Kathleen (1979). *Women and Participation in Rural Development: A Framework for Project Design and Policy-Oriented Research.* Ithaca, N.Y.: Cornell University, Rural Development Committee.

Stavis, Benjamin (1979). *Agricultural Extension for Small Farmers.* East Lansing: Michigan State University, Department of Agric. Economics, Rural Development Working Paper No. 3.

Stiefel, Matthias, et al. (1981). *Dialogue About Participation 1*. Geneva: UNRISD.

Stren, Richard (1980). "Squatting and the State Bureaucracy: A Case Study of Tanzania." Paper presented at the ASA Annual Meeting, Philadelphia, October.

Szal, Richard J., ed. (1979). "Popular Participation, Employment and the Fulfillment of Basic Needs." *International Labor Review*, 118,1,Jan-Feb.: 27-38.

Tendler, Judith (1981). "Fitting the Foundation Style: The Case of Rural Credit." Rosslyn, Va.: Inter-American Foundation.

Tilakaratna, S. (1982). *Grass Roots Self-Reliance in Two Rural Locations in Sri Lanka: Organizations of Betel and Coir Yarn Producers*. Geneva: ILO, WEP 10/WP24.

UNICEF (1981). "Integrating People's Participation into Country Programs." New York: UNICEF, Program Development and Planning Division.

_____ (1978). "Participatory Research and Basic Needs." Geneva: *Assignment Children* No. 41.

United Nations, Department of Social and Economic Affairs (1978). *A Manual and Resource Book for Popular Participation Training*. 4 volumes. ST/ESA/66.

_____ (1975). *Popular Participation in Decision Making for Development*, ST/ESA/31.

Uphoff, Norman, et al. (1979). *Feasibility and Application of Rural Development Participation: A State-of-the-Art Paper*. Ithaca, N.Y.: Cornell University, Rural Development Committee.

Vanek, Jaroslav (1971). *The Participatory Economy*. Ithaca, N.Y.: Cornell University Press.

Varia (1981). "Can Participation Enhance Development?" Issue *NFE Exchange* No. 20. East Lansing: Michigan State University, Institute for International Studies in Education.

Vyasulu, Vinod (1981). "Alternative Development Strategies for Koraput." *IFDA Dossier*, 26, November/December:29-40.

Waddimba, Joje (1979). *Some Participative Aspects of Programmes to Involve the Poor in Development*. Geneva: UNRISD, 79.7.

Wallman, Sandra, ed. (1977). *Perceptions of Development*. London: Cambridge University Press.

Wanigesekera, Earle (1977). "Popular Participation and Local Level Planning in Sri Lanka." *Marga Quarterly Journal*, 4,4:37-77.

Warren, Donald I. (1981). *Helping Networks: How People Cope with Problems in Urban Communities*. Notre Dame, Ind.: University of Notre Dame.

Wellstone, Paul (1978). *How the Rural Poor Got Power: Narrative of a Grass-Roots Organizer*. Amherst: University of Mass. Press.

Wesseler, Matthias, ed. (1981). *Participatory Learning and Rural Development – Working Papers*. Witzenhausen/FRG: Deutsches Institut für Tropische und Subtropische Landwirtschaft.

Whyte, William F. (1981). *Participatory Approaches to Agricultural Research and Development: A State-of-the-Art Paper*. Ithaca, N.Y.: Cornell University, Rural Development Committee.

II.B. Food Systems and Rural Development: Classics, Theory and Multiregional Works

Abasiekong, Edet M. (1982). *Integrated Rural Development in the Third World: Its Concepts, Problems, and Prospects*. Smithtown, N.Y.: Exposition Press.

Agarwal, Bina (1981). *Agricultural Modernization and Third World Women: Pointers from the Literature and an Empirical Analysis*. Geneva: ILO, WEP 10/WP21.

Arbeitsgruppe Bielefelder Entwicklungssoziologen, eds. (1979). *Subsistenzproduktion und Akkumulation*. Saarbrucken: Verlag Breitenbach.

Bailey, F. G., ed. (1973). *Debate and Compromise: The Politics of Innovation*. Totowa, N.J.: Rowman and Littlefield.

Barlett, Peggy F., ed. (1980). *Agricultural Decision Making: Anthropological Contributions to Rural Development*. New York: Academic Press.

Berdichewsky, Bernardo, ed. (1979). *Anthropology and Social Change in Rural Areas*. The Hague: Mouton.

Berger, John (1979). *Pig Earth*. New York: Pantheon.

——— (1978). "Towards understanding peasant experience." *Race & Class*, XIX, 4:345-59.

Berthelot, J., and Ravignon, F. de (1981). *Les sillons de la faim*. Paris: L'Harmattan.

Chambers, Robert, et al., eds. (1981). *Seasonal Dimensions to Rural Poverty*. London: Frances Pinter.

Clammer, John, ed. (1978). *The New Economic Anthropology*. London: Macmillan.

Clay, Jason W. (1979). "The Articulation of Non-Capitalist Agricultural Production Systems with Capitalist Exchange Systems." Unpublished Ph.D. dissertation, Cornell University. (Case study on Brazil.)

Clayton, E., and Petry, F., eds. (1981). *Monitoring Systems for Agricultural and Rural Development Projects*. Rome: FAO, Economic and Social Development Paper No. 12 (N.B.: Forthcoming volumes on experiences in French, Spanish, and Arabic speaking worlds will be published in those languages.)

Copans, Jean (1975). *Anthropologie et imperialisme*. Paris: Maspero.

Crawford, Paul R. (1982). *AID Experience in Agricultural Research: A Review of Project Evaluations*. Washington: AID, PPC, Office of Evaluation, Program Evaluation Discussion Paper No. 13.

Dahl, Gudrun, and Hjort, Anders (1976). *Having Herds: Pastoral Herd Growth and Household Economy*. Stockholm: University of Stockholm, Department of Anthropology.

Dahlberg, Kenneth (1979). *Beyond the Green Revolution: The Ecology and Politics of Global Agricultural Development*. New York: Plenum.

Deere, Carmen D., and deLeal, Magdalena L. (1980). *Women in Agriculture: Peasant Production and Proletarianization in Three Andean Regions*. Geneva: ILO, WEP 10/WP13.

Dorner, Peter, ed. (1977). *Cooperative and Commune: Group Farming in the Economic Development of Agriculture*. Madison: University of Wisconsin Press.

Dumont, René (1978). *Paysans écrasés, terres massacres*. Paris: Laffont.
_____ (1957, 1954 in Fr.). *Types of Rural Economy: Studies in World Agriculture*. London: Methuen. (N.B.: These are but a small sample of more than 50 years of first-hand research by the world authority in agricultural development.)
Dumont, René, and Cohen, Nicholas (1980). *The Growth of Hunger: A New Politics of Agriculture*. Salem, N.H.: Marion Boyars.
Dumont, René, and Mazoyer, Marcel (1969). *Développement et socialismes*. Paris: Seuil.
Écosystémes forestiers tropicaux (1980). Paris: UNESCO.
Elwert, Georg, and Wong, Diana (1980). "Subsistence Production and Commodity Production in the Third World," *Review*, III,3:501-22.
Equipe Ecologie et Anthropologie des Sociétés Pastorales (1979). *Pastoral Production and Society*. Cambridge: Cambridge University Press.
Esman, Milton, et al. (1978). *Landlessness and Nearlandlessness in Developing Countries*. Washington: AID, DSB, Office of Rural Development.
Fahm, Lattee (1980). *The Waste of Nations: The Economic Utilization of Human Waste in Agriculture*. Montclair, N.J.: Allanheld, Osmun.
Feder, Ernest (1980). "The Odious Competition Between Man and Animal Over Agricultural Resources in Underdeveloped Countries," *Review*, III, 3:463-500.
Furst, Peter T. (1978). "Spirulina." *Human Nature*, March: 60-65.
Galli, Rosemary, ed. (1981). *The Political Economy of Rural Development: Peasants, International Capital, and the State*. Albany: State University of New York Press.
George, Susan (1981). *Les stratégies de la faim*. Paris: Grunauer-Chaix.
_____ (1977). *How the Other Half Dies: The Real Reasons for World Hunger*. Montclair, N.J.: Allanheld, Osmun.
Ghai, D., et al., eds. (1981). *Overcoming Rural Underdevelopment: Proceedings of a Workshop on Alternative Agrarian Systems and Rural Development, Arusha*. Geneva: ILO.
Ghai, Dharam, et al., eds. (1979). *Agrarian Systems and Rural Development*. New York: Holmes & Meier.
Goodman, David, and Redclift, Michael (1982). *From Peasant to Proletarian: Capitalist Development and Agrarian Transitions*. New York: St. Martin's Press.
Griffin, Keith (1978). *International Inequality and National Poverty*. New York: Holmes & Meier.
_____ (1976). *Land Concentration and Rural Poverty*. New York: Holmes & Meier.
_____ (1974). *The Political Economy of Agrarian Change*. Cambridge, Mass.: Harvard University Press.
Griffin, Keith, et al. (1977). *Poverty and Landlessness in Rural Asia*. Geneva: ILO, WEP.
Gow, David, et al. (1979). *Local Organizations and Rural Development: A Comparative Reappraisal*. Washington, D.C.: Development Alternatives, Inc.
Harle, Vilho, ed. (1978). *The Political Economy of Food*. Farnborough, England: Saxon House.

Harwood, Richard R. (1979). *Small Farm Development: Understanding and Improving Farming Systems in the Humid Tropics*. Boulder, Colo.: Westview Press.

Helias, Pierre-Jakez (1975). *Le cheval d'orgueil*. Paris: Librairie Plon. (English trans., 1978. *The Horse of Pride: Life in a Breton Village*. New Haven, Conn.: Yale University Press.)

Heyer, Judith, et al. (1981). *Rural Development in Tropical Africa*. London: St. Martin's.

Hill, Polly (1981). *Dry Grain Farming Families: Hausaland (N. Nigeria) and Karnataka (India) Compared*. Cambridge: Cambridge University Press.

Hodson, Dennis F. (1981). "The Administration and Activities of a Young Organization of Rural Workers in India." *Agricultural Administration*, 1,8:307-20.

Huizer, G., and Mannkeim, B., eds. (1979). *The Politics of Anthropology*. The Hague: Mouton.

Jackson, Tony, and Eade, Deborah (1982). *Against the Grain: The Dilemma of Project Food Aid*. Oxford: OXFAM.

Jacoby, Erich H., and Charlotte F. (1971). *Man and Land: The Essential Revolution*. New York: Alfred A. Knopf.

de Janvry, Alain (1982). *The Agrarian Question and Reformism in Latin America*. Baltimore, Md.: Johns Hopkins University Press.

Johnston, Bruce F., and Clark, William C. (1982). *On Designing Strategies for Rural Development: A Policy Analysis Perspective*. Baltimore, Md.: Johns Hopkins University Press.

Kahn, Joel S., and Llobera, Josep R. (1981). *The Anthropology of Pre-Capitalist Societies*. Atlantic Highlands, N.J.: Humanities Press.

Lappé, Frances Moore, and Collins, Joseph (1979, 2nd ed.). *Food First: Beyond the Myth of Scarcity*. New York: Ballantine Books.

LeFort, Claude (1978). *Les formes de l'histoire: Essais d'anthropologie politique*. Paris: Gallimard.

Lehmann, David, ed. (1974). *Agrarian Reform and Agrarian Reformism*. London: Faber and Faber.

Leonard, David (1977). *Reaching the Peasant Farmer: Organization Theory and Practice in Kenya*. Chicago: University of Chicago Press.

Le Roy Ladurie, Emmanuel (1978, 1975 in Fr.). *Montaillou: The Promised Land of Error*. New York: George Braziller.

Longhurst, Richard, ed. (1981). "Rapid Rural Appraisal: Social Structure and Rural Economy." Special issue of *IDS Bulletin*, 12,4:1-54.

Manniche, Peter, ed. (1970, 1978). *Rural Development in Denmark and the Changing Countries of the World*. Oxford: Pergamon Press.

Meillassoux, Claude (1981). *Maidens, Meal, and Money*. Cambridge: Cambridge University Press (1975, in French).

_____ (1977). *Terrains et théories*. Paris: Anthropos.

National Academy of Science (1981a). *Energy for Rural Development*. Washington, D.C.: National Academy Press.

_____ (1981b). *Food, Fuel, and Fertilizer from Organic Waste*. Washington, D.C.: National Academy Press.

_____ (1981c). *The Water Buffalo*. Washington, D.C.: National Academy Press.

_____ (1981d). *The Winged Bean*. Washington, D.C.: National Academy Press.

_____ (1979). *Tropical Legumes*. Washington, D.C.: National Academy Press.

_____ (1978). *Postharvest Food Losses in Developing Countries*. Washington, D.C.: National Academy Press.

_____ (1977). *Non-Conventional Proteins and Foods*. Washington, D.C.: National Academy Press.

_____ (1975). *Underexploited Tropical Plants with Promising Economic Value*. Washington, D.C.: National Academy Press.

Paige, Jeffery M. (1975). *Agrarian Revolution: Social Movements and Export Agriculture in the Underdeveloped World*. New York: Free Press.

Palmer, Robin, and Parsons, Neil, eds. (1977). *The Roots of Rural Poverty in Central and Southern Africa*. Berkeley: University of California Press.

Pearse, Andrew (1980). *Seeds of Want, Seeds of Plenty: Social and Economic Implications of the Green Revolution*. New York: Oxford University Press.

Perelman, Michael (1977). *Farming for Profit in a Hungry World: Capital and the Crisis*. Montclair, N.J.: Allanheld, Osmun.

Potter, Jack M., et al., eds. (1967). *Peasant Society: A Reader*. Boston: Little, Brown.

Reining, Priscilla, and Lenkerd, Barbara, eds. (1980). *Village Viability in Contemporary Society*. Boulder, Colo.: Westview Press.

Schofield, Sue (1979). *Development and the Problems of Village Nutrition*. London: Croom Helm.

Sen, Amartya (1981). *Poverty and Famines: An Essay on Entitlement and Deprivation*. London: Oxford University Press.

Shaner, W. W., et al. eds. (1982). *Farming Systems Research and Development*. Boulder, Colo.: Westview Press.

Siffin, William (1979). "Administrative Problems and Integrated Rural Development." Bloomington: University of Indiana, PASITAM.

Smith, William E., et al (1980). *The Design of Organizations for Rural Development Projects: A Progress Report*. Washington: IBRD, Staff Working Paper 375.

Sutlive, Vinson H., ed. (1981). *Where Have All the Flowers Gone? Deforestation in the Third World*. Williamsburg, Va.: College of William and Mary, Department of Anthropology, Studies in Third World Societies, No. 13.

Uri, Pierre (1981). *Aider le tiers-monde à se nourrir lui-même*. Paris: Economica.

Vallianatos, Evan G. (1976). *Fear in the Countryside: The Control of Agricultural Resources in the Poor Countries by Nonpeasant Elites*. Cambridge: Ballinger.

Whyte, William F. (1975). *Organizing for Agricultural Development: Human Aspects in the Utilization of Science and Technology*. New Brunswick, N.J.: Transaction Books.

Wolf, Eric (1969). *Peasant Wars of the Twentieth Century*. New York: Harper & Row.

_____ (1966). *Peasants*. Englewood Cliffs, N.J.: Prentice-Hall.

II.C. Health, Education, Population, Environment
  Women in Development
  Other Marginalized Groups
  Cultural and Legal Communication

Allman, James, ed. (1978). *Women's Status and Fertility in the Muslim World*. New York: Praeger.

Anderson, Lascelles, and Windham, Douglas, eds. (1982). *Education and Development: Issues in the Analysis and Planning of Postcolonial Societies*. Lexington, Mass.: Lexington Books.

Asante, Molefe Kete, et al., eds. (1979). *Handbook of Intercultural Communication*. Beverly Hills, Calif.: Sage.

Baetz, Reuben, ed. (1975). *Development and Participation: Implications for Social Welfare*. New York: Columbia University Press.

Beneria, Lourdes, ed. (1982). *Women and Development: The Sexual Division of Labour in Rural Societies*. New York: Praeger.

Black, Naomi, and Cottrell, Ann. B., eds. (1981). *Women and World Change: Equity Issues in Development*. Beverly Hills, Calif.: Sage.

Bock, John, and Papagiannis, George, eds. (1982). *Nonformal Education and National Development*. New York: Praeger.

Bourguignon, Erika, ed. (1980). *A World of Women: Anthropological Studies of Women in the Societies of the World*. New York: Praeger.

Bozeman, Adda (1971). *The Future of Law in a Multicultural World*. Princeton, N.J.: Princeton University Press.

Buvinić, Mayra, and Youssef, Nadia (1978). *Women-Headed Households: The Ignored Factor in Development Planning*. Washington, D.C.: International Center for Research on Women for AID.

Conde, J., et al. (1979). *The Integrated Approach to Rural Development Health and Population*. Paris: OECD.

Crouch, B. R., and Chamala, S. (1981). *Extension Education and Rural Development*. Chichester: John Wiley.

Le Développement culturel: Expériences régionales (1981). Paris: UNESCO.

Doyal, Lesley (1979). *The Political Economy of Health*. London: Pluto Press.

Dunlop, David (1982). *Toward a Health Project Evaluation Framework*. Washington: AID, PPC, Evaluation Special Study No. 8.

Easterlin, Richard, ed. (1980). *Population and Economic Change in Developing Countries*. Cambridge, Mass.: National Bureau of Economic Research.

Eberstadt, Nick, ed. (1981). *Fertility Decline in the Less Developed Countries*. New York: Praeger.

Ellen, Roy (1982). *Environment, Subsistence and System: The Ecology of Small-Scale Social Formations*. Cambridge: Cambridge University Press.

Etienne, Mona, and Leacock, Eleanor (1980). *Women and Colonization: Anthropological Perspectives*. New York: Praeger.

Fahim, Hussein, ed. (1982). *Indigenous Anthropology in Non-Western Countries*. Durham, N.C.: Carolina Academic Press.

Foster, George, et al. (1978). *Long-Term Field Research in Social Anthropology*. New York: Academic Press.

Freire, Paulo (1978). *Pedagogy in Process: Letters to Guinea-Bissau*. New York: Seabury Press.

_____ (1973). *Education for Critical Consciousness*. New York: Seabury Press.

_____ (1970). *Pedagogy of the Oppressed*. New York: Seabury Press.

Fry, Christine L., ed. (1981). *Dimensions of Aging, Culture, and Health*. New York: Praeger.

_____ (1980). *Aging in Culture and Society: Comparative Viewpoints and Strategies*. New York: Praeger.

Fugelsang, Andreas (1982). *About Understanding: Ideas and Observations on Cross-Cultural Communication*. Uppsala: Dag Hammarskjold Foundation.

Gailey, Christine W., and Etienne, Mona (1982). *Women and the State in Pre-Industrial Societies: Anthropological Perspectives*. New York: Praeger.

Georges, Robert A., and Jones, Michael O. (1980). *People Studying People: The Human Element in Fieldwork*. Berkeley: University of California Press.

Goodland, Robert (1982). *Tribal Peoples and Economic Development: Human and Ecological Considerations*. Washington, D.C.: IBRD.

Greenberg, David F., ed. (1981). *Crime & Capitalism: Readings in Marxist Criminology*. Palo Alto, Calif.: Mayfield.

Huston, Perdita (1979). *Third World Women Speak Out*. New York: Praeger.

Ingersoll, Jasper, et al. (1981). *Social Analysis of AID Projects: A Review of the Experience*. Washington: AID/PPC/PDPR.

JASPA (1981). *Ensuring Equitable Growth: A Strategy for Increasing Employment, Equity, and Basic Needs Satisfaction*. Addis Ababa: ILO/JASPA (Jobs and Skills Program for Africa).

Johnson, E. A. J. (1970). *The Organization of Space in Developing Countries*. Cambridge, Mass.: Harvard Univeristy Press.

Lathem, Willoughby, ed. (1979). *The Future of Academic Community Medicine in Developing Countries*. New York: Praeger.

Leonor, M. D., and Richards, P. J. (1982). *Target Setting for Basic Needs: The Operation of Selected Government Services*. Geneva: ILO.

Luckham, Robin, ed. (1981). *Law and Social Enquiry: Case Studies of Research*. Uppsala: SIAS.

Lyons, R. F. (1981). *The Organization of Education in Remote Rural Areas* (Sudan and Nepal). Paris: International Institute for Educational Planning.

Meillassoux, Claude (1981, 1975 in Fr.). *Maidens, Meal, and Money*. Cambridge: Cambridge University Press.

Michael, Donald N. (1973). *On Learning to Plan and Planning to Learn: The Social Psychology of Changing Toward Future-Responsive Societal Learning*. San Francisco, Calif.: Jossey-Bass.

Minkler, Meredith, and Cox, Kathleen (1980). "Creating Critical Consciousness in Health: Applications of Freire's Philosophy and Methods to the Health Care Setting." *International Journal of Health Services*, X,2:311-22.

Morsy, Zaghloul, ed. (1979). *Learning and Working*. Paris: UNESCO.

Newland, Kathleen (1979). *The Sisterhood of Man*. New York: W. W. Norton.

Obbo, Christine (1980). *African Women: Their Struggle for Economic Independence*. London: Zed Press.

O'Connor, Ronald W., ed. (1980). *Managing Health Systems in Developing Areas: Experiences from Afghanistan*. Lexington, Mass.: D. C. Heath.

Palmer, Ingrid, and Buchwald, Ulrike von (1980). *Monitoring Changes in the Conditions of Women − A Critical Review of Possible Approaches*. Geneva: UNRISD, 80.1.

Preston, D. A., ed. (1980). *Environment, Society and Rural Change in the Third World*. Chichester: John Wiley.

Rensburg, Patrick van (1981). "Education and Culture for Liberation." *Development Dialogue*, 1:138-50.

Ribes, Bruno, ed. (1981). *Domination or Sharing? Endogenous Development and the Transfer of Knowledge*. Paris: UNESCO.

Rizzi, Felice (1981). *Educazione nei paesi del Terzo Mundo*. Brescia: La Scuola.

Rodgers, G., and Standing, G., eds. (1981). *Child Work, Poverty, and Underdevelopment: Issues for Research in Low-Income Countries*. Geneva: ILO.

Ross, Eric B., ed. (1980). *Beyond the Myths of Culture: Essays in Cultural Materialism*. New York: Academic Press.

Sanday, Peggy R. (1981). *Female Power and Male Dominance: On the Origins of Sexual Inequality*. Cambridge: Cambridge University Press.

Sarri, Rosemary, and Hasenfeld, Yeheskel, eds. (1978). *The Management of Human Services*. New York: Columbia University Press.

Schmidt, Stephen W., et al., eds. (1977). *Friends, Followers, and Factions: A Reader in Political Clientage*. Berkeley: University of California Press.

Schultz, Theodore M. (1981). *Investing in People*. Berkeley: University of California Press.

Silverman, Milton, et al. (1982). *Prescriptions for Death: The Drugging of the Third World*. Berkeley: University of California Press.

Smock, Audrey C. (1981). *Women's Education in Developing Countries: Opportunities and Outcomes*. New York: Praeger.

Somavía, Juan (1981). "The Democratization of Communications: From Minority Social Monopoly to Majority Social Representation." *Development Dialogue* 2:13-29.

Turner, David H., and Smith, Gavin, eds. (1979). *Challenging Anthropology: A Critical Introduction to Social and Cultural Anthropology*. Toronto: McGraw-Hill.

Wallman, Sandra, ed. (1977). *Perceptions of Development*. Cambridge: Cambridge University Press.

Weekes-Vagliani, Winifred (1980). *Les femmes dans le développement: quatre études de cas*. Paris: OECD.

Wolfson, Margaret S. (1979). *Nouvelles approches aux problèmes de population*. Paris: OECD.

Young, Kate, et al., eds. (1981). *Of Marriage and the Market: The Subordination of Women from an International Perspective*. London: CSE Books.

II.D. Energy, Appropriate Technology
    Credit, Infrastructure
    Urban Development
    Poverty Measurement

Abu-Lughod, Janet, and Hay, Richard, eds. (1980). *Third World Urbanization*. London: Methuen.

Anderson, G. William, and Vandervoort, C. (1981). *Rural Roads Evaluation Summary Report*. Washington: AID, PPC, Office of Evaluation, Program Evaluation Report 5.

ARTEP (1981). *Employment Expansion Through Local Resource Mobilization*. Bangkok: ILO/ARTEP (Asian Regional Team for Employment Promotion).

Biro, Andras (1981). "The Local Space: A Privileged Instance of Development." *Development Dialogue*, 1:103-13.

Boyle, Godfrey, and Harper, Peter, eds. (1976). *Radical Technology*. London: Marion Boyars.

Brokensha, D. W., et al., eds. (1980). *Indigenous Knowledge Systems and Development*. Washington, D.C.: University Press of America.

Bromley, Ray, and Gerry, Chris, eds. (1979). *Casual Work and Poverty in Third World Cities*. Chichester: John Wiley.

Cohen, Robin, et al., eds. (1979). *Peasants and Proletarians: The Struggle of Third World Workers*. New York: Monthly Review Press.

Connell, John, and Lipton, Michael (1979). *Assessing Village Labour Situations in Developing Countries*. Delhi: Oxford University Press.

Cooley, Mike (1980). *Architect or Bee? The Human/Technology Relationship*. Boston: South End Press.

Daly, Herman E., and Umaña, Alvaro F., eds. (1981). *Energy, Economics, and the Environment*. Boulder, Colo.: Westview Press.

Dauber, Roslyn, and Cain, Melinda L., eds. (1980). *Women and Technological Change in Developing Countries*. Boulder, Colo.: Westview Press.

Dear, Michael, and Scott, Allen, eds. (1981). *Urbanization and Urban Planning in Capitalist Society*. London: Methuen.

Dorf, Richard, and Hunter, Yvonne, eds. (1978). *Appropriate Visions: Technology, the Environment and the Individual*. San Francisco, Calif.: Boyd & Fraser.

Edquist, Charles and Olle (1979). *Social Carriers of Techniques for Development*. Stockholm: SAREC.

Evans, Donald, and Adler, Laurie, eds. (1979). *Appropriate Technology for Development: A Discussion and Case Histories*. Boulder, Colo.: Westview Press.

Farbman, Michael, ed. (1981). *The PISCES Studies: Assisting the Smallest Economic Activities of the Urban Poor*. Washington: AID, Bur. for Science and Technology, Office of Urban Development.

Fergany, Nader (1981). *Monitoring the Condition of the Poor in the Third World: Some Aspects of Measurement*. Geneva: ILO, WEP 10-6/WP52.

Gilbert, Alan, and Gugler, Josef (1982). *Cities, Poverty and Development: Urbanization in the Third World*. Oxford: Oxford University Press.

HABITAT, ed. (1981). *Residential Circumstances of the Urban Poor in Developing Countries*. New York: Praeger.

Howell, John, ed. (1980). *Borrowers and Lenders: Rural Financial Markets and Institutions in Developing Countries*. London: Overseas Development Institute.

Hugon, Philippe, ed. (1980). "Secteur informel et petite production marchande dans les villes du Tiers Monde." *Revue Tiers Monde*, No. 82, avril-juin (entire issue).

Irvine, John, et al. (1979). *Demystifying Social Statistics*. London: Pluto Press.

King, Alexander, and Cleveland, Harland, eds. (1980). *Bioresources for Development: The Renewable Way of Life*. Oxford: Pergamon Press.

Lloyd, Peter (1979). *Slums of Hope: Shanty Towns in the Third World*. Harmondsworth, England: Penguin.

Lockeritz, William, ed. (1978). *Agriculture and Energy: Proceedings of a Conference*. New York: Academic Press.

Long, Franklin A., and Oleson, A., eds. (1980). *Appropriate Technology and Social Values – A Critical Appraisal*. Cambridge, Mass.: Ballinger.

McAnany, Emile G., ed. (1980). *Communications in the Rural Third World*. New York: Praeger.

McRobie, George (1981). *Small Is Possible*. New York: Harper & Row.

Makhijani, Arjun, and Poole, Alan (1975). *Energy and Agriculture in the Third World*. Cambridge, Mass.: Ballinger.

Mangin, William, ed. (1970). *Peasants in Cities: Readings in the Anthropology of Urbanization*. Boston: Houghton Mifflin.

Max-Neef, Manfred (1981). "The 'Tiradentes' Project: Revitalization of Small Cities for Self-Reliance." *Development Dialogue*, 1:115-37.

Miller, Duncan (1979). *Self-Help and Popular Participation in Rural Water Systems*. Paris: OECD.

Morazé, Charles, ed. (1980). *Le Point Critique*. Paris: PUF and IEDES.

Nicol, Davidson, and D'Onofrio-Flores, Pamela, eds. (1981). *Scientific-Technological Change and the Role of Women in Development*. Boulder, Colo.: Westview Press.

Norman, Colin (1981). *The God That Limps: Science and Technology in the Eighties*. New York: W. W. Norton.

Perlman, Janice E. (1976). *The Myth of Marginality: Urban Poverty and Politics in Rio de Janeiro*. Berkeley: University of California Press.

Ramesh, Jairam, and Weiss, Charles, eds. (1979). *Mobilizing Technology for World Development*. New York: Praeger.

Roberts, Bryan (1978). *Cities of Peasants: The Political Economy of Urbanization in the Third World*. Beverly Hills, Calif.: Sage.

Safa, Helen I., ed. (1981). *Towards a Political Economy of Urbanization in Third World Countries*. Oxford: Oxford University Press.

Schumacher, E. F. (1979). *Good Work*. New York: Harper & Row.

_____ (1973). *Small is Beautiful: Economics as if People Matter*. New York: Harper & Row.

Stohr, W. B., and Fraser Taylor, D. R., eds. (1981). *Development from Above or Below: The Dialectics of Regional Planning in Developing Countries*.

Chichester, England: John Wiley.

Wionczek, Miguel S., et al., eds. (1981). *Energy in the Transition from Rural Subsistence*. Boulder, Colo.: Westview Press.

III. Organization Studies: Bureaucracy or Participation

III.A. General Systems and Organization Theory

Abrahamsson, Bengt (1977). *Bureaucracy or Participation: The Logic of Organization*. Beverly Hills, Calif.: Sage.

Agger, Robert A. (1978). *A Little White Lie: Institutional Divisions of Labor and Life*. New York: Elsevier.

Beer, Stafford (1979). *The Heart of Enterprise*. New York: John Wiley & Sons.

_____ (1975). *Platform for Change*. London: John Wiley & Sons.

Bennis, Warren (1966). *Beyond Bureaucracy*. New York: McGraw Hill.

Berne, Eric (1963). *The Structure and Dynamics of Organizations and Groups*. New York: Grove Press.

Borich, Gary D., and Jemelka, Ron P. (1982). *Programs and Systems: An Evaluation Perspective*. New York: Academic Press.

Britan, Gerald M. (1981). *Bureaucracy and Innovation: An Ethnography of Policy Change*. Beverly Hills, Calif.: Sage.

Britan, Gerald M., and Cohen, Ronald, eds. (1980). *Hierarchy and Society: Anthropological Perspectives on Bureaucracy*. Philadelphia: Institute for the Study of Human Issues (hereafter ISHI).

Cherns, Albert, ed. (1976). *Sociotechnics*. London: Malaby Press.

Clegg, Stewart, and Dunkerly, David (1980). *Organization, Class, and Control*. London: Routledge & Kegan Paul.

Himmelstrand, Ulf, ed. (1981). *Spontaneity and Planning in Social Development*. Beverly Hills, Calif.: Sage.

Hodges, Donald C. (1981). *The Bureaucratization of Socialism*. Amherst: University of Massachusetts Press.

Hummel, Ralph (1977). *The Bureaucratic Experience*. New York: St. Martin's Press.

Jacoby, Henry (1973, 1969 in Ger.). *The Bureaucratization of the World*. Berkeley: University of California Press.

Kanter, Rosabeth M. (1977). *Men and Women in Corporations*. New York: Basic Books.

Kaufman, Herbert (1971). *The Limits of Organizational Change*. University: University of Alabama Press.

Kharasch, Robert N. (1973). *The Institutional Imperative*. New York: Charterhouse Books.

Klapp, Orrin E. (1978). *Opening and Closing: Strategies of Information Adaptation in Society*. Cambridge: Cambridge University Press.

Lammers, Cornelis J., and Hickson, David J., eds. (1979). *Organizations Alike and Unlike: International and Interinstitutional Studies in the Sociology of Organizations*. London: Routledge & Kegan Paul.

Lehman, Meir M. (1980). "Programs, Life Cycles, and Laws of Software Evolution." *Proceedings of the IEEE*, 68,9:1061-80.

Merkle, Judith (1980). *Management and Ideology: The Legacy of the International Scientific Management Movement*. Berkeley: University of California Press.

Miller, James G. (1978). *Living Systems*. New York: McGraw Hill.

Mlinar, Zdravko, and Teune, Henry, eds. (1978). *The Social Ecology of Change*. Beverly Hills, Calif.: Sage.

Perrow, Charles (1980). "Organization Theory in a Society of Organizations." Livermore, Colorado: Red Feather Institute for Advanced Studies in Sociology, Paper No. 62.

Pfeffer, Jeffrey, and Salancik, Gerald R. (1978). *The External Control of Organizations: A Resource Dependence Perspective*. New York: Harper & Row.

Pressman, Jeffrey L., and Wildavsky, Aaron B. (1979, 2nd ed.). *Implementation*. Berkeley: University of California Press.

Ramos, Alberto G. (1981). *The New Science of Organizations*. Toronto: University of Toronto Press.

Stout, Russell (1980). *Management or Control: The Organizational Challenge*. Bloomington: Indiana University Press.

Sztompka, Piotr (1979). *Sociological Dilemmas: Toward a Dialectic Paradigm*. New York: Academic Press.

____ (1974). *System and Function: Toward a Theory of Society*. New York: Academic Press.

Salamin, Graeme, and Thompson, Kenneth, eds. (1980). *Control and Ideology in Organizations*. Cambridge, Mass.: MIT Press.

Schein, Edgar (1980, 3rd ed.). *Organizational Psychology*. Englewood Cliffs, N.J.: Prentice-Hall.

Scott, William G., and Hart, David K. (1979). *Organizational America*. Boston: Houghton Mifflin.

Teune, Henry, and Mlinar, Zdravko (1978). *The Developmental Logic of Social Systems*. Beverly Hills, Calif.: Sage.

Weber, Max (1964 ed.). *The Theory of Social and Economic Organization*. New York: Free Press.

Zaltman, Gerald, and Duncan, Robert (1977). *Strategies for Planned Change*. New York: John Wiley & Sons.

III.B. Participation in Social Programs: Issues of Community Organizing and Planning

Barnett, Stanley A., and Engel, Nat (1982). *Effective Institution Building: A Guide for Project Designers and Project Managers Based on Lessons Learned from the AID Portfolio*. Washington: AID/PPC/E, Program Evaluation Discussion Paper 11.

Bjorkman, James W. (1979). *Politics of Administrative Alienation in India's Rural Development Programs*. Delhi: Ajanta Publications.

Black, J. E., et al. (1977). *Education and Training for Public Sector Management in the Developing Countries*. New York: Rockefeller Foundation.

Caiden, Naomi, and Wildavsky, Aaron (1974, 1980). *Planning and Budgeting in Poor Countries*. New Brunswick, N.J.: Transactions Books.

Carmichael, Douglass (1976-77). Unpublished papers on the quality of work life in the World Bank, Washington, D.C.

Chaturvedi, H. R. (1977). *Bureaucracy and the Local Community: Dynamics of Rural Development*. Columbia, Mo.: South Asia Books.

Chekki, Dan A., ed. (1980). *Participatory Democracy in Action: International Profiles of Community Development*. New Delhi: Vikas.

_____ (1979). *Community Development: Theory and Method of Planned Change*. New Delhi: Vikas.

Conyers, Diana (1982). *An Introduction to Social Planning in the Third World*. Chichester, England: John Wiley.

Cox, Fred M., et al., eds. (1979, 3rd ed.). *Strategics of Community Organization*. Itasca, Ill.: F. E. Peacock.

_____ (1977). *Tactics and Techniques of Community Practice*. Itasca, Ill.: F. E. Peacock.

Craig, Gary (1982). *Community Work and the State*. Boston: Routledge & Kegan Paul.

Crane, Barbara B., and Finkle, Jason L. (1981). "Organizational Impediments to Development Assistance: the World Bank's Population Program." *World Politics*, 33:516-53.

Day, Peter (1981). *Social Work and Social Control*. London: Tavistock.

Dore, R., and Mars, Z., eds. (1981). *Community Development*. London: Croom Helm.

Duller, H. J. (1982). *Development Technology*. London: Routledge & Kegan Paul.

Esman, Milton J. (1980). "Development Assistance in Public Administration: Requiem or Renewal." *Public Administration Review*, 40,5:426-31.

_____ (1978). "Development Administration and Constituency Organization." *Public Administration Review*, 38,2:166-72.

Fischer, Constance T., and Brodsky, Stanley L. (1978). *Client Participation in Human Services: The Prometheus Principle*. New Brunswick, N.J.: Transaction Books.

Fox, Frederick V., et al. (1976). "Designing Organizations to be Responsive to their Clients," pp. 53-72 in Kilman, Ralph H., et al., eds. *The Management of Organization Design*, volume one. New York: North-Holland.

Gellar, Sheldon (1976). "Development Models, Development Administration, and the Ratched-McMurphy Model: A View from the Bottom," pp. 11-25 in Hopkins, Jack W., ed., *Administration for Development: A Comparative Perspective on the Middle East and Latin America*. Bloomington: School of Public and Environmental Affairs, University of Indiana.

Gittell, Marilyn (1980). *Limits to Citizen Participation*. Beverly Hills, Calif.: Sage.

Gow, David D., et al. (1979). *Local Organizations and Rural Development: A Comparative Reappraisal*. 2 volumes. Washington: DAI.

Heginbotham, Stanley (1975). *Cultures in Conflict: The Four Faces of Indian Bureaucracy*. New York: Columbia University Press.

Helmers, F. Leslie (1979). *Project Planning and Income Distribution*. The Hague: Martinus Nijhoff.

Honadle, George, and Klauss, Rudi, eds. (1979). *International Development Administration: Implementation Analysis for Development Projects*. New York: Praeger.

Imboden, N. (1980). *Managing Information for Rural Development Projects*. Paris: OECD.

Korten, David C., ed. (1979a). *Population and Social Development Management: A Challenge for Management Schools*. Caracas, Venezuela: Istituto de Estudios Superiores de Administracion.

—— (1979b). "Toward a Technology for Managing Social Development." Harvard School of Public Health, expanded version.

Laar, Aart van de (1980). *The World Bank and the Poor*. The Hague: Martinus Nijhoff.

Loveman, Brian (1976). "The Comparative Administration Group, Development Administration, and Antidevelopment." *Public Administration Review*, 36,6:616-21.

March, James G., and Olsen, Johan P. (1976). *Ambiguity and Choice in Organizations*. Bergen, Norway: Universitetsforlaget.

Marson, D. Brian (1971). "Dissimilar Value Commitments and the Dynamics of Development Administration." *Thai Journal of Development Administration*, XI,4:607-21.

Mickelwait, Donald R., et al. (1979). *New Directions in Development: A Study of U.S. AID*. Boulder, Colo.: Westview Press.

Montgomery, John D. (1979). "The Populist Front in Rural Development: or Shall We Eliminate the Bureaucrats and Get On with the Job." *Public Administration Review*, 39,1:58-65.

Morgan, E. Philip (1980). "Managing Development Assistance: Some Effects with Special Reference to Southern Africa." *SADEX*, 2,1:1-17.

Nef, J., and Dwivedi, O. P. (1981). "Development Theory and Administration: A Fence Around an Empty Lot." *The Indian Journal of Public Administration*, XXVII,1:42-66.

Parston, Gregory (1980). *Planners, Politics, and Health Services*. London: Croom Helm.

Paul, Samuel (1982). *Managing Development Programs: The Lessons of Success*. Boulder, Colo.: Westview Press.

Resnick, Herman, and Patti, Rino, eds. (1980). *Change from Within: Humanizing Social Welfare Organizations*. Philadelphia: Temple University Press.

Rothman, Jack (1974). *Planning and Organizing for Social Change*. New York: Columbia University Press.

Rothman, Jack, et al. (1976). *Promoting Innovation and Change in Organizations and Communities*. New York: John Wiley & Sons.

Siffin, William J. (1979). "Administrative Problems and Integrated Rural Development." Bloomington: University of Indiana, PASITAM Design Study.

Smith, William E., et al. (1980). *The Design of Organizations for Rural Development Projects – A Progress Report*. Washington: World Bank Staff Working Paper No. 375.

Stevens, Phillips (1978). "Social Science Involvement in African Development Planning." *African Studies Review*, XXI,3:1-6.

Tendler, Judith (1982). *Turning Private Voluntary Organizations Into Development Agencies: Questions for Evaluation*. Washington: AID/PPC/E, Program Evaluation Discussion Paper 12.

_____ (1975). *Inside Foreign Aid*. Baltimore: Johns Hopkins University Press.

Thomas, David N. (1976). *Organizing for Social Change*. London: George Allen & Unwin.

Thomas, Theodore H. (1977). "Innovation in Organization Structure: Normative Implications of Participatory Styles." Unpublished Ph.D. dissertation, University of California at Los Angeles.

_____ (1973). "People Strategies for International Development: Administrative Alternatives to National Political and Economic Ideologues." *Journal of Comparative Administration*, 5,1(May):87-107.

Thomas, Theodore H., and Brinkerhoff, Derick (1978). "Devolutionary Strategies for Development Administration." Washington, D.C.: American Society for Public Administration, SICA Occasional Paper No. 8.

UNDP (1979). *Comprehensive Development Planning*. New York: UNDP, Evaluation Study No. 1.

Warren, Roland (1977). *Social Change and Human Purpose: Toward Understanding and Action*. Chicago: Rand McNally.

Warwick, Donald P. (1977). "Planning as Transaction and Dealing with Bureaucratic and Political Contexts." Cambridge, Mass.: Harvard Center for Studies of Education and Development. June, unpublished.

III.C. Participation in Social Programs: Issues of Implementation and Evaluation

Argento, Gerrit, et al. (1981). *Interim Evaluation of DS/RAD Project 936-5300, Organization and Administration of Integrated Rural Development*. Washington: AID, OS/MD, February.

Aslanian, Carol B., ed. (1981). *Improving Educational Evaluation Methods*, Beverly Hills, Calif.: Sage.

Attkisson, C. Clifford, et al., eds. (1978). *Evaluation of Human Service Programs*. New York: Academic Press.

Blalock, Hubert M. (1982). *Conceptualization and Measurement in the Social Sciences*. Beverly Hills, Calif.: Sage.

Bloom, Martin, and Fischer, Joel (1982). *Evaluating Practice: Guidelines for the Accountable Professional*. Englewood Cliffs, N.J.: Prentice-Hall.

Conner, Ross F. (1981). *Methodological Advances in Evaluation Research*. Beverly Hills, Calif.: Sage.

Cronbach, Lee J. (1980). *Toward Reform of Program Evaluation: Aims, Methods, and Institutional Arrangements*. San Francisco, Calif.: Jossey Bass.

Culbert, Samuel, and McDonough, John (1980). *The Invisible War: Pursuing Self-Interests at Work*. New York: John Wiley & Sons.

Datta, Louis-Ellin (1981). *Evaluation in Change: Meeting New Governmental Needs*. Beverly Hills, Calif.: Sage.

Dunsire, Andrew (1978). *Implementing in a Bureaucracy*. New York: St. Martin's Press.

Filstead, William J. (1981). "Using Qualitative Methods in Evaluation Research." *Evaluation Review*, 5,2:259-68.

Freeman, Howard E., and Solomon, Marian A., eds. (1981). *Evaluation Studies – Review Annual 6*. Beverly Hills, Calif.: Sage.

Goodsell, Charles T., ed. (1981). *The Public Encounter: Where State and Citizen Meet*. Bloomington: Indiana University Press.

House, Ernest R. (1980). *Evaluating with Validity*. Beverly Hills, Calif.: Sage.

Ingle, Marcus D. (1979). "Implementing Development Programs: A State-of-the-Art Review." Washington: AID, DSB, Office of Rural Development.

——— (1977). "Organizational Determinants of Rural Equality: An Exploratory Study of Development Project Information-Processing and the Distribution of Socio-Economic Benefits in Less Developed Countries." Unpublished Ph.D. dissertation, Syracuse University, Maxwell School.

Judd, Charles M., and Kenny, David A. (1981). *Estimating the Effects of Social Intervention*. Cambridge: Cambridge University Press.

Kline, Elliott H., and Buntz, C. Gregory (1979). "On the Effective Use of Public Sector Expertise: Or Why the Use of Outside Consultants Often Leads to the Waste of In-House Skills." *Public Administration Review*, 39,5:226-29.

Langbein, Laura I. (1980). *Discovering Whether Programs Work*. Santa Monica, Calif.: Goodyear.

Leistritz, F. Larry, and Murdock, Steven H. (1981). *The Socioeconomic Impact of Resource Development Methods for Assessment*. Boulder, Colo.: Westview.

Levine, Robert A., et al., eds. (1981). *Evaluation Research and Practice: Comparative and International Perspectives*. Beverly Hills, Calif.: Sage.

Levitan, Sar A., and Wurzburg, Gregory (1979). *Evaluating Federal Social Programs: An Uncertain Art*. Kalamazoo, Mich.: W. E. Upjohn Institute for Employment Research.

Meyers, William R. (1981). *Evaluation Enterprise: A Realistic Appraisal of Evaluation Careers, Methods, and Applications*. San Francisco, Calif.: Jossey Bass.

Nachmias, David, ed. (1980). *The Practice of Policy Evaluation*. New York: St. Martin's Press.

Patton, Michael Quinn (1981). *Creative Evaluation*. Beverly Hills, Calif.: Sage.

Perloff, Robert and Evelyn, eds. (1980). *Values, Ethics, and Standards in Evaluation*. San Francisco, Calif.: Jossey Bass.

Rossi, Peter H., and Freeman, Howard E. (1982, 2nd ed.). *Evaluation: A Systematic Approach*. Beverly Hills, Calif.: Sage.

Rothman, Jack (1980). *Social R+D: Research and Development in the Human Services*. Englewood Cliffs, N.J.: Prentice-Hall.

Sieber, Sam D. (1981). *Fatal Remedies: The Ironies of Social Intervention*. New York: Plenum.

Smith, Nick L., ed. (1982). *Communication Strategies in Evaluation*. Beverly Hills, Calif.: Sage.

____ (1981a). *Metaphors for Evaluation: Sources of New Methods*. Beverly Hills, Calif.: Sage.

____ (1981b). *New Techniques for Evaluation*. Beverly Hills, Calif.: Sage.

Strachan, Harry W. (1978). "Side-Effects of Planning in the Aid Control System." *World Development*, 6,4:467-78.

Warwick, Donald (1975). *A Theory of Public Bureaucracy: Politics, Personality and Organization in the State Department*. Cambridge, Mass.: Harvard University Press.

Williams, Walter (1980). *The Implementation Perspective: A Guide for Managing Social Service Delivery Programs*. Berkeley: University of California Press.

Williams, Walter, and Elmore, Richard, eds. (1976). *Social Program Implementation*. New York: Academic Press.

Worsley, Peter, ed. (1971). *Two Blades of Grass: Rural Cooperatives in Agricultural Modernization*. Manchester: Manchester University Press.

Zappulla, Elio (1982). *Evaluating Administrative Performance: Current Trends and Techniques*. Belmont, Calif.: Star.

III.D. Participation in the Industrial Organization

Abrahamsson, Bengt, and Brostrom, Anders (1980). *The Rights of Labor*. Beverly Hills, Calif.: Sage.

Aronowitz, Stanley (1973). *False Promises. The Shaping of American Working Class Consciousness*. New York: McGraw Hill.

Braverman, Harry (1974). *Labor and Monopoly Capital: The Degradation of Work in the Twentieth Century*. New York: Monthly Review Press.

Burns, Tom R., et al., eds. (1979). *Work and Power: The Liberation of Work and the Control of Political Power*. Beverly Hills, Calif.: Sage.

Comisso, Ellen (1979). *Workers' Control Under Plan and Market: Implications of Yugoslav Self Management*. New Haven, Conn.: Yale University Press.

Edwards, Richard (1979). *Contested Terrain: The Transformation of the Workplace in the Twentieth Century*. New York: Basic Books.

Espinosa, Juan G., and Zimbalist, Andrew S. (1978). *Economic Democracy: Workers' Participation in Chilean Industry 1970-1973*. New York: Academic Press.

Derossi, Flavia (1982). *The Technocratic Illusion: A Study of Managerial Power in Italy*. Armonk, N.Y.: M. E. Sharpe.

Hecksher, Charles C. (1981). "Democracy at Work: In Whose Interests? The Politics of Worker Participation." Unpublished Ph.D. dissertation, Harvard University.

Horvat, Branko, et al., eds. (1975). *Self-governing Socialism: A Reader*. 2 volumes. White Plains, N.Y.: International Arts and Sciences Press.

Jones, Derek C., and Svejnar, Jan, eds. (1982). *Participatory and Self-Managed Firms: Evaluating Economic Performance.* Lexington, Mass.: Lexington Books.

Kester, Gerard (1980). *Transition to Workers' Self-Management: Its Dynamics in the Decolonizing Economy of Malta.* The Hague: Institute for Social Studies.

Macarov, David (1982). *Worker Productivity: Myths and Reality.* Beverly Hills, Calif.: Sage.

Mason, Ronald (1982). *Participatory and Workplace Democracy: A Theoretical Development in Critique of Liberalism.* Carbondale: Southern Illinois University Press.

Meidner, Rudolph (1978). *Employee Investment Funds: An Approach to Collective Capital Formation.* London: Allen & Unwin.

Mertz, Herbert (1979). *Workers' Capitalism: The Fusion of Free Enterprise and Socialism.* Gaithersburg, Md.: New Visions Press.

Monat, Jacques (1981). *Workers' Participation in Decision Within Undertakings.* Geneva: ILO.

Nightingale, Donald V. (1982). *Workplace Democracy: An Inquiry into Employee Participation in Canadian Work Organizations.* Toronto: University of Toronto Press.

Pfeffer, Richard M. (1979). *Working for Capitalism.* New York: Columbia University Press.

Schweickart, David (1980). *Capitalism or Worker Control? An Ethical and Economic Appraisal.* New York: Praeger.

Thames, Cindy (1981). "How Kollmorgen keeps managers farsighted and yet responsive." *Electronic Business*, November:100-2.

Thomas, Henk, and Logan, Chris (1982). *Mondragon: An Economic Analysis.* London: George Allen & Unwin.

Vanek, Jaroslav (1977). *The Labor Managed Economy.* Ithaca, N.Y.: Cornell University Press.

Vanek, Jaroslav, ed. (1975). *Self-Management: Economic Liberation of Man.* Harmondsworth, England: Penguin.

IV.   Representative Samples of Recent Modernization/Growth Writings

IV.A. Economic History, Growth Theory, and Philosophy

Alhadeff, David A. (1982). *Microeconomics and Human Behavior: Toward a New Synthesis of Economics and Psychology.* Berkeley: University of California Press.

Almond, Gabriel, et al., eds. (1982). *Progress and Its Discontents.* Berkeley: University of California Press.

Ayres, Robert (1979). *Uncertain Futures.* New York: John Wiley & Sons.

Bairoch, Paul (1978, Eng.). *The Economic Development of the Third World Since 1900.* Berkeley: University of California Press.

Balassa, Bela (1982). *Development Strategies in Semi-Industrial Economics*. Baltimore, Md.: Johns Hopkins University Press for the World Bank.

Barney, Gerald O. (1980-81). *The Global 2000 Report to the President of the U.S.* 3 volumes. Elmsford, N.Y.: Pergamon Press.

Bauer, P. T. (1981). *Equality, the Third World, and Economic Delusion*. Cambridge, Mass.: Harvard University Press.

_____ (1976, 2nd ed.). *Dissent on Development: Studies and Debates in Development Economics*. London: Weidenfeld and Nicholson.

Berg, Robert, et al. (1981). *Accelerated Development in Sub-Saharan Africa: An Agenda for Action*. Washington: World Bank.

Brown, Lester (1981). *Building a Sustainable Society*. New York: W. W. Norton.

Camps, Miriam (1981). *Collective Management: The Reform of Global Economic Organizations*. New York: McGraw Hill.

Carens, J. H. (1981). *Equality, Moral Incentives, and the Market*. Chicago: University of Chicago Press.

Chenery, Hollis, et al. (1979). *Structural Change and Development Policy*. Oxford: Oxford University Press for the World Bank.

Chenery, Hollis, and Syrquin, Moises (1975). *Patterns of Development 1950-1970*. New York: Oxford University Press for the World Bank.

Chenery, Hollis, et al. (1974). *Redistribution with Growth*. Oxford: Oxford University Press for the World Bank.

Clayre, Alasdair, ed. (1980). *The Political Economy of Cooperation and Participation*. Oxford: Oxford University Press.

Cohen, Benjamin (1973). *The Question of Imperialism*. New York: Basic Books.

Cohen, John M., and Uphoff, Norman (1980). "Participation's Place in Rural Development: Seeking Clarity through Specificity." *World Development*, 8,3:213-35.

Corea, Gamani (1980). *Need for Change*. New York: Pergamon Press.

Crozier, Michel J., et al. (1975). *The Crisis of Democracy*. New York: New York University Press for the Trilateral Commission.

Douglas, Mary, and Wildavsky, Aaron (1982). *Risk and Culture: An Essay on the Selection of Technological and Environmental Dangers*. Berkeley: University of California Press.

Friedrich Ebert Foundations, eds. (1981). *Towards One World? International Responses to the Brandt Report*. London: Temple Smith.

Gerschenkron, Alexander (1965). *Economic Backwardness in Historical Perspective*. New York: Praeger.

Gersovitz, Mark, et al., eds. (1982). *The Theories and Experience of Economic Development: Essays in Honor of Sir W. Arthur Lewis*. London: George Allen & Unwin.

Greenwald, Douglas, ed. (1982). *Encyclopedia of Economics*. New York: McGraw Hill.

Goldthorpe, J. E. (1975). *The Sociology of the Third World: Disparity and Involvement*. Cambridge: Cambridge University Press.

Hagan, Everett E. (1962). *On the Theory of Social Change*. Homewood, Ill.: Dorsey Press.

Hansen, Roger D. (1979). *Beyond the North-South Stalemate*. New York: McGraw Hill.

Huntington, Samuel (1976). *No Easy Choice: Political Participation in Developing Countries*. Cambridge, Mass.: Harvard University Press.

——— (1968). *Political Order in Changing Societies*. New Haven, Conn.: Yale University Press.

Kahn, Herman (1979). *World Economic Development 1979 and Beyond*. New York: William Morrow.

Kristensen, Thorkil (1982, 2nd ed.). *Development in Rich and Poor Countries*. New York: Praeger.

Laszlo, Ervin, ed. (1977). *Goals for Mankind*. New York: E. P. Dutton for the Club of Rome.

Lipton, Michael (1977). *Why Poor People Stay Poor: Urban Bias in World Development*. Cambridge, Mass.: Harvard University Press.

MacGreevey, William P. (1980). *Third World Poverty*. Lexington, Mass.: Lexington Books.

Maddison, Angus (1982). *Phases of Capitalist Development*. Oxford: Oxford University Press.

Mason, Edward, and Asher, Robert (1973). *The World Bank Since Bretton Woods*. Washington, D.C.: Brookings Institution.

May, Brian (1981). *The Third World Calamity*. London: Routledge and Kegan.

Mellor, John (1976). *The New Economics of Growth: A Strategy for India and the Developing World*. Ithaca, N.Y.: Cornell University Press.

Morawetz, David (1977). *Twenty-Five Years of Economic Development 1950-1975*. Washington: World Bank.

Olson, Mancur (1965). *The Logic of Collective Action: Public Goods and the Theory of Groups*. Cambridge, Mass.: Harvard University Press.

Owens, Edgar, and Shaw, Robert (1974). *Development Reconsidered*. Lexington, Mass.: Lexington Books.

Pearson, Lester B., ed. (1969). *Partners in Development: Report of the Commission on International Development*. New York: Praeger.

Powell, G. Bingham (1982). *Contemporary Democracies: Participation, Stability, and Violence*. Cambridge, Mass.: Harvard University Press.

Powelson, John P. (1979). *A Select Bibliography on Economic Development, with Annotations*. Boulder, Colo.: Westview Press.

Reynolds, Lloyd G. (1977). *Image and Reality in Economic Development*. New Haven, Conn.: Yale University Press.

Rondinelli, Dennis, and Ruddle, Kenneth (1978). *Urbanization and Rural Development: A Spatial Policy for Equitable Growth*. New York: Praeger.

Rossi, Ino, ed. (1980). *People in Culture: A Survey of Cultural Anthropology*. New York: Praeger.

Rostow, Walter W. (1980). *Why the Poor Get Richer and the Rich Slow Down*. Austin: University of Texas Press.

——— (1978). *The World Economy: History and Prospects*. Austin: University of Texas Press.

Sachs, Ignacy (1979). *Pour une économie politique du développement: Etudes du planification*. Paris: Flammarion.

Samuelson, Paul (1982). *Foundations of Economic Analysis*. Cambridge, Mass.: Harvard University Press.

Singer, Hans, and Ansari, Javed (1982, 3rd ed.). *Rich and Poor Countries*. London: George Allen & Unwin.

Streeten, Paul (1982). *First Things First: Meeting Basic Human Needs*. Oxford: Oxford University Press for the World Bank.

Streeten, Paul, and Jolly, Richard, eds. (1981). *Recent Issues in World Development*. Oxford: Pergamon Press.

Tinbergen, Jan, ed. (1976). *RIO – Reshaping the International Order*. New York: E. P. Dutton for the Club of Rome.

Todaro, Michael (1977). *Economic Development in the Third World*. London: Longman.

Usher, Dan (1981). *The Economic Prerequisite to Democracy*. New York: Columbia University Press.

Verba, S., et al. (1979). *Participation and Political Equality: A Seven-Nation Comparison*. Cambridge: Cambridge University Press.

Ward, Barbara (1979). *Progress for a Small Planet*. New York: W. W. Norton.

Weaver, James, and Jameson, Kenneth P. (1978). *Economic Development: Competing Paradigms – Competing Parables*. Washington, D.C.: AID, Development Studies Program, Occ. Paper 3.

Zuvekas, Clarence (1980). *Economic Development: An Introduction*. New York: Macmillan.

IV.B. Macro and International Economics

Abi-Saab, George, ed. (1981). *The Concept of International Organization*. Paris: UNESCO.

Al-Shaikhly, Salah, ed. (1982). *Development Financing*. Boulder, Colo.: Westview Press.

Aronson, Jonathan D. (1977). *Money and Power: Banks and the World Monetary System*. Beverly Hills, Calif.: Sage.

Audretsch, David, and Kindleberger, Charles, eds. (1983). *Multinational Corporations in the 1980's*. forthcoming.

Berg, Elliott, et al. (1981). *Accelerated Development in Sub-Saharan Africa: An Agenda for Action*. Washington IBRD.

Bird, Graham (1978). *The International Monetary System and the Less Developed Countries*. London: Macmillan.

Bitterman, Henry J. (1973). *The Refunding of International Debt*. Durham, N.C.: Duke University Press.

Bolling, Landrum (1982). *Private Foreign Aid: U.S. Philanthropy in Relief and Development*. Boulder, Colo.: Westview Press.

Bosson, Rex, and Varon, Bension (1977). *The Mining Industry and the Developing Countries*. New York: Oxford University Press.

Bye, Maurice, and Destanne de Bernis, Gérard (1976). *Relations économiques internationales*. Paris: Dalloz.

Center for Strategic and International Studies, ed. (1981). *World Trade Competition: Western Countries and Third World Markets.* New York: Praeger.

Clarkson, S. (1979). *The Soviet Theory of Development: India and the Third World in Marxist Leninist Scholarship.* London: Macmillan.

Clark, William (1981). "Robert McNamara at the World Bank." *Foreign Affairs,* 60,1:167-84.

Cline, William, ed. (1979). *Policy Alternatives for a New International Economic Order.* New York: Praeger.

Coats, Warren L., and Khatkhate, Deena R., eds. (1980). *Money and Monetary Policy in Less Developed Countries.* Oxford: Pergamon Press.

Currie, Lachlan (1981). *The Role of Economic Advisers in Developing Countries.* Westport, Conn.: Greenwood.

Davis, Stanley M. (1979). *Managing and Organizing Multinational Corporations.* New York: Pergamon Press.

Dolman, Antony, J. (1981). *Resources, Regimes, World Order.* Oxford: Pergamon Press.

Donaldson, Robert H., ed. (1981). *The Soviet Union in the Third World: Successes and Failures.* Boulder, Colo.: Westview Press.

Franck, Thomas M., and Weisband, Edward (1980). *Foreign Policy By Congress.* New York: Oxford University Press.

Franco, Larry G., and Seiber, Marilyn J. (1979). *Developing Country Debt.* Oxford: Pergamon Press.

Frey-Wouters, Ellen (1980). *The European Community and the Third World: The Lomé Convention and its Impact.* New York: Praeger.

Finger, Seymour M., and Harbert, Joseph R., eds. (1982). *U.S. Policy in International Institutions.* Boulder, Colo.: Westview Press.

Goldberg, Ray A., and McGinty, Richard C., eds. (1979). *Agri-business Management for Developing Countries — Southeast Asian Corn System and American and Japanese Trends Affecting It.* Cambridge, Mass.: Ballinger.

Gordenker, Leon (1976). *International Aid and National Decisions: Development Programs in Malawi, Tanzania, and Zambia.* Princeton, N.J.: Princeton University Press.

Halderman, John (1982). *The Political Role of the United Nations: Advancing the World Community.* New York: Praeger.

Hansen, Roger, et al. (1982). *U.S. Foreign Policy and the Third World: Agenda 1982.* New York: Praeger. (An annual from the Overseas Development Council in Washington.)

Hossain, Kamal, ed. (1980). *Legal Aspects of the New International Economic Order.* London: Frances Pinter.

Hürni, Bettina (1980). *The Lending Policy of the World Bank in the 1970's: Analysis and Evaluation.* Boulder, Colo.: Westview Press.

Ingham, Barbara (1981). *Tropical Exports and Economic Development: New Perspectives on Producer Response in Three Low-Income Countries.* New York: St. Martin's Press.

Jones, Leroy P., ed. (1982). *Public Enterprise in Less-Developed Countries.* Cambridge: Cambridge University Press.

Killick, Tony (1978). *Development Economics in Action: A Study of Economic Policies in Ghana*. New York: St. Martin's Press.

Kitchen, Helen, ed. (1976). *Africa: From Mystery to Maze*. Lexington, Mass.: Lexington Books.

Kostecki, M. M., ed. (1982). *State Trading in International Markets*. New York: St. Martin's Press.

Krasner, Stephen D. (1978). *Defending the National Interest: Raw Materials Investments and U.S. Foreign Policy*. Princeton, N.J.: Princeton University Press.

Laszlo, Ervin, et al. (1980). *The Obstacles to the New International Economic Order*. New York: Pergamon Press for United Nations Institute for Training and Research.

Lees, Francis, and Eng, Maximo (1975). *International Financial Markets*. New York: Praeger.

Lewis, John P., et al. (1979). *Development Co-operation 1979 Review*. Paris: OECD.

Mathieson, John (1981). *Basic Needs and the New International Economic Order: An Opening for North-South Collaboration in the 1980's*. Washington: Overseas Development Council, Working Paper No. 4.

Megateli, Abderrahmane (1980). *Investment Policies of National Oil Companies: A Comparative Study of Sonatrach, Nioc, and Pemex*. New York: Praeger.

Mikesell, Raymond F. (1979). *The World Copper Industry*. Baltimore, Md.: Johns Hopkins University Press.

Montavon, R., et al. (1979). *The Role of Multinational Companies in Latin America: A Case Study in Mexico*. London: Saxon House.

Mortimer, Robert A. (1980). *The Third World Coalition in Third World Politics*. New York: Praeger.

Nicol, Davidson, et al., eds. (1981). *Regionalism and the New International Economic Order*. Oxford: Pergamon Press.

Odell, John S. (1982). U.S. *International Monetary Policy: Markets, Power, and Ideas as Sources of Change*. Princeton, N.J.: Princeton University Press.

Olson, Robert K. (1981). U.S. *Foreign Policy and the New International Economic Order*. Boulder, Colo.: Westview Press.

Pierre, Andrew J. (1982). *The Global Politics of Arms Sales*. Princeton, N.J.: Princeton University Press.

Reubens, Edwin P., ed. (1981). *The Challenge of the New International Economic Order*. Boulder, Colo.: Westview Press.

Rittberger, Volker, ed. (1981). *Science and Technology in a Changing International Order*. Boulder, Colo.: Westview Press and UNITAR.

Richardson, Neil (1978). *Foreign Policy and Economic Dependence*. Austin: University of Texas Press.

Rothstein, Robert (1981). *The Third World and U.S. Foreign Policy: Cooperation and Conflict in the 1980's*. Boulder, Colo.: Westview Press.

____ (1979). *Global Bargaining: UNCTAD and the Quest for a New International Economic Order*. Princeton, N.J.: Princeton University Press.

Rousseau, Rudolph R. (1976). "Factors Affecting Decisions of the United States Senate on Bilateral and Multilateral Foreign Assistance Legislation,

1965-1974." Unpublished Ph.D. dissertation, Brandeis University Fletcher School of Law and Diplomacy.

Salda, Anne C. M. (1980). "The International Monetary Fund, 1978-9: A Selected Bibliography." *IMF Staff Papers*, 27,2(June):380-436.

Sanford, Jonathan (1982). *U.S. Foreign Policy and Multilateral Development Banks*. Boulder, Colo.: Westview Press.

Schiffer, Jonathan (1981). "The Changing Post-War Pattern of Development: The Accumulated Wisdom of Samir Amin." *World Development*, 9,6:515-37.

Sengupta, Arjun, ed. (1980). *Commodities, Finance, and Trade: Issues in North-South Negotiations*. London: Frances Pinter.

Shelp, Ronald K. (1981). *Beyond Industrialization: Ascendancy of the Global Service Economy*. New York: Praeger.

Singh, Jyoti S. (1982, 2nd ed.). *A New International Economic Order: Toward a Fair Redistribution of the World's Resources*. New York: Praeger.

Stevens, Christopher (1979). *Food Aid and the Developing World*. New York: St. Martin's Press.

Stewart, Frances, and Sengupta, Arjun (1982). *International Financial Cooperation: A Framework for Change*. London: Frances Pinter.

Szyliowicz, Joseph, ed. (1981). *Technology and International Affairs*. New York: Praeger.

Touscoz, Jean, ed. (1978). *Transfert de technologie, sociétés transnationales et nouvel ordre économique international*. Paris: PUF.

Turner, Louis, and McMullen, Neil (1982). *The Newly Industrializing Countries: Trade and Adjustment*. London: George Allen and Unwin.

U.S. Congress. House of Representatives. Committee on Banking, Finance, and Urban Affairs (H.C. Banking) (1980). *To Amend the Bretton Woods Agreement Act. . . .* Washington: Government Printing Office. (Committee hearings February-April.)

U.S. Congress. House of Representatives (1980). "International Monetary Fund Quota Increase." *Congressional Record*, H9027-H9050 and H9130-H9143, September 17-18.

U.S. Department of the Treasury (1982). *United States Participation in the Multilateral Development Banks in the 1980's*. Washington, D.C.: Government Printing Office.

Voll, Sarah P. (1980). *A Plough in Field Arable: Western Agri-business in Third World Agriculture*. Hanover, N.H.: University Press of New England.

Wallerstein, Mitchel (1980). *Food for War – Food for Peace: United States Food Aid in a Global Context*. Cambridge, Mass.: MIT Press.

Weintraub, Sidney, et al. (1981). *Economic Coercion and U.S. Foreign Policy*. Boulder, Colo.: Westview Press.

Wellons, P. A. (1977). *Borrowing by Developing Countries on the Euro-Currency Market*. Paris: OECD.

Williams, Maurice, et al. (1978). *Development Cooperation 1978 Review*. Paris: OECD (N.B.: One of this annual publication.)

IV.C. Micro Growth Topics: Food and Rural Growth, Health, Education, Population, Infrastructure, Energy, Technology, Urban Growth

Anthony, Kenneth, et al. (1979). *Agricultural Change in Tropical Africa*. Ithaca, N.Y.: Cornell University Press.

Arnon, I. (1981). *Modernization of Agriculture in Developing Countries*. Chichester, England: John Wiley & Sons.

Baetz, Reuben, ed. (1975). *Development and Participation*. New York: Columbia University Press.

Balaam, David N., and Carey, Michael J., eds. (1981). *Food Politics: The Regional Conflict*. London: Croom Helm.

Bates, Robert (1981). *Markets and States in Tropical Africa*. Berkeley: University of California Press.

Bates, Robert H., and Lofchie, Michael F., eds. (1980). *Agricultural Development in Africa*. New York: Praeger.

Bathrick, David O. (1981). *Agricultural Credit for Small Farm Development: Policies and Practices*. Boulder, Colo.: Westview Press.

Belshaw, Cyril S. (1976). *The Sorcerer's Apprentice: An Anthropology of Public Policy*. Oxford: Pergamon Press.

Benor, Daniel, and Harrison, James (1977). *Agricultural Extension: The Training and Visit System*. Washington: World Bank.

Berg, Alan (1981). *Malnourished People: A Policy View*. Washington: World Bank.

Berry, R. Albert, and Cline, William R. (1979). *Agrarian Structure and Productivity in Developing Countries*. Baltimore, Md.: Johns Hopkins University Press for the ILO.

Bhatia, Ramesh (1980). "The World Bank, Energy Prices, and Agricultural Development." Washington: IBRD, Economics and Policy Division, AGREP Division Working Paper No. 37.

Busch, Lawrence, and Lacy, William B. (1982). *Science, Agriculture, and the Politics of Research*. Boulder, Colo.: Westview Press.

Christensen, Cheryl, et al. (1981). *Food Problems and Prospects in Sub-Saharan Africa: The Decade of the 1980's*. Washington: U.S. Department of Agriculture.

Chuta, Enyinna, and Liedholm, Carl (1979). *Rural Non-Farm Employment: A Review of the State of the Art*. East Lansing, Michigan: Michigan State University, Department of Agricultural Economics, Rural Development Paper No. 4. (N.B.: Several ongoing series of rural development papers.)

Coombs, Philip H. (1981a). *New Strategies for Improving Rural Family Life*. Essex, Conn.: International Council for Educational Development.

——— (1981b). *Future Critical World Issues in Education: A Provisional Report of Findings*. Essex, Conn.: International Council for Educational Development.

Crawford, Paul R. (1982). *AID Experience in Agricultural Research: A Review of Project Evaluations*. Washington: DAI.

Cronan, D. S. (1980). *Underwater Minerals*. New York: Academic Press.

Cusack, David F., ed. (1982). *Agroclimate Information for Development: Reviving the Green Revolution*. Boulder, Colo.: Westview Press.

Daines, Samuel (1979). *Agrobusiness and Rural Enterprise Project Analysis Manual*. Washington: AID, DSB, Office of Agriculture.

Davis, Russell G. (1980). *Planning Education for Development*. 2 volumes. Cambridge, Mass.: Harvard University Press.

Diwan, Romesh, and Livingston, Dennis (1979). *Alternative Development Strategies and Appropriate Technology*. New York: Pergamon Press.

Douglas, Johnson E. (1980). *Successful Seed Programs: A Planning and Management Guide*. Boulder, Colo.: Westview Press.

Dunkerley, Joy, et al. (1981). *Energy Strategies for Developing Nations*. Washington, D.C.: Resources for the Future.

Foster, John, et al. (1981). *Energy for Development: An International Challenge*. New York: Praeger.

Gibbons, John H., ed. (1981). *Background Papers for Innovative Biological Technologies for Lesser Developed Countries*. Washington, D.C.: U.S. House of Representatives, Foreign Affairs Committee and Office of Technology Assessment.

Gilbert, E. H., et al. (1980). *Farming Systems Research: A Critical Appraisal*. East Lansing: Michigan State University, Dept. of Agricultural Economics, Rural Development Paper No. 6.

Glaser, William, and Habers, Christopher (1978). *The Brain Drain: Emigration and Return*. Oxford: Pergamon Press.

Goering, Theodore J., et al. (1981). *Agricultural Research: Sector Policy Paper*. Washington: World Bank.

Golladay, Frederick (1980). *Health Sector Policy Paper*. Washington: IBRD.

Halperin, Rhoda, and Dow, James, eds. (1977). *Peasant Livelihood: Studies in Economic Anthropology and Cultural Ecology*. New York: St. Martin's Press.

Hansen, Gary E., ed. (1981). *Agricultural and Rural Development in Indonesia*. Boulder, Colo.: Westview Press.

Harris, David R., ed. (1980). *Human Ecology in Savanna Environments*. New York: Academic Press.

Honadle, George, et al. (1980). *Integrated Rural Development: Making it Work?* Washington: Development Alternatives, Inc. for AID.

Jedlicka, Allen (1977). *Organizing for Rural Development: Risk Taking and Appropriate Technology*. New York: Praeger.

Johnson, Glenn, and Maunder, Allen, eds. (1981). *Rural Change: The Challenge for Agricultural Economists*. Montclair, N.J.: Allanheld, Osmun.

Leichter, Howard M. (1979). *A Comparative Approach to Policy Analysis: Health Care Policy in Four Nations*. Cambridge: Cambridge University Press.

Lele, Uma (1975). *The Design of Rural Development: Lessons from Africa*. Baltimore, Md.: Johns Hopkins University Press.

Lloyd, Peter (1982). *A Third World Proletariat?* London: George Allen & Unwin.

Morgan, Robert, et al. (1979). *Science and Technology for Development: The Role of U.S. Universities*. New York: Pergamon Press.

Moris, Jon (1981). *Managing Induced Rural Development*. Bloomington: University of Indiana, International Development Institute.

Migdal, Joel S. (1974). *Peasants, Politics, and Revolution: Pressures Toward Political and Social Change in the Third World*. Princeton, N.J.: Princeton University Press.

Nelson, Joan M. (1979). *Access to Power: Politics and the Urban Poor in Developing Nations*. Princeton, N.J.: Princeton University Press.

Norman, Colin (1981). *The God that Limps: Science and Technology in the Eighties*. New York: W. W. Norton.

Noor, Abdun (1981). *Education and Basic Human Needs*. Washington: IBRD, SWP450.

Pimental, David, ed. (1980). *Handbook of Energy Utilization in Agriculture*. Boca Raton, Fla.: CRC Press.

Pimental, David, and Perkins, John, eds. (1980). *Pest Control: Cultural and Environmental Aspects*. Boulder, Colo.: Westview Press.

Pischke, J. D. Von, et al. (1981). *The Political Economy and Specialized Farm Credit Institutions in Low-Income Countries*. Washington: IBRD, WP446.

Reutlinger, Shlomo (1982). "World Bank Research on the Hunger Dimension of the Food Problem." *World Bank Research News*, 3,1:3-9.

Reynolds, Lloyd, ed. (1975). *Agriculture in Development Theory*. New Haven, Conn.: Yale University Press.

Roberts, Hayden (1979). *Community Development*. Toronto: University of Toronto Press.

Rogers, Everett M. (1969). *Modernization Among Peasants: The Impact of Communication*. New York: Holt, Rinehart.

Russell, Clifford, and Nicholson, Norman K., ed. (1981). *Public Choice and Rural Development*. Washington, D.C.: Resources for the Future.

Sabot, R. H., ed. (1981). *Migration and the Labor Market in Developing Countries*. Boulder, Colo.: Westview Press and the World Bank.

Sagasti, Francisco (1979). *Technology, Planning, and Self-Reliant Development*. New York: Praeger.

Sang, Yung C. (1981). *Aquaculture Economics: Basic Concepts and Methods of Analysis*. Boulder, Colo.: Westview Press.

Staveren, J. M. Van, and van Dusseldorp, D. B. W. M. (1980). *Framework for Regional Planning in Developing Countries*. Wageningen, Netherlands: International Institute for Land Reclamation and Improvement.

Stewart, Frances (1978). *Technology and Development*. London: Macmillan.

Stifel, Laurence D., et al., eds. (1982). *Social Sciences and Public Policy in the Developing World*. Lexington, Mass.: Lexington Books.

Storms, Doris (1979). *Training and Use of Auxiliary Health Workers: Lessons from Developing Countries*. Washington, D.C.: American Public Health Association.

Tomek, William G., and Robinson, Kenneth L. (1981, 2nd ed.). *Agricultural Product Prices*. Ithaca, N.Y.: Cornell University Press.

Turner, Alan, ed. (1980). *The Cities of the Poor: Settlement Planning in Developing Countries*. New York: St. Martin's Press.

Uphoff, Norman T., et al. (1979). *Feasibility and Application of Rural Development Participation: A State-of-the-Art Paper*. Ithaca, N.Y.: Cornell University, Rural Development Committee.

Valdes, Alberto, ed. (1981). *Food Security for Developing Countries*. Boulder, Colo.: Westview Press.

Vyas, V. S., et al. (1977). *Rural Asia: Challenge and Opportunity*. New York: Praeger for the Asian Development Bank.

Wang, Jaw-Kai, and Hagan, Ross E. (1980). *Irrigated Rice Production Systems: Design Procedures*. Boulder, Colo.: Westview Press.

Wilde, John C. de, et al. (1967). *Experiences with Agricultural Development in Tropical Africa*. Baltimore, Md.: Johns Hopkins University Press.

Woods, Richard G., ed. (1981). *Future Dimensions of World Food and Population*. Boulder, Colo.: Westview Press.

Young, Michael, et al. (1980). *Distance Teaching for the Third World*. London: Routledge & Kegan Paul.

IV.D. Administration of Growth Project Implementation and Evaluation of Growth Measurement

Adulbhan, P., and Sharif, N. (1979). *Systems Modelling in Developing Countries*. Oxford: Pergamon Press.

Blitzer, Charles R., et al., eds. (1975). *Economic Wide Models and Development Planning*. Oxford: Oxford University Press.

Booz, Allen & Hamilton, Inc. (1978). "Study of Selected Aspects of the Project Assistance Cycles." Washington: AID/otr-C-1689, October 13.

Bottrall, Anthony F. (1981). *Comparative Study for the Management and Organization of Irrigation Projects*. Washington: IBRD, SWP458.

Bridier, Manuel, and Michaelof, Serge (1980). *Guide pratique d'analyse de projets*. Paris: Economica.

Bryant, Coralie, and White, Louise G. (1981). *Managing Development in the Third World*. Boulder, Colo.: Westview Press.

Casley, D. J., and Lury, D. A. (1981). *Data Collection in Developing Countries*. Oxford: Oxford University Press.

Cochrane, Glynn (1979). *The Cultural Appraisal of Development Projects*. New York: Praeger.

Crozier, Michel (1964, 1963 in Fr.). *The Bureaucratic Phenomenon*. Chicago: University of Chicago Press.

Daines, Samuel R. (1979). *Impact Evaluation of the Haiti Small Farmer Improvement Project*. Washington: Practical Concepts and USAID/Haiti.

—— (1977). *An Overview of Economic and Data Analysis Techniques for Project Design and Evaluation*. Washington: AID, DSP.

Deboeck, Guido, and Rubin, Deborah (1980). *Selected Case Studies on Monitoring and Evaluation of Rural Development Projects. VI Eastern Africa, V2*

East Asia and the Pacific. Washington: IBRD, Agriculture and Rural Development Department.

Delp, P., et al. (1977). *Systems Tools for Project Planning*. Bloomington: Indiana University, PASITAM.

Development Project Management Center (1979). *Elements of Project Management*. Washington: AID, DSB, Office of Rural and Administrative Development.

Diamond, William, and Raghavan, V. S., eds. (1982). *Aspects of Development Bank Management*. Baltimore: Johns Hopkins University Press for the World Bank.

Downs, Anthony (1967). *Inside Bureaucracy*. Boston: Little, Brown.

Gant, George F. (1979). *Development Administration*. Madison: University of Wisconsin Press.

Goodman, Louis J., and Love, Ralph N., eds. (1980). *Project Planning and Management*. New York: Pergamon Press.

____ (1979). *Management of Development Projects: An International Case Study Approach*. New York: Pergamon Press.

Grindle, Merilee, ed. (1980). *Politics and Policy Implementation in the Third World*. Princeton, N.J.: Princeton University Press.

Hageboeck, Molly (1979). *Manager's Guide to Data Collection*. Washington: AID, PPC.

Hageboeck, Molly, et al. (1980). *Evaluating the Impact of AID Projects*. Washington, D.C.: Practical Concepts, Inc.

Hirschman, Alberto (1967). *Development Projects Observed*. Washington, D.C.: Brookings Institution.

Hoole, Francis W. (1978). *Evaluation Research and Development Activities*. Beverly Hills, Calif.: Sage.

IBRD (1981a). *A Handbook on Monitoring and Evaluation of Agriculture and Rural Development Projects*. Washington, D.C.: World Bank.

____ (1981b). *Concordance to Project Performance Audit Reports. . . .*, Report 3625, September 30, unpublished.

Imboden, N. (1978). *A Management Approach to Project Appraisal and Evaluation: With Special Reference to Non-Directly Productive Projects*. Paris: OECD.

Jedlicka, Allen D. (1977). *Organization for Rural Development: Risk Taking and Appropriate Technology*. New York: Praeger.

Kazen, Felisa M. (1978). *Definitions and Measurements of Poverty*. Washington, D.C.: Academy for Educational Development.

Kilby, Peter (1979). "Evaluating Technical Assistance." *World Development*, 7,3:309-23.

Knight, Peter T., ed. (1980). *Implementing Programs of Human Development*. Washington: IBRD, Working Paper No. 403.

Kubr, Milan, ed. (1982). *Managing a Management Development Institution*. Geneva: ILO.

Lindenberg, Marc, and Crosby, Benjamin (1981). *Managing Development: The Political Dimension*. West Hartford, Conn.: Kumarion Press.

MacArthur, J. D., and Amin, G. A. (1979). *Cost-Benefit Analysis and Income Distribution in Developing Countries*. Oxford: Pergamon Press.

McHale, Vincent E., et al., eds. (1980). *Evaluating Transnational Programs in Government and Business*. New York: Pergamon Press.

McKelvey, Bill (1982). *Organizational Systematics: Taxonomy, Evolution, Classification*. Berkeley: University of California Press.

March, James, and Simon, Herbert (1958). *Organizations*. New York: John Wiley & Sons.

Mehmet, Ozay (1978). *Economic Planning and Social Justice in Developing Countries*. New York: St. Martin's Press.

Meier, Gerald M. (1982). *Pricing Policy for Development Management*. Baltimore, Md.: Johns Hopkins University Press for the World Bank.

Mickelwait, Donald R., et al. (1978a). *Information for Decisionmaking in Rural Development*. Washington, D.C.: Development Alternatives (for AID/DSB).

—— (1978b). *The "New Directions" Mandate: Studies in Project Design, Approval, and Implementation*. Washington, D.C.: Development Alternatives (for AID/DSB).

Morris, Morris D. (1979). *Measuring the Condition of the World's Poor: The Physical Quality of Life Index*. New York: Pergamon Press.

Perrett, Heli, and Lethem, Francis, J. (1980). *Human Factors in Project Work*. Washington: World Bank, Working Paper 397.

Ralston, Lenore, et al. (1981). *Voluntary Efforts in Decentralized Management*. Berkeley, Calif.: University of California, Institute for International Studies, Project on Managing Decentralization.

Simon, Herbert (1976, 3rd ed.). *Administrative Behavior*. New York: Free Press.

Smith, Kenneth F. ed. (1980). *Design and Evaluation of AID-Assisted Projects*. Washington: AID, Office of Personnel Management, Training and Development Division.

Squire, Lyn, and van der Tak, Herman (1975). *Economic Analysis of Projects*. Baltimore, Md.: Johns Hopkins University Press for the World Bank.

Soumelis, Constantin G. (1977). *Project Evaluation Methodologies and Techniques*. Paris: UNESCO.

Thompson, Mark (1980). *Benefit-Cost Analysis for Program Evaluation*. Beverly Hills, Calif.: Sage.

U.S. Congress. House of Representatives. Committee on Government Operations (1981). *AID's Administrative and Management Problems in Providing Foreign Economic Assistance*. Washington, D.C.: Government Printing Office.

Waterston, Albert (1965). *Development Planning*. Baltimore, Md.: Johns Hopkins University Press for the World Bank.

Wildavsky, Aaron (1979). *Speaking Truth to Power: The Art and Craft of Policy Analysis*. Boston: Little, Brown.

V. Latin America

V.A. Regional and South American Topics

Aguiar, Neuma, ed. (1979). *The Structure of Brazilian Development*. New Brunswick, N.J.: Transaction Books.

Alexander, Robert J. (1982). *Romulo Betancourt and the Transformation of Venezuela*. New Brunswick, N.J.: Transaction Books.

Alschuler, Lawrence R., ed. (1982). *Dependent Agricultural Development and Agrarian Reform in Latin America*. Ottawa: Editions de l'Université d'Ottawa.

Arango Condono, Gilberto (1978). *Estructura economica colombiana*. Bogota: ANIF.

Araujo, Ana Maria (1980). *Tupamaras: Des Femmes de L'Uruguay*. Paris: Des Femmes.

Arroyo, Gonzalo, ed. (1981). *Les firmes transnationales et l'agriculture en Amérique latine*. Paris: Anthropos.

Aspelin, Paul, and dos Santos, Silvio Coelho (1981). *Indian Areas Threatened by Hydroelectric Projects in Brazil*. Copenhagen: IWGIA (International Work Group for Indigenous Affairs) Document 44. (N.B.: 43 previous studies on threatened indigenous peoples and *IWGIA Newsletter*.)

Asturias, Miguel Angel (1977). *Edicion critica de las obras completas de Miguel Angel Asturias*. 19+ volumes. Madrid: Closas-Orcoyen.

_____ (1973). *Eyes of the Interred*. New York: Delacorte Press.

_____ (1971). *Green Pope*. New York: Delacorte Press.

_____ (1968). *Strong Wind*. New York: Delacorte Press. (N.B.: The Banana Republic trilogy, three of many novels and other works on the human condition in rural Central America.)

Berry, Albert R., et al., eds. (1980). *Politics of Compromise: Coalition Government in Colombia*. New Brunswick, N.J.: Transaction Books.

Black, Jan K. (1977). *United States Penetration of Brazil*. Philadelphia: University of Pennsylvania.

Bourque, Susan C., and Warren, Kay Barbara (1981). *Women of the Andes: Patriarchy and Social Change in Two Peruvian Towns*. Ann Arbor: University of Michigan.

Bourricaud, Francois (1970). *Power and Society in Contemporary Peru*. New York: Praeger.

Brundenius, Claes, and Lundahl, Mats, eds. (1982). *Development Strategies and Basic Needs in Latin America*. Boulder, Colo.: Westview Press.

Brush, Stephen B. (1977). *Mountain, Field, and Family: The Economy and Human Ecology of an Andean Valley*. Philadelphia: University of Pennsylvania Press.

Bunster, Ximena, and Chaney, Elsa (1982). *Sellers and Servants: Working Women in Lima, Peru*. New York: Praeger.

Burbach, Roger, and Flynn, Patricia (1980). *Agri-business in the Americas*. New York: Monthly Review Press.

Butari, Juan J. (1979). *Employment and Labor Force in Latin America: A Review at National and Regional Levels*. Rio de Janeiro: ECIEL.

Cajka, Francis R. (1979). "Peasant Commercialization in the serrianiás of Cochabamba Bolivia." Unpublished Ph.D. dissertation, University of Michigan.

Canak, William Leigh (1981). "National Development in Columbia: Accumulation, Crisis, and the State." Unpublished Ph.D. dissertation, University of Wisconsin.

Cardoso, Fernand H., and Faletto, Enzo (1979, 1971 in Sp.). *Dependency and Development in Latin America*. Berkeley, Calif.: University of California Press.

CEPAL (1981). *Latin American Development in the 1980's*. Santiago: CEPAL (ECLA: Economic Commission for Latin America). (N.B.: This is the central document in a set of five studies by the secretariat of this UN agency.)

Chamoux, Marie-Noelle (1981). *Indiens de la Sierra. La communauté paysanne au Mexique*. Paris: L'Harmattan.

Chevalier, Jacques (1982). *Civilization and the Stolen Gift: Capital, Kin, and Cult in Eastern Peru*. Toronto: University of Toronto Press.

Cleaves, Peter S., and Scurrah, Martin J. (1980). *Agriculture, Bureaucracy, and Military Government in Peru*. Ithaca, N.Y.: Cornell University Press.

Crahan, Margaret, ed. (1982). *Human Rights and Basic Needs in the Americas*. Washington, D.C.: Georgetown University Press.

Cuche, Denys (1981). *Pérou nègre*. Paris: L'Harmattan.

Cueva, Agustin (1981). *The Process of Political Domination of Ecuador*. New Brunswick, N.J.: Transaction Books.

Danns, George K. (1982). *Domination and Power in Guyana: A Study of the Police in a Third World Context*. New Brunswick, N.J.: Transaction Books.

Dew, Edward (1978). *The Difficult Flowering of Surinam: Ethnicity and Politics in a Plural Society*. The Hague: Martinus Nijhoff.

Dietz, Henry A. (1980). *Poverty and Problem-Solving Under Military Rule: The Urban Poor in Lima, Peru*. Austin: University of Texas Press.

Dominguez Company, Francisco (1981). *Estudios sobre instituciones locales hispano americas*. Caracas: Academia National de la Historia.

Dowbor, Ladislav (1982). *La formation du capitalisme dépendant au Brésil*. Paris: Anthropos.

Ducantenzeiler, Graciela (1982). *Syndicats et politique en Argentine, 1955-1973*. Montréal: Presses de l'Universite de Montréal.

Dumont, René, and Mottin, M. F. (1981). *Le mal-développement en Amérique latine*. Paris: Seuil.

Duncan, Kenneth, and Rutledge, Ian, eds. (1977). *Land and Labour in Latin America: Essays on the Development of Agrarian Capitalism in the Nineteenth and Twentieth Centuries*. Cambridge: Cambridge University Press.

Eglin, Jean, and Théry, Hervé (1982). *Le pillage de l'Amazonie*. Paris: Maspero.

Fagen, Richard R., ed. (1979). *Capitalism and the State in U.S.-Latin American Relations*. Stanford, Calif.: Stanford University Press.

Fals Borda, Orlando (1971). *Cooperatives and Rural Development in Latin America*. Geneva: UNRISD.

Faucher, Philippe (1981). *Le Brésil des militaires*. Montréal: Presses de l'Université de Montréal.

Feder, Ernest (1971). *The Rape of the Peasantry: Latin America's Landholding System*. Garden City, N.Y.: Doubleday.

Figueroa, Adolfo (1951). *La economia campesina de la Sierra del Peru*. Lima: Pontificia Universidad Catolica del Peru.

Fitzgerald, E. V. K. (1979). *The Political Economy of Peru: Economic Development and the Restructuring of Capital*. Cambridge: Cambridge University Press.

_____ (1976). *The State and Economic Development: Peru since 1968*. Cambridge: Cambridge University Press.

Foweraker, Joe (1981). *The Struggle for Land: A Political Economy of the Pioneer Frontier in Brazil from 1930 to the Present Day*. Cambridge: Cambridge University Press.

Franco, Rolando (1981). *Planificacion social en America Latina y el Caribe*. Santiago: ILPES/UNICEF (Latin American Institute for Economic and Social Planning/UNICEF).

Galofre, Fernando (1981). *Pobreza critica en la ninez*. Santiago: CEPAL/UNICEF.

Gangotena G., Francisco (1981). "Peasant Social Articulation and Surplus Transference: An Ecuadorean Case." Unpublished Ph.D. dissertation, University of Florida.

Garcia, Marcos A., and Martins, Antonio J., eds. (1981). *Etat et société en Amérique Latine*. Brussels: Editions de l'Université de Bruxelles.

Gardner, James A. (1980). *Legal Imperialism: American Lawyers and Foreign Aid in Latin America*. Madison: University of Wisconsin.

Gil, Frederico G., et al., eds. (1979). *Chile at the Turning Point: Lessons of the Socialist Years, 1970-1973*. Philadelphia: ISHI.

Golbert, Albert S., and Gingold, Yenny N. (1982). *Latin American Laws and Institutions*. New York: Praeger.

Hall, Anthony (1978). *Drought and Irrigation in Northeast Brazil*. Cambridge: Cambridge University Press.

Handelman, Howard (1975). *Struggle in the Andes*. Austin: University of Texas Press.

Healy, Kevin J. (1979). "Power, Class and Rural Development in Southern Bolivia." Unpublished Ph.D. dissertation, Cornell University; and (1982, Spanish version) *Caciques y patrones: Una experiencia de desarollo rural en Bolivia del sur Le Paz*: CERES.

Hennelly, Alfred, S. J., and Langan, John, S. J., eds. (1982). *Human Rights in the Americas: The Struggle for Concensus*. Washington, D.C.: Georgetown University Press.

Hewlett, Sylvia Ann (1980). *The Cruel Dilemmas of Development: Twentieth-Century Brazil*. New York: Basic Books.

Hewlett, Sylvia A., and Weinert, Richard, eds. (1982). *Brazil and Mexico: Patterns in Late Development*. Philadelphia: Institute for the Study of Human Issues.

Hintzen, Percy Claude (1981). "Capitalism, Socialism and Socio-Political Confrontation in Multi-Racial Developing States: A Comparison of Guyana and Trinidad." Unpublished Ph.D. dissertation, Yale University.

Humphrey, John (1982). *Capitalist Control and Workers' Struggle in the Brazilian Auto Industry*. Princeton, N.J.: Princeton University Press.

Hurtado, Osvaldo (1980, 1977 in Sp.). *Political Power in Ecuador*. Albuquerque: University of New Mexico Press.

Indianité, ethnocide, indigénisme en Amérique latine (1982). Paris: Centre National de Recherches Scientifiques (hereafter CNRS).

Kaufman, Edy (1981). *Uruguay in Transition*. New Brunswick, N.J.: Transaction Books.

Klein, Herbert (1982). *Bolivia: Evolution of a Multi-Ethnic Society*. London: Oxford University Press.

Leal, Magdalena Leon de, ed. (1980). *Mujer capitalismo agrario: Estudio de cuatro regiones colombianas*. Bogota: Asociacion Colombiana par el Estudio de la Poblacion.

Leeds, Anthony (1973). "Political, Economic, and Social Effects of Producer and Consumer Orientations toward Housing in Brazil and Peru: A Systems Analysis," pp. 181-215 in Rabinowitz, Francine F., and Trueblood, Felicity M., eds. *National-local Linkages: The Interrelationships of Urban and National Policies in Latin America*. Beverly Hills, Calif.: Sage.

Lowy, Michael, ed. (1980). *Le Marxisme en Amérique latine: Anthologie*. Paris: Maspero.

Luzuriaga, Carlos, and Zuvekas, Clarence (1980). "Income Distribution and Poverty in Rural Ecuador: A Survey of the Literature, 1950-1979" (353 pages). Washington: AID, Latin America and USDA.

McClintock, Cynthia (1981). *Peasant Cooperatives and Political Change in Peru*. Princeton, N.J.: Princeton University Press.

McDonough, Peter (1981). *Power and Ideology in Brazil*. Princeton, N.J.: Princeton University Press.

Malloy, James M., ed. (1977). *Authoritarianism and Corporatism in Latin America*. Pittsburgh, Pa.: University of Pittsburgh Press.

Mariategui, Jose Carlos (1971). *Seven Interpretive Essays on Peruvian Reality*. Austin: University of Texas Press.

Martin, Juan (1981). *Desarrollo regional argentino: La agricultura*. Santiago: CEPAL, Cuadernos.

Martiniere, Guy (1978). *Les Amériques latines, une histoire économique*. Grenoble: Presses Universitaries de Grenoble.

Mitchell, Simon, ed. (1981). *The Logic of Poverty: The Case of the Brazilian Northeast*. London: Routledge & Kegan Paul.

Moran, Emilio F. (1981). *Developing the Amazon*. Bloomington: Indiana University Press.

Pando, Jose Antonio Encinas del, ed. (1980). *Gastos militares y desarrollo en America del Sur*. Lima: Centro de Investigaciones Economicas y Sociales de la Universidad de Lima.

Pearse, Andrew (1976). *The Latin American Peasant*. London: Frank Cass.

Piel, Jean (1970). "The Place of the Peasantry in the National Life of Peru in the Nineteenth Century." *Past and Present*, No. 46(February):108-33.

Prebisch, Raul (1981). *Capitalismo periferico: crisis y transformacion*. Mexico City: El Fondo De Cultura Economica. (N.B.: Most recent of many important works: English translation in progress.)

Rodney, Walter (1981). *A History of the Guyanese Working People, 1881-1905*. Baltimore, Md.: Johns Hopkins University Press.

Schoultz, Lars (1981). *Human Rights and United States Policy toward Latin America*. Princeton, N.J.: Princeton University Press.

Schuyler, George (1980). *Hunger in a Land of Plenty* (Venezuela). Cambridge, Mass.: Schenkman.

Shoemaker, Robin (1981). *The Peasants of El Dorado: Conflict and Contradiction in a Peruvian Frontier Settlement*. Ithaca, N.Y.: Cornell University Press.

Singelmann, Peter (1980). *Structures of Domination in Peasant Movements in Latin America*. Columbia: University of Missouri Press.

Smith, Brian (1982). *The Church and Politics in Chile*. Princeton, N.J.: Princeton University Press.

Smith, Nigel J. H. (1982). *Rainforest Corridors: The Transamazon Colonization Scheme*. Berkeley: University of California Press.

Standing, Guy, and Szal, Richard (1979). *Poverty and Basic Needs: Evidence from Guyana and the Philippines*. Geneva: ILO.

Stavenhagen, Rudolfo (1981). *Between Underdevelopment and Revolution: A Latin American Perspective*. New Delhi: Abhinav Publications.

Stein, William W. (1975). "The Peon Who Wouldn't: A Study of the Hacienda System at Vicos." *Papers in Anthropology* (University of Oklahoma, Department of Anthropology), 16,2:78-135.

_____ (1974). "Countrymen and Townsmen in the Callejon de Huaylas, Peru: Two Views of Andean Social Structure." State University of New York at Buffalo, Council on International Studies, Special Studies No. 51.

_____ (1972). "Race, Culture, and Social Structure in the Peruvian Andes." Buffalo: State University of New York at Buffalo, Department of Anthropology.

Stephens, Evelyne (1980). *The Politics of Workers' Participation: The Peruvian Approach in Comparative Perspective*. New York: Academic Press.

Strachan, Lloyd W. (1981). "Capitalism and the Peasant Northwest Parana, Brazil." Unpublished Ph.D. dissertation, University of Wisconsin.

Sulmont, Denis (1980). *El movimiento obrero peruano (1890-1980): Resena historica*. Lima: Tarca.

Taussig, Michael T. (1980). *The Devil and Commodity Fetishism in South America*. Chapel Hill: University of North Carolina Press.

Thomas, Vinod (1978). "The Measurement of Spatial Differences in Poverty: The Case of Peru." World Bank Staff Working Paper No. 273.

Thorp, Rosemary, ed. (1979). *Inflation and Stabilization in Latin America*. London: Macmillan.

Uricoechea, Fernando (1980). *The Patrimonial Foundations of the Brazilian Bureaucratic State*. Berkeley: University of California Press.

Wachtel, Nathan (1977). *The Vision of the Vanquished: The Spanish Conquest of Peru through Indian Eyes*. Sussex: Harvester Press.

Waisman, Carlos H. (1982). *Modernization and the Working Class: The Politics of Legitimacy*. Austin: University of Texas Press.

White, Richard A. (1978). *Paraguay's Autonomous Revolution, 1810-1840*. Albuquerque: University of New Mexico Press.

Wiarda, Howard J. (1982, 2nd ed.). *Politics and Social Change in Latin America: The Distinct Tradition*. Amherst: University of Massachusetts Press.

____ (1981). *Corporatism and National Development in Latin America*. Boulder, Colo.: Westview Press.

Wilson, James W. (1979). "Freedom and Control: Workers' Participation in Management in Chile, 1967-1975." Unpublished Ph.D. dissertation, Cornell University.

Wilson, Patricia Ann (1975). "From Mode of Production to Spatial Formation: The Regional Consequences of Dependent Industrialization in Peru." Unpublished doctoral dissertation, Cornell University.

Yates, Michael James (1981). "Colonists and Campesinos: Small-Scale Agricultural Production and Rural Life in Eastern Paraguay." Unpublished Ph.D. dissertation, Columbia University.

Yepes, Jose A. G. (1981). *The Challenge of Venezuelan Democracy*. New Brunswick, N.J.: Transaction Books.

Zandstra, H., et al. (1979). *Caqueza: Living Rural Development*. Ottawa: International Development Research Centre.

Zuvekas, Clarence (1977). "An Annotated Bibliography of Agricultural Development in Bolivia." AID, Latin America and USDA. (N.B.: Zuvekas was the principal editor of a multicountry series on Latin American agriculture, including Bolivia, Colombia, Costa Rica, Caribbean Region, Guyana, Haiti, Honduras, Ecuador, Guatemala, Paraguay, and Peru. The largest are cited separately.)

V.B. Central American and Caribbean Topics

Adams, Richard N. (1970). *Crucifixion by Power: Essays on Guatemalan National Social Structure, 1944-1966*. Austin: University of Texas Press.

Alas, Higinio (1982). *El Salvador: Por qué la insurrección?* San Jose, Costa Rica: Central American Human Rights Commission.

Alibar, France, and Lembeye-Boy, Pierrette (1982). *Le couteau seul: la condition féminine aux Antilles*. Paris: Editions Caribéennes/L'Harmattan.

Anselin, Alain (1979). *L'émigration antillaise en France, du Bantoustan au getto*. Paris: Anthropos.

Armstrong, Robert, and Shenk, Janet (1982). *El Salvador: The Face of Revolution*. Boston: South End.

Aventurin, Elzéa F. (1982). *Guadeloupe échouée*. Paris: Nouvelles Editions Africaines.

Barenstein, Jorge (1981). *El análisis de la burocracia estatal desde la perspectiva Weberiana: Los administradores en el sector público mexicano*. Mexico City: CIDE.

Barkin, David (1978). *Desarrollo regional y reorganizacion campesina: la Chontalpa como reflejo del problema agropecuairo mexicano*. Mexico City: Editorial Nueva Imagen.

Beckford, George, ed. (1975). *Caribbean Economy: Dependence and Backwardness*. Kingston, Jamaica: Institute of Social and Economic Research.

Birdwell, D. B. (1979). "Cycles of Power: Social Organization in a Belizean Village." Unpublished Ph.D. dissertation, Southern Methodist University.

Black, George (1981). *Triumph of the People: The Sandinista Revolution in Nicaragua*. London: Zed Press.

Bonniol, Jean-Luc (1980). *Terre-de-haut des Saintes*. Paris: Editions Caribéennes.

Brossat, Alain, and Maragnes, Daniel (1981). *Les Antilles dans l'impasse?* Paris: L'Harmattan.

Brodsky, Harold, et al. (1978). "The Small Farmer in Jamaican Agriculture: An Assessment of Constraints and Opportunities." Kingston: USDA, OICD and USAID/Jamaica.

Browning, David (1971). *El Salvador: Landscape and Society*. Oxford: Clarendon Press.

Buhrer-Solal, J. C., and Levenson, C. B. (1980). *Le Guatemala et ses populations*. Paris: PUF.

La Caraibe meancée. Environnement et développement dans les grandes et petites Antilles (1980). Paris: Karthala.

Carvajal, Manuel J. (1979a). "Bibliography of Poverty and Related Topics in Costa Rica." Washington: AID, Latin America and USDA (2,056 items).

_____ (1979b). "Report on Income Distribution and Poverty in Costa Rica." Washington: AID, Latin America and USDA.

Cline, William R., and Delgado, Enrique, eds. (1978). *Economic Integration in Central America*. Washington, D.C.: Brookings Institution.

Collins, Joseph (1982). *What Difference Could a Revolution Make? Farming and Food in the New Nicaragua*. San Francisco, Calif.: Institute for Food and Development Policy.

Cook, Scott (1982). *Zapotec Stoneworkers: The Dynamics of Rural Small Commodity Production in Modern Mexican Capitalism*. Washington, D.C.: University Press of America.

Cross, M., and Marks, A., eds. (1979). *Peasants, Plantations and Rural Communities in the Caribbean*. Guilford: University of Surrey, Department of Sociology; and Leiden: Royal Institute of Linguistics and Anthropology.

Crusol, Jean (1980). *Economies insulaires de la Caraibe*. Paris: Editions Caribéennes.

Davis, Shelton H., and Hodson, Julie (1982). *Witnesses to Political Violence in Guatemala: The Suppression of a Rural Development Movement*. Boston: OXFAM-America.

Dominguez, Jorge (1978). *Cuba: Order and Revolution*. Cambridge, Mass.: Harvard University Press.

Dominguez, Jorge, ed. (1982a). *Cuba: Internal and International Affairs*. Beverly Hills, Calif.: Sage.

_____ (1982b). *Mexico's Political Economy: Challenges at Home and Abroad*. Beverly Hills, Calif.: Sage.

EPICA (1982). *Grenada: The Peaceful Revolution*. Washington, D.C.: EPICA Task Force.

Erickson, Frank, et al. (1979). "An Annotated Bibliography of Agricultural Development in Jamaica." Washington: AID, Latin America and USDA (197 pages).

Espejo, Paz (1980). *Des femmes du Nicaragua*. Paris: Des Femmes.

Esteva, Gustavo (1982). *The Struggle for Rural Mexico*. South Hadley, Mass.: J. F. Bergin.

Fass, Simon (1980). *The Economics of Survival: A Study of Poverty and Planning in Haiti*. Washington: AID, DSB, Office of Urban Development.

Feder, Ernest (1978). *Strawberry Imperialism: An Enquiry into the Mechanisms of Dependency in Mexican Agriculture*. Mexico City: Editorial Campesina.

Feinberg, Richard, ed. (1982). *Central America: International Dimensions of the Crisis*. New York: Holmes & Meier.

Fletcher, L. B., and Graber, E. (1980). *Economic Growth, Equity and Agricultural Development in the Dominican Republic*. Ames: Iowa State University, Department of Economics and Sociology, International Studies in Economics No. 12.

Flores Macal, Mario (1978). *Orígenes de las formas de dominación en El Salvador*. San Jose: Universidad de Costa Rica.

Gilhodes, Pierre (1978). *Paysans du Panama*. Paris: Presses de la Fondation Nationale des Sciences Politiques (hereafter FNSP).

Girault, Christian A. (1980). "Habitatants, speculateurs et exportateurs: Le commerce du café en Haiti." Unpublished Ph.D. dissertation, McGill University.

Goldsmith, A. A. (1981). "The Politics of Rural Stagnation. Development Policy, Local Organizations, and Agrarian Change in Jamaica." Unpublished Ph.D. dissertation, Cornell University.

Griffiths, John and Peter, eds. (1981). *Cuba: the Second Decade*. London: Writers and Readers.

Grindle, Merilee S. (1977). *Bureaucrats, Politicians, and Peasants in Mexico: A Case Study in Public Policy*. Berkeley: University of California Press.

Gudeman, Stephen (1978). *The Demise of a Rural Economy* (Panama). London: Routledge & Kegan Paul.

Guess, George M. (1979). "Bureaucracy and the Unmanaged Forest Commons In Costa Rica: Or Why Development Does Not Grow on Trees." Washington: AID, DSB, Office of Rural Development.

Henry, Paget, and Stone, Carl, eds. (1981). *The Newer Caribbean: Decolonization, Democracy, and Development*. Philadelphia: ISHI.

Hewitt de Alcantara, Cynthia (1976). *Modernizing Mexican Agriculture: Socioeconomic Implications of Technological Change 1940-1970*. Geneva: UNRISD.

Horowitz, Irving, ed. (1981, 4th ed.). *Cuban Communism*. New Brunswick, N.J.: Transaction Books.

Hurbon, Laennec (1980). *Culture et dictature en Haiti: L'imaginaire sous contrôl*. Paris: L'Harmattan.

Immerman, Richard H. (1982). *The CIA in Guatemala: The Foreign Policy of Intervention*. Austin: University of Texas.

Jackson, D. R. (1980). "The Communal Co-operative Experience: An Example from El Salvador." Unpublished Ph.D. dissertation, University of Wisconsin.

Jamail, Milton H. (1980). *The United States-Mexico Border: A Guide to Institutions, Organizations, and Scholars*. Tucson: University of Arizona, Latin America Area Center.

Johnson, Roberta A. (1980). *Puerto Rico: Commonwealth or Colony?* New York: Praeger.

Keith, Nelson Willoughby (1981). "A Development Strategy in Historico-Structural Perspective: Dependence, Dependency Management, and the Bauxite Policies in Jamaica." Unpublished Ph.D. dissertation, Rutgers University.

Labelle, Micheline (1978). *Idéologie de couleur et classes sociales en Haiti*. Montréal: Les Presses Universitaires de Montréal.

Lundahl, Mats (1979). *Peasants and Poverty: A Study of Haiti*. London: Croom Helm.

Manley, Michael (1982). *Jamaica: Struggle in the Periphery*. London: Writers and Readers.

de Márquez, Viviane B., ed. (1979). *Dinámica de la empresa mexicana: Perspectives politicas, economicas y sociales*. Mexico City: El Colegio de Mexico.

Menjivar, Rafael (1977). *Crisis del desarrollismo: Caso El Salvador*. San Jose: Editorial Universitario Centro-america.

_____ (1969). *Reforma agraria: Guatemala, Bolivia and Cuba*. San Salvador: Universitaria de El Salvador.

Mesa-Lago, Carmelo (1981). *The Economy of Socialist Cuba: A Two-Decade Appraisal*. Albuquerque: University of New Mexico Press.

Mottin, Marie France (1980). *Cuba quand même: Vies quotidiennes dans la révolution*. Paris: Seuil.

O'Sullivan-Ryan, J. (1978). "Rural Development Programs and the Problem of Marginality in the Western Highlands of Guatemala." Unpublished Ph.D. dissertation, Stanford University.

Payne, A. J. (1980). *The Politics of the Caribbean Community 1961-79*. New York: St. Martin's Press.

Pena, G. de la (1980). *Herederos de promesas: Agricultura, politica y ritual en los Altos de Morelos*. Mexico City: Ediciones de la Casa Chata.

Pena, Guillermo de la (1982). *A Legacy of Promises: Agriculture, Politics, and Ritual in the Morelos Highlands of Mexico*. Austin: University of Texas.

Post, Ken (1978). *Arise Ye Starvelings: The Jamaican Labor Rebellion of 1938 and Its Aftermath*. The Hague: Martinus Nijhoff.

Ramirez, Rafael L., and Deliz, Wenceslao, S., eds. (1980). *Crisis y critica de las ciencias sociales en Puerto Rico*. Rio Pedro: University of Puerto Rico, Centro de Investigaciones Sociales.

Ronceray, Hubert de (1980). *Sociologie du fait haitien*. Quebec: Presses de l'Université de Québec.

Salas, Louis (1979). *Social Control and Deviance in Cuba*. New York: Praeger.

Sanderson, S. E. (1981). *Agrarian Populism and the Mexican State: The Struggle for Land in Sonora*. Berkeley: University of California Press.

Schlesinger, Stephen, and Kinzer, Stephen (1981). *Bitter Fruit: The Untold Story of the American Coup in Guatemala*. New York: Doubleday.

Seligson, Mitchell A. (1980). *Peasants of Costa Rica and the Development of Agrarian Capitalism*. Madison: University of Wisconsin Press.

Sharpe, Kenneth E. (1977). *Peasant Politics: Struggle in a Dominican Village*. Baltimore, Md.: Johns Hopkins University Press.

Simon, L. R., and Stephens, J. C. (1981). *El Salvador Land Reform 1980-1981: Impact Audit*. Boston: OXFAM.

Smith-Hinds, William L. (1980). "Commitment and Community in a Honduran Campesino Organization. Unpublished Ph.D. dissertation, University of Notre Dame.

Stavrakis, O. (1979). "The Effect of Agricultural Change upon Social Relations and Diet in a Village in Northern Belize." Unpublished Ph.D. dissertation, University of Minnesota.

Stone, Carl (1980). *Democracy and Clientalism in Jamaica*. New Brunswick, N.J.: Transaction Books.

Vellinga, Menno (1979). *Economic Development and the Dynamics of Class: Industrialization, Power and Control in Monterrey, Mexico*. Assen, Netherlands: Van Gorcum.

Walker, Thomas W., ed. (1981). *Nicaragua in Revolution*. New York: Praeger.

Warman, Arturo (1980, 1976 in Sp.). *"We Come to Object": The Peasants of Morelos and the National State*. Baltimore, Md.: Johns Hopkins University Press.

Weber, Henri (1981). *Nicaragua: The Sandinista Revolution*. London: Verso.

Weir's Agricultural Consulting Services, Jamaica (1980). *Small Farming in the Less Developed Countries of the Commonwealth Caribbean*. Barbados: Caribbean Development Bank.

Womack, John (1969). *Zapata and the Mexican Revolution*. New York: Alfred A. Knopf.

Young, J. C. (1981). *Medical Choice in a Mexican Village*. New Brunswick, N.J.: Rutgers University Press.

Zuvekas, Clarence (1978a). *Agriculture Development in Haiti*. Washington: AID.

_____ (1978b). "Land Tenure, Income, and Employment in Rural Haiti: A Survey." AID, Latin America and USDA. (N.B.: See note on Zuvekas in his cite, 1977, on Bolivia.)

VI.   Sub-Saharan Africa

VI.A. Multiregional Studies

Adedeji, Adebayo, ed. (1981). *The Indigenization of African Economies*. New York: Holmes & Meier.

Amin, Samir, ed. (1975). *L'agriculture africaine et le capitalisme*. Paris: Anthropos.

Animation et développement en milieu rural (1981). Paris: Centre G.-Pompidou.

Babu, Mohamed (1981). *African Socialism or Socialist Africa?* London: Zed Press.

Bay, Edna, ed. (1982). *Women and Work in Africa.* Boulder, Colo.: Westview Press.

Bernstein, Henry (1979). "African Peasantries: A Theoretical Framework." *Journal of Peasant Studies* (London), 6,4:412-43.

Biarnès, Pierre (1980). *L'Afrique aux Africains: 20 ans d'indépendance en Afrique noire francophone.* Paris: Armand Colin.

Braganca, Aquino de, and Wallerstein, Immanuel, eds. (1982). *The African Liberation Reader.* 3 volumes. London: Zed Press.

Chaliand, Gerard (1980). *L'enjeu africain. Stratégies des puissances.* Paris: Seuil.

Le Concept de pouvoir en Afrique (1982). Paris: UNESCO.

Constantin, Francois, et al. (1979). *Les entreprises publiques en Afrique noire: Sénégal, Mali, Madagascar.* Paris: Pedone.

Crosby, Edward, et al., eds. (1981). *The African Experience in Community Development: Continuing Struggles in Africa and the Americas.* Reynoldsburg, Ohio: Advocate.

Crummey, D. E., and Stewart, C. C., eds. (1981). *Modes of Production in Africa: The Precolonial Era.* Beverly Hills, Calif.: Sage.

Davidson, Basil (1978). *Let Freedom Come: Africa in Modern History.* Boston: Little, Brown.

—— (1974). *Can Africa Survive? Arguments Against Growth Without Development.* Boston: Little, Brown. (N.B.: Two basic works of the many by the man who, more than any other, taught the West that Africa does, indeed, have a history.)

Development Group for Alternative Policies (1982, rev. ed.). *The African Development Foundation: A New Institutional Approach to U.S. Foreign Assistance to Africa.* Washington: D-GAP.

Dogbe, Yves-Emmanuel (1982). *Lettre ouverte aux pauvres d'Afrique.* Le Mée-sur-Seine, France: Akpagnon.

Dumont, René, and Mottin, Marie-France (1980). *L'Afrique étranglé.* Paris: Seuil.

Dupriez, Hughes (1981). *Paysans d'Afrique noire.* Brussells: Terres et Vie.

—— (1979). *Integrated Rural Development Projects Carried Out in Black Africa with EDF Aid: Evaluation and Outlook for the Future.* Brussels: Commission of the European Communities.

Ergas, Zecki (1977). *La troisième métamorphose de l'Afrique Noire, essai sur l'économie politique de l'education et le développement rural.* Geneva: Médecine et Hygiène.

Fafunwa, A. Babs, and Aisiku, J. U. (1982). *Education in Africa: A Comparative Survey.* London: George Allen & Unwin.

Forje, John W. (1979). *The Rape of Africa at Vienna: African Participation in the 1979 UN Conference on Science and Technology for Development.* Lund: AV-Centralen.

Franke, Richard W., and Chasin, Barbara H. (1980). *Seeds of Famine.* Montclair, N.J.: Allanheld, Osmun.

Fransman, Martin, ed. (1982). *Industry and Accumulation in Africa*. London: Heinemann.

Gentil, Dominique (1979). *Les practiques coopératives en milieu rural Africain*. Sherbrooke, Quebec: Université de Sherbrooke, Centre d'Etudes en Economie Coopérative.

Gosselin, Gabriel (1978, 1980). *L'Afrique désenchantée: Théorie et politique du développement*. 2 volumes. Paris: Anthropos.

Gutkind, Peter C. W., et al., eds. (1978). *African Labor History*. Beverly Hills, Calif.: Sage.

Gutkind, Peter C. W., and Wallerstein, Immanuel, eds. (1977). *The Political Economy of Contemporary Africa*. Beverly Hills, Calif.: Sage.

Gutkind, Peter, and Waterman, Peter, eds. (1977). *African Social Studies: A Radical Reader*. New York: Monthly Review Press.

Halpern, Manfred (1976). "Changing Connections to Multiple Worlds: The African as Individual, Tribesman, Nationalist, Muslim, Christian, Traditionalist, Transformer, and as a World Neighbor, Especially with Israel and the Arabs," pp. 9-44 in Kitchen, Helen. *Africa: From Mystery to Maze*. Lexington, Mass.: Lexington Books.

Harris, Richard, ed. (1975). *The Political Economy of Africa*. Cambridge, Mass.: Schenkman.

Heyer, Judith, et al., eds. (1981). *Rural Development in Tropical Africa*. London: Macmillan.

Ki-Zerbo, J., et al., eds. (1980). *UNESCO General History of Africa*. Berkeley: University of California Press, projected 8 volumes.

Klein, Martin A., ed. (1980). *Peasants in Africa: Historical and Contemporary Perspectives*. Beverly Hills, Calif.: Sage.

Lanning, Greg, and Mueller, Marti (1979). *Africa Undermined*. Harmondsworth, England: Penguin.

Maîtrise de l'espace agraire et développement en afrique tropicale: Logique paysanne et rationalité technique (Actes du Colloque d'Ouagadougou, 4-8 décembre 1978) (1979). Paris: Office de la Recherche Scientifique et Technique Outre-Mer (hereafter ORSTOM).

Markovitz, Irving L. (1977). *Power and Class in Africa*. Englewood Cliffs, N.J.: Prentice-Hall.

Mazrui, Ali (1976). *A World Federation of Cultures: An African Perspective*. New York: Free Press.

Mbuyinga, Elenga (1982). *Pan Africanism or Neocolonialism? : The Bankruptcy of the OAU*. London: Zed Press.

Meunier, R., and Gouiric, N. (1980). *Etudes africaines en Europe*. 2 volumes. Paris: Karthala.

Mtewa, Mekki (1980). *Public Policy and Development Politics: The Politics of Technical Expertise in Africa*. Washington, D.C.: University Press of America.

Ouali, Kamadi (1982). *Intégration africaine*. Paris: Economica.

Palmberg, Mai, ed. (1978). *Problems of Socialist Orientation in Africa*. Uppsala: SIAS.

Pastoral Production and Society: Proceedings of an International Meeting on Nomadic Pastoralism (1979). Cambridge: Cambridge University Press.

Rodney, Walter (1974). *How Europe Underdeveloped Africa*. Washington, D.C.: Howard University Press.

Rosberg, Carl G., and Callaghy, Thomas M., eds. (1979). *Socialism in Sub-Saharan Africa: A New Assessment*. Berkeley: University of California, Institute of International Studies.

Rweyemamu, J., ed. (1980). *Industrialization and Income Distribution*. Dakar: CODESIRA Book Service.

Samoff, Joel (1980). "Underdevelopment and Its Grass Roots in Africa," *Canadian Journal of African Studies*, 14,1:5-36.

Sandbrook, Richard (1982). *The Politics of "Basic Needs": Urban Aspects of Assaulting Poverty in Africa*. Toronto: University of Toronto Press.

Sandbrook, Richard, and Cohen, Robin, eds. (1975). *The Development of an African Working Class*. Toronto: University of Toronto Press.

Schwartz, Alf (1980). *Colonialistes, africanistes et Africains*. Montréal: Nouvelle Optique.

Schwartz, Alf, ed. (1981). *Les Faux Prophètes de l'Afrique ou l'Afr(eu)canisme*. Québec: Presses de l'Université de Laval.

Shaw, Timothy, ed. (1981). *Alternative Futures for Africa*. Boulder, Colo.: Westview Press.

Shaw, Timothy M., and Heard, Kenneth A., eds. (1979). *The Politics of Africa: Dependence and Development*. New York: Holmes & Meier.

Sylvester, Anthony (1981). *Arabs and Africans: Co-operation for Development*. London: Bodley Head.

Temu, Arnold, and Swai, Bonaventure (1981). *Historians and Africanist History: A Critique*. London: Zed Press.

Walker, Anne, et al. (1981). *Information Kit for Women in Africa*. New York: International Women's Tribune Centre, Inc. and Addis Ababa: African Training and Research Center for Women.

Young, Crawford (1982). *Ideology and Development in Africa*. New Haven, Conn.: Yale University Press.

_____ (1976). *The Politics of Cultural Pluralism*. Madison: University of Wisconsin Press.

Young, Crawford, et al. (1981). *Cooperatives and Development: Agricultural Politics in Ghana and Uganda*. Madison: University of Wisconsin Press.

VI.B. West and Equatorial Africa

Adams, Adrian (1977). *Le long voyage des gens du Fleuve* (Senegal). Paris: Maspero. (N.B.: Her articles in Section 2A.)

Alschuler, Lawrence (1980). "Multinationals and the Development of Periphery Capitalism in the Ivory Coast (1960-1975)." Ottawa: University of Ottawa, Institute for International Cooperation, Paper No. 808.

Amin, Samir (1973). *Neocolonialism in West Africa*. New York: Monthly Review Press.

_____ (1969). *Le monde des affaires sénégalais*. Paris: Minuit.

_____ (1968). *Le développement du capitalisme en Côte d'Ivoire*. Paris: Minuit.

_____ (1965). *Trois experiences africaines de développement: le Mali, la Guinée et le Ghana*. Paris: PUF.

Amin, Samir, ed. (1974). *Modern Migrations in West Africa*. London: Oxford University Press.

Amin, Samir, and Coquery Vidrovitch, Catherine (1969). *Histoire économique du Congo, 1880-1968*. Paris: Anthropos.

Baier, Stephen (1980). *An Economic History of Central Niger*. New York: Oxford University Press.

Barbier, Maurice (1982). *Le conflit du Sahara occidental*. Paris: L'Harmattan.

Barbier, Jean-Claude, et al. (1980). *Complexes agro-industriels au Cameroun*. Paris: ORSTOM.

Barclay, A. H., et al. (1979). *The Development Impact of Private Voluntary Organizations. Kenya and Niger*. Final Report. Washington: DAI.

Bayart, Jean-Francois (1979). *L'état au Cameroun*. Paris: FNSP.

Beckman, Bjorn (1976). *Organizing the Farmers: Cocoa Politics and National Development in Ghana*. Uppsala: SIAS.

Belasco, Bernard (1980). *The Entrepreneur as Culture Hero: Preadaptions for Nigerian Economic Development*. New York: Praeger.

Belloncle, Guy (1981). *Le tronc d'arbre et le caiman: Carnets de brousse maliens*. Paris: L'Harmattan.

_____ (1980a). *Femmes et développement en Afrique Sahélienne*. Paris: Ouvrières/Economie.

_____ (1980b). *Jeunes ruraux du Sahel: Une expérience de formation de jeunes alphabetisés au Mali*. Paris: L'Harmattan.

_____ (1978). *Cooperatives et développement en Afrique noire sahélienne*. Sherbrooke, Quebec: Université de Sherbrooke.

Bellot, Jean-Marc (1980). "Kel Tamasheq du Gourma Nigerien et Peul du Torodi: Sociétés agro-pastorales en mutation (République du Niger)." Thèse de III cycle, Université de Bordeaux.

Benini, A. A. (1980). *Community Development in a Multi-ethnic Society: the Upper River Division of the Gambia, West Africa. With Minor Comparative Studies from Upper Volta and Benin*. Bielefelder Studien der Entwicklungssoziologie, No. 8. Saarbrucken: Verlag Breitenbach.

Bequele, Assefa (1980). "Poverty, Inequality and Stagnation – The Ghanaian Experience." Geneva: ILO, WEP 10-6/WP33.

Bernus, Edmond (1981). *Touaregs nigeriens: Unité culturelle et diversité régionale d'un peuple pasteur*. Paris: ORSTOM.

Berron, Henri (1981). *Tradition et modernisme en pays langunaires de basse Côte d'Ivoire (Ivoiriens et étrangers)*. Paris: Ophrys.

Bertrand, Hughues (1975). *Le Congo, formation sociale et mode de développement économique*. Paris: Maspero.

Bienen, Henry, and Diejomaoh, V. P., eds. (1981). *The Political Economy of Income Distribution in Nigeria*. New York: Holmes & Meier.

Biersteker, Thomas J. (1978). *Distortion or Development? Contending Perspectives on the Multinational Corporation* (Nigeria). Cambridge, Mass.: MIT Press.

Billaz, René, and Diawara, Y. (1982). *Enquêtes en milieu rural sahélien*. Paris: PUF.

Bledsoe, Caroline (1980). *Women and Marriage in Kpelle Society*. Stanford, Calif.: Stanford University Press.

Boormans, Maurice (1977). *Statut personnel et famille au Maghreb de 1940 à nos jours*. Paris: Mouton.

Boubacar, Diarra Sadek (1974). "Political Change, Rural Transformation and Development Administration: The Politics of Change and Development in Francophone Africa with Special Reference to the Upper Volta." Unpublished Ph.D. dissertation, University of Minnesota.

Bourgi, Albert (1979). *La politique francaise de coopération en Afrique: le cas du Sénégal*. Dakar: Nouvelles Editions Africaines.

Bourgoin, Henri, and Guillaume, Philippe (1979). *Côte d'Ivoire, économie et société*. Paris: Stock.

Bray, Mark (1982). *Universal Primary Education in Nigeria: A Study of Kano State*. London: Routledge & Kegan Paul.

Brokensha, David, et al. (1977). *The Anthropology of Rural Development in the Sahel: Proposals for Research*. Binghampton, N.Y.: Institute for Development Anthropology.

Buijtenhuijs, Robert (1978). *Le Frolinat et les révoltes populaires du Tchad, 1965-1976*. The Hague: Mouton.

Chambas, M. I. (1980). "The Politics of Agriculture and Rural Development in the Upper Region of Ghana." Unpublished Ph.D. dissertation, Cornell University.

Charlick, Robert B. (1982). *Animation Rurale – A Technique for Participatory Rural Development*. Ithaca, N.Y.: Cornell University, Rural Development Committee. (N.B.: Other forthcoming volumes, country specific, on Upper Volta, Cameroon, and Niger.)

_____ (1977). "Planification et évaluation des activités d'information et d'organisation rurale dans le cadre du projet de productivité du Department de Niamey." Niamey: USAID, December.

_____ (1976). "The Niamey Regional Productivity Project – Analysis of the Social Soundness of the Design." Washington: USAID, September.

_____ (1974). "Power and Participation in the Modernization of Rural Hausa Communities." Unpublished Ph.D. dissertation, University of California at Los Angeles.

Chassey, F. de (1978). *Mauritanie 1900-1975, de l'ordre colonial à l'ordre néo-colonial entre Maghreb et Afrique Noire*. Paris: Anthropos.

_____ (1977). *L'étrier, la houe et le livre: "Sociétés traditionnelles" au Sahara et au Sahel occidental*. Paris: Anthropos.

Cissé, Moussa Cola, et al. (1982). *Le Mali, le paysan et l'Etat*. Paris: L'Harmattan.

Cohen, Abner (1981). *The Politics of Elite Culture: Explorations in the Dramaturgy of Power in a Modern African Society* (Sierra Leone). Berkeley: University of California Press.

Collins, Paul, ed. (1981). *Administration for Development in Nigeria*. New Brunswick, N.J.: Transaction Books.

Colvin, Lucie, et al. (1981). *The Uprooted of the Western Sahel: A History of Migrants' Quest for Cash in the Senegambia.* New York: Praeger.

Conti, Anna (1979). "Capitalist Organization of Production Through Non-Capitalist Relations: Women's Role in a Resettlement Project in Upper Volta." *Review of African Political Economy,* 15/16:75-92.

Copans, Jean (1980). *Les marabouts de l'arachide: La confrerie mouride et les paysans du Sénégal.* Paris: Le Sycomore.

Couty, Ph., and Halaire, A. (1981). *De la carte aux systèmes: Vingt ans d'études agraires au sud du Sahara (ORSTOM 1960-1980).* Paris: ORSTOM.

C.R.E.S.M. (1979). *Introduction à la Mauritanie.* Paris: CNRS.

—— (1977). *Problèmes agraires au Maghreb.* Paris: CNRS.

Damiba, Pierre-Claver, and Schrumpf, Paul (1981). *Quel avenir pour le Sahel?* Lausanne: P. M. Favre.

Delgado, Christopher L. (1979). *Livestock Versus Foodgrain Production in Southeast Upper Volta.* Ann Arbor: University of Michigan, CRED.

Derrien, Jean-Maurice (1982). *Conditions de travail et sousdéveloppement: les industries agro-alimentaires au Sénégal et au Togo.* Paris: CNRS.

Diop, Abdoulaye-Bara (1981). *La société Wolof.* Paris: Karthala.

Dorjahn, Vernon R., and Isaac, Barry L., eds. (1979). *Essays on the Economic Anthropology of Liberia and Sierra Leone.* Philadelphia: Institute for Liberian Studies.

Dowse, Frank (1979). *Aspects of Ghanaian Development: Studies in Political Sociology.* London: Frank Cass.

Dunn, John, ed. (1978). *West African States: Failure and Promise.* Cambridge: Cambridge University Press.

Dunn, J., and Robertson, A. F. (1974). *Independence and Opportunity: Political Change in Ahafo.* Cambridge: Cambridge University Press.

Edoh, Anthony Adem (1979). "Decentralization and Local Government Reforms in Ghana." Unpublished Ph.D. dissertation, University of Wisconsin (Madison).

Enger, Warren J. (1979). *Niger Agricultural Sector Assessment.* Niamey: USAID/Niger, 2 volumes.

Ernst, Klaus (1976). *Tradition and Progress in the African Village: Non-capitalist Transformation of Rural Communities in Mali.* New York: St. Martin's Press.

Faure, Y.-A., and Medard, J. F., eds. (1982). *Etat et bourgeoisie en Côte-d'Ivoire.* Paris: Karthala.

Fernandez, James (1982). *Bwiti: An Ethnography of the Religious Imagination in Africa (Gabon).* Princeton, N.J.: Princeton University Press.

Fieloux, Michele (1980). *Les sentiers de la nuit: Les migrations rurales lobi de la Haute-Volta vers la Côte-d'Ivoire.* Paris: ORSTOM.

Franke, Richard W., and Chasin, Barbara H. (1980). *Seeds of Famine: Ecological Destruction and the Development Dilemma in the West African Sahel.* Montclair, N.J.: Allanheld, Osmun.

Gastellu, J. M. (1981). *L'égalitarianisme économique des Serer du Sénégal.* Paris: ORSTOM.

Gay, John (1975). "Decision-Making in Traditional Agriculture Among the Kpelle of Liberia." Rome: FAO, unpublished report for LIR/73/014/A/01/12.

Geschiere, Peter (1982). *Village Communities and the Authority of the State: Changing Relations in Maka Villages (S.E. Cameroon) Since 1900.* London: Routledge & Kegan Paul.

Goody, Esther N. (1982). *Parenthood and Social Reproduction: Fostering and Occupational Roles in West Africa.* Cambridge: Cambridge University Press.

Goody, Jack (1980). "Rice-burning and the Green Revolution in Northern Ghana." *Journal of Development Studies,* 16,1:136-55.

Graham, Ronald (1982). *Monopoly Capital and African Development: The Political Economy of the World Aluminum Industry.* London: Zed Press.

Gregory, Joel W. (1974). "Underdevelopment, Dependency and Migration in Upper Volta." Unpublished Ph.D. dissertation, Cornell University.

Gugler, Josef, and Flanagan, William G. (1978). *Urbanization and Social Change in West Africa.* Cambridge: Cambridge University Press.

Hart, David (1980). *The Volta River Project.* Edinburgh: Edinburgh University Press (via Columbia University Press).

Hart, Keith (1982). *The Political Economy of West African Agriculture.* Cambridge: Cambridge University Press.

Higgott, Richard (1980). "Structural Dependence and Decolonisation in a West African Landlocked State: Niger." *Review of African Political Economy,* 17(Jan.-Apr.):43-58.

Hlophe, Stephen (1979). *Class, Ethnicity, and Politics in Liberia.* Washington, D.C.: University Press of America.

Honadle, George H. (1978). "Organization Design for Development Administration: A Liberian Case Study of Implementation Analysis for Project Benefit Distribution." Unpublished Ph.D. dissertation, Syracuse University.

Howard, Rhoda (1979). *Colonialism and Underdevelopment in Ghana.* New York: Africana.

Hull, Galen (1980). "Strategies for Development for the Rural Enterprise Development Project in the Eastern Region ORD of Upper Volta." Washington: Partnership for Productivity and AID/Ouagadougou.

Jones, William I. (1976). *Planning and Economic Policy Socialist Mali and Her Neighbors.* Washington, D.C.: Three Continents Press.

Joshi, H., et al. (1981). *Abidjan: Urban Development and Employment in the Ivory Coast.* Geneva: ILO.

Kane, C. H., ed. (1982). *Enfants et jeunes au Sahel.* Dakar: ENDA/UNICEF.

Kennedy, Paul T. (1980). *Ghanaian Businessmen: From Artisan to Capitalist Entrepreneur in a Dependent Economy.* Munich and London: Weltforum-Verlag.

Kraus, Jon (1979). "Strikes and Labour Power in Ghana." *Development and Change,* 10,2:259-86.

Ladouceur, Paul A. (1979). *Chiefs and Politicians: The Politics of Regionalism in Northern Ghana.* London: Longman.

Lahuec, Jean-Paul (1980). *Le terroir de Zaonghu: Les Mossi de Koupela (Haute-Volta).* Paris: ORSTOM.

Lateef, Noel V. (1980). *Crisis in the Sahel: A Case Study in Development Cooperation*. Boulder, Colo.: Westview Press.

Lewis, Barbara C. (1980). "Political Variables and Food and Food Price Policy in West Africa." Washington: AID and USDA, Contract Rpt. 53-319,R-0-99.

Liniger-Goumez, Max (1980). *La Guinée equatoriale, un pays méconnu*. Paris: L'Harmattan.

Manning, Patrick (1982). *Slavery, Colonialism and Economic Growth in Dahomey, 1640-1960*. Cambridge: Cambridge University Press.

Masini, Jean, et al. (1979). *Les multinationales et le développement, trois entreprises et al Côte d'Ivoire*. Paris: PUF.

Mayson, D. T., and Sawyer, A. (1979). "Labour in Liberia." *Review of African Political Economy*, 14:3-15.

Mendonsa, Eugene L. (1982). *The Politics of Divination* (Ghana). Berkeley: University of California Press.

Minko, Henri (1981). *La fiscalité gabonnaise de développement*. Paris: Novelles Editions Africaines.

Mondjannagni, Alfred-Comain (1977). *Campagnes et villes au Sud de la République Populaire du Benin*. The Hague: Mouton.

Nicolas, Guy (1981). *Dynamique de l'Islam au sud du Sahara*. Paris: Orientalistes de France.

Nihan, Georges, and Demol, Erik (1982). *Le secteur non structuré "moderne" de Yaoundé (République-Unie du Cameroun)*. Geneva: ILO.

Nnoli, Okwudiba, ed. (1981). *Path to Nigerian Development*. Dakar: CODESRIA Books.

O'Brien, Rita Cruise, ed. (1979). *The Political Economy of Underdevelopment: Dependence in Senegal*. Beverly Hills, Calif.: Sage.

Palau Marti, Monserrat (1982). *Société et réligion au Benin*. Paris: Anthropos.

Peace, Adrian (1979). *Choice, Class, and Conflict: A Study of Southern Nigerian Factory Workers*. Atlantic Highlands, N.J.: Humanities Press.

Pearson, Scott R., et al. (1981). *Rice in West Africa: Policy and Economics*. Stanford, Calif.: Stanford University Press.

Peil, Margaret (1981). *Cities and Suburbs: Urban Life in West Africa*. New York: Holmes & Meier.

Pellow, Deborah (1977). *Women in Accra: Options for Autonomy*. Algonac, Michigan: Reference.

Price, Robert M. (1975). *Society and Bureaucracy in Contemporary Ghana*. Berkeley: University of California Press.

Rey, Pierre-Philippe (1977). "Le Systeme politique mossi et les migrations: A propos de trois textes de J. Capron et J. M. Kohler." *Journal des Africanistes*, 47,1:115-24.

_____ (1971). *Colonialisme, néo-colonialisme et transition au capitalisme: exemple de la "Comilog" au Congo-Brazzaville*. Paris: Maspero.

Reyna, Stephen P., ed. (1980). *Sahelian Social Development*. Abidjan: USAID, REDSO.

Richard, Philippe and Baudet (1980). "La Politique céréalière voltaique et le role de l'office national des céréales." Paris: SEDES and CCCE.

Rivière, Claude (1978). *Classes et stratification en Afrique: le cas guinéen.* Paris: PUF.

Rocheteau, Guy (1982). *Pouvoir financier et indépendence économique en Afrique: Le cas du Sénégal.* Paris: Karthala.

Sawadogo, Abdoulaye (1977). *L'agriculture en Côte d'Ivoire.* Paris: PUF.

Schott, John R., ed. (1978). *An Experiment in Integrated Rural Development: The Mampong Valley Social Laboratory in Ghana.* New York: International Institute of Rural Reconstruction.

Schumacher, Edward J. (1975). *Politics, Bureaucracy, and Rural Development in Senegal.* Berkeley: University of California Press.

Shepherd, A. W. (1979). "The Development of Capitalist Rice Farming in N. Ghana." Unpublished Ph.D. dissertation, Cambridge University.

Smale, Melinda (1980). *Women in Mauritania: The Effects of Drought and Migration on their Economic Status and Implications for Development Programs.* Washington: AID, Office of Women in Development.

Snyder, Francis G. (1981). *Capitalism and Legal Change: Transformation of an African Society* (Senegal). New York: Academic Press.

Spittler, G. (1978). *Herrschaft über Bauern: Staatliche Herrschaft und islamisch-urbane Kultur in Gobir.* Frankfort: Campus.

Stuumlautrzinger, U. (1980). *Der Baumwollanbau im Tschad: Zur Problematik landwirtschaftlicher Exportproduktion in der Dritten Welt.* Zurich: Atlantis Verlag.

Swanson, Richard A. (1979). *Gourmantché Agriculture.* 2 parts. Fada N'Gourma: AID IRD Project, Eastern ORD, BAEP.

Tardits, Claude (1980). *Le royaume bamoum.* Paris: Armand Colin.

Thomson, James T. (1979). "Capitation in Colonial and Post-Colonial Niger: Analysis of the Effects of an Imposed Head Tax System on Rural Political Organization," pp. 201-21 in Burman, S. B., and Harrell-Bond, B. E., eds. *The Imposition of Law.* New York: Academic Press.

―― (1977). "Ecological Deterioration: Local Level Rule-Making and Enforcement Problems in Niger," pp. 57-79 in Glantz, M.H., ed. *Desertification: Environmental Degradation in and around Arid Lands.* Boulder, Colo.: Westview Press.

Thomson, J. T. (1975). "Law, Legal Processes, and Development at the Local Level in Hausa Speaking Niger: A Trouble Case Analysis of Rural Institutional Inertia." Unpublished Ph.D. dissertation, University of Indiana.

Toure, Abdou (1982). *La Civilisation quotidienne en Côte-d'Ivoire.* Paris: Karthala.

Trouvé, J., and Bessat, C. (1980a). *Les liens entre migrations rurales et politiques gouvernementales* (Upper Volta). Geneva: ILO, WEP 10-6/WP29.

―― (1980b). *L'exode rural des jeunes et les politiques gouvernementales de développement: L'expérience camérounaise.* Geneva: ILO, WEP 10-6/WP38.

Werlin, Herbert H. (1979). "The Consequences of Corruption: The Ghanaian Experiences," pp. 247-60, and "The Roots of Corruption: The Ghanaian Enquiry," pp. 381-400 in Ekpo, Monday U., ed. *Bureaucratic Corruption in Sub-Saharan Africa.* Washington: University Press of America.

Williams, Gavin (1980). *State and Society in Nigeria*. Lagos: Afrographika; and London: Spokesman Books.

VI.C. Central and Southern Africa

Adam, Herbert, and Giliomee, Hermann (1979). *Ethnic Power Mobilized: Can South Africa Change?* New Haven, Conn.: Yale University Press.

Bender, Gerald J. (1978). *Angola Under the Portuguese: The Myth and the Reality*. Berkeley: University of California Press.

Bezy, Fernand, et al. (1981). *Accumulation et sous-développement au Zaire (1960-1980)*. Louvain-la-Neuve, Belgium: Presses de l'Université de Louvain.

Bohning, W. R., ed. (1981). *Black Migration to South Africa*. Geneva: ILO.

Bozzoli, Belinda (1981). *The Political Nature of a Ruling Class: Capital and Ideology in South Africa 1890-1933*. London: Routledge & Kegan Paul.

Bratton, Michael (1980). *The Local Politics of Rural Development: Peasant and Party-State in Zambia*. Hanover, N.H.: University Press of New England.

Chonchol, Maria Edy (1980). *Guide bibliographique du Mozambique: Environnement naturel, développement et organisation villageoise*. Paris: L'Harmattan.

Clarence-Smith, W. G. (1980). "Class Structure and Class Struggles in Angola in the 1970's." *Journal of Southern African Studies*, 7,1:109-26.

Clarke, Duncan G. (1980). *Foreign Companies and International Investment in Zimbabwe*. Salisbury, Zimbabwe: Mambo Press.

_____ (1978). *The Unemployment Crisis*. London: CIIR, Series, From Rhodesia to Zimbabwe, No. 3.

Colclough, Christopher, and McCarthy, Stephen (1980). *The Political Economy of Botswana: A Study of Growth and Distribution*. Oxford: Oxford University Press.

Danaher, Kevin (early 1983). *South Africa and the United States: The Progression of a Relationship*. Washington, D.C.: Institute for Policy Studies.

Daniere, Andre, et al. (1981). "Rwanda: Short Assessment of the Education Sector." Kigali: USAID/Rwanda.

Faaland, J., et al. (1979). *Report of the Special Programming Mission to Botswana*. Rome: International Fund for Agricultural Development.

Freedman, Jim (1979). "East African Peasants and Capitalist Development: The Kiga of Northern Ruanda," pp. 245-60 in Turner, David H., et al., eds. *Challenging Anthropology: A Critical Introduction to Social and Cultural Anthropology*. Toronto: McGraw-Hill.

Ghai, Dharam, and Radwan, Samir (1980). *Growth and Inequality: Rural Development in Malawi, 1964-1978*. Geneva: ILO, WEP 10-6/WE35.

Gould, David J. (1980). *Bureaucratic Corruption and Underdevelopment in the Third World: The Case of Zaire*. New York: Pergamon Press.

Gran, Guy, ed. (1979). *Zaire: The Political Economy of Underdevelopment*. New York: Praeger.

_____ (1978). "Zaire 1978: The Ethical and Intellectual Bankruptcy of the World-System." *Africa Today*, 25,4:5-24.

Green, Reginald, et al., eds. (1982). *Namibia: The Last Colony*. London: Longman.

Greenberg, Stanley B. (1980). *Race and State in Capitalist Development: Comparative Perspectives*. New Haven, Conn.: Yale University Press.

Guichaoua, André (1981). "Surpeuplement et stratégies migratoires des paysans au Burundi." Geneva: ILO, WEP 10-6/WP46.

Hare, A. Paul, et al., eds. (1979). *South Africa: Sociological Analyses*. Cape Town: Oxford University Press.

Head, Bessie (1981). *Serowe: Village of the Rainwind*. London: Heinemann Educational Books.

Houyoux, Joseph (1973). *Budgets ménagers, nutrition, et mode de vie à Kinshasa*. Kinshasa: Presses de l'Université du Zaire.

ILO/JASPA (1979). *Options for a Dependent Economy: Development, Employment, and Equity Problems in Lesotho*. Addis Ababa: ILO/JASPA.

Isaacman, Allen (1978). *A Luta Continua: Creating a New Society in Mozambique*. Binghampton: State University of New York at Binghampton, Fernand Braudel Center.

Jolly, Richard, ed. (1981). *Basic Needs in an Economy Under Pressure: Findings and Recommendations of an ILO/JASPA Basic Needs Mission to Zambia*. Addis Ababa: ILO/JASPA.

Kalibwami, Justin (1979). *Le Rwanda face à son avenir: Etudes socio-politiques*. Paris: L'Harmattan.

Kowet, Donald K. (1978). *Land, Labour Migration and Politics in Southern Africa: Botswana, Lesotho, and Swaziland*. Uppsala: SIAS; and New York: Africana.

Kuper, Adam (1982). *Wives for Cattle*. London: Routledge & Kegan Paul.

Lemarchand, René (1982). *The World Bank in Rwanda: The Case of OVAPAM*. Bloomington: University of Indiana, Occasional Paper in Rural Development.

_____ (1970). *Rwanda and Burundi*. New York: Praeger.

Marcum, John (1969, 1978). *The Angolan Revolution*. 2 volumes. Cambridge, Mass.: MIT Press.

Magubane, Bernard M. (1979). *The Political Economy of Race and Class in South Africa*. New York: Monthly Review Press.

Mayer, Philip, ed. (1981). *Black Villagers in an Industrial Society: Anthropological Perspectives on Labour Migration in South Africa*. London: Oxford University Press.

Mezger, Dorothea (1980). *Copper in the World Economy*. New York: Monthly Review Press.

Morris, W. H. (1979). "A Report on Agricultural Production, Marketing, and Crop Storage in Rwanda." Kigali: USAID/ Kigali.

Msukwa, L. A. H. (1981). *Meeting the Basic Health Needs of Rural Malawi*. Swansea, Wales: University College of Swansea, Centre for Development Studies. (N.B.: This is one of 14 (1977) from their monograph series. See also their occasional paper series, 1-13 [1977-].)

Mugomba, Agrippah, and Nyaggah, Mougo, eds. (1980). *Independence Without Freedom: The Political Economy of Colonial Education in Southern Africa*.

Santa Barbara, Calif.: ABC-Clio.

Munslow, Barry (1983). *Mozambique: The Revolution and Its Origins.* London: Longman.

Murray, Martin, ed. (1982). *South African Capitalism and Black Political Opposition.* Cambridge, Mass.: Schenkman.

Newbury, M. Catharine (1980). "Ubureetwa and Thangata: Catalysts to Peasant Political Consciousness in Rwanda and Malawi." *Canadian Journal of African Studies*, 14,1:97-111.

_____ (1978). "Ethnicity in Rwanda: The Case of Kinyaga." *Africa*, 48,1:17-40.

_____ (1975). "The Cohesion of Oppression: A Century of Clientage in Kinyanga, Rwanda." Unpublished Ph.D. dissertation, University of Wisconsin.

Nsekela, Amon J., ed. (1981). *Southern Africa: Towards Economic Liberation.* London: Rex Collings.

Nzongola-Ntalaja (1975). "Urban Administration in Zaire: A Study of Kananga, 1971-3." Unpublished Ph.D. dissertation, University of Wisconsin, Madison.

Ollawa, Patrick E. (1979). *Participatory Democracy in Zambia: The Political Economy of National Development.* Devon: Arthur H. Stockwell.

Palmer, Robin, and Parsons, Neil, eds. (1977). *The Roots of Rural Poverty in Central and Southern Africa.* Berkeley: University of California Press.

Perrings, Charles (1979). *Black Mineworkers in Central Africa.* New York: Africana.

Poewe, Karla O. (1981). *Matrilineal Ideology: Male-Female Dynamics in Luapula, Zambia.* New York: Academic Press.

Riddell, Roger (1979). "Prospects for Land Reform in Zimbabwe, *Rural Africana*, 4-5:17-31.

_____ (1978a). *Alternative to Poverty.* London: CIIR, Series, From Rhodesia to Zimbabwe, No. 1.

_____ (1978b). *The Land Question.* London: CIIR, Series, From Rhodesia to Zimbabwe, No. 2.

Saul, John S., and Gelb, Stephen (1981). *The Crisis in South Africa: Class Defense, Class Revolution.* New York: Monthly Review Press.

Schatzberg, Michael G. (1980). *Politics and Class in Zaire: Bureaucracy, Business and Beer in Lisala.* New York: Africana.

Scudder, Thayer, and Colson, Elizabeth (1980). *Secondary Education and the Formation of an Elite: The Impact of Education on Gwembe District, Zambia.* New York: Academic Press.

Searle, Chris (1981). *We're Building the New School! Diary of a Teacher in Mozambique.* London: Zed Press.

Stockwell, John (1978). *In Search of Enemies: A CIA Story.* New York: W. W. Norton.

Stoneman, Colin (1978). "Foreign Capital and the Reconstruction of Zimbabwe." *Review of African Political Economy*, 11:62-83.

_____ (1976). "Foreign Capital and the Prospects for Zimbabwe," *World Development*, 4,1:25-58.

Stoneman, Colin, ed. (1981). *Zimbabwe's Inheritance.* London: Macmillan.

SWAPO (1981). *To Be Born a Nation: The Liberation Struggle for Namibia.* London: Zed Press.

Toit, Darcy du (1981). *Capital and Labour in South Africa: Class Struggles in the 1970's*. London: Routledge & Kegan Paul.

Tordoff, William, ed. (1980). *Administration in Zambia*. Manchester University Press.

Turok, Ben, ed. (1979). *Development in Zambia: A Reader*. London: Zed Press.

Vail, Leroy, and White, Landag (1980). *Capitalism and Colonialism in Mozambique: A Study of Quelimane District*. London: Heinemann Educational Books.

Binsbergen, William M. J. Van (1981). *Religious Change in Zambia: Exploratory Studies*. London: Routledge & Kegan Paul.

Vanderlinden, Jacques, ed. (1980). *Du Congo au Zaire, 1960-1980: Essai de Bilan*. Brussels: Centre de Recherche et d'Informations Socio-Politiques.

Williams, T. D. (1979). *Malawi: Politics of Despair*. Ithaca, N.Y.: Cornell University Press.

Winai-Stom, G. (1975). "The Influence of Multinational Corporations on Lesotho's Politics and Economics," *The African Review*, 5,4:473-97.

VI.D. East Africa, the Horn, and Indian Ocean Islands

Abate, Alula, and Kiros, Fassil (1980). *Agrarian Reform, Structural Changes and Rural Development in Ethiopia*. Geneva: ILO 10-6/WP37.

Abubaker, Gafer S. (1979). "Rural Participation in Program Phases: A Case of Resettlement and Rural Development of Khasm El Girba (New Halfa) Project (1959-1976), Democratic Republic of Sudan." Unpublished Ph.D. dissertation, State University of New York at Albany.

Barclay, A. H. (1981). *Evaluation of the Abyei Development Project, Sudan*. Washington: DAI.

Barkan, Joel, and Okumu, John, eds. (1979). *Politics and Public Policy in Kenya and Tanzania*. New York: Praeger.

Barnett, Tony (1979). "Why Are Bureaucrats Slow Adopters?: The Case of Water Management in the Gezira Scheme." *Sociologia Ruralis*, 10,1:60-70.

____ (1977). *The Gezira Scheme: An Illusion of Development*. London: Frank Cass.

Benedict, Marion and Burton (1982). *Men, Women, and Money in Seychelles*. Berkeley: University of California Press.

Bouillon, Antoine (1982). *Madagascar, le colonisé et son âme*. Paris: L'Harmattan.

Carlsen, J. (1980). *Economic and Social Transformation in Rural Kenya*. Uppsala: SIAS.

Cliffe, L., et al., eds. (1977). *Government and Rural Development in East Africa*. The Hague: Martinus Nijhoff.

Cliffe, Lionel, et al., eds. (1975). *Rural Cooperation in Tanzania*. Dar es Salaam: Tanzania Publishing House.

Coulson, Andrew (1982). *Tanzania 1800-1980: A Political Economy*. Oxford: Oxford University Press.

Coulson, Andrew, ed. (1980). *African Socialism in Practice – The Tanzanian Experience*. London: Spokesman Books.

Desjeux, Dominique (1979). *La question agraire à Madagascar: administration et paysannat de 1895 à nos jours*. Paris: L'Harmattan.

El Hadari, A. M. (1975). "Some Socio-Economic Aspects of Farming in the Nuba Mountains, Western Sudan." *Eastern Africa Journal of Rural Development*, 7,1/2:157-76.

El Hassan, Idris Salim (1980). "On Ideology: The Case of Religion in Northern Sudan." Unpublished Ph.D. dissertation, University of Connecticut.

Fenet, Alain, et al. (1979). *La question de L'Erythrée*. Paris: PUF.

Freyhold, Michaela von (1979). *Ujamaa Villages in Tanzania: Analysis of a Social Experiment*. New York: Monthly Review Press.

Geist, Judith K. (1981). "Coastal Agrarian Underdevelopment and Regional Imbalance in Kenya." Unpublished Ph.D. dissertation, University of California at Berkeley.

Halliday, Fred, and Molyneux, Maxine (1981). *The Ethiopian Revolution*. London: Verso.

Heyer, Judith, et al., eds. (1976). *Agricultural Development in Kenya: An Economic Reassessment*. Nairobi: Oxford University Press.

Hyden, Goran (1980). *Beyond Ujamaa in Tanzania: Underdevelopment and an Uncaptured Peasantry*. Berkeley: University of California Press.

Iliffe, John (1975). *A Modern History of Tanganyika*. Cambridge: Cambridge University Press.

ILO (1976). *Growth, Employment, and Equity: A Comprehensive Strategy for the Sudan*. Geneva: ILO.

ILO/JASPA (1977). *Economic Transformation in a Socialist Framework: An Employment and Basic Needs Oriented Development Strategy for Somalia*. Addis Ababa: ILO/JASPA.

Joinet, Bernard (1981). *Tanzanie, manger d'abord*. Paris: Karthala.

Kaplinsky, Raphael, ed. (1978). *Readings on the Multinational Corporation in Kenya*. Nairobi: Oxford University Press.

Kim, K. S., et al., eds. (1977). *The Political Economy of Tanzania*. London: Heinemann Educational Books.

Kitching, Gavin (1980). *Class and Economic Change in Kenya: The Making of an African Petite-Bourgeoisie*. New Haven, Conn.: Yale University Press.

Kjekshus, Helge (1977). *Ecology Control and Economic Development in East African History*. Berkeley: University of California Press.

Kottak, Conrad P. (1980). *The Past in the Present: History, Ecology, and Cultural Variation in Highland Madagascar*. Ann Arbor: University of Michigan Press.

Langdon, Steven (1981). *Multinational Corporations in the Political Economy of Kenya*. New York: St. Martin's Press.

Lewis, I. M. (1982, 2nd ed.). *A Pastoral Democracy: A Study of Pastoralism and Politics Among the Northern Somali of the Horn of Africa*. New York: Holmes & Meier.

Livingstone, Ian (1981). *Rural Development, Employment, and Incomes in Kenya*. Addis Ababa: ILO/JASPA.

Mamdani, Mahmood (1976). *Politics and Class Formation in Uganda*. New York: Monthly Review Press.

Mannick, A. R. (1979). *Mauritius: The Development of a Plural Society*. Nottingham, England: Spokesman Books.

McCall, Michael K. (1980). "The Diffusion of Regional Underdevelopment: Articulation of Capital and Peasantry in Sukumaland, Tanzania." Unpublished Ph.D. dissertation, Northwestern University.

Mittelman, James H. (1981). *Underdevelopment and the Transition to Socialism: Mozambique and Tanzania*. New York: Academic Press.

_____ (1976). *Ideology and Politics in Uganda. From Obote to Amin*. Ithaca, N.Y.: Cornell University Press.

Mwansasu, Bismarck U., and Pratt, Cranford, eds. (1979). *Towards Socialism in Tanzania*. Toronto: University of Toronto Press.

Ng'ang'a, D. Mukaru, et al. (1981). "Kenya: The Agrarian Question." Special issue of *Review of African Political Economy* (N.B.: its bibliography).

Obbo, Christine (1980). *African Women: Their Struggle for Economic Independence*. London: Zed Press.

O'Brien, John J. (1980). "Agricultural Labor and Development in Sudan." Unpublished Ph.D. dissertation, University of Connecticut.

Pavageau, Jean (1981). *Jeunes paysans sans terres. L'exemple malgache*. Paris: L'Harmattan.

Raikes, P. (1978). "Rural Differentiation and Class Formation in Tanzania." *Journal of Peasant Studies*, 5,3:285-325.

Research and Information Centre on Eritrea (1982). *Bibliography on Eritrea*. Rome: Research and Information Centre on Eritrea.

Resnick, Idrian (1981). *The Long Transition: Building Socialism in Tanzania*. New York: Monthly Review Press.

Rweyemamu, Justinian (1973). *Underdevelopment and Industrialization in Tanzania*. Nairobi: Oxford University Press.

Samoff, Joel (1979). "The Bureaucracy and the Bourgeoisie: Decentralization and Class Structure in Tanzania." *Comparative Studies in Society and History*, 25,1:30-62.

_____ (1974). *Tanzania: Local Politics and the Structure of Power*. Madison: University of Wisconsin Press.

Samoff, J. and R. (1976). "The Local Politics of Underdevelopment," *African Review*, 6,1:69-97.

Saul, John S. (1979). *The State and Revolution in Eastern Africa*. New York: Monthly Review Press.

Selassie, Bereket H. (1980). *Conflict and Intervention in the Horn of Africa*. New York: Monthly Review Press.

Sherman, Richard (1980). *Eritrea: The Unfinished Revolution*. New York: Praeger.

Shivji, Issa G. (1975). *Class Struggles in Tanzania*. New York: Monthly Review Press.

Simmons, Adele S. (1982). *Modern Mauritius: The Politics of Decolonization*. Bloomington: Indiana University Press.

Stichter, Sharon (1982). *Migrant Labour in Kenya: Capitalism an African Response 1895-1975*. New York: Longman.

Swainson, Nicola (1980). *The Development of Corporate Capitalism in Kenya, 1918-1977*. Berkeley: University of California Press.

Veen, J. J. de (1981). *The Rural Access Roads Programme: Appropriate Technology in Kenya*. Geneva: ILO.

Waterbury, John (1979). *Hydropolitics of the Nile Valley*. Syracuse, N.Y.: Syracuse University Press.

Zaki, Elsayed A. A. (1980). "An On-Going Evaluation of the Planning, Implementation, and Tenancy (Farm) Size of the Rahad Irrigation Project of the Sudan." Unpublished Ph.D. dissertation, Michigan State University.

_____ (1978). *Wisdom from the Nile: A Collection of Folk-Stories from Northern and Central Sudan*. Oxford: Clarendon Press.

VII.   North Africa and the Middle East

Abdalah Hanna (1978). *al-Qadiya al-zira'iya wa-l-harakat al-fallahiya fi Suriya wa Lubnan*. Beirut: (N.B.: The agricultural question and the peasant movement in Syria and Lebanon, first two of five planned volumes of a very important work.)

Abdel-Khalek, Gouda, and Tignor, Robert, eds. (1982). *The Political Economy of Income Distribution in Egypt*. New York: Holmes & Meier.

Abed, B. K. (1979). "The Social Organization of Production and Reproduction in Rural Tunisia." Unpublished Ph.D. dissertation, Pennsylvania State University.

Abrahamian, Ervand (1982). *Iran Between Two Revolutions*. Princeton, N.J.: Princeton University Press.

Abu-Lughod, Janet (1980). *Rabat: Urban Apartheid in Morocco*. Princeton, N.J.: Princeton University Press.

Algar, Hamid, ed. (1981). *Islam and Revolution: Writings and Declarations of Imam Khomeini*. Berkeley, Calif.: Mizan Press.

Ali, Ahmet (1981). *Développement économique en Turquie*. Paris: Anthropos.

Allan, J. A. (1981). *Libya: The Experience of Oil*. London: Croom Helm.

Allman, James, ed. (1978). *Women's Status and Fertility in the Muslim World*. New York: Praeger.

Al-Otaiba, Mana Saeed (1980). *Le pétrole et l'économie des Emirats arabes unis*. Paris: Hachette-Classique.

Amin, Samir (1982). *Irak et Syrie: 1960-1980*. Paris: Minuit.

_____ (1980). *L'économie arabe contemporaine*. Paris: Minuit.

'Awdi, Hammud (1980). *al-Madkhal al-ijtima'i fi dirasat al-tarikh wa-l-turath al-'Arabi*. Cairo: (Social and economic interpretation of Arab history and heritage in Yemen.)

Badillo, Dominique (1980). *Stratégies agro-alimentaires pour l'Algérie*. Paris: Edisud.

Balta, Paul, et al. (1982). *L'Algérie des Algériens, vingt ans après*. Paris: Ouvrières.

Banisadr, Abol-Hassan (1980). *Quelle révolution pour l'Iran?* Paris: Fayolle.

Batatu, Hanna (1979). *The Old Social Classes and the Revolutionary Movements of Iraq*. Princeton, N.J.: Princeton University Press.

Beck, Lois, and Keddie, Nikki, eds. (1978). *Women in the Muslim World*. Cambridge, Mass.: Harvard University Press.

Bedrani, Slimani (1982). *L'agriculture algérienne depuis 1966: Etatisation ou privatisation*. Paris: Economica.

Benhouria, Tahar (1980). *L'économie algérienne*. Paris: Maspero.

Benissad, Mohamed Elhocine (1980). *Economie du développement de l'Algérie (1962-1978): sous-développement et socialisme*. Paris: Economica.

Berberoglu, B. (1982). *Turkey in Crisis: From State Capitalism to Neocolonialism*. London: Zed Press.

Berque, Jacques (1980). *L'Islam au défi*. Paris: Gallimard.

Bertrand, Jean-Pierre, et al. (1980). *L'industrie libanaise et les marchés arabes du Golfe*. Lyon: Presses de l'Université de Lyon.

Birks, J. S., and Sinclair, C. A. (1980a). *Arab Manpower*. New York: St. Martin's Press.

____ (1980b). *International Migration and Development in the Arab Region*. Geneva: ILO.

Bruinessen, M. M. van (1978). *Agha, Shaikh and State: On the Social and Political Organization of Kurdistan*. Utrecht: University of Utrecht Press.

Cantori, Louis J., and Harik, Iliya, eds. (1981). *Local Politics and Development in the Middle East*. Boulder, Colo.: Westview Press.

Chaliand, Gerard, ed. (1980, 1978 in Fr.). *People Without a Country: The Kurds and Kurdistan*. London: Zed Press.

Chikh, Slimani (1981). *Le Maghreb et l'Afrique sub-saharienne*. Paris: CNRS.

Les classes moyennes au Maghreb (1981). Paris: CNRS.

Cohen, John M., and Lewis, David B. (1979). "Rural Development in the Yemen Arab Republic: Strategic Issues in a Capital Surplus Labor Short Economy." Cambridge, Mass.: Harvard Institute for International Development, Development Discussion Paper No. 52. (N.B.: Good bibliography of Western language material.)

Deeb, Marius K. and Mary Jane (1982). *Libya Since the Revolution: Aspects of Social and Political Development*. New York: Praeger.

DERSA (1981). *L'Algérie en débat*. Paris: Maspero, Collection Cedatim.

Dessouki, Ali E. H., ed. (1982). *Islamic Resurgence in the Arab World*. New York: Praeger.

Donohur, John J., and Esposito, John L., eds. (1982). *Islam in Transition: Muslim Perspectives*. Oxford: Oxford University Press.

Dubar, Claude, and Nasr, Salim (1976). *Les classes sociales au Liban*. Paris: Presses de FNSP.

Eickelman, Dale F. (1981). *The Middle East: An Anthropological Approach*. Englewood Cliffs, N.J.: Prentice-Hall.

Elfathaly, Omar I., et al. (1980). *Political Development and Social Change in Libya*. Farnborough, England: Gower.

—— (1978). *Political Development and Bureaucracy in Libya*. Farnborough, England: Gower.

El Mallakh, Ragaei, and Atta, Jacob K. (1982). *The Absorptive Capacity of Kuwait: Domestic and International Perspectives*. Lexington, Mass.: Lexington Books.

El Saadaoui, Naoual (1981). *Ferdaous, une voix en enfer*. Paris: Des Femmes.

El Saadewi, Nawal (1980). *The Hidden Face of Eve: Women in the Arab World*. London: Zed Press.

Esposito, John L., ed. (1980). *Islam and Development*. Syracuse, N.Y.: Syracuse University Press.

First, Ruth (1974). *Libya: The Elusive Revolution*. Harmondsworth, England: Penguin.

Fischer, Michael (1980). *Iran: From Religious Dispute to Revolution*. Cambridge, Mass.: Harvard University Press.

Frankel, William (1980). *Israel Observed: An Anatomy of the State*. London: Thames & Hudson.

Freiha, Adel A. (1980). *L'armée et l'état au Liban (1945-1980)*. Paris: Librairie Generale de Droit et de Jurisprudence.

Gangaroso, Eugene, ed. (1980). *Human Resources for Primary Health Care in the Middle East*. Beirut: American University of Beirut Press.

Gazzo, Yves (1980). *Pétrole et développement: Le cas libyen*. Paris: Economica.

Geertz, Clifford, et al. (1979). *Meaning and Order in Moroccan Society*. Cambridge: Cambridge University Press.

Gellner, E., ed. (1981). *Islam: société et communauté*. Paris: CNRS.

Gitelman, Zvi (1982). *Becoming Israelis: Political Resocialization of Soviet and American Immigrants*. New York: Praeger.

Golany, G., ed. (1979). *Arid Zone Settlement Planning: The Israeli Experience*. Oxford: Pergamon Press.

Gran, Peter (1979). *Islamic Roots of Capitalism: Egypt 1760-1840*. Austin: University of Texas Press.

Graz, Liesl (1980). *L'Irak au présent*. Paris: Trois Continents.

Haddad, Yvonne H. (1982). *Contemporary Islam and the Challenge of History*. Albany: State University of New York Press.

Haghigat, Chapour (1980). *Iran: la révolution inachevée et l'ordre américain*. Paris: Anthropos.

Halliday, Fred (1979). *Iran: Dictatorship and Development*. Harmondsworth, England: Penguin.

Hallwood, Paul, and Sinclair, Stuart (1981). *Oil, Debt, and Development: OPEC in the Third World*. London: George Allen & Unwin.

Hasen, Bent, and Radwan, Samir (1982). *Employment Opportunities and Equity in a Changing Economy: Egypt in the 1980's*. Geneva: ILO.

Hinnebusch, R. A. (1979). "Party and Peasant in Syria." *Cairo Papers in Social Science*, 3,1:1-112.

Hooglund, Eric J. (1982). *Land and Revolution in Iran, 1960-1980*. Austin: University of Texas Press.

Ibrahim, Saad Eddin (1982). *The New Arab Social Order: A Study of the Social Impact of Oil Wealth*. Boulder, Colo.: Westview Press; and London: Croom Helm.

Idris, Yusuf (1978). *The Cheapest Nights and Other Stories*. London: Owen. (N.B.: A classic on urban Egypt.)

Ikram, Khalid, et al. (1980). *Egypt: Economic Management in a Period of Transition*. Baltimore: Johns Hopkins University Press for the World Bank.

Ismael, Jacqueline (1982). *Kuwait: Social Change in Historical Perspective*. Syracuse, N.Y.: Syracuse University Press.

Karpat, Kemal H., ed. (1982, 2nd ed.). *Political and Social Thought in the Contemporary Middle East*. New York: Praeger.

Katouzian, Homa (1981). *The Political Economy of Modern Iran, 1926-1979*. New York: New York University Press.

Kazemi, Farhad (1980). *Poverty and Revolution in Iran: The Migrant Poor, Urban Marginality and Politics*. New York: New York University Press.

Keddie, Nikki R. (1981). *Roots of Revolution: An Interpretive History of Modern Iran*. New Haven, Conn.: Yale University Press.

Kerr, Malcolm H., and Yassin, El Sayed, eds. (1982). *Rich and Poor States in the Middle East: Egypt and the New Arab Order*. Boulder, Colo.: Westview Press.

Keyder, Caglar (1981). *The Definition of a Peripheral Economy: Turkey 1923-1929*. Cambridge: Cambridge University Press.

Khader, Bichara, ed. (1982). *Monde arabe et développement économique*. Paris: Le Sycomore.

Khalek, Gouda Abdel, and Tignor, Robert, eds. (1981). *Political Economy of Income Distribution in Egypt*. New York: Holmes & Meier.

Kour, Z. H. (1979). *The Development of Aden and British Relations with Neighboring Tribes, 1839-1972*. London: Frank Cass.

Lackner, Helen (1978). *A House Built on Sand: A Political Economy of Saudia Arabia*. London: Ithaca Press.

Leca, J., et al. (1979). *Développements politiques au Maghreb*. Paris: Ed du CNRS.

Lee, C. E. (1979). "Nomads, Farmers, and Migrant Labor in Southern Tunisia." Unpublished Ph.D. dissertation, University of Wisconsin.

Leveau, Remy (1976). *Le fellah marocain, défenseur du trône*. Paris: Presses de la Fondation Nationale des Sciences Politiques.

Longuenesse, Elisabeth (1977). "La classe ouvrière en Syrie, une classe en formation." Unpublished Ph.D. dissertation, René Descartes Université (Paris).

Looney, Robert E. (1982). *Saudia Arabia's Development Potential: Application of an Islamic Growth Model*. Lexington, Mass.: Lexington Books.

Mahfuz, Naguib (1973). *God's World: An Anthology of Short Stories*. Minneapolis, Minn.: Bibliotheca Islamica.

_____ (1966). *Midaq Alley Beirut: Khayats* (also 1976, Washington, D.C.: Three Continents Press). (N.B.: One of a classic trilogy on urban Egypt.)

Mali, Habib El (1978). *Surplus économique et développement, le cas de l'économie marocaine*. Paris: Cujas.

Mas, P. de (1978). *Marges marocaines: limites de la cooperation au développement dans une région peripherique: le cas du Rif*. The Hague: NUFFIC/IMWOO/REMPLOD.

Massialas, Byron, and Jarrar, Samir (1982). *Educational Issues in the Middle East*. New York: Praeger.

Mars, L. (1980). *The Village and the State: Administration, Ethnicity and Politics in an Israeli Cooperative*. Farnborough, England: Gower.

Mazur, Michael P. (1979). *Economic Growth and Development in Jordan*. Boulder, Colo.: Westview Press.

Migdal, Joel S. (1980). *Palestinian Society and Politics*. Princeton, N.J.: Princeton University Press.

Naipaul, V. S. (1981). *Among the Believers: An Islamic Journey*. New York: Random House.

Niblock, Tim, ed. (1980). *Social and Economic Development in the Arab Gulf*. London: Croom Helm.

Oualalou, Fathallah (1981). *Propos d'économie marocaine*. Paris: Soc. Marocaine des Editeurs Réunis.

Peneff, Jean (1981). *Industriels algériens*. Paris: Ed du CNRS.

Perennes, Jean-Jacques (1980). *Structures agraires et décolonisation. Les oasis de l'oued R'hir (Algérie)*. Paris: L'Harmattan.

Richards, Alan (1981). *Egypt's Agricultural Development 1800-1980: Technical and Social Change*. Boulder: Westview Press.

Rivier, François (1981). *Croissance industrielle dans une économie assistée: le cas jordanien*. Lyon: Presses Universitaires de Lyon.

_____ (1980). *Industries et politique industrielle en Egypte*. Lyon: Presses Universitaires de Lyon.

Rodinson, Maxime (1982). *Marxism and the Modern World*. New York: Monthly Review Press.

Sabagh, Georges (1981). "Demographic Research on the Middle East in the 1970s." *MESA Bulletin*, XV,2:6-27.

Said Amer, Tayeb (1982). *Le développement industriel de l'Algérie*. Paris: Anthropos.

Said, Edward (1978). *Orientalism*. New York: Pantheon.

Salamah, Adib Najib (1980). *al-kanisa fi mujtama' al-qaryah*. Cairo (Role of Coptic churches in Egyptian villages).

Samarbakhsh, A. G. (1980). *Socialisme en Irak et en Syrie*. Paris: Anthropos.

Sanasarian, Eliz (1982). *The Women's Movement in Iran: From 1900 to Today*. New York: Praeger.

Sanderson, Lilian P. (1981). *Against the Mutilation of Women: the Struggle Against Unnecessary Suffering*. London: Ithaca Press.

Sayigh, Rosemary (1979). *Palestinians: From Peasants to Revolutionaries*. London: Zed Press.

Schnetzler, Jacques (1981). *Le développement algérien*. Paris: Masson.

Seddon, David (1981). *Moroccan Peasants*. Hamden, Conn.: Archon Books.

Sharkawi, Abdel Rahman (1962). *Egyptian Earth*. London: Heinemann Educational Books. (N.B.: Classic novel of rural Egypt.)

Shoukri, Ghali (1981). *Egypt: Portrait of a President – Sadat's Road to Jerusalem*. London: Zed Press.

Sid-Ahmed, Abdelkader (1980). *L'OPEP, passé, présent et perspectives*. Paris: Economica.

Springborg, Robert (1982). *Family, Power, and Politics in Egypt: Sayad Bey Marei – His Clan, Clients, and Cohorts*. Philadelphia: University of Pennsylvania Press.

Tapper, Richard (1979). *Pasture and Politics: Economics, Conflict, and Ritual Among Shah-Sevan Nomads of Northwestern Iran*. New York: Academic Press.

Thio, K. S. (1979). *L'efficacité de la planification agricole en Tunisie*. Wageningen, Netherlands: Landbouwhogeschool.

Toumi, Mohsen (1978). *Tunisie, pouvoirs et luttes*. Paris: Le Sycomore.

Uca, Mehmet (1982). *Workers' Participation and Self-Management in Turkey: Evaluating the Past and Considering the Future*. The Hague: Institute of Social Studies, Research Report No. 13.

Van Dam, Nikolaos (1981, 2nd ed.). *The Struggle for Power in Syria: Sectarianism, Regionalism and Tribalism in Politics, 1961-1980*. London: Croom Helm.

Vieille, Paul (1975). *La féodalité et l'état en Iran*. Paris: Anthropos.

Waddams, Charles (1980). *The Libyan Oil Industry*. Baltimore, Md.: Johns Hopkins University Press.

Weekes, Richard V., ed. (1978). *Muslim Peoples: A World Ethnographic Survey*. Westport, Conn.: Greenwood Press. (N.B.: Basic bibliography.)

Westerlind, P. B. (1979). "From Farm to Factory: The Economic Development of the Kibbutz." Unpublished Ph.D. dissertation, University of California, Santa Barbara.

Wikan, Unni (1982). *Behind the Veil in Arabia: Women in Oman*. Baltimore, Md.: Johns Hopkins University Press.

____ (1980). *Life Among the Poor in Cairo*. London: Methuen.

Wilkinson, J. C. (1977). *Water and Tribal Settlement in South-East Arabia: A Study of the Aflaj of Oman*. Oxford: Clarendon Press.

Wright, John (1982). *Libya: A Modern History*. Baltimore, Md.: Johns Hopkins University Press.

Vernoux, Joseph (1981). *Iran des Mollah. La révolution introuvable*. Paris: Anthropos.

Yasar, Kemal (1974). *Iron Earth, Copper Sky*. London: Collins and Harvill. (N.B.: Premier novelist on rural Turkey.)

Yefsah, Abdelkader (1982). *Le processus de légitimation du pouvoir militaire et la construction de l'état en Algérie*. Paris: Anthropos.

Zabarah, Mohammed A. (1982). *Yemen: Traditionalist vs. Modernity*. New York: Praeger.

Zartman, L. William, et al. (1982). *Political Elites in Arab North Africa: Moroc-co, Algeria, Tunisia, Libya, and Egypt*. New York: Longman.
Zurcik, E. (1981). "Theoretical Considerations for a Sociological Study of the Arab State." *Arab Studies Quarterly*, 3,3:229-57.

VIII. South and East Asia

Ahern, Emily M., and Gates, Hill, eds. (1982). *The Anthropology of Taiwanese Society*. Stanford, Calif.: Stanford University Press.
Alexander, K. C. (1981). *Peasant Organizations in South India*. New Delhi: Indian Social Institute.
Amin, Samir (1981). *L'avenir du maoisme*. Paris: Minuit.
Anderson, Robert S., et al, eds. *Science, Politics, and the Agricultural Revolution in Asia*. Boulder, Colo.: Westview Press.
Andors, Stephen (1977). *China's Industrial Revolution: Politics, Planning, and Management, 1949 to the Present*. New York: Pantheon.
Bailleau-Lajoinie, Simone (1980). *Conditions de femmes en Afghanistan*. Paris: Editions Sociales.
Baker, Christopher J. (1982). *An Indian Rural Economy 1880-1955: The Tamilnad Countryside*. Oxford: Oxford University Press.
Banerjee, Sumanta (1981). *India's Simmering Revolution: The Naxalite Uprising*. London: Zed Press.
Barker, Randolph, and Sinha, Radha P., eds. (1982). *The Chinese Agricultural Economy*. Boulder, Colo.: Westview Press.
Barnett, A. Doak (1981). *China's Economy in Global Perspective*. Washington, D.C.: Brookings Institution.
Bhatty, Zarina (1980). *Economic Role and Status of Women: A Case Study of Women in the Beedi Industry in Allahabad*. Geneva: ILO, WEP 10/WP15.
Binswanger, Hans, et al., eds. (1980). *Rural Household Studies in Asia*. Singapore: Singapore University Press.
Blaikie, Piers, et al. (1980). *Nepal in Crisis: Growth and Stagnation at the Periphery*. Oxford: Clarendon Press.
Bliss, C. J., and Stern, N. H. (1982). *Palanpur: The Economy of an Indian Village*. London: Oxford University Press.
Chaliand, Gerard, ed. (1982). *Guerrilla Strategies: An Historical Anthology from the Long March to Afghanistan*. Berkeley: University of California Press.
Charsley, Simon (1982). *Culture and Sericulture: Social Anthropology and Development in a South Indian Livestock Industry*. New York: Academic Press.
Cheema, J. K. (1981). "Coordinative and Participative Linkages: Towards an Organizational Understanding of Constraints to Rural Development" (Punjab). Unpublished Ph.D. dissertation, University of Michigan.
Chu, Godwin C., and Hsu, Francis L. K., eds. (1979). *Moving a Mountain: Cultural Change in China*. Honolulu: University of Hawaii Press.
Committee on Scholarly Communication with the People's Republic of China (1980). *Animal Agriculture in China*. Washington, D.C.: National Academy Press.

Creevey, L. E. (1980). *Planning for Integrated Rural Development: Community Shops in Sri Lanka*. Philadelphia: University of Pennsylvania Press.

Croll, Elizabeth (1982). *The Family Rice Bowl: Food and the Domestic Economy in China*. Geneva: UNRISD.

Dasgupta, Biplab (1977). *Agrarian Change and the New Technology in India*. Geneva: UNRISD.

Day, Richard H., and Singh, Indeijit (1977). *Economic Development as an Adaptive Process: The Green Revolution in the Indian Punjab*. Cambridge: Cambridge University Press.

Delloye, Isabelle (1981). *Des femmes d'Afghanistan*. Paris: Des Femmes.

Dhanagare, D. N. (1982). *Peasant Movements in India, 1920-1950*. Oxford: Oxford University Press.

Dixon, John (1981). *The Chinese Welfare System*. New York: Praeger.

Dupree, Louis (1980). *Afghanistan*. Princeton, N.J.: Princeton University Press.

Dutt, Ashok K., and Noble, Allan G., eds. (1982). *India: Cultural Patterns and Processes*. Boulder, Colo.: Westview Press.

Etienne, Gilbert (1978). *Progrès agricole et maitrise de l'eau: le cas du Pakistan*. Paris: PUF.

Faaland, Just, ed. (1980). *Aid and Influence: The Case of Bangladesh*. New York: St. Martin's Press.

Farmer, B. H., ed. (1980). *Green Revolution? Technology and Change in Rice-Growing Areas of Tamil Nadu and Sri Lanka*. London: Macmillan.

Fei, John C. H., et al. (1980). *Growth with Equity: The Taiwan Case*. New York: Oxford University Press for the World Bank.

Franda, Marcus (1979). *Small is Politics: Organizational Alternatives in India's Rural Development*. New York: John Wiley & Sons.

Frankel, Francine (1978). *India's Political Economy, 1947-1977*. Princeton, N.J.: Princeton University Press.

Fürer-Haimendorf, Christoph von (1982). *Tribes of India: The Struggle for Survival*. Berkeley: University of California Press.

Gaborieau, Marc (1978). *Le Népal et ses populations*. Bruxelles: Editions Complexes.

Gardezi, H., and Rashid, J. (1982). *The Political Economy of Pakistan: Readings in Dependence*. London: Zed Press.

Gough, Kathleen (1982). *Rural Society in Southeast India*. Cambridge: Cambridge University Press.

Gray, J., and White, G. (1982). *China's New Development Strategy*. New York: Academic Press.

Griffin, Keith, and Saith, Ashwani (1982). *Growth and Equality in Rural China*. Geneva: ILO.

Gunatilleke, Godfrey, et al., eds. (1982). *Ethical Dimensions of Development in Asia*. Lexington, Mass.: Lexington Books.

Hameed, N. D. Abdul, et al. (1977). *Rice Revolution in Sri Lanka*. Geneva: UNRISD.

Harding, Harry (1982). *Organizing China: The Problem of Bureaucracy 1949-1976*. Stanford, Calif.: Stanford University Press.

Hardt, John, ed. (1978). *Chinese Economy Post-Mao: A Compendium of Papers*. Washington, D.C.: Government Printing Office. (N.B.: A Joint Economic Committee publication once every three to four years.)

Hariss, John (1981). *Capitalism and Peasant Farming: Agrarian Structure and Ideology in Northern Tamil Nadu*. Oxford: Oxford University Press.

Hartmann, Betsy, and Boyce, James (1979). *Needless Hunger: Voices from a Bangladesh Village*. San Francisco, Calif.: Institute for Food and Development Policy.

Harzard, B. P. (1981). *Peasant Organization and Peasant Individualism: Land Reform, Cooperation, and the Chinese Communist Party*. Bielefelder Studien des Entwicklungssoziologie No. 14. Saarbrucken: Verlag Breitenbach.

Hawkins, John, ed. (1982). *Education and Social Change in the People's Republic of China*. New York: Praeger.

Hayami, Yujiro, et al., eds. (1979). *Agricultural Growth in Japan, Taiwan, Korea, and the Philippines*. Honolulu: University of Hawaii Press.

Hinton, William (1966). *Fanshen: A Documentary of Revolution in a Chinese Village*. New York: Random House.

Hossain, M. (1981). *Conscientizing Rural Disadvantaged Peasants in Bangladesh: Intervention Through Group Action; a Case Study of Proshika*. Dacca: Civil Officers' Training Academy.

Hossain, Monowar, et al. (1981). *Rural Industries Study Project – Final Report*. Dacca: Bangladesh Institute of Development Studies.

Hsiung, James C. (1981). *Contemporary Republic of China: The Taiwan Experience 1950-1980*. New York: Praeger.

Huang Shu-Min (1982). *Agricultural Degradation: Changing Community Systems in Rural Taiwan*. Washington, D.C.: University Press of America.

Jahan, Rounaq, and Papanek, Hanna, eds. (1979). *Women and Development: Perspectives from South and Southeast Asia*. Dacca: Bangladesh Institute of Law and International Affairs.

Juergensmeyer, Mark (1982). *Religion as Social Vision: The Movement Against Untouchability in 20th-Century Punjab*. Berkeley: University of California Press.

Kantowski, Detlef (1980). *Sarvodaya: The Other Development*. Delhi: Vikas.

Khan, A. R. (1978). *The Comilla Model and the Integrated Rural Development Programme of Bangladesh: An Experiment in "Co-operative Capitalism."* Geneva: ILO, WEP10-6/WP20.

Kim, Han-Kyo, ed. (1980). *Studies on Korea. A Scholar's Guide*. Honolulu: University of Hawaii Press.

Kumar, Dharma, and Desai, Meghnad (1982). *The Cambridge Economic History of India, Vol. 2: 1751-c1970*. Cambridge: Cambridge University Press.

Kurian, Rachel (1981). *The Position of Women Workers in the Plantation Sector in Sri Lanka*. Geneva: ILO, WEP 10/WP18.

Lele, Jayant (1982). *Elite Pluralism and Class Rule: Political Development in Maharashtra, India*. Toronto: University of Toronto Press.

Lucas, AnElissa (1982). *Chinese Medical Modernization: Policy Continuity Across Revolutionary Periods*. New York: Praeger.

Maclachlan, Morgan D. (1982). *Why They Did Not Starve: Biocultural Adaption in a South Indian Village*. Philadelphia: ISHI.

Mahmud, Wahiduddin, ed. (1981). *Development Issues in an Agrarian Economy – Bangladesh*. Dacca: Center for Administrative Studies.

Mies, Maria (1982). *The Lacemakers of Narsapur: Indian Housewives in the World Market*. London: Zed Press.

Misra, B. D., et al. (1982). *Organization for Change: A System Analysis of Family Planning in Rural India*. Ann Arbor: University of Michigan Press.

Moulder, Frances V. (1977). *Japan, China and the Modern World Economy*. Cambridge: Cambridge University Press.

Nafziger, E. Wayne (1978). *Class, Caste, and Entrepreneurship: A Study of Indian Industrialists*. Honolulu: University of Hawaii Press.

Nossiter, T. J. (1982). *Communism in Kerala*. Berkeley: University of California Press.

O'Connor, Ronald W., ed. (1980). *Managing Health Systems in Developing Areas: Experiences from Afghanistan*. Lexington, Mass.: Lexington Books.

Okhawa, Kazushi, and Key, Bernard, eds. (1981). *Asian Socioeconomic Development: A National Accounts Approach*. Honolulu: University of Hawaii Press.

Ozama, Terutomo (1979). *Multinationalism, Japanese Style*. Princeton: N.J.: Princeton University Press.

Park, Chong Kee, ed. (1981a). *Essays on the Korean Economy – Volume III Macroeconomic and Industrial Development in Korea*. Honolulu: University of Hawaii Press.

_____ (1981b). *Essays on the Korean Economy – Volume IV: Human Resources and Social Development*. Honolulu: University of Hawaii Press.

Perkins, Dwight (1977). *Rural Small-Scale Industry in the People's Republic of China*. Berkeley: University of California Press.

Plucknett, Donald L., and Beemer, Halsey L., eds. (1981). *Vegetable Farming Systems in the People's Republic of China*. Boulder, Colo.: Westview Press.

Ponnambalam, Sutchi (1980). *Dependent Capitalism in Crisis: The Sri Lankan Economy 1948-1980*. London: Zed Press.

Raychaudhuri, Tapan, and Habib, Irfan, eds. (1982). *The Cambridge Economic History of India, Volume I: c1200-c1750*. Cambridge: Cambridge University Press.

Richard, Peter, and Gooneratne, Wibert (1981). *Basic Needs, Poverty, and Government Policies in Sri Lanka*. Geneva: ILO.

Rix, Alan (1980). *Japan's Economic Aid*. New York: St. Martin's Press.

Rudra, Ashok (1981). *The Basic Needs Concept and Its Implementation in Indian Development Planning*. Bangkok: ILO/ARTEP.

Sayeed, Khalid B. (1980). *Politics in Pakistan: The Nature and Direction of Change*. New York: Praeger.

Schendel, Willem van (1981). *Peasant Mobility: The Odds of Life in Rural Bangladesh*. Assen, The Netherlands: Van Gorcum.

Schregle, Johannes (1982). *Labour Relations and Development in Southern Asia: Problems and Prospects*. Geneva: ILO.

Schurmann, Franz (1968). *Ideology and Organization in Communist China*. Berkeley: University of California Press.

Sebstad, Jennifer (1982). *Struggle and Development Among Self-Employed Women: A Report on the Self-Employed Women's Association Ahmedabad, India*. Washington: AID, DSB, Office of Urban Development.

Selden, Mark (1981). "The Inner Logic of Chinese Development." *Review*, 5,3:487-503.

Selden, Mark, and Lippitt, Victor, eds. (1982). *The Transition to Socialism in China*. Armonk, N.Y.: M. E. Sharpe.

Sen, Anupam (1982). *The State, Industrialization and Class Formations in India: A Neo-Marxist Perspective on Colonialism, Underdevelopment and Development*. London: Routledge & Kegan Paul.

Shirk, Susan L. (1982). *Competitive Comrades: Career Incentives and Student Strategies in China*. Berkeley: University of California Press.

Shue, Vivienne (1980). *Peasant China in Transition: The Dynamics of Development Toward Socialism 1949-1956*. Berkeley: University of California Press.

Silva, K. M. de (1982). *A History of Sri Lanka*. Berkeley: University of California Press.

Silva, S. D. B. de (1982). *The Political Economy of Underdevelopment* (South Asia focus). London: Routeldge & Kegan Paul.

Simon, Denis F. (1982). *Taiwan, Technology Transfer, and Transnationalism: The Political Management of Dependency*. Boulder, Colo.: Westview Press.

Skjonsberg, Else (1982). *A Special Caste? Village Women in Sri Lanka*. London: Zed Press.

Sobhan, Rehman, and Ahmad, Muzaffer (1981). *Public Enterprise in an Intermediate Regime: A Study in the Political Economy of Bangladesh*. London: Zed Press.

Somjee, A. H. (1979). *The Democratic Process in a Developing Society*. London: Macmillan.

Srinivas, M. N. (1976). *The Remembered Village*. Berkeley: University of California Press.

Stavis, Benedict (1978). *The Politics of Agricultural Mechanization*. Ithaca, N.Y.: Cornell University Press.

Stevens, Robert D., et al., eds. (1976). *Rural Development in Bangladesh and Pakistan*. Honolulu: University of Hawaii Press.

Stokes, Eric (1978). *The Peasant and the Raj: Studies in Agrarian Society and Peasant Rebellion in Colonial India*. Cambridge: Cambridge University Press.

Tissier, Patrick (1978). *L'education en Chine Populaire*. Paris: Maspero.

――― (1976). *La Chine: transformations rurales et développement socialiste*. Paris: Maspero.

United Nations/ESCAP (1982). *Food Supply and Distribution in Asia and the Pacific: Medium-Term Outlook and Regional Co-operation*. Bangkok: UN/ESCAP, E/ESCAP/246.

Vohra, Dewan C. (1980). *India's Aid Diplomacy in the Third World*. New Delhi: Vikas.

Vylder, Stephen de (1982). *Agriculture in Chains: Bangladesh – A Case Study in Contradictions and Constraints*. London: Zed Press.

Wade, Robert (1981). *Irrigation and Agricultural Politics in South Korea*. Boulder, Colo.: Westview Press.

Whyte, Robert, and Orr, Pauline (1982). *The Women of Rural Asia*. Boulder, Colo.: Westview Press.

Wilson, Richard W., et al., eds. (1982). *Moral Behavior in Chinese Society*. New York: Praeger.

____ (1979). *Value Change in Chinese Society*. New York: Praeger.

Xue Muqiao (1982). *Problemes économique du socialisme en Chine*. Peking: Editions en Langues Étrangères.

Yang, Martin M. C. (1970). *Socio-Economic Results of Land Reform in Taiwan*. Honolulu: University of Hawaii Press.

Zeidenstein, Sondra, and Abdullah, Tahrunnessa (1981). *Village Women of Bangladesh*. Oxford: Pergamon Press. (N.B.: This is No. 4 of a Pergamon series on women in development in South Asia.)

IX.   Southeast Asia and the Pacific

Afendras, Evangelos, and Kuo, Eddie, eds. (1980). *Language and Society in Singapore*. Singapore: Singapore University Press.

Allen, M. R., ed. (1982). *Vanuatu: Politics, Economics, and Ritual in Island Melanesia*. New York: Academic Press.

Amarshi, Azeem, et al. (1979). *Development and Dependency: The Political Economy of Papua New Guinea*. Melbourne: Oxford University Press.

Anand, R. P., and Quisumbing, Purificacion V., eds. (1981). *ASEAN: Identity, Development, and Culture*. Honolulu: University of Hawaii Press.

Anderson, Benedict (1978). "The Study of the Thai State: The State of Thai Studies," in Ayal, Eliezer, ed. *The Study of Thailand: Analyses of Knowledge, Approaches, and Prospects in Anthropology, Art History, Economics, History, and Political Science*. Athens, Ohio: Ohio University, Center for International Studies.

Asian Development Bank (1978). *Rural Asia: Challenge and Opportunity*. New York: Praeger.

Banks, David J. (1982). *Malay Kinship*. Philadelphia: ISHI.

Barnett, Anthony (1982). *The Cambodian Revolutions*. New York: Schocken Books.

Bello, Walden, et al. (1982). *Development Debacle: The World Bank in the Philippines*. San Francisco: Institute for Food and Development Policy.

Bhati, U. N. (1976). *Some Social and Economic Aspects of the Introduction of New Varieties of Paddy in Malaysia*. Geneva: UNRISD.

Booth, Anne, and McCawley, Peter, eds. (1982). *The Indonesian Economy During the Soeharto Era*. New York: Oxford University Press.

Castillo, G. T. (1979). *Beyond Manilla: Philippine Rural Problems in Perspective.* Ottawa: International Development Research Centre.

Collier, William L. (1976). *Agricultural Evolution in Java: Decline of Shared Poverty.* Bogor, Indonesia: Indonesian Agro-Economic Survey.

Condominas, George (1982). *L'Espace social à propos de l'Asie du Sud-Est.* Paris: Flammarion.

Corrèze, Françoise (1982). *Vietnamiennes au quotidien.* Paris: L'Harmattan.

Coward, E. Walter, ed. (1980). *Irrigation and Agricultural Development in Asia.* Ithaca, N.Y.: Cornell University Press.

DeKoninck, Rodolphe (1979). "The Integration of the Peasantry: Examples from Malaysia and Indonesia." *Pacific Affairs*, 52,2:265-91.

Deyo, Frederic C. (1981). *Dependent Development and Industrial Order: An Asian Case Study.* New York: Praeger.

Doré, Amphay (1980). *Le partage du mékong.* Paris: Encre.

Dulykasem, Uthai (1981). "Education and Ethnic Nationalism: A Study of the Muslim-Malays in Southern Thailand." Unpublished Ph.D. dissertation, Stanford University.

Eder, James (1982). *Who Shall Succeed? Agricultural Development and Social Inequality on a Philippine Frontier.* Cambridge: Cambridge University Press.

Elliott, David W. P., ed. (1981). *The Third Indochina Conflict.* Boulder, Colo.: Westview Press.

Elliott, David (1978). *Thailand: Origins of Military Rule.* London: Zed Press.

——— (1976). "Revolutionary Reintegration: A Comparison of the Foundation of Post-Liberation Political Systems in North Vietnam and China." Unpublished Ph.D. dissertation, Cornell University.

Feeny, David H. (1982). *The Political Economy of Productivity: Thai Agricultural Development.* Vancouver: University of British Columbia Press.

Fisk, E. K., and Rani, Osman, eds. (1982). *The Political Economy of Malaysia.* Oxford: Oxford University Press.

Forest, Alain (1980). *Le Cambodge et la colonisation francaise: Histoire d'une colonisation sans heurts.* Paris: L'Harmattan.

Fujimoto, A. A. (1982). *Land Tenure and Income Sharing among Malay Peasants.* Singapore: Singapore University Press.

Geertz, Clifford (1963). *Agricultural Involution: The Processes of Ecological Change in Indonesia.* Berkeley: University of California Press.

Gibbons, David S., et al. (1980). *Agricultural Modernization, Poverty, and Inequality: The Distributional Impact of the Green Revolution in Regions of Malaysia and Indonesia.* Farnborough, England: Saxon House.

Golay, Frank H., et al. (1969). *Underdevelopment and Economic Nationalism in Southeast Asia.* Ithaca, N.Y.: Cornell University Press.

Gran, Guy (1979). "Vietnam in Pursuit of Development: Socialist Promise, Natural Calamities, and Permanent Learning." *Cultures et développement*, XI,2:261-81.

——— (1975). "Vietnam and the Capitalist Route to Modernity: Village Cochinchina, 1880-1940." Unpublished Ph.D. dissertation, University of Wisconsin.

——— (1974). *Vietnam: The Human Costs of the American Aid Program.* Washington, D.C.: Indochina Resource Center.

Grijpstra, Bouwe (1976). *Common Efforts in the Development of Rural Sarawak, Malaysia*. Assen, Netherlands: Vangorcum.

Hall, D. G. E. (1981, 4th ed.). *A History of South East Asia*. New York: St. Martin's Press.

Hart, Gillian (1978). "Labour Allocation Strategies in Rural Javanese Households." Unpublished Ph.D. dissertation, Cornell University.

Hasan, Parves (1978). "Economic Perspectives on Southeast Asia and East Asia." Washington: IBRD discussion paper, unpublished.

Hayami, Yujiro, and Kikuchi, Masao (1982). *Asian Village Economy at the Crossroads: An Economic Approach to Institutional Change*. Baltimore, Md.: Johns Hopkins University Press.

Hodgkin, Thomas (1981). *Vietnam: The Revolutionary Path*. New York: St. Martin's Press.

Houtart, François, and Lemercinier, Genevieve (1982). *Sociologie d'une commune vietnamienne*. Paris: L'Harmattan and C.R.S.R., Université Catholique de Louvain.

Husken, Frans (1979). "Landlords, Sharecroppers, and Agricultural Labourers: Changing Labour Relations in Rural Java." *Journal of Contemporary Asia*, 9,2:140-51.

Indochina Resource Center (1980). "Thailand Plays the Great Power Game." *Southeast Asia Chronicle*, 69:1-32. (N.B.: Sample country focus of its ongoing publication.)

International Agrarian Studies Group – Asia (IASG) (1979). "Report on Thailand." Bangkok: IASG for the FAO 1979 conference in Rome.

Jackson, Karl D., and Pye, Lucian W., eds. (1978). *Political Power and Communication in Indonesia*. Berkeley: University of California Press.

Joliffe, Jill (1979). *East Timor: Nationalism and Colonialism*. Brisbane: University of Queensland Press.

Jomo, K. S. (1983). *Class Formation in Malaysia: Capital, the State, and Uneven Development*. Kuala Lumpur: Oxford University Press.

Kahn, Joel S. (1982). "From Peasants to Petty Commodity Production in Southeast Asia." *Bulletin of Concerned Asian Scholars*, 14,1:3-15.

Kattenburg, Paul M. (1981). *The Vietnam Trauma in American Foreign Policy, 1945-1975*. New Brunswick, N.J.: Transaction Books.

Kerkvliet, Benedict (1977). *The Huk Rebellion: A Study of Peasant Revolt in the Philippines*. Berkeley: University of California Press.

Kiernan, Ben, ed. (1982). *Peasants and Politics in Kampuchea, 1942-1980*. Armonk, N.Y.: M. E. Sharpe.

Kunstadter, Peter, et al., eds. (1978). *Farmers in the Forest: Economic Development and Marginal Agriculture in Northern Thailand*. Honolulu: University of Hawaii Press.

Leenhardt, Maurice (1979; 1947 in Fr.). *Do Kamo: Person and Myth in the Melanesian World*. Chicago: University of Chicago Press.

Le Thanh Khoi (1978). *Socialisme et développement au Vietnam*. Paris: PUF.

MacAndrews, Colin, and Chia Lin Sien, eds. (1982). *Too Rapid Rural Development: Perceptions and Perspectives from Southeast Asia*. Athens, Ohio: Ohio University Press.

MacDougall, J. (1975). "Technocrats as Modernizers: the Economists of Indonesia's New Order." Unpublished Ph.D. dissertation, University of Michigan.

McCoy, Alfred W., and de Jesus, Edilberto, eds. (1982). *Philippine Social History: Global Trade and Local Transformations.* Honolulu: University of Hawaii Press.

McDonald, Hamish (1981). *Suharto's Indonesia.* Honolulu: University of Hawaii Press.

McFarlane, Bruce, ed. (1979). *A Political Economy of S.E. Asia in the 1980's* (A 1979 Stockholm Conference). Adelaide, Australia: Veriken Press.

McMichael, Joan, ed. (1976). *Health Care for the People: Studies from Vietnam.* Nottingham, England: Spokesman Books.

Marr, David G. (1981). *Vietnamese Anticolonialism 1885-1925.* Berkeley: University of California Press.

—— (1971). *Vietnamese Tradition on Trial, 1920-1945.* Berkeley: University of California Press.

Meesook, Oey Astra (1979). "Income, Consumption and Poverty in Thailand, 1962/3 to 1975/6." Washington: World Bank, Staff Working Paper 364.

Morrell, David, and Samudavanija, Chai-anan (1980). *Political Conflict in Thailand: Reform, Reaction, Revolution.* Cambridge, Mass.: Oelgeschlager, Gunn & Hain.

Multatuli (1982). *Max Havelaar: or the Coffee Auctions of the Dutch Trading Company.* Amherst: University of Massachusetts Press.

Murray, Charles A. (1977). *A Behavioral Study of Rural Modernization: Social and Economic Change in a Thai Village.* New York: Praeger.

Mus, Paul (1952). *Viet-Nam: Sociologie d'une guerre.* Paris: Seuil.

Owen, Norman (1983). *Prosperity Without Progress: Manila Hemp and Material Life in the Colonial Philippines.* Berkeley: University of California Press.

Palmer, Ingrid (1978). *The Indonesian Economy Since 1965.* London: Frank Cass.

—— (1977). *The New Rice in Indonesia.* Geneva: UNRISD.

—— (1976). *The New Rice in Asia.* Geneva: UNRISD.

—— (1975). *The New Rice in the Philippines.* Geneva: UNRISD.

Peluso, Nancy Lee (1981). *Survival Strategies of Rural Women Traders or a Woman's Place Is in the Market: Four Case Studies from Northwestern Sleman in the Special Region of Yogyakarta.* Geneva: ILO, WEP 10/WP17.

Permtanjit, Grit (1981). "Political Economy of Capitalist Development: Study of the Limits of the Capacity of the State to Rationalize in Thailand." Unpublished Ph.D. dissertation, University of Pennsylvania.

Phongparchit, Pasuk (1980). *Rural Women of Thailand: From Peasant Girls to Bangkok Masseuses.* Geneva: ILO, WEP 10/WP14.

Porter, Gareth D. (1976). "Imperialism and Social Structure in Twentieth Century Vietnam." Unpublished Ph.D. dissertation, Cornell University.

Popkin, Samuel (1979). *The Rational Peasant: The Political Economy of Rural Society in Vietnam.* Berkeley: University of California Press.

Quiminal, Catherine (1982). *"Le Kampuchea": Viet-Nam – Cambodge, guerre et indépendance.* Paris: Anthropos.

Rosenberg, David A., ed. (1979). *Marcos and Martial Law in the Philippines*. Ithaca, N.Y.: Cornell University Press.

Scott, James (1976). *The Moral Economy of the Peasant: Rebellion and Subsistence in Southeast Asia*. New Haven, Conn.: Yale University Press.

Sivaraksa, Sulak (1980). *Siam in Crisis*. Bangkok: Komol Keemthong Foundation.

Silverstein, Josef (1980). *Burmese Politics*. New Brunswick, N.J.: Rutgers University Press.

Spiro, Melford E. (1970, 1982). *Buddhism and Society: A Great Tradition and Its Burmese Vicissitudes*. Berkeley: University of California Press.

Steinberg, David (1982). *Burma's Road Toward Development: Growth and Ideology Under Military Rule*. Boulder, Colo.: Westview Press.

Steinberg, David J., et al. (1971). *In Search of Southeast Asia: A Modern History*. New York: Praeger.

Strange, Heather (1981). *Rural Malay Women in Tradition and Transition*. New York: Praeger.

Trullinger, James W. (1980). *Village at War: An Account of Revolution in Vietnam*. New York: Longman.

Turton, Andrew, et al. (1978). *Thailand: Roots of Conflict*. London: Spokesman Books.

Weinstein, Franklin B. (1976). *Indonesian Foreign Policy and the Dilemma of Dependence*. Ithaca, N.Y.: Cornell University Press.

Wertheim, William F. (1964). *East-West Parallels: Sociological Approaches to Modern Asia*. The Hague: Van Hoeve.

_____ (1959, 2nd ed.). *Indonesian Society in Transition*. The Hague: Van Hoeve.

Westermeyer, Joseph (1982). *Poppies, Pipes, and People: Opium and Its Use in Laos*. Berkeley: University of California Press.

Williams, Colen and Satato (1980). "Socio-Political Constraints on Primary Health Care: A Case Study from Java." *Development Dialogue*, 1:85-101.

Young, Kevin, et al. (1980). *Malaysia: Growth and Equity in a Multiracial Society*. Baltimore, Md.: Johns Hopkins University Press for the World Bank.

X. Development Reference Guides

Agency for International Development, Bureau for Technical Assistance (1976-77). *Research Literature for Development*. 2 volumes. Washington: AID. (Listing of AID contract reports.)

Altbach, Philip G., et al. (1982). *International Bibliography of Comparative Education*. New York: Praeger.

Altbach, Philip G., and Rathgeber, Eva-Maria (1980). *Publishing in the Third World: Trend Report and Bibliography*. New York: Praeger.

America in Asia: Research Guides on United States Economics in Pacific Asia (1979). Hong Kong: Asia/North American Communications Center.

Anderson, T. J., ed. (1980). *Land Tenure and Agrarian Reform in East and Southeast Aisa: An Annotated Bibliography*. Boston: G. K. Hall.

Ball, Nicole (1981). *World Hunger: A Guide to the Economic and Political Dimensions*. Oxford: Clio Press.

Barr, Kenneth (1979). "Long Waves: A Selective Annotated Bibliography." *Review*, II,4:675-718.

Bechtel, Rosanna M. (1980). *Salus: Low-Cost Rural Health Care and Health Manpower Training. An Annotated Bibliography with Special Emphasis on Developing Countries*. Ottawa: International Development Research Centre. (N.B.: This is No. 5 of *the* annual reference guide for health development literature.)

Benya, Larry, et al. (1977). *Managing Decentralization: An Annotated Bibliography*. Syracuse, N.Y.: Maxwell Training and Development Programs, Syracuse University.

Bergquist, Charles W. (1979). *Alternative Approaches to the Problem of Development: A Selected and Annotated Bibliography*. Durham, N.C.: Carolina Academic Press.

Beudot, Françoise (1976-80). *Elements for a Bibliography of the Sahel Drought*. 5 volumes and 2,217 citations. Paris: OECD.

Blanchard, J. Richard, and Farrell, Lois, eds. (1981). *Guide to Sources for Agricultural and Biological Research*. Berkeley: University of California Press.

Bloomfield, B. C., ed. (1980). *Middle East Studies and Libraries*. London: Mansell.

Borremans, Valentina (1979). *Guide to Convivial Tools*. New York: R. R. Bowker Co. (Library Journal Special Report No. 13.)

Brownstone, David, and Gorton, Carruth (1982, 2nd ed.). *Where to Find Business Information*. New York: John Wiley & Sons.

Butenschøn, C. A., ed. (1981). *Norwegian Development Research Catalogue*. Fantoft, Norway: Christian Michelsen's Institute for Science and Intellectual Freedom, Dept. of Social Science and Development.

Cadett, Melissa L. (1981). *Food Aid and Policy for Economic Development: An Annotated Bibliography and Directory*. Sacramento, Calif.: Trans. Tech. Management Press.

Cohen, John M., et al. (1978). *Participation at the Local Level: A Working Bibliography*. Ithaca, N.Y.: Cornell University, Rural Development Committee, Bibliography Series No. 1.

Cordeiro, Daniel R. (1979). *A Bibliography of Latin American Bibliographies: Social Sciences and Humanities*. Metuchen, N.J.: Scarecrow Press.

Cox, Robert W. (1979). "Ideologies and the New International Economic Order: Reflections on Some Recent Literature." *International Organization*, 33, 2:257-302.

Currey, Bruce, et al. (1981). *Famine: A First Bibliography*. Westport, Conn.: Greenwood.

Curutchet, Mirina (1981). *Draft Bibliography on Human Settlement: Volume 1 Developing Countries with Emphasis on Eastern Africa*. Lund: University of Lund, Dept of Building Function Analysis, Working Paper No. 1.

Cyriax, G. R. (1981). *World Index of Economic Forecasts*. New York: Facts on File.

Darrow, Ken, et al. (1981). *Appropriate Technology Sourcebook, Volume II*. Stanford, Calif.: Volunteers in Asia.

―― (1977). *Appropriate Technology Sourcebook, Volume I*. Stanford, Calif.: Volunteers in Asia.

Delancey, Mark W. (1981). *African International Relations: An Annotated Bibliography*. Boulder, Colo.: Westview Press.

Delorme, Robert L. (1981). *Latin America: Social Science Information Sources: 1967-1979*. Santa Barbara, Calif.: ABC-Clio.

Dimitrov, D., ed. (1981). *World Bibliography of International Documentation. Volume 1. International Organizations. Volume 2. Politics and World Affairs*. Pleasantville, N.Y.: UNIFO.

Diwan, Romesh K., and Livingston, Dennis (1979). *Alternative Development Strategies and Appropriate Technology: Science Policy for an Equitable World Order*. Elmsford, N.Y.: Pergamon Press.

Feller, Gordon, et al., eds. (1981, 3rd ed.). *Peace and World Order Studies: A Curriculum Guide*. New York: Institute for World Order, Transnational Academic Program.

Fortmann, Louise (1979). *Tillers of the Soil and Keepers of the Hearth: A Bibliographic Guide to Women and Rural Development*. Ithaca, N.Y.: Cornell University, Rural Development Committee.

Garcia-Bouza, Jorge (1980). *A Basic-Needs Analytical Bibliography*. Paris: OECD.

Gaudier, Maryse (1980). *Les besoins essentieles, bibliographie analytique/Basic Needs, Analytical Bibliography*. Geneva: Institut International d'Etudes Sociales.

Gellar, Sheldon (1981). "Planning, Management, and Participatory Development Issues in Irrigation Projects: A Select Annotated Bibliography." Paris: CILSS and OECD.

―― (1982). *Development by and for the People: A Select Annotated Bibliographical Guide to Participatory Development Issues*. Paris: Club de Sahel CILSS.

Gleditsch, N. P., et al., eds. (1980). *Johan Galtung: A Bibliography of His Scholarly and Popular Writings*. Oslo: International Peace Research Institute.

Graham, Ann H., and Woods, Richard D. (1981). *Latin America in English-Language Reference Books: A Selected, Annotated Guide*. New York: Special Libraries Association.

Grimwood-Jones, Diana (1979, 2nd ed.). *Middle East and Islam: A Bibliographical Introduction*. Zug, Switzerland: Inter Documentation.

Hale, P. R., and Williams, B. D., eds. (1977). *Liklik Buk: A Rural Development Handbook Catalogue for Papua New Guinea*. Wewak, Papua New Guinea: Wirui Press.

Holdcroft, Lane E. (1977). *The Rise and Fall of Community Development in Developing Countries, 1950-65: A Critical Analysis and an Annotated Bibliography*. East Lansing: Michigan State University, Department of Agricultural Economics.

ILO (1981). *Guide to Tools and Equipment for Labour Based Road Construction*. Geneva: ILO.

International Land Development Consultants (Arnhem, Netherlands) (1981). *Agricultural Compendium for Rural Development in the Tropics and Subtropics*. Amsterdam: Elsevier.

Ives, Jane H., and Ashford, Nicholas A., eds. (1981). *International Occupational Safety and Health Resource Catalogue*. New York: Praeger.

Jacquemot, P., ed. (1981). *Economie et sociologie du Tiers-monde: Un guide bibliographique et documentaire*. Paris: L'Harmattan.

Kirchbach, Friedrich von (1980). *Annotated Bibliography on Transnational Corporations in the ASEAN Area*. Bangkok: UN/ESCAP, Joint CTC/ESCAP Unit on TNC's, Working Paper No. 10. (N.B.: Other papers in this important ongoing series are focussed on specific countries and industries.)

Kubr, Milan, and Vernon, Ken (1981, 2nd ed.). *Management, Administration, and Productivity: International Directory of Institutions and Information Sources*. Geneva: ILO.

Lambert, Claire M., ed. (1978). *Village Studies: Data Analysis and Bibliography*. London: Mansell for the University of Sussex, Institute of Development Studies. (N.B.: Volume 1 covers India 1950-1975; Volume 2 covers the rest of the Third World 1950-1975. Both are partially annotated.)

Lifchitz, Edgardo (1980). *Bibliografia analitica sobre empresas transnacionales/ Analytical Bibliography on Transnational Corporations*. Mexico: ILET.

Lipnack, Jessica, and Stamps, Jeffrey (1982). *Networking: The First Report and Directory*. Garden City, N.Y.: Doubleday. (N.B.: The New Age/social change movement in the U.S.)

Marien, Michael, ed. (1982). *Future Survey Annual 1980-81*. Washington, D.C.: World Future Society.

Meghdessian, Samira R. (1980). *The Status of the Arab Woman: A Select Bibliography*. Westport, Conn.: Greenwood.

Nicholas, David (1981). *The Middle East – Its Oil, Economics and Investment Policies: A Guide to Sources of Financial Information*. London: Mansell.

Nunn, G. Raymond (1980). *Asia: Reference Works; A Select Annotated Guide*. London: Mansell.

O'Connor, Anthony M. (1981). *Urbanization in Tropical Africa: An Annotated Bibliography*. Boston: G. K. Hall.

OECD (1981). *Directory of Non-Governmental Organizations in OECD Member Countries Active in Development Cooperation*. Paris: OECD.

Palme, Gabriel (1978). "Dependency: A Formal Theory of Underdevelopment or a Methodology for the Analysis of Concrete Situations of Underdevelopment." *World Development*, 6,7/8:881-924.

Patterson, Maureen (1982). *South Asian Civilization: A Bibliographic Synthesis*. Chicago: University of Chicago Press.

Paulston, Rolland G. (1978). *Changing Educational Systems: A Review of Theory and Experience*. Washington: IBRD.

Research Centre for Cooperation with Developing Countries (1980). *Economic Cooperation and Integration Among Developing Countries: A Select Annotated Bibliography*. Ljublana, Yugoslavia.

Rondinelli, Dennis A., and Palia, Aspy (1976). *Development Planning and Implementation in Developing Countries*. Honolulu: East-West Technology and

Development Institute, East-West Center.

Sable, Martin H. (1981). *The Latin American Studies Directory*. Detroit, Mich.: Blaine Ethridge Books.

Saito, Shiro, et al. (1979). *Southeast Asia Research Tools*. 9 volumes. Honolulu: University of Hawaii, Asian Studies Program.

Savary, Julien (1982). *Les multinationales francaises*. Paris: PUF.

Sheehy, Eugene P., ed. (1980, 9th ed.). *Guide to Reference Books – Supplement*. Chicago: American Library Association.

_____ (1976, 9th ed.). *Guide to Reference Books*. Chicago: American Library Association.

Singer, Philip, and Titus, Elizabeth (1980). *Resources for Third World Health Planners*. Buffalo, N.Y.: Trado-Medic Books.

Smith, Margo L., and Damien, Yvonne M. (1981). *Anthropological Bibliographies: A Selected Guide*. South Salem, N.Y.: Redgrave Publishing Co.

Stout, Russell (1980). *Organizations, Management, and Control* (An annotated bibliography). Bloomington: Indiana University Press.

UNESCO (1980, 5th ed.). *World List of Social Science Periodicals*. Paris: UNESCO.

_____ (1979, 2nd ed.). *World Directory of Social Science Institutions*. Paris: UNESCO.

Union for Radical Political Economics (1977). *Reading Lists in Radical Political Economics*. New York: URPE (Vol. 3, Winter).

United Nations, Centre on Transnational Corporations (1979a). *Bibliography on Transnational Corporations*. New York: UN, ST/CTC/4.

_____ (1979b). *International Directory of Data Bases Relating to Companies*. New York: UN, ST/CTC/7.

Wilhelm, Laurence (1978, 2nd ed.). *Le risque de famine au Sahel: Revue de la littérature*. Geneva: UNRISD/78/C,27.

Wilson, David E. (1979). *National Planning in the United States: An Annotated Bibliography*. Boulder, Colo.: Westview Press.

Yanarella, Ernest J. and Ann-Marie (1982). *Energy and Social Sciences: A Bibliographic Guide to the Literature*. Boulder, Colo.: Westview Press.

Index

African Development Foundation, 44
Agency for International Development (AID), 35-39, 46-55, 63-81, 233-60, 310-14; AID—state policy conflict over farm prices, 74; blueprint project design approach, 233-60 (*see* project design); bureaucratic imperatives to continue in Zaire, 80-81; contradictions of its legislative mandate, 46-51; development goals in Zaire, 63-64; evaluation process, 295-96; North Shaba Maize Project, 59-81; oversight by Congress, 51-52, 55; Philippine Small Scale Irrigation Project, 298, 311-12; as prisoner of national security state, 35-39; Rahad Irrigation project, 299, 312-13; in Zaire, 59-81, 247
aid flows: contemporary, limits, 5; in context of world economy, 26-28; use in participatory development, 4
aid project cycle (*see* project design, project implementation, and evaluation in development)
Akchi experiment, 351
arms race, 349-52; process of ending by systems engineering, 351-52; weakness of underorganized citizens against, 350-51; world-system utility of, 350, 351
Asian Development Bank, 309

Bangladesh, 55, 254, 274, 285-86; Comilla project, 254, 274; local bureaucratic inventives, 285
Bank of International Settlements, 26
base organizations, 146, 162-75, 178-79; basic principles of community organizing, 163; decision making in small groups, 169-72; handling human inequality equitably, 171-72; harmony and struggle paths, 162-63; importance of small size, 168; limits to consensus, adversarial, and consociational methods of deciding, 170; linkage to larger world, 179-81; logic of organizing poor, 162; maturity of in relation to evaluative capacity, 318-20; overall handicaps of mobilized poor, 178; reasons for participation, 164-65, 173-75; standard versus participatory, 164-65, 173-75; unresolved practical dilemmas, 172
Belgium, 131, 133: role in Zaire debt discussions, 131-32
Bergsten, Fred, 54
Bhoomi Sena movement (India), 157, 163-64, 200
Blumenthal, Erwin, 132
Brandt Commission report, 5, 19
Brazil, 84

CAPs (Agrarian Production Cooperative in Peru), 217-19
Central Intelligence Agency, 40-41: role in development miseducation, 40-41
children in development, 159-60
Chile, 341
citizenship, 1-3, 20-23, 150-61, 178-79, 321, 324-35; building historical consensus as a mobilization tool, 331-32; *conscientization* as process for creating, 157-61; educating for self-reliance, 333; elite bias in defining history, 150; elite bias in defining human nature and need, 150-53; elite processes of departicipatory

About the Author

Guy Gran is an independent development consultant in Washington, D.C. and Adjunct Professor of Comparative Politics in the School of Government and Public Administration of American University. In times past, he applied years of Vietnamese studies to the public policy process, testified many times before congressional committees, and played a central role in changing U.S. policy toward Indochina between 1973 and 1975. His first book *Zaire: The Political Economy of Underdevelopment* (an edited collection: Praeger, 1979) is a study of how *not* to proceed with development. He received a Ph.D. in comparative world history from the University of Wisconsin in 1975.